ISLAMIC JURISPRUDENCE, ISLAMIC LAW, AND MODERNITY

RESOURCES IN ARABIC AND ISLAMIC STUDIES

series editors

Joseph E. Lowry
Devin J. Stewart
Shawkat M. Toorawa

international advisory board

Maaike van Berkel
Kristen Brustad
Antonella Ghersetti
Ruba Kana'an
Wen-chin Ouyang
Tahera Qutbuddin

Number 15
Islamic Jurisprudence, Islamic Law, and Modernity

ISLAMIC JURISPRUDENCE, ISLAMIC LAW, AND MODERNITY

MOHAMMAD H. FADEL

LOCKWOOD PRESS
Columbus, Georgia
2023

ISLAMIC JURISPRUDENCE, ISLAMIC LAW, AND MODERNITY

ISBN 978-1-957454-79-5

Cover design by Susanne Wilhelm.

Cover image: Joaquín Sorolla, *Hall of the Ambassadors, Alhambra, Granada* (1909). Public domain, via Wikimedia Commons

Library of Congress Cataloging-in-Publication Data

Names: Fadel, Mohammad H., author.
Title: Islamic jurisprudence, Islamic law, and modernity / Mohammad H. Fadel.
Description: Columbus, Georgia : Lockwood Press, 2023. | Series: Resources in Arabic and Islamic studies; 15 | Includes bibliographical references and index. | Contents: Nature, revelation, and the state in pre-modern Sunni theological, legal, and political thought — Islamic law reform : between reinterpretation and democracy — The implications of Fiqh al-aqalliyyāt (jurisprudence of minorities) for the rights of non-Muslim minorities in Muslim-majority countries — Islamic jurisprudence — The social logic of Taqlīd and the rise of the mukhtaṣar — "Istafti qalbaka wa in aftāka al-nāsu wa aftūka :" the ethical obligations of the muqallid between autonomy and trust — "Istiḥsān is nine-tenths of the law" : the puzzling relationship of Uṣūl to Furū' in the Mālikī Madhhab — Is historicism a viable strategy for Islamic law reform? the case of 'Never shall a folk prosper who have appointed a woman to rule them' — Islamic law, gender, and the family — Two women, one man : knowledge, power, and gender in medieval Sunni legal thought — Reinterpreting the guardian's role in the Islamic contract of marriage : the case of the Mālikī school — Political liberalism, Islamic family law, and family law pluralism — Adoption in Islamic law — Islamic law and the market — Ribā, efficiency, and prudential regulation : preliminary thoughts — Ethics and finance : an Islamic perspective in the light of the purposes of Islamic Sharī'a.
Identifiers: LCCN 2023024494 (print) | LCCN 2023024495 (ebook) | ISBN 9781957454795 (hardcover) | ISBN 9781957454023 (adobe pdf)
Subjects: LCSH: Islamic law. | Dhimmis (Islamic law)—Islamic countries. | Taqlīd. | Malikites. | Domestic relations (Islamic law) | Adoption (Islamic law)
Classification: LCC KBP250 .F33 2023 (print) | LCC KBP250 (ebook) | DDC 340.5/9—dc23/eng/20230609
LC record available at https://lccn.loc.gov/2023024494
LC ebook record available at https://lccn.loc.gov/2023024495

Printed in the United States of America on acid-free paper.

Contents

Series Editors' Preface vii
Acknowledgments ix
Introduction xi

Islamic Law and the State

1. Nature, Revelation and the State in Pre-Modern Sunni Theological, Legal and Political Thought 3
2. Islamic Law Reform: Between Reinterpretation and Democracy 25
3. The Implications of *Fiqh al-Aqalliyyāt* (Jurisprudence of Minorities) for the Rights of Non-Muslim Minorities in Muslim-Majority Countries 67

Islamic Jurisprudence

4. The Social Logic of *Taqlīd* and the Rise of the *Mukhtaṣar* 87
5. "*Istafti qalbaka wa in aftāka al-nāsu wa aftūka*": The Ethical Obligations of the *Muqallid* between Autonomy and Trust 123
6. "*Istiḥsān* Is Nine-Tenths of the Law": The Puzzling Relationship of *Uṣūl* to *Furūʿ* in the Mālikī *Madhhab* 143
7. Is Historicism a Viable Strategy for Islamic Law Reform? The Case of 'Never Shall a Folk Prosper Who Have Appointed a Woman to Rule Them' 157

Islamic Law, Gender, and the Family

8. Two Women, One Man: Knowledge, Power, and Gender in Medieval Sunni Legal Thought 195
9. Reinterpreting the Guardian's Role in the Islamic Contract of Marriage: The Case of the Mālikī School 219
10. Political Liberalism, Islamic Family Law, and Family Law Pluralism 237
11. Adoption in Islamic Law 273

Islamic Law and the Market

12. *Ribā*, Efficiency, and Prudential Regulation: Preliminary Thoughts 293
13. Ethics and Finance: An Islamic Perspective in the Light of the Purposes of Islamic *Sharīʿa* 337

Bibliography of Mohammad H. Fadel's Published Works 373
Index 377

Series Editors' Preface

Mohammad Hossam Fadel, the leading exponent of a Rawlsian perspective on Islamic law and governance, has produced an impressive body of innovative, theoretically grounded, and provocative scholarship. His work on Islamic law and Islamic legal history ranges from medieval institutions and the history of Islamic legal interpretation to urgent problems of modernist receptions and re-assessments of Islamic legal doctrine. He received a Ph.D. from the University of Chicago in Near Eastern Languages and Civilizations and a J.D. from the University of Virginia School of Law. After two federal judicial clerkships he worked as an attorney for a major law firm in Manhattan. In 2006 he joined the Faculty of Law at the University of Toronto, where he is currently a professor of law and was for a decade Canada Research Chair for the Law and Economics of Islamic Law.

Although Professor Fadel's intellectual concerns focus to a large degree on the compatibility of the Islamic legal tradition with modern liberal political sensibilities and institutions (what he calls "conditions of modernity" in his Introduction), his research and writing have also focused on premodern Islamic legal thought and institutions. His explorations of issues in commercial law, problems of gender hierarchy, and dimensions of interpretive authority in premodern contexts, for example, underpin arguments that stress the flexible, subtle, and contingent aspects of Islamic law. Those properties of Islamic law, for Professor Fadel, render it suitable, once properly understood, for communities characterized by self-government, by emerging ideas about equality, and by market capitalism.

A frequent point of reference in Professor Fadel's work is the political philosopher John Rawls. Professor Fadel's "Rawlsian-inflected-approach" (as he calls it) leads him to read the Islamic legal tradition politically. His reading is not a search for top-down, 'authentically' Islamic structures of governance. Rather, by teasing out jurists' assumptions, often latent, about the political, the economic, or the familial, and interpreting the legal doctrines the jurists articulate on the basis of those assumptions, he emphasizes those doctrines' sophistication, potential adaptability, and thus the ways in which they thereby retain continuing viability. Although his readings of Islamic legal sources suggest that those sources remain relevant to a society in which there may be substantial but legitimate disagreements over matters of law and morality, equally his Rawlsian approach reminds us that premodern Muslim jurists formulated Islamic law also under conditions of substantial disagreement over matters of law and morality, and also over questions of religion, politics, theology, and metaphysics.

Drawing on his expertise in the Mālikī school of legal thought, Professor Fadel has recently collaborated (with Connell Monette) on what will likely become the standard translation of the *Muwaṭṭa*ʾ (Harvard University Press, 2019), the legal treatise produced by Mālik ibn Anas (d. 795), the eighth-century CE scholar after whom the Māliki school is named. The *Muwaṭṭa*ʾ is one of the very earliest preserved complete Islamic law texts. It is critically important for the early history of Islamic law in all its dimensions and also the foundation of the work of Mālikī jurists from the early ninth century CE up through today.

The studies published in this volume give an excellent overview of the concerns and approaches that animate Professor Fadel's scholarship. They illustrate well his interests in Islamic law as a domain of Islamic political thought, in law-and-economics perspectives on Islamic commercial law, in the problem of gender hierarchy in Islamic law, and more generally in the ways Islamic law might be deployed in pluralistic and secularized societies today.

Professor Fadel's scholarship benefits from and continues the legacy of those path-breaking historians of Islamic law who re-invigorated its study in the 1980s—notably, Wael Hallaq, Sherman Jackson, Baber Johansen, David Powers, Susan Spectorsky, Jeanette Wakin, Bernard Weiss, Aron Zysow, and others—and put Islamic legal studies and Islamic legal history on a modern academic footing. We are excited to present this collection to scholars and to the interested public.

Joseph E. Lowry
Devin J. Stewart
Shawkat M. Toorawa

Acknowledgments

In the course of an academic career, one incurs debts, scholarly and personal, that overwhelm one's capacity to discharge them. Writing as someone who, in the words of the Muslim jurists, is *mustaghraq al-dhimma*—a person whose capacity to bear any further obligations has been exhausted—I have been blessed to owe too much to far too many. I will never be able to repay what my teachers, friends, colleagues and most importantly, my family, have freely given me over my lifetime. This book, however, would have been impossible without the valuable assistance of my two research assistants, Faizan Malik and Ghassan Osmat, each of whom worked diligently to help me prepare this anthology. I also wish to single out my wife, Reem Elsobky, whose presence in my life catalyzed so much of my work and brought me untold personal joy. Without her resilience, patience, and encouragement, I could not have accomplished what I did. I do hope, in the spirit of the saying "the alms due in respect of knowledge is spreading it," that this work satisfies in part the obligations a scholar owes to knowledge. My numerous errors, of course, are fully my own and I hope no one holds any of my numerous teachers responsible for them, whether real or imagined.

Introduction

This collection of thirteen articles spans almost two decades of writing. During this time, I completed a PhD at the University of Chicago (1995) and a JD at the University of Virginia (1999), served as a law clerk in a United States federal district court and in a United States court of appeals (1999–2001), and practiced law in New York on Wall Street in the immediate aftermath of the collapse of the tech bubble and 9/11 (2001–2005). I only "resumed" my academic career in January 2006, when I was fortunate enough to be hired by the University of Toronto Faculty of Law. The fact that I was able to return to the academy so long after having completed my PhD and even my JD can only be explained by the enduring impact that the "war on terror" had on universities in North America. While the national security state's expanded interest in all things Muslim had its inevitable and obvious impact in fields such as international relations and language studies, it is also had downstream effects in encouraging universities to expand their humanistic offerings on Islam and Muslims. Perhaps the post-9/11 expansion in the humanistic study of Islam in North American universities was intended as an act of liberal resistance to the Manichean "you're with us or against us" world view that the Bush administration adopted in the immediate aftermath of the atrocities of 9/11 and the subsequent US invasions of Afghanistan and Iraq. Whatever the motivations for the expansion of interest in Islamic Studies in the post-9/11 era, I can say, with not a little bit of embarrassment, that it certainly made my return to academia much easier than it might otherwise have been.

While the history of Islamic reformism has always been deeply entangled in various political projects, promoting modes of Islam compatible with liberal sensibilities became a central foreign policy priority of the United States.[1] As a result of the greater political salience of Islamic reform movements, Islam came to occupy an important part of public political discourse in liberal democracies. Far removed from the arcane debates about the historical provenance of texts and careful readings of thousand year old texts that were the bread and butter of my training as a student in the Department of Near Eastern

1. Cheryl Benard, *Civil Democratic Islam: Partners, Resources, and Strategies* (Santa Monica, CA: Rand, National Security Research Division, 2003); Saba Mahmood, "Secularism, Hermeneutics, and Empire: The Politics of Islamic Reformation," *Public Culture* 18, no. 2 (2006): 323–47, https://doi.org/10.1215/08992363-2006-006.

Languages and Civilizations at the University of Chicago, public intellectuals—who often had little to no training in Islamic Studies—began to engage in very public debates about the role of religion in politics generally, and Islam particularly, whether Islam was compatible with modernity, and whether the religious freedom afforded to Muslim citizens of liberal democracies would serve to integrate them as citizens, or instead offer them the means to create antiliberal, separatist enclaves *within* liberal democracies.[2] In such an environment, a person with my credentials—a degree in Islamic Studies and a JD—proved to be a convenient interlocutor.

Even as I was practicing law in Manhattan, I was asked to lecture at various law schools on Islamic law on topics such as Islam, democracy, liberalism and terrorism.[3] American law schools began to express a desire to bring in scholars who could teach their students at least the rudimentary outlines of Islamic law, even if, for the most part, such instructors were hired only as adjuncts or special visitors. Scholars from disciplines such as law and religion and political theory began to seek out Muslim collaborators to involve them in public intellectual projects and specialized inquiries. For example, *The Boston Review* invited Khaled Abou El Fadl to publish an essay on these questions that resulted in his work, *Islam and the Challenge of Democracy*, along with the short responses of a group interdisciplinary scholars (including myself) with expertise in law and religion, international relations, political theory and Islamic Studies to comment on the piece.[4] I will have more to say about my short response to Abou El Fadl's essay below, but here I wish simply to point out that the post-9/11 environment made issues of Islamic reform that Muslim intellectuals had long grappled with publicly salient in a heretofore unprecedented manner. What had largely been discussions between Muslim intellectuals with a few interested non-Muslim observers on the margins was now catapulted into a central part of mainstream public discourse. This increased academic interest in Islamic law, along with the relative dearth of Muslim interlocutors, offered me opportunities to pursue my scholarly interests even as I continued to practice law, such as contributing to a law review article on the classical conceptions of adoption in Christianity, Judaism and Islam.[5]

---

2. See, e.g., Mark Lilla, *The Stillborn God: Religion, Politics, and the Modern West* (New York: Vintage Books, 2008); Mark Lilla, "The Politics of God," *The New York Times*, August 19, 2007, sec. Magazine, https://www.nytimes.com/2007/08/19/magazine/19Religion-t.html.

3. For example, New York University School of Law held a panel discussion on November 6, 2001, not even a month after the events of 9/11, on the topic of "Law and Religion After September 11th: Perspectives on Islam and Islamism," in which I was one of the speakers along with Noah Feldman.

4. Khaled Abou El Fadl, *Islam and the Challenge of Democracy*, ed. Joshua Cohen and Deborah Chasman (Princeton, NJ: Princeton University Press, 2004).

5. Daniel Pollack et al., "Classical Religious Perspectives of Adoption Law," *The Notre Dame Law Review* 79, no. 2 (2004): 693–753.

I was also fortunate that my colleagues in Islamic legal studies had not written me off, even though I had seemingly left the humanities for law school immediately after defending my dissertation. The late anthropologist of Islam, Elizabeth Fernea, graciously invited me to participate in a conference in 1998 at the University of Texas on the contemporary relationship of religion and feminism in the Abrahamic religions. Frank Vogel, then a professor at Harvard Law School, invited me to participate as a commentator in a January 1999 conference on the Muslim marriage contract at Harvard Law School, even though I was still a law student at the time. The late Bernard Weiss of the University of Utah invited me to participate in a workshop he organized in September 1999 that brought together many of the leading scholars of Islamic law from North America and Europe for an intensive weekend of papers, discussions, hiking and academic fellowship. The last decade of the 1990s witnessed a veritable renaissance in Islamic legal studies. What had been a dormant field, effectively left for dead at the hands of colonial era Orientalists, had once again become a subject of intense study, debate and creativity. This was reflected in the increasing numbers of new generations of scholars and graduate students who were interested in Islamic law. As a result, the academic study of Islamic law was transformed from the domain of a small clique of scholars into a flourishing subdiscipline within Islamic Studies, with its own flagship journal publishing cutting edge scholarship on Islamic law, *Islamic Law & Society*.

That I was present at the University of Chicago when this transformation took place and so was well-positioned to benefit from the renewed academic interest in Islamic law was purely serendipitous. Indeed, my decision to study Islamic law itself was largely accidental, or at least, it was not something I had envisaged when I began my graduate studies. I began my PhD program in the fall of 1989 with no idea of what I wanted to study, only that I wanted to continue my study of Arabic. Although the obvious path for me at the time, given my undergraduate major in Government and Foreign Affairs, was to continue to law school, I had foresworn that route. I instead chose to continue my study of Arabic. Although I began my study of Arabic with the sole aim of satisfying the College of Arts and Science's two-year foreign language requirement, even after I fulfilled my University's graduation requirements I continued to study Arabic, largely out of a desperate desire to believe that I had actually gained some competence in Arabic. Fortunately, I studied enough undergraduate Arabic to gain acceptance into CASA, the Consortium of Arabic Study Abroad's year-long program at the American University in Cairo. CASA both enabled me to spend a year focused exclusively on the study of Arabic and to meet a new generation of scholars of Islamic Studies and Arabic Literature, including, but not limited to, Sherman Jackson, who was the Executive Director of CASA while I was there and would later serve as an important mentor to me, and Shawkat Toorawa, one of the editors of the series of works appearing under the title "Resources in Arabic and Islamic Studies." I doubt I would have enjoyed any success as a scholar without both the excellent Arabic instruction I received at CASA and the opportunities CASA provided me to develop lifelong relationships with a rising generation of new scholars in the field.

As a graduate student, however, I did not really turn to Islamic law as a field of study until it was time for me to prepare a dissertation proposal. Aside from a reading class with Professor Fred Donner in which we read selections from the basic Ḥanafī text *Mukhtaṣar al-Qudūrī*, I spent my first three years of graduate school taking a diverse set of classes, largely without thought to the requirement of writing a dissertation. Every quarter, however, I always managed to take a class with the late Jaroslav Stetkevych. I had the pleasure of reading with him Arabic poetry spanning the entire history of the Arabic language, from the pre-Islamic period to modern poetry. We also read together from the works of medieval linguistic theoreticians like Ibn al-Athīr's *al-Mathal al-Sā'ir* and Ibn Jinnī's *Fiqh al-Lugha*. He also taught the mandatory class on classical Arabic grammar, of course using Wright's *A Grammar of the Arabic Language*. Professor Wadad al-Kadi's classes introduced me to the great figures of Islamic intellectual history and political thought. Through numerous editing exercises in different classes I took with her, she instilled in me our responsibility to be scrupulous with, and faithful to, our textual sources.

Although my course work as a graduate student had very little direct relationship to my dissertation or my future work as a scholar, it gave me the tools I needed to become a successful scholar: mastery of the Arabic language, respect for the literary tradition, and a desire to be worthy successors to the figures whose works we carefully studied. When I finally had to put together a dissertation proposal in my fourth year of course work, however, I returned to my undergraduate roots in political science: I became attracted to the study of Islamic law as a topic out of my natural interest in law as a social institution directly involved in the daily governance of society. I found many of the prevailing claims about Islamic law at the time to be quite puzzling, such as the claim that medieval Islamic law was not relevant for the governance of Muslim societies and that it had remained essentially unchanged for a period approaching a millennium until western modernity came along to disturb its deep slumber. Accordingly, I decided that I would study a text or author from the later Middle Ages precisely because the prevailing wisdom was that there was nothing of interest to be learned from studying post-Ayyubid Muslim jurists.

Being at the University of Chicago also gave me the opportunity to take a class at the University of Chicago Law School. I took a course on legal interpretation with Judge Frank Easterbrook, not realizing at the time that he was one of the giants of the 20th-century American legal academy and one of its most influential federal appellate judges. That course introduced me for the first time to legal scholarship outside the narrow domain of Islamic law and seeded in my mind for the first time the possibility that attending law school might further my scholarly interests in Islamic law.

Professor Sherman Jackson proved very helpful in directing me at this point in my studies, introducing me to an Azharī teacher of Mālikī fiqh who taught introductions to fiqh classes to CASA students at AUC. I spent one summer with that teacher reading chapters of ritual law from the Mālikī text *al-Sharḥ al-Ṣaghīr* of the 18th-century Egyptian

Mālikī, Abū al-Barakāt Aḥmad al-Dardīr.[6] I would later read almost the entirety of the text with that teacher a few years later when I returned to Egypt on a Fulbright-Hays dissertation writing fellowship. I also managed to spend a semester at McGill University's Institute of Islamic Studies, where Professor Wael Hallaq generously permitted me to take a class he was teaching on the *Muwāfaqāt* of Shāṭibī. The semester I spent at McGill allowed me to learn directly from the scholar most responsible for the revival of the study of Islamic law in North America. Not only was I able to benefit greatly from Professor Hallaq's vast learning, I was also able to spend that semester reading intensively the secondary literature on Islamic law in preparation for writing a dissertation. Professor Hallaq also generously agreed to serve as an outside member of my dissertation committee. This was very important for me because at the time no one at the University of Chicago, despite the strength of its program, could claim expertise in Islamic law, particularly in the later periods that were the subject of my dissertation. Finally, as a graduate student at the University of Chicago, I was fortunate enough to form what would become life-long professional relationships with colleagues who would become some of the most accomplished scholars in contemporary Islamic Studies, such as Ebrahim Moosa and Marion Katz. My work has profited enormously from having such a broad set of intellectually challenging colleagues working on a broad range of interesting questions from different perspectives.

Islamic Law as a Political Commitment

Unlike most scholars who studied Islamic law in the latter part of the last century, I was not interested in Islamic law as a religious question. I was instead motivated to study Islamic law from the political perspective, to understand it as a tool of governance and social organization. Of course, according to much of the secondary literature of the time, whatever "Islamic law" was, it was most certainly not a tool of governance, or at least not an effective one. The view that prevailed in English-language scholarship was that Islamic law, while at one time—perhaps at the beginning of the Abbasid dynasty—was an effective tool of governance, its ideological character as a "religious law" meant that it was either too idealistic, too inflexible, or both, to serve as an effective instrument of governance over the years. Its religious character doomed it to function as an unattainable utopian ideal. The function of jurists was not to supply rules for the orderly governance of society, but rather to defend the theological ideal of a perfect religious

6. Aḥmad ibn Muḥammad Dardīr and Aḥmad ibn Muḥammad Ṣāwī, *Al-Sharḥ al-Ṣaghīr ʿalā Aqrab al-Masālik ilā Madhhab al-Imām Mālik Wa Bi'l-Hāmish Ḥāshiyat al-Shaykh Aḥmad b. Muḥammad al-Ṣāwī al-Mālikī*, ed. Muṣṭafā Kamāl Waṣfī (Cairo: Dār al-Maʿārif, 1972).

law. Whether it effectively regulated Muslim society, scholarship had told us, was not a principal concern for Muslim jurists.[7]

Because I wished to test these claims in my dissertation, I needed to study texts from the postclassical period that focused on practical matters rather than on the theological questions that in my opinion dominated the study of Islamic law.[8] I settled on the study of adjudication because I thought studying courts would allow me to focus directly on the questions that most concerned me: was Islamic law in the postclassical period one characterized by a religious spirit of idealism indifferent to the practical needs of the law as a system of governance, or did it, in fact, address itself to the practical questions of daily life that we routinely expect legal systems to address? Given the fact that I had already begun to study Mālikī fiqh in Egypt, I decided it made sense for my dissertation to focus on Mālikī doctrines of adjudication, and so my attention fell on the late 8th/14th century figure of Ibn Farḥūn (d. 799/1397), author of an encyclopedic treatise on adjudication, *Tabṣirat al-Ḥukkām*.[9] One of the most challenging aspects of writing the dissertation was that it was essentially impossible to understand the rules governing courts and judges without understanding the substantive law that judges were expected to apply. This meant that I had to become much more familiar with the substantive content of

---

7. See, for example, Joseph Schacht, Introduction to Islamic Law (Oxford: Clarendon, 1964) and Noel Coulson, *A History of Islamic Law*, The New Edinburgh Islamic Surveys : NEIS (Edinburgh: Edinburgh University Press, 2022), https://doi.org/10.1515/9781474465892. For an overview of scholarship on the relationship of Islamic law to the state, see Mohammad Fadel, "State and Sharia," in *The Ashgate Research Companion to Islamic Law*, ed. Rudolph Peters and P. J. Bearman, Ashgate Research Companion (Farnham, Surrey: Ashgate, 2014), 93–107.

8. Theology impacted the study of Islamic law in several ways. First, the historiography of Islamic law was dominated by debates regarding *when* certain sources became theologically authoritative, e.g., the practice (*al-sunna*) of the Prophet Muḥammad, and the authenticity of various texts found in early works of Islamic law, whether reports attributed to the Prophet Muḥammad or other early figures of the Muslim community. Second, Islamic law scholarship was characterized by its view that Islamic law, because it was a "religious law," suffered from an especially prominent gap between its "theory and practice," with scholarship centered around exposing this structural "feature" of Islamic law. Third, Islamic law scholarship in the 80s and 90s had become almost single-mindedly focused on the problem of originality versus stagnation in postclassical Islamic law. This debate took place largely under the rubric of whether the "gate of *ijtihād*" had really been closed. Although it had long been taken for granted that Muslim theological commitments forced medieval Muslim jurists to disclaim any right to interpret the law for themselves, Wael Hallaq robustly challenged this view in a 1984 article titled "Was the Gate of Ijtihād Closed." His argument provoked great interest and reinvigorated scholars' interest in the works of Muslim jurists in later centuries. Wael B. Hallaq, "Was the Gate of Ijtihad Closed?," *International Journal of Middle East Studies* 16, no. 1 (1984): 3–41, https://doi.org/10.1017/S0020743800027598.

9. Mohammad Fadel, "Ibn Farḥūn," *Encyclopaedia of Islam, THREE*, January 1, 2018, https://referenceworks.brillonline.com/entries/encyclopaedia-of-islam-3/ibn-farhun-COM_30773?lang=en; Ibrāhīm ibn ʿAlī Ibn Farḥūn, *Tabṣirat al-Ḥukkām fī Uṣūl al-Aqḍīyah ... wa-Manāhij al-Aḥkām*, ed. Ṭāhā ʿAbd al-Raʾūf Saʿd, 2 vols. (Cairo: Maktabat al-Kulliyyāt al-Azhariyya, 1986).

Mālikī fiqh than I had been. Fortunately, I was awarded a Fulbright-Hays Dissertation Writing fellowship for 1993–1994 which enabled me to spend a year in Egypt working on my dissertation. I was able to use this time, in part, to complete reading *al-Sharḥ al-Ṣaghīr* under the guidance of the very same Azharī shaykh that Professor Jackson had introduced me to in previous years. I would go to his home three days a week and we would read, together, the text of *al-Sharḥ al-Ṣaghīr*, line by line, occasionally referring to al-Ṣāwī's notes on the text, known as *Bulghat al-Sālik*, that was printed alongside Dardīr's. After having read a primary text of Mālikī fiqh, more or less from cover to cover under the tutelage of an Azharī, I was now in a position to navigate Ibn Farḥūn's text, begin a more systematic exploration of Mālikī substantive law, and complete my dissertation, *Adjudication in the Mālikī Madhhab: A Study of Legal Process in Medieval Islamic Law*.[10]

The relatively profound engagement I had with substantive Mālikī law during my dissertation would have a profound impact on both my scholarship and my own views on Islamic legal reform in modernity. Growing up as an Arab-American-Muslim in the postcivil rights era South inevitably had an impact on the way I viewed the world, both as an American and as a Muslim. Firmly committed to the idea of the United States as a constitutional democracy based on the equality of all citizens, and born into a religiously observant Egyptian-Arab Muslim family, my understanding of Islam was always shaped by my experience of American political ideals. When I confronted contradictions between the ideals of American democratic liberalism and Islamic doctrines, my visceral reaction—as was the reaction of most American-Muslims of my generation—was to dismiss these problematic historical Islamic doctrines as either historical rules that no longer had any relevance, ancient rules that lacked sufficient grounding in the Quran to bind us today, or simply products of poor reasoning. Like most liberal-minded American-Muslims, I found in the theory of *ijtihād* what appeared to be a magical elixir, a tool that could be used to resolve any apparent conflict between my commitment to the liberal politics of America and my private commitments as a Muslim by simple decree.

One of the immediate effects of studying Mālikī fiqh was to disabuse me of the simplistic ideas I had about Islamic law before I started graduate school. As a lay Muslim, I naively understood Islamic law to be a "simple" matter of textual interpretation, and if the rule was problematic, it was probably either because the text was misunderstood or in the case of a rule based on a hadith, because the hadith was inauthentic. Studying Islamic law—both its jurisprudence (*uṣūl al-fiqh*) and substantive law—convinced me that Islamic law was anything but simple. To the contrary, it was an intellectually sophisticated project that was worthy of sustained scholarly engagement. This was rapidly becoming clear with respect to jurisprudence: the works of scholars such as Wael

10. Mohammad Hossam Fadel, "Adjudication in the Maliki Madhhab: A Study of Legal Process in Medieval Islamic Law" (ProQuest Dissertations Publishing, 1995), https://search.proquest.com/docview/304244838?pq-origsite=primo.

Hallaq,[11] Bernard Weiss,[12] Aron Zysow,[13] Jeanette Wakin[14] and others had taken our understanding of Islamic jurisprudence well-beyond the tragic, four-source Shāfiʿī triumphalism described by Joseph Schacht.[15] But scholars had also begun to pay attention to substantive law in the postclassical period: scholars such as Baber Johansen,[16] Sherman Jackson,[17] Brinkley Messick,[18] Khaled Abou El Fadl[19] and David Powers[20] had all published works on postclassical Islamic substantive law that demonstrated that it was not, contrary to popular belief, a sterile period of unthinking deference but a time full of interesting legal problems and scholars interested in solving them, even if that meant changing an "unchanging" law.

My dissertation—with its close attention to substantive legal doctrines—fell neatly into this new current of Islamic law research that was beginning to take Islamic law as something more than a handmaiden to theology and saw in it something that could be appreciated as law on its own terms. This approach to Islamic law served me well when I began law school in the fall of 1996. Rather than viewing law school as interrupting my academic vocation, I thought of law school more as an extended postdoc, where I

---

11. See, for example, Wael B. Hallaq, *A History of Islamic Legal Theories: An Introduction to Sunnī Uṣūl al-Fiqh* (Cambridge: Cambridge University Press, 1997).

12. Bernard G. Weiss, *The Search for God's Law: Islamic Jurisprudence in the Writings of Sayf al-Din al-Amidi* (Salt Lake City: University of Utah Press, 1992).

13. Aron Zysow, *The Economy of Certainty: An Introduction to the Typology of Islamic Legal Theory*, Resources in Arabic and Islamic Studies 2 (Atlanta: Lockwood Press, 2013).

14. Jeanette Wakin, "Interpretation of the Divine Command in the Jurisprudence of Muwaffaq Al-Dīn Ibn Qudāmah," in *Islamic Law and Jurisprudence*, ed. Nicholas Heer and Farhat Ziadeh (Seattle: University of Washington Press, 1990).

15. I describe Schacht's theory of Islamic jurisprudence, and Shāfiʿī's role in it as "tragic," because Schacht sees in Shāfiʿī both the ideological triumph of the "Islamic" in Islamic law and the roots for its sociological demise: in articulating its religious grounds so powerfully, Shāfiʿī guaranteed that Islamic law could not be a sociologically adaptive legal system. Mālik ibn Anas, *Al-Muwaṭṭa': The Recension of Yaḥyā b. Yaḥyā al-Laythī (d. 234/848)*, trans. Mohammad H. Fadel and Connell Monette, Harvard Series in Islamic Law 8 (Cambridge: Program in Islamic Law, Harvard Law School, 2019), 20–21.

16. Baber Johansen, *The Islamic Law on Land Tax and Rent: The Peasants' Loss of Property Rights under the Hanafite Doctrine*, Exeter Arabic and Islamic Series. (London: Croom Helm, 1988).

17. Sherman A. Jackson, *Islamic Law and the State: The Constitutional Jurisprudence of Shihāb al-Dīn al-Qarāfī*, Studies in Islamic Law and Society 1 (Leiden; Brill, 1996).

18. Brinkley Morris Messick, *The Calligraphic State: Textual Domination and History in a Muslim Society / Brinkley Messick.*, Comparative Studies on Muslim Societies 16 (Berkeley: University of California Press, 1993).

19. Khaled Abou El Fadl, "Islamic Law and Muslim Minorities: The Juristic Discourse on Muslim Minorities from the Second/Eighth to the Eleventh/Seventeenth Centuries," *Islamic Law and Society* 1, no. 2 (1994): 141–87, https://doi.org/10.2307/3399332.

20. David Stephan Powers, *Law, Society, and Culture in the Maghrib, 1300–1500*, Cambridge Studies in Islamic Civilization (Cambridge: Cambridge University Press, 2002).

got the opportunity to throw myself into the study of law for its own sake, whereas my experience studying Islamic law and even speaking about in the context of Near Eastern studies always brought back concerns that were of tangential significance to what was the most important question for me: How did Islamic law function as a system of law in premodern Muslim societies? My three years in law school afforded me an opportunity to think about law much more abstractly and much more systematically than my training in graduate school ever did. I found myself constantly engaged in comparing common law doctrines with their analogues in Islamic law. This might seem obvious in the first-year "common law" mandatory classes of contracts, torts, property and criminal law, but I also found that what I was learning in other subjects, such as civil procedure, administrative law, and remedies were also highly relevant to understanding Islamic substantive law.

My experience in law school convinced me that studying law, far from being a diversion for those interested in Islamic law, or at best something nice to do if one could, was rather the sine qua non for understanding Islamic law. Just as knowledge of Arabic was commonly recognized as indispensable to be a serious scholar of Islamic law, so too I had come to believe that expertise in legal reasoning was necessary to gain a proper understanding of substantive Islamic legal doctrine that was chock full of technical legal language that made no sense to the uninitiated. While I still viewed myself as ideologically committed to a reformist understanding of Islamic law, I had come to understand that simplistic appeals to *ijtihād* could not possibly be effective in effecting the reform that modernist Muslims sought. Instead of viewing Islamic law as an obstacle to reform, I came to the conclusion that the most effective means of reforming Islamic law was through appeals to norms internal to Islamic law itself rather than to abstract values such as justice or beauty or equality, despite the centrality of these as moral values to the Islamic tradition.[21]

My experience in law school was also formative to my future academic career by reintroducing me to John Rawls. As an undergraduate, we read selections from Rawls's *Theory of Justice*[22] in my political theory seminar, but for whatever reason, I never encountered him again in my coursework. In law school, however, I was introduced to Rawls's later

---

21. There are many Muslims who advocate for reform of the historical rules of Islamic law by making appeals to moral values that are believed to be superior to the particular rules of substantive law that contradict or are in tension with modern liberal norms. See, for example, Khaled Abou El Fadl, *Speaking in God's Name: Islamic Law, Authority and Women* (Oxford: Oneworld, 2001); Khaled Abou El Fadl, *The Search for Beauty in Islam: A Conference of the Books* (Lanham, Md: Rowman & Littlefield, 2006); and, Ziba Mir-Hosseini et al., eds., *Gender and Equality in Muslim Family Law: Justice and Ethics in the Islamic Legal Tradition*, Library of Islamic Law 5 (London: I.B. Tauris, 2013).

22. John Rawls, *A Theory of Justice*, Harvard Paperback (Cambridge: Belknap Press of Harvard University Press, 1971).

work, *Political Liberalism*,[23] through my role on the Virginia Law Review. That year, the Virginia Law Review published a lengthy article applying Rawls's views on associations to self-governing communities in the context of American federalism.[24] That experience introduced me to Rawls as a theorist of democratic pluralism, and not just a theorist of liberal democracy. I immediately saw that his approach to reconciling incommensurate philosophical and theological commitments in the setting of liberal constitutional democracies held great relevance not only for understanding intra-Muslim pluralism, but also the place of Muslims and Islam in liberal democracies.

I began to articulate my now Rawlsian-inflected approach to Islamic law reform succinctly in my reply to Khaled Abou El Fadl's essay, *Islam and the Challenge of Democracy*.[25] There, I expressed reservations about what I described as his "top-down approach" to legal reform that begins with abstract moral norms and then derives from them particular rules. I instead advocated a "bottom-up approach" pursuant to which one "begins with well-established legal rules, moral principles, and theological truths" to make the case that the reformist position being advocated best vindicates the historical principles of Islamic law, morality and theology.[26] Finally, I emphasized the need to articulate arguments that are not only persuasive to the adherents of a particular group of Muslims, but are potentially attractive to Muslims with whom one does not necessarily share the same theological assumptions. From the perspective I was advocating, historical Islamic law, morality and theology served as an important reservoir of arguments in furtherance of the reformist project, not as the obstacle standing in the way of reform. It has been the task of my scholarship to demonstrate why I believe this is the case.

Reading Islamic Law Politically, not Theologically or Religiously

Throughout much of the 20th century, Islamic law scholars argued that Islamic law, by its nature, was "immutable" because it was an expression of divine will. This was commonly expressed by denying Islamic law the status of law at all, with the first important Orientalist scholar of Islamic law, Christiaan Snouck Hurgronje, declaring it to be a "deontology," not law, because it promiscuously mingled "religion, ethics and politics in an unsystematic way."[27] Accordingly, it was incapable of adapting to changing circum-

---

23. John Rawls, *Political Liberalism*, John Dewey Essays in Philosophy. No. 4 (New York: Columbia University Press, 1993).

24. Mark D. Rosen, "The Outer Limits of Community Self-Governance in Residential Associations, Municipalities, and Indian Country: A Liberal Theory," *Virginia Law Review* 84, no. 6 (1998): 1053–1144, https://doi.org/10.2307/1073695.

25. Mohammad Fadel, "Too Far from Tradition," in Khaled Abou El Fadl, *Islam and the Challenge of Democracy*, ed. Joshua Cohen and Deborah Chasman (Princeton: Princeton University Press, 2004), 81–86.

26. Fadel, 85.

27. Baber Johansen, *Contingency in a Sacred Law: Legal and Ethical Norms in the Muslim fiqh*, Studies

stances, a feature that precipitated a crisis for Islamic law with the onset of modernity. Baber Johansen argued persuasively against the stereotype of Islamic law as an undifferentiated set of duties using the evidence of Ḥanafī substantive law, which, as he showed in various studies, systematically differentiated among various social spheres through the law itself.[28] For example, the law of duress (*ikrāh*) helped to mark the boundaries between the social domain of the market from the domain of the household insofar as the absence of duress was a requirement for licit market transactions but was irrelevant in determining the validity of actions related to the household. Accordingly, even though a sale made under duress was invalid, a coerced divorce was effective despite the absence of voluntariness.[29] Johansen further argues, again quite persuasively, that one of the major accomplishments of the Muslim jurists was to carve out for the legal a domain that was distinct from the "ethical, religious and political."[30]

The first step in creating a distinctly legal domain was accomplished by systematically distinguishing theology from law, a process that began in earnest during the early Abbasid period in the 3rd/9th centuries.[31] Because jurists are only concerned with the evaluation of human acts from a legal perspective, important theological questions of ontology, rational belief and divine power are of little or no relevance to the development of legal doctrine.[32] But their exclusive focus on the observable features of human actions also meant that the legal domain was distinguished from the ethical and the religious domains, each being relegated to what Johansen calls the *forum internum* of the individual.[33] Even in the case of ritual law, Muslim jurists were only concerned with the external features of the proper performance of Islamic ritual, not bothering to discuss the inward psychological dimension of ritual which, despite its centrality, is unobservable and therefore beyond the jurisdiction of the jurist.[34]

---

in Islamic Law and Society 7 (Leiden: Brill, 1999), 43. Professor Johansen gives an excellent history of western scholarship of Islamic law, from its origins with Hurgronje, Max Weber's incorporation of Islamic law into his universal theory of sociology as an exemplar of "sacred law," to the work of Goldziher and Schacht (Johansen, 42–62). For a more recent overview of western scholarship on Islamic law, and how western scholars conceive of its relationship to religion, ethics and law, see Marion Holmes Katz, *Wives and Work: Islamic Law and Ethics before Modernity* (New York: Columbia University Press, 2022), 22–27.

28. Johansen's interpretation of Ḥanafī fiqh is not without its critics. See, for example, Talal Asad, *Formations of the Secular: Christianity, Islam, Modernity*, Cultural Memory in the Present. (Stanford: Stanford University Press, 2003), 245.

29. Johansen, *Contingency in a Sacred Law*, 63–64.

30. Johansen, 61.

31. Johansen, 23–24, 33.

32. Johansen, 24–25.

33. Johansen, 35–36.

34. Johansen, 35.

Consider juristic discussion of the intention (*al-niyya*) that Mālikīs consider a condition for the validity of the ritual washing (*wuḍūʾ*) that precedes performance of regular rituals, like prayer. Al-Dardīr provides three variations of the formula of the intention: that the worshiper intend either (1) removal of the cause precluding performance of the ritual (*rafʿ al-ḥadath*); (2) making permitted what had been prohibited by a precluding cause (*istibāḥat mā manaʿahu [al-ḥadath]*); or (3) performance of a ritual obligation (*adāʾ al-farḍ*). Not only is there no specific verbal formula associated with this obligation, but it is also preferable for the worshiper *not* to utter anything evincing his intention "because the essence of intentions lies in the heart and the tongue has no relationship to it (*al-awlā tark al-talaffuẓ bi-dhālika li-anna ḥaqīqat al-niyya al-qaṣd bi'l-qalb lā ʿalāqata li'l-lisān bihā*)."[35] His commentator, al-Ṣāwī, comments on al-Dardīr's claim that the intention lies in the heart by noting that this serves two purposes. The first is to distinguish worship from customary matters (*tamyīz al-ʿibādāt ʿan al-ʿādāt*) which, in contrast to worship, require parties to verbalize their intent, i.e., parties to a contract of sale must *manifest* their intent to trade, whether by words or conduct, for a valid sale to be concluded.[36] The second is to distinguish one ritual performance from another (*wa baʿḍ al-ʿibādāt ʿan baʿḍ*).[37] The jurists' approach to humility in worship is similarly perfunctory: the highly technical approach to intention in ritual one finds in works of Islamic law is replicated in their discussion of humility (*khushūʿ*) in ritual prayer. Surprisingly, humility is not considered an essential element (*rukn*) of the ritual prayer but is instead described as one of the commendable features (*al-mandūbāt*) of prayer, along with mindfulness of God's greatness (*istiḥḍār ʿaẓamat allāh taʿālā*).[38]

It is this technical treatment of the private dimension of religious practice that perhaps led some western scholars of Islam to even deny Islam the status of religion. Johansen quotes G. H. Bousquet as following Hurgronje's lead when he wrote in his article about worship (*ʿibāda*) in the *Encyclopaedia of Islam* that worship in Islam is nothing more than a set of duties prescribed by God on human beings which are "described in minute detail" by jurists. They are not means intended to bring the worshiper closer to God as is the case with other religions.[39] This interpretation of Islamic ritual, however, ignores the existence of *other* Islamic sciences that specialized in the internal dimension of religion. Even as the jurists treat the concept of the religious intention functionally, pietists like the Ḥanbalī Ibn Rajab (d. 795/1393) wrote extensively on the centrality of intention to

35. Dardīr and Ṣāwī, *Al-Sharḥ al-Ṣaghīr ʿalā Aqrab al-Masālik Ilā Madhhab al-Imām Mālik Wa Bi'l-Hāmish Ḥāshiyat al-Shaykh Aḥmad b. Muḥammad al-Ṣāwī al-Mālikī*, 1:115.

36. Dardīr and Ṣāwī, 3:14.

37. Dardīr and Ṣāwī, 1:115.

38. Dardīr and Ṣāwī, 1:323.

39. Johansen, *Contingency in a Sacred Law*, 44–45.

the spiritual life of the Muslim.[40] Similarly, if the jurists seem indifferent to engaging in a meaningful discussion of what humility in prayer requires and how that relates to a worshiper's performance of prayer, works like Abū Ḥāmid al-Ghazālī's *The Revivification of the Religious Sciences* focus extensively on such questions.[41] The determination of jurists to identify, and then defend, a domain of the legal distinct from the theological, the ethical, and the religious, not only protected the autonomy of the law from these other disciplines. It also created legitimate space for private religion to flourish beyond the reach of the law.

Muslim jurists therefore distinguished law, fiqh, both from theology, on the one hand, and religion and ethics, on the other hand. Theology, as Johansen explains it, is concerned with the rational vindication of the truths of Islam.[42] Ethical duties are distinct from legal duties insofar as they are absolute, constitute the *forum internum* between a person and God, and can only be publicly adjudicated by God in the next life, although individuals are always in a position to know whether their own actions are in conformity with their ethical obligations. Because the legal domain is limited to the external, its conclusions by contrast, are always contingent and relative, with the omnipresent possibility that even valid legal judgments miss the mark from the (true) ethical perspective, which is known only to God and the parties to the dispute.[43] The fiqh's reductive treatment of religion is suggestive of a *civic* or *public religion* rather than a private religion of salvation.[44] Ibn Farḥūn, for example, in explaining the legal perspective of ritual, justifies it functionally, as a means for "disciplining the soul (*kasr al-shahawāt*)."[45] For that reason, it is appropriate that rituals be included in a system that "serves as a normative reference for a universally valid system of justice"[46] that seeks to secure a comprehensive conception of human flourishing.[47]

Just as classical orientalists erred by reducing the Muslim idea of religion to the jurists' political treatment of religion in works of law, one must take care not to infer from the claim that fiqh represents a domain autonomous from the ethical and the religious,

---

40. See, for example, his commentary on the famous hadith, "Deeds are judged by their intentions (*innamā al-aʿmāl bi'l-niyyāt*)." 'Abd al-Raḥmān ibn Aḥmad Ibn Rajab, *Jāmi' al-'ulūm wa-al-ḥikam*, ed. Muḥammad al-Aḥmadī Abū al-Nūr (Cairo: Maṭābi' al-Ahrām al-tijāriyya, 1969), 1:55–96.

41. Ghazālī, *Iḥyā' 'ulūm al-dīn*, 4th ed. (Beirut: Dār al-Kutub al-'Ilmīyah, 2005), 1:189–201 (discussing the psychological dispositions that a worshiper must cultivate in order to benefit from prayer and other Islamic rituals).

42. Johansen, *Contingency in a Sacred Law*, 26.

43. Johansen, 36.

44. Ronald Beiner, in his book *Civil Religion: a Dialogue in the History of Political Philosophy*, defines "civil religion" as "the appropriation of religion by politics for its own purposes." Ronald Beiner, *Civil Religion: A Dialogue in the History of Political Philosophy* (Cambridge: Cambridge University Press, 2011), 1.

45. Ibn Farḥūn, *Tabsirat al-Ḥukkām Fī Usūl al-Aqḍīyah ... Wa-Manāhij al-Aḥkām*, 2:138.

46. Johansen, *Contingency in a Sacred Law*, 26.

47. Ibn Farḥūn, *Tabsirat Al-Ḥukkām Fī Usūl al-Aqḍīyah ... Wa-Manāhij al-Aḥkām*, 2:138.

that the fiqh, for that reason, is somehow devoid of Islamic morality. We can defend the necessary connection between fiqh and Islamic morality, however, without resurrecting late 19th- and 20th-century ideas that Islamic law did not distinguish between the ethical and the legal.[48] Johansen, for example, argues that one way in which the fiqh functionally differentiated among social spheres was precisely through the significance of the ethical dimension of the domain being regulated: because of the heightened ethical demands related to lawful sexual intercourse, strict compliance with the formalities of contracting marriage were required to be satisfied before intercourse could be licit, in contrast to commercial contracts, in regard to which Ḥanafī jurists recognized that the illicit nature of a substance such as wine did not preclude a Muslim from enjoying *some* rights with respect to it.[49]

More generally, we can say that law *always* takes a moral perspective on human action. If we take this feature of law for granted, then Islamic law is no different than other legal systems in taking a moral perspective on human action. But—and this is what distinguishes law from other kinds of moral discourses—the moral judgment of the law is based on the law's particular perspective on the conduct at issue.[50] Rather than claiming that law is distinct from morality, it is more accurate to say that law represents a particular form of morality that is limited compared to other, thicker conceptions of morality. Islamic law therefore is "religious" not only in the sense that its material sources are drawn, ultimately, from revelation,[51] but also because its morality derives its sense of right and wrong from revelation. Nevertheless, the morality of the fiqh is a more specialized and limited morality than the comprehensive morality of Islam as a religion. For Sunni fiqh, it is the political morality of the community of believers mutually committed to upholding Islamic conceptions of the good, i.e., commanding the right and prohibiting the wrong,[52] on an assumption of the fundamental political equality of the members of that community. The theological rejection of prophetic leadership after the death of the Prophet Muḥammad creates the space for the normative contingency in both knowing the law in its ideal form and in its application to particular persons that Johansen

48. Wael B. Hallaq, *Sharīʿa: Theory, Practice, Transformations* (Cambridge: Cambridge University Press, 2009), 2 (stating Islamic law's failure to distinguish law from morality, far from being a defect as suggested by its western critics, was one of its great virtues, and perhaps rendered it superior to western law along numerous dimensions).

49. Johansen, *Contingency in a Sacred Law*, 64 ("The law clearly gives differential ethical and religious evaluation to the ownership in different spheres of the law.").

50. Scott Shapiro, *Legality* (Cambridge: Belknap Press of Harvard University Press, 2011), 186 ("The legal point of view of a certain system ... is a theory that holds that the norms of that system are morally legitimate and obligating.").

51. Johansen, *Contingency in a Sacred Law*, 33.

52. Michael Cook, *Commanding Right and Forbidding Wrong in Islamic Thought* (Cambridge: Cambridge University Press, 2000).

identifies as giving rise to the distinctive structures of Sunni law and its relationship to theology, ethics and religion. The political significance of this particular Sunni theological commitment is perhaps most clearly evident when contrasted to the classical Imāmī Shīʿa rejection of *ijtihād* as a means to know the law,[53] and their readiness to permit judges to rule based on the private knowledge of the judge, rather than limit judges to facts established by the laws of evidence.[54]

What does it mean to say that the fiqh represents the political morality of the community of Muslims in contrast to the thicker moral demands of religion? This statement is a recognition that the distinctive feature of the fiqh as a set of moral ideals is its connection with the possibility of political enforcement, ordinarily through the judiciary, but also potentially through the police powers (*siyāsa*) of the ruler.[55] It is the prospect of coercive enforcement that gives the epistemological uncertainty inherent in the law ethical valence in the legal institutions of Sunnism. The Ḥanafīs give theoretical recognition to the different ethical requirements of the political and the religious in their distinction between two different ideas of human inviolability (*ʿiṣma*), the first related to their status as servants of God and the second related to their status as subjects of an empirical legal order. The former is known as *al-ʿiṣma al-muʾaththima* and the latter is known as *al-ʿiṣma al-muqawwima*.[56]

---

53. Zysow, *The Economy of Certainty*, 283; Rodrigo Adem, "Classical Naṣṣ Doctrines in Imāmī Shīʿism: On the Usage of an Expository Term," *Shii Studies Review* 1, no. 1–2 (2017): 42–71, https://doi.org/10.1163/24682470-12340002. The substantial majority of Shīʿa scholars in later centuries, known as the *uṣūlīs*, however, came to accept the legitimacy of *ijtihād*. Classical Shīʿa skepticism toward *ijtihād* persisted among what became a minority trend within Shīʿism known as the *akhbārīs*.

54. "المسألة الثامنة / علم القاضي هل هو من وسائل الإثبات في باب القضاء كالبيّنة / كتاب القضاء للسيد الخوئي (قده) – مدرسة الفقاهة," https://www.eshia.ir/feqh/archive/text/alerazi/feqh/32/330202/ ("The apparent sense of the noble verses [of the Quran] require judgment in accordance to what is true in itself. Accordingly, knowledge of it [i.e., the truth] is a means [of judgment] and requires, necessarily, the inference that it is valid for a judge to rule in accordance with it [i.e., his own knowledge of the truth in itself]. It is a proof in itself and does not need any proof to demonstrate that it [i.e., the judge's knowledge of the truth in itself] is admissible evidence. Accordingly, it is valid for a judge, in reaching his verdict, to rely on his own knowledge that this is just, correct and fair ("*al-āyāt al-sharīfa tabqā ẓāhira fī luzūm al-ḥukm bi'l-ḥaqq al-thābit wāqiʿan wa fī nafs al-amr fa-yakūn al-ʿilm bihi ʿilman ṭarīqiyyan wa mustalziman li-jawāz al-qaḍāʾ bihi wa al-ḥukm ʿalā ṭibqihi wa huwa ḥujja bi-dhātihi wa lā yaḥtāj fī ithbāt ḥujjiyyatihi ilā iltimās dalīl ākhar fa-yajūz li'l-qāḍī an yastanida fī al-ḥukm ilā ʿilmihi bi-anna hādhā ʿadl wa ḥaqq wa qisṭ*")). Cf. Dardīr and Ṣāwī, *Al-Sharḥ al-Ṣaghīr 'alā Aqrab al-Masālik Ilā Madhhab al-Imām Mālik Wa Bi'l-Hāmish Ḥāshiyat al-Shaykh Aḥmad b. Muḥammad al-Ṣāwī al-Mālikī*, 4:230 (*wa lā yastanid al-ḥākim fī ḥukmihi li-ʿilmihi bal lā budda min bayyina aw iqrār* ("The judge, in rendering his verdict, may not rely on his own knowledge [of the truth in itself]; rather, there must be either proof [i.e., witnesses or oaths] or an admission"). Al-Ṣāwī comments on this rule, noting that it applies even if the judge is a master-jurist (*mujtahid*) or saint with access to the unseen (*wa law kāna min ahl al-kashf*).

55. Johansen, *Contingency in a Sacred Law*, 3.

56. Muḥammad ibn 'Abd al-Wāḥid Ibn al-Humām et al., *Sharḥ Fatḥ al-qadīr* (Cairo: Muṣṭafā al-Bābī al-

The first form of inviolability arises simply by virtue of a person embracing Islam, and it is foundational to our natures as servants of God. Violation of another person's moral inviolability results in sin, and although violation of another person's moral inviolability is not sufficient to result in any practical legal remedies, it is the foundation on which all deterrence rests.[57]

The second kind of inviolability, which I refer to as *remedial* inviolability, rather than protecting the moral inviolability of persons, protects their status as things, i.e., it treats humans as *though* they were property by imposing monetary compensation as a remedy for injuries to their body, and for that reason, it *completes* their moral inviolability.[58] These two different grounds for inviolability, although related to one another, are governed by different logics. The moral inviolability of the person depends on the deterrence that arises from knowledge that one is answerable to God for one's conduct, and therefore is appropriate for the person's *forum internum*. Remedial inviolability, by contrast, by treating human beings as though they were property, is based on their corporeal equality and fungibility (*tamāthul*).[59] Because remedial inviolability only deals with part of our humanity—in contrast to moral inviolability which views us from the perspective of our true nature as servants of God—it is appropriate that the rules of law that Muslim judges apply are limited to the *forum externum*.[60]

A Mother's Obligation to Nurse Her Newborn Children as a Case Study in Reading Islamic Law Politically

This discussion, so far, has been highly abstract. Accordingly, it will be helpful at this point to take an example from the fiqh to illustrate what it means to read Islamic law from the political point of view. I will use the example of whether a mother has a duty to nurse her newborn, comparing the approaches of the Ḥanafīs and the Mālikīs, respectively.[61]

Ḥalabī, 1972), 6:27–28.

57. Ibn al-Humām et al., 6:27 (*al-ʿiṣma aṣluhā al-muʾaththima li-ḥuṣūl aṣl al-zajr bihā* ("Inviolability originates in moral inviolability because the foundation of deterrence lies in it").

58. Ibn al-Humām et al., 6:28 ([*al-ʿiṣma*] *al-muqawwima kamāl fīhi* "remedial inviolability completes it [i.e., inviolability]").

59. Ibn al-Humām et al., 6:29.

60. Johansen, *Contingency in a Sacred Law*, 36.

61. Marion Katz, in her recent book, has discussed the views of different Muslim jurists with respect to a married mother's obligation to nurse her own newborn. See Marion Holmes Katz, *Wives and Work: Islamic Law and Ethics before Modernity* (New York: Columbia University Press, 2022), 52–53 (citing Mālik's views in the *Mudawwana*) and 137–41 (discussing al-Sarakhsī's views on this question and related questions in the *Mabsūṭ*).

The Ḥanafīs make it clear that the mother has a *moral* duty, i.e., a religious duty, to nurse her child. Ibn Nujaym (d. 1005/1596), author of *al-Nahr al-Fāʾiq*, explains in his commentary that the rule stating that a mother is not to be compelled to nurse her newborn (*lā tujbar ummuhu li-turḍiʿ*) is directed to judges: "meaning, judicially (*yaʿnī qaḍāʾan*)." Nevertheless, her *forum internum* is bound by a religious obligation to nurse her child, because it being akin to the father's duty to provide maintenance for the mother and the child (*wa in lazimahā diyānatan li-annahā ka'l-nafaqa wa hiya ʿalā al-ab*).[62] In a situation where the mother refuses to nurse her newborn, the father is obliged to hire a wet nurse for the newborn, but the mother, as long as she is married to the father or her divorce is not yet final, may not, after having refused to nurse her child, agree to do so for a wage (*wa yastaʾjir man turḍiʿuhu . . . lā ummahu law mankūḥa aw muʿtadda*).[63] Ibn Nujaym explains this rule as follows:

> Such a contract would not be valid because she owes a duty to nurse her child by virtue of an express command, but if she refused to do so, she is excused because of the possibility that she is incapable carrying out this duty. When she agreed to do so for a wage, however, her capacity to nurse became manifest. Doing so therefore becomes obligatory for her, and it is not permissible to take a wage to perform a pre-existing duty.[64]

The refusal to permit the mother to receive a wage for nursing *her* newborn child is consistent with the Ḥanafī conception of the household as a domain of social life that excludes the logic of the market. She either performs them *gratis* in recognition of their moral binding character, or she refuses to do so, and is legally deemed excused before the courts, but not before God.[65] But note that the rule invalidating any attempt by the wife/mother to profit from her contributions to the household does not apply if she performs that very same labor outside her own household. With respect to *other* households, she

62. ʿUmar ibn Ibrāhīm Ibn Nujaym, *al-Nahr al-Fā'iq: Sharḥ Kanz al-Daqā'iq*, ed. Aḥmad ʿIzzū ʿInāya (Beirut: Dār al-Kutub al-ʿIlmiyya, 2002), 2:518.

63. Ibn Nujaym, 2:519.

64. Ibn Nujaym, 2:519 (*lā yajūz dhālika li-anna al-irḍāʿ mustaḥaqq ʿalayhā bi'l-naṣṣ fa-in imtanaʿat ʿudhirat li-iḥtimāl ʿajzihā ghayr annahu bi'l-ajr ẓaharat qudratuhā fa-kāna al-fiʿl wājiban ʿalayhā wa lā yajūz akhdh al-ujra ʿalayhi*).

65. Explicating the details of Ḥanafī family law are beyond the scope of this essay, but for more details on Ḥanafī resistance to assimilating the norms of marital exchange to those that regulate commercial exchange, see Baber Johansen, "The Valorization of the Human Body in Muslim Sunni Law," *Princeton Papers: Interdisciplinary Journal of Middle Eastern Studies* 4 (1996): 77–112 and Hina Azam, *Sexual Violation in Islamic Law: Substance, Evidence, and Procedure*, Cambridge Studies in Islamic Civilization (Cambridge: Cambridge University Press, 2015), https://doi.org/10.1017/CBO9781316145722 (especially chapter 4). See also, Kecia Ali, *Marriage and Slavery in Early Islam* (Cambridge: Harvard University Press, 2010), 89 (noting the absolute refusal of Ḥanafīs to countenance giving a wife a right of divorce (*ṭalāq*) for her husband's failure to maintain her).

is permitted to pursue her interests as a seller of her own labor. Accordingly, the Ḥanafīs express no objection to a wife taking a wage for nursing the newborn of a *cowife*, because that is a household independent from her own.[66] Finally, the refusal to recognize the validity of an employment contract in the setting of the household is also consistent with a more general feature of Ḥanafī fiqh that prohibits someone from taking a wage (*ajr*) for fulfilling a preexisting, religious duty. Accordingly, the Ḥanafīs take the position that it is impermissible to take a wage for teaching the Quran or fiqh to the public because this is a preexisting duty of religion.[67]

The Mālikīs, with their greater readiness to assimilate the transactional features of the marital relationship to commercial life, take a different approach. They agree with the Ḥanafīs that the married mother of a newborn is under a duty to nurse the child without claiming a wage. This duty, however, stems from her contract with her husband and is not a freestanding duty derived from religion. The content of the duty, therefore, is subject to variation by custom, as evidenced by the fact that upper class women are exempt from this duty.

> A married mother . . . is obliged to nurse her newborn children without receiving a wage unless she is of high status.[68]

Mālikī authorities, moreover, affirm the justiciability of this obligation, presumably because, like any other contractual duty, it may be enforced by a judge in a proper proceeding.[69] Later Mālikī authorities affirm that a high-status woman, however, *if* she agrees to nurse her newborn children, *may* take a wage for her services. This rule confirms that in the Mālikī view, the mother's obligation to nurse originates contractually, not as part of the mandatory, divinely imposed obligations of marriage.[70]

---

66. Ibn Nujaym, *al-Nahr al-Fā'iq*, 2:519.

67. Abū Bakr ibn Mas'ūd Kāsānī, *Kitāb Badā'i' al-Ṣanā'i' fī Tartīb al-Sharā'i'*, 2nd Edition (Beirut: Dar al-Kutub al-'Ilmiyya, 1986), 4:191; Katz, *Wives and Work*, 140–41.

68. See Muḥammad b. Yūsuf Mawwāq, *al-Tāj wa'l-Iklīl*, on the margin of Muḥammad ibn Muḥammad Ḥaṭṭāb, Khalīl ibn Isḥāq al-Jundī, and Muḥammad ibn Yūsuf Mawwāq, *Mawāhib al-Jalīl li-Sharḥ Mukhtaṣar Khalīl.*, 3rd ed. (Beirut: Dār al-Fikr, 1992), 4:213 (*wa ʿalā al-umm al-mutazawwija . . . raḍāʿ waladihā bi-lā ajr illā li-ʿuluww qadr*).

69. Ḥaṭṭāb, Khalīl ibn Isḥāq al-Jundī, and Mawwāq, 4:213 (Mawwāq, quoting Mālik from the *Mudawwana* as saying "a married woman can be ordered to nurse her newborn children without receiving a wage unless she is not someone who nurses on account of her high status, in which case it becomes the husband's obligation ("*tujbar dhāt al-zawj ʿalā raḍāʿ waladihā bi-lā ajr illā an takūna mimman lā turḍiʿ li-sharafihā fa-dhālika ʿalā al-zawj*").

70. Ḥaṭṭāb, Khalīl ibn Isḥāq al-Jundī, and Mawwāq, 4:213; Dardīr and Ṣāwī, *Al-Sharḥ al-Ṣaghīr 'alā Aqrab al-Masālik Ilā Madhhab al-Imām Mālik Wa Bi'l-Hāmish Ḥāshiyat al-Shaykh Aḥmad b. Muḥammad al-Ṣāwī al-Mālikī*, 2:754.

If the father lacks the means to hire a wet nurse, or the newborn refuses to nurse from any woman other than his mother, the Ḥanafīs and Mālikīs both concur that necessity trumps the mother's rights. In these two cases, if the mother fails to nurse the newborn, the child is exposed to the risk of death, and for that reason, both schools agree she can be compelled to nurse the newborn.[71] Because of the contractual nature of the duty in Mālikī fiqh, however, the mother may nevertheless still demand a wage for her services, e.g., if she is an upper-class woman who would not ordinarily be expected to nurse her newborn children, she has separated from husband following a final divorce (*bāʾin*), or she is a widow and the newborn has inherited property from its father.[72]

Reading these rules from a political perspective rather than a religious one discloses interesting differences between these two schools of law. The Ḥanafīs construe the mother-child relationship as part of a divinely imposed, mandatory set of religious obligations, and so the mother's duty to nurse her newborn, in the first instance, is owed to God. Because it is a duty owed to God, its primary mechanism of enforcement is the *forum internum*, not the *forum externum* represented by the judiciary. The religious nature of the duty is recognized by crediting the woman's claim of incapacity to fulfill the duty. Recognition of the priority of the *forum internum* in this case has the effect of creating a zone of bodily autonomy for the mother: because she is answerable to God for her religious duties, the coercive institutions of the law must credit her good faith when she claims lack of capacity.

The religious nature of the duty, however, nevertheless receives recognition in Ḥanafī fiqh by prohibiting the mother of the newborn from claiming a wage in the event she does nurse her newborn child, whether or not the newborn is willing to nurse from a woman other than its mother. Her revealed willingness to nurse for a wage rebuts the law's presumption that she lacked the capacity to nurse. By demanding a wage, it is as if she exited, voluntarily, from the hidden world of the *forum internum* and entered the corporeal world of bodies where judicial coercion is appropriate. By so doing she removes her conduct from the realm where only moral inviolability is relevant and moves it into the realm of objects, where remedial inviolability is properly invoked. Likewise, when the newborn refuses to nurse from any other woman, and its life is at risk if the mother does not nurse the child, the law of necessity trumps the otherwise applicable principle of the autonomy of the mother's *forum internum*. Necessity preempts the mother's moral autonomy and authorizes a judge to adopt the logic of the *forum externum* to coerce her,

71. Ibn Nujaym, *al-Nahr al-Fāʾiq*, 2:518–19; Ḥaṭṭāb, Khalīl ibn Isḥāq al-Jundī, and Mawwāq, *Mawāhib al-Jalīl li-Sharḥ Mukhtaṣar Khalīl.*, 4:213–14; and, Dardīr and Ṣāwī, *Al-Sharḥ al-Ṣaghīr ʿalā Aqrab al-Masālik Ilā Madhhab al-Imām Mālik Wa Bi'l-Hāmish Ḥāshiyat al-Shaykh Aḥmad b. Muḥammad al-Ṣāwī al-Mālikī*, 2:754.

72. Ḥaṭṭāb, Khalīl ibn Isḥāq al-Jundī, and Mawwāq, *Mawāhib al-Jalīl li-Sharḥ Mukhtaṣar Khalīl.*, 4:213–14; Dardīr and Ṣāwī, *Al-Sharḥ al-Ṣaghīr ʿalā Aqrab al-Masālik Ilā Madhhab al-Imām Mālik Wa Bi'l-Hāmish Ḥāshiyat al-Shaykh Aḥmad b. Muḥammad al-Ṣāwī al-Mālikī*, 2:754.

not to perform her religious duty to nurture the newborn, but to save the life of the newborn by nursing it.

Mālikīs, by contrast, view the obligation a mother owes to her newborn as arising out of her obligations under the marriage contract, and for that reason, it is owed in the first instance to the husband. It accordingly lapses upon her separation from her husband by divorce. After separation, all mothers, regardless of social status, are entitled to a wage for nursing.[73] As long as the marriage contract remains intact, however, most women are obliged to nurse their newborn children as an incident of the contract, and if they refuse to do so, a Muslim judge can compel them to perform their contractual obligation. We know that this is a contractual obligation, and not a religious one, because upper-class women are exempt from this duty by virtue of prevailing social custom that frees upper class women from this burden.[74] Because upper-class women are not obliged to nurse their children as an entailment of the marriage contract, if they *do* nurse their newborn, they may take a wage in consideration for these services because there is no preexisting obligation to do so, in contrast to Ḥanafī teaching on the subject. Likewise, because of the absence of a preexisting religious duty, she is also entitled to claim a wage when necessity compels her to nurse her newborn. Mālikī doctrine also creates a zone of autonomy for the wife, but in this case, it is contractual autonomy rather than religious autonomy. What is it stake in the Mālikī treatment of the obligation toward the newborn is the mother's contractual freedom, not her religious duty to God.

The contrasting Ḥanafī and Mālikī treatments of the mother's obligation to nurse her newborn reveals an interesting feature of the role of religion in Islamic law. Contrary to common stereotypes of religion serving a totalizing function in Islamic law, it was the Ḥanafī recognition of the mother's duty as a religious duty in the first instance that created the corresponding zone of bodily autonomy by rendering the obligation nonjusticiable. By contrast, because the Mālikīs view the duty as a contractual obligation in the first instance, the duty to nurse originates in the corporeal world of objects—the domain where remedial inviolability reigns supreme—and so the mother's decisions are all cognizable in a court. As a result, the Mālikī system only grants her the autonomy over her body that Ḥanafī law grants her if she has sufficient social standing to bargain for that autonomy. On the other hand, it affords her the positive right to monetize her care work within the household, if she has sufficient bargaining power to do so.[75] Counterintui-

73. Dardīr and Ṣāwī, *Al-Sharḥ al-Ṣaghīr ʿalā Aqrab al-Masālik Ilā Madhhab al-Imām Mālik Wa Bi'l-Hāmish Ḥāshiyat al-Shaykh Aḥmad b. Muḥammad al-Ṣāwī al-Mālikī*, 2:754 (stating that a woman whose divorce has become final (*al-bāʾin*) is under no obligation to nurse).

74. Dardīr and Ṣāwī, 2:754. As al-Dardīr puts it, the woman who is exempted from the duty of nursing is "she who is of the upper echelons of society whose custom is not to have their women nurse their children (*kānat min ashrāf al-nās alladhīna shaʾnuhum ʿadam irḍāʿ nisāʾihim awlādahunna*)."

75. This is true even for the majority of women for whom custom would render nursing an obligation

tively, the greater secularity of Mālikī fiqh on the question of nursing newborns results in a practical *reduction* of the woman's bodily autonomy but produces a theoretical increase in her market autonomy.

The distinction within Islamic law of obligations amenable to enforcement through political intervention and those enforceable primarily via individual conscience is not unique to Ḥanafism. One sees the same dynamic at play, for example, in Mālik's rule regarding a dying person's declaration that he seeks to pay accumulated, but unpaid, sums of the alms-tax (*zakāt*), or to fulfill unperformed obligatory vows entailing the payment of property for a pious purpose, obligations which are not in principle, justiciable: Mālik recognizes the effectiveness of such a declaration, even deeming it a debt, thereby giving it greater priority than the dying person's other testamentary dispositions, but he limits the effectiveness of such declarations to one-third of the dying person's estate. His refusal to treat deathbed declarations as the equivalent of commercial debts was intended to prevent individuals from deferring performance of those religious obligations that require the payment of property until such time as they are on their deathbeds when their property has effectively passed to their heirs. Just as the immunity a mother of a newborn enjoys from judicial enforcement of her moral obligation to care for her newborn in Ḥanafī fiqh has the incidental effect of precluding her from enforcing a contract to nurse, so too the immunity a Muslim enjoys from having a court enforce his obligations to pay *zakāt* on his monetary savings (*al-amwāl al-bāṭina*)[76] or his monetary obligations arising out of broken oaths (*yamīn*) or unfulfilled pious vows (*nudhūr*)[77] in Mālikī fiqh precludes him from using judicial process to fulfill his religious obligations postmortem at the expense of his heirs.[78]

We should not be surprised that Islamic law is quite careful in differentiating between nonjusticiable religious obligations and obligations that are amenable to judicial enforcement. The example of the obligations a wife-mother owes to her newborn is a particular example of a more general feature of the political in the premodern Muslim world as Ghazālī described it in the *Revivification of the Religious Sciences*. There, Ghazālī identified four different kinds of politicians: the prophet, the ruler, the scholar and the preacher. Prophetic politics is the highest form of the political because its jurisdiction extends to the body and the soul of everyone. The jurisdiction of rulers, by contrast,

---

of the marriage contract to the extent they successfully inserted in their marriage contract a provision relieving them of this obligation.

76. Sulaymān ibn Khalaf Bājī, *Kitāb al-Muntaqā Sharḥ Muwāṭṭa' Imām Dār al-Hijra Sayyidinā Mālik ibn Anas* (Beirut: Dār al-Kitāb al-ʿArabī, 1979), 2:94.

77. Some oaths and vows are amenable to judicial enforcement, for example, oaths to divorce a specific wife or manumit a particular slave. See, for example, Dardīr and Ṣāwī, *Al-Sharḥ al-Ṣaghīr ʿalā Aqrab al-Masālik Ilā Madhhab al-Imām Mālik Wa Bi'l-Hāmish Ḥāshiyat al-Shaykh Aḥmad b. Muḥammad al-Ṣāwī al-Mālikī*, 2:224. Most oaths and vows, however, were not judicially enforceable.

78. Mālik ibn Anas, *Al-Muwaṭṭa'*, 227, hadith no. 685 and 263–64, hadith no. 838.

is limited to the bodies of their subjects. Scholars and preachers, by contrast, have no jurisdiction over the bodies of the subjects, but only over their minds and hearts, either through demonstration or rhetorical persuasion.[79] The religious lives of human beings, which represent their true purposes, however, are inextricably connected to their corporeal existence. This feature of human life requires the existence of just law to ensure that people have the means to pursue the higher ends that religion imposes on them. It is the function of scholars to *teach* rulers these principles of justice that secure the worldly conditions that allow humans to pursue their true, religious ends.[80] It should not be surprising, therefore, that the positive rules of Islamic law reflect these structural features of Islamic politics as Ghazālī describes them.

An Overview of the Articles in This Anthology

The articles in this anthology cover a representative range of my interests from the last twenty years, with pieces in the domains of Islamic law and the state, Islamic jurisprudence, Islamic law and gender, Islamic law and the family, and Islamic law and the market. Despite the seemingly disparate range of topics these articles are united by the theme of demonstrating the compatibility between the political commitments implicit in Islamic jurisprudence and law and the requirements of self-government under law under the conditions of modernity. The "conditions of modernity" include democracy, gender egalitarianism and market capitalism. The various articles included in this anthology explore these questions, in a very broad sense, through unpacking the tension inherent in Islamic law between its mandatory character—insofar as some of its rules are nonwaivable—and its freedom-producing character insofar as it confers powers on legal agents to design their own rules and institutions.

This paradox of the law—that it both imposes on us positive duties and therefore restricts our negative freedom *and* empowers us to create domains of freedom where we are secure to enjoy our negative freedom—is perhaps best exemplified in the Sunni doctrine of the caliphate. According to Sunnis, the means by which the ruler of the juridical community of the Muslims is selected is through the choice (*ikhtiyār*) of the Muslims themselves. But Muslims are *not* free to refuse to establish such a ruler. The duty to establish a juridical existence for the Muslim community is itself a mandatory rule of law. The fact that jurists considered this obligation to be a collective one (*farḍ kifāya*), moreover, in no way undermines the legal consequences of this obligation. The insistence on the absolute nature of the obligation to establish a legal order representing the Muslim community is not evidence of a Muslim failure to understand the difference between religion

79. Ghazālī, *The Book of Knowledge; Being a Translation with Notes of the Kitab al-'Ilm of al-Ghazzali's Ihya' 'Ulum al-Din* (Lahore: Ashraf, 1962), 21.

80. Ghazālī, 33–34.

and politics. Rather, it reflects their understanding that the existence of a legal order is an indispensable *enabling condition* for the way of life Islamic law promotes to be fulfilled.

If an Islamic theory of self-government is conceivable, it must emerge from debates about the state and the relationship of law to the community's freedom to order its own affairs. Accordingly, I have approached the question of the caliphate and Islamic constitutional law from the perspective of the resources it offers for a project of self-government. In so doing, I take a tack that is in tension with much contemporary scholarship on Islamic law that believes that Islamic law has nothing meaningful to say about the state. The prevailing view is that the political is either exogenous to Islamic law, a view best represented among contemporary scholars of Islamic law by Wael Hallaq,[81] or a domain of radically failed aspiration represented by an unbridgeable gap between theory and practice.[82] In my view, the ubiquity of the state and its representatives in Islamic law, in both ritual law (*ʿibādāt*) and transactional law (*muʿāmalāt*), make such a position untenable. It is, moreover, impossible to understand Islamic law *without* understanding the political theory of Sunnism. Sunni political theory in turn depends on certain theological commitments. The first article in the anthology, *Nature, Revelation and the State in Pre-Modern Sunni Theological, Legal and Political Thought*, gives an overview of my attempt to sketch the relationship between Sunni theology, including the Sunni conception of reason and revelation, to their theory of the state as the legal representative (*wakīl*) of the Muslim community and the powers it enjoys.

The second article, *Islamic Law Reform: Between Reinterpretation and Democracy*, builds on that introduction to give a much more detailed, juridical account of the normative state in Sunni legal thought by carefully reading various doctrines of positive law that

81. Mohammad Fadel, "A Tragedy of Politics or an Apolitical Tragedy?," *Journal of the American Oriental Society* 131, no. 1 (2011): 109–27, 115.

82. Indeed, even the most important modern Arab jurist, the Egyptian ʿAbd al-Razzāq al-Sanhūrī, subscribed to the view that the prevalence of despotic forms of rule impeded the development of a significant body of Islamic public law. ʿAbd al-Razzāq Aḥmad Sanhūrī, *Maṣādir al-Ḥaqq fī al-Fiqh al-Islāmī: Dirāsa Muqārana bi'l-Fiqh al-Gharbī* (Beirut: Dār al-Fikr, 1953), 37, n.2. Earlier in his career, however, he outlined a plan to reconceptualize Islamic law using the categories of private law and public law in the civil law tradition based on the distinction in Islamic law between the rights of God (*ḥaqq allāh*) and the rights of man (*ḥaqq al-ʿabd*). ʿAbd al-Razzāq al-Sanhūrī, "al-Dīn wa'l-Dawla fī'l-Islām," *Majallat al-muḥāmāt al-sharʿiyya* 1,1 (1929), 8–14. I am indebted to Samy Ayoub for these references. For an overview of contemporary scholarship on the historiography of Islamic law and the state, see Fadel, "State and Sharia." For a recent interpretation of Ibn Taymiyya as representing an attempt to overcome the problem of failed aspiration in Sunni political thought, see Ovamir Anjum, *Politics, Law and Community in Islamic Thought: The Taymiyyan Moment*, Cambridge Studies in Islamic Civilization (Cambridge: Cambridge University Press, 2012). For a notable exception to the dominant trend that sees the historical Muslim state as outside the normative Islamic legal order, see Samy Ayoub, *Law, Empire, and the Sultan: Ottoman Imperial Authority and Late Ḥanafī Jurisprudence*, Oxford Islamic Legal Studies (New York: Oxford University Press, 2020).

involve the state and its officials to demonstrate the symmetry between the rules jurists developed to regulate public officials and those that applied to private persons based on doctrines of agency and fiduciary duty. The article attempts to show that whatever jurists' subjective views regarding the legitimacy of their rulers from an ideal Islamic perspective, they regulated public officials using normative legal categories that imposed on them the duties of agents and fiduciaries. This approach functioned both to limit the legal effects of their decision and to authorize them to act in legally binding ways, provided they exercised those powers in a manner consistent with the conduct of agents and fiduciaries of the community. The article argues that such a theory of the state effectively recognizes the legitimacy of positive legislation as morally binding on the Muslim community, even in circumstances where revealed law would not make the legislated conduct obligatory (or prohibited). It therefore suggests that the most efficacious route for Islamic legal reform is not creative reading of revelation through a revisionist approach to jurisprudence (*uṣūl al-fiqh*), but rather effective democratic self-government, insofar as the latter ideal best represents the Sunni political ideal of state as representative of the community. Legitimate legislation from this perspective is the exercise of the community's freedom to pursue its collective good, not the coercive enforcement of a particular view of revelation.

The third article, *The Implications of* Fiqh al-Aqalliyyāt *(Jurisprudence of Minorities) for the Rights of Non-Muslim Minorities in Muslim-Majority Countries*, develops the idea of *fiqh al-aqalliyyāt* as applied to Muslim minorities to consider what the arguments justifying dispensations for Muslim minorities might mean for non-Muslim minorities in the Muslim world. It argues that the very same reasons that justify dispensations for Muslim minorities under non-Muslim rule apply *a fortiori* to recognizing dispensations with respect to historical rules governing non-Muslim populations. Although the article does not make the claim explicitly, its conclusions are consistent with the constitutional idea, elaborated in the first two articles of the anthology, of the Muslim state as a self-governing state insofar as the political doctrine of equality of citizenship can be seen as furthering the rational good of the Muslim community.

The anthology, after making the case for the primacy of the state in understanding legal order, then transitions to four pieces on Islamic jurisprudence: *The Social Logic of* Taqlīd *and the Rise of the Mukhtaṣar*; Istafti qalbaka wa in aftāka al-nās wa aftūka: *the Ethical Obligations of the* Muqallid *Between Autonomy and Trust*; "Istiḥsān *is Nine-Tenths of the Law*": *the Puzzling Relationship of* Uṣūl *to* Furūʿ *in the Mālikī* Madhhab; and *Is Historicism a Viable Strategy for Islamic Legal Reform? The Case of 'Never Shall a Folk Prosper Who Have Appointed a Woman to Rule Them.'* Each one of these articles engages a question of jurisprudence, but from a distinctively practical perspective. The first article takes up the issue of *taqlīd*—the institution of deference to *mujtahids*—that was almost universally held responsible for the alleged "decline" and "stagnation" of Islamic law in the medieval period. It makes the argument that *taqlīd* as an institution is better understood not from the perspective of "originality," but rather from the perspective of a legal system that requires a minimum baseline of stability in its rules in order to function as a legal system.

The second article speaks to two problems that potentially arise under the system of *taqlīd* as described by Islamic jurisprudence from the perspective of democratic self-government. The first is whether the distinction in Islamic jurisprudence between the *mujtahid*—the master-jurist who is both able and duty-bound to derive laws directly from revelation independently—and the *muqallid*—everyone else lacking those credentials—necessarily implies that nonexperts have no role to play in the production and maintenance of the legal order. The second is whether the distinction between the master-jurist and the non-expert allows for nonjurists to have moral motivations to follow the law independent of the epistemological reasons that lead them to defer to the views of master-jurists. Both of these questions raise important issues with respect to both democracy and Islam: if the vast majority of Muslims are excluded from a role in law-making, but are relegated to law-takers, it would seem that Islamic law would foreclose the possibility of democratic self-rule by denying the majority of people the capacity for moral self-governance. The second question is relevant to the rule of law because it touches on the likelihood that the majority of people will or will not have intrinsic motivations to follow the law.

The third of the four jurisprudential pieces explores a broad theoretical question that used to trouble scholars of Islamic law for some time: the relationship of jurisprudence to substantive law, i.e., did the theoretical doctrines set forth in works of jurisprudence effectively "produce" the observed rules of Islamic law, or is jurisprudence largely an exercise in post hoc rationalization of doctrines that were already extant?[83] It does so through exploring the doctrine of *istiḥsān* in Mālikī jurisprudence in the context of the Mālikī law of pledges (*ruhūn*). The aim of the paper was to demonstrate that despite Shāfiʿī's anti-*istiḥsān* polemics, Mālikī jurists continued to endorse *istiḥsān* without embarrassment, and that it continued to play an important role in developing substantive law, particularly in the context of commercial law, in which the reasonable commercial needs of creditors and debtors played an important role in developing the substantive doctrines of Mālikī fiqh governing this body of law. The larger point of the paper is to suggest that the triumph of textualism that is commonly associated with Shāfiʿī's theory of the sources of the law should not be assumed to be consistent with the historical rules of Islamic law and that the substantive rules of law instead developed largely according to their own internal logic rather than the formal rules that Shāfiʿī and his successors in jurisprudence outlined in works on legal theory. This is particularly true in rules governing property relations, as the article attempts to show in connection with the Mālikī law of pledges. Analyzing the continued jurisprudential relevance of the doctrine of *istiḥsān*

83. Omar Farahat, "Reason-Giving and the Duty to Obey: Perspectives from Classical Islamic Jurisprudence," *The Journal of Law and Religion* 36, no. 1 (2021): 8, https://doi.org/10.1017/jlr.2020.52.

in the post-Shāfiʿī period in connection with a branch of the law of property foreshadows later pieces in the anthology dealing with the potential applicability of Islamic law to contemporary market relations.

The last jurisprudential piece is similar to the second article insofar as it takes a specific problem that is of concern to contemporary Muslims—the prospect of active female participation in the public life of the community—and analyzes it in light of a famous text that could be read to preclude that possibility through the mediation of an important debate in jurisprudence: whether the apparent sense of a general term (*al-lafẓ al-ʿāmm*) can be restricted in light of its particular circumstances (*khuṣūṣ al-sabab*). One way of understanding this jurisprudential controversy is through the relatively familiar controversy within statutory interpretation between the plain sense of a statute and the reasonable intent of the statute considering the historical circumstances, including debates of the legislators, that accompanied the rule's adoption.[84] Of course, this problem is more acute in the context of interpreting revealed texts which are not drafted in the form of clear statutes.

In contrast to the approach taken by some Muslim feminists to this text, I do not challenge either its historicity or its normativity. The article, after describing different positions taken on the question of whether the plain sense of a revealed text can be circumscribed by its historical circumstances, explores how Muslims preserved and read this text in light of this jurisprudential controversy. The article tells a story of how early Muslim sources tended toward preserving a rich narrative framework which places the Prophetic pronouncement at issue in a very specific theopolitical context, but with the passage of time, Muslim authors lost interest in the specific theopolitical context of the prophetic utterance and instead embedded it in an increasingly androcentric discourse that held a dim view of women playing any public role. The article documents how this one text was put to different uses in different literary contexts, arguably giving it different meanings in so doing. In an increasingly androcentric cultural context, however, jurisprudential canons such as "weight is given to the generality of the expression, not the particularity of its circumstances," could justify forgetting the original narrative context of the report, even though, in practice, jurists honored such canons more in the breach than in the keeping. It is not surprising, therefore, that by the late medieval period, the text is routinely reproduced without any apparent consciousness of the narrative cir-

84. The tension between plain sense interpretation of statutes versus a purposive approach to statutory interpretation based on a postulated legislative intent is one of the most important controversies in contemporary American jurisprudence. This debate is further complicated by whether legislative history is a helpful guide to determining legislative intent. See, for example, Lawrence M. Solan, "Private Language, Public Laws: The Central Role of Legislative Intent in Statutory Interpretation," *The Georgetown Law Journal* 93, no. 2 (2005): 427–86; Frank H. Easterbrook, "What Does Legislative History Tell Us?," *Chicago-Kent Law Review* 66, no. 2 (1990): 441–50; David A. Strauss, "'Statutes' Domains' and Judges' Prerogatives," *The University of Chicago Law Review* 77 (2010): 1261–74.

cumstances in which it first appeared. But the article is not simply about one report, albeit one that carries a lot of weight in contemporary Muslim anti-women discourses. It attempts to set out a method for dealing with such elements in the tradition by approaching them with what one might call a "proportional approach" that focuses only on the legally relevant elements of the controversy, and carefully avoids entangling itself in additional controversies.

The last six articles in the anthology all deal with particular questions of Islamic substantive law in three different areas, Islam and gender, Islamic family law, and Islamic commercial law. There are four articles on gender and the family: *Two Women, One Man: Knowledge, Power and Gender in Medieval Islamic Thought*; *Reinterpreting the Guardian's Role in the Islamic Contract of Marriage: the Case of the Mālikī School*; *Political Liberalism, Islamic Family Law, and Family Law Pluralism*; and *Classical Religious Perspectives of Adoption Law*. The two articles on Islamic commercial law are: Ribā, *Efficiency and Prudential Regulation: Preliminary Thoughts* and *Ethics and Finance: An Islamic Perspective in the Light of the Purposes of Islamic* Sharīʿa.

The first article explores the tensions in Islamic law and jurisprudence surrounding the treatment of women's statements. It makes the case that Sunni thought determines standards of admissibility of female statements not based on preexisting assumptions about gender and the capacity of a person to be a credible source, but by the institutional context and the closeness or distance of the decision to the prospect of coercion. Where there is little to no prospect of coercive power being deployed as a consequence of a woman's statement, gender becomes irrelevant to evaluating the admissibility of her statement, but where coercion is the immediate result of a statement, such as a witness to a murder, gender becomes salient and may lead to the exclusion of female statements in their entirety. The Sunni treatment of female statements, therefore, is less a window into gendered theories of epistemology than it is into gender and medieval Sunni political theory.

The second article explores the technical doctrines of Mālikī law governing the role of the guardian (*walī*) in the marriage contract. By focusing on the question of the minor's capacity, the article draws attention to the importance in Mālikī doctrine between the mature virgin (*al-bikr al-rashīda*) and the immature virgin, on the one hand, and discriminatory *empirical* presumptions on when boys and girls can be presumed to have the capacity to look after their own affairs independently. The article shows that in the case of the never married, but mature female, Mālikī doctrine makes the consent of her natural guardian to her marriage contract redundant. It also shows that the Mālikī rule permitting the guardian to compel his minor daughter's marriage after she attains physical puberty contradicts Mālikī teachings regarding the noncompellability of the marriage of an adult who lacks capacity due to an inability to manage his own affairs (*al-safīh*). By reading the rules of guardianship closely, the article suggests plausible routes for viewing these rules from a gender-neutral perspective.

While the second article is primarily concerned with paving the way for internal Islamic legal reform, the third article is focused primarily on demonstrating how classical Islamic family law—or certain versions of it—meets minimum requirements of gender equality to satisfy Rawlsian standards of a just family. The article explains that Rawls' conception of the family permits a degree of pluralism in the internal organization of the family, including the possibility for families based on gender hierarchy that is "voluntary." It then gives an overview of salient doctrines of Islamic family law, comparing and contrasting Ḥanafī and Mālikī positions on questions of particular concern to liberal family law. It also discusses pluralism in the family from an Islamic perspective, identifying different vectors of Islamic family law pluralism: pluralism between Muslim and non-Muslim conceptions of marriage; intra-Muslim pluralism regarding the rights and obligations of the parties to a marriage contract; idiosyncratic demands of Muslims as manifested in bargained-for terms in their individual marriage contracts; and, pious motivations that might be relatively indifferent to viewing marriage solely as a legal institution. It concludes with the argument that Islamic marriage contracts ought to be fully justiciable in the context of liberal family laws that permit a wide range of privately negotiated marital contracts, and that Islamic arbitration of such contracts is an ideal institution for regulating Muslim family disputes from the perspective of political liberalism.

The last article is an excerpt from a coauthored piece that deals with adoption in classical Rabbinic, Canon and Islamic law. My contribution to the article deals with the rights of children and parents in classical Islamic law by exploring Islamic law's prohibition of adoption. It explores these questions in connection with the Islamic institution of fosterage—*kafāla*—and argues that Islamic law's particular rules regarding the rights of parents and children exhibits a tension between safeguarding the interests of the child (*maṣlaḥat al-ṭifl*) and viewing the parent's obligations toward the child through the lens of a central principle of commercial law, that the right to profit is incidental to the risk of loss (*al-kharāj bi'l-ḍamān*). The article concludes with suggestions for modifying classical rules about adoption and fosterage in light of modern concerns while giving effect to classical legal values to the extent practicable.

The first article on *ribā*, Ribā, *Efficiency and Prudential Regulation*, gives a doctrinal survey of the most important features of the *ribā* doctrine, and seeks to make clear that it is best understood as a set of doctrines, not a single doctrine, and that it should not be confused with interest, insofar as Islamic law permitted various contracts that include, implicitly at least, an interest charge. The article makes the case that a coherent theory of *ribā* is required in order to place modern Islamic finance on secure jurisprudential footing and save it from the problem of "shariʿa arbitrage," i.e., synthesizing conventional financing contracts through the intermediation of two or more contractual forms recognized as legitimate by classical Islamic law. The article suggests that because *ribā* consists of various doctrines, they should not all be subject to the same level of legal skepticism. Some forms of *ribā*, particularly the form singled out for the Quran's condemnation, should never be tolerated, while other forms specified in Prophetic practice and juristic doctrine admit exceptions based on need. This fact suggests that Islamic law's regulation of these secondary forms of *ribā*—including interest on loans—is prudential rather than categorical, and on that basis, modern Islamic law should be able to incorporate much of conventional finance on a more principled basis rather than using the subterfuges favored by contemporary practitioners of Islamic finance.

The last article in the anthology, *Ethics and Finance*, gives an overview of relevant Islamic law doctrines to questions of modern finance broadly, not just *ribā*. Appealing to different kinds of profit-seeking contracts and altruistic contracts, and precedents for public financing, the article makes the claim that Islamic ethical discourse on questions of finance seeks to distinguish, expressly, profit-seeking domains from altruistic domains, and that it does not, as a legal matter, give preference to one or the other. Rather, it affords persons legal means to pursue *both* profit-seeking ends and altruistic ends, but it prohibits persons from comingling these two different kinds of activities. Moreover, the article also makes the case that one of the aims of the rules of Islamic law is to promote efficient use of resources, something that justifies rules encouraging the productive use of savings rather than hoarding, in addition to rules discouraging wasteful investment. The article relies on evidence from Islamic jurisprudence as well as Islamic substantive law to support its positions.

Bibliography

Abou El Fadl, Khaled. *Islam and the Challenge of Democracy.* Edited by Joshua Cohen and Deborah Chasman. Princeton: Princeton University Press, 2004.

———. "Islamic Law and Muslim Minorities: The Juristic Discourse on Muslim Minorities from the Second/Eighth to the Eleventh/Seventeenth Centuries." *Islamic Law and Society* 1, no. 2 (1994): 141–87. https://doi.org/10.2307/3399332.

———. *The Search for Beauty in Islam: A Conference of the Books.* Lanham, Md: Rowman & Littlefield, 2006.

———. *Speaking in God's Name: Islamic Law, Authority and Women.* Oxford: Oneworld, 2001.

Adem, Rodrigo. "Classical Naṣṣ Doctrines in Imāmī Shīʿism: On the Usage of an Expository Term." *Shii Studies Review* 1, no. 1–2 (2017): 42–71. https://doi.org/10.1163/24682470-12340002.

Ali, Kecia. *Marriage and Slavery in Early Islam.* Cambridge: Harvard University Press, 2010.

Anjum, Ovamir. *Politics, Law and Community in Islamic Thought: The Taymiyyan Moment.* Cambridge Studies in Islamic Civilization. Cambridge: Cambridge University Press, 2012.

Asad, Talal. *Formations of the Secular: Christianity, Islam, Modernity.* Cultural Memory in the Present. Stanford: Stanford University Press, 2003.

Ayoub, Samy. *Law, Empire, and the Sultan: Ottoman Imperial Authority and Late Ḥanafī Jurisprudence.* Oxford Islamic Legal Studies. New York: Oxford University Press, 2020.

Azam, Hina. *Sexual Violation in Islamic Law: Substance, Evidence, and Procedure.* Cambridge Studies in Islamic Civilization. Cambridge: Cambridge University Press, 2015. https://doi.org/10.1017/CBO9781316145722.

Bājī, Sulaymān ibn Khalaf. *Kitāb al-muntaqā sharḥ Muwāṭṭa' Imām dār al-hijrah sayyidinā Mālik ibn Anas.* 7 vols. Beirut: Dār al-Kitāb al-ʿArabī, 1979.

Beiner, Ronald. *Civil Religion: A Dialogue in the History of Political Philosophy.* Cambridge: Cambridge University Press, 2011.

Benard, Cheryl. *Civil Democratic Islam: Partners, Resources, and Strategies*. Santa Monica, CA: RAND, National Security Research Division, 2003.

Cook, Michael. *Commanding Right and Forbidding Wrong in Islamic Thought*. Cambridge: Cambridge Edinburgh University Press, 2000.

Coulson, Noel. *A History of Islamic Law*. The New Edinburgh Islamic Surveys : NEIS. Edinburgh: University Press, 2022. https://doi.org/10.1515/9781474465892.

Daniel Pollack, Moshe Bleich, Charles J Reid Jr, and Mohammad H Fadel. "Classical Religious Perspectives of Adoption Law." *The Notre Dame Law Review* 79, no. 2 (2004): 693–753.

Dardīr, Aḥmad ibn Muḥammad, and Aḥmad ibn Muḥammad Ṣāwī. *Al-Sharḥ al-Ṣaghīr ʿalā Aqrab al-Masālik Ilā Madhhab al-Imām Mālik Wa Bi'l-Hāmish Ḥāshiyat al-Shaykh Aḥmad b. Muḥammad al-Ṣāwī al-Mālikī*. Edited by Muṣtafā Kamāl Waṣfī. Miṣr: Dār al-Maʿārif, 1972.

Easterbrook, Frank H. "What Does Legislative History Tell Us?" *Chicago-Kent Law Review* 66, no. 2 (1990): 441–50.

Fadel, Mohammad. "Adjudication in the Maliki Madhhab: A Study of Legal Process in Medieval Islamic Law." ProQuest Dissertations Publishing, 1995. https://search.proquest.com/docview/304244838?pq-origsite=primo

——. "Ibn Farḥūn." *Encyclopaedia of Islam, THREE*, January 1, 2018. https://referenceworks.brillonline.com/entries/encyclopaedia-of-islam-3/ibn-farhun-COM_30773?lang=en

——. "State and Sharia." In *The Ashgate Research Companion to Islamic Law*, edited by Rudolph Peters and P. J. Bearman, 93–107. Ashgate Research Companion. Farnham, Surrey: Ashgate, 2014.

——. "A Tragedy of Politics or an Apolitical Tragedy?" *Journal of the American Oriental Society* 131, no. 1 (2011): 109–27.

Farahat, Omar. "Reason-Giving and the Duty to Obey: Perspectives from Classical Islamic Jurisprudence." *The Journal of Law and Religion* 36, no. 1 (2021): 5–28. https://doi.org/10.1017/jlr.2020.52.

Ghazālī. *The Book of Knowledge: Being a Translation with Notes of the Kitab al-ʿIlm of al-Ghazzali's Ihya' ʿUlum al-Din*. Lahore: Ashraf, 1962.

——. *Iḥyāʾ ʿulūm al-dīn*. 4th ed. Beirut: Dār al-Kutub al-ʿIlmīyah, 2005.

Hallaq, Wael B. *A History of Islamic Legal Theories: An Introduction to Sunnī Uṣūl al-Fiqh*. Cambridge: Cambridge University Press, 1997.

——. *Sharīʿa: Theory, Practice, Transformations*. Cambridge: Cambridge University Press, 2009.

——. "Was the Gate of Ijtihad Closed?" *International Journal of Middle East Studies* 16, no. 1 (1984): 3–41. https://doi.org/10.1017/S0020743800027598.

Ḥaṭṭāb, Muḥammad ibn Muḥammad, Khalīl ibn Isḥāq al-Jundī, and Muḥammad ibn Yūsuf Mawwāq. *Mawāhib al-Jalīl li-sharḥ Mukhtaṣar Khalīl*. 3rd ed. 6 vols. Beirut: Dār al-Fikr, 1992.

Ibn al-Humām, Muḥammad ibn ʿAbd al-Wāḥid, ʿAlī ibn Abī Bakr Marghīnānī, Muḥammad ibn Maḥmūd Bābartī, Aḥmad Qāḍī Zādah, and Saʿd Allāh ibn ʿIsā Saʿdī Chalabī. *Sharḥ Fatḥ al-qadīr*. 10 vols. Cairo: Muṣṭafā al-Bābī al-Ḥalabī, 1972.

Ibn Farḥūn, Ibrāhīm ibn ʿAlī. *Tabsirat Al-Ḥukkām Fī Usūl al-Aqḍīyah ... Wa-Manāhij al-Aḥkām*. Edited by Ṭāhā ʿAbd al-Raʾūf Saʿd. 2 vols. Cairo: Maktabat al-Kulliyyāt al-Azhariyya, 1986.

Ibn Nujaym, ʿUmar ibn Ibrāhīm. *al-Nahr al-fāʾiq: sharḥ Kanz al-daqāʾiq*. Edited by Aḥmad ʿIzzū ʿInāya. Beirut: Dār al-Kutub al-ʿIlmiyya, 2002.

Ibn Rajab, ʿAbd al-Raḥmān ibn Aḥmad. *Jāmiʿ al-ʾulūm wa-al-ḥikam*. Edited by Muḥammad al-Aḥmadī Abū al-Nūr. Cairo: Maṭābiʾ al-Ahrām al-tijāriyya, 1969.

Jackson, Sherman A. *Islamic Law and the State: The Constitutional Jurisprudence of Shihāb al-Dīn al-Qarāfī*. Studies in Islamic Law and Society 1. Leiden: Brill, 1996.

Johansen, Baber. *Contingency in a Sacred Law: Legal and Ethical Norms in the Muslim fiqh*. Studies in Islamic law and society 7. Leiden: Brill, 1999.

——. *The Islamic Law on Land Tax and Rent: The Peasants' Loss of Property Rights under the Hanafite Doctrine*. Exeter Arabic and Islamic Series. London: Croom Helm, 1988.

——. "The Valorization of the Human Body in Muslim Sunni Law." *Princeton Papers: Interdisciplinary Journal of Middle Eastern Studies* 4 (1996): 77–112.

Kāsānī, Abū Bakr ibn Mas'ūd. *Kitāb badā'i' al-ṣanā'i' fī tartīb al-sharā'i'*. 2nd ed. 7 vols. Beirut: Dar al-Kutub al-'Ilmiyya, 1986.

Katz, Marion Holmes. *Wives and Work: Islamic Law and Ethics before Modernity*. New York: Columbia University Press, 2022.

Lilla, Mark. "The Politics of God." *The New York Times*, August 19, 2007, sec. Magazine. https://www.nytimes.com/2007/08/19/magazine/19Religion-t.html.

——. *The Stillborn God: Religion, Politics, and the Modern West*. New York: Vintage Books, 2008.

Mahmood, Saba. "Secularism, Hermeneutics, and Empire: The Politics of Islamic Reformation." *Public Culture* 18, no. 2 (2006): 323–47. https://doi.org/10.1215/08992363-2006-006.

Mālik ibn Anas. *Al-Muwaṭṭa': The Recension of Yaḥyā b. Yaḥyā al-Laythī (d. 234/848)*. Translated by Mohammad H. Fadel and Connell Monette. Harvard Series in Islamic Law 8. Cambridge: Program in Islamic Law, Harvard Law School, 2019.

Messick, Brinkley Morris. *The Calligraphic State: Textual Domination and History in a Muslim Society / Brinkley Messick*. Comparative Studies on Muslim Societies 16. Berkeley: University of California Press, 1993.

Mir-Hosseini, Ziba, Kari Vogt, Lena Larsen, and Christian Moe, eds. *Gender and Equality in Muslim Family Law: Justice and Ethics in the Islamic Legal Tradition*. Library of Islamic Law 5. London: I.B. Tauris, 2013.

Powers, David Stephan. *Law, Society, and Culture in the Maghrib, 1300–1500*. Cambridge Studies in Islamic Civilization. New York: Cambridge University Press, 2002.

Rawls, John. *Political Liberalism*. John Dewey Essays in Philosophy 4. New York: Columbia University Press, 1993.

——. *A Theory of Justice*. Harvard Paperback. Cambridge: Belknap Press of Harvard University Press, 1971.

Rosen, Mark D. "The Outer Limits of Community Self-Governance in Residential Associations, Municipalities, and Indian Country: A Liberal Theory." *Virginia Law Review* 84, no. 6 (1998): 1053–1144. https://doi.org/10.2307/1073695.

Sanhūrī, 'Abd al-Razzāq Aḥmad. *Maṣādir al-ḥaqq fī al-fiqh al-Islāmī: dirāsa muqarana bi-al-fiqh al-gharbī*. Beirut: Dār al-Fikr, 1953.

Schacht, Joseph. *Introduction to Islamic Law*. Oxford: Clarendon, 1964.

Shapiro, Scott. *Legality*. Cambridge: Belknap Press of Harvard University Press, 2011.

Solan, Lawrence M. "Private Language, Public Laws: The Central Role of Legislative Intent in Statutory Interpretation." *The Georgetown Law Journal* 93, no. 2 (2005): 427–86.

Strauss, David A. "'Statutes' Domains' and Judges' Prerogatives." *The University of Chicago Law Review* 77 (2010): 1261–74.

Wakin, Jeanette. "Interpretation of the Divine Command in the Jurisprudence of Muwaffaq Al-Dīn Ibn Qudāmah." In *Islamic Law and Jurisprudence*, edited by Nicholas Heer and Farhat Ziadeh. Seattle: University of Washington Press, 1990.

Weiss, Bernard G. *The Search for God's Law: Islamic Jurisprudence in the Writings of Sayf al-Din al-Amidi.* Salt Lake City: University of Utah Press, 1992.

Zysow, Aron. *The Economy of Certainty: An Introduction to the Typology of Islamic Legal Theory*. Resources in Arabic and Islamic Studies 2. Atlanta: Lockwood, 2013.

"المسألة الثامنة / علم القاضي هل هو من وسائل الإثبات في باب القضاء كالبيّنة / كتاب القضاء للسيد الخوئي (قده) – مدرسة الفقاهة." https://www.eshia.ir/feqh/archive/text/alerazi/feqh/32/330202/.

Islamic Law and the State

1
NATURE, REVELATION AND THE STATE IN PRE-MODERN SUNNI THEOLOGICAL, LEGAL AND POLITICAL THOUGHT

Mohammad Fadel

INTRODUCTION

[271] The pre-modern Islamic theological, legal and political tradition—understood for purposes of this paper as the period between the 9th and 18th centuries—represents a complex synthesis of pre-Islamic Arabian, Near Eastern, Central Asian and Hellenistic traditions with the revelation given to Muhammad ibn ʿAbd Allāh (d. 632) in seventh century Western Arabia. The Islamic tradition, therefore, is multifaceted, incorporating ancient Greek and Hellenistic philosophy, pre-Islamic Near Eastern wisdom traditions, the heroic values of Arabian paganism, and notions of divine kingship found in Turko-Iranian Central Asian traditions. This synthesis manifested itself in numerous literary genres, including, speculative philosophy (*falsafa*) in the ancient Greek and Hellenistic traditions, rationalist theology (*kalām*), traditionalist theology (*ʿaqīda*) and law (*fiqh*), and belle-lettres (*adab*), each of which offered a distinctive point of view on questions of nature, revelation, law and the state. It would be an error, moreover, to assume that impermeable barriers separated these various disciplines and approaches to understanding the world. Not only were many Muslim authors polymaths, and therefore composed works in several of these traditions, but there can be little doubt that the views expressed, and the tastes developed, in these various domains regularly crossed the self-defined boundaries of their respective genres and intruded into the domains of others, if only because pre-modern Muslim intellectuals would have had at least some exposure to these vari-

This article was originally published in *The Muslim World*, vol. 106, no. 2, Apr. 2016, pp. 271–290.

I would like to thank Professors Afifi al-Akiti and Joshua Hordern for inviting me to participate in this project of *New Conversations in Islamic and Christian Political Thought*, and for Professor al-Akiti's tireless work in editing my contributions. I would also like to thank the other participants for the lively exchange of ideas and spirit of intellectual fellowship that prevailed in both Oxford and Cambridge.

ous different traditions, all of which, one way or another, contributed, even if in varying degrees, to the formation of an 'Islamic' *weltanschauung*.[1]

[272] It goes without saying, therefore, that it would be impossible to provide an exhaustive survey of the Islamic tradition with respect to perspectives regarding nature, revelation and the state; moreover, it would be absurd to attempt to reduce the pluralism of the Islamic tradition on these questions to one *Islamic* position on nature, revelation and the state. Accordingly, this paper will limit itself to the Sunni theological and legal traditions on these matters, with the caveat that even with this qualification there is the real risk of obscuring the richness and diversity of thought on these questions within the Sunni theological and legal traditions. Nevertheless, I will focus on the idea of divine law and its relationship to nature as articulated by the majority of Sunni Muslim theologians in the discipline of theological ethics (*uṣūl al-fiqh*) and Sunni positive law (*fiqh*), and the Sunni conception of the state, the outlines of which, I argue, can be discovered through a careful reading of various doctrines of Sunni positive law. This paper's relatively narrow focus on law stands in sharp contrast to the papers of my interlocutors and fellow contributors, Joan Lockwood O'Donovan and Russell Hittinger, whose papers,[2] despite their differences, both seem to share a certain regret at the increasing turn toward legalism in Christian theology as a result of the transition to modernity. The prominence of a legal approach to ethics in the Islamic tradition from its earliest days, as well as the post-Enlightenment Christian tradition, may perhaps offer an interesting window into considering the long-term developments of Abrahamic traditions as they evolved out of late Antiquity, through the Middle Ages and into modernity, but weaving together such a narrative is too ambitious for this paper.[3] At the same time, the kind of integration between law, theology and philosophy suggested by the papers of Joan Lockwood O'Donovan and

1. The great Shāfiʿī authors, al-Māwardī (d. 1058) and al-Ghazālī (d. 1111), as well as the Mālikī jurist and philosopher, Ibn Rushd (d. 1198; Lat. Averroes), are exemplars of the broad range of interests that preoccupied medieval Muslim intellectuals. Al-Māwardī, for example, although known primarily as a Shāfiʿī jurist, also wrote an important work on ethics from a secular perspective, *Adab al-dunyā wa-l-dīn* [Ethics of Secular and Religious Life], as well as works on political ethics from the Iranian mirror of princes tradition. Al-Ghazālī, too, wrote numerous philosophical, theological and mystic works as well as works of law. Averroes, although known primarily in the Latin West in his role as a commentator on Aristotle, was also a prominent Mālikī jurist in his own right, authoring an important treatise of comparative law, *Bidāyat al-mujtahid wa-nihāyat al-muqtaṣid*, and in legal theory and theology, *al-Kashf ʿan manāhij al-adilla.*

2. Joan Lockwood O'Donovan, 'Law and Moral Community in Pre-Modern Christian Thought: Continuity and Discontinuity in the Western Tradition', *The Muslim World*, 106:2 (2016): 291–305; F. Russell Hittinger, 'Natural Law and Wisdom Traditions', *The Muslim World*, 106:2 (2016): 313–336.

3. On this possibility, see Armando Salvatore, *The Public Sphere: Liberal Modernity, Catholicism, Islam* (New York: Palgrave, 2007), esp. chaps. 3 and 4, where the author argues that medieval Catholicism and Sunni Islam played crucial roles in creating a lay system of public reasoning that paved the way for the formation of the liberal public sphere.

Hittinger as being the natural desideratum of Christianity is not something completely unfamiliar to the Islamic tradition, take, for example works such as *al-Dharīʿa ilā makārim al-sharīʿa* [The Means to Understanding the Virtues of the Revealed Law] of al-Rāghib al-Iṣfahānī (d. 1108 or 1109) or the *Iḥyā' ʿulūm al-dīn* [Reviving the Religious Sciences] of al-Ghazālī (d. 1111), both of which give an account of Islamic ethics from a broader philosophical, indeed, Aristotelian, perspective. Incorporating the ethical, theological and political theories of the Muslim philosophers such as al-Fārābī (d. *ca.* 950), Ibn Sīnā (d. 1037; Lat. Avicenna) and Ibn Rushd (d. 1198; Lat. Averroes), among others, is also, unfortunately, beyond the scope of this article and must be left for another day. But since [273] this article grows out of the desire to initiate 'new conversations' in Islamic and Christian political thought, it is encouraging to know that there remains much ground on which those new conversations can be pursued fruitfully. For now, however, the conversation will be limited to Sunni Muslim conceptions of revealed law, its relationship to nature, and the relationship of revealed law to the state.

SUNNI THEOLOGICAL DEBATES ON THE NATURE OF DIVINE LAW BETWEEN REASON AND REVELATION

While scholars continue to contest many of the details of early Islamic legal history, there is little dispute that Islamic substantive law, *fiqh*, preceded a theoretical account of the origins of the law. The discipline that attempts to account for the law's origins is known as *uṣūl al-fiqh*, literally, the 'foundations of understanding'. It is useful to dwell, if only for a moment, on the literal meaning of this term, itself a compound noun. The second noun, *fiqh*, although it came to designate 'law', literally means 'understanding', and it is that sense which the Qur'an uses when it rhetorically asks, 'What ails those people? They scarcely comprehend (*yafqahūna*) even a single statement!',[4] and when it says 'We have certainly prepared Hell for many of the jinn and human-kind; they have hearts but do not use them to understand (*yafqahūn*)'.[5] The word *uṣūl*, on the other hand, is a plural of the noun *aṣl*, which means 'origin', or 'root', or in the case of a tree, its 'trunk', as compared to its branches, which in Arabic is *furūʿ* (sing. *farʿ*). The compound noun *uṣūl al-fiqh*, therefore, refers to how we come to understand divine law, it being understood that our 'understanding', our *fiqh* of divine law, is a product of a certain approach to understanding. The method which we use to understand divine law constitutes our *uṣūl*, the roots of the law, while the conclusions reached by the good faith application of our method of inquiry are merely the 'branches' that grow out of these methodological principles.

4. Qur'an 4:78 (al-Nisāʾ): *fa-mā li-hāʾulāʾi al-qawmi lā yakādūna yafqahūna ḥadīthan.*

5. Qur'an 7:179 (al-Aʿrāf): *wa la-qad dharaʾnā li-jahannama kathīran min al-jinni wa-l-insi la-hum qulūbun lā yafqahūna bi-hā.*

Although the branches are derivative in this metaphor, it is the branches which represent the actual rules regulating the behavior of Muslims, individually, and collectively.

The other crucial point is that 'understanding' from the Qur'anic perspective is subjective: it takes place at the level of each individual, and the goal of revelation is to produce individuals whose hearts 'understand' revelation. This subjective perspective on law in turn manifests itself in the Muslim jurists' definition of *fiqh* as knowledge of how the divine lawgiver judges the actions of those subject to the law (*mukallafūn*).[6] It is therefore a theological conception of the law insofar as its primary concern is understanding how God judges human action; it is only secondarily concerned with law in the [274] sense of regulating human conduct from the perspective of what is good for humans from a human perspective, although as we shall see, Muslim jurisprudence developed theories whereby there was a presumed identity between what God demanded of humans and what the actual good of humans as humans is. But, the main point is that the 'understanding' which is the desideratum of Muslim legal inquiry is not, in the first instance, an 'understanding' of what humans should want considered solely as humans, but rather what humans should want from the perspective of humans as servants of God. It is therefore a theocentric conception of law and ethics. *Uṣūl al-fiqh*, meanwhile, is primarily the meta-theory that governs our inquiry into our understanding of divine law, from whence it can be discovered, the tools of reasoning that can be used in interpreting its material sources, to the extent reasoning on such matters is permitted, and determining who is qualified to engage in such reasoning.[7]

In this context, we are interested in the extent to which Sunni theologians understood nature to be an independent source of knowledge of divine law. Muslim jurists took up this issue largely in connection with their answers to two highly-contested questions. The first question was the status of human actions before the advent of revelation (*ḥukm al-ashyāʾ qabla wurūd al-sharʿ*), and the second was whether pure reason could determine the essential goodness or evilness of actions (*al-taḥsīn wa-l-taqbīḥ al-ʿaqliyyayn*).[8] Oversimplifying, Sunni Muslim jurists and theologians divided into two camps on these questions, largely as a result of the extent to which they believed that moral knowledge was generated exclusively through divine revelation or whether reason was also a source of moral knowledge. The Ashʿarīs generally affirmed that revelation was the exclusive

6. Accordingly, al-Ghazālī defines *fiqh* as 'an expression for the knowledge of the established revelatory rules governing actions of persons with moral capacity (*ʿibāra ʿan al-ʿilm bi-l-aḥkām al-sharʿiyya al-thābita li-afʿāl al-mukallafīn*); al-Ghazālī, *al-Mustaṣfā* (Beirut: *Dār al-Kutub al-ʿIlmiyya*, 1993), 5.

7. Al-Ghazālī defines *uṣūl al-fiqh* as 'an expression of the proofs of these rules [of *fiqh*] and knowledge of how they indicate the particular rules [as a matter of inference] as a general matter, not in their particulars (*ʿibāra ʿan adillat hādhihī al-aḥkām wa ʿan maʿrifat wujūh dalālatihā ʿalā l-aḥkām*); al-Ghazālī, *Mustaṣfā*, 5.

8. For a good overview of the main features of this debate, along with translations of important texts in the debate, see Kevin Reinhart, *Before Revelation* (Albany, NY: State Univ. of New York Press, 1995).

source of moral knowledge, while the Muʿtazilīs took the view that pure reason was a source of at least *some* moral knowledge. If a jurist or theologian was a Muʿtazilī, or sympathetic to some Muʿtazilī ethical doctrines, he would be likely to affirm the proposition that even prior to the advent of revelation, human beings could adopt a presumption that their actions were morally permissible (*ibāḥa*), at least where no apparent harm would ensue as a result of the conduct, and that human beings were subject to at least *some* moral obligations for which they could be fairly accountable before God, such as the obligation to thank a benefactor, to save a drowning person from death, and the sinfulness of oppression.[9] Ashʿarīs, on the other hand, or those sympathetic to them, took the position that before the advent of revelation, human action was not governed [275] by any norm of divine law (*lā ḥukm*), and moreover, that pure reason is incapable of making true judgments regarding good and evil, and therefore, no obligation under divine law exists prior to revelation's communication of such obligations.[10]

We should not, however, exaggerate the differences in these ethical theories, nor misunderstand what was at stake. Both sets of theologians were concerned primarily with knowledge of the content of divine law. Accordingly, when the Ashʿarīs denied that pure reason could generate knowledge of an obligation, what they had in mind was an obligation toward God. This is clear from Ghazālī's discussion of whether pure reason is sufficient to generate an obligation of gratitude to a benefactor, e.g., God, before revelation, and concludes that it cannot because it is impossible for reason to know whether God desires humans to show gratitude to Him through worship at all.[11]

The general Ashʿarī skepticism of the utility of reason in discovering the content of *divine* law, however, is irrelevant to whether or not they believed reason was also an unreliable guide for *human* law-making. Indeed, there is plenty of evidence that numerous Ashʿarī theologians affirmed the reliability of human reason as a guide to discerning good and evil from a humanistic perspective. For example, the twelfth century Syrian Ashʿarī theologian and Shafiʿī jurist, ʿIzz al-Dīn ibn ʿAbd al-Salām (d. 1262) expressly stated that human reason is generally sufficient to allow humans to discover their own, secular goods, unaided by revelation, and in most cases—at least outside of devotional matters—there will be a happy congruence between what revelation commands and

9. Abū l-Ḥusayn al-Baṣrī (d. 1085) may be taken as a representative figure of the Muʿtazilī position on these matters. See Abū l-Ḥusayn al-Baṣrī, *al-Muʿtamad fī uṣūl al-fiqh*, ed. Khalīl al-Mays (Beirut: Dār al-Kutub al-ʿIlmiyya, 1983), 315–22.

10. Ghazālī may be taken as a representative figure of the Ashʿarī position granting revelation a monopoly of moral knowledge. See, al-Ghazālī, *Mustaṣfā*, 45.

11. Al-Ghazālī, *Mustaṣfā*, 49–50 (pure reason is unable to discern whether God would punish us or reward us for showing gratitude to Him in the form of worship prior to revelation commanding us to do one or the other).

what human reason discovers.[12] The great Central Asian Shafiʿī jurist and theologian, Fakhr al-Dīn al-Rāzī (d. 1209), affirmed reason as grounds for interpersonal obligation, while denying that what reason recognizes as obligatory for human beings necessarily binds God insofar as human beings, *qua* human beings, have objective needs that can't be ignored, while God, because of his omnipotence, has no needs and therefore cannot be limited by rational judgments.[13]

Rāzī's explanation of the relationship of reason to divine law suggests that the medieval debates between Muʿtazilīs and Ashʿarīs were more about divine freedom rather than the reliability or competence of human reason as such in knowing good and evil. The important point is that even from the perspective of Ashʿarīs, human reason was in principle a reliable guide to what constituted good behavior, but one could not trust one's reasoned conclusions in the absence of revelation from God confirming those judgments.

[276] The Ashʿarī critique of Muʿtazilī 'rationalist' ethics is not so much a rejection of rationalism in ethics as it is a criticism of the Muʿtazilīs for making assumptions about the nature of good that themselves could not be justified on the basis of pure reason. Revelation, according to the Ashʿarīs, itself provides the basis for believing that our rational understanding of good and evil—when confirmed by revelation—provides a reliable basis for human understanding of divine law. The perceived congruence between reason and revelation, however, is not a matter of rational necessity, but by virtue of divine grace (*faḍl*). Having come to the conclusion that reason was potentially a reliable tool in discovering divine law, and with revelation's actual negation of the doubts that pure reason would have regarding its ability to know divine law, Ashʿarī theologians, beginning as early as Ghazālī, if not earlier, set about understanding divine law as *though* it were consistent with the conclusions of natural reason, and so articulated a theory of revelation that argued that divine law, as an empirical matter, confirmed by a thorough induction of revelation, furthered five universal ends (*al-Maqāṣid al-kulliyya*): the protection of religion (*dīn*), life (*ḥayāt*), property (*māl*), progeny (*nasl*) and mind (*ʿaql*).

They also argued that these five universal ends of revealed law were not particular to Islamic law, but were characteristic of all the pre-Islamic revealed laws and represented values that were also held in common with Greek philosophy (*falsafa*). Differences found among various cases of revealed law as well as differences between revealed law generally and philosophy was primarily the result of different weightings of the same goods rather than representing categorical incommensurability.[14] The most systematic articu-

12. ʿIzz al-Dīn ibn ʿAbd al-Salām, *Qawāʿid al-aḥkām fī maṣāliḥ al-anām*, 2 vols. (Beirut: *Dār al-Maʿrifa*, 1968), 1:4.

13. Fakhr al-Dīn al-Rāzī, *Mafātīḥ al-ghayb*, 32 vols. (Cairo: al-Maṭbaʿa al-Bahiyya al-Miṣriyya, 1934–62) 20:174.

14. Mohammad Fadel, 'The True, the Good and the Reasonable', *Canadian Journal of Law and Jurispru-*

lation of the *Maqāṣid* understanding of revealed law and how we humans are to understand it rationally comes in the work of the eminent Andalusian Muslim jurist, al-Shāṭibī (d. 1388) as articulated in his work of theoretical jurisprudence, *al-Muwāfaqāt*.[15] The theory of revealed law's universal ends in turn has been taken up eagerly in the modern era by Muslim reformers who seek to use the meta-theory of *Maqāṣid* to justify various reforms of Islamic substantive law that go beyond the historical doctrines of Islamic law.[16]

THEORETICAL JURISPRUDENCE AND THE PROBLEM OF LEGAL INDETERMINACY

Muslim theology, over its long history, sought a synthesis between a conception of law that was revealed in a more or less determinate body of texts, on the one hand, and a conception of law that was consistent with the conclusions of natural reason, on the [277] other. This did not mean, however, that all important issues were resolved. Indeed, their shared conception of divine law—whether it was contained exclusively in revealed texts, as in the Ashᶜarī conception, or whether reason's conclusions operated in an independent and complementary fashion to revealed texts, as in the Muᶜtazilī conception—required careful attention to the words of revelation. I am aware of no Muslim theologian, for example, that claimed that the results of natural reasoning could abrogate an express command of revelation. Accordingly, whether a jurist was sympathetic to the Ashᶜarī or Muᶜtazilī understanding of the relationship of nature to divine law, all Muslim jurists agreed that texts were an indispensable source for understanding the content of divine law. From this perspective, therefore, it is unsurprising that much of *uṣūl al-fiqh* is concerned with questions of epistemology, both as a general matter, and with the specific problem of how to obtain knowledge of divine law. Another shared assumption which was crucial to the subsequent development of *uṣūl al-fiqh* was that the texts of revelation were not themselves divine law, but rather served as *evidence* (*adilla*; sing. *dalīl*) of the content of divine law, and accordingly, the detailed content of divine law inevitably required the use of human inference and reasoning (*istidlāl*).

Generic accounts of *uṣūl al-fiqh* often present it as little more than the so-called four source theory, namely, that Muslim jurists recognized four material sources from which divine law might be discovered: the Qur'an; the normative practice of the Prophet Muhammad, known as the *sunna*; consensus, known as *ijmāᶜ*; and finally, analogy, known

dence 5 (2008): 55–6. For a detailed treatment of the various theories articulated by medieval Muslim jurists that sought to reconcile revelation with reason, see Anver Emon, *Islamic Natural Law Theories* (New York: Oxford University Press, 2010).

15. Al-Shāṭibī, *al-Muwāfaqāt fī uṣūl al-sharīᶜa*, ed. ᶜAbdallāh Dirāz, 4 vols. (Beirut: *Dār al-Maᶜrifa*, 1975).

16. For an overview of the place of the *maqāṣid* in the reasoning of modern Muslim reformers, see Andrew March, 'Theocrats Living Under Secular Law: An External Engagement with Islamic Legal Theory', *Journal of Political Philosophy* 19:1 (2011): 34–8.

as *qiyās*. But reducing *uṣūl al-fiqh* to the 'four source' theory not only reduces this discipline to a question of what are the material sources of divine law, it also is misleading insofar as it fails to identify the more controversial and substantive debates found in *uṣūl al-fiqh* related to questions such as the nature of language, hermeneutics, how the material sources themselves are defined, how they are to be weighed in the event of conflict, who is authorized to derive judgments regarding the content of divine law, and what is the epistemological/theological/ontological status of such judgments, on the assumption that human judgment is an admissible procedure for understanding and deriving divine law from revelation in the first place. Behind the superficial agreement among Sunnis to consider these four material sources as containing indicants of divine law lay substantial disagreement on nearly all these other questions.

As a practical matter, while Sunni jurists were in broad agreement as to the admissibility of the so-called 'four sources' in legal reasoning, what constituted normative Prophetic practice, how consensus ought to be defined, and what kinds of analogy, to say nothing of when analogy was admissible, were matters of deep and abiding controversy. The only material source that was non-controversial was the first source, the Qur'an, but although there was no controversy as to the contents of the Qur'an, nor any doubts that it had been reliably transmitted over time from the Prophet Muhammad to the present day, there were substantial disagreements as to how its legal provisions (which themselves constituted only a small part of its text) should be understood. These deep methodological disagreements no doubt were significant in producing the epistemological bent of *uṣūl al-fiqh*. The epistemological focus of *uṣūl al-fiqh* is reflected in the juristic [278] taxonomy of indicants of divine law in relation to two variables: historical certainty with respect to its attribution to the Lawgiver (*thubūt*), and interpretive certainty with respect to the Lawgiver's intended meaning (*dalāla*).

Accordingly, any jurist who attempts to use a text as evidence for a particular rule of divine law had first to establish, as a historical matter, that the text in question could be appropriately attributed to the Lawgiver. This was not problematic with respect to the Qur'an according to Muslim jurists because of the fact that its text reached us through such a large and widely-dispersed number of individuals that it was inconceivable that the unity of the text they transmitted could be explained either as a coincidence or a conspiracy. The only explanation for the observed unity of the Qur'anic text was that it had a single source, specifically, the Prophet Muhammad. Muslim jurists referred to any historical report that met the prerequisites of widespread and concurrent historical transmission as *mutawātir* and believed that it produced certain knowledge of past events (with *tawātur* referring to the concept of widespread and concurrent transmission).

Aside from the Qur'an, however, no other texts containing indicants of the divine law could satisfy this requirement. Historical reports about the Prophet's teachings and practices could only be known by the transmissions of particular individuals. For that reason, Muslim jurists referred to these reports as 'reports of individuals' (*āḥād*; sing. *aḥad*). These individual reports could not be guaranteed either to be free from error or even not to be products of outright fabrication. Accordingly, a recipient of a report was under an obligation to investigate the likelihood that its claimed attribution to the Prophet Muhammad was reasonable before it would be admissible as an indicant of divine law. While Muslim scholars by the third Islamic century (ninth century CE) developed critical techniques intended to sort reliable reports from those that were not, jurists insisted that because of the mode of the transmission of these reports, individual reports could never claim more than a *probable* attribution to the Lawgiver, even in the best of circumstances. Accordingly, the particular texts documenting the historical teachings of the Prophet Muhammad could only produce a probable opinion (*ẓann*) regarding the content of divine law, even in cases where the purported teachings found in the report are themselves textually clear. Consensus, although in theory an infallible source of knowledge regarding the content of divine law, suffered from conceptual ambiguities, and because it was essentially a claim about the past, claims of consensus were always subject to doubt regarding the veracity of the claim.[17]

Disputes regarding the veracity of the attribution of various reports to the Prophet Muhammad or the occurrence of consensus played an important role in generating controversy among Muslim jurists about the content of divine law. Just as important, however, were disputes as to the meaning of various revealed texts. In other words, jurists might agree that a particular text was validly attributed to the Prophet Muhammad, but [279] they might nevertheless derive different legal inferences from the reported statement or practice.[18] Interpretive disputes among the jurists could be a product of numerous factors, such as differing hermeneutical understandings of the text, or the extent to which extra-textual circumstances should be taken into account in understanding the text. Out of a recognition that jurists in good faith could come to different legal conclusions about the meanings of texts held in common, or about which sources of divine law should be considered dispositive on particular issues, Sunni jurists distinguished between rules based on the considered opinion (*ẓann*) of a qualified jurist (*mujtahid*), and those rules that were known of necessity to be constitutive of divine law and therefore were not dependent on the reasoning of specialized interpreters. Jurists referred to such rules using various names, such as 'that which is known to be part of the law by necessity (*al-maʿlūm min al-dīn bi-l-ḍarūra*)', or 'conclusive rules (*aḥkām qaṭʿiyya*)', to contrast them from the speculative rules developed by the jurists through legal reasoning.

Accordingly, the epistemological strength of a particular rule was a function of two different variables, one historical and the other interpretive. A text could be definitive in terms of its attribution to the Lawgiver, in which case it would be referred to as having certainty with respect to attribution (*qaṭʿī al-thubūt*), or its attribution to the Lawgiver

17. For an overview of the doctrine of consensus, see Wael Hallaq, 'On the Authoritativeness of Sunni Consensus', *International Journal of Middle East Studies* 18:4 (1986): 427–54.

18. See, for example, Fadel, 'The True, the Good and the Reasonable', 59–60.

could be probable (*ẓannī*). Otherwise, its attribution to the Lawgiver might be considered improbable (*ḍaʿīf*), or without basis, i.e., forged (*mawḍūʿ*). As a general rule, the contents of divine law could only be derived from texts whose historical attribution to the Lawgiver were either certain or probable. Texts were also divided semantically in accordance with the clarity or ambiguity of their meaning. Accordingly, a text that bore no semantic ambiguity was referred to as certain with respect to its meaning (*qaṭʿī al-dalāla*), while texts which communicated a likely meaning, but also conveyed a secondary possible intent were referred to as probable with respect to its meaning (*ẓannī al-dalāla*). Only if a text were certain with respect to both variables could one conclude that the rule produced was itself certain. Otherwise, the rule only represented a *probable* determination of the content of divine law.

Most rules of Islamic law, as a result, could only claim to be probable rulings, at least according to the Sunnis. Equally important in this context, however, was that because these derivative rules were merely probable, they were also non-uniform, insofar as different jurists arrived at different conclusions regarding the content of divine law as applied to specific cases. The willingness of Sunnis to countenance probable conclusions as valid expressions of the content of divine law, combined with a plurality of qualified legal interpreters (*mujtahid*), eventually produced a system of normative pluralism, whereby these different conceptions of divine law—which could often substantially conflict on derivative matters (derivative at least from the perspective of theology)—existed side by side in a system of mutual recognition that can be accurately characterized as normative pluralism. It was a pluralistic conception of divine law simply by virtue of the [280] fact that numerous competing opinions existed at any time; this system of pluralism was normative because it was inherent to the entire project of Islamic law conceived of as a project of human interpretation of divine revelation that did not allow for any living human being, after the death of the Prophet Muhammad, to claim direct access to divine law. While Sunni jurists were divided as to whether a single correct rule corresponding to the actual content of divine law existed for all cases, such that only one of the expressed opinions of the jurists was correct and the others wrong, they agreed that even on the assumption that only one of the different opinions of the jurists could be the correct opinion, it was impossible to know which of the various opinions was the correct one. They also agreed that those jurists who were mistaken were not only *not* morally culpable for their good faith error, but that they would also be positively rewarded on the basis of their good-faith, but mistaken, effort to discover God's rule for the case.[19]

19. Muslim jurists are divided on this question into two camps. Those who held that there was a single correct legal rule for each case and that all other opinions were erroneous conceptions of divine law were known as *al-mukhaṭṭiʾa*. The second group of jurists, known as *al-muṣawwiba*, opined that in the absence of an express rule found in revelation, Muslims were subject to a meta-ethical norm to exercise judgment in good faith (*ijtihād*) to determine the status of the indeterminate act in light of what was

While Sunnis believed that acting in conformity with a probable conception of divine law, at least from the perspective of a morally-competent individual, was sufficient to live a morally acceptable life before God, it meant that, from a political perspective, divine law, on its own, could not serve as a basis for adjudicating most quotidian disputes, at least in circumstances where disputants had a good faith basis for believing that they were each acting in conformity with divine law. This pluralistic conception of divine law as it applied to practical matters of secular life no doubt gave great impetus for Muslim jurists to theorize the role of a state as prerequisite for rendering divine law an effective tool of social governance. I now turn to this topic.

THE PLACE OF THE STATE IN SUNNI CONCEPTIONS OF DIVINE LAW

From a theological perspective, the diverse answers that Muslim jurists gave to quotidian legal questions, such as the formulas that were used to initiate various civil transactions, or to contract or dissolve marriages, were all equally plausible conceptions of divine law, and accordingly, individuals were morally entitled to act on the basis of such opinions from a religious perspective. But what would happen if there were an interaction between two individuals with contrasting, and in that particular case, incompatible conceptions of divine law? Ghazālī for example, gives the hypothetical of a husband [281] and wife, each of whom is a qualified independent interpreter of the law, who disagree as to whether a certain utterance made by the husband constitutes a binding expression of divorce. Because both the husband and wife are each qualified interpreters of revelation, they are morally obliged to follow the results of their own reasoning, but in following the meta-ethical principle that applies in areas where revelation fails to provide an express rule, the two are at loggerheads: the husband insists she is his wife, while the wife insists she is now divorced. It is impossible to reconcile these two views because, unlike a contract dispute, for example, the wife cannot simply compromise her claim, for to do so would cause her, from her perspective, to be engaged in illicit cohabitation.

The solution, Ghazālī tells us, is that they must submit their dispute to a judge (*qāḍī*), and the judge's interpretation of the law becomes binding on them both.[20] Ghazālī's solution—adopt the reasoning of the judge—raises its own problems, among them, how is it possible that a ruling of the judge can effect a *pro tanto* repeal of the otherwise applicable meta-ethical norm that individuals—in cases where no express rule of revelation controls—are under an obligation to follow their own good faith moral reasoning based on a

---

expressly contained in revelation. In all cases determined by good faith judgment, the ethical obligation is to follow the results of one's good faith interpretation, if one was a qualified interpreter of revelation (*mujtahid*), or to follow the reasoning of a qualified interpreter of revelation, if one was not qualified to interpret revelation independently (*muqallid*); Fadel, 'The True, the Good and the Reasonable', 44–7.

20. Al-Ghazālī, *Mustaṣfā*, 356–57.

comparison of the case at hand with cases which revelation had conclusively resolved? While this is an essentially theological problem, Ghazālī's solution also raises an institutional problem: who is this figure, the *qāḍī*, and by virtue of what authority is his judgment given authority to pre-empt the good faith moral judgments of other individuals who, by hypothesis, are also acting in good-faith, and have a *prima facie* claim to be acting in a lawful manner?

Muslim jurists had long disputed whether a judge's verdict could alter the underlying moral rule that governed the disputed case, but over time, and certainly by the fourteenth century, they had generally come to the view that the judge's ruling conclusively resolved the dispute between the parties, not only in terms of the parties' rights and obligations in this world, but also as a moral matter between the parties and God.[21] As explained by al-Qarāfī (d. 1285), the moral effect of a judge's decision not only bound the disputants, it also bound the rest of the world, meaning that jurists who, prior to the judge's resolution of the dispute, would have been entitled to opine that a certain transaction or marriage was invalid, for example, were obligated to adopt the judge's reasoning *for that case*, and recognize the validity of that transaction or marriage, despite the fact that they had previously believed it to be invalid. For example, suppose an adult, but never-previously married woman, freely enters into a marriage with an eligible suitor, but without the prior consent of her father, who is present in the town. According to a majority of Muslim jurists, such a marriage would be invalid, because a condition of validity of such a marriage is the consent of the woman's father. Suppose, however, the father brings a suit to invalidate the marriage, and the case is heard by a judge who [282] believes that an adult woman, whether or not previously married, is free to enter into a marriage contract without her father's consent, and upholds the marriage. In this case, his ruling not only conclusively establishes the moral validity of this marriage as between the couple and the bride's father, but it also stops jurists who believe that marriages concluded by a never-previously married woman require the father's consent from opining that their marriage is invalid. Rather, if they are asked about the validity of that woman's marriage, they must say, 'It is a valid marriage, because a judge has ruled that it is valid'.[22]

But the conclusion to clothe judicial decisions with moral authority that superseded the pre-political interpretive authority of divine law was itself a product of several centuries of theological, moral and legal debate, and was in no way a doctrinally inevitable outcome, at least as viewed from the perspective of the earliest Muslim community. Judges, then, had the paradoxical authority to resolve conclusively quotidian disputes in

21. For an overview of the various debates on the moral effects of judge's ruling, see Mohammad Fadel, 'Forum, Exterior (*Ẓāhir*), and Interior Forum (*Bāṭin*)', in Stanley N. Katz (ed.), *Oxford International Encyclopedia of Legal History*, 6 vols. (New York: Oxford Univ. Press, 2009), 3:97–8.

22. Sherman Jackson, *Islamic Law and the State: The Constitutional Jurisprudence of Shihāb al-Dīn al-Qarāfī* (New York: Brill, 1996), 171–74.

accordance with divine law despite the fact that divine law, on its face, did not provide conclusive answers to those quotidian disputes. The authority to do so, however, was not by virtue of some inherent quality in the judges, or something about their function that was oracular, but rather by virtue of the combination of having been validly appointed to the office of judge *and* their adherence to the rule of law by ruling in accordance only with established rules of evidence and valid rules of substantive law. It was only as a result of the maturation of Sunni thinking about the nature of public order, as evidenced in works such as *al-Aḥkām al-sulṭāniyya* [The Ordinances of Government] of the aforementioned al-Māwardī, and its relationship to the public order, that the morally constitutive role of the state could be explicitly theorized.

But, how could a stable rule of law have arisen if, according to the epistemological assumptions of *uṣūl al-fiqh*, legal disputes were generally resolved only by a probable conception of divine law which admitted the plausibility of numerous solutions to the same issue? Indeed, many jurists argued that a qualified interpreter of the law, a *mujtahid*, was obliged to review his own reasoning each time a case was presented to him to insure that he or she had not changed his or her mind as a result of new information.[23] Under such a norm, it would be hard to see how a stable body of rules could emerge that would support the rule of law. The solution, again, was political: because theological doctrines did not permit recognition of a human authority that could determine which conflicting view was the 'correct' conception of divine law, Sunni jurists in the Middle Ages applied the doctrine of 'deference', *taqlīd*, to place a limit on the spectre of legal indeterminacy and put a limit on legal pluralism. By the thirteenth century, if not earlier, judges had ceased being *mujtahid*s, and instead were *muqallid*s, jurists who [283] practiced deference to previous authorities, and were bound to uphold the rules of prior masters.[24] Judges who applied rules that were not approved by established authorities were likely to have their rulings overturned, while judges who respected established legal doctrines could be certain that their rulings would be respected under the Islamic legal principle which is similar to *res judicata*: that a prior judicial ruling based on a reasonable interpretation of the law (*ijtihād*) is not to be overturned by a subsequent court based on a different interpretation of the law (*ijtihād*).

In addition to the effective reduction of legal pluralism by reducing the scope for novel interpretations of revelation, Muslim jurists in the Late Middle Ages also articulated a doctrine that enabled a reviewing court to overturn a prior decision in situations

23. Mohammad Fadel, '*Istafti qalbaka wa in aftāka al-nāsu wa aftūka*': The Ethical Obligations of the Muqallid between Autonomy and Trust', in A. Kevin Reinhart and Robert Gleave (eds.), *Islamic Law in Theory: Studies in Jurisprudence in Honor of Bernard Weiss* (Boston: Brill, 2014), 109–10.

24. For an account of how the Islamic judicial system evolved from one based on independent legal reasoning to one rooted in deference to prior doctrine, see Mohammad Fadel, 'The Social Logic of Taqlīd and the Rise of the Mukhtaṣar', *Islamic Law and Society* 3:2 (1996): 193.

where the prior court issued a ruling based on a rule that could not be justified within the constraints of the shared interpretive assumptions of the Sunni jurists themselves. Accordingly, if a judge's decision contradicted consensus, an *a fortiori* analogy, a clear scriptural text (*naṣṣ*) or general legal principles, it was to be overturned.[25] This principle no doubt had the effect of reducing differences among the different Sunni authorities, or at a minimum, helped reduce the scope of legal differences to those that had been previously recognized as legitimate by the jurists themselves. While the rise of *taqlīd*, and the various doctrines designed to reduce the scope for different interpretations of divine law could be described as non-political doctrines, their effectiveness was dependent upon the fact that judicial rulings were enforceable only to the extent that they adhered to these doctrines. It is unlikely that such doctrines could have gained any long-term traction if, in fact, they were not supported by the state that appointed judges and enforced their decisions against recalcitrant parties.

The quotidian application of divine law, and its ability to act as an effective moral regulator of the social world, therefore, could not proceed without a state which appointed judges, without whom it would have been impossible to provide conclusive rules in circumstances where mere interpreters could only provide guesses, reasonable guesses to be sure, but guesses nonetheless, regarding the specific content of divine law. At the same time, the existence of the state was necessary to insure that the interpretive project of the discovery of divine law by human interpretation did not degenerate into an irresponsible cacophony of arbitrary opinion by allowing for the best-reasoned and best-attested opinions to crystallize into law that was publicly recognized and enforced. The state, in an important sense, was a prerequisite to the effective functioning of divine law in the Sunni conception as a system for the resolution of quotidian disputes. But did the Sunnis have a conception of the state that went beyond merely a neutral arbiter of divine law among its citizens? As I will argue below, the answer is yes: Sunni jurists, certainly by the fourteenth century, had developed a theory of the state that allowed it to [284] play a positive role in improving (*iṣlāḥ*) the community under the doctrine of *siyāsa sharʿiyya*, statecraft in accordance with divine law.[26] The next section takes up this topic in greater detail.

25. Jackson, *Islamic Law and the State*, 107.

26. As a historical matter, it was not until the modern era when Muslim states began using the power of *siyāsa sharʿiyya* expansively in an effort to transform Muslim societies. Prior generations of rulers had used this power sparingly, and largely to regulate state interests, such as taxation and land use, and in the field of criminal law. Until the nineteenth century, therefore, Muslim law could be fairly described as having been developed and applied largely by judges and jurists, not rulers.

SHARᶜIYYA, POSITIVE LAW AND SELF-GOVERNMENT IN SUNNI LAW

Thus far, we have seen how the ideal of divine law, because it is not specified in a fashion that operationalizes it at a quotidian level, requires the establishment of a state that at a minimum could provide a legitimate forum for the resolution of the disputes that inevitably break out, even among properly motivated moral subjects. Significantly, later Sunni jurists did not merely recognize the authority of courts as a *de facto* necessity born out of the pragmatic need to bring an end to secular strife and conflict, but also that the decisions of judges, if they were the result of a valid procedure that applied reasonable conceptions of divine law, were also morally significant, even in the absence of the possibility of coercive enforcement. The question we wish to address in this section is how such a state to which is entrusted the administration of divine law can come into existence.

Sunni Muslims rejected two perfectionist models of a state under divine law, instead adopting a conception of a state built upon the idea of a community made up of the adequately virtuous. The two models that I contrast to the Sunni model of the state belong to the Khawārij and the Shiᶜa, respectively. Despite the radical differences between the Khawārij's conception of the state and that of the Shiᶜa, they both shared a commitment to the rule of the most virtuous. The Khawārij, so-called because 'they departed' (*kharajū*) from the camp of ᶜAlī b. Abī Ṭālib (d. 661), the fourth rightly-guided caliph in Sunni doctrine, and the first Imam of the Shiᶜa, when ᶜAlī agreed to submit his dispute over the caliphate with Muᶜāwiya b. Abī Sufyān (d. 680), the then governor of Syria and the would-be avenger of his cousin, ᶜUthmān b. ᶜAffān (d. 656), the third Sunni caliph who was murdered at the hands of rebels, to an arbitrator for resolution. For the Khawārij, ᶜAlī, by agreeing to submit this political dispute to human resolution, substituted human law for divine law, and thereby forfeited his right to claim authority over the Muslim community.[27] For the Shiᶜa, by contrast, only a divinely-designated descendant of the Prophet Muhammad was a legitimate ruler of the Muslim community, and any ruler who rejected the authority of the Imam was, by definition, a usurper.

[285] The Khawārij conception of authority was highly egalitarian insofar as any Muslim was eligible to rule the community, provided he was the most virtuous member of the community. The puritanical Khawārij commitment to political perfection was manifest not only at the time the community's leader was selected; indeed, if the ruler subsequently committed a violation of divine law, for example, by substituting human law for divine law as had occurred in their interpretation of ᶜAlī's willingness to arbitrate the conflict with Muᶜāwiya, it became an obligation of the Muslim community to topple

27. Indeed, the slogan by which the Khawārij became famous was 'Judgement belongs only to God' (*lā ḥukma illā li-llāh*).

the faithless leader.[28] The Shi‘a in contrast to the Khawārij believed that only a divinely-inspired figure who, by virtue of divine grace, was capable of perfectly interpreting and applying the law was entitled to govern and that anyone lacking this feature would, by definition, be a usurper. An infallible Imam was needed from the Shiʿi perspective because, in their opinion, it was the only solution to the problem of crafting authority against the background of human equality. While the Khawārij reconciled the problem of justifying political authority among a community of equals by demanding that the ruler be the most virtuous in terms of knowledge of and adherence to the law, the Shi‘a solved the same political problem by positing an infallible figure, the Imam, who attained his position through his status as a descendant of the Prophet Muhammad and who was deemed to have perfect knowledge of the law.[29] For the Sunnis, by contrast, every human being of sound intellect (*ʿaql*) and moral integrity (*ʿadl*), was capable of having a *reasonable* understanding of divine law by virtue of the universal accessibility of revelation and of reasonably conforming with the law's demands without the mediation of extraordinary humans.

As Ibn ʿAbd al-Salām, the thirteenth-century Shāfiʿī jurist put it, no human being by nature possessed a superior claim to obedience than any other human being. The Sunnis, unlike both the Khawārij and the Shiʿa, turned away from the rule of the most virtuous, and solved the political problem of authority among equals by positing a self-governing community that could appoint an agent—the *caliph*—who would be entrusted to administer the law and the community's affairs, and insofar as he was an agent of the community, he could be held accountable to the community through the law for his conduct. The basic outlines of this solution are found in the law of the caliphate. The Sunni doctrine of the caliph as agent of the Muslim community first developed in the context of the various theological debates that swirled around the institution among various Muslim theologians long after the historical events that created the historical institution of the caliphate had already taken place and after sectarian differences had become established. Although Muslim jurists, in the course of developing substantive [286] Islamic law, articulated rules governing the constitution and exercise of power by public officials, it was not until the eleventh century that Muslim jurists wrote systematic treatises on the law of the caliphate when the Shāfiʿī jurist Māwardī and his Ḥanbalī contemporary, Abū Yaʿlā al-Farrāʾ (d. 1066); both authored treatises with the same title, *al-Aḥkām al-sulṭāniyya* [The Ordinances of Government].

---

28. For an overview of the development of Khārijī political and theological doctrines, see Adam Geiser, *Muslims, Scholars, Soldiers: The Origin and Elaboration of the Ibāḍī Imamate Traditions* (New York: Oxford Univ. Press, 2011).

29. For a classical elaboration of the Shiʿi defense of their position on the Imāmate, see al-Ḥillī, *al-Bāb al-Ḥādī ʿAshar: A Treatise on the Principles of Shiʿite Theology*, trans. William McElwee Miller (London: Royal Asiatic Society, 1958), 62–8.

While there is substantial overlap in both works—indeed some passages are reproduced in both works verbatim—there are, nevertheless, important differences in the two works that perhaps led to Māwardī's work eclipsing that of Abū Yaʿlā's. Perhaps the most important reason behind the greater fame of Māwardī's work is that as a Shafiʿī jurist, Māwardī's work was able to take advantage of the geographically broader dispersal of Shafiʿī jurists relative to the comparatively limited presence of Ḥanbalī jurists in the medieval Islamic world. The celebrated Ḥanafī jurist, Abū Bakr al-Kāsānī (d. 1191), although he did not author an independent treatise on the caliphate, nevertheless also confirmed the idea of the principal-agent relationship as the defining feature of the Sunni conception of political authority. In his discussion of the appointment and dismissal of judges and governors, there is a passage which deserves to be quoted at length:

> The difference between an agent who serves a natural principal [and a judge] is that the agent [of a natural principal] acts solely under the authority of the natural principal and solely for his interests and so [upon the death of the natural principal], the principal's legal capacity terminates and the agent is dismissed by operation of law. The judge, however, does not act under the authority of the caliph and for his interests; rather, he acts under the authority of the Muslims for their interests. The caliph is nothing more than their messenger [with] respect [to appointing and dismissing judges] and for that reason is not personally liable, just like agents in all other contracts. . . And since the caliph is an agent, his acts are effectively the acts of the Muslim public, and their authority persists after the death of the caliph and so the judge continues in his office. When the caliph dismisses a judge or a governor, however, the dismissal is effective, even though they are not dismissed by operation of law upon the caliph's death, because he is not, in reality, dismissed by the caliph, but rather by virtue of the authority of the Muslim community, on account of what we already mentioned: the caliph obtained his office by virtue of the Muslim community's appointment of him, and it is the Muslim community, conceptually, that authorized him to replace one public official with another because their well-being depends on that. Accordingly, his authority to dismiss officials, conceptually, is derived from them as well.[30]

---

30. *Wa-wajh al-farq anna al-wakīl yaʿmal bi-wilāyat al-muwakkil wa-fī khāliṣ ḥaqqihi ayḍan waqad baṭalat ahliyyatu l-wilāya fa-yanʿazil al-wakīl wa-l-qāḍī lā yaʿmal bi-wilāyat al-khalīfa wa-fī ḥaqqihi bal bi-wilāyat al-muslimīn wa-fī ḥuqūqihim wa-innamā l-khalīfa bi-manzilat al-rasūl ʿanhum li-hādhā lam talḥaqhu al-ʿuhda ka-l-rasūl fī sā'ir al-ʿuqūd. . .wa idhā kāna rasūlan kāna fiʿluhu bi-manzilat fiʿl ʿāmmat al-muslimīn wa-wilāyatuhum baʿda mawt al-khalīfa bāqiya fa-yabqā al-qāḍī ʿalā wilāyatihi. . .inna al-khalīfa idhā ʿazala al-qāḍī aw al-wālī yanʿazil bi-ʿazlihi wa lā yanʿazil bi-mawtihi li-annahu lā yanʿazil bi-ʿazl al-khalīfa ayḍan ḥaqīqatan bal bi-ʿazl al-ʿāmma li-ma dhakarnā anna tawliyatahu bi-tawliyat al-ʿāmma wa-l-ʿāmma wallawhu al-istibdāl maʿnan li-taʿalluq maṣlaḥatihim bi-dhālika fa-kānat wilāyatuhu minhum maʿnan fī l-ʿazl ayḍan*; al-Kāsānī, *Badāʾiʿ al-ṣanaʾiʿ fī tartīb al-sharāʾiʿ*, 7 vols. (Cairo: Maṭbaʿat al-Jamāliyya, 1910), 7:16.

[287] In any case, Sunni jurists adopted the language of agency to describe the nature of the political relationship between the caliph and the community, and it is through the lens of the agency relationship that the mutual rights and obligations of public officials and individuals in the Muslim community are structured. The relationship of agency does this in two ways: first, it limits the power of the ruler by making a distinction between authorized conduct and unauthorized conduct. Just as a natural principal is only bound by the authorized actions of his agent, so too the Muslim community is bound only by the caliph's *authorized* actions. Because public officials are not authorized to commit illegal acts, any action or command of a public official that is contrary to law loses its status as a public act and becomes, as a result, a legal nullity. From a moral perspective, this principle was articulated in the juristic principle, 'No obedience in sin'.[31] This moral principle was also reinforced by the formal doctrine of agency law, which rendered void any agency agreement whose object was an unlawful act. Applying this principle to the agency agreement between the Muslim community and the caliph, it follows that the Muslim community lacks the power to appoint a caliph to pursue illegal ends, and so it is inconceivable that a caliph, or any other public official who acts unlawfully could claim to be acting pursuant to delegated power in such a circumstance; instead, a public official acting unlawfully, from a formal jurisprudential perspective, is relying on the brute force of personal power rather than the delegated authority of the community.

The refusal of Muslim jurists to recognize the legality of illegal actions was operationalized in various ordinary rules of law, such as the rules governing the transfer of public property to private individuals,[32] and the rules of liability for tort.[33] The principle that stepping outside of the scope of his delegated authority renders a public official the legal equivalent of a private person is explicitly affirmed by the renowned thirteenth century Ḥanbalī jurist, Ibn Qudāma, who, in his analysis of unlawful killing, expressly compares the liability of an individual who kills another in compliance with what he knows to be the illegal command of someone acting under color of law to someone who complies, even as a result of coercion, with the command of someone *not* acting under color of law, saying that the illegal command of the public official renders him the legal

31. The Arabic expression is *lā ṭāʿata li-makhlūq fī maʿṣiyat al-khāliq*.

32. Al-Sarakhsī (d. 1096), for example, gives the case of a ruler who attempts to transfer public property to a private person in a fashion that would be harmful to the public good. In this case, any member of the public is given the right to challenge the transfer before a court on the grounds that the ruler lacks authority to harm the public good; al-Sarakhsī, *Kitāb al-Mabsūṭ*, 30 vols. (Beirut: Dār al-Maʿrifa, 1913), 23:183.

33. For this reason, a subordinate public official who knowingly orders the death of someone he knows to be innocent, or knowingly executes an innocent person, is liable to the victim's next of kin, even if he is following the order of a superior public official. Ibn Qudāma, al-*Mughnī*, 10 vols. (Cairo: Maktabat al-Jumhūriyya al-ʿArabiyya, 1964), 8:366.

[288] equivalent of a private person who never has the authority to kill another, even if that other person is legally deserving of capital punishment.

But, the principles of agency law which prevented public officials from acting legitimately outside the scope of the law also functioned to bind the community affirmatively in cases where the public official *did* act within the scope of his authority. In other words, when a public official exercised discretion in a manner that was consistent with the terms of the agency relationship, individual Muslims became duty bound to obey such discretionary commands, even though they were not, in the first instance, obligatory from the perspective of divine law as set out in revelation. Accordingly, and as made clear in Māwardī's and Abū Yaʿlā's discussion of the contract of the caliphate, participation in this contract was obligatory (*wājib*), and the ruler was entitled to fight those who refused obedience as rebels (*bughāt*). The contract of the caliphate, therefore, created a notion of *rightful* coercion that public officials could wield against those individuals who refused to obey the law, such as a defendant in a lawsuit who refused to appear voluntarily before a judge when summoned.[34]

Public officials also had the power to make general law and thereby resolve certain disputes among the jurists that were not amenable to resolution as a matter of juristic interpretation. One particularly important example of this from the post-thirteenth century era was the decision by rulers, when appointing judges, to limit their jurisdiction to specific doctrines of law, such that, if they ruled on the basis of rules outside of those designated in their appointment, their judgments would be overturned, even if the substantive rule which the judge relied on was a legitimate interpretation of divine law from the perspective of interpretation.[35] In the Ottoman era, it was not uncommon for rulers to designate specifically which rule of law—among a variety of interpretively legitimate solutions—would be recognized in courts, not on the grounds that the ruler knew the divine will better than the jurists, but rather in the name of the public good.[36] Like Hobbes' sovereign, the Sunni ruler had the authority to undo the knots of interpretation that had accumulated in the law by virtue of 'making what ends he will'.

The Sunni ruler, however, unlike Hobbes' sovereign, was always restricted in choosing ends that the divine law had authorized; moreover, he could not contravene the ends of divine law, nor could he claim to determine conclusively which particular interpretation of divine law was, in fact, correct; instead, his jurisdiction was limited to determining which rule was most appropriate for the public good (*al-maṣlaḥa al-ʿamma*).

---

34. Farhat Ziadeh, 'Compelling a Defendant's Appearance at Court in Islamic Law', *Islamic Law and Society* 3:3 (1996): 305.

35. Fadel, 'The Social Logic of Taqlīd', 229–30.

36. Rudolph Peters, 'What Does it Mean to be an Official *Madhhab*? Ḥanafism and the Ottoman Empire', in Peri Bearman et al. (eds.), *The Islamic School of Law: Evolution, Devolution, and Progress* (Cambridge, Mass.: Harvard Law School, 2005), 152–53.

The authority to cut the Gordian knot could be exercised even outside the context of judicial appointments, such as in the imposition of price-control regulations. The [289] legitimacy of price-controls was deeply contested among pre-modern Sunni jurists, with many jurists holding the opinion that they were an unlawful interference in a merchant's property rights. Some jurists, however, upheld price-controls in certain circumstances if they were viewed as reasonable and necessary to secure the public good. Where the ruler decided to issue price controls in accordance with the criteria established by those jurists who authorized them, however, it became a moral *and* prudential obligation to obey the command, even on the part of those individuals who, in good faith, believed that the revealed law did not permit price controls. Although individuals have the right, indeed, the duty, to disobey the ruler to the extent his command results in sin, mere disagreement with the content of a public official's command is not grounds for disobedience if the individual can comply with the command without committing a sin. In the case of price controls, a merchant commits no sin by selling to the public at a price designated by the ruler, even if that price is less than the price he would have charged in the absence of that restraint.[37]

In all cases where a public official is exercising coercive power, he is not doing so in the name of a *true* conception of divine law that is uniquely accessible to him; rather, the right to coerce stems from his status as a lawful representative of the community who has been entrusted to use political judgment (*al-siyāsa*) to further the public good within the constraints of divine law, hence giving rise to the appellation, *siyāsa sharʿiyya*, sometimes translated as "religious politics," but more aptly understood as politics within the bounds of divine law. Under that power, the public official is not limited to merely upholding the pre-political order of rights, perhaps in the fashion suggested by Joan Lockwood O'Donovan's Christian monarch, but could also encompass any 'action through which the people are [brought] closer to prosperity'.[38] The discretion given to public officials to pursue the public good, and the moral obligation on the part of individual Muslims to obey lawful exercises of discretion, can only be understood as resulting from the relationship of agency that Sunnis posited existed between the Muslim community and their rulers.

CONCLUSION

Sunni Islam offers a complex tradition of theological, legal and political thought that attempts to synthesize commitments to following divine law as manifested in a particular revelation with naturalistic assumptions that revelation, as an empirical matter, furthers

37. Ibn Ḥajar al-Haytamī, *al-Fatāwā al-Kubrā*, 4 vols. in 2 (Beirut: Dār Ṣādir, 2000), 1:235–36.
38. Mohammad Fadel, 'Adjudication in the Mālikī Madhhab: A Study of Legal Process in Medieval Islamic Law' (PhD diss., Univ. of Chicago, 1995), 83.

ends that are reasonably intelligible to human beings' nature as rational beings. The idea of a kind of deep harmony between divine law as indicated in revealed texts with human beings' natural ends supported egalitarian assumptions regarding the accessibility of divine law to ordinary human beings. Because we are all equally situated, or [290] substantially so, with respect to knowledge of divine law, we are, as a theological matter, entitled to our own reasonable interpretations of the content of divine law, at least with respect to its secondary and tertiary rules. The pluralism inherent in the Sunni conception of divine law, however, also generated a contrary impulse, namely, the desire to create a state that could make divine law effective as a tool for the resolution of the quotidian disputes that arose within the Muslim community. Unlike other Muslim conceptions of the state, Sunni theologians and jurists conceived of the state as an institution made up of individuals of ordinary integrity who, because of their knowledge of divine law and their status as lawful representatives of the Muslim community, could resolve particular disputes that broke out among members of the community in a morally conclusive fashion and could also pursue the public good of the community, coercing the recalcitrant in appropriate circumstances. It must be emphasized that the Sunni theological and juristic tradition emphasized in this essay is not the only tradition of theological, juristic and political thought within historical Islam, nor even is it the exclusive tradition within Sunnism. I do suggest, however, that it is the dominant Sunni interpretation of law, nature and the state, and provides an appropriate basis for productive conversation with our Christian interlocutors.

2

ISLAMIC LAW REFORM: BETWEEN REINTERPRETATION AND DEMOCRACY

Mohammad Fadel

[44] Conventional accounts of modern Islamic history begin with the Muslim encounter with the European imperialist. It is easy to understand why the Napoleonic invasion of Egypt might be chosen as a convenient line of demarcation marking the beginning of a new system of governance in the traditional Arab heartlands of Islam. It did, after all, serve as a catalyst for a radical and ambitious attempt to reshape the political, administrative, and legal, infrastructure of the Ottoman Empire in what ultimately proved to be a failed attempt to stave off European domination, a project that came to be known as al-tanẓīmāt. On the other hand, it also imposes risks of obscuring long-term developments in the governance—including the role of law—in the Arab provinces of the Ottoman Empire causing us to believe that the post-Napoleonic legal and administrative reforms of the Tanẓīmāt were without precedent in Islamic legal norms.

Mid-twentieth century Islamic law scholars generally held positive views of the Tanẓīmāt, and Islamic legal reform, derived from the widely-shared perception that blind adherence to Islamic traditions and law, posed insurmountable obstacles to the ability of Muslim societies to enter the modern era. Writers of that era almost universally believed that Islamic law, as a religious law, was essentially immutable and therefore unable to adapt to the radically new circumstances of modernity; accordingly, reforms such as the Tanẓīmāt were absolutely necessary for the progress of Muslim societies.[1] Scholars such as Joseph Schacht took for granted that the Tanẓīmāt-era legal and administrative reforms, and the 20th-century legal reforms enforced by successor states to the Ottomans were not Islamic in any meaningful sense, but that did not detract from the necessity of those reforms. Schacht hoped that future generations of Muslim jurists could creatively assimilate what was essentially non-Islamic law under a yet to be developed modern con-

This article is based on the Coulson Memorial Lecture delivered at the School of Oriental and African Studies on 19 March 2015.

1. See, for example, J.N.D. Anderson, "Is the *Sharīʿa* Doomed to Immutability?" 56,1 *The Muslim World* 10–13 (1966).

ception of Islamic law, [45] much in the same way that he claimed that early Muslim jurists Islamized non-Islamic law in the first one hundred and fifty years of Islamic history.[2]

More recent Islamic law scholars, such as Wael Hallaq[3] and Noah Feldman,[4] also express skepticism of the Islamic bona fides of the 19th- and 20th-century legal reforms. Unlike previous generations of scholars, however, they are sharply critical of the effects of the legal reforms. For both Hallaq and Feldman, the displacement of the traditional law-finding methods of the *ʿulamāʾ* in favour of centralised legislation, along with their replacement with state bureaucrats as the administrators of the law, represented catastrophic developments, not only for the integrity of Islamic law as a jurisprudential system, but for the possibility of non-tyrannical government. For these scholars, the substitution of positive law for the traditional Sharīʿa inevitably led to the rise of tyrannies in the post-Ottoman Arab successor states, with all effective power vested in all-powerful executives, whether kings or presidents.

Regardless of the substantive disagreements between older and newer generations of scholars on the merits of the Tanẓīmāt, both critics and supporters appear to share a common assumption regarding what makes a rule Islamic in contrast to non-Islamic, namely: if a rule can be found in the historical doctrines of Islamic law as articulated by the schools of Islamic law, or can be derived using the reasoning techniques developed by theoretical jurisprudence, *uṣūl al-fiqh*, it is "Islamic." A rule that originates in the will of the state, by contrast, is "secular" and therefore is non-Islamic, and of dubious Islamic legitimacy. Indeed, it remains dogma that there is no conceptual room for human legislation in Islamic jurisprudence. Accordingly, instances of decrees and statutes in pre-modern Muslim history are deviations from the requirements of ideal Islamic legal theory, concessions to bitter reality, not a principled recognition of the legitimacy of non-divine law.[5] The notion that a Muslim polity makes and applies rules that are Islamic but the product of human political deliberation rather than revealed strikes most scholars as absurd.[6] According to this interpretation of Muslim legal modernity, what Muslims need, is a new [46] hermeneutic, a new *uṣūl al-fiqh*, capable of generating modern Islamic norms by introducing new methods of scriptural interpretation.[7]

The division in the eyes of modern scholars of Islamic law between normative jurisprudence and raw political power in turn produced two contradictory conceptions of legality in the historical Muslim world, the rules of *fiqh*, which were developed by the

2. Joseph Schacht, "Problems of Modern Islamic Legislation," 12 *Studia Islamica* (1960), pp. 199–29.

3. Wael Hallaq, *Sharīʿa: Theory, Practice, Transformations* (New York: Cambridge University Press, 2009) (Part III).

4. Noah Feldman, *The Fall and Rise of the Islamic State* (Princeton: Princeton University Press, 2008).

5. See, e.g., Schacht, p. 110.

6. Schacht, for example, dismissed the quest of modernist Arab lawyers for a "secular Islamic legislation" as a "contradiction in adjecto," pp. 120–21.

7. Schacht, p. 129; Hallaq, pp. 500–42.

jurists through the rational interpretation of revelation, on the one hand, and the rules of *siyāsa*, which were articulated by political authorities in reliance on their irresistible political power and pragmatic considerations of necessity, on the other.[8] Only the first body of rules is properly Islamic; the second, by contrast, is secular, even despotic, and exists outside the normative bounds of proper Islamic law. The rules of *siyāsa*, according to many scholars, including Professor Coulson himself, represent the failure of the rule of law and the inevitable concession of an unrealistically utopian conception of law to the immoral demands of power, and not a workable synthesis between revealed and secular law-making.[9] *Siyāsa* therefore represents a jurisprudential embarrassment to Islamic law: while the jurists produced a sophisticated science of theoretical jurisprudence that grounded their activity and justified it from the perspective of divine law, no equivalent effort seems to have been undertaken for *siyāsa*. Accordingly, the secondary literature largely describes *siyāsa* as though it were simply a product of necessity and arbitrary and despotic power; moreover, *siyāsa*'s persistence and expansion throughout Muslim history after the early ʿAbbāsid period was indicative not only of the existence of a Schmittian state of exception in historical Muslim societies, but also that this state of exception was an enduring feature of post-ʿAbbāsid Muslim societies which could not legitimately adapt to changing circumstances because, among other reasons, the nature of Islamic law as a divine law precluded the legitimacy of human legislation.

Nevertheless, Tanẓīmāt-era writers such as Rifāʿa Rāfiʿ al-Ṭahṭāwī, Khayr al-Dīn al-Tūnisī and Rashīd Riḍā, write about positive law, *qānūn*, with no sense of embarrassment, or fear that it undermined Islamic conceptions of political legitimacy. Their works on political and moral reform, such as Tahṭāwī's [47] *al-Murshid al-Amīn*,[10] al-Tūnisī's *Taqwīm al-Masālik*,[11] and Riḍā's *al-Khilāfa*,[12] all assumed the necessity and legitimacy of rules derived from practical reason without recourse to the principles of *uṣūl al-fiqh*. Ṭahṭāwī, for example, calls on the ruler, *mutawallī al-aḥkām*, to adopt rational rules which, from a Sharīʿa perspective, fell into any of the various ethical categories of Islamic law other than the *ḥarām*, so long as the rules the ruler formulated were appropriate to achieve the goal of *tamaddun* (civilization), and satisfied certain formal requirements, including, equality and non-arbitrariness in application. Al-Tūnisī also assumed that rules devel-

---

8. For an overview of conventional accounts of the relationship of Islamic law to the Muslim state, see Mohammad Fadel, "State and *Sharīʿa*," in *The Ashgate Research Companion to Islamic Law*, edited by Peri Bearman and Rudolph Peters (Surrey: Ashgate, 2014), pp. 29–42.

9. Noel J. Coulson, "The State and the Individual in Islamic Law," in *The Traditional Near East*, edited by J. Stewart-Robinson (Englewood Cliffs, NJ: Prentice Hall, 1966), pp. 122–35.

10. Rifāʿa Rāfiʿ al-Ṭahṭāwi, *al-Murshid al-Amīn li'l-Banāt wa'l-Banīn* (Cairo: al-Majlis al-Aʿlā li-l-Thaqāfa, 2002).

11. Khayr al-Dīn al-Tūnisī, *Aqwam al-Masālik fī Maʿrifat Aḥwāl al-Mamālik* (Tunis: al-Dār al-Tūnisiyya li-l-Nashr, 1972).

12. Muḥammad Rashīd Riḍā, *al-Khilāfa* (Cairo: al-Zahrāʾ li-l-Iʿlām al-ʿArabī, 1988).

oped through practical reason (not interpretation) were part of the Sharīʿa, because the principles of the Sharīʿa could not be made effective without their proper specification in accordance with the variable demands of time and place. Practical reason, therefore, was indispensable to the proper articulation of the Sharīʿa and accordingly, a modern articulation of the Sharīʿa demanded the incorporation of modern scientific knowledge in order to make its ordinances effective. It was on those grounds that he criticized the jurists of his day for preferring to study classical texts of law in their seminaries with little practical relevance to contemporary Muslim society rather than formulating rules that could effectively govern their contemporary societies. Rashīd Riḍā vehemently criticized those jurists who denied a legitimate role for positive law in Islamic jurisprudence as being ignorant of the fact that Islamic law—insofar as it regulates secular life—seeks the well-being of human beings in this life, and does not seek to impose on them a particular manner of living or organization of society. In other words, Rashīd Riḍā criticized Muslim jurists and theologians who opposed reforms while conflating rules of secular life—which are not determined by revelation but by human ends—with those of ritual observance.[13]

Neither Ṭahṭāwī nor Tūnisī, however, explain why ordinary Muslims should follow the rational rules that they advise the rulers to adopt. Riḍā, although he does not dwell on the problem of why people should follow non-revealed law, makes the curious comment that all rules in an Islamic polity are either a rule provided by revelation, or the considered view of the community (*raʾy al-umma*), [48] without explaining why the considered view of the community provides a moral basis for obligation.[14] While neither Taḥṭāwī nor Tūnisī explicitly make such a claim, they also, in their own way, endorse a conception of popular participation in governance. Ṭahṭāwī recognises the importance of widespread internalization of the law as a condition for the law's effectiveness, achieved only when the people have a genuine and voluntary commitment to upholding its provisions, while Tūnisī is concerned that sufficient numbers of people are properly motivated to defend the law from invasion by public officials.

For writers of that era, the task of reformers was both to make the state more effective and to reduce the arbitrary power of public officials by strengthening the rule of law. Popular participation in this project was but a means to achieve each of these ends. To what extent, however, did these goals have any roots in historical Islamic jurisprudence, or should we understand the proposals of these reformers as just another iteration of the classical binary division between the jurists' law (*fiqh*) and the rulers' law (*siyāsa*)? Put differently, does pre-Nahḍa Islamic law provide a moral justification for the binding

13. For an overview of their views on positive law, Islamic law, and political reform in the Arab world, see Mohammad Fadel, "Modernist Islamic Political Thought and the Egyptian and Tunisian Revolutions of 2011," 3 *Middle East Law and Governance* (2011), pp. 94–104.

14. Riḍā, p. 9.

character of the rational positive law that the Nahḍa-era reformers called for? If so, could a properly conceived understanding of political life, derived from substantive Islamic law itself, provide an alternative basis for a Muslim legal modernity and dispense with the need for a "new" *uṣūl al-fiqh*?

Answers to these questions require re-examination of various rules and doctrines of historical Islamic law as articulated by Sunnī jurists in an attempt to identify a cognizable body of 'public law' and to theorise the structure of this historical body of rules. This article aims to demonstrate that Sunnī jurists prior to the 19th century had already articulated a substantial body of rules that provide a coherent basis to public law. The Sunnī conception of public law was not formulated as a matter of ad hoc responses to particular historical circumstances as conventional understandings of *siyāsa* suggest, but was rather the product of a moral commitment to the normative political principle that the caliph is an ideal public agent (*wakīl*) acting on behalf of an ideal principal (*aṣl* or *muwakkil*), the Muslim community.[15] A fortiori, the relationship of all lesser officials to persons within their jurisdictions were also bound by the same ideals. This agency principle validates exercises of authority by rendering the agent's authorized acts binding on the community, and invalidates the agent's unauthorized acts by rendering them non-binding on the [49] community. The content of Sunnī public law is simply the terms on which public officials have been authorized to act on behalf of their principal, the Muslim community.

In short, pre-19th century Sunnī law understood public authority (*wilāya*) as a special instance of the fiduciary duties of the general law of agency (*wikāla*). Viewed from this perspective, the positive law of the state, i.e., *siyāsa*, does not represent an alternative system of law distinct from *fiqh*. *Siyāsa* is rather the result of the deliberations of an idealized agent acting to further the rational good of his principal, the Muslim community. To the extent that the actions of actual rulers fulfill this ideal by satisfying the legal rules applicable to a public conception of agency, the rules bind the Muslim community, not by virtue of the ruler's decree being a "true" interpretation of revelation (as would be the case were the ruler understood to be a *mujtahid*, such as Mālik or Abū Hanīfa), but because a principal, in this case, the Muslim community, is bound by the duly authorized actions of his agent.

The relationship of agency between the ruler and the ruled led pre-19th century jurists to deploy general principles of fiduciary law to regulate the rights and duties of both public officials and the governed. The fiduciary requirement that applied to public officials sharply distinguished the rules governing their activities from the actions of natural persons who, all things being equal, were free to act out of self-interest. As set out in

15. Sunnī jurists refer to the Muslim community using a variety of terms, such as *ʿāmmat al-muslimīn*, *jamāʿat al-muslimīn*, *al-muslimīn*, or *al-jamāʿa*. Sometimes they may even use other terms that are not specifically inflected by religion, such as "the people," *al-nās*.

the ideal theory of the caliphate by writers such as al-Māwardī and al-Farrāʾ,[16] legitimate authority was constituted through a delegation of authority, initially, from the Muslim community to the caliph, and thereafter, from the caliph, to lesser public officials. The fiduciary duty of the agent to his principal to use his discretionary authority exclusively for the principal's interest (*maṣlaḥat al-muwakkil*), not the agent's own interest, was then extended to the powers delegated to lesser public officials.[17] This fiduciary conception of public law, in turn, justified both the limited nature of the public official's authority, and the moral duty of obedience (*ṭāʿa*) on the part of individuals subject to the public official's jurisdiction (*wilāya*). Moreover, the fiduciary principle applied to organize relations of the ruler to the governed whether the ruler had been appointed de jure, and therefore became an agent of the public by virtue of consent (*ʿaqd*), or achieved his position by [50] conquest (*al-mutaghallib*), in which case the law retroactively deemed him to have been appointed to his position by virtue of necessity (*ḥākim al-ḍarūra*).[18]

Whether Muslims ought to pursue reforms in the way they read revelation or pursue reform through democratic politics, is not merely an academic question. The relationship of Islamic law to democratic politics and popular sovereignty has become deeply contentious and divisive in the Arab world, and even threatens the possibility of non-authoritarian political life. It is also leaving its mark in contemporary Muslim religious thought where Muslim publics, having apparently abandoned any hope in politics, are now seeking to accomplish the substantive reform of the norms of the jurists' law through what are often far-fetched interpretations of revelation. Yet, as this article will argue, many of the substantive reforms which are rightly demanded could be accomplished in a morally compelling fashion if promulgated through the positive law of a properly constituted representative state, without any need to advance implausible claims about the meaning of revelation.[19]

---

16. Abū al-Ḥasan ʿAlī b. Muḥammad b. Ḥabīb al-Māwardī, *al-Aḥkām al-Sulṭāniyya* (Beirut: Dār al-Kutub al-ʿIlmiyya, n.d.); Abū Yaʿlā Muḥammad b. al-Ḥusayn al-Farrāʾ, *al-Aḥkām al-Sulṭāniyya* (Beirut: Dār al-Kutub al-ʿIlmiyya, 1983).

17. 3 *al-Sharḥ al-Ṣaghīr*, Abū al-Barakāt Aḥmad b. Muḥammad b. Aḥmad al-Dardīr, ed. Muṣṭafā Kamāl Waṣfī (*Dār al-Maʿārif*: Cairo, n.d.), p. 508 (an agent is obliged to act for the benefit of the principal (*wa faʿala al-wakīl al-maṣlaḥa wujūban . . . li-muwakkilihi*)).

18. See, for example, 5 al-Khaṭīb al-Shirbīnī, *Mughnī al-Muḥtāj ilā Maʿrifat Maʿānī Alfāẓ al-Minhāj* (Beirut: Dār al-kutub al-ʿilmiyya, 1994), p. 423.

19. A good example of implausible interpretations of revelation are attempts to interpret the use of the verb *ḍa-ra-ba* in the notorious "beating" verse, 4:34, to mean "go away" instead of "beat." Neal MacFarquhar, "Verse in Koran on Beating Wife Gets New Translation," *N.Y. Times*, March 25, 2007, available at http://www.nytimes.com/2007/03/25/world/americas/25iht-koran.4.5017346.html?pagewanted=all&_r=0. If, on the other hand, positive law, in certain circumstances is capable of generating moral duties that are non-scriptural, as this article argues, then the adoption of positive law prohibiting the exercise of such a right would provide a moral basis for prohibiting wife-beating regardless of enduring controversies regarding the correct meaning of the verse.

The emphasis on the need for a new "*uṣūl al-fiqh*" is based on the erroneous premise that the rights and obligations set out by the jurists in their law represent an immutable set of pre-political rights and obligations. If that were correct, then the only way to overcome the historical legacy of the jurists' law is to present an alternative articulation of these pre-political rights and obligations through a new interpretation of the sources of Islamic law. In short, this reform strategy proposes to substitute a new jurists' law for the jurists' law of old.

If such a view represents mistaken political theory, however, and it is the case that Muslims may legitimately revise the pre-political rights and duties established by the jurists' law through legitimate representative politics, then the most felicitous route for effective reform is not interpretive, but political. Properly representative states, based on the argument presented in this article, are entitled to promulgate morally binding positive law which goes beyond the pre-political rights and duties of the jurists' law. Were such states to exist, they could promulgate a reform agenda through positive law that could claim [51] a much firmer basis for legitimacy than controversial claims about the true meaning of revelation. It is the task of this article to explain why such a political approach is well-grounded in historical doctrines of Sunnī law. This article begins by excavating the content of Sunnī public law by focusing on the rules that govern the behavior of public officials, whether by conferring upon the public official a positive power to act in a fashion that affects the rights of another, or by imposing a rule that acts to constrain his power to so affect the rights of another. This very distinction, between public versus non-public, assumes that Muslim jurists distinguished a public sphere from a non-public sphere, a claim which some may find to be a controversial claim in itself. Accordingly, I also analyze rules that establish the public/private distinction and describe some of the legal rules which seek to preserve the integrity of each sphere. After establishing the distinctive features of the public sphere and the private sphere, I then discuss the rules governing the legitimate exercise of public functions. I conclude with a discussion on the implications for the legitimacy of positive legislation and its radical potential for reforming the historical rules of the jurists' law.

Accordingly, I begin with an inquiry into jurisdictional law: the rules that create various jurisdictions (*wilāyāt*/s. *wilāya*), the various powers that are incidental to the creation of a valid jurisdiction, the substantive norms that regulate how those powers are to be exercised, and the obligations of individuals who fall under the authority of various jurisdictions to adhere to the decisions of public officials. As I will try to show, Sunnī jurisdictional law arose in response to the problem of how the exercise of power over an equal can ever be justified. The answer Sunnī jurists gave was that such a power can only be morally justified to the extent that the ruler behaved as an ideal representative of the ruled. The moral ideal of the principal-agent relationship is the fundamental structural principle of Sunnī public law. Therefore, the principles of agency law serve both to limit the authority of public officials and to authorize them to regulate affirmatively the lives of those properly subject to their jurisdiction.

1. THE PROBLEM OF OBEDIENCE, THE CALIPHATE AND THE BIRTH OF SUNNĪ PUBLIC LAW

1.1. The "Independence Principle," Legitimate Authority, and Usurpers

The egalitarian theological assumptions of Sunnism posed a problem for political ordering. If all persons were morally equal (or substantially so) insofar as each of them was in principle capable of understanding God's law, and each of them would be individually accountable to God for his or her adherence to divine teachings, and none of them could claim a special knowledge of that law [52] that was inaccessible to anyone else, religious doctrine could not provide an obvious answer to the question of who should assume the mantle of political leadership. Indeed, the 12th-century Muslim theologian al-ʿIzz b. ʿAbd al-Salām succinctly articulated the political consequences of Sunnī theological doctrines by stating that "no human is more worthy of obedience than another" and that it is only God who is entitled to an unqualified duty of obedience.[20] Obedience is only consistent with human equality to the extent that God has authorized a duty of obedience.

One of the divinely-authorized exceptions to the principle of non-obedience is the obligation to obey public officials: "the Imams, judges and governors." Even as Ibn ʿAbd al-Salām affirmed that obedience to political authorities is an exception to the independence principle, he called into question that very principle by declaring that no such duty is owed to "the ignorant kings and princes until the subject of the command (*al-maʾmūr*) can ascertain that the command is permitted by revelation."[21] By this qualification, Ibn ʿAbd al-Salām effectively introduced into the moral calculus the difference between power and authority. It is only legitimate Imams, judges and rulers who are morally entitled to obedience. Illegitimate rulers, by contrast, possessed power but lacked authority, and accordingly, no moral duty of political obedience existed with respect to "ignorant kings and princes." If a moral duty of obedience arose in such cases, it is only because the subject has ascertained independently that the command may be followed without the risk of disobeying God. Illegitimate rulers, then, may be obeyed provided that their commands can be determined to be lawful ex post. As a matter of principle, however, sinful commands can never produce a moral duty of obedience, as that would amount to a contradiction of divine sovereignty.[22]

---

20. ʿIzz al-Dīn ibn ʿAbd al-Salām, 2 *Qawāʿid al-Aḥkām fī Maṣāliḥ al-Anām* (Beirut: Dār al-Maʿrifa, n.d.), p. 157.

21. Ibid.

22. The prohibition against complying with unlawful commands is not categorical, but is rather subject to a prudential standard (*darʾ mafsada*), the details of which are beyond the scope of this article. This article is concerned exclusively with the jurists' conception of ideal theory. Ibid.

1.2. The Contract of the Caliphate and Sunnī Ideals of Legitimate Authority

What, however, provides a person with legitimate authority and distinguishes him from the mere possessor of naked power that is illegitimate? The answer to this question lies in the Sunnī theory of the caliphate. Modern scholarship, [53] both Muslim and non-Muslim, has typically dismissed Sunnī writings on the caliphate as little more than post hoc justification of the political status quo, an expression of utopian dreams disconnected from political realities, or an abject surrender to the arbitrary power of military forces that came to dominate Muslim polities with the long and gradual decline of the effective power of the ʿAbbāsid caliphate.[23]

This reading of pre-modern Sunnī writing on the caliphate partially misrecognizes the function of Sunnī writing on the caliphate, particularly in the context of intra-Muslim theological polemics. As one Sunnī theologian put it, the caliphate is properly a legal topic, not a theological one.[24] Another reason for the quick dismissal of Sunnī writing on the caliphate is what can only be termed an anachronistic bias in favour of formal democratic procedures. Patricia Crone, for example, noted with disappointment the failure of Sunnīs to establish representative institutions that could have checked the arbitrary power of government, even though such an institutional innovation would not have been too difficult to achieve given their theological and juridical doctrines.[25]

Modern scholarship, then, has largely focused on what is perceived to be absent from Sunnī discussions of the caliphate, rather than attempting to understand the salient political principles that Sunnī jurists actually affirmed. Even though Sunnī jurists were lawyers and not political philosophers, it is nevertheless possible to draw out the immanent principles of their political thought through a careful reading of the substantive rules they produced.

In approaching a text like al-Māwardī's *al-Aḥkām al-Sulṭāniyya* in this way, the reader must take care to stand back from the potentially tedious detail with which the author discusses legal minutia and focus instead on the structural features of his presentation of those rules. The most important of these is the contractual foundation of the caliphate. This feature of Māwardī's text is well-recognized by modern scholars. Instead of attempting to understand the consequences of this idea for the moral and legal regulation of the state, however, modern scholarship has focused on empirical questions, such as whether his contractual account of the state is a satisfactory historical account of the Muslim state in its various stages of development, or alternatively, they have decried the

23. Fadel, "Sharia and the State," *supra* note 8.

24. Saʿd al-Dīn al-Taftazānī, 5 *Sharḥ al-Maqāṣid*, edited by ʿAbd al-Raḥmān ʿUmayra (Beirut: ʿĀlam al-Kutub, 1989), p. 232.

25. Patricia Crone, *God's Rule: Government and Islam* (New York: Columbia University Press, 2004), p. 277.

failure of Muslims to operationalize this potentially democratic [54] idea by specifying institutional modalities to make this contract of governance effective. In this context, however, I am not concerned with empirical objections to Māwardī's theory of the state, but rather the extent to which the idea of contract animates Sunnī law's approach to the problem of governance generally, and to the extent possible, determine what the ideal content of that contract is.

It is indisputable that for Māwardī, contract is the exclusive means by which authority can come into existence. Not only is the initial act of the selection of a ruler called a contract—the contract of the caliphate (or the imamate) (*ʿaqd al-khilāfa* or *ʿaqd al-imāma*), all subsequent appointments of public officials are also described as contracts of appointment (*ʿaqd tawliya*). Like any contract, it is entered into by two parties. The contract of the caliphate can take two forms: (i) the contract takes place between electors (*ahl al-ḥall wa'l-ʿaqd*) and the successful candidate for the caliphate; and (ii) the contract takes place between the incumbent caliph and the person the incumbent designated as his successor (*walī al-ʿahd*). In both cases, the party selecting the caliph, i.e., the electors in the first procedure, and the incumbent caliph in the second procedure, is obliged to select a candidate in light of a comprehensive list of qualifications made up of moral, martial and personal virtues, knowledge of religious law and charismatic descent from the Prophet's tribe of Quraysh.[26] The party selecting the caliph (or the incumbent designating his own successor) is permitted to select a lesser-qualified candidate even if a better-qualified candidate is available, if the lesser qualified candidate is minimally qualified. The party selecting the caliph (or the caliph when he selects his successor) can prefer one quality, e.g., martial valor to piety or learning, if it is a time of external or internal threat to the state, or vice-versa in a time of peace.

Neither the electors, nor the caliph, in exercising their powers of selection, however, are free to ignore the qualifications of the candidates and simply select the candidate who is most appealing to their private preferences. The duty of electors and caliphs to choose exclusively from among legally satisfactory candidates arises from the fact that they are acting in a representative capacity on behalf of the entirety of the Muslim community, and not in their personal capacity. Māwardī makes express reference to the representational aspect of their role in his discussion of the rules governing the removal of incumbent rulers:

> [55] "The Imam who has appointed a successor may not dismiss his successor in the absence of legal cause even though he may dismiss his other appointees at will. He may dismiss them at will because he appointed them in furtherance of his own rights, while he appointed his successor in furtherance of the right of

26. Later jurists, however, were willing to dispense with this requirement provided the other qualifications were satisfied. See, 5 al-Shirbīnī, pp. 422–23.

the Muslims. Accordingly, he lacks the power to dismiss him just as the electors may not dismiss the caliph to whom they have pledged loyalty in the absence of legal cause."[27]

The idea that the Muslim community is the actual party in interest to the contract also manifests itself in other rules of al-Māwardī's *Aḥkām*. One example is the continuing validity of the appointments of judges and governors despite the death or removal of the caliph who appointed them. Because judges and regional governors are appointed to further the interests of the Muslim community rather than the personal interests of the caliph, the validity of their appointments continues despite the death of the incumbent caliph who appointed them.[28]

Leaving aside the philosophical problem of how to define the Muslim community, and whether it is distinct from the actual, empirical Muslims living at the time any particular caliph is selected, as a practical matter, al-Māwardī, along with practically all other Sunnī and non-Sunnī Muslim authorities, saw that formation of a state, and loyal adherence to it, was an obligation that bound all Muslims. It was of course a collective obligation (*farḍ kifāya*) and not a personal one (*farḍ ʿayn*) to participate in the formation of the caliphate, but according to Māwardī one could not escape the subsequent obligation of obedience by claiming non-participation in the contract. And indeed, Māwardī's language—"everyone in the community is obliged" (*ʿalā kāffat al-umma*)—makes clear that every Muslim is under an obligation to perform the contract once it is formed. Those who refuse to recognize the caliph's authorities are rebels (*ahl al-baghy*) and may be legitimately subdued by force of arms to compel their obedience.[29] The mandatory nature of the caliphate's contract therefore plays a crucial role in constituting the public order over which the caliph exercises exclusive authority as representative of the Muslim community.

[56] This right of the caliph and by extension, the Muslim community, to compel the obedience of the recalcitrant is implicit in Māwardī's description of the operative provisions of the contract of the caliphate. According to Māwardī, the contract of the caliphate entails a delegation from the entirety of the community of the administration of public affairs to the caliph, a responsibility which is entrusted to him in his capacity as the community's exclusive agent over its public affairs:

> "Everyone in the community is obliged to delegate [administration] of common affairs to him, without any interference in his [jurisdiction] or opposition

27. Al-Māwardī, p. 12.

28. Al-Māwardī, p. 37 (continued validity of the appointment of a governor made by the caliph, despite the caliph's death) and p. 96 (the continued validity of the judge's appointment despite the death of the appointing caliph).

29. Al-Māwardī, p. 74.

> so that he can perform that which has been entrusted to him with respect to [attaining the general] welfare and [establishing the orderly] administration of [public] institutions."[30]

The obligatory nature of the contract confirms both its necessity and its fiduciary character. Accordingly, it is not surprising that the jurists interpreted the powers vesting in the caliph as powers that must be exercised only for the good of the community, which as mentioned previously, is the legal party in interest to the contract with the caliph. The notion that the contract exists exclusively for the benefit of the community is implicit in the operative verbs Māwardī chooses to describe the grant of authority to the caliph: he uses the verb *wukkila*—the passive voice for the verb used to appoint an agent—rather than, for example, *mullika*—the passive voice for the verb used to express the idea of transferring dominion over something, to express the nature of the [57] relationship between the caliph and the Muslim community.[31] Unsurprisingly, therefore, he understands obedience as arising out of a relationship of reciprocity:

> "When the Imam discharges the rights of the community which we have previously described [in the terms of this contract], he is entitled to their obedience and succour."[32]

30. *ʿAlā kāffat al-umma tafwīḍ al-umūr al-ʿāmma ilayhi min ghayr iftiyāt ʿalayhi wa lā muʿāraḍa li-yaqūma bi-mā wukkila ilayhi min wujūh al-maṣāliḥ wa tadbīr al-aʿmāl.* Ibid., p. 17. Al-Māwardī includes ten matters of "common affairs" that the caliph must undertake and over which he presumably exercises exclusive jurisdiction: protection of religious orthodoxy; resolution of private disputes and enforcement of legal judgments so that "justice prevails, the unjust cannot transgress and the oppressed are not weak"; public security, "so that the people can pursue their livelihoods and disperse securely in their journeys, without fear for their selves or their goods"; application of the mandatory penalties of criminal law (*al-ḥudūd*) so that "God's prohibitions are protected from violation and the rights of His servants are protected from damage and destruction"; fortifying the frontiers to deter enemy attacks; waging war against non-Muslims who refuse to embrace Islam or enter into a relationship of protection (*dhimma*) with the Islamic state; collecting lawful taxes; distributing public funds in an appropriate and timely fashion; appointment of suitable and competent delegates to public offices of the state; and, supervision of the affairs of state. Ibid. p. 18.

31. In describing the operative terms of the contract, for example, Māwardī uses the verb "entrusted" (*wukkila*) to describe the relationship of the caliph to the Muslim community, on the one hand, and the matters over which the caliph can exercise power. A person who has been entrusted by another to discharge some task is known as a *wakīl* or agent in Islamic law, and owes duties of loyalty to the party delegating to him the powers to so act. Likewise, the term used to describe the caliph's designated successor is *walī al-ʿahd*, which literally means "trustee of the covenant." The designated successor, in other words, is *entrusted* with the covenant that the incumbent caliph has undertaken in favor of the Muslim community. Significantly, Muslim jurists never used the verb *mallaka*, to give dominion, or any of its cognates, to describe the contractual relationship between the Muslim community and public officials.

32. Ibid. p. 19.

The contract of the caliphate establishes a public order that is distinct from a private order. The public order comes into existence via a delegation of authority from the community to the caliph. The caliph or the imam then further delegates powers to various public office holders, all of whom are acting, in one way or another, in a fiduciary capacity as a representative for all or some of the Muslim community. The individual persons making up the Muslim community, when they delegate their powers to the caliph, simultaneously renounce any competence they might have over managing public affairs, at least insofar as they are private individuals and are not properly appointed by the caliph to exercise some public power. Respect for the public order is obligatory, and those who refuse to recognize it may be legitimately fought to compel their obedience under the applicable laws of rebellion. *Mutatis mutandis*, lesser officials, such as governors, judges and tax collectors, provided they are acting lawfully, are entitled to compel individuals to obey their commands.

1.3. Duress and Sunnī Acquiescence to Usurpation

Māwardī's description of the rules regarding selection of the caliph, and terms governing his appointment, might usefully be analogized to the concept of "ideal theory." Māwardī's *Aḥkām* also includes provisions of "non-ideal" theory, i.e., what happens when the public sphere is taken over in part or in whole forcibly by usurpation. His theories regarding how the law should deal with usurpers has generally not met with much sympathy from modern commentators. Nevertheless, I have sought, at least partially, to rehabilitate Māwardī's [58] treatment of these circumstances by tying his analysis of non-ideal theory to the ideals informing his ideal doctrine of the caliphate. The salient feature in Māwardī's treatment of usurpers—whether the usurpation takes place at the level of the caliph or the governor—is the refusal to take a categorical position, whether in favour of the usurper or against him. Instead, the reaction is provisional and equivocal and rooted in prudence: to the extent that the usurper is willing to rule in accordance with the law, then his actions become legitimate, even if the usurpation, until such time as the caliph offers recognition of the de facto ruler, is not. Only where there is a complete and open break by the usurper with the legitimate public order does a categorical rupture take place. Crucially, however, the willingness to tolerate, and potentially rehabilitate usurpers, is not on account of deference to the usurper, but rather to further the interests of the law and the interests of the people which it protects.[33] Accordingly, the usurper obtains recognition only to the extent that he acts as though he were legitimately selected or appointed. Māwardī's treatment of the usurper, and his provisional willingness to rehabilitate him certainly paves the way for the legitimacy of the ruler by necessity, *ḥākim*

33. Al-Māwardī, pp. 39–40.

al-ḍarūra. Yet it also ensures that the usurper can only function as a ruler to the extent that ex post he observes the rule of law, including, the fiduciary ideal of representation regulating his relationship to the ruled.

1.4. Conclusion

Māwardī's conception of the caliphate provides a template for legality that entails the creation of a public sphere through the idea of a contract of delegation from the abstract idea of the Muslim community to its public agent, the caliph. The relationship created by this contract is a fiduciary one based on an ideal of representation, and pursuant to that idea, the caliph, and the officials appointed, directly or indirectly by the caliph, all stand in a fiduciary relationship with those whom they rule. The fiduciary ideal of representation entails both a power to use discretion on behalf of the governed, and places a limitation on that power. Because the principal is the Muslim community, public officials may only exercise the discretion vested in them in accordance with the law and in the public interest. The idea of government as standing in a fiduciary relationship of representation also responds to the theo-political premise of the moral equality of human beings. Human equality means that none are entitled to the obedience of their fellows. Obedience to an order that is constituted by law, and seeks their common good, not the particular good of the persons making the command, however, does not result in unjustifiable [59] obedience to another person. It is rather tantamount to compliance with a universal moral ideal that binds equally all humans.

2. THE SUNNĪ LAW OF AGENCY, GUARDIANSHIP AND FIDUCIARY DUTIES

As the previous section made clear, al-Māwardī's discussion of the caliphate in *al-Aḥkām al-Sulṭāniyya* structures the relationship of the caliph—and the public order he represents—as existing in a principal-agent relationship with the Muslim community. His use of explicit terms of agency to describe the formation of the relationship, i.e., *tawkīl* and *tafwīḍ*, and his use of explicit terms of representation, i.e., *niyāba*, to describe the function of public officials, as when he described the electors as acting in a representative capacity for the Muslim community rather than for themselves as individuals, make the role of this relationship in al-Māwardī's understanding of the legal basis of the caliphate clear. He also used the term *wilāya*—authority—to describe the jurisdiction of public officials, a term that is also used to describe both the authority a natural agent enjoys by virtue of a contract of agency with a natural principal and the authority the law grants to a guardian (*walī*) over a ward (*mūlā ʿalayhi*). The next section of this article (Section III) describes how the ideals of the law of agency, as well as the rules governing the conduct of a guardian, operate in the context of public law. Before one can recognize fully the links between Sunnī principles of private law and the principles of Sunnī public law, a brief digression into the private law of agency and guardianship is necessary.[34] This section, therefore, addresses the salient elements of the Sunnī private law of agency and guardianship.

The agency relationship is contractual, consisting of a principal (*al-muwakkil*),[35] an agent (*al-wakīl*), a right (*ḥaqq*), and manifestation of the relationship (*ṣīgha*). It effects a delegation (*niyāba*) that runs from the principal/delegator (*al-munīb*) to the delegate (*al-munāb*).[36] The scope of the delegation of authority may be unqualified, e.g., "I appoint you as my unrestricted agent (*wakkaltuka wikāla mufawwaḍa*)" or "for all of my affairs (*fī jamī*ᶜ *umūrī*)." Alternatively, it may be restricted by express language or by circumstantial [60] evidence to a particular transaction or class of transactions. In either case, the agent's assent is required before the agency relationship becomes effective.[37]

Given the object of an agency relationship is a "right" of the principal, there is an internal limitation on the scope of an agency relationship: it cannot be used to discharge what are inherently personal religious obligations, such as performance of the mandatory pilgrimage (*ḥajj al-farīḍa*), daily prayers (*al-ṣalāt*), or an oath of innocence in a lawsuit (*yamīn*), nor can it be used in the furtherance of an illegal or sinful act (*ma*ᶜ*ṣiya*).[38] Other authors describe this internal limitation on the scope of an agency relationship as resulting from the requirement that a prerequisite of a valid delegation (*niyāba*) is the personal right of the principal to perform the act which is the object of the delegation.[39] The Ḥanafī jurist, Abū Bakr al-Kasānī takes the same approach, stating that because the agent's authority derives entirely from the principal's own authority, the agent's authority to act is necessarily limited to those actions the principal could legitimately perform himself.[40]

The agency relationship, if it is restricted, also includes an extrinsic, contractual limitation as manifested in the principal's instructions to the agent. Whether the agency is restricted or unrestricted, however, the agent is bound to act in the interest of the principal.[41] Accordingly, when the agent violates the principal's contractually-imposed limitations on her authority, or fails to act in the interest of the principal, the agent's

34. I use private law to refer to those rules that regulate the relations of natural persons *and* the rules that govern endowments (*awqāf*/ s. *waqf*).

35. The principal may also be referred to as *al-aṣl*.

36. 3 Aḥmad b. Muḥammad b. Aḥmad al-Dardīr, *al-Sharḥ al-Ṣaghīr* 501.

37. Ibid. p. 506.

38. Ibid. pp. 503–4.

39. 5 Muḥammad b. Muḥammad b. ᶜAbd al-Raḥmān al-Ḥaṭṭāb, *Mawāhib al-Jalīl li-Sharḥ Mukhtaṣar Khalīl* (Beirut: Dār al-Fikr, 1992, 3rd ed.), p. 190.

40. 6 Abū Bakr al-Kāsānī, *Badā*ᵓ*i*ᶜ *al-Ṣanā*ᵓ*i*ᶜ (Beirut: Dār al-Kutub al-ᶜIlmiyya, 1986, 2nd ed.), p.620 (*ammā alladhī yarji*ᶜ *ilā al-muwakkil fa-huwa an yakuna mimman yamliku fi*ᶜ*l mā wukkila bihi bi-nafsihi li-anna al-tawkīl tafwīḍ mā yamlikuhu min al-taṣarruf ilā ghayrihi fa-mā lā yamlikuhu bi-nafsihi kayfa yaḥtamil al-tafwīḍ ilā ghayrihi*).

41. 3 al-Dardīr, p. 508 (*wa fa*ᶜ*ala al-wakīl al-maṣlaḥa*).

action binds only the agent, and not the principal.[42] Because the agent is duty-bound to act in the best interests of the principal, the agent is prohibited from self-dealing i.e., using his [61] authority to enter into transactions for her own private benefit, except in exceptional circumstances.[43] The obligation to act in the interests of the principal also precludes the agent from acting on non-arm's length terms (*muḥābāt*) in favour of those with whom he has, for example, a personal tie. Thus, an agent who sells on credit is permitted to offer the debtor an extension of the term for commercial reasons beneficial to the principal, e.g., to solicit additional business from the debtor, but not as a personal favour to the debtor.[44] If an agent leases real property on a non-arm's length basis, the principal maintains the right to invalidate the contract before performance begins. Once performance has begun, however, the agent is liable to the principal for the difference between the contract rent and the fair rent.[45]

When the agent satisfies the conditions of the agency agreement, i.e., by acting within the scope of the agreement and in conformity with the interest of the principal, however, the agent's action is attributed to the principal simply by virtue of the representation (*al-niyāba*) that is the legal effect of the agency relationship.[46] Likewise, the agent, so long as third parties know him to be an agent, is personally immune from the contractual claims of those whom he deals with on behalf of the principal. Accordingly, the purchaser of a good who claims a defect (*ʿayb*) in the good, or if the purchaser's title to the good was successfully challenged by the true owner (*istiḥqāq*), the principal bears liability, not

42. Ibid. p. 510. In Ḥanafī and Mālikī doctrine, however, the principal retains the option to ratify an action of the agent that violates her instructions or otherwise was not in her interests. Al-Kāsānī also points out that if the agent were to contradict his principal's instructions in a way *beneficial* (*khilāf ilā khayr*) to the principal, e.g., the principal orders the agent to sell her goods for $1,000, but the agent in fact sells it for $1,100, the agent's action binds the principal because her action, although it appears to contravene the principal's instructions, is in fact in accordance with her instructions, and it can be assumed that principal implicitly would have requested the agent to sell at the higher price and so he was acting pursuant to the principal's authority (*li-annahu āmir bihi dalālatan fa-kāna mutaṣarrifan bi-tawliyat al-muwakkil*). 6 Al-Kāsānī, p. 624.

43. 3 al-Dardīr, p. 512.

44. 4 Mālik b. Anas, *al-Mudawwana al-Kubrā* (Beirut: Dār al-Fikr, n.d.), p. 40.

45. 7 Muḥammad b. ʿAbdallāh al-Kharshī, *Sharḥ Mukhtaṣar Khalīl li'l-Kharshī* (Beirut: Dār al-Fikr, n.d.), p. 48.

46. The Mālikī text, *al-Sharḥ al-Ṣaghīr*, does not even bother to make this point explicit, contenting itself instead to point out what actions, if taken by the agent, preclude the ordinary effect of an agent's actions, namely, binding the principal. The Ḥanafī al-Kāsānī, however, makes this point explicit, stating that "among the legal effects of an agency relationship is the establishment of the authority to act within the scope of the agency (*wa li'l-wikāla aḥkām minhā thubūt wilāyat al-taṣarruf alladhī tanāwalahu al-tawkīl*)." 6 al-Kāsānī, p. 23.

the agent.[47] The agent also enjoyed immunity from tort claims incurred in the course of performing his duties, with recourse to be had against the principal.[48]

[62] Finally, an agency relationship comes to a conclusion, and the agent is divested of authority to act on behalf of the principal, upon the first to occur of (i) the principal's removal of the agent, (ii) the principal's death, or (iii) in the case of a restricted agency, the agent's completion of the object of the agency agreement.[49]

Sunnī jurists extended the principles regulating the principal-agent relationship to non-consensual relationships such as that of the executor of an estate or guardian of an orphan (*al-waṣī*) and the supervisor of an endowment (*nāẓir al-waqf*) to regulate the relationship between the executor and the heirs, the guardian and the orphan, and the supervisor of the endowment and the endowment's beneficiaries. They justified the extension of the principles of agency law to these non-consensual relationships on the grounds that each of the orphan's guardian, the estate's executor and the endowment's supervisor acts on behalf of a third-party (*al-taṣarruf ʿan al-ghayr*). Accordingly, persons in acting in such capacities are the functional equivalent of an agent (*bi-manzilat al-wakīl*), and so it is appropriate that the duties of an agent attach to them.[50]

Indeed, even fathers were subject to the fiduciary principals of agents with respect to their dealings with their minor children. For example, neither the father nor the guardian of an orphan was permitted to admit the validity of a claim against a minor child,[51] nor could he waive a right of a minor.[52] Al-Kāsānī's explanation of the limits of paternal authority illuminate the centrality of the child's right and that the father's rights as the guardian of the minor child are limited to actions that preserve or vindicate the child's rights. Accordingly, al-Kāsānī wrote:

> Among the prerequisites for the validity [of a waiver of right to retaliation] is that the waiver (*ʿafw*) comes from the person possessed of the right (*ṣāḥib al-ḥaqq*) because it amounts to abandonment of the claim (*isqāṭ al-ḥaqq*), and abandonment of the claim where there is no claim is an absurdity (*muḥāl*). Accordingly, waiver is not valid from a stranger (*ajnabī*) because of the absence of a claim, nor from the father nor from the grandfather in a case of retaliation (*qiṣāṣ*) due to the minor because the claim belongs to the minor, not to them. Indeed, they have authority [63] only to

47. 3 al-Dardīr, p. 508 (*wa ṭūliba al-wakīl bi'l-ʿuhda min ʿayb fīmā bāʿahu li-muwakkalihi aw istiḥqāq mā lam yaʿlam al-mushtarī bi'annahu wakīl*).

48. 6 al-Kāsānī, p. 27 (describing a case where the agent of an investment partnership (*al-muḍārib*) uses the partnership capital to invest in a slave, and the slave then accidentally kills a third party and concluding that liability falls on the investors and not their agent).

49. 3 al-Dardīr, p. 523 (*wa'-nʿazala al-wakīl mufawwaḍan aw lā . . . bi-mawt muwakkilihi aw bi-ʿazlihi . . . wa yanʿazil ghayr al-mufawwaḍ bi-tamām mā wukkila fīhi*).

50. 7 al-Kharshī, p. 48.

51. 6 al-Kāsānī, p. 24. (*al-ab wa'l-waṣī . . . lā yamlik al-iqrār ʿalā al-ṣaghīr bi'l-ijmāʿ*).

52. 5 al-Kāsānī, p. 151.

> vindicate rights belonging to the minor (*innamā lahumā wilāyat istīfāʾ ḥaqq wajaba l'l-ṣaghīr*). Another reason is that their authority is limited to the good of the minor and a waiver [of his claim] is a pure harm [to the minor] because it is an abandonment of the right in its entirety, so they do not possess this right (*wa li'anna wilāyatahumā muqayyada bi'l-naẓar li'l-ṣaghīr wa'l-ʿafw ḍarar maḥḍ li'annahu isqāṭ al-ḥaqq aṣlan wa ra'san fa-lā yamlikānihi*).[53]

For the Mālikīs, the fiduciary obligations of the agent were also used to analyze the duties of the father with respect to his management of his minor children's property. Accordingly, while the law gave him the right to manage their property so long as they remained minors, he was liable for misusing their property, such as cases involving self-dealing, where he buys or sells their property to or for himself, or cases involving favoritism to third-parties, where he buys or sells their property to third parties on a non-arm's length basis.[54] The same fiduciary principles also applied to limit the father's discretion in connection with his actions as guardian for his daughter's marriage.[55] Jurists applied the same principles to the trustee of an endowment (*nāẓir al-waqf*).[56] Accordingly, if the trustee leases the endowment's property on a non-arm's length basis, the beneficiaries of the endowment are entitled either [64] to rescind the lease or affirm it, if it has yet to be performed (*in lam yafut*), or sue the trustee for the difference between the contract rent and the fair rent (*ujrat al-mithl*), if it has been performed. The trustee, moreover, has no right of recourse against the lessee, who can only be liable for the difference between the contract rent and the fair rent if the trustee is insolvent.[57]

---

53. Ibid.

54. The general approach of the Mālikīs was to presume that the father's actions with respect to his minor children's property was consistent with their interests until proof of the contrary is produced (*bayʿ al-ab ʿalā ṣighār banīhi wa abkār banātihi maḥmūl ʿalā al-naẓar ḥattā yathbuta khilāfuhu*). 5 al-Mawwāq, *al-Tāj wa'l-Iklīl* (Beirut: Dār al-Fikr, 1992, 3rd ed.), p. 69. Where evidence of self-dealing exists, however, the Mālikīs disagree on the proper remedy, with some arguing for rescission of the self-dealing transaction, and others arguing for holding the father monetarily liable to the child for the fair value (*qīma*) of the property. 5 al-Ḥaṭṭāb, p. 69. The same parental duty to act in the best interest of the minor in dealing with the minor's property also applies to the father when acting as a guardian for his daughter's marriage.

55. See, for example, 4 Shihāb al-Dīn al-Qarāfī, *al-Dhakhīra*, edited by Muḥammad Abū Khubza (Beirut: Dār al-Gharb al-Islāmī, 1994), p. 253, who said "whoever exercises authority over marriage, or anything else, arbitrary acts are not permissible for him by consensus; rather, he is obliged to follow the best interests of the ward (*man waliya wilāyat al-nikāḥ aw ghayrihi lā yajūz lahu al-taṣarruf bi'l-tashahhī ijmāʿan bal tajib murāʿāt maṣlaḥat al-mūlā ʿalayhi*)."

56. The trustee of an endowment would initially be appointed by the endowment's founder, and successor trustees would be appointed in accordance with the terms of the endowment, or if there was a failure to appoint a trustee in accordance with the terms of the endowment, the court could appoint a trustee. The beneficiaries of the endowment, however, did not select the trustee, and for this reason, the relationship between the trustee and the beneficiaries is non-consensual.

57. 4 al-Dardīr, p. 64; 4 Aḥmad al-Ṣāwī, *Ḥāshiyat al-Ṣāwī ʿalā al-Sharḥ al-Ṣaghīr* ed. Muṣṭafā Kamāl Waṣfī (*Dār al-Maʿārif*: Cairo, n.d.), p. 64.

3. THE REPRESENTATIONAL/FIDUCIARY IDEAL AND SUNNĪ PUBLIC LAW

The previous section outlined the structure of the Sunnī private law of agency, and how its fiduciary norms were transferred to non-consensual relationships in which one person has authority (*wilāya*) to act (*al-taṣarruf*) on behalf of a third person, whether in the context of the father-child relationship, the guardian-orphan relationship, or the relationship of an endowment's trustee with the beneficiaries. Below, I argue that Sunnī jurists analogously applied the fiduciary norms that applied to contractual agents and the norms governing non-consensual fiduciary relationships, to analyze the relationship between public officials and the public, thus giving legal and moral content to a Sunnī ideal of public law.[58] One especially clear case of the use of a private law norm to develop a rule of public law is in the case of liability for trespass on public property. The Ḥanafī rule is that whoever builds a structure on public property without the permission of the ruler is strictly liable for any injuries that result from that structure to members of the public. Al-Kāsāni, for example, in explaining the legal basis for this rule, expressly analogizes it to the applicable principles of liability arising out of trespass in private law. Thus, he argues that public goods (*maṣāliḥ ʿāmmat al-muslimīn*) are a right that belongs to the public (*mā yarjiʿ ilā maṣāliḥ al-muslimīn kāna ḥaqqan lahum*), and that the administration of [65] such public goods lies within the jurisdiction of the ruler (*al-tadbīr fī amr al-ʿāmma ilā al-imām*). Accordingly, to dig a well in a public path, or any other structure, without the ruler's permission is akin to digging a well on a private person's property without the owner's permission (*kāna al-ḥafr fīhi bi-ghayr idhn al-imām ka'l-ḥafr fī dār insān bi-ghayr idhn ṣāḥib al-dār*), in which case the well-digger, under principles of private trespass, would be liable for any injuries or deaths that may occur. Accordingly, someone who builds a structure on public property without the ruler's permission is committing a trespass on public property and so should be held strictly liable for any injuries or deaths resulting from the trespass.[59]

58. Sunnī jurists used several terms to express the idea of a public official, such as *sulṭān*, *khalīfa*, *imām*, *walī al-amr* (pl. *awliyāʾ al-umūr*). They also used several terms to express the idea of the public, such as *al-ʿāmma*, *ʿāmmat al-muslimīn*, *jamāʿat al-muslimīn*, *al-kāffa*, and *al-muslimīn*. For an overview of these various terms in Sunnī substantive law, see Mohammad Fadel, "Public Authority (*Sulṭān*) in Islamic Law," in *The Oxford International Encyclopedia of Legal History*, edited by Stanley N. Katz (Oxford University Press, on line edition, 2009). available at: https://www.oxfordreference.com/display/10.1093/acref/9780195134056.001.0001/acref-9780195134056-e-663?rskey=nvAikt&result=661.

59. 7 al-Kāsānī, p. 278. The position cited above is the prevalent doctrine of the Ḥanafī school and is based on what is known as *ẓāhir al-riwāya*. The minority position is represented by the view of Abū Yūsuf, one of Abū Ḥanīfa's two most important disciples, who held that no liability would attach to the private person if the action, e.g., digging a well, was in fact for the public good, in which case the public implicitly authorized the action (*mā kāna min maṣāliḥ al-muslimīn kāna al-idhn bihi thābitan dalālatan wa'l-thābit dalālatan ka'l-thābit naṣṣan*). Ibid.

Various cases presented below give an overview of how Sunnī jurists, using what they considered appropriate and analogous cases from private law, constructed an ideal of government based on a combination of the representational and fiduciary ideals that structured the private law of agency and the fiduciary norms that underlay the relationship of various kinds of guardians to their respective beneficiaries. My analysis begins with rules affirming that the caliph, and by extension, lesser public officials, function as agents of the Muslim community. From there, I proceed to establish that Sunnī jurists distinguished, as a conceptual matter, a distinctively public sphere that was differentiated from the private sphere by virtue of special rules that applied to the former, and that the only persons authorized to act in that domain were duly appointed public officials. In other words, not only did Sunnī jurists distinguish conceptually between the public and private spheres as separate legal domains, they recognized that public officials possessed exclusive authority over the administration of that domain. I then show how the juridical distinction between the public sphere and the private sphere places an internal limit on the power of public officials by precluding them from exercising the private rights of natural persons. I conclude by showing that Sunnī jurists applied the same substantive standards that governed the discretionary actions of fiduciaries in the private law context to the discretionary actions of public officials, thus setting up the next section of the article, in which I consider the place of positive law (*amr*) in the jurisprudence of pre-modern Sunnī jurists.

3.1. Explicit Affirmations of the Representative and Fiduciary Character of the Caliphate

[66] Abū Bakr al-Kāsānī, in his magnum opus, *Badāʾiʿ al-Ṣanāʾiʿ*, expressly affirms the representative nature of the contract of the caliphate, and asserts that the caliph, as a legal matter, acts solely as a public agent for the Muslim community. His articulation of this proposition leaves no room for doubt that Sunnī jurists viewed the caliph as an agent of the Muslim community; that his powers are delegated from the community; that those powers are exercised for the benefit of the community, i.e., the "public," and not for his private benefit; and, that his lawful actions are, from a legal perspective, the actions of the community.[60] Al-Kasānī distinguishes the rules governing the dismissal of a judge from those governing the dismissal of the agent of a natural principal by noting that judges are not divested of authority when the caliph (or other official) who appointed him dies or is removed from office. He accounts for this difference by noting that the caliph who appointed the judge does not stand in a principal-agent relationship with the judge. Rather, the judge's true principal is the Muslim community; it is from their authority and not the caliph's personal authority that the judge's authority derives.[61] Because the

60. 7 al-Kasānī, p. 16.

61. *Al-qāḍī lā yaʿmal bi-wilāyat al-khalīfa wa fī ḥaqqihi bal bi-wilāyat al-muslimīn wa fī ḥuqūqihim*. Ibid.

Muslim community does not perish, the judge's appointment continues to be valid despite the death or removal from office of the official who appointed him.[62] Indeed, Kāsānī states expressly that the caliph's role in both appointing and dismissing public officials is simply that of a messenger (*rasūl*) acting on behalf of the community, because in both cases, whether that of appointment or dismissal, the actual party doing the appointing and dismissing is the Muslim community.[63] The caliph, as messenger of the community, simply expresses the will of the community. Accordingly, his actions are effectively—and in the eyes of the law—community actions. Whether appointing or dismissing judges, the caliph in each case exercises power delegated to him from the Muslim public; he possess the specific power of appointment and dismissal because the rational good of the public cannot be achieved unless the caliph has such powers.[64] [67] The fact that the caliph is a representative of the Muslim public (*ʿāmmat al-muslimīn*) also accounts for other rules of substantive law, one of which Kāsāni mentions in passing—the immunity of public officials from ordinary principles of tort. Kāsānī explains that because the caliph is an agent of the community, "he is immune from liability in the same manner as other agents in contractual dealings,"[65] the general principle being that liability arising out of an agent's authorized activities is borne by the principal who authorized the conduct, and not the agent.[66]

Kāsānī in this passage expressly affirms two other crucial principles of Sunnī public law. The first is that because the caliph is an agent, the powers the caliph exercises can only consist of powers that are delegated to him from the Muslim community. The second is that such powers as have been delegated to the caliph on behalf of the Muslim community are derivative of what is necessary and proper to achieve their rational good as a community, and can only be exercised in furtherance of that good. The idea of the caliph as the agent of the Muslim community, however, also includes within it the important limitation that an agent only has authority to act to the extent that the principal itself could have acted directly. Accordingly, because the principal is the Muslim community, the caliph lacks authority to contravene the Sharīʿa, which is itself constitutive of the Muslim community. As explained below, this means that public officials lack authority to issue commands that contravene the Sharīʿa, and if they do, such orders, all things being equal, are effectively legal nullities.

---

62. *Wilāyatuhum baʿda mawt al-khalīfa bāqiya fa-yabqā al-qāḍī ʿalā wilāyatihi*. Ibid.

63. *Innamā al-khalīfa bi-manzilat al-rasūl ʿanhum . . . wa idhā kāna rasūlan kāna fiʿluhu bi-manzilat fiʿl ʿāmmat al-muslimīn . . . inna al-khalīfa idhā ʿazala al-qāḍī aw al-wālī yanʿazil bi-ʿazlihi wa lā yanʿazil bi-mawtihi li-annahu lā yanʿazil bi-ʿazl al-khalīfa ḥaqīqatan bal bi-ʿazl al-ʿāmma*. Ibid.

64. *Tawliyatahu bi-tawliyat al-ʿāmma wa'l-ʿāmma wallawhu al-istibdāl dalālatan li-taʿalluq maṣlaḥatihim bi-dhālika fa-kānat wilāyatuhu minhum maʿnan fi'l-ʿazl ayḍan*. Ibid.

65. *Li-dhālika lam talḥaqhu al-ʿuhda ka'l-rasūl fī sāʾir al-ʿuqūd*. Ibid.

66. Supra n. 47 and n. 48.

3.2. Protecting the Exclusive Jurisdiction of the Public Sphere in Sunnī Substantive Law

Māwardī's theory of the caliphate noted that the very act of delegation of authority over public affairs also entailed a simultaneous divesture of any power individuals might have to exercise power over public life, describing any attempts to interfere with the caliph's exercise of those delegated powers as an invasion into public decision making (*iftiyāt*). This concept, *iftiyāt*, was already a term of art in early Sunnī jurisprudence,[67] and while it is not clear whether [68] Māwardī used it in its technical legal sense or simply in its ordinary sense, it is nevertheless the case that for Sunnī jurists, private enforcement of the law was criminalized as an invasion of the public order, or *iftiyāt*. Jurists used this doctrine to enforce the exclusive jurisdiction of the state over sensitive matters such as the enforcement of criminal law or the right of retaliation in tort law. Mālikīs, for example, held that a private arbitrator who exceeded his jurisdiction by ruling in matters of criminal law was subject to criminal punishment (*adab*) if his decision is carried out, even if the decision was substantively correct.[68] For the same reason, the next of kin of a murder victim, if he kills the murderer without a prior judicial ruling, is guilty of the crime of *iftiyāt*, taking the law into his own hands.[69]

Even though private persons were not permitted to exercise public powers directly, they could apply to courts to protect their interests as members of the public from government abuse or neglect. The great Ḥanafī Central Asian jurist, al-Sarakhsī, for example, authorized individual members of the public to bring suit to enjoin transfers of public property to private individuals if such a transfer would cause an injury to the public. In recognizing this claim, Sarakhsī argued that because the ruler's authority over public interests was limited to vindicating the rights of the public, he lacked authority to take actions that undermined those rights.[70]

The public, according to Kāsāni, could also resort to the judiciary in defense of public rights against invasion from private persons. Public nuisance provides another excellent case of how private law remedies were adapted to provide a remedy for the violation of a

67. See, for example, Ibn Farḥūn, 2 *Tabṣirat al-Ḥukkām* (Cairo: Maktabat al-Kulliyyāt al-Azhariyya, 1986), p. 185, quoting an early Mālikī authority as saying that a man who kills a stranger he finds having intercourse with his wife is liable for intentional murder, unless he can produce witnesses who testify to the fact of vaginal penetration. Even if he establishes this defense, however, the husband would still be liable criminally for interfering in the state's jurisdiction (*wa innamā ʿalayhi al-adab min al-sulṭān li-iftiyātihi ʿalayhi bi-taʿjīl qatlihi*).

68. See, for example, 4 al-Dardīr, pp. 199–200.

69. See, for example, ibid., 4:336 (negating the guardian's right to kill the murderer in retaliation without the prior permission of the judge, and subjecting him to criminal punishment if he does, but exempting him from retaliation if he can prove that the person he killed was in fact the killer).

70. *Li'l-sulṭān wilāyat al-naẓar dūn al-iḍrār bi'l-ʿāmma . . . wa fī mā yaḍurru bi-him li-kulli wāḥid minhum an yamnaʿa fa'l-imām . . . lahu wilāyat istīfāʾ ḥaqq al-ʿāmma lā wilāyat al-ibṭāl.* 23 Shams al-Dīn al-Sarakhsī, *Kitāb al-Mabsūṭ* (Beirut: Dār al-Maʿrifa, 1913), p. 183.

public right. For example, if a person builds a private structure on his own property that threatens to collapse and cause an injury to his neighbour, under ordinary principles of private law, the neighbour must first give notice to the owner of the structure and demand that he repair it before the owner becomes liable for losses should the structure subsequently collapse onto the neighbour's property. Where the faulty structure threatens to collapse onto public property, this rule of prior notice presents a problem: because it is extremely unlikely that the person who gives notice to the owner [69] of the decrepit property that his structure needs repair will be the person who is injured should it collapse, the requisite nexus between the person giving notice and the injury which is required in the law of private nuisance is absent. Accordingly, Kāsānī instead transforms the claim of injury into one belonging to the public, not the specific person who is injured, and accordingly, any adult member of the public can serve notice on the owner on behalf of the rest of the public, because in so doing, he is vindicating a right of the public which they share in common. Once any member of the public gives notice to the owner, then any member of the public who is subsequently injured by the structure's collapse has standing to sue the owner for his or her injury.[71]

3.3. Protecting the Private Sphere from the Public Sphere

Implicit in Māwardī's notion of delegation of public powers to the caliph is that individuals retain their powers over their private affairs. The Andalusian Mālikī jurist, Abū Bakr b. al-ʿArabī (d. 1148), relies on the limited nature of the delegation of power to the ruler to explain why the ruler may waive the criminal punishment of a highway robber who surrenders voluntarily, but not the personal claims of the defendant's victims. The justification for this distinction, Ibn al-ʿArabī explains, is that the Imam is not an agent for specific persons in regard to their specific rights; rather, he is their representative only with respect to their common and abstract rights, which have not been identified as belonging to any particular person.[72] [70] The Imam's jurisdiction as public agent, there-

---

71. *Wa ammā sharāʾiṭ al-wujūb fa-minhā al-muṭālaba bi'l-naqḍ ḥattā law saqaṭa qabla al-muṭālaba fa-ʿaṭaba bihi shayʾ lā ḍamān ʿalā ṣāḥib al-ḥāʾiṭ li-anna al-ḍamān yajib bi-tark al-naqḍ al-mustaḥaqq li-anna bihi yaṣīr mutaʿaddiyan fī al-tasbīb ilā al-itlāf wa lā yathbut al-istiḥqāq bi-dūn al-muṭālaba wa ṣūrat al-muṭālaba hiya an yataqaddama ilayhi wāḥid min ʿaraḍ al-nās fa-yaqūl lahu 'inna ḥāʾiṭaka hādhā māʾil aw makhūf fa-irfaʿhu.' Fa idhā qāla lahu dhālika lazimahu rafʿuhu li-anna hādhā ḥaqq al-ʿāmma fa-idhā qāma bihi al-baʿḍ ṣāra khaṣman ʿan al-bāqīn, sawāʾ kāna alladhī taqaddama ilayhi musliman aw dhimmiyyan ḥurran aw ʿabdan . . . bālighan aw ṣabiyyan baʿda an kāna ʿāqilan.* 7 al-Kāsānī, p. 283.

72. *Wa ammā man qāla fī ḥuqūq al-ādamiyyīn inna al-imām lā yatawallā ṭalabahā wa innamā yaṭlubuhā arbābuhā wa huwa madhhab Mālik fa-ṣaḥīh li-anna al-imām laysa bi-wakīl li-muʿayyanīn min al-nās fī ḥuqūqihim al-muʿayyana wa innamā huwa nāʾibuhum fī ḥuqūqihim al-mujmala al-mubhama allatī laysat bi-muʿayyana.* 2 Al-Qāḍī Abū Bakr b. al-ʿArabī, *Aḥkām al-Qurʾān*, edited by Muḥammad ʿAbd al-Qādir ʿAṭā (Beirut: Dār al-Kutub al-ʿIlmiyya, 2003), pp. 102–3.

fore, does not extend to private claims that specific, natural persons have against other specific, natural persons. While the public has a common right in the application of the criminal law, their rights to compensation are individual to each of them, and accordingly, the Imam lacks authority to pursue or waive those claims, in accordance with the limited jurisdiction of his office.

3.4. The Fiduciary Principle and the Principle of Public Rationality in Sunnī Public Law

I have tried to make the case that Sunnī jurists transferred the fiduciary principles of agency and guardianship from the context of private law to the conduct of the caliph and lesser public officials. The cases discussed above were intended to affirm the normative view among the jurists that although the caliph, and the lesser officials he appointed, were the exclusive agents of the community with respect to the community's public affairs, individuals maintained exclusive authority over their private rights. Yet the question of how public officials should exercise their powers over public affairs has yet to be addressed. The analogy to the private law of agency and that of guardians, however, suggests that their actions must be consistent with the well-being of the public in order for their actions to be valid. In other words, one would expect that the actions of public officials according to Sunnī jurisprudence, if they are to be deemed valid, must meet a standard of rationality as determined from the perspective of the public.

The 13th-century Egyptian Mālikī jurist, Shihāb al-Dīn al-Qarāfī (d. 684/1285), in fact, does just that, expressly arguing that actions of public officials, in order for them to be valid, must be rational from the perspective of the public. Moreover, he deems this requirement of rationality to be jurisdictional, which is consistent with this article's argument that the normative basis of the powers of public officials was their status as fiduciaries for the public. Accordingly, he stated in *al-Furūq* that:

> Regarding the difference between the actions of public officials which are given effect in the law and those which are not . . . the first category [of actions that are invalid] are those actions which were not included in their original jurisdiction. You should know that whoever exercises authority over another, from the caliph down to the guardian of an orphan, is not authorized to act except to attain a good or to ward off a harm in accordance with God most High's statement "Do not approach the property of the orphan except in the fairest manner . . ."[73] and because of the [71] statement of the Prophet Muḥammad, may God's peace and blessings be upon him, "Any person who is given authority over any of my community's affairs, and fails to exercise that authority in good faith for their benefit, is forbidden entry to Paradise." Accordingly, caliphs and governors have no jurisdiction to act except in accordance with the requirements of

73. *Al-Isrāʾ*, 17:34.

> good-faith judgment. Decisions that reduce well-being are never "in the fairest manner," but rather are their opposite. The authority conferred by virtue of holding public office therefore is limited to acts that produce either an absolute increase in well-being or a net gain in overall well-being, or to acts that prevent an absolute loss of well-being or prevent a net loss in overall well-being.[74]

The public rationality requirement arises out of the fiduciary relationship that office holders have with respect to those who fall under their jurisdiction. Whenever a public official is called upon to exercise a power in furtherance of the interests of a specific person, e.g., when a judge is required to act as a guardian in the marriage of an orphan girl, he is bound by the requirement of rationality, as determined from the perspective of the person on whose behalf the authority is exercised. When a public official exercises public power, then its rationality must be determined from the perspective of the public.

The same principle applies when public officials exercise authority over particular members of the public. Accordingly, while an adult woman or her natural guardian is entitled to waive the legal condition of the social suitability of the prospective groom, the judge is not, and he must only marry her to a husband who is at least her social peer.[75] Likewise, when a judge acts as a guardian over a minor who has the right to seek damages (*diya*) or retaliation (*qiṣāṣ*) against a tortfeasor, the judge is not permitted to waive the minor's [72] claim, even though a tort victim is in principle always free to waive his claims to damages or retaliation and forgive the tortfeasor outright (*ʿafw*) in order to seek religious reward.[76] Natural persons, by contrast, acting with respect to their own property, are not subject to such a standard, and are free to act with respect to their own property in a fashion that is not, from an objective perspective, beneficial.[77]

---

74. *Iʿlam anna kulla man waliya wilāya al-khilāfa fa-mā dūnahā ilā waṣiyy lā yaḥillu lahu an yataṣarrafa illā bi-jalb maṣlaḥa aw darʿ mafsada li-qawlihi taʿālā 'lā taqrabū māl al-yatīm illā bi'l-latī hiya aḥsan' wa li-qawlihi ʿalayhi al-salām 'man waliya min umūr ummatī shayʾan thumma lam yajtahid lahum wa lam yanṣaḥ fa'l-janna ʿalayhi ḥarām' fa-yakūn al-aʾimma wa'l-wulāt maʿzūlīn ʿammā laysa fīhi badhl al-jahd wa'l-marjūḥ abadan laysa bi'l-aḥsan bal al-aḥsan ḍiddahu wa laysa al-akhdh bihi badhlan li'l-ijtihād bal al-akhdh bi-ḍiddihi . . . wa takūn al-wilāya innamā tatanāwal jalb al-maṣlaḥa al-khāliṣa aw al-rājiḥa wa darʾ al-mafsada al-khāliṣa aw al-rājiḥa.* 4 Shihāb al-Dīn al-Qarāfī, *al-Furūq* (Beirut: ʿĀlam al-kutub, n.d.), p. 39. See also, 1 Shihāb al-Dīn Aḥmad b. Muḥammad Makkī, *Ghamz ʿUyūn al-Baṣāʾir fī Sharḥ al-Ashbāh wa'l-Naẓāʾir* (Beirut: Dār al-Kutub al-ʿIlmiyya, 1985), p. 369 (the actions of the Imam bind the public only if they are in the public good (*al-qāʿida al-khāmisa: taṣarruf al-imām ʿalā al-raʿiyya manūṭ bi'l-maṣlaḥa*)); and, 1 Jalāl al-Dīn al-Suyūṭī, *al-Ashbāh wa'l-Naẓāʾir* (Beirut: Dār al-Kutub al-ʿIlmiyya, 1990), p. 121.

75. 1 al-Suyūṭī, p. 121.

76. Ibid; 7 al-Kāsānī, p. 246.

77. 4 al-Qarāfī, p. 39 (an individual with respect to his own property is free to do with it what he wishes, even if his actions are not objectively beneficial to him).

3.5. Tort Law at the Intersection Between Public Law and Private Law

Tort law provides another important context for determining the interaction between public law and private law. Public officials, including judges and officers entrusted with executing judgments, could, in the course of performing their tasks, violate the rights of others, e.g., by criminally punishing the wrong defendant, or erroneously taking or destroying property from a private person without legal cause. Ordinarily, such actions would precipitate the aggrieved party's right to seek a remedy against the person who was the proximate cause of the wrong. Application of the ordinarily applicable tort rule to the actions of public officials might reasonably deter individuals from serving in offices that might lead them to commit such torts with regular frequency.[78]

Conversely, too lenient a standard would undermine the rule of law by excusing government officials from liability for unlawful actions. In resolving this tension, Muslim jurists adapted the principles that apply to private conduct to public officials by granting public officials a presumptive right to assume [73] the validity of governmental actions. However, this presumption would be removed in situations where the government official knew that the conduct in question was illegal.

Their treatment of unlawful killing under the colour of law illustrates the interdependence of private and public standards of liability in the legal thought of late medieval Muslim jurists, and how a different standard of liability was articulated for those acting under the colour of law from that which applied to private persons. Ibn Qudāma, the 13th century Damascene Ḥanbalī jurist, explained the remedy for unlawful killing under colour of law in the following terms:

> Were a public official [*al-sulṭān*] to command a [subordinate] person [to kill another], and so he does kill that other person, if the killer knew that the deceased was not subject to a lawful death sentence, the subordinate is subject to retaliation (*al-qiṣāṣ*), but not the superior official (*al-āmir*), because he [i.e., the killer]

78. Al-ʿIzz b. ʿAbd al-Salām, 1 *Qawāʿid al-Aḥkām fī Maṣāliḥ al-Anām*, p. 91 (placing liability on the treasury instead of the judge's family on account of the fact that application of the ordinary rule of tort liability with respect to misappropriation of property would unreasonably require the judge and his extended family to bear liabilities of actions performed for the benefit of the public). He applies the same reasoning to excuse the public executioner from liability for mistakenly putting to death innocent people because to apply the ordinary rule in this circumstance would deter anyone from accepting the position of executioner. Ibid., p. 90. Where the judge mistakenly, but in good faith, puts someone to death, or amputates a limb or the like, the Shāfiʿīs disagree whether liability should be borne personally by the judge or the treasury. 2 Ibn ʿAbd al-Salām, p. 67. The Ḥanafīs, however, place liability for such errors on the public treasury on the grounds that the judge was acting for the benefit of the public. 6 Muḥammad b. Idrīs al-Shāfiʿī, *Kitāb al-Umm* (Beirut: Dār al-Maʿrifa, 1990), p. 190 (*wa qad qāla ghayrunā min al-mashriqiyyīn al-ʿaql ʿalā bayt al-māl li-anna al-sulṭān innamā yuʾaddib li-jamāʿat al-muslimīn fīmā fīhi ṣalāḥuhum fa'l-ʿaql ʿalayhim fī bayt mālihim*).

> lacks a legal excuse for his action. . . . Accordingly, the subordinate official is subject to retaliation, exactly as would be the case if the superior was not a public official. If [the subordinate] did not know that [the deceased was subject to an unlawful death sentence], then liability attaches to the superior official. In this case, the [subordinate] who was commanded [to carry out the unlawful order] is excused because he is under an obligation of obedience to the Imam in respect of acts that are not sinful, and the legal presumption is that the Imam's rulings are just. If the person commanding the killing is not acting under colour of law, but is simply a member of the public, for example, and [the commanded person] killed [the other person], he is liable for intentional killing in all cases, whether or not he has knowledge [of the victim's actual innocence] because he is never under an obligation of obedience to the person who issued the command. Ordinary persons never have authority to kill, in contrast to public officials, who can apply capital punishment in cases of apostasy, adultery, and highway robbery, if the highway robber has committed murder ... An ordinary person never has authority over any of these matters.[79]

[74] Ibn Qudāma's analysis begins with asking whether the issuer of the command is acting under colour of law. If so, the person carrying out the command has a presumptive defense from liability insofar as he is entitled to assume that the orders of public officials are consistent with law. If, however, he comes to know that an order to kill lacks legal basis, he becomes personally responsible for the conduct because the order, once known to be illegal, is stripped of its authority, even if the public official coerces the subordinate.[80] In effect, it becomes the legal equivalent of an order to kill issued by a person who is not acting under colour of law. Private persons, as Ibn Qudāma's analysis makes clear, never have authority to kill another person, whether or not their victim is substantively guilty of even the most heinous crimes known to the legal system. In the absence of coercion,

79. *Wa law amara al-sulṭān rajulan fa-qatala ākhara fa-in kāna al-qātil yaʿlam annahu lā yastaḥiqq qatluhu fa'l-qiṣāṣ ʿalayhi dūna al-āmir li-annahu ghayr maʿdhūr fī fiʿlihi . . .fa-lazimahu al-qiṣāṣ ka-mā law amarahu ghayr al-sulṭān; wa in lam yaʿlam dhālika fa'l-qiṣāṣ ʿalā al-āmir dūn al-maʾmūr li-anna al-maʾmūr maʿdhūr li-wujūb ṭāʿat al-imām fīmā laysa bi-maʿṣiya wa'l-ẓāhir annahu lā yaʾmur illā bi'l-ḥaqq; wa in amarahu ghayr al-sulṭān min al-raʿiyya bi'l-qatl fa-qatala fa'l-qawad ʿalā al-maʾmūr bi-kulli ḥāl ʿalima aw lam yaʿlam li-annahu lā yalzamuhu ṭāʿatuhu wa laysa lahu al-qatl bi-ḥāl bi-khilāf al-sulṭān fa-inna ilayhi al-qatl li'l-ridda wa'l-zinā wa qaṭʿ al-ṭarīq idhā qatala al-qāṭiʿ . . . wa hādhā laysa ilayhi shayʾ min dhālika.* 8 Muwaffaq al-Dīn ʿAbdallāh b. Aḥmad b. Muḥammad Ibn Qudāma, *al-Mughnī* (Cairo: Maktabat al-Jumhūriyya al-ʿArabiyya, 1964), p. 366. See also, 5 al-Khaṭīb al-Shirbīnī, *Mughnī al-Muḥtāj ilā Maʿrifat Maʿānī Alfāẓ al-Minhāj* (Beirut: Dār al-Kutub al-ʿIlmiyya, 1994), p. 539 (applying same framework to liability of executioner who kills an innocent man). See, also, 4 al-Ḥaṭṭāb, p. 250 *(kull mā umira bi-fiʿlihi ẓulman min qatl aw qaṭʿ aw jald aw akhdh māl wa huwa yakhāf in lam yafʿalhu nazala bihi mithl dhālika fa-lā yafʿaluhu fa'in faʿalahu lazimahu al-qiṣāṣ wa'l-ghurm).*

80. While Muslim jurists permit prudential considerations to authorize deviations from the law in many circumstances, a defense of necessity is never admissible in the case of killing another.

the subordinate is exclusively responsible for the victim's death, not the commanding official. The illegal nature of the command renders it a legal nullity, which means that the subordinate, from a legal perspective, becomes the sole proximate cause of the unlawful killing.

Jurists also adapted private law principles applicable to compensation for wrongful death to allocate liability between the public and private persons in cases where the identity of the killer was unknown. When the body of a murder victim was found in a particular section of town, the Ḥanafī doctrine of *qasāma* required fifty of the people living in that area (*ahl al-maḥalla*) to swear oaths that they neither were responsible for killing the deceased, nor did they have knowledge of the killer's identity, whereupon the people of that area would be liable to the deceased's next of kin for payment of compensation (*diya*) for wrongful killing.[81] If the murder victim, however, is found in a public [75] place, such as the town's cathedral mosque (*al-masjid al-jāmiʿ*), public streets (*shawāriʿ al-ʿāmma*), bridges (*jusūr al-ʿāmma*) or market places (*sūq al-ʿāmma*), no oaths are administered because no particular person or group of persons is responsible for the safety of public places. Rather, the public, insofar as it is the beneficiary of these places, is collectively responsible for their protection, [82] and since it would be impossible to oblige everyone to take an oath, no oaths are required and compensation is due from the treasury, because the property of the treasury is the property of the public.[83]

Shifting the obligation of compensation from private persons to the public, therefore, seems a straightforward application of the more general principle of Islamic property law that distributes losses based on the principle that risk of loss follows the possibility of profit (*al-kharāj bi'l-ḍamān*). Since it is the public that nominally controls public spaces and is the beneficiary of public facilities, it becomes liable for losses occurring in such places.

4. IS THERE SPACE FOR LEGISLATIVE POWER IN SUNNĪ PUBLIC LAW?

The above sections explained how Muslim jurists applied the jurisdictional limitations implicit in the idea of the contract of the caliphate to establish an ideal of rule of law that included distinctive public and private spheres, each with its own appropriate set of norms. A central feature of the Sunnī conception of the rule of law was that the norms of

81. 7 al-Kāsānī, 286. The theory behind this remedy is that owners or possessors of land have a duty to provide protection (*ḥifẓ*) to those on the land. They therefore become liable to pay compensation for anyone murdered on their land if the true killer cannot be found. Ibid, p. 289.

82. *wa tajib al-diya ʿalā bayt al-māl li-anna tadbīr hādhi al-mawādiʿ wa maṣlaḥatahā ilā al-ʿāmma fa-kāna ḥifẓuhā ʿalayhim fa-idhā qaṣṣarū ḍammanū bayt al-māl mālahum fa-yuʾkhadh min bayt al-māl*. 7 al-Kāsānī, 290.

83. *wa idhā kāna fī yad al-ʿāmma fa-ḥifẓuhu ʿalā al-ʿāmma lākin lā sabīl ilā ījāb al-qasāma ʿalā al-kull wa amkana ījāb al-diya ʿalā al-kull li-imkān al-istīfāʾ minhum bi'l-akhdh minhum bi'l-akhdh min bayt al-māl li-anna māl bayt al-māl māluhum fa-kāna al-akhdh min bayt al-māl istīfāʾan minhum*. 7 al-Kāsānī, 289.

private law could be extended to regulate the actions of public officials based on an implicit analogy between the Muslim community and that of a natural person. Sunnī jurists treated the Muslim community as a legal person, having its own rights and capable of bearing obligations. All the above cases, however, assumed that the rights and potential obligations of the collective Muslim community were determined by the pre-political norms of the jurists' law. Below I discuss the extent to which Sunnī jurists recognized the authority of public officials to regulate the conduct of individuals through statute as a kind of law-making activity distinct from the jurists' law, and what the jurisprudential basis for that activity could be. [76] Qarāfī, in his work *al-Iḥkām fī Tamyīz al-Fatāwā ʿan al-Aḥkām wa Taṣarrufāt al-Qāḍī wa'l-Imām*, identified three different sources of rules in Islamic law.[84] The first is the interpretive work of jurists who, relying on their specialized training, interpret the indicants of revelation (*al-adilla al-sharʿiyya*) to formulate general legal rules (*aḥkām ʿāmma*) which they communicate to the public through the institution of the legal opinion (*al-fatwā*).[85] The legal opinion, even though formulated as a universal rule, does not communicate a binding rule except with respect to those individuals who choose to adhere to the opinion in question. The non-binding nature of a legal opinion, combined with the fact of differences of opinion regarding the proper meaning of revelation, meant that numerous and at times contradictory fatwas theoretically governed the same set of facts. The activity of jurists, because it is interpretive, is purely that of law-finding and is constitutive of the jurists' law. In the event of a dispute, the fact that the jurists' law generated numerous plausible answers to the same legal question meant that the disputants might in good faith contest the legal norm properly applicable to their dispute. Resolution of such disputes required the litigants to take their claims to a judge (*al-qāḍī* or *al-ḥākim*) whose role in such situations was to originate (*inshāʾ*) a particular rule (*ḥukm khāṣṣ*) that put an end to that particular dispute. In so doing, the judge must rely on the legal opinion of a recognized authority, i.e., an opinion of one of the established schools of law, a requirement which created a link between the theoretical, general law-finding of the jurists, and the practical, particular law-making of the judges.[86] A properly constituted judicial ruling established the "law of the case"[87] for that dispute, and conclusively resolved the controversy (*ikhtilāf*), both for secular and religious pur-

84. Shihāb al-Dīn al-Qarāfī, *al-Iḥkām fī Tamyīz al-Fatāwā ʿan al-Aḥkām wa Taṣarrufāt al-Qāḍī wa'l-Imām*, edited by ʿAbd al-Fattāḥ Abū Ghudda (Aleppo: Maktab al-Maṭbūʿāt al-Islāmiyya, 1967). For one interpretation of Qarāfī's legal and constitutional theories, see Sherman Jackson, *Islamic Law and the State: The Constitutional Jurisprudence of Shihāb al-Dīn al-Qarāfī* (Brill: New York, 1996).

85. A jurist who communicates legal norms to the public is called a *muftī*.

86. Judges also differed from muftis insofar as the latter interpreted revealed indicants, while the former heard the evidence of the litigants (*al-ḥijāj*) which, as a general matter, consist of witness testimony, admissions or oaths.

87. For an overview of the contemporary operation of the "law of the case" doctrine in United States federal courts, see Wright & Miller, *Federal Practice and Procedure* § 4478, *Law of the Case*.

poses, between the parties. It also precluded anyone who held a different conception of the law prior to the judge's decision from contesting the applicable rule once the judge had ruled.

[77] For example, in a dispute involving a woman who contracts a marriage without the permission of her family in reliance on the Ḥanafī rule recognizing such a marriage and her guardian, who seeks to invalidate that marriage contract in reliance on the Mālikī rule that does not recognize the validity of such a marriage, the judge's decision in her favor establishes the validity of her marriage as the law of the case. This decision not only forever resolved the dispute as between the two litigants, but it also foreclosed dissenting muftis, e.g., Mālikīs, from continuing to give legal opinions declaring that their marriage was invalid.[88] The judge's ruling, however, only resolved the dispute with respect to those particular litigants. Subsequent disputes arising out of the same facts, but involving different litigants must be resolved anew by the particular judge before whom the case is brought. In other words, the system of judge-made law which Qarāfī described was capable of only making law interstitially and in the context of particular disputes; judges' rulings lacked general, precedential impact.

Al-Qarāfī, however, also identifies a third sources of rules, one which he calls *taṣarruf bi'l-imāma*. I will provisionally translate this term as an "administrative act," although al-Qarāfī catalogues several instances of this power that would not easily qualify as "administrative" in contemporary parlance, e.g., a judge's determination of the level of maintenance owed to an ex-wife from her former husband. It is an exercise of the power of the Imam, the general police power of the public (*al-siyāsa al-ʿāmma*) that is vested in the caliph through the delegation to him of authority over public affairs and public policy, and from him is then delegated to various public officials.[89] Public officials with general jurisdiction, when they exercise their administrative powers, interpret the empirical domain of the public good (*al-maṣlaḥa al-ʿāmma*), and seek the preponderant good of the community, an activity which is distinct both from the law-finding of muftis, which relies on scriptural evidence (*al-adilla*), and the interstitial law-making of judges, which relies on the particular evidence of litigants (*al-ḥujja*).[90] [78] An administrative act might be general by its terms, insofar as it applied to everyone in the jurisdiction, for example, a decree regarding market place regulations, or it might be particular, for example, a judicial order setting the amount of maintenance due a nursing mother from

---

88. For an overview of the various debates on the moral effects of judge's ruling, see Mohammad Fadel, "Forum, Exterior (Zahir), and Interior Forum (Batin)," *Oxford Encyclopedia of Legal History*, ed. Stanley N. Katz (Baber Johansen, Islamic Law editor) (2009).

89. *Al-imām huwa alladhī fuwwiḍat ilayhi al-siyāsa al-ʿāmma fi'l-khalāʾiq*. Al-Qarāfī, *al-Iḥkām*, p. 93. Al-Qarāfī says elsewhere in the *Iḥkām* that the office of the caliph contains within it "the capacity to exercise . . . general political authority (*tatanāwal . . . ahliyyat al-siyāsa al-ʿāmma*)." Ibid, p. 157.

90. *Taṣarruf al-imāma . . . yaʿtamid al-maṣlaḥa al-rājiḥa aw al-khāliṣa fī ḥaqq al-umma wa hiya ghayr al-ḥujja wa'l-adilla*. Ibid, p. 41.

her former husband, or the punishment applicable to a particular criminal. Administrative acts, unlike fatwas, are binding, but unlike the particular judgments of judges, they are not conclusive, and may be prospectively revised or even repealed by the very public official who issued the act or another public official who obtains jurisdiction over the matter.[91] In each of these cases, the relevant decision maker issues an order based on his determination of what is in the best interest (*al-aṣlaḥ* or *al-aḥsan*) of those under his jurisdiction, or other relevant empirical consideration, but in no case is the decision based on interpretation either of revealed texts or admissible evidence produced by litigants. Because such determinations are necessarily relative and vary depending upon circumstances, the content of such orders needs to be revised when circumstances subsequent to the original order change sufficiently as to make the original order inconsistent with the law's purposes.[92] Unlike a judge, the public official in this context is not applying the legal norm of a fatwa to the particular evidence presented in a particular dispute, but is rather formulating rules through the exercise of his practical reason, exercised in accordance with a broad legal standard, such as, in the case of a judge presiding over a maintenance suit, "provide a nursing woman an appropriate amount of maintenance in light of her reasonable needs and the reasonable capacity of the father," or in a sentencing proceeding, "determine an appropriate punishment for this defendant based on the seriousness (or lack thereof) of his crime, the need (or lack thereof) to deter him or others like him, from similar conduct, and the prospect of rehabilitating him," or in the case of a city's ruler, making a decision to set maximum prices for basic staple goods in the public markets, provided that in doing so the decision maker believes that setting maximum prices is necessary for the public good.

Qarāfī, however, did not discuss the relationship of the administrative powers of public officials to the jurists' law. According to Qarāfī, it is ordinarily the case that individuals are entitled to act in pursuit of their own interests without the prior permission of the state so long as in doing so they are acting in [79] conformity with the rules set out in the jurists' law. This third category of rules, however, potentially creates a tension between the norms of the jurists' law which are generated through interpretation of revelation (the domain of the jurists) and rule-making in the name of the public good (the domain of public officials). We have seen that jurists developed particular understandings that governed the validity of these administrative acts, for example, that they be consistent with rational good of the public, but what if these rules, or some of them, even if they satisfied the requirement of public rationality, circumscribed one or more of the rules

91. Accordingly, a judge could revise a prior maintenance order, whether by enhancing it or reducing it, as appropriate in light of the circumstances. In the case of a criminal sentence, as long as the punishment has not been served, a subsequent judge who came to have jurisdiction over the prisoner could reduce the punishment.

92. See n. 74, *supra*.

recognized as validly part of the jurists' law, or even prohibited an action entirely that was otherwise in conformity with it, such as a decree of the ruler prohibiting marriages without the consent of the natural guardian, despite the fact that the well-established rule of the Ḥanafī school permitted it?[93] Did such a decree bind individual Muslims in the relevant jurisdiction where the decree applied, or were they free to ignore it and continue to act in conformity with the jurists' rule? Qarāfī did not attempt to provide systematic answers to these questions. Jurists of subsequent generations in the Mamluk and Ottoman eras, however, offered answers to the relationship of administrative acts to the jurists' law by asking whether it was obligatory to obey a ruler's decree if it purports to render obligatory an act that was non-obligatory as a matter of jurists' law, or prohibited an action that the jurists' law permitted. While the jurists' law included five ethical categories of judgments—obligatory, forbidden, supererogatory, disfavoured and permitted—judges were permitted to issue judicial rulings based on only three of these categories, the obligatory, the forbidden and the permitted.

Clearly, an administrative act that ordered commission of a forbidden act, or omission of an obligatory act, all things being equal, was invalid, while an administrative act ordering performance of an obligatory act, or prohibiting a forbidden act, was redundant. Administrative acts only represent a true third source of rules if they could legitimately compel an individual to perform, or refrain from performing, an act that, from the perspective of the jurists' law, was either disfavoured, permitted or merely supererogatory. Whether public officials had such authority was controversial at various points in Islamic [80] history,[94] but jurists of Ottoman-era Egypt and Syria, however, had generally come to the conclusion that such commands could be morally binding, provided they satisfied various conditions, even though the actions commanded were not obligatory from the perspective of the jurists' law.

This conclusion is consistent with what was described in the previous section. Namely, that insofar as the jurists imagined the Muslim community to be the functional equivalent of a collective person whose rights and obligations could be analogized to those of a natural person, it followed that just as a natural person could lawfully perform acts that were either supererogatory or disfavoured when it was in his interest to do so, similarly the collective person of the Muslim community may "decide" to act in a certain way, even if divine law did not compel it to do so in the first instance, provided that certain conditions were met that were intended to ensure that the command, in fact, was

93. The Ottomans, despite being Ḥanafīs, did in fact issue a rule prohibiting women from contracting their own marriages. Rudolph Peters, "What Does it Mean to be an Official *Madhhab*? Ḥanafism and the Ottoman Empire," in Peri Bearman et al. (eds.), *The Islamic School of Law: Evolution, Devolution, and Progress* (Cambridge, Mass.: Harvard Law School, 2005), 152–53.

94. See Yossef Rapoport, "Royal Justice and Religious Law: *Siyāsah* and Shariʿah Under the Mamluks," 16 *Mamluk Studies Review* (2012), pp. 71–102, 92–97.

properly "public" and therefore attributable to the Muslim community and not simply the arbitrary personal decision of the decision maker. From this perspective, the valid commands of the caliph, and other public officials, when exercising the administrative power of the public, are an expression of the public's will, and it is for that reason that they become morally binding. To put it differently, while the common belief that rights recognized in the jurists' law are pre-political is substantially correct, there is little basis for the further inference that the ruler has no authority to make rules that revise, restrict or even prohibit the exercise of such rights, provided that in so doing, the ruler is acting in a properly "public" fashion.[95]

I have been able to identify five jurisdictional conditions that jurists mentioned as prerequisites (*shurūṭ*) to the legal validity of a positive command (*amr*) that regulates the activities of private persons that are also regulated by the jurists' law. Two were subjective and three were objective:

(i) [81] the public official issuing the command had to have a good-faith subjective belief that the command was lawful, i.e., not sinful, even if what was commanded was not mandatory.[96]

(ii) the person to whom the command is directed, from his subjective perspective, must be able to comply with the command without committing a sin.[97]

(iii) the subject of the command must lie within the public domain and not the private.[98]

---

95. One might object that according to the juristic principle, *al-sulṭān walī man lā walī lahu*, the ruler only exercises general jurisdiction over persons who lack both full capacity and a natural guardian. Accordingly, the ruler lacks authority to act on behalf of those who have full capacity. Mālikī jurists, however, have affirmed the principle that the ruler, in fact, has authority over everyone, even those with natural guardians and enjoy full capacity. See 3 al-Ḥaṭṭāb, p. 432 (denying the implied restriction of the judge's ability to act as an adult woman's marriage guardian in circumstances where her father is alive and present, because the judge is the guardian of everyone; *qawluhu 'walī man lā walī lahu' mafhūmuhu man lahu walī fa-laysa bi-walī lahā wa laysa kadhālika bal al-qāḍī walī kull wāḥid*).

96. 2 Ibn Ḥajar al-Haytamī, *al-Fatāwā al-Fiqhiyya al-Kubrā* (Cairo: al-Maktaba al-Islāmiyya, n.d.), pp. 235–36 (obedience is obligatory if the ruler believes the command is lawful); Ibn Qudāma, p. 366 (if the ruler issues a command which he believes is illegal, and it is carried out, the ruler is personally liable).

97. See, for example, 7 al-Kāsānī, p. 100 (orders of the ruler should be obeyed unless they are known to be sinful); 4 al-Ḥaṭṭāb, p. 250 (if the ruler orders a person to kill, amputate or unjustly appropriate property, he must not obey the command, and if he does, he is liable for retaliation (*qiṣāṣ*) and the value of the unlawfully seized item (*al-ghurm*)); see also, al-Shirbīnī, 5:539; see also, 8 Ibn Qudāma, p. 366. Ibn Qudama in this case limited this requirement to a person with an independent capacity to interpret the law; non-specialists, on the other hand, were entitled to adopt the legal reasoning of the public official who had issued the command, at least in cases whose legality was a matter of legal reasoning (*ijtihād*).

98. See, for example, 1 Muḥammad b. Aḥmad b. ʿArafa, *Ḥāshiyat al-Dasūqī ʿalā al-Sharḥ al-Kabīr* (Beirut: Dār al-Fikr, n.d.), pp. 406–7 (*iʿlam anna maḥalla kawn al-imām idhā amara bi-mubāḥ aw mandūb tajib ṭāʿatuhu idhā kāna mā amara bihi min al-maṣāliḥ al-ʿāmma*); 2 Sulaymān b. Muḥammad b. ʿUmar, *Ḥāshiyat al-Bijirmī ʿalā al-Khaṭīb* (Beirut: Dār al-Fikr, 1995), p. 238 (duty to obey a command mandating the performance

(iv) the command, from a substantive perspective, must be rationally-related to achieving the public good, either absolutely or relatively.[99]

(v) [82] the public official must be acting within the jurisdictional terms of his appointment.[100] Accordingly, a judge appointed to hear family law cases in Cairo, for example, could not divorce a woman in Damascus, even if his verdict was substantively correct, nor could he invalidate a contract of sale in Cairo, even if, as a matter of substantive law, the contract is universally recognized as unenforceable.

Qarāfī adds that the actions of a public official are not valid if they are tainted by a conflict of interest.[101] If these conditions are satisfied, and the decision maker is untainted by a conflict of interest, the administrative act is valid and binding, both from a moral perspective and a prudential one.

One historical example of juristic treatment of law-making by government officials is found in a legal opinion issued by a 15th-century Shāfiʿī jurist in the Mamlūk era, issued in response to a question concerning the legality of a recently promulgated price-control regulation.[102] The mufti concluded that the petitioner, who was apparently a follower of the Shāfiʿī school of law, was morally bound to follow a controversial price-control regulation, even though the petitioner believed such a regulation to be unlawful. The mufti reasoned that so long as the ruler had a good-faith belief that the rule was permissible—and that would be satisfied in this case given the fact that the Mālikī school of law permitted such regulations—and that the petitioner could comply with the rule without committing a sin, the rule bound him, morally and prudentially, because foregoing the exercise of a right is not the same thing as committing a sin. What is unexplained in Ibn Ḥajar's opinion, however, is why compliance with a valid command is a moral obligation

---

of an act that revealed law classifies as permissible becomes obligatory only if it relates to the public good, like refraining from smoking); 3 *Ḥāshiyat al-Imām ʿAbd al-Ḥamīd al-Shirwānī ʿalā Tuḥfat al-Muḥtāj* (Beirut: Dār Iḥyāʾ al-Turāth al-ʿArabī, n.d.), 69 and 71 (same). There appears to be a difference of opinion between Mālikī and Shāfiʿī jurists with respect to commands of the ruler directing the public to perform supererogatory acts of devotion: the Mālikīs deny any effect to such commands because they are not connected to the public good, while the Shāfiʿīs seem to hold that they become obligatory by virtue of the ruler's command to perform them. They are in agreement, however, that with respect to the command to perform (or refrain from) an act that the revealed law deems permissible, the command must relate to the public good before it becomes an obligation.

99. 4 al-Qarāfī, *al-Furūq*, p. 39 supra n. 74; 1 Makkī, p. 373.

100. Ibid., p. 40 (*fa-yulḥaq bihi al-qaḍāʾ min al-qāḍī bi-ghayr ʿamalihi fa-innahu lā tatanāwaluhu al-wilāya li-anna ṣiḥḥat al-taṣarruf innamā yustafād min ʿaqd al-wilāya wa ʿaqd al-wilāya innamā yatanāwal manṣiban muʿayyanan wa baladan muʿayyanan fa-kāna maʿzūlan ʿammā ʿadāhu lā yanfudh fīhi ḥukmuhu wa qālahu Abū Ḥanīfa wa'l-Shāfiʿī wa Aḥmad ibn Ḥanbal . . . wa mā ʿalimtu fīhi khilāfan*).

101. Ibid., p. 43 (*al-qāʿida anna al-tuhma taqdaḥ fī al-taṣarrufāt ijmāʿan min ḥaythu al-jumla*).

102. 2 Ibn Ḥajar al-Haytamī, *al-Fatāwā al-Fiqhiyya al-Kubrā*, pp. 235–36.

(*fī'l-sirr*), and not just a prudential one (*fī'l-jahr*).[103] After all, the merchant is not bound to accept the moral reasoning of the Mālikī school that this rule, as an abstract matter, is a permissible [83] exercise of public power as an indisputable matter of revealed law. Nor was there a particular decision by a judge that resolved a particular dispute between this merchant and a prospective customer that would have determined judicially the validity of the price-control regulation. It seems that when the public official exercises his administrative powers lawfully, he acts as an agent of the public. As a result, his actions bind the members of the public in the same way that the authorized actions of a private agent bind the principal. In short, as Kāsānī suggested, the lawful actions of the ruler are really the actions of the community, and the petitioner, as a member of the community, is obliged to act in conformity with the legal decisions of the community, at least so long as compliance with such decisions does not entail sin.

The same explanation must also lie behind why a judicial ruling becomes the law of the case, binding not only the parties to the dispute, but also requiring dissenting muftis who could have legitimately dissented prior to the judicial ruling, to affirm the judge's decision. Late medieval authorities such as al-Qarāfī argued for the view that the judge's decision in a particular case was morally, as well as politically, decisive. This overturned older doctrine which held that a judicial ruling could not change the underlying moral norm governing the particular dispute. This later development, however, failed to provide an explanation for why individuals could be compelled to appear before a judge, and despite this element of coercion, that the judge's decision had these moral features.[104] The answer can be found in the morality of arbitration: there, it is obvious that the arbitrator's power to resolve the dispute is based on the consent of the two disputants. It is the combination of their consent to submit to the arbitrator's decision and the substantive correctness of the norms applied by the arbitrator that makes the decision morally salient.

The same principle must explain the moral salience of a judge's decision in Islamic law and why the judge's decision is morally different than being compelled to obey a legal opinion which one subjectively denies: it is our general consent to the jurisdiction of judges, combined with their application of reasonably just norms, which produces morally salient decisions, even if we may subjectively reject the validity of particular rules that judges adopt from time to time. One without the other would not be enough; both

103. Ibid. (distinguishing the obligation to obey inwardly (*fī'l-sirr*) and outwardly (*fī'l-jahr*)). Other jurists apply the terms *bāṭin* and *ẓāhir* to express the same notions of inward and outward compliance. See, for example, 3 *Ḥāshiyat al-Shirwānī*, p. 71. The difference is not inconsequential from the perspective of the rule of law: If obedience in this case were only a prudential obligation, the merchant would be free to ignore it if he could do so without risking detection, for example.

104. The fact that a litigant can be compelled to appear before a judge creates a scenario that does not seem to differ substantially from a person being compelled to follow a legal opinion whose validity he subjectively rejects.

are necessary. The legitimacy of judges' jurisdiction, unlike that of an arbitrator, however, cannot depend on the specific consent of the litigants; however, parties can be reasonably deemed to have consented to the judges' jurisdiction insofar as the [84] judges were appointed pursuant to some kind of consensual process, based on an appropriate consideration of our own rational good. The contract of the caliphate attempts to solve this problem by providing a theory of jurisdiction that ultimately derives its authority from a universal delegation from the community to the ruler who then acts as its agent in creating the various sub-jurisdictions of the state, including those of the judiciary. We can be compelled to appear before judges because the decision to appoint them was, in some kind of morally meaningful way as suggested by Kāsānī, our own decision because it was taken on our behalf in accordance with substantively just norms and procedurally appropriate means.[105]

From a substantive perspective, the binding decisions of judges are explained by reference to the fact that they are applying norms of divine law in a procedurally valid way, but how then to account for the binding nature of rules such as a general price-setting regulation imposed in times of market scarcity, despite the fact that we are legitimately entitled to dispute the merits of such a rule as a proper understanding of divine law? Here, the answer is that the administrative act represents a legitimate exercise of the public will. It is legitimate procedurally, because it issues from a properly authorized agent, and it is legitimate substantively because (i) it does not command the violation of a mandatory norm of divine law, and (ii) it is rationally related to a question of the public good, not the private business of traders. Just as principals are bound by the decisions of their agents taken within the scope of their authority in private law, the principals, the "citizens," are bound by the decisions of their public agents taken within the scope of their authority when they lawfully exercise the administrative powers that have been delegated to them.

Public administrative acts then ought not to be understood as commands, or as exercises in the interpretation of divine law backed by coercive force, but as expressions of the public's will to exercise its collective freedom in a particular way. As it is morally obligatory to participate as a member of the public, the public is entitled to coerce those members who refuse to cooperate with its validly-expressed will, whether that is manifested in the appointment of particular persons as judges, or in particular decrees, regardless of one's subjective consent to either of these particular decisions. The mere fact that the public's [85] will is subject to prospective revision—the salient feature of an

105. Accordingly, the caliph is not free to appoint whoever he wishes to the post of judge, but is required to appoint only candidates who are ethically, temperamentally, and professionally qualified for the position. In other words, Islamic law's requirements for the office of judge represent a reasonable approximation of the kind of abstract qualifications we would want to see in a judge before we would be willing to recognize his decisions as binding.

administrative act which distinguishes it from a judicial ruling—does not mean that an individual can defy the expression of the public will prior to such time as it expresses a change in its will.

Does the authority to issue morally binding commands pursuant to a proper procedure, constitute a genuine recognition of a legislative power by late medieval and early modern Muslim jurists? As already noted in the introduction to this article, western scholarship on Islamic law has refused to recognize a legitimate role for legislation in Islamic law, albeit recognizing a place for "administration." Unfortunately, scholars who deny the existence of a legislative power in Islamic law while affirming the existence of "administration" do not explain the criteria by which they distinguish legislation from mere administration. Perhaps they intend the following thought: Islamic law mandates, for example, that the state collect alms (*zakāt*) but does not provide institutional specifics regarding how this mandate is to be discharged. The Imām's role would therefore be to provide rules to give effect to this pre-existing legal obligation.

Under this conception, legitimate administration might be understood as the promulgation of rules that are ancillary to achieve an already existing obligation under divine law, as if divine law includes something akin to the United States constitution's "necessary and proper" clause. When scholars say that Islamic law does not recognize a legitimate role for legislation then, what might be meant is that in the absence of a pre-existing norm of divine law, there is no legitimate means for the state to promulgate binding law because it would be creating a binding norm that is not firmly tied to a revealed norm. However this requires accepting a very narrow conception of divine law that itself is contrary to how Sunnī jurists understood divine law. Consider, for example, the Mālikī view that the Muslim community is obligated to establish institutions that provide for the flourishing of all the arts and crafts necessary for human civilization to flourish.[106] If that is accepted as a principle of divine law, it becomes almost inconceivable that any legitimate endeavor of government would be deemed outside of the domain of divine law. Indeed, one can even speak of a merger between divine law and human law, at least at this level of abstraction.[107] At this point, then, it seems the distinction between [86] administration and legislation is semantic and not substantive. This article argues that late medieval and early modern Muslim jurists recognized the right of rulers to make morally binding norms for those under their jurisdiction in circumstances

106. See, for example, 4 al-Mawwāq, p. 539 (stating that promoting the "important crafts" (*al-ḥiraf al-muhimma*) are a collective obligation (*farḍ kifāya*) of the Muslim community) and 3 al-Kharshī, p. 110 (same).

107. In this respect, it might be helpful to compare pre-19th century Muslim conceptions of the relationship of *qānūn* to *sharʿ* with Thomas Hobbes' enigmatic position that the civil law and the natural law are co-extensive. See Ross Harrison, "The Equal Extent of Natural and Civil Law," in *Hobbes and the Law*, edited by David Dyzenhaus and Thomas Poole (New York: Cambridge University Press, 2012), pp. 22–38.

based on considerations of the public good and not based on a correct understanding of revelation. This seems to me to be a clear case of law-making, i.e., legislation, rather than law-finding, and therefore sufficient to establish, on a provisional basis at least, the jurisprudential legitimacy of statutory law, from the internal perspective of the jurists' law itself, even in circumstances where that statutory law supplements the requirements of the jurists' law, restricts its applications or even pre-empts it entirely, so long as the conditions for valid statutory commands are satisfied.

5. ISLAMIC PUBLIC LAW, AND DEMOCRACY AND LEGAL REFORM

In one of Rashīd Riḍā's more daring jurisprudential arguments, he argued that while there was nothing objectionable in an individual Muslim's adherence to traditional legal doctrines, whether substantively or hermeneutically, those traditional interpretive methods depended for their efficacy on individual assent to their teachings. Therefore, they were incapable of producing general public law that was capable of undertaking the broad social, economic and political reforms to Muslim society needed to overcome their relative weakness in the face of European imperialism.[108] Only positive law legislated by a state that enjoyed legitimacy could address the broad structural problems related to the public good. He accordingly advocated for a merging of religious and political authority, whereby political authorities would be involved in the interpretation of religious law by placing the public good as the paramount concern of legal hermeneutics, and religious authorities would be involved in political life by monitoring political authorities to ensure that their decisions were consistent with the public good.

The primary means of reform would be positive legislation, for which he introduced the neologism *ishtirāʿ*—a cognate of Sharīʿa, the Arabic word for revealed law—to distinguish legislative activity from the historical interpretive activity of the traditional jurists.[109] But, it seems that the chief difference between his conception of modern Islamic legislation, *ishtirāʿ*, and the tradition-[87]al activity of interpretation, *ijtihād*, was that the former would be a collective exercise, while the latter was an individualistic exercise. Even for Riḍā, however, it appears that the goal of what he called *ishtirāʿ* was to find the appropriate rule of divine law, not to determine the content of the public will. His theory of law-finding differed from the classical view insofar as it would incorporate modern circumstances, give due weight to considerations of the public good, and incorporate the deliberations of a corporate body of sufficiently-trained jurists. His belief was that given the proper, i.e., legitimate, institutional framework, decisions of such a deliberative

---

108. Muḥammad Rashīd Riḍā, *al-Khilāfa* (Cairo: al-Zahrāʾ li'l-Iʿlām al-ʿArabī, 1988), p. 98.
109. Ibid., p. 101.

body would be accepted as universally authoritative and thereby be an effective means to pursue the public good.[110]

While Riḍā's critique of traditional conceptions of law and political legitimacy were trenchant in many respects, his solution—effectively, the creation of a collective body of jurists who, through a collective exercise in legal interpretation, albeit one that emphasized the public good more than fidelity to revealed text, would find the appropriate Islamic rule—raises its own troubling implications. Specifically, it suggests that legislation—*ishtirāᶜ*—is a kind of hermeneutical law-finding activity, whose outcome, at the end, is no more than a legal opinion, a fatwa. If that is the case, however, on what grounds does it command obedience? To the extent that the claim is that it should be followed because it is either a true conception of divine law, or more modestly, the best conception of divine law, it reintroduces the problem of religious despotism which Riḍā had been so keen to eliminate from Muslim religious life, albeit in perhaps a less arbitrary form to the extent that such interpreters may be accountable to the public through democratic procedures such as elections and the fact that they reach their conclusions deliberatively rather than individually.

On the other hand, the proposition that governmental bodies, particularly elected ones, claim to apply divine law has caused some prominent Muslim legal scholars to condemn attempts to incorporate Islamic law into modern legal systems as a distortion of Islamic law, which, in their view, is essentially an interpretive project and cannot, by its nature, be reduced to the commands of a state. To protect the integrity of Islamic law as a system of revealed law, it is crucial, therefore, that it be removed in its entirety from governance so that it exists outside the realm of politics and serves only as a pure aspirational ideal or as a source for individual morality.[111] This concern—that a state's claim to be applying Islamic law is metaphysically untenable and thus at bottom a [88] misappropriation of divine prerogative—and the concern that statutory law lacks Islamic integrity because it is not a product of authentic Islamic legal reasoning—are a result of the same error into which Riḍā fell, namely, the belief that a modern state applying Islamic law is essentially acting as a master-jurist (*mujtahid*), charged with the task of finding the correct interpretation of divine law, with the difference that it has either sufficient legitimacy to win voluntary compliance with its opinions, or it possesses the necessary coercive resources to compel compliance with its views regarding the correct conception of divine law. The model of law-making which I have identified in the late Sunnī tradition, by contrast, understands positive law as expressions of the public will that meet Islamic conditions of validity and not as interpretations of divine will; it offers a theory of law-

110. Ibid., p. 104.

111. See, for example, Khaled Abou El Fadl, *Islam and the Challenge of Democracy* (Princeton: Princeton University Press, 2015) and Abdullahi an-Naᶜim, *Islam and the Secular State* (Cambridge: Harvard University Press, 2008).

making in a modern Muslim-majority polity based on political deliberation about the public good at its center rather than a process of law-finding through scriptural interpretation (however defined). One example should make clear the difference in approach. In 2000 Egypt passed a law granting women the right to divorce at will on condition that they waive any monetary claims they might have against their husbands, particularly, their claim to unpaid dower.[112] This statute substantially reformed the historical doctrine of *khulᶜ*, or wife-initiated divorce for a consideration, as understood in the jurists' law. While all four Sunnī schools of law recognized the validity of this kind of divorce, they had required the husband's consent.[113] In justifying passage of this law, the Egyptian government engaged in an act of law-finding, relying on a revisionist interpretation of revelation, arguing that the most relevant Prophetic precedents omit any requirement that that the husband consent to the divorce. While there is no reason to doubt the good faith of the Egyptian legal officials who offered this revisionist interpretation of the relevant precedents, the law did contravene a well-established consensus among all schools of law that the husband's consent was required, and consensus itself is a source of revealed law according to the Sunnīs. Moreover, the modest achievements of the law are themselves a reflection of the limited gains that [89] can be made by applying a law-finding approach that depends almost entirely on reinterpretation of precedent.[114]

If statutes of this kind were instead understood to be a reflection of a public will that is informed by, but not bounded by, textual precedent, a much bolder approach to the reform of family law could be undertaken that is not dependent on revealed precedent. In this case, for example, and that of family law more generally, it is well-established that the parties to the contract can include conditions, including, conditions regarding termination of the marriage, that go beyond the default rules of the marriage contract. The state, as the legitimate and exclusive agent of the public, clearly has the authority to insert mandatory conditions in the marriage contract regulating, among other things, the terms on which marriages can be dissolved, provided that those conditions otherwise satisfy the conditions for valid legislation. On the theory I advocate, the Law of 2000 would be justified not on the grounds that it is the best understanding of the various Prophetic reports regarding *khulᶜ*, but rather that the state, as the lawful agent of the public,

112. For details, see Oussama ᶜArabi, *Studies in Modern Islamic Law and Jurisprudence* (London: Kluwer Law International, 2001), pp. 169–88.

113. For an overview of the law of *khulᶜ*, see Mohammad Fadel, "Political Liberalism, Islamic Law and Family Law Pluralism: the Contrasting Cases of New York and Ontario," in *Marriage and Divorce in a Multi-Cultural Context: Reconsidering the Boundaries of Civil Law and Religion*, ed. Joel Nichols (Cambridge: Cambridge University Press, 2011).

114. For a criticism of the limitations of the 2000 *Khulᶜ* Law, see Mohammad Fadel "Judicial institutions, the legitimacy of Islamic state law and democratic transition in Egypt: Can a shift toward a common law model of adjudication improve the prospects of a successful democratic transition?," *International Journal of Constitutional Law* (2013), Vol. 11 No. 3, 646, 660–61.

has inserted as a mandatory condition in all marriage contracts, the conditional right of the wife to a *khul*ᶜ upon her agreement to relinquish all monetary claims against her husband in order to further the public interest by providing an effective and reasonably fair means for the prompt dissolution of unhappy marriages.

A proper jurisprudential understanding of legislation as the expression of the public will and not discovery of divine law would also resolve the potential democratic deficit in demands that states apply Islamic law: if the role of the government is to act as an agent for a properly constituted public will, legitimacy comes from adequately representing that public will, not from the law-finding skill of legislators through interpretation. And if the state acts as an agent for the public, and occupies the position of a fiduciary toward the public, it follows that to the extent possible, the public itself should be regularly consulted regarding the performance of its agent. Moreover, it also follows from the theory of the state that I have articulated that Islamic law does not bind the publics of contemporary Muslim states to particular historical institutions, but leaves them free to adopt any set of institutions that are more effective in representing their will as the principal to whom the government, as its agent, must answer. The idea of the state as acting in an essentially fiduciary [90] capacity toward the government also places substantial internal limitations on state power that go well-beyond simply prohibiting it from making laws that compel the commission of sin. It requires that all government acts be tested for procedural validity and substantive validity as being in the public interest.[115]

It is true that the public will in this conception would be bounded by revelation in important respects insofar as presumably there would be substantive limits on what could constitute valid legislation. That problem, however, is not dissimilar from the familiar paradox inherent in establishing constitutional limitations on popular sovereignty. Indeed, the theory of the state articulated in this paper provides an answer to the majoritarian dilemma insofar as the relationship of agency that ties the people to the state limits both the powers of the state and the "people." Just as the state may not perform any act not properly authorized by the people, the people are precluded from authorizing the state to commit crimes because a principal in Islamic law lacks the power to appoint an agent to commit an unlawful act. Such a conception of Islamic law-making, by making public deliberation rather than interpretation central to the state's legislative projects, might also bridge the gap between Islamists and non-Islamists in post-authoritarian societies insofar as the latter fear that demands for Islamic law will exclude democratic deliberation from the political process and replace it with debates about the correct interpretation of Islamic law.

115. In this respect, it is interesting to note that Thomas Hobbes also seemed to have articulated a theory of state authority in terms of a fiduciary relationship which a recent author has argued provides a firmer basis for modern democracy than the consent-based theory of the social contract. See Evan Fox-Decent, *Sovereignty's Promise: the State as Fiduciary* (New York: Oxford University Press, 2011).

By divorcing the question of positive law from interpretation of revelation, and instead resting it on the legitimate expression of public will, we make it clear that collective deliberation about the good of the political community is a constitutive feature of Islamic law, and that Islamic law does not exist as some free-floating set of rules outside the political community, confronting it only with the binary choice of compliance or non-compliance on a take-it or leave-it basis. The notion that law must serve the good of the community, and that it must be a valid expression of the public will, provides a solid basis for a political project that seeks to reconcile historical conceptions of Islamic legality with modern conceptions of democracy and human rights, or at a minimum, one that is more solid than one which either resolves the problem of Islamic law and democracy and human rights, either by collapsing one into the other, or by excluding one or the other from the norms of the political community.

3
THE IMPLICATIONS OF *FIQH AL-AQALLIYYĀT* (JURISPRUDENCE OF MINORITIES) FOR THE RIGHTS OF NON-MUSLIM MINORITIES IN MUSLIM-MAJORITY COUNTRIES

Mohammad Fadel

[83] INTRODUCTION: WHEN CAN NON-MUSLIMS BE BOUND BY ISLAMIC LAW?

Islamic law has shown concern with the rights and obligations of Muslims living outside the territory of an Islamic state virtually from the moment that the Prophet (S) established a city-state in Madina. The Qur'an, for example, stated that the Muslims of Madina did not have any *political* obligations toward Muslims who had not performed hijra, unless those Muslims sought their help on account of religious persecution. Even in that case, however, the Muslims of Madina were excused from such an obligation if they were bound by a treaty of peace to the tribe that was guilty of persecuting Muslims in their midst. (Qur'an, 8: 72). Conversely, Islamic law was also concerned with the rights and obligations of non-Muslims living in the territory of an Islamic state, a concern that also began with the establishment of an Islamic state in Madina. Thus the Charter of Madina set out a system of mutual rights and obligations that bound the people of Madina together in certain common pursuits regardless of their religion, while reserving only particular obligations to those Madinese who were Muslims.[1] It is important to note in this regard that the Charter of Madina pre-dates the concept of *dhimma* in consideration for payment of a tax, *jizya*, which is alluded to in *Sūrat al-Tawba*. (Qur'an, 9: 29). [84] Whether considering the obligations of Muslims in an Islamic state toward Muslims living in a non-Islamic state, or the obligations of non-Muslims to an Islamic state, Islamic law deemed the existence of a compact, or agreement, to be decisive. This distinction,

This article was originally published as a chapter in *The Question of Minorities in Islam: Theoretical Perspectives and Case Studies*, edited by Mohamed El-Tahir El-Mesawi (Kuala Lumpur: The Other Press, 2015), pp. 83–106

1. Ali Bulaç, "The Medina Document," in *Liberal Islam: a Reader*, ed. Charles Kurzman (New York: Oxford University Press, 1998), pp. 169–178.

i.e. between individuals who are governed by a compact and individuals who are simply governed by Islamic law on its own terms, gave rise to the historical conceptions of the *dār al-islām* and *dār al-ḥarb*, the former being a territory in which Islamic law applies of its own by virtue of the existence of a Muslim community possessing control over a certain territory with the ability to defend it against hostile invaders (*manaʿa*). By virtue of a combination of their political independence and moral commitment to Islam, a legitimate basis is given to enforcing law against Muslims.[2]

BUT WHAT ABOUT NON-MUSLIMS WHO RESIDE IN THAT TERRITORY?

On what basis could Islamic law legitimately apply to them? While they could in principle enjoy the political benefits of residence in an Islamic state, they could not, because of their failure to be Muslims, share in its moral commitments, and accordingly, their commitments to following Islamic law were necessarily political rather than moral, meaning, their obligation to follow Islamic law was an incident to the terms of the political agreement they entered into with the Islamic state. To be clear, non-Muslims were morally obliged to obey Islamic law in the sense that God would hold them culpable for failing to adhere to Islam in general,[3] but we are concerned here with another issue: to what extent did Muslim jurists believe it legitimate to hold non-Muslims liable in this world for breaching the substantive obligations of Islamic law?

As evidenced by the controversies among Muslims jurists regarding the extent to which non-Muslims resident in an Islamic state were bound by the substantive rules of Islamic law, it was clear that non-Muslims were subject to only *some* rules of Islamic law, but not all. The general answer given by Muslim jurists was [85] that non-Muslims could legitimately be expected to obey those rules of Islamic law which were not based exclusively on an assumption of belief in Islam. Accordingly, non-Muslims could not be held liable for failing to perform Islamic rituals. Likewise, the application of *ḥudūd* to non-Muslims was controversial: some, like Imām Mālik, exempted non-Muslims from the *ḥadd* of *zinā* (fornication and adultery) on the grounds that the main purpose of this *ḥadd* was repentance, and accordingly it would be nonsensical to apply it to someone who does not accept Islam as true. Others permitted applying the *ḥadd* of *zinā* to non-Muslims such as Christians and Jews on the grounds that adultery was forbidden to them under their own religions, and accordingly, they were being punished for conduct that they themselves held to be immoral pursuant to their own beliefs. As for ordinary criminal law—*taʿzīr*—I

---

2. Mohammad Fadel, "International Law, Regional Developments: Islam," in *The Max Planck Encyclopedia of Public International Law* (*www.mpepil.com*), edited by ed. Dr. Frauke Lachenmann et al. (Oxford), p. 10.

3. See Badr al-Dīn Muḥammad b. Bahādur b. ʿAbdallāh al-Zarkashī, *al-Baḥr al-Muḥīṭ*, ed. Muḥammad Muḥammad Tāmir (Beirut: Dār al-Kutub al-ʿIlmiyya, 2000), vol. 1, p. 36.

know of no dispute that this body of law applied equally to non-Muslims and Muslims. So robust was the conviction that *ta'zīr* applied to Muslims and non-Muslims alike that Imām Mālik, despite his argument that non-Muslims were not subject to the *ḥadd* for adultery, held they could be punished for adultery under the principle of *taʿzīr*. Similarly, Imām Mālik treated the *ḥadd* punishments for *sariqa* and *ḥirāba* as forms of *taʿzīr* in order to apply them to non-Muslims, arguing that these punishments are necessary for the protection of property and life, an interest binding both Muslims and non-Muslims. Likewise, civil law—property, contract and tort—applied equally to Muslims and non-Muslims although tort law, according to all the Sunnī madhhabs other than the Ḥanafīs, provided different levels of compensation in cases of wrongful death in cases where the victim was a non-Muslim.[4]

I provide this brief background simply to point out that the question of the extent to which non-Muslims in an Islamic state are politically subject to Islamic law is a question that has preoccupied Muslim jurists from the earliest days of Muslim legal thinking, and Muslim jurists recognized that the application of Islamic law to non-Muslims required a different kind of [86] justification than that justifying its application to Muslims. Application of Islamic law to Muslims was simply derivative of their acceptance of Islam as being true. For non-Muslims, the justification had to be more complex, and accordingly, Muslim jurists struggled in formulating principled limits to the application of Islamic law to non-Muslims. And while they generally proceeded to analyze this problem using a case-by-case method, it is clear that they sought out a rationale that would be legitimate from the perspective of non-Muslims. In other words, they articulated reasons for the application of Islamic law to non-Muslims which they thought non-Muslims could reasonably accept for their own reasons.

Accordingly, non-Muslims could legitimately be expected to be subject to Islamic civil law because pursuant to those doctrines they receive the benefits of trade and protection from assault; they were exempt from Islamic ritual law because it would be absurd to ask someone to pray in a fashion whose format they subjectively reject as false; they were subject to the *taʿzīr* rules of Islamic criminal law because *taʿzīr* rules, unlike *ḥadd* rules, are based on the public interest, not solely the vindication of the claims of God, and thus does not imply any belief in Islam as such; and, they were exempt from Islamic requirements of marriage formation and dissolution since they had their own *beliefs* that governed the legitimacy of marriage formation and dissolution. In short, Islamic law strove to provide shared justifications for the application of Islamic law to non-Muslims in circumstances where shared belief in Islam could not provide the basis for legitimacy.

4. Mohammad Fadel, "The True, the Good and the Reasonable: The Theological and Ethical Roots of Public Reason in Islamic Law," 21, 1 *The Canadian Journal of Law & Jurisprudence* 5, 61–65 (2008).

MUSLIMS LIVING IN NON-MUSLIM TERRITORY, *FIQH AL-AQALLIYYĀT* AND DEMOCRATIC CITIZENSHIP

Muslim jurists, just as they articulated theories for binding non-Muslims to a subset of the rules of Islamic law, also theorized the conditions under which Muslims could live in a non-Islamic state, or put differently, what were the conditions that rendered emigration from a non-Islamic state to an Islamic one obligatory. This too was a question that entered Muslim juristic discourse from the earliest days of Islam. As was the case with the question of the extent to which Islamic law could bind non-Muslims, so too Muslim jurists differed on the question regarding the conditions [87] on which a Muslim could live in a non-Islamic state. Some jurists articulated a strong rule prohibiting it outright, e.g. the Mālikīs, while others, e.g. the Ḥanafīs and the Shāfiʿīs, produced a more nuanced position which permitted Muslims to continue living in a non-Islamic state if certain minimum conditions were satisfied regarding the ability of Muslims resident there to manifest Islam (*iẓhār al-dīn*). Muslim jurists conceptualized the legal basis on which Muslims would live in a non-Islamic state using concepts similar to that which they used in analyzing the relationship of non-Muslims to the Islamic state: because of the absence of shared belief, the relationship had to be set forth pursuant to the terms of an agreement (*ʿaqd*). Just as the relationship of *dhimma* was contractual and included mandatory and permissive terms, so too the agreement of security pursuant to which Muslims could legitimately live in a non-Islamic state had to meet certain minimum conditions, i.e. the ability to manifest Islam, but it could go beyond that as well. In the pre-modern period, however, Muslim jurists were mainly concerned with ascertaining whether the minimum conditions for the security of Muslims and the practice of Islam were satisfied so that the Muslim community in question could remain where they were or whether they were under an obligation to emigrate to a territory more hospitable to the practice of Islam.[5]

In the modern period this historical tradition for analyzing the status of Muslims living in non-Islamic territories has formed the basis of the *fiqh al-aqalliyyāt*—the jurisprudence of Muslim minorities.[6] It is my belief that the doctrinal developments being articulated in the domain of the *fiqh al-aqalliyyāt*—at least with regards to Muslim minorities living in democratic states—should be increasingly relevant to Muslims' understandings of the rights of non-Muslims in Islamic states. [88] At the outset it should be understood that the modern relationship of citizen is radically different than the relationship of se-

5. Khaled Abou el Fadl, "Islamic Law and Muslim Minorities: the Juristic Discourse on Muslim Minorities from the Second/Eighth to the Eleventh/Seventeenth Centuries," 1,2 *Islamic Law and* Society (1994), pp. 141–187.

6. See Andrew March, *Islam and Liberal Citizenship: The Search for an Overlapping Consensus* (New York: Oxford University Press, 2009).

curity which dominated pre-modern Islamic conceptions of the relationship between Muslims and a non-Islamic state. In the latter relationship Muslims promised the non-Islamic state to refrain from violence and obey the non-Islamic state's law in exchange for an undertaking by the non-Islamic state to recognize the inviolability of Muslims' religion, lives and property. So too, the contract of *dhimma* that Islamic law offered to non-Muslims is extremely circumscribed in scope relative to the modern conception of citizen: thus, pursuant to the relationship of *dhimma*, the Islamic state agreed to protect the non-Muslim from outside aggression as well as to grant her all the substantive protections of Islamic law internally in exchange for the *dhimmī*'s undertaking to obey Islamic law to the extent that it applied to him.[7]

Because neither the Muslim living in a non-Islamic state nor a *dhimmī* living in an Islamic state had any political rights to participate in the government, however, the relationship described by pre-modern Muslim jurists of the Muslim to a non-Islamic state, and of a *dhimmī* to an Islamic state, resembles modern discussions of alienage more than it does citizenship.

The defining feature of citizenship is that it creates a relationship that is not only vertical in the sense that it is between the individual and the state, but also another horizontal relationship that extends to other citizens through a relationship of equality and shared responsibility for collective governance of the state. A Muslim living in a non-Islamic state pursuant to a grant of security, by way of contrast, was in a subordinate position relative to the legal order there. So too a *dhimmī* in the Islamic state was subordinate because he suffered numerous political disabilities: not only was a *dhimmī* ineligible for public office, but even in areas of civil law he suffered certain forms of inequality, at least according to some Muslim schools of law.

As a citizen of a non-Islamic state, however, the minority Muslim is now an equal and not only enjoys equal rights but is also bound by the same legal duties as those that apply to the non-Muslim majority. Likewise, the non-Muslim *dhimmī*, once he becomes a [89] citizen of the Islamic state, is assumed to be in a position of equality with the majority Muslim population. Or, to put it differently, in a modern state, the concept of citizen is *non-sectarian*, and accordingly, rights and duties apply to all citizens simply by virtue of their status as citizens without regard to their religious beliefs.[8]

7. Fadel, supra note 2.

8. Humayun Kabir, the great, post-independence Indian Muslim politician observed that "In Muslim political thought . . . lawgivers had allowed for two kinds of situations, a situation in which there is a Muslim ruler and a large number of non-Muslim subjects and also the situation in which there is a non-Muslim ruler and Muslim subjects. But Muslim political thought had not provided for the situation which developed in India today, the situation in which *Muslims are citizens in a secular State*. In this situation, they are neither the sole rulers nor merely the ruled. We can put it another way and say that they are the rulers and ruled simultaneously. They are not merely ruled, but neither are they merely rulers. They are rulers and the ruled at the same. Further they are not rulers by themselves;

It is the defining feature of democratic citizenship that because of the relationship of equality inherent in the idea of citizenship, laws must respect the equality of the citizens, with the consequence that laws, to be legitimate, must be of such character that they are capable of being justified to the citizens in terms they can understand and accept as individuals having an equal share of public sovereignty. Again, to contrast this feature of modern citizenship to the pre-modern relationship of protection, becoming a "citizen" of the non-Islamic state would have required the Muslim to abandon Islam, because in states such as Catholic Spain, Catholicism defined the state. Likewise, for a *dhimmī* to be an equal to a Muslim, he would have to abandon his religion and become a Muslim. In democratic citizenship, however, such requirements are deemed to be impermissible because it is believed that it is impossible to justify adherence to one religion on grounds that are consistent with the equality of the citizens, meaning, it is impossible for the state to provide compelling reasons that all citizens can accept to make them adhere to the same religion, unlike, for example, a law that regulates their secular well-being, as is the case with legislation pertaining to traffic laws or laws regulating the market.

[90] Democracy then requires a basis for *shared* justification as a condition for laws to be legitimate. This condition—the need for shared justification—places limits on the kinds of laws democracies can legitimately promulgate. This desire for a shared basis of justification provides an important point of overlap between modern democratic conceptions of legitimacy and pre-modern Islamic conceptions of legitimacy. I have already discussed the limitations Muslim jurists placed on the application of Islamic law to non-Muslims and how that should be understood as a resolution of the problem of legitimacy: on what grounds is it legitimate to require non-Muslims to adhere to Islamic conceptions of justice? The answer Muslim jurists gave was that it is just to hold them to Islamic standards when those standards are comprehensible to them without regard to the truth of Islam. In a similar fashion democratic legislation is considered to be just—even as against the minority who rejected the legislation at issue—because it is limited to matters which all citizens can reasonably accept regardless of whether they profess the truth of certain controversial metaphysical doctrines, e.g. the truth of Christianity.

Accordingly, the possibility of democratic citizenship—rather than mere protection, i.e. alienage—presented Muslim communities living in democratic societies both new possibilities and new challenges. On the positive side of the ledger, the prospect of democratic citizenship offered them the possibility to share positively in the governance of their societies on a basis of equality with non-Muslim citizens. Democratic citizenship also made Muslims' position within non-Islamic states more secure: as citizens instead of aliens, they enjoyed inviolable rights that could not be compromised, e.g. they could not be deported. At the same time, however, their obligations to non-Islamic states would

they are rulers in association with people of many different religions." Humayun Kabir, "Minorities in a Democracy." *Liberal Islam*, supra note 1, p. 150.

correspondingly increase: whereas under a regime of alienage they were freer to negotiate what specific commitments they would make to their host state, whether in terms of service in national armies or even the right to apply Islamic law to their family disputes (often times effected through doctrines of private international law), as citizens they would be treated as any other citizen and would only be entitled to exemptions from national law to the same extent as other non-Muslim citizens enjoyed such exemptions.

[91] MUSLIM REACTIONS TO THE DEMANDS OF DEMOCRATIC CITIZENSHIP

Because democratic citizenship is a richer relationship than the mere protection contemplated by Muslim jurists in the pre-modern period, whether Muslims could in good faith accept the offer of citizenship raised novel issues in Islamic law. These issues have occupied the attention of a good many Muslim jurists since the early part of the 20th century. The most fundamental issue is that of loyalty (*walāʾ*) to the non-Islamic state. It was certainly settled doctrine in the pre-modern period that a Muslim could not give *walāʾ* to a non-Islamic state, and that doing so was a virtual repudiation of Islam. On the other hand, in the pre-modern period states were not democratic, and many in fact were organized around adherence to a specific religion, e.g. Catholicism, or after the Reformation, a national church, e.g. The Church of England.[9]

Given this reality, it is easy to understand why Muslim jurists would conclude that a Muslim who pledged loyalty to such a state necessarily repudiated Islam. That this should also be the case for democratic citizenship does not appear to be clear: a democratic state makes no religious demands on its citizens in the sense that it does not require citizens to profess one faith or even faith in general. Accordingly, and unlike the case of Hapsburg Spain, Muslims could become citizens and retain their adherence to Islam, at least in a prima facie sense. The pre-modern discourse, however, was concerned with more than just the ability to maintain the name of Islam; it also was desirous of protecting the dignity (*ʿizza*) of Muslims and Islam, and was concerned that by living in a non-Islamic state, a Muslim would subject himself to humiliation (*dhull*) because the legal system of the non-Islamic state would not protect his dignity. Finally, there was the concern that by living under the protection of a non-Islamic state, a Muslim would become subject to the "rules of infidelity" [92] (*aḥkām al-kufr*), something that would entail both humiliation and injustice. In analyzing whether it is permissible for Muslims to be citizens of democratic states, Muslim jurists writing in the field of *fiqh al-aqalliyyāt* have had to analyze these three issues in the light of two concerns: the first is determining what was the purpose (*al-maqṣūd*) of the various rules of Islamic substantive law which either prohibited or discouraged residence in non-Islamic states, and the second is deter-

9. See generally, Andrew March, "Islamic Foundations for a Social Contract in Non-Muslim Liberal Democracies," 101,2 *American Political Science Review*, pp. 235–252 (2007).

mining the nature of kinds of claims democratic states can legitimately make upon Muslims, and whether a Muslim could accept those obligations consistently with his Islamic commitments. Starting with the first question, that of *walāʾ*, Muslim jurists developed a distinction between *walāʾ* as a political concept and *walāʾ* as a religious one. They argued that what Islam prohibits is expressing loyalty to falsehood.[10]

Accordingly, a Muslim could not have loyalty to a Catholic State any more than he could have loyalty to the Roman Catholic Church, because in both cases he would be endorsing falsehood. Democratic constitutions, however, do not require loyalty in this sense. Rather than requiring loyalty to a specific religious doctrine, citizenship requires loyalty to a set of principles that are accepted as just and which form the basis of the state's legal system, most notably, its constitution. This kind of loyalty is acceptable because it does not contradict loyalty to Islam as a religious doctrine. In other words, loyalty to a system of law that is not derived from a false metaphysical doctrine but is instead limited to just principles of law does not require Muslims to reject their belief in Islam or their continued religious solidarity with the Muslim community and accordingly is consistent with Islamic commitments. So too the kind of love and affection that arise between Muslims and non-Muslims living together in a just society is also permitted because it is love and affection that is civic in nature and born of mutual cooperation for one another's welfare; it does not require or imply acceptance or recognition of the legitimacy of whatever false views non-Muslims hold about God.[11] The terms of democratic citizenship, however, do far more than simply allow[93] Muslims to be citizens without renouncing Islam. The inherent limits of legislation in a democratic state ensure that Muslims, at a minimum, will be permitted to fulfill certain fundamental Islamic obligations, specifically, the open fulfillment of the most fundamental ritual obligations of Islam (*al-shaʿāʾir*) as well as open teaching of Islamic doctrines to both Muslims and non-Muslims (*daʿwa*). Norms of democratic legitimacy are also responsive to Muslim concerns about dignity: because democratic states respect the norm of equality in legislation, Muslims can be assured that they will not be singled out for a set of specific norms intended to stigmatize them as separate from, and as less worthy than other non-Muslim citizens.

Finally, democratic legislation does not result in Muslims' submission to *aḥkām al-kufr* because the rules governing a democratic state are the product of the deliberative assemblies of the citizens who apply their collective reasoning as citizens to questions of the public good, not questions of religious belief. Such assemblies therefore are not the equivalent of an ecclesiastical council promulgating rules for their followers pursuant to false religious doctrine. In other words, because democratic citizenship does not make claims on a Muslim that require him to repudiate Islam, whether explicitly or implicitly, pledging loyalty to a democratic state as embodied in the terms of democratic citizenship does not

10. Id. 249.
11. Id. 250

constitute a repudiation of Islam in a way that pledging loyalty to a Catholic regime or a Communist regime, for example, might. Implicit in this theoretical justification of Muslim citizenship in democratic states is several assumptions. Perhaps the most fundamental is that Islam can not only survive, but flourish in a pluralist regime simply by virtue of its inherent appeal as a rational doctrine.

Accordingly, a Muslim community in a democratic state will be able to pass on Islam to future generations by teaching them about Islam using methods of rational persuasion. The survival of the Muslim community in a democratic state therefore does not depend on the threat of coercive state sanctions to deter Muslims from exiting the community. Not only is the inherent appeal of Islamic teachings assumed to be sufficient to preserve the Muslim community over time, so too Muslim jurists assume [94] that they are sufficient to attract non-Muslims to Islam on condition that Muslims are in fact given a fair opportunity to present their beliefs to non-Muslim society, a condition guaranteed by democratic society. Second, Muslim jurists assume the existence of a certain kind of justice that is not derivative of religious conceptions, including Islamic conceptions, but instead can be derived from rational deliberation. This assumption is implicit in the justification of democratic politics as a legitimate kind of lawmaking in contrast to false claims of other religions which claim an ability to disclose the will of God to human beings, e.g. the Catholic Church. Yūsuf al-Qaraḍāwī, for instance, refers to such a non-sectarian conception of justice in a fatwa of his in which he explains how it is possible for Muslims to engage in *political cooperation* with non-Muslims despite the fact that non-Muslims entertain false beliefs about God.[12] Al-Qaraḍāwī gives many reasons, some of which amount to explaining why difference in belief does not constitute an obstacle as such to political cooperation, but he also explains that it is the Muslims' love of justice (*qisṭ*) which motivates them to cooperate productively with non-Muslims, despite the latter's adherence to false doctrines.[13]

While al-Qaraḍāwī does not explain what he means by justice in that fatwa, it can safely be assumed that it must entail a form of justice that is autonomous of revelation, or else it would not form a common basis for cooperation with non-Muslims. At the same time, however, its autonomy from revelation does not mean that is repugnant to revelation. Rather, this system of non-sectarian, rational justice must in a certain sense be consistent with Islamic conceptions of justice or else Muslims could not appeal to it. What then would be the relationship of this autonomous version of justice to Islamic conceptions of justice that derive directly from our knowledge of God's will as revealed in the Qur'an and Sunna? It seems that the answer is that it *supplements* the non-sectarian conception of justice which is common to human beings regardless of their religious (or non-religious) commitments. In the first instance, this supplementary knowledge binds Muslims in their interactions with one another because they have shared [95] knowledge of these addition-

12. Yūsuf al-Qaraḍāwī, 3 *Fatāwā Muʿāṣira* (Beirut: al-Maktab al-Islami, 2003), pp. 189–191.
13. Ibid.

al (religious) obligations. Obviously, this includes such requirements of Islamic law as ritual law and rules regarding the etiquette of intra-Muslim personal relationships. Negatively, this places limits on the kinds of demands non-sectarian justice can make upon Muslims, in particular, it cannot claim to compel Muslims to disobedy God. What is significant about these arguments is that they go beyond narrow utilitarian-based justifications for Muslim citizenship in non-Islamic (but democratic) states. A utilitarian argument would run along the lines of the following: it is distasteful or even prohibited for Muslims to accept citizenship in a democratic state because it requires them not only to tolerate a non-Islamic state, but also to support it actively. Nevertheless, these harms are outweighed by the benefits accruing to Muslims from living in a democratic state, at least until such time as Muslims are present there in large enough numbers that would allow them to Islamize the host regimes' legal systems more thoroughly so as to make them more systematically compatible to Islamic substantive law. In other words, the kinds of justifications recently articulated by Muslim jurists in connection with the concept of *fiqh al-aqalliyyāt* go well beyond a justification that rests on a conception of necessity that is, at least conceptually, only temporary and will be revised once the circumstances giving rise to the necessity (the minority condition) are resolved, i.e. Muslims become a majority of the population or otherwise obtain political power.

NON-MUSLIMS IN MODERN MUSLIM-MAJORITY STATES

If democratic states fulfill a certain moral ideal of political society that is compatible with Islamic commitments in a non-contingent manner, however, the question arises as to whether the justifications for Islamic endorsement of democratic citizenship set out in the *fiqh al-aqalliyyāt* discourse are not applicable to states with Muslim majorities? While Muslim states, as a matter of their national legal systems, have made much progress in creating legal systems based on equal citizenship, they can still be criticized for retaining substantial elements of sectarianism in their legal systems that are substantially inconsistent with the democratic [96] ideal of *equal* citizenship. The most obvious traces of sectarianism in the legal systems of Muslim states are constitutional declarations that the state's religion is Islam, a statement that immediately gives the polity a sectarian character; other instances of *de jure* sectarianism in Muslim states include rules imposing religious tests for certain public offices, e.g. that the president or the prime minister must be Muslim; and, provisions in a state's constitution affirming that the Islamic Sharīʿa is "a" or "the" principal source of the state's legislation. Less controversial, but still problematic, are the existence of sectarian-based personal status laws pursuant to which the applicable rules of family law are determined by the sectarian identity of the citizen rather than his status simply as citizen. (In other words, many Muslim states lack a law of personal status that applies to all of its citizens, and instead, applies different laws to its citizens depending on how the state classifies their sectarian identity.) While this is often times in conformity with the wishes of the non-Muslim minority, it can often be inconsistent with the equal citizenship rights of non-Muslims. Thus, a non-Muslim woman who otherwise cannot obtain a divorce because of her sectarian identity has an incentive to convert to Islam solely to obtain the benefit of a divorce, which might be immediate if her husband refuses to convert to Islam as well during her *ʿidda*, or deferred in the event of his conversion by petitioning for a judicial divorce as a Muslim woman. The ideals of equal citizenship in this circumstance would appear to require recognition of a right to a judicial divorce simply on the grounds of her status as a citizen without regard to her sectarian affiliation which, as a matter of her subjective belief, she may or may not accept.

Another way to understand this point is that the concept of equal citizenship requires a positive conception of toleration, not simply a negative one. While pre-modern Islamic law accepted a negative concept of toleration, meaning that it would allow non-Muslims to preserve many aspects of their ways of life even though Muslims believed them to be erroneous, Islamic law did not contemplate positive tolerance of non-Islamic ways of life in a manner that the views of non-Muslims in the Islamic state should be included in formulating the laws of the Islamic state. Another way of putting this is that under traditional Islamic conceptions of [97] toleration of non-Muslims, non-Muslims did not have any right to formulate the terms of the general rules of society, and to that extent, they were completely objects of the law rather than its subjects. This is evidenced by numerous rules of pre-modern Islamic law, e.g. the bar on non-Muslims serving as witnesses in court (*shuhūd*); the prohibition on non-Muslims being judges; and, the prohibition on Muslims serving as a policy-making minister (*wazīr tafwīḍ*). Even the right to grant security to a non-Muslim from a hostile state—a right guaranteed to even Muslim slaves, women and minors—was denied to non-Muslim *dhimmīs*.

The political marginalization of non-Muslims eventually led to severe problems in historical Islamic states such as the Ottoman Empire, most prominently in the form of a sectarian consciousness that allowed outside powers to manipulate one group against another to further its own imperialist interests, even leading to extension of the infamous capitulations to non-Muslims who were nominally citizens of Islamic states.[14] For this reason, one of the main objects of legal reform in the Ottoman Empire was to create a more unified legal system that would be in greater conformity with the ideal of equal citizenship with the goal of creating national solidarity that transcended sectarian affiliation, something that was deemed necessary if Islamic states were to resist (or liberate themselves from) imperialist encroachment. Throughout the 19th century, haltingly at first, and then more systematically, Muslim governments took steps to narrow the distinction between Muslims and non-Muslims in their legal systems. Mehmet 'Ali Pasha in Egypt, for example, after introducing universal conscription quickly decided to impose that obligation on Egypt's Christians as well as its Muslims. The Ottomans, through

14. Fadel, *supra* note 2.

the Tanzimat reform, likewise enshrined legal equality for Muslims and non-Muslims throughout its territories and also began to require non-Muslims to serve in its armies.[15]

While the political reforms of the nineteenth and twentieth centuries were often driven by practical necessity and had a [98] certain *ad hoc* character to them, a more systematic approach to this problem of reconciling Islamic commitments to justice with a non-sectarian conception of justice was one of the driving factors behind the new Egyptian civil code. According to ʿAbd al-Razzāq al-Sanhūrī, Egypt could not be genuinely independent unless its legal system had an organic tie to its indigenous legal system, i.e. the Sharīʿa. At the same time, however, its legal system had to be modern and thus required a recasting of the substantive values of historical Islamic law that would make them workable for the needs of a modern Islamic state. Significantly, al-Sanhūrī believed that non-Muslim jurists were equally competent in working out the details of a modernized Islamic civil code. This was because, in al-Sanhūrī's opinion, Islamic law was a universal legal system that had to be able to justify its rules to both Muslims and non-Muslims.[16]

Its rules regarding the interactions of citizens, however, had to be revised to make them compatible with modern life, both substantively, and in terms of their justifications. One of the methodological innovations al-Sanhūrī introduced in the course of his attempt to develop a modern Islamic law code was the principle that, because Islamic law is universally valid, it was capable of adopting any principle of law that was not repugnant to its fundamental commitments. This principled accommodation of non-Muslims in the juristic project of a modern Islamic code is reminiscent of justifications offered by Muslim jurists as to why Muslims can accept the terms of democratic citizenship in good faith: because democratic commitments do not require Muslims to affirm articles of faith, for example, that are repugnant to Islam, its results are substantially equivalent to Islamic conceptions of justice. Al-Sanhūrī's desire to include non-Muslims in his project of a renewed and modernized Islamic legal system, however, was also in his view good practical politics. He recognized the danger [99] to national independence that alienated religious minorities posed, and accordingly, he believed that those elements within the Egyptian religious establishment who opposed full integration of the Copts into the structure of the Egyptian state were just as dangerous to the future of Islam as those Egyptian intellectuals who had become secularists in the mould of Kamal Atatürk.[17]

---

15. See, for example, Butrus Abu-Manneh, "The Islamic Roots of the Gulhane Rescript," 34 *Die Welt des Islams* (1994), pp. 173–203.

16. For more on Sanhūrī and his contributions to modern Islamic law, see Enid Hil, "The Place and Significance of Islamic Law in the Life and Work of ʿAbd al-Razzāq al-Sanhūrī, Egyptian Jurist and Scholar," Parts I and II, 3,1 *Arab Law Quarterly* (1988), pp. 33–64 and 3,2 *Arab Law Quarterly* (1988), pp. 182–218 and ʿAmr Shalakany, "Between Identity and Distribution: Sanhūrī, Genealogy and the Will to Islamise," 8,2 *Islamic Law and Society*, pp. 201–244 (2001).

17. See, for example, Nādiya al-Sanhūrī and Tawfīq al-Shāwī, *al-Sanhūrī min Khilāl Awrāqihi al-Shakhṣiyya* (Cairo: Dār al-Shurūq, 2002), pp. 134–135 and pp. 150–151.

IMPLICATIONS OF *FIQH AL-AQALLIYYĀT* FOR NON-MUSLIMS IN MUSLIM MAJORITY STATES

Sanhūrī, despite his brilliance as a scholar of comparative law and his substantial expertise in Islamic law, in the final analysis lacked the Islamic scholarly credentials to carry the day, and as is well-known, there continues to be substantial controversy whether Sanhūrī's code is sufficiently Islamic. What is significant from the perspective of this paper, however, is that the current discourse of *fiqh al-aqalliyyāt* provides substantial normative justification for Sanhūrī's project of generating a modern system of Islamic law that is able to win the support of all citizens, whether or not Muslim. Just as Sanhūrī imagined an abstract body of substantive Islamic law that he described as universal and immutable but whose practical and detailed manifestations could change based on time and place, so too jurists involved in the practice of *fiqh al-aqalliyyāt* go beyond the particular historical rulings of Islamic law and try to derive from them abstract rules that allow them to argue that the principles protected by these abstract rules are in fact being satisfied by democratic principles.

So, the question naturally arises: if it is permissible to argue that the fundamental goals of Islam are met in a democratic society, why should democratic constitutions be limited to non-Muslim states? Isn't it the case that if Muslim-majority countries adopted legal orders that satisfied standards of democratic legitimacy that such polities would be equally capable to satisfy the requirements of Islam for a just order, if not more so? The concluding part of this Article will make the case that indeed, just as Muslim jurists [100] have argued that democratic states satisfy the goals of Islam with respect to political organization, so too would a democratic legal order satisfy Muslims' obligations even in contexts where they are majorities.

The first step in making this case is that the distinction between the obligations of Muslims in a minority context and when they are in a majority context ought not to be relevant from the perspective of what Islam deems to be the minimum conditions required for a state to earn the political loyalty of Muslims.

Giving too much weight to the empirical fact that Muslim minorities are politically weak at the present time reflects the continued influence of the juristic division of the world between *dār al-islām* and *dār al-ḥarb*, a classification that has come under increasing criticism by Muslim jurists in the post-World War II era. As Wahba al-Zuḥaylī argued in his book *Islam and International Law*,[18] the fact that contemporary international law guarantees the most valuable rights in the eyes of Islam—namely, the right to preach Islam peacefully without active opposition by governments who are to take an officially neutral position vis-à-vis Islam—means that offensive jihad is no longer an Islamic require-

---

18. Wahba al-Zuḥaylī, *al-ʿAlāqāt al-Duwaliyya fi al-Islām: Muqarāna bi-l-Qanūn al-Dawlī al-Ḥadīth* (Beirut: Muʾassasat al-Risāla, 1981).

ment. He goes on to argue that the spread of norms of peaceful relations among states, religious freedom, the self-determination of peoples and the prohibition against aggressive war means that the world has become the equivalent of one territorial jurisdiction (*dār*), implying that law (at least public law) ought to be universal. Accordingly, what is significant to the *fiqh al-aqalliyyāt* arguments is not the numbers of Muslims in a given non-Islamic state, for if that were the case their obligations would vary depending on the percentage of Muslims in the general population; rather, what is significant is whether the legal order of the state itself guarantees the security of Muslims and guarantees their ability to practice, teach and call to Islam. Once those conditions are satisfied, Muslims are *Islamically* bound to maintain their ties of loyalty to that state even if they gain numbers and thus become politically more powerful.

The same argument applies to states in which Muslims comprise a majority of the population: if the state provides the same [101] guarantees then the interests of Islam are sufficiently protected and there is no need for the state to be structured expressly as an instrumentality for the protection of Islam or Muslims. Just as Zuḥaylī argued that the need for offensive jihad has been rendered obsolete because of the realities of the post-World War II international order, namely, its protection of the independence and sovereignty of states, its commitments to human rights, and governments' neutrality with respect to Islam,[19] it would seem that the need to have a state dedicated to the protection of Islam would also be obsolete. Ironically, this argument is confirmed by various rules that in the pre-modern period prohibited non-Muslims from exercising power (*wilāya*) over Muslims.

The juristic assumption motivating this rule was that the non-Muslim would rule based on his or her own (false) conceptions of religion, not that he would be applying just law. This would imply that where a non-Muslim citizen is applying or enforcing the rules of what is a just legal system, the mere fact that its officials are non-Muslims does not transform the legal system into an unjust order. The fact that the disbelief of legal officials is not relevant to the justice of the non-Islamic legal order is obvious in the case of western democracies which despite the fact that the overwhelming majority of its political decision makers are not Muslim, the jurists who have developed the *fiqh al-aqalliyyāt* discourse have not allowed that fact to derogate from the normative justness of these countries' political and legal institutions. There is also pre-modern Islamic precedent in support of this approach: while al-Māwardī holds that non-Muslims are not eligible to serve as *wazīr tafwīḍ*, they are eligible to serve as *wazīr tanfīdh*. The reason is that the former exercises discretion in the name of the Muslim community, whereas the latter simply enforces rules that Muslims themselves have already made.

The same analysis applies to non-Muslim citizens of a democratic state: whether or not Muslims are majority or minority of that population, all legal officials are bound to enforce a law that applies to all citizens and that is the product of their collective

19. Fadel, *supra* note 2.

deliberation. Such an official, whether he is a Christian, Jew, Hindu [102] or Buddhist, is bound to apply this body of democratic law and is not permitted to apply his or her own religious conception of what is true or right. If such an official did so, it would constitute an *abuse* of power for which the law would provide a remedy. In short, a democratic state provides protections against the threat that non-Muslims would use their political power to discriminate against, dominate, or persecute Muslims. If that fact can be relied upon to legitimate Muslims' residence in democratic states in which they are the minority, it applies *a fortiori* to states where Muslims are the majority since minoritarian religious communities would be extremely concerned, from a practical perspective, to do anything that would suggest they wish to use their political power to oppress Muslims. In short, if we accept the conclusion of the emerging discourse of *fiqh al-aqalliyyāt* that democratic political life is sufficient to protect the interests of Islam and Muslims where they are a minority, then *a fortiori* it is sufficient to protect them in circumstances where they constitute the majority. In this latter situation they are even in less need of special privileges from the state to maintain the health of the Muslim community, teach Islamic doctrines, and call others to it. Not only does consistent application of the principles espoused in the *fiqh al-aqalliyyāt* discourse require their application also to states in which Muslims form the majority, so too does prudent politics. Muslim-majority states should recognize that the existence of flourishing and prosperous Muslim communities in the developed world is in the interests of Muslim-majority countries. Yet, the failure of Muslim-majority countries to adhere to the equality requirements of democracy serves to undermine the ability of Muslim citizens of non-Muslim states to exercise fully their rights as citizens. Elements of those countries hostile to Islam and Muslims use the persistence of political discrimination against non-Muslims and rules criminalizing or penalizing civilly apostasy are used to argue that Muslims are not morally committed to the prevailing democratic order and therefore are not entitled to its protections. Even though such an argument reduces Muslims to a group rather than treating them as individuals, and as such represents a violation of democratic commitments to equality, this argument has gained and is continuing to gain traction, especially in Europe. Indeed, the European Court of Human [103] Rights in two decisions, *Refah Party v. Republic of Turkey*[20] and *Shahin v. Turkey*[21] has essentially taken the position that Islam is inherently anti-democratic and therefore governments are permitted to take steps to regulate it that would not be permissible with respect to other religions or associations. Recently, a prominent Oxford-based philosopher of law, John Finnis, has begun to make open calls for European govern-

20. *Refah Partisi (The Welfare Party) and Others v. Turkey*, nos. 41340/98, 41342/98, 41343/98 and 41344/98, CHR 2003-II-(13.2.03) (Feb. 13, 2003).

21. *Layla Sahin v. Turkey*, no. 44774/98 (Nov. 10, 2005).

ments to create incentives for Muslims to leave Europe, again based on the argument that Islam is inherently opposed to democratic politics.[22]

Public discussion of such policies, even if they are not adopted in the short-term, are extremely dangerous, not just for the long-term interests of Muslim communities living in the west, but also for international relations. To the extent that jurists like al-Zuḥaylī have argued that doctrines such as *dār al-ḥarb* and offensive jihad are obsolete, it was based on the notion that non-Islamic states are capable of treating their Muslim citizens with respect and equality. To the extent non-Muslim states adopt laws that are overtly hostile to Islam and Muslims, however, al-Zuḥaylī's argument concerning the secure place of Islam in today's world will appear less and less convincing to Muslims who might begin to listen to more radical voices.

Given the fact that the underlying logic of *fiqh al-aqalliyyāt*'s justification of democracy also applies to Muslim-majority states, and the importance of diffusing even the appearance of a conflict of civilizations, it appears critical that Muslim-majority states take decisive steps to incorporate their non-Muslim citizens into the decision-making structure of their states in a manner consistent with democratic norms of equality. The Islamic movements in Muslim states too should make this one of their own priorities. Many individuals in Islamic movements have benefitted from the freedoms of liberal democracy; they should have the unique combination of theory and practice to carry the day against elements in [104] the Islamic movement who would wish to continue, if not enhance, the marginalization of non-Muslims for the domestic politics of Muslim-majority states.

CONCLUSION

Islamic law, from the earliest days of the Prophet's (S) migration to Madina, has been careful to distinguish between the rules that are applicable in Muslim territory and non-Muslim territory. Islamic law permitted Muslims to live in non-Muslim territory provided certain conditions were met, specifically, that Muslims could manifest their religion. Conversely, Islamic law allowed non-Muslims to live permanently in Islamic territory as protected persons provided they agreed to abide by the non-religious elements of Islamic law. In the post-World War II era, with the spread of international law, human rights and global norms of governance, the rights of individual citizenship have supplanted the rights of communities. Accordingly, Muslims living outside of Islamic territory enjoy, theoretically at least, rights equal to those of their non-Muslim countrymen. In return, however, Muslims are expected to bear equally the duties of citizenship in the non-Muslim state. The new circumstances in which Muslim minorities find themselves,

22. John Finnis, *Endorsing Discrimination Between Faiths: A Case of Extreme Speech?* at 12 (2008), available at http://www.ssrn.com/abstract=1101522.

particularly in western democratic countries has given rise to a new juristic discourse known as *fiqh al-aqalliyyāt*. This body of jurisprudence has attempted to normalize the relationship of Muslim minorities as citizens to their states of citizenship, even though the majority of the population is non-Muslim.

Significantly, jurists engaged in this discourse have stressed the fact that the array of rights guaranteed in democracies are sufficient to insure that Muslims can live there with honor and [105] dignity, and the right to manifest Islam, including, by calling others to it. On this basis, they have agreed that the presence of Muslim minorities as citizens of democratic states is religiously permissible. On the other hand, the same logic these jurists have used to legitimate the presence of Muslim citizens in non-Muslim countries implies that even in Muslim-majority situations, a democratic state that is religiously neutral, provided it is otherwise just, ought to be sufficient to protect the honor and dignity of Muslims, and their right to manifest Islam and call others to it. This calls into question the need for an explicitly Islamic state to protect Muslims' interests as Muslims. To the extent that we accept *fiqh al-aqalliyyāt* as representing a legitimate interpretation of the Sharīʿa for Muslims living as minorities, it would seem that Muslim majorities should also be required to treat non-Muslims with the same level of equality that they demand of non-Muslims when Muslims are the minority. Not only is this demand normatively just, at least in light of the claims of *fiqh al-aqalliyyāt*, it is also good policy: in today's interconnected world, which some jurists have said ought really be deemed one legal jurisdiction (*dār*), it undermines the security and well-being of Muslim minorities for Muslim majority jurisdictions to claim a right to subject non-Muslim minorities to discriminatory legislation—such as qualifications for public office or access to divorce—while demanding that Muslim minorities enjoy the same rights that their non-Muslim majority co-citizens enjoy. While this would represent a departure from the traditional logic of the relationship of *dhimma*, it would nevertheless be consistent with the higher goals (*maqāṣid*) of Islamic law which seeks to maintain peaceful co-existence with [106] non-Muslims who are prepared to live in peace and mutual respect with Islam.

Islamic Jurisprudence

4

THE SOCIAL LOGIC OF *TAQLĪD* AND THE RISE OF THE *MUKHTAṢAR*

Mohammad Fadel

INTRODUCTION

[193] Modern scholarship treating the history of Islamic law, both Muslim and Western, has given the *ijtihād/taqlīd* dichotomy a central position in explaining the dynamic of Islamic law's development. Despite sharp differences regarding the historical importance each concept played, the majority of authors agree, at least implicitly, that legal progress was almost exclusively a function of the freedom jurists enjoyed to exercise independent reasoning, *ijtihād*. Both Muslim and Western writers have privileged *ijtihād* because of its associations with independent rational thought. These authors have also disparaged *taqlīd*, either explicitly or implicitly, on the presumption that the natural telos of the Islamic legal system, based as it is upon the interpretive efforts of individual jurists, was the production of independent interpreters of the law, *mujtahids*. It is no surprise that a *muqallid* is understood as a jurist who fails to reach the rank of *ijtihād* and whose work in the legal system and his role in it are derivative at best and slavish at worst.[1]

[194] Disagreement among modern scholars regarding the *ijtihād/taqlīd* dichotomy, then, is not so much a disagreement about the nature of each as much as it is a disagreement about whether or not *ijtihād* ever came to an end, and if it did, when.[2] That modern historians

---

This article was originally published in *Islamic Law and Society* vol. 3, no. 2, 1996, pp. 193–233.

1. Schacht, for example, defined *taqlīd* as "the unquestioning acceptance of the doctrines of established schools and authorities." Joseph Schacht, *An Introduction to Islamic Law* (Oxford: Oxford University Press, 1964), 71.

2. Thus, authors like Coulson and Schacht tend to assert that Islamic law became subject to *taqlīd* in the 4th/10th century, while Hallaq and Makdisi either deny that *ijtihād* came to an end or assert that it met its demise only at a relatively late period. Hallaq has been the most persistent modern scholar in criticizing inherited views regarding the cessation of *ijtihād* and has demonstrated, for example, that the issue of whether or not an age could be devoid of an independent interpreter of the law *(mujtahid)* did not appear as an issue in works of legal theory *(uṣūl al-fiqh)* prior to the 7th/13th century. For the various positions on this issue, see N. J. Coulson, *A History of Islamic Law* (Edinburgh: Edinburgh University Press, 1964), 80; Schacht, An *Introduction* 70–71; Wael Hallaq, "Was the Gate of *ijtihād* Closed?," *International Journal of Middle East Studies*, 16 (1984), 3–41. See also George Makdisi, *The Rise of Colleges: Institutions of*

of Islamic law differ little regarding the intellectual inferiority of *taqlīd* to *ijtihād* is evident from the different explanations given for the existence of *taqlīd*. Coulson explained *taqlīd* to be a result of a type of exhaustion that was inevitable given the material sources of Islamic law.[3] Schacht attributed the rise of *taqlīd* to a belief in the near perfection of the law as it had been formulated by previous jurists, combined with a pessimistic view regarding the relative competence of succeeding jurists.[4] Hallaq has argued that debates over the permissibility of *ijtihād* "reflected the uncertainty of Muslim jurists regarding the originality of their legal minds."[5]

Hallaq also has produced evidence that even for Muslim legal theorists of the pre-modern era, *taqlīd* was more than a negative phenomenon—it was an apocalyptic sign of the end of religious knowledge and a harbinger of the final destruction of the Muslim community.[6] Both modern Western scholars of Islamic law and many Muslim jurists throughout the pre-modern period, it appears, reached similar [195] conclusions, although for different reasons, regarding the intellectual inferiority of *taqlīd* to *ijtihād*.[7]

This privileging of *ijtihād* is also evident in the writings of 20th-century Muslim legal historians. Al-Ḥajawī referred to the period of Islamic jurisprudence between the 5th/11th and the 14th/20th century as "the stage of old age and senility approaching non-existence (*ṭawr al-shaykhūkha wa al-haram al-muqrib min al-ʿadam*)."[8] Al-Zarqā' was more charitable than al-Ḥajawī, dating the decadence (*inḥiṭāṭ*) of jurisprudence in the Islamic world to the middle of the 6th/12th century.[9] For both authors, "decadence" was the direct result of the cessation of *ijtihād*. Al-Jīdī, likewise, made a causal link between the cessation of *ijtihād*

Learning in Islam and the West (Edinburgh: Edinburgh University Press, 1981), 285, 290–91, where the author argued that the door of *ijtihād* was never closed, although increased governmental pressures beginning in the 7th/13th century, especially through the office of the paid *muftī*, greatly restricted the scope of *ijtihād*. For a summary of the different positions regarding the *ijtihād/taqlīd* debate, see R. Stephen Humphreys, *Islamic History: A Framework for Inquiry* (rev. ed., Princeton: Princeton University Press, 1991), 212.

3. Coulson, *A History* 81.

4. Schacht, *An Introduction* 70–71.

5. Wael Hallaq, "Considerations on the Function and Character of Sunni Legal Theory," *Journal of the American Oriental Society*, 104 (1984), 689.

6. Wael Hallaq, "On the Origins of the Controversy about the Existence of *Mujtahids* and the Gate of *Ijtihad*," *Studia Islamica*, 63 (1986), 129–41.

7. Hallaq, "Was the Gate of *Ijtihād* Closed," 20.

8. Muḥammad b. al-Ḥasan al-Ḥajawī al-Tha'ālibī, *al-Fikr al-sāmī fī tārīkh al-fiqh al-islāmī*, ed. ʿAbd al-ʿAzīz b. ʿAbd al-Fattāḥ al-Qārī (al-Madīna al-Munawwara: al-Maktaba al-ʿIlmiyya, 1396), 1 vol., containing vols. 1 and 2 of original work, 12–13. The characteristic feature of this last age is the death of *ijtihād*. This should be contrasted with the "Time of Youth (*ṭawr al-shabāb*)" characterized by the flourishing of *ijtihād*.

9. Muṣṭafā Aḥmad al-Zarqā', *al-Fiqh al-islāmī fī thawbihi al-jadīd: al-madkhal al-fiqhī al-ʿāmm*, Part 1 (6th ed., Damascus: Damascus University Press, n.d.), 122–23.

and the "decadence" of jurisprudence.[10] Therefore, these authors dismissed the larger part of Islamic legal history on the assumption that it lacked anything of interest because it was dominated by *taqlīd*.[11] Their dismissive treatment of post-4th/10th century Islamic jurisprudence recalls Coulson's characterization of later Islamic jurisprudence as being slavish both in form and content.[12]

While the prevailing interpretation of the relationship between *ijtihād* and *taqlīd* in Islamic legal history no doubt has its attractions, it suffers from an idealist approach to the study of law—namely, that law as an intellectual enterprise can be understood without regard to the institutional context within which it develops. This is ironic because the problem of the continuity of *ijtihād* was originally posed as a problem within the context of the sociology of Islamic law. Weber argued that [196] the cessation of *ijtihād* prevented Muslim societies from regulating themselves through the vehicle of formal law. Denied the right to develop the law, an ever-increasing sphere of Muslim society was regulated by "concrete, ethical or other practical valuations"[13] whose chronic instability prevented the rational calculation of consequences necessary for the rise of capitalism.[14] Although the law, in principle, was complete and left no room for legitimate changes, Weber argued that customary and secular laws, which were illegitimate from the perspective of Islamic law, filled the void left behind by a rigid "ideal code."[15]

Jackson's recent work on the Mālikī jurist Shihāb al-Dīn al-Qarāfī attempts to transcend the prevailing idealist discourse by explaining the rise of *taqlīd* as an attempt by jurists to limit government manipulation of the legal system.[16] His most important contribution to this debate has been to suggest that *taqlīd* was more than a mere absence of *ijtihād*; he argues that the relationship of *taqlīd* to *ijtihād* can only be understood if one takes into account the

---

10. ʿUmar al-Jīdī, *Muḥāḍarāt fī tārīkh al-madhhab al-mālikī fī al-gharb al-islāmī* (Rabāṭ: Manshūrāt ʿUkāẓ, 1407/1987), 131.

11. For example, al-Ḥajawī stated that a decision not to include the biographies of any Mālikī jurists subsequent to Khalīl b. Isḥāq would have been fair, "for most of them were his followers. Thus, from the time of Khalīl until now, jurisprudence has reached the stage of dissolution *(inḥilāl al-quwā)*, decrepitude *(shiddat al-ḍaʿf)*, senility and destruction beyond which there is only non-existence *(ʿadam)*." Muḥammad b. al-Ḥasan al-Ḥajawī al-Thaʿālibī, *al-Fikr al-sāmī fī tārīkh al-fiqh al-islāmī*, 4 vols. (Rabāṭ: Maṭbaʿat Idārat al-Maʿārif, 1340/1926, completed at Fās: Maṭbaʿat al-Baldiyya, 1345/1931), 4:79.

12. Coulson, *A History*, 84; Jīdī, 131; al-Ḥajawī, Rabāṭ ed., 4:79; al-Zarqā', 162–63.

13. Max Weber, *Economy and Society*, ed. Guenther Roth and Claus Wittich, 2 vols. (Berkeley: University of California Press, 1978), 2:976.

14. Ibid., 823.

15. Weber thus notes that "sacred law could not be disregarded; nor could it, despite many adaptations, be really carried out in practice," Ibid., 821. Also see Bryan S. Turner, *Weber and Islam* (London: Routledge & Kegan Paul, Ltd., 1974), 115.

16. Sherman Jackson, "In Defense of Two-Tiered Orthodoxy" (Ph. D. diss., University of Pennsylvania, 1991), 11. See also idem, *Islamic Law and the State: The Constitutional Jurisprudence of Shihāb al-Dīn al-Qarāfī* (Leiden: E.J. Brill, 1996).

role each was assigned within the legal process—a society's institutionalized means for the resolution of disputes.[17]

When we attempt to understand *ijtihād* and *taqlīd* as an issue in the sociology of Islamic law, as suggested by Weber, and with reference to the legal process of pre-modern Muslim societies, as suggested by Jackson, many interesting issues emerge. Among these is the comprehensiveness of *taqlīd*. Another is legal change. Presumably, if a regime of *taqlīd* was sufficiently comprehensive, so that most situations were regulated by a rule, and if *taqlīd* allowed for legitimate, recognizable legal change, many of Weber's objections to it would be satisfied. A third issue, closely related to the question of legal change, is the relationship of law to fact, and whether or not interpretation of fact was considered *ijtihād* or *taqlīd*. Another critical issue is the determination of what constituted a rule in a system governed by *ijtihād* and what constituted a rule in a *taqlīd*-based system.

[197] Because I cannot deal with all these issues in one essay, I shall focus my attention here on the relationship of legal rules to *ijtihād* and *taqlīd*. Rules are indisputably central to any legal process. An important feature of all functioning legal systems is stable rules, or at least the claim to possess them; however, the subjective process of *ijtihād*, as we shall see, could furnish only opinions, and even those opinions were subject to change in the light of a *mujtahid*'s subsequent *ijtihād*. Most scholars who privilege *ijtihād* over *taqlīd* rarely account for the cost of this instability to the legal system. In my opinion, *taqlīd*, viewed from the perspective of the sociology of law and the legal process, is best understood as an expression of the desire for regular and predictable legal outcomes, akin to what modern jurisprudence terms the "rule of law": the ideal that legal officials are bound to pre-existing rules.

Unlike *ijtihād*, reaching a legal rule through *taqlīd* was an objective process supervised by members of a legal school (*madhhab*) who insured that the outcome conformed to the group's rule. The spread of *taqlīd* at the expense of *ijtihād* should be viewed as reflecting the triumph of the ideal of the rule of law over the ideal of judicial discretion, rather than as representing a qualitative decline in legal scholarship or a lack of originality. Because *taqlīd* arose to satisfy a social need for uniformity in the law, it must be judged in light of its own social logic—its success in creating uniform rules. *Taqlīd*, therefore, was an alternative method of deriving legal norms, a method that replaced the subjective conscience of the legal interpreter (*al-mujtahid*) with the group sensibilities of the legal school (*madhhab*).

Taqlīd was not a magical solution to the legacy of indeterminacy created by *ijtihād*. Because contradictory opinions were often attributed to the same *mujtahid*, and because his followers often reached contradictory conclusions regarding unprecedented cases, indeterminacy was also a serious problem within a *madhhab*. With time, however, the various opinions found within a school were evaluated, and only one came to be considered the rule of a school. These rules, moreover, beginning in the 7th/13th century, were compiled into works known as *mukhtaṣars*, "abridgements." The function of these works was sim-

17. Jackson, "In Defense," 179.

ply to provide the rule of the school for a given case. Therefore, Islamic law underwent a long-term evolution from a legal system that relied almost exclusively on the discretion of legal officials, whether judges or *muftīs*, to one that relied almost exclusively on pre-existing rules. Islamic law after the 7th/13th century occupied a middle point between the two competing ideals that characterized European legal history: the [198] judge-made common law of England and the code-law of the Continent.[18] Islamic law in the age of *mukhtaṣars*, therefore, can best be described as a codified common law.[19]

LEGAL INDETERMINACY IN ISLAMIC LAW

Being a jurists' law[20] the problem of rule-indeterminacy was acute in Islamic law. This was complicated by the fact that Islamic law was ideologically grounded in the unique revelatory experience of the Prophet Muhammad. Because this revelation taught both that God was the ultimate Lawgiver and that revelation had ceased after Muhammad, Islamic law was cut off from its primary Lawgiver immediately upon the death of the Prophet.[21] This meant that rule-making activity could continue only through judicial interpretation of the original rules provided by the revelation. Over time, the science of legal theory (*uṣūl al-fiqh*) was developed to aid jurists in their efforts to extend the scope of the law.[22] The conclusions provided by this interpretive science were admitted by the jurists themselves, however, to be only probable.[23] Legal theory recognized only one means by which a jurist's probable interpretation could become an incontrovertible rule: the principle of consensus (*ijmāᶜ*). That consensus could in fact function in this manner was not universally admitted.[24] What seems more likely was that the institution of consensus did serve to place

18. Martin Shapiro, *Courts: A Comparative and Political Analysis* (Chicago: The University of Chicago Press, 1981), 126.

19. Although most of my examples are drawn from the Mālikī school, the developments undergone by the Mālikī school after the 6th/12th century were a response to structural problems, and therefore, they are illustrative of long-term trends in Islamic law. This discussion, therefore, will also be of relevance to understanding later developments in the Ḥanafī and Shāfiᶜī schools.

20. Schacht, *Introduction*, 209.

21. This was the case only for Sunni Muslims. Shiᶜī Muslims accepted the principle of an infallible ruler, or Imām, who could provide Muslims with rules that were substantively representative of the Divine Will.

22. See, for example, Joseph Schacht, *The Origins of Muhammadan Jurisprudence* (Oxford: Clarendon Press, 1950), and idem, *Introduction*, 37–48; George Makdisi, "The Juridical Theology of Shāfiᶜī Origins and Significance of *Uṣūl al-fiqh*," *Studia Islamica*, 59 (1984), 5–47; Coulson, *History*, 9–73.

23. For a general introduction to the problem of probability in Islamic law, see Aron Zysow, "The Economy of Certainty" (Ph.D. diss., Harvard University, 1984). On the role of interpretation in the development of Islamic law, see Bernard Weiss, "Interpretation in Islamic Law," *American Journal of Comparative Law*, 26 (1978), 199–212.

24. See Bernard Weiss, "The Primacy of Revelation in Classical Islamic Legal Theory as Expounded by

an upward limit on legal [199] indeterminacy by prohibiting the introduction of new legal solutions.[25] Therefore, while the science of legal theory rationalized the process by which legal interpretation was to be carried out, interpretation, by itself, could not succeed in creating definitive new rules unless a particular interpretation, against huge odds, was able to generate a consensus among the jurists. Negatively, *ijtihād* could show what could not be the rule. Positively, it could only point to what could be the rule. In the absence of consensus, then, all positions held by qualified interpreters of the law (*mujtahids*) were deemed equally correct in practice.[26]

Weiss has suggested that *taqlīd*, which requires non-jurists to follow a jurist, was introduced as the solution to the problem of indeterminacy which no set of neutral principles of interpretation seemed to be able to solve.[27] This suggestion has the virtue of offering an explanation of the necessary role that *taqlīd* had to play in the operation of the legal system instead of simply viewing it as a negative phenomenon. But Weiss' suggestion is ultimately unsatisfactory, for while it assigns to *taqlīd* a legitimate role in the legal system, it views it as binding only upon the lay person. Although a lay person may be comforted to know that his religious obligation towards God is fulfilled whenever he follows the opinion of a qualified interpreter of the law, this does nothing to fulfill his desire for a stable rule of law that would enable him to know, in advance, the probable worldly consequences of his actions. Because theoreticians of the law such as al-Ghazālī maintained that a lay person's religious obligation was to follow the opinion of a *mujtahid*, whenever that *mujtahid* changed his or her mind, the follower was religiously obliged to amend his or her behavior so that it would be in accord with the new opinion of the *mujtahid*.[28]

Sayf al-Āmidī," *Studia Islamica*, 59 (1984), 79–109; Zysow, 198–281; Wael Hallaq, "On the Authoritativeness of Sunni Consensus," *International Journal of Middle East Studies*, 18 (1986), 427–54.

25. Jackson, "In Defense," 92.

26. This question was known in legal theory as *taṣwīb al-mujtahidīn*, literally, "taking [the opinions of] qualified jurists to be correct." While jurists and theologians disagreed as to the details of what this issue meant, there was general agreement, even among those who believed that there was a "correct" rule for every case, that in controversial areas of the law, human beings did not have access to which opinion was actually the correct one. Therefore, in practice everyone agreed that all opinions issued by qualified interpreters of the law were equally likely, ultimately, to be the correct rule for the case at hand. See Zysow, 460–61.

27. Weiss argued that consensus was actually of no legal relevance because of the principle that "considered opinion is binding in matters of law *(al-ẓann wājib al-iʿtibār fī al-sharʿ)*." Thus, he opined that the opinion of the jurist had the practical force of law whether or not it enjoyed consensus. Weiss, "Interpretation in Islamic Law," 204, and "The Primacy of Revelation," 96.

28. Thus, al-Ghazālī gave the example of a man who married a woman based on a *mujtahid's* opinion that this marriage was legal. If that *mujtahid* later changed his or her mind and determined that that marriage was illegal, then the same man was required to divorce his wife, based upon the revised opinion of his *mujtahid*. Abū Ḥāmid Muḥammad b. Muḥammad al-Ghazālī, *al-Mustaṣfā fī ʿilm al-uṣūl* (Beirut: Dār

[200] Al-Ghazālī's doctrine of *taqlīd* could provide legitimacy only for actions performed in the past; an individual could not be secure that in the future he would not be required to renounce prior obligations or agreements in the event that his *mujtahid* changed his or her mind regarding the permissibility of that act. Clearly, for *taqlīd* to serve as the basis of a positive law that could alleviate the problems of legal indeterminacy, it had to be the *taqlīd* of dead jurists, since only they could never change their minds. Moreover, because a judge's political legitimacy is intimately connected with the belief that his judgments are a result of pre-existing rules, it would be most unusual to find that a situation of radical rule-indeterminacy would be allowed to persist over generations without some type of intervention aimed at guaranteeing some stability in legal rules.[29]

THE HIERARCHIES WITHIN A LEGAL SCHOOL

In an attempt to minimize the effects of indeterminacy upon the legal system, Muslim jurists, with inter-school variations, divided jurists into several distinct classes. The Ḥanafīs, according to Abū Zahra, divided the jurists of a school into seven categories.[30] The Shafiʿī jurist Ibn al-Ṣalāḥ divided jurists into two categories, independent (*mustaqill*)[31] and affiliated (*muntasib*).[32] He further divided this latter group into four categories, giving a total of five.[33] Al-Qarāfī, according to Jackson, divided the jurists of the Mālikī school into three categories, excluding the independent interpreter of the law, the *mujtahid*.[34] Al-Ḥajawī and al-Jīdī also mentioned a similar tripartite division for the Mālikīs.[35]

[201] While one of the functions of these divisions was to create a hierarchy within the school based on the extent to which doctrine had been mastered, its most important function seems to have been the regulation of juristic communication with the non-legal world.[36] The legitimacy of a jurist's communication of the law to the non-legal world

al-Kutub al-ʿIlmiyya, 1413/1993), 367; also see Abū ʿAmr ʿAbd al-Raḥmān b. al-Ṣalāḥ, *Fatāwā wa masāʾil ibn al-Ṣalāḥ*, ed. ʿAbd al-Muʿṭī Amīn Qalʿajī, 2 vols. (Beirut: Dār al-Maʿrifa, 1406/1986), 1:45.

29. For the importance to judicial legitimacy of the appearance that the judge is ruling based on pre-existing rules, see Shapiro, *Courts* 1–64.

30. The highest level was the jurist who interpreted directly from the sources of the law, *al-mujtahid fī al-sharʿ*, or alternatively, *al-mujtahid al-mustaqill*. The lowest ranking jurist was the one who knew only the doctrine of the school. See Muḥammad Abū Zahra, *Muḥāḍarāt fī tārīkh al fiqh al-islāmī* (Cairo: Dār al-Fikr al-ʿArabī, n.d.), 128.

31. Ibn al-Ṣalāḥ, 21.

32. Ibid., 29.

33. Ibid., 29–36.

34. The first level was the transmission *(naql)* of a case whose solution was mentioned explicitly in an authoritative manual of the school, while the second level of transmission was a report of the well-known rule *(naql al-mashhūr)* of the school. See Jackson, "In Defense," 155–63.

35. Al-Ḥajawī, Rabāṭ ed., 4:214; al-Jīdī, 98.

36. Cf. Hallaq, "Was the Gate of *Ijtihād* Closed?," 29–30.

depended solely on that jurist's position within his school's hierarchy. As we shall see, this hierarchy was constitutive of the legitimacy of legal communications in both the realms of legal opinions (*fatāwā*) and the decisions (*aḥkām*) of judges.

The main reason that led both Ibn al-Ṣalāḥ and al-Qarāfī to discuss these internal hierarchies was to identify which cases fell under the competency of which jurists. Al-Qarāfī, for example, divided the Mālikī jurists of his day into those who have studied the introductory books of the school's doctrine, those who have knowledge regarding the various opinions of the school, and those who, in addition to having complete knowledge of the school's doctrine, also knew the science of legal methodology. The first category of jurists was allowed to respond only to cases whose rules had been explicitly treated in the introductory books of the school. Al-Qarāfī would not allow such a jurist to answer questions which appeared to be governed by a general rule, for fear that such a rule may, in fact, be restricted or qualified in another, more advanced book of the school.[37] The second category of jurists, despite their superior knowledge of the school and their knowledge of the different opinions within it, could answer questions based only on the well-established (*mashhūr*) opinion of the school.[38] It was only the last class, i.e., the jurists who had also mastered the science of legal methodology (*uṣūl al-fiqh*), that was empowered to issue legal opinions regarding unprecedented cases.[39]

Ibn al-Ṣalāḥ provided a parallel description of the powers of the different grades of jurist within the Shāfiʿī school. A jurist of the lowest rank could issue opinions only for those cases mentioned explicitly in the books of the school (*masṭūrāt madhhabihi, manṣūṣāt imāmihi*). Unlike al-Qarāfī, Ibn al-Ṣalāḥ gave this class of jurist some freedom of interpretation, allowing him to perform the "no difference" (*lā fāriq*) analogy as well as to reply to cases governed by the well-established [202] and well-regulated general rules of the school.[40] The second and third categories of jurists identified by Ibn al-Ṣalāḥ both had the right to create new doctrine through interpretation, the difference between them being that the former's opinions were incorporated into the doctrine of the school, while the opinions of the latter class were not.[41] The highest category of membership in a school, according to Ibn al-Ṣalāḥ, was

37. Shihāb al-Dīn al-Qarāfī, *al-Furūq*, 4 vols. (Beirut: ʿĀlam al-Kutub, n.d.), 2:107.

38. Ibid.

39. Ibid., 2:108. Presumably, a jurist from this class would also be allowed to issue legal opinions based on opinions other than the *mashhūr.*

40. An example of the "no difference" analogy is that a legal official of this class can give an opinion regarding a female slave based on the explicit rule governing a male slave. He gave no example for an event governed by a well-regulated general rule whose applicability to the novel case was so clear that it was permissible for this jurist to give an opinion based on it, however. See Ibn al-Ṣalāḥ, 36.

41. Ibn al-Ṣalāḥ called the second class *aṣḥāb al-wujūh wa al-ṭuruq.* Ibn al-Ṣalāḥ, 32. While the third class did not have a name, he referred to the jurists of this class as those who, while not quite the equal of the previous class in learning, nevertheless were well-versed in the law and were allowed, in the course of issuing legal opinions, to create new doctrine. Although the opinions of these jurists were

that jurist who, although himself an independent interpreter of the law, became famous as a disciple of another jurist because he adopted the latter's method and propagated it.[42]

While Ibn al-Ṣalāḥ allowed slightly more freedom to the jurists of his school than al-Qarāfī was willing to grant Mālikī jurists, the former, despite his credentials as a transmitter of hadith, was only willing to permit a jurist of the highest rank to contradict the school's substantive rules based on hadiths that appeared contrary to the established doctrine of that jurist's school. Although it is well known that al-Shāfiʿī is reported to have said, "If you find something in my book contrary to the *sunna* of the Prophet (S), adopt the *sunna* of the Prophet (S) and abandon what I have said," Ibn al-Ṣalāḥ found this position dangerous, saying:

> This is not a trivial matter, for it is not permissible for every jurist to apply independently what he takes to be a proof from the hadith. Among the Shāfiʿīs who took this path are those who followed a hadith that Shāfiʿī had abandoned intentionally, despite the fact that he [viz., al-Shāfiʿī] knew it [to be formally] valid, out of consideration for some obstacle (*māniʿ*) [to its application] of which he was aware but which was not manifest to others, like Abū al-Walīd Mūsā b. Abī al-Jārūd[43] (d. 3d/9th century).[44]

[203] Therefore, it was only the jurist whose "tools of *ijtihād* have been perfected" who possessed the requisite authority to reason independently based on a hadith.[45] If another independent interpreter of the law upheld the position supported by the hadith in question, though, the follower of al-Shāfiʿī was permitted to adopt that other interpreter's opinion for that one case. Ibn al-Ṣalāḥ stressed that it was the other independent interpreter's use of the hadith which permitted a lower ranking jurist to follow it, not the latter's individual interpretation of the text in question.[46]

Ibn Rushd (the Grandfather) divided the Andalusian legal community of his age into three classes (*ṭawāʾif*, sing. *ṭāʾifa*). The first, and one assumes the majority, was that group of jurists who accepted the doctrine of Mālik and his followers unquestioningly. Their knowledge of the law was limited to the memorization of the legal opinions of Mālik and his followers without a deep understanding of these opinions (*dūn al-tafaqquh*). As a result of

---

collected and studied, "the affiliation of them [viz. their opinions for novel cases] to the school does not reach the same rank as the opinions of the *aṣḥāb al-wujuh*, nor are they as strong as they are." Ibn al-Ṣalāḥ, 36.

42. Ibid., 29

43. He was a student of al-Shāfiʿī whose death date is not known with precision. See Ibn Qāḍī Shuhba, *Ṭabaqāt al-shāfiʿiyya*, ed. ʿAbdal-Ḥafīẓ Khān, 4 vols. (Ḥaydarabad al-Dakkan, al-Hind: Maṭbaʿat Majlis Dāʾirat al-Maʿārif al-ʿUthmāniyya, 1978–80), 1:22.

44. Ibn al-Ṣalāḥ, 54.

45. Ibid., 58.

46. Ibid., 59.

this, they were unable to distinguish valid opinions (*al-ṣaḥīḥ*) of the school from invalid opinions (*al-saqīm*). While this class corresponded roughly to the lowest class of jurists identified by al-Qarāfī, Ibn Rushd denied them the right to issue legal opinions, "for they have no knowledge about the validity of anything of that [which they have memorized of the opinions of Mālik and his followers]."[47] They could, however, follow these opinions in their private lives (*fī khāṣṣatihā*) as long as there was no *muftī* to consult; likewise, they could relate the opinions of Mālik and his followers to others if there were no *muftī*s in the town. In this latter case, the questioner was following the jurist only in his transmission of an opinion; the opinion being followed remained that of Mālik or one of his followers.[48] It seems, then, that Ibn Rushd refused to consider the simple act of transmission as being tantamount to a *fatwā*.[49]A *fatwā* had to be constituted by some type of knowledge, something that this first class of jurists lacked.

The second class, unlike the first, held the doctrine of Mālik and his followers to be correct based on their knowledge of the validity of the [204] texts and principles[50] upon which Mālik and his followers based their doctrines. Because of their superior legal knowledge, they were able to determine which opinions were consistent with the overall principles and texts of the school and which opinions were beyond the pale (*al-saqīm al-khārij*). This class was entitled to issue legal opinions as long as the validity of the rule being communicated was clear in its mind (*idhā kānat qad bānat lahā* [*al-ṭā'ifa*] *ṣiḥḥatuhu*). They were not empowered, however, to issue legal opinions for novel cases, because they had not perfected the tools necessary for legal interpretation (*ijtihād*).[51] Their jurisdiction did not extend, then, beyond the right to choose among the various opinions found within the Mālikī schoo1.[52] While this class roughly corresponded to the second class of jurists identified by al-Qarāfī, there is a slight difference, for, while Ibn Rushd allowed jurists of this class to select which opinion of the school they would use in their legal opinions, al-Qarāfī limited them to that opinion of the school which was *mashhūr*.

The third class of jurists was distinguished from the second by the fact that, in addition to their complete knowledge of the school's doctrine, they also were knowledgeable

47. Muḥammad b. Muḥammad al-Ḥaṭṭāb, *Mawāhib al-jalīl*, 6 vols. (3d ed., Beirut: Dār al-Fikr, 1412/1992), 6:94.

48. Ibid., 6:94–95.

49. Hallaq refers to this phenomenon as "*al-iftā' bi-l-ḥifẓ*" (replying based on memory), whose status as a *fatwā* is questionable. See Wael Hallaq, "From *Fatwās* to *Furū*ᶜ: Growth and Change in Islamic Substantive Law," *Islamic Law and Society*, 1,1 (1994), 54.

50. I have used "texts and principles" as a translation for the Arabic term *uṣūl*, which is ambiguous, sometimes referring to the basic texts of the school which served as the basis for the development of the school's positive doctrines, at other times referring to "principles," i.e., that Mālik gives the *ᶜamal* of Madina greater weight than a *hadith*. See Wael Hallaq, "Was al-Shafiᶜī the Master Architect of Islamic Jurisprudence?," *International Journal of Middle East Studies*, 25 (Nov. 1993), 587–605.

51. Al-Ḥaṭṭāb, 6:94–95.

52. This kind of *muftī* was termed by al-Ḥajawī as *mujtahid fatwā*. Al-Ḥajawī, 4:214.

regarding the science of legal methodology, and therefore, not only knew how to derive the legal school's existing doctrine from the original sources of the law, but also were entitled to issue opinions for novel cases. In regard to the material used by this class of jurists in their legal interpretation, Ibn Rushd made clear that it included the original sources of Islamic law—the Qurʾān, the Sunna, and the Consensus.

> As for the third group, this is the one who may generally (*ʿumūman*) issue legal opinions based upon interpretation (*ijtihād*) and analogy based on the texts (*uṣūl*) which are the Book, the Sunna and the Consensus of the Community, based on the concept (*maʿnā*) joining the text to the case (*al-nāzila*) and [analogy] based on what has been produced from them [viz., the texts] (*wa ʿalā mā qīsa ʿalayhā*), if analogies have already been done on them [viz., the texts].[53]

[205] This latter type of interpretation, analogy based on analogy, was what al-Qarāfī termed "*takhrīj*," translated by Jackson as extrapolation. Therefore, while both Ibn Rushd and al-Qarāfī agreed that this class of jurist was allowed to create new doctrine, they disagreed in regard to the raw material he could use in his interpretation. Whereas al-Qarāfī limited him to the texts of the school, Ibn Rushd allowed him to use the original sources of the law as well.[54]

If these jurists expressed a desire to regulate the practice of issuing legal opinions that were, in general, non-binding, it should come as no surprise that they wished to regulate the rules by which a judge resolved cases. Indeed, Ibn Rushd's discussion of the three classes of jurists was prompted by a question (*istiftāʾ*) regarding the legitimacy of rulings handed down by judges who were not qualified to interpret the law. Ibn Rushd stated unequivocally in that *fatwā* that if the judge had not reached the rank of *muftī*, i.e., the rank which allowed the jurist to create new doctrine by interpretation, "he may only rule based upon an explicit rule."[55] If he failed to find such a rule for the case before him, he must postpone his decision until he received a *fatwā* from a qualified jurist providing him with the legal rule to be applied in the case. Should he rule without the opinion of a qualified interpreter of the law, his ruling must be reviewed:

---

53. Al-Ḥaṭṭāb, 6:94–95.

54. This is implied in a statement of al-Qarāfī's made in the *Dhakhīra* as quoted by al-Ḥaṭṭāb, where the former states that the jurist who has mastered the texts of his school and its rules "is affiliated to his school in the same way that an independent interpreter of the law is affiliated to the texts of the Law and its rules. Thus, it is permissible for that [jurist] to extrapolate and use analogy as long as its stipulations have been met just as it was for the independent interpreter." Ibid., 6:92. In contrast to both Ibn Rushd and al-Qarāfī, another important Andalusian jurist, al-Qāḍī Ibn al-ʿArabī, forbade extrapolation based on the texts of the school and required that solutions to novel cases be derived exclusively from revelation. See Ibn Farḥūn, *Kashf al-niqāb al-ḥājib min muṣṭalaḥ ibn al-ḥājib*, ed. Ḥamza Abū Fāris and ʿAbdal-Salām al-Sharīf (Beirut: Dār al-Gharb al-Islāmī, 1990), 107.

55. Al-Ḥaṭṭāb, 6:93.

> Thus, this judge must do the following with respect to those cases for which he can find no explicit rule from Mālik or one of his followers whose validity is clear to him: he is only to decide it based on a legal opinion of one qualified to interpret [the law] ... if he finds him in his town, [then he should consult him]; if not, he must seek him out in other towns. Should he rule based on his [own] opinion, but is not authorized to do so (*wa lā raʾya lahu*), or [should he rule] based on the opinion of one who is not authorized to hold a legal opinion (*aw bi-raʾy man lā raʾya lahu*), his judgment is suspended until [it is] reviewed. The ruler should order the judge, if he is not qualified to interpret [the law], ... [206] not to rule in any matter requiring interpretation without consulting with one qualified to interpret [the law].[56]

Another Andalūsī jurist, al-Qāḍī Ibn al-ʿArabī (d. 543/1148), was equally adamant about the rules a *muqallid*-jurist could use in his decisions:

> In this case [viz., where the judge is a *muqallid*] he may only rule based on the legal opinion of the scholar whom he follows, where the case is [governed] by an explicit rule. If he makes an analogy based on it [viz., his Imām's legal opinion] or says, "This implies that," then he has transgressed [his jurisdiction].[57]

Al-Qarāfī's treatment of the discretionary powers of a *muqallid*-judge was just as restrictive as that of Ibn Rushd and Ibn al-ʿArabī:

> Just as the *muqallid* is forbidden to extrapolate in respect to something that is not [already] a position of the scholars and he is forbidden to investigate the original sources of the law, and he is obliged to act only on the basis of a scholar's opinion . . . the same holds true for this [*muqallid*-judge], and that is what is intended by what was [said] previously regarding the stipulations of judgeship: that he not extrapolate [new rules] and that he rule based only on explicit rules.[58]

Despite the agreement of these three jurists regarding the necessity of restricting a *muqallid*-judge's power to the application of pre-existing rules, and his dependence on the legal opinion of a qualified jurist in novel cases, the concept of what constituted an explicit rule (*al-manṣūṣ*) remained ambiguous and undefined.[59] Thus, implicit in Ibn Rushd's *fatwā* cited above is his belief that the judge was of sufficient rank to discriminate among the different positions in the school, since the explicit rule that he used could have been formulated by either Mālik or one of his followers.[60] If this is true, the existence of mul-

56. Ibid. See David Powers, "On Judicial Review in Islamic Law," *Law and Society Review*, 26,2 (1992), 317.

57. Al-Ḥaṭṭāb, 6:92.

58. Ibid., 92–93.

59. Ibn Farḥūn defined *naṣṣ* as that statement "whose wording is such that it is at the extremity of clarity and obviousness." Ibn Farḥūn, *Kashf al-niqāb*, 99.

60. Ibn Rushd came very close to saying this explicitly in a later section of the same *fatwā*: "the rule

tiple and often contradictory opinions within a school would have given such a judge considerable freedom to create rules *in situ* in all controversial areas of the law.

[207] Given that al-Qarāfī's use of *manṣūṣ* with regard to the judge was synonymous with his use of the term with respect to *muftīs*[61] his conceptualization of the relationship between the judge's position in the legal hierarchy and the legitimacy of his rulings also leads to some difficult questions. Jackson's analysis of al-Qarāfī's use of *manṣūṣ* almost certainly implies something approximating "case" or "precedent," suggesting that the jurist of the lowest rank in al-Qarāfī's hierarchical model could reply to a question only when he was certain that it was the exact replica of the case mentioned in the introductory books of the school that he had studied.[62] Al-Qarāfī, as mentioned, explicitly denied to the jurist of the lowest-tier the right to apply general, unqualified rules to unknown fact situations because of the possibility that these rules, although they appear general and unqualified in the introductory books of the school, were in fact, often restricted and qualified in other, more advanced legal texts.[63] This places severe limitations on the *muqallid*-judge or *muftī*, for the legal relevance of the same facts may change over time, especially if the ruling is dependent upon a custom, or if an advance in knowledge renders a prior application of that rule obsolete.[64] We must conclude, therefore, that in al-Qarāfī's mind, only a jurist who was at least of the second grade was qualified to sit on the bench.[65]

The case of a middle-tiered jurist in al-Qarāfī's system is also problematic. While this judge in principle was bound to the *mashhūr*, not every jurist had the requisite training

---

has been stated previously regarding those whom we have described as belonging to that group which knows the validity of Mālik's doctrine but has not reached the level of knowledge enabling it to perform analogy of new cases to established ones." Al-Ḥaṭṭāb, 6:93.

61. Ibid., 93.

62. According to al-Qarāfī, the case must not be "similar to it, and not analogous to it; nay it exactly." Jackson, 156.

63. See note 37.

64. This is implied in al-Qarāfī's argument that it is illegitimate to practice *taqlīd* in regard to an assessment of a fact. Shihāb al-Dīn Aḥmad b. Idrīs al-Qarāfī, *Kitāb al-iḥkām fī tamyīz al-fatāwā ʿan al-aḥkām wa taṣarrufāt al-qāḍī wa al-imām*, ed. ʿAbdal-Fattāḥ Abū Ghudda (Aleppo: Maktabat al-Maṭbūʿāt al-Islāmiyya, 1387/1967), 201–2. He also argued that the means of knowing a fact in the external world for an individual are infinite and cannot be determined by the law. Al-Qarāfī, *al-Furūq*, 1:128. For a summary of his arguments and their implication for the law, see Jackson, "In Defense," 146.

65. This is only true if the books to which al-Qarāfī refers fail to inform the novice which rules are bound to particular customs and which are not. This may or may not have been the case, but al-Qarāfī fails to tell us the titles of the *mukhtaṣars* that were used by beginning jurists. Until we have an answer to the question of which books beginning students of the law studied, it is difficult to answer how al-Qarāfī imagined it possible for a low-ranking jurist to be able to answer any question at all, which, of course, might have been his intention. The identification of the *mukhtaṣars* of the school at that time is a question that is beyond the scope of this essay.

to recognize which opinion of the [208] school actually constituted the *mashhūr*. Furthermore, if the *mashhūr* was a pre-existing rule, one assumes that there must be some relationship between it and the *manṣūs* that regulated the first-tier jurist. If this is true, then what was the difference between the two, other than that perhaps the jurist of the second tier had more freedom to apply general and unqualified rules to new fact situations?

Therefore, while Ibn Rushd, al-Qarāfī and al-Qāḍī Abū Bakr all desired to limit the discretionary powers of low ranking judges and *muftīs*, the rules of the *madhhab* had yet to be organized in a way that could guarantee the achievement of this goal.[66] Given the numerous opinions extant in the Mālikī school, a more formal system of regulation had to be created to ensure that the discretion of lower ranking jurists was sufficiently restricted.

LEGAL INDETERMINACY WITHIN A SCHOOL OF LAW, THE DOCTRINE OF *TAKHYĪR* AND THE FORMALIZATION OF *TAQLĪD*

I have argued that one of the main incentives for a move to a legal system that relied on *taqlīd* was to avoid the inevitable indeterminacy in the law that resulted from independent interpretation of revelation by individuals. While *taqlīd*, defined as following the doctrine of an eponym/Imām, was not a magical cure for indeterminacy, it at least deferred the problem of theological indeterminacy to the next life, and the question of legal (in the sense of *madhhab*-law) indeterminacy became a purely secular matter.[67] Thus, whereas an independent interpreter of the law was required to ask what God's rule was, the jurist who was a follower of an Imām had only to discover what his Imām's rule was, and was allowed to ignore the question of what actually constituted God's rule for the question at hand.[68]

[209] Following the opinion of a qualified independent interpreter of the law was not a simple task, however, for the legal doctrine of the eponyms did not exist in

66. Although al-Qarāfī mentions that the *muqallid*-judge is allowed to rule based on the *mashhūr*, he nowhere states, as far as I know, that he is bound to rule by it; *al-Iḥkām*, 79.

67. Thus, al-Qarāfī notes that adjudication can occur only over disputes regarding worldly affairs: [*al-ḥukm*] *yaqaᶜ fīhi al-nizāᶜ fī maṣāliḥ al-dunyā*. *Al-Iḥkām*, 23–24; he adds that it is absurd to imagine adjudication regarding controversial issues of the law or procedures or principles of legal methodology because these are concerns of the other world: *al-qaḍā' fī al-madārik muḥāl li-anna al-nizāᶜ fīhā laysa min maṣāliḥ al-dunyā bal maṣāliḥ al-ākhira wa-taqrīr qawāᶜid al-sharᶜ wa-uṣūl al-fiqh kulluhu min hādhā al-bāb*. *Al-Iḥkām*, 69; also see Jackson, "In Defense," 182–83.

68. This is implied when al-Qarāfī states that "the judge, if he is *a muqallid*, is allowed to issue a legal opinion based on the *mashhūr* of his school and to rule based on it *even if it does not seem valid in his mind*, relying on his Imām's opinion in respect to the strength of the rule applied in the ruling (emphasis added)." *Al-Iḥkām*, 79.

the form of explicit, positive legal rules. Before one could follow the opinion of Mālik on a certain case, one had to discover, or more accurately, in many cases, reconstruct, what his opinion on a given case was. While the followers of each eponym inevitably had particular problems in the creation of a coherent doctrine that could be attributed to the founder of their respective schools, several obstacles were common to all the schools. The first was the historical problem of attribution of a doctrine to the eponym. Because the eponyms had changed their minds on certain cases over their careers, different disciples, depending on the period of their study with the eponym, transmitted different doctrines. To this must be added the possibility that different students could have committed errors in the transmission of their master's doctrine.[69] At the same time the problem of linguistic indeterminacy inhered in the texts of the eponyms just as it did in the texts of revelation. Perhaps the fact that the eponyms were merely jurists, however, mitigated this fact, for it allowed eponyms to address legal issues more directly than revelation did.

More significant for the long term problem of legal indeterminacy, interpretation of the eponym's doctrine was carried out in the context of a group, whereas interpretation of revelation, because of its religious dimension, necessarily had to be individualistic.[70] As a result of this shift to group interpretation, a community of speakers was created that was empowered with the ability to distinguish "correct" statements from "incorrect" statements based on the conventions of that community.[71] This implied that under a system of *taqlīd* it was possible to [210] declare statements to be "correct" or "incorrect" within the conventions of that particular school; this was not possible under a system of *ijtihād*.

69. Another source of error resulted from confusion in the names of the transmitters of Mālik's doctrine, where two transmitters might have the same name, but one is a more outstanding student than the other. See al-Qāḍī ʿIyāḍ, *Tartīb al-madārik*, 8 vols. (Rabāṭ: Wizārat al-Awqāf wa-al-Shuʾūn al-Islāmiyya, 1965–1983), 1:16. Another source of error was corruption of texts in their transmission. One of the reasons for the popularity of Ibn Rushd's commentary on the *ʿUtbiyya* was his competence as an editor and his ability to account for the conflicting transmissions for the same case. See al-Mukhtār b. Ṭāhir al-Talīlī, *Ibn Rushd wa kitābuhu muqaddimāt* (Libya: al-Dār al-ʿArabiyya li-l-Kitāb, 1988), 419.

70. For *taqlīd* being a type of group interpretation, see Jackson, 3–4 and 175.

71. According to Wittgenstein, words do not have intrinsic meanings, and even speakers themselves cannot know for certain the meaning of their own words. For example, we cannot be certain when a speaker says "dog" that he did not actually mean "dangerous animals" unless that question was actually present in the speaker's mind at the time of the utterance. Just as his listeners could not be certain, neither could the speaker himself be certain that he did not actually mean "dangerous animals." According to Wittgenstein, then, meaning is actually generated by a community that has shared, conventional notions about language. For this reason meaning cannot be created by the speaker, for the meaning of his utterance is determined by the manner in which the community of speakers responds to it. For the implications of Wittgenstein's language skepticism on the thought of some American jurists, see Frank Easterbrook, "Statutes' Domains," *University of Chicago Law Review*, 50 (1983), 534–36. For a synopsis of Wittgenstein's arguments regarding language and the need for a community of speakers, see Saul Kripke, *Wittgenstein on Rules and Private Language* (Cambridge: Harvard University Press, 1982).

This shift from individual interpretation of revelation to group interpretation of an eponym's doctrine was marked by a significant shift in what H.L.A. Hart termed the "rule of recognition."[72] For example, the "rule of recognition" attributed to Mālik by Ibn Hishām (d. 606/1209) reflected the fact that Mālik was an independent interpreter of the law, and assumed that judges were also independent interpreters of the law:

> Mālik said: the judge should rule based on [those provisions of] the Book of God that have neither been abrogated, nor that have been explicitly contradicted by the *sunna*. If he does not find [the solution] in the Book of God, then [he should rule] based on that which is unanimously attributed to the Messenger of God, practice having been in accord with it. If he fails to find [the solution there], then [he should rule] based on that which has been reported about the [opinions of the] Companions, if they were in agreement. If they disagreed, he rules according to that [opinion] which is in accord with practice in regard to that [question]. If he does not find it, then [he should rule] based on that which has been reported about the [opinions of the] Followers. If he does not find [the solution there] then [he should rule] based on that which the scholars have agreed upon. If he does not find [the solution there] then he should exercise his independent judgment and make an analogy based on that which he knows from them [viz., the scholars]. If [the case] is problematic for him, he should consult jurists who are worthy of consultation because of their religiosity, their intelligence, and their understanding. If they contradict each other, he should consider which [opinion] is most likely correct and rule based on it. If he should reach an opinion contrary to their opinion, he should not rule, suspend judgment and gain more information. Then, he should rule on that [case] based on what he perceives most likely to be correct. He has the [211] right to rule based on his own opinion if he is their equal, but not if he is beneath them [in learning]. If he is unable to reach a conclusion, he should leave it and not rule on something about which he entertains a doubt. [73]

Here, Mālik clearly assumed that the judge was interpreting the law directly from revelation. Only if he failed to find a solution there did he proceed to the ancillary sources of the law. Given the state of Islamic law in the 2nd/8th century, it is not surprising that Mālik would assume that the judge was a *mujtahid*; it is surprising to discover that a jurist

72. The "rule of recognition" is the "master rule" by which a person can discover the rule regulating a certain case. Thus, in developed legal systems, the rule of recognition is very complex. A "rule of recognition" does not refer to rules by reference to a text or list, "but to some general characteristic possessed by the primary rules." If more than one general characteristic is used as identifying criteria, provisions are made for resolving the conflicts between different rules by arranging an order of superiority. Hart, 92–93.

73. Ibn Hishām, *al-Mufīd li-l-ḥukkām fī mā yaʿriḍ lahum min nawāzil al-aḥkām,* Arab League Manuscript Institute, #35 *Fiqh Mālikī,* 3r.

as late as Ibn Shās (d. 610/1213) subscribed to an ideology of judicial *ijtihād* and failed to provide a "rule of recognition" regulating the judicial activities of a *muqallid* jurist. Thus, in the chapter on adjudication from his *Jawāhir*, Ibn Shās states:

> Regarding that [which the judge uses] in his rulings: he rules [based] only on proof. Muḥammad b. ʿAbd al-Ḥakam said, "The judge rules by that which is in the Book of God, may He be glorified. If he does not find [the solution] in the Book of God, then in the *sunna* of His Prophet, may God bless him and grant him peace. If it is not in the *sunna* of God's messenger, may God bless him and grant him peace, then he rules by that which his Companions, may God be pleased with them, ruled. If there is nothing regarding the case there, and there is no consensus, then he is to apply his individual reasoning after that.[74]

In the chapter entitled *al-maqḍī bihi* ("that by which judgment is rendered"), Ibn Farḥūn (d. 799/1396) outlined two parallel "rules of recognition," one for judges who were *mujtahids* and the second for *muqallids*. The first is very similar, though not as detailed, to the one attributed to Mālik by Ibn Hishām mentioned above. It also resembles that attributed by Ibn Shās to Muḥammad b. ʿAbd al-Ḥakam (d. 268/881). For jurists who were *muqallids*, however, Ibn Farḥūn outlined a procedure that was qualitatively different from that governing the behavior of *mujtahids*: instead of seeking the law from its sources, they were obliged to seek a scholar's *fatwā* regarding what the law was.[75]

[212] While there was no disagreement regarding the obligation of the *muqallid*-judge to consult a legal expert, controversy existed among Muslim jurists of all schools in regard to the *muqallid*-judge's obligation when he was faced with contradictory opinions attributed to his Imām or to his Imām's followers. Ibn Farḥūn reported three positions on this issue within the Mālikī school. The first was that he must follow the opinion of the most learned of them, the second was that he must follow the opinion of the majority of them, and the third was that he was free to rule based on any of the opinions as long as he was, in doing so, not behaving arbitrarily. This latter position was known as

---

74. Ibn Shās, *ʿIqd al-jawāhir al-thamīna, Kitāb al-aqḍiya,* Arab League Manuscript Institute, uncatalogued *Fiqh Mālikī* 12, 7a, counting from the first folio of *Kitāb al-aqḍiya.*

75. Ibn Farḥūn does not preface his discussion of this procedure saying that it is for independent interpreters of the law. However, after having completed that discussion, he begins the next topic by saying, "If the judge is not an independent interpreter [of the law], however, then . . . ." Ibn Farḥūn, *Tabṣirat al-ḥukkām fī uṣūl al-aqḍiya wa-manāhij al-aḥkām*, 2 vols. (Cairo: al-Qāhira al-Ḥadītha li'l-Ṭibāʿa, 1406/1986), 1:65–66. Furthermore, it should not be understood from this that Ibn Farḥūn was the first jurist to create a "rule of recognition" for the *muqallid*-judge; rather, his was the earliest and most detailed exposition of such a rule that I have found for the Mālikīs.

takhyīr. Ibn Farḥūn described the first opinion as "the most valid (*aṣaḥḥ*)."[76] Ibn al-Ṣalāḥ also mentioned that when a jurist of the Shāfiʿī school was faced with a case that had more than one opinion attributed to al-Shāfiʿī or his followers, he was not allowed to choose one of the two; rather, he had to determine which of "the two is the weightier and the more valid, grasping this from the basic texts of his school without violating the rules of his school by adopting another's [rules]. This is [only permissible] if he is capable of interpretation within his school; if he is not, he must transmit it [the rule] from one of those qualified to weigh [opinions] from among the leading scholars of the school."[77] Another Shāfiʿī jurist, Abū ʿAbd Allāh Muḥammad al-Sulamī, who wrote a treatise devoted entirely to this issue,[78] reported that although such famous Shāfiʿī jurists as al-Māwardī, al-Juwaynī and al-Ghazālī supported the doctrine of *takhyīr*,[79] the Shāfiʿī jurist was bound to establish which of the different opinions within the school was weightier. Some Mālikī jurists of the 6th/12th century were also known to have [213] advocated the doctrine of *takhyīr*. Ibn Shās quoted Abū Bakr al-Ṭarṭūshī (d. 520/1126) as saying:

> No Muslim is obliged to follow [the opinion] of the one to whose doctrine he is affiliated in regard to legal cases and judgments. Thus, one who is a Mālikī is not obliged in his legal rulings to follow the opinion of Mālik, and, it is likewise for the rest of the schools. Indeed, he rules based on whatever rule that his reasoning leads him to.[80]

Although Qarāfī was ambivalent toward this doctrine, he seems to have accepted its legitimacy as long as the process was performed with integrity.[81]

---

76. In actuality there were only two positions: Is the *muqallid,* when faced with more than one position in the school, required to determine which of the different opinions is weightier, or may he select one of the competing opinions? Whether he chose to follow the opinion of the most accomplished jurist or the opinion supported by the greatest number was a disagreement on how the jurist is to *weigh* the competing opinions. Ibn Farḥūn, 1:65.

77. Ibn al-Ṣalāḥ, 1:61.

78. *Kitāb farāʾid al-fawāʾid wa-taʿāruḍ al-qawlayn li-mujtahid wāḥid,* Arab League Manuscript Institute, *Fiqh Shāfiʿī,* #247. While I was unable to identify the full name of this author, he lived after Ibn al-Ṣalāḥ as is evident from the author's reference to him on folio 21r.

79. Ibid., 19a, 20r.

80. While al-Ṭarṭūshī was talking about *takhyīr* at the level of the different schools, *a fortiori* he would have supported it within a single school, al-Ḥaṭṭāb, 6:93. The text in *al-Jawāhir* of Ibn Shās is the same as that quoted by al-Ḥaṭṭāb with this significant variant. Where al-Ḥaṭṭāb's transmission of Abu Bakr al-Ṭarṭūshī's statement reads, "the opinion of Mālik *(qawl Mālik),*" the manuscript of *al-Jawāhir* reads, "the opinions of Mālik *(aqwāl mālik),*" thus making clearer that he was against those who would limit a judge's choice to one of the different opinions within one school. Ibn Shās, 2a. This text is also quoted in Buhrām's commentary on Khalīl, Dār al-Kutub al-Miṣriyya, in his gloss on Khalīl's statement "*wa-ḥakama bi-qawli muqalladihi.*"

81. Ibn Farḥūn, *al-Tabṣira,* 1:74–75.

Later jurists, both Mālikīs and Shāfiʿīs, rejected the doctrine of *takhyīr* unanimously, despite the fact that it appeared to those jurists to be the doctrine most consistent with the science of legal methodology, and the fact that earlier authorities of the school had permitted it. The reason these jurists gave for the necessity that the different opinions within a school must be subjected to a process of evaluation and weighing had nothing to do, moreover, with the issue of whether or not every independent interpreter of the law was correct; instead, practical considerations relating to the application of the law were paramount in their minds when they rejected *takhyīr*. Prompted by his distaste for the doctrine of *takhyīr*, Ibn al-Ṣalāḥ related an incident that he attributed to the famous Mālikī jurist al-Bājī (d. 474/1081) which, in his mind, illustrated the danger of this doctrine:

> The case of one who uses [*takhyīr*] is like the case (*sabīl*) of one of the Mālikī jurists about whom the Mālikī Abū al-Walīd al-Bājī related that he [viz., the unnamed Mālikī jurist] would say, "Whenever my friend is involved in a court case (*ḥukūma*), friendship requires that I issue the *fatwā* based on the transmission that suits him." Al-Bājī also related on the authority of someone whom he trusts that during his [viz., the unnamed source's] absence, he was involved in a case, and a group of jurists, meaning prominent (*min ahl al-ṣalāḥ*) Mālikī jurists, issued *fatwās* harmful to him. When he returned he asked them [about their [214] opinions], and they said, "We did not know that it concerned you," and they then gave *fatwās* based on the transmission in agreement with his interests. Al-Bājī said, "This is something about which Muslims whose [opinions] are taken into account in [determining the existence of] Consensus have no disagreement: it is not permissible."[82]

This incident, while clearly a caricature of the position of those who argued for *takhyīr*, nevertheless, dramatically demonstrates that the freedom afforded judges and *muftīs* under this doctrine could severely undermine public confidence in the integrity of legal decisions and opinions. Al-Qarāfī, while resigned to the fact that in many areas of the law, the *muftī* or the judge would be forced to choose a position without actually being able to evaluate the strength of the rule he chose,[83] warned the legal class against the temptations of choosing positions arbitrarily:

> It is not appropriate for the *muftī*, whenever there are two positions regarding a case, one of which is strict, and the other lenient, to give *fatwās* to the general populace according to the strict rule while giving the elite among the rulers opinions based on the lenient position. That is close to wickedness (*fusūq*),

82. Ibn al-Ṣalāḥ, 1:63. Ibn Farḥūn also quoted the same passage from Ibn al-Ṣalāḥ, Ibn Farḥūn, *al-Tabṣira*, 1:72–73.

83. Ibn Farḥūn, *al-Tabṣira*, 1:75.

> treachery (*khiyāna*) in religion and manipulation of the Muslims. That is [also] evidence of the heart's being empty of awe, respect and fear of God, and its being alive with frivolity and love of position and ingratiation to creatures instead of to the Creator. We seek refuge in God from the attributes of the heedless—and the judge is like the *muftī* in regard to this [point].[84]

While al-Qarāfī's warning focused on the religious consequences of the manipulation of legal indeterminacy by jurists, later Mālikī jurists, like Ibn ʿAbd al-Salām (d. 749/1348), argued against *takhyīr* based solely on its consequences for the functioning of the judicial system. Thus, after observing that the doctrine of *takhyīr* was more consistent with the practice of the ancients, Ibn ʿAbd al-Salām states:

> The more appropriate course in my estimation in regards to the judge is that he be bound to one doctrine (*ṭarīqa*), and whenever he has followed an eponym, that he should not abandon it [viz., the eponym's doctrine] for another's [doctrine], because that leads to suspicion that he is partial to one of the litigants, and because of what has been transmitted regarding the prohibition about rendering two contradictory rulings for the same case.[85]

[215] Similarly, Buhrām (d. 805/1402) argued that "were the judge to rule based on an opinion other than it [viz., the opinion of his eponym], he would be accused of injustice and arbitrary rule."[86]

Thus, while the supporters of *takhyīr* stipulated that the choice should not be arbitrary or motivated by self-interest, later jurists seem to have rejected the doctrine precisely because no objective standard could be created to test the integrity of the choice made by the judge or the *muftī*. The only solution was the creation of a new "rule of recognition," one which would regulate the manner by which *muqallid* judges and *muftīs* would choose among the contrary opinions present in each jurist's school.

MUKHTAṢARS AND THE FORMALIZATION OF LEGAL DOCTRINE

The importance of the 7th/13th century in the history of Islamic law lay in the effort to formalize the doctrine of the legal schools, an effort that culminated in the attempt to form unequivocal legal rules within each *madhhab*. We find for the Shāfiʿī school two important works, *al-Ghāya al-quṣwā fī dirāyat al-fatwā* of al-Qāḍī al-Bayḍāwī (d. 685/1286) and the *Minhāj* of al-Nawawī (d. 672/1273). The most significant feature of these works

84. Ibid., 1:74.

85. Al-Ḥaṭṭāb, 6:93.

86. Buhrām, *Sharḥ Buhrām ʿalā mukhtaṣar Khalīl*, Dār al-Kutub al-Miṣriyya, *Fiqh Mālikī*, 254, *bāb al-qaḍāʾ*, on his gloss on Khalīl's statement, "*wa-ḥakama bi-qawli muqalladihi.*" This manuscript is unnumbered, but the relevant section can be found easily since his commentary includes the text of Khalīl's *mukhtaṣar.*

is the attempt to develop a systematic set of technical terms whose purpose was to classify the legal status of the different opinions within the Shāfiʿī school. The editor of al-Bayḍāwī's work made the important observation that despite the fact that these two works were contemporaneous, the technical terms used by each author were different, in some cases even the opposite of what the other used.[87] The editor inferred from this the plausible conclusion that the terminological differences in the two works are most likely explained by the fact that these two works were the first attempt to introduce technical terms regulating the different opinions within the Shāfiʿī school; as a result, it was inevitable that there would be ambiguity in their use.[88] It [216] is also worth noting that both authors, working independently in different areas of the Muslim world, wrote texts remarkably similar in purpose: the clarification of Shāfiʿī doctrine for the jurists of the lowest tier of the schoo1.[89]

Likewise for the Mālikīs, the 7th/13th century witnessed the first attempt to classify the opinions of the school systematically at the hands of Ibn al-Ḥājib (d. 646/1248) in his abridgment (*mukhtaṣar*) of the Mālikī school known as *Jāmiʿ al-ummahāt*.[90] Like the previously mentioned works of the Shāfiʿī school, this work is also characterized by a sophisticated technical vocabulary that seems to have been the creation of the author himself. That the terms used by Ibn al-Ḥājib were intimately connected to the structure of the work was taken for granted by Ibn al-Ḥājib's commentators. Ibn Farḥūn devoted an entire work, *Kashf al-niqāb al-ḥājib min muṣṭalaḥ Ibn al-Ḥājib*, to the question of Ibn al-Ḥājib's technical language. Some of Ibn al-Ḥājib's terms that Ibn Farḥūn chose to explain include, but are not limited to, the *mashhūr*, *ashhar*, *ṣaḥīḥ*, *aṣaḥḥ*, *al-ẓāhir*, *al-wāḍiḥ*, *al-ijrā'*, *al-istiqrā'*, and *al-madhhab*.[91] The fact that the famous Mālikī *mukhtaṣar* which preceded Ibn al-Ḥājib's, known as *ʿIqd al-jawāhir al-thamīna*, or more simply, *al-Jawāhir*, seems to be free of any systematic use of these or other terms corroborates my hypothesis that Ibn al-Ḥājib was the first to organize the opinions of the Mālikī school according to the requirements of

87. Al-Bayḍāwī, for example, used the term *al-aṣaḥḥ* to signify which opinion of al-Shāfiʿī was the rule of the school and reserved the term *al-aẓhar* to signify which opinion of al-Shāfiʿī's followers represented the doctrine of the school. Al-Nawawī did the opposite, that is, he used *al-aṣaḥḥ* to refer to the opinions of al-Shāfiʿīs followers and reserved *al-aẓhar* to indicate which of al-Shāfiʿī's opinions represented the doctrine of the school. ʿAbd Allāh b. ʿUmar al-Bayḍāwī, *al-Ghāya al-quṣwā fī dirāyat al-fatwā*, ed. ʿAlī Muḥyī al-Dīn ʿAlī al-Qara Dāghīd (Dammām: Dār al-Iṣlāḥ, 1982), 110.

88. Ibid., 111. The editor of this work, ʿAlī Muḥyī al-Dīn, noted that many of the terms used by both al-Nawawī and al-Bayḍāwī had been in use prior to their books, but not as technical terms.

89. Ibid., 119.

90. ʿUthmān b. ʿAmr b. Abī Bakr, known as Ibn al-Ḥājib. The work remains in manuscript. It should be noted that Ibn al-Ḥājib's work pre-dates those of al-Bayḍāwī and al-Nawawī by several years, possibly making it the first work of its kind in Islamic jurisprudence. For the reaction of his contemporaries to his book, see Ibn Farḥūn, *al-Dībāj al-mudhahhab fī maʿrifat aʿyān al-madhhab*, ed. Muḥammad al-Aḥmadī Abū al-Nūr, 2 vols. (Cairo: Maktabat Dār al-Turāth, n.d.), 2:86–89.

91. Ibn Farḥūn, *Kashf al-niqāb* 210–11.

a technical language whose ultimate purpose was to clarify which opinions of the school were its authoritative rules.[92]

While any attempt to interpret Ibn al-Ḥājib's work without direct access to the text is bound to be speculative, it is possible to put forward some plausible theories about the text based on quotations taken from it found in later works, as well as Ibn Farḥūn's own reading of it.[93] That Ibn Farḥūn went to such great lengths in order to explain the [217] terms used by Ibn al-Ḥājib is evidence that the work cannot be understood without an attempt to understand his technical vocabulary. At the same time Ibn Farḥūn demonstrated that Ibn al-Ḥājib was occasionally inconsistent in his use of the book's terms.[94] There are several ways to explain this inconsistency. The first is to claim that the author did so intentionally in order to conceal his own interpretations of the *madhhab*'s doctrine. Another is to claim that the complexity of the project was such that he was bound to make mistakes in certain areas of the book. A third is to deny that Ibn al-Ḥājib himself had equally rigorous notions for all of his categories. Thus, while a term such as "*mashhūr*" may be consistent throughout the book, a term like "*madhhab*" may have been used less systematically, due to the differing importance of each for the book's structure. I incline more to the second explanation: being the first of its kind, the book was bound to incorporate much of the terminological confusion that had characterized an earlier period of jurisprudence when terms such as "*mashhūr*" and "*aṣaḥḥ*," "*ẓāhir*" and "*aẓhar*" had been used informally. The source of this confusion was intimately related to the plethora of opinions within each legal schoo1.[95] When Ibn Farḥūn was writing his commentary on Ibn al-Ḥājib, over six hundred years had passed since the death of Mālik. With the exception of his *Muwaṭṭa'*, Mālik did not write books of law. Instead, his legal opinions, which were essentially *fatwās*, were transmitted by his disciples, whom al-Qāḍī ʿIyāḍ numbered as exceeding one hundred, all of whom studied directly under Mālik and transmitted his doctrines.[96] Eventually later jurists within the Mālikī tradition discriminated among

92. This conclusion is based on my reading of the chapter on Adjudication *(Kitāb al-aqḍiya)* of *al-Jawāhir* from a manuscript taken from the Arab League Manuscript Institute. It is possible that in other chapters of the book he experimented with a technical vocabulary.

93. One finds quotes from Ibn al-Ḥājib's work scattered throughout *Tabṣirat al-ḥukkām*. Likewise, al-Ḥaṭṭāb and al-Mawwāq often quote from Ibn al-Ḥājib's text in the course of their respective commentaries on the *mukhtaṣar* of Khalīl. Ibn Farḥūn himself authored a commentary on Ibn al-Ḥājib's *mukhtaṣar*, entitling it *Tashīl al-muhimmāt fī sharḥ jāmiʿ al-ummahāt*, the introduction of which has been published under the title of *Kashf al-niqāb al-ḥājib min muṣṭalaḥ Ibn al-Ḥājib*.

94. See, for example, Ibn Farḥūn, *Kashf al-niqāb*, 118.

95. For a discussion of the different types of opinions in the Mālikī school, see Jackson, 167–75.

96. Al-Qāḍī 1/4 vol. 3, table of contents.

Mālik's students, settling upon Ibn al-Qāsim as the most reliable transmitter of Mālik's doctrine, and the *Mudawwana* as the most reliable source of Mālik's doctrine.[97]

Like Mālik, Ibn al-Qāsim did not write any books. Instead, his own version of Mālik's teaching was transmitted by second generation Mālikī jurists such as Asad Ibn al-Furāt (d. 213/828), Saḥnūn, Ibn Ḥabīb (d. 238/852) and al-ʿUtbī (d. 255/868). These were the jurists [218] who authored the works that were later to become known in the Mālikī legal school as the *ummahāt* (sing. *umm*), the source books of Mālikī jurisprudence.[98]

In practice, it was impossible to rely solely on Ibn al-Qāsim's teachings, for there were many issues of law for which Ibn al-Qāsim could not attribute an opinion to Mālik. This obliged later jurists to use the opinions of Mālik's other disciples, who often attributed positions to Mālik on precisely those cases for which Ibn al-Qāsim had not been able to provide a solution. More importantly, however, Ibn al-Qāsim's privileged position as the authoritative transmitter of Mālik's doctrine seems to have been developed at a later date.[99] Presumably, for the first centuries of Mālikī jurisprudence, opinions had been evaluated on the basis of their individual worth and not on the authority of the transmitter of that opinion.

As a result, the many contradictory positions attributed to Mālik by his various disciples often became recognized as law in different areas of the territory in which Mālikism was represented. Disagreements among Mālik's disciples were often significant and contentious. Apparently in frustration at the extent of his own disagreements with Ashhab (d. 204/819) regarding Mālik's doctrine, Ibn al-Qāsim is reported to have said, "It is as if Ashhab and I had studied with two different scholars."[100] This, combined with the fact that centers of Mālikism were scattered throughout al-Andalus, North Africa, Egypt and ʿIrāq, led to a considerable divergence of opinions within the school, especially when later jurists were faced with the need to create new doctrine to solve unprecedented cases. In many centers of Mālikism, then, the actual rules recognized by local judges and *muftīs* were often at variance with the doctrine of Ibn al-Qāsim, although they could have been based on the teachings of other prominent disciples of Mālik such as Ashhab. Any attempt to create uniform doctrine was bound to be laden with difficulties. [219] The historical fact of intra-school controversy helps to explain why the doctrine of *takhyīr*

---

97. For arguments regarding why Ibn al-Qāsim was the most reliable transmitter of Mālik's doctrine, see Ibn Farḥūn, *al-Tabṣira,* 1:66–69.

98. Although Asad was counted by al-Qāḍī ʿIyāḍ as a student of Mālik, he did not study with him for a lengthy period of time, and his book, *al-Asadiyya,* which served as the basis for Saḥnūn's *Mudawwana,* was a result of his study with Ibn al-Qāsim. Al-ʿUtbī's book is known as *al-Mustakhraja,* and Ibn Ḥabīb's work is known as *al-Wāḍiḥa.* The fourth source book of Mālikī law is the book of Muḥammad b. al-Mawwāz, a third generation Mālikī who studied with the students of Ibn al-Qāsim. His book is called *Kitab Muḥammad,* or simply, *al-Mawwāziyya.* See al-Ṭalīlī, 357–66.

99. This is a largely unwritten chapter of Mālikī law that deserves independent treatment.

100. al-Qāḍī ʿIyāḍ, 3:250.

was rejected. Practically speaking, how was it possible for the Mālikī school to create uniform doctrine out of this admittedly rich, but often contradictory, legal heritage? It had of course taken steps to minimize the dangers of this indeterminacy by restricting powers of interpretation to upper-level jurists, as discussed above. However, given a context of contradictory positions attributed to Mālik and his colleagues, how was a jurist to proceed without at least being forced to choose one among the several competing opinions within the school? The most important concept used by Mālikī jurists of the post 7th/13th century to resolve this problem was that of the *mashhūr*.

THE MASHHŪR AND THE CRYSTALIZATION OF LEGAL DOCTRINE[101]

According to Ibn Farḥūn, the function of Ibn al-Ḥājib's technical vocabulary was to separate "opinions" found within the school from the school's actual rule to be used both by judges and *muftīs*. If Ibn Farḥūn's interpretation of *Jāmiʿ al-ummahāt* is accurate, the text operated at two levels, the first addressed to the jurists of the first-tier and the second to middle level jurists.[102] The first level was directed toward those jurists whom al-Qarāfī and Ibn Rushd had identified as being allowed to communicate only an explicit text (*manṣūṣ*) of the school. These jurists, according to Ibn Farḥūn, were bound to rule and issue *fatwās* based exclusively on the *mashhūr* of the schoo1.[103] As noted, however, al-Qarāfī had used this term to describe the opinion used by the middle-tiered jurist in his legal opinions. Al-Qarāfī's use of the term is problematic in the light of Ibn Farḥūn's usage: according to the former, a jurist was empowered to use the *mashhūr* opinion only after a fair amount of training in the law;[104] according to the latter, the *mashhūr* was that opinion in the school that bound jurists who lacked the right to interpret the texts of the school.

Whereas for al-Qarāfī, a jurist's discovery of the *mashhūr* appears to have been mediated through interpretation, presumably based on that jurist's subjective evaluation of the strength of the different rules of the school, the *mashhūr* for Ibn Farḥūn functioned in an authoritarian manner, binding only the jurists of the lowest-tier who could not, [220] legitimately, interpret legal doctrine. How, then, did the *mashhūr* evolve from an interpretive term to an authoritarian one? The answer, it seems, was the identification of the *mashhūr* opinion by post-7th/13th jurists with the historical concept of "Mālik's last opinion (*al-qawl al-marjūʿ ilayhi*)."

101. Compare my account of the *mashhūr* with Jackson, "In Defense," 167–78, and Hallaq, "From *Fatwās to Furūʿ*," 53–54.

102. Although speaking of a "first" level and a "second" level, I do not imply a hierarchy or a division parallel to "apparent (*ẓāhir*)" and "hidden (*bāṭin*)."

103. Ibn Farḥūn, *al-Tabṣira,* 1:66.

104. Hallaq, "From *Fatwās* to *Furūʿ*," 54.

Prior to Ibn Farḥūn the term *mashhūr* seems to be have been used in a manner close to its denotative linguistic meaning: the commonly accepted rule of the school.[105] Ibn Farḥūn's use of this concept, however, was based on its later conventional meaning as "Mālik's last opinion." That Ibn Farḥūn accepted the basic affinity of the *mashhūr* to the notion of "Mālik's last opinion" is evinced by the fact that he used the two terms interchangeably, at one time saying that the *muqallid*-judge was bound to rule by the *mashhūr* in all contexts of controversy within the school, while at other times saying that he was bound to rule by Mālik's final position in all controversial cases.[106] Furthermore, we find Ibn Farḥūn quoting a *fatwā* from Abū Muḥammad ʿAbd Allāh b. ʿAlī b. Samārā (d. 647/1249),[107] who stated that whenever there were contradictory texts attributed to Mālik, the obligation of the *mujtahid* (meaning the *mujtahid* within the confines of the Mālikī school) was to determine which of the texts represented Mālik's final position on the subject. Applying this principle anachronistically to the work of earlier Mālikī jurists, Ibn Samārā assumed that the opinions of early Mālikī jurists, like Muḥammad b. al-Mawwāz (d. 269/882), al-Qāḍī Ismāʿīl (d. 282/895), Ibn Abī Zayd al-Qayrawānī (d. 386/996) and their peers, represented their efforts to determine what constituted Mālik's last opinion on a given case, based either on considerations of history or on interpretation of the texts of the school itself.[108]

This reading of the activities of the earlier Mālikī jurists attempted to apply the doctrine of abrogation (*naskh*) to the opinions of an independent interpreter of the law. Indeed, the author of the *fatwā* cited above made explicit reference to the concept of abrogation in defending his argument.[109] This argument was not unique to the Mālikīs. Ibn al-Ṣalāḥ made the same argument: wherever two positions are attributed to al-Shāfiʿī, the jurist must follow the second of the two positions, or [221] what was known in the Shāfiʿī school as the "new" opinion in contrast to the "old," because the former "abrogates the previous [opinion]."[110] Similarly, al-Sulamī described the relationship of a *mujtahid*'s second opinion to his first as one of abrogation, the later abrogating the earlier.[111] More importantly, he argued that the relationship between two contradictory texts must be either one of abrogation or of suspended judgment, for it is impossible to believe that al-Shāfiʿī held two contradictory positions simultaneously.[112]

105. Ibid.; Jackson, "In Defense," 168.

106. Ibn Farḥūn , *al-Tabṣira,* 1:66 and 1:70.

107. His name appears in the *Nayl al-ibtihāj* as "Ibn Satārī," Aḥmad Bābā al-Tunbuktī, *Nayl al-ibtihāj bi-taṭrīz al-dībāj,* ed. ʿAbd Allāh al-Harāma (Tripoli, Libya: Kulliyyāt al-Daʿwa al-Islāmiyya, 1989), 214–15.

108. Ibn Farḥūn, *al-Tabṣira,* 1:67.

109. Ibid.

110. Ibn al-Ṣalāḥ, 1:60.

111. Al-Sulamī, 12r.

112. Ibid., 18a, 19r.

The implications of al-Sulamī's argument were the same for all schools: the different positions attributed to the independent interpreters of the law were all valid instances of *ijtihād*, but each independent interpreter could have held only one of the contradictory opinions at any one time. Therefore, the obligation of the *muqallid* was to follow the last opinion of the independent interpreter, because, prima facie, his last statement represented a retraction of his previous statements. His previous positions could no longer be described as the eponym's *ijtihād*, and subsequently could not serve as the basis for *taqlīd*.[113]

Given the use of the doctrine of abrogation to the opinions of *mujtahids*, it is not difficult to see how the *mashhūr* became associated with the default rule of the school, even though the term probably originated as representing the jurist's effort to determine which opinion of the school was most in accord with the school's overall principles. However, even if one attempted to claim that Mālik's last opinion on a case and the *mashhūr* opinion of the school were one and the same, that still did not eliminate the need for historical and interpretive efforts to determine which of the opinions attributed to Mālik represented his last word on the matter.

The final evolution of the term *mashhūr* was achieved through the figure of Ibn al-Qāsim. Later Mālikī jurists argued that in all probability Ibn al-Qāsim's reports of Mālik's doctrine were a reliable source of the eponym's final positions on controversial issues, and should [222] therefore be considered, all things being equal, the rule of the school.[114] In his chapter regarding the rules which a judge was to apply in court, Ibn Farḥūn developed a "rule of recognition" rooted in the history of the school that served to regulate the activities of the jurist of the lowest rung. The purpose of his "rule of recognition" was to isolate, among all the opinions attributed to Mālik, which was the *mashhūr*. This was the privileged opinion of the school because it was taken conventionally to be Mālik's final word on a given issue. Ibn Farḥūn also assimilated his own concept of the *mashhūr* as being historically determined to Ibn al-Ḥājib's use of the term in his *Jāmiᶜ al-ummahāt*.[115]

113. This question was based on the issue taken from legal methodology discussed earlier, where it was resolved that a *muqallid* is obliged to change his actions whenever the opinion of the Imām whom he follows changes, see note 28. Thus, Ibn al-Ṣalāḥ maintained that Shāfiᶜī's "old doctrine is no longer an opinion of al-Shāfiᶜī, and therefore, their [viz., jurists within the Shāfiᶜī *madhhab*] choice of the old in them [some twenty cases according to Ibn al-Ṣalāḥ] is of the same genus of that we have [already] mentioned: one of them choosing an opinion from a school other than the Shāfiᶜī school whenever his [own] reasoning *(ijtihād)* leads him to that." Ibn al-Ṣalāḥ, 1:68.

114. Ibn Farḥūn, *al-Tabṣira*, 1:67–68.

115. Whether or not Ibn al-Ḥājib understood the *mashhūr* in the same manner as Ibn Farḥūn is irrelevant to the present discussion. In any case, a future study might attempt a comparison of the rules declared by Ibn al-Ḥājib to be the *mashhūr* with the opinions of Mālik attributed to Mālik in the basic sources of Mālikī law such as the *Mudawwana* and the *ᶜUtbiyya*. Such an empirical study of the *mashhūr*

Ibn Farḥūn distinguished among the various transmissions of Ibn al-Qāsim's doctrines. Thus, while we are told that Ibn al-Qāsim's opinion in the *Mudawwana* of Saḥnūn is superior to the opinions expressed by other disciples of Mālik in that same work, the opinions of these different scholars are superior to Ibn al-Qāsim's opinions expressed in other books. One jurist justified this elevation of the *Mudawwana* over the other books of the school on the grounds of its superior mode of transmission.[116] On the other hand, Abū Ṭāhir Ibrāhīm b. ʿAbd al-Ṣamad Ibn al-Bashīr (d. 526/1131) attributed the superiority of the *Mudawwana* to its composite composition: unlike the other source books of the school, it contained the legal reasoning of three jurists, Ibn al-Qāsim, Asad Ibn al-Furāt and Saḥnūn.[117]

Whatever the case may be, Ibn Farḥūn gave Ibn al-Qāsim's opinion in the *Mudawwana* the default status of being the *mashhūr* of the school, going so far as to say that the expression *madhhab al-mudawwana* is the equivalent of *mashhūr*.[118] For this reason, Ibn Farḥūn took Ibn al-Ḥājib's use of the term *ashhar* to be synonymous with *madhhab* [223] *al-mudawwana*, explaining that the author did not use the more common term *mashhūr* in these contexts because of the fact that later jurists had described many of their own independent opinions, or the opinions of jurists other than those of Ibn al-Qāsim in the *Mudawwana*, as being the *mashhūr*. By using the comparative form, Ibn al-Ḥājib clarified which opinion was the actual rule of the school, and, hence, should be applied by judges and *muftīs*.[119]

Ibn Farḥūn was certainly not the first to equate Ibn al-Qāsim's transmission of Mālik's positions in the *Mudawwana* as representing the school's rule in a given area of law, as is evident from Ibn Samārā's *fatwā* cited above. Indeed, Ibn Sahl (d. 486/1093) reported that in 5th/11th century Cordoba, Ibn al-Qāsim and the *Mudawwana* had already gained recognition by the legal establishment as the authoritative sources of Mālikī legal practice.[120]

---

would contrast nicely with the ideological perspective given by Ibn Farḥūn that is being presented in this context.

116. Ibid., 1:70. Al-Qāḍī ʿAbd al-Wahhāb al-Baghdādī (d. 422/1031) attributed the greater reliability of the *Mudawwana* to the fact that it was Saḥnūn who transmitted it. Al-Qāḍī ʿIyāḍ, 3:246. For more information regarding the history of the *Mudawwana's* transmission, see the biography for Asad Ibn al-Furāt, 3:291 and the biography of Saḥnūn, 4:45, also in *al-Tartīb*. It should be noted that al-Qāḍī ʿIyāḍ, while recognizing the importance of al-ʿUtbī's work *al-Mustakhraja*, charged that it was full of errors and rare cases, 4:253–54.

117. Al-Talīlī, 365.

118. Ibn Farḥūn, *al-Tabṣira*, 1:71.

119. Ibn Farḥūn , *al-Tabṣira*, 1:72 and *Kashf al-niqāb al-ḥājib*, 89.

120. Text: *al-muʿawwal fīmā yuftā bihi mimmā jarat al-aḥkām ʿalayhi qawl Ibn al-Qāsim lā siyyamā al-wāqiʿ minhu fī al-mudawwana thumma ʿalā mā waqaʿa fīhā li-ghayrihi hādhā alladhī samiʿnāhu qadīman fī majālis shuyūkhinā alladhīna intafaʿnā bihim wa in kāna alladhīna adraknāhum min shuyūkhinā alladhīna kānat al-futyā tadūr ʿalayhim bi-Qurṭuba rubbamā istahtarū fī al-ikhtiyār ilā mā waqaʿa fī ghayrihā. Mukhtaṣar fatāwā al-Burzulī,* Aḥmad b. ʿAbd al-Raḥmān al-Qarawī, known as Ḥalūlū, Arab League Manuscript Institute, 29 *Fiqh Mālikī*, 1r.

Likewise, in the following century Ibn al-Ḥājj (d. 529/1134) was reported to have said that in his town, Seville, with the exception of five rules, only the opinions of Ibn al-Qāsim were used in legal opinions.[121] Despite this, Ibn Farḥūn seems to have been one, if not the first, of the Mālikī jurists who succeeded in providing a theoretical basis justifying Ibn al-Qāsim's privileged position among Mālik's disciples. It is clear, however, that Ibn al-Qāsim was elevated to this position principally in order to remove the indeterminacy from which the Mālikī school suffered.

Ibn Farḥūn claimed that one of the main purposes of the book of Ibn al-Ḥājib was to transmit which opinion constituted the *mashhūr* rule of the school, understood as Mālik's final opinion, which in turn was the rule to be used by *muftīs* and judges.[122] If this is true, it may explain the popularity of the work—instead of the *muqallid*-judge having to engage in the historical interpretation necessary to arrive at Mālik's last position on a given topic of law, he could simply rely on Ibn al Ḥājib's report of what that rule was. While this interpretation seems plausible, it fails to explain why Ibn al-Ḥājib also included in his work non-*mashhūr* opinions—whether attributed to Mālik, Ibn al-Qāsim, or other [224] disciples of Mālik—graded by terms such as *ṣaḥīḥ* and *ẓāhir*, which, in contrast to the *mashhūr*, applied to the substance of an opinion rather than to its pedigree. The most likely answer to this question is that these non-*mashhūr* opinions were included for the sake of the middle-tiered jurist, i.e., that jurist who was qualified to choose opinions of the eponym that he later retracted based on the jurist's own detailed knowledge of the eponym's doctrine. Therefore, while a jurist from the lowest tier was not free to apply the *ṣaḥīḥ* opinion if it conflicted with the *mashhūr*, a second or third tier jurist almost certainly could.[123]

MUKHTAṢAR KHALĪL: THE APEX OF CODIFICATION IN THE MĀLIKĪ SCHOOL[124]

My argument that Ibn al-Ḥājib's *Jāmiʿ al-ummahāt* was an effort at codifying Mālikī doctrine is largely based on Ibn Farḥūn's commentary on the author's technical terms. Based on Ibn Farḥūn's analysis of those terms, I argued that Ibn al-Ḥājib's text operated on two levels: the

121. Ibid.

122. Ibn Farḥūn, *Kashf al-niqāb*, 64–65 and 89.

123. Ibn Farḥūn, *Kashf al-niqāb*, 64–65.

124. In using the term codification, I am referring to the function of the text within the Mālikī legal system. While it is true, as far as I know, that neither the *Jāmiʿ al-ummahāt* nor the *Mukhtaṣar Khalīl* were promulgated as codes by the state, both texts, especially the latter, share an essential feature of law codes—the desire to have an authoritative statement of the law. Having said that, however, one should not believe that state officials were not interested in these texts. For example, the ʿAlawī Sulṭān Muḥammad b. ʿAbd Allāh (d. 1204/1790) of the Maghrib required that legal rulings and opinions be derived only from certain commentaries of Khalīl. He also banned the teaching of certain commentaries in favor of others. Al-Jīdī, 137. Moreover, Mālikī jurists behaved as though *Mukhtaṣar Khalīl* was their authoritative source of legal doctrine, requiring *muftīs* to review it once a year. Ibrāhīm al-Laqqānī,

first, based on the *mashhūr*, was designed to present the doctrine of the school to the lowest level jurist in such a way as to save him the difficulty of extracting it from the school's primary texts (*ummahāt*), and the second, based on terms such as the *ṣaḥīḥ*, was directed toward second and third level jurists who could legitimately use non-*mashhūr* opinions of the school by performing a type of *ijtihād* based on the original texts of the school. Despite the enormous success enjoyed by *Jāmiᶜ al-ummahāt*, the fact that it operated on these two levels seemed to make it unnecessarily cumbersome: if it were written for the lowest level jurist, he did not need the secondary opinions of the school, while the upper-level jurists certainly did not need Ibn al-Ḥājib's work to become familiar with the school's secondary doctrines.

[225] Scarcely a century passed before the next logical step toward a more univocal expression of Mālikī doctrine was achieved. An Egyptian Mālikī jurist, Khalīl b. Isḥāq al-Jundī (d. 749/1348 or 767/1365), authored what was destined to become the most important work for post-8th/14th Mālikism—so unrivaled in fame that it became known simply as *Mukhtaṣar Khalīl*, "The Abridgment of Khalīl." Ibn Farḥūn, who as a student had attended some of Khalīl's lectures in law, Arabic language and hadith, made the important observation that what distinguished Khalīl's work from Ibn al-Ḥājib's was precisely its univocal nature. Not surprisingly, the work gained its univocal nature from the fact that, according to Ibn Farḥūn, it restricted itself to the *mashhūr* of the school while ignoring the school's other opinions.[125] As a result of this feature, the book rapidly became popular with students of law, who studied it eagerly.[126]

The *Mukhtaṣar* of Khalīl, in contrast to the more discursive works of the school, included only legal rules, and hence served the needs of *taqlīd* perfectly.[127] Khalīl stated explicitly in the introduction of his work that his book's function was "to clarify what is used in giving legal opinions."[128] As a result, the book lacked much of the sophisticated technical language developed by Ibn al-Ḥājib.[129]

Manār ahl al-fatwā wa qawāᶜid al-iftā' bi-l-aqwā, ed. Ziyād Muḥammad Maḥmūd Ḥumaydan (Beirut: Dār al-Aḥbāb, 1412/1992), 220; al-Jīdī, 104.

125. Ibn Farḥūn, *al-Dībāj*, 1:358.

126. Khalīl b. Isḥāq al-Jundī died in 749/1348 according to Ibn Farḥūn, while al-Tunbuktī maintained that his probable death date was 767/1365. It should be noted that Khalīl himself also wrote one of the most influential commentaries on Ibn al-Ḥājib's work, *al-Tawḍīḥ*. See *al-Dībāj*, 1:357–58.

127. What I mean by "only rules," is that he does not argue for the "correctness" of the rules, nor does he provide any commentary which would introduce the opinions of different jurists.

128. Al-Ḥaṭṭāb, 1:24. Also see Hallaq, "From *Fatwās* to *Furūᶜ*," 58.

129. Instead of the several terms used by Ibn al-Ḥājib, Khalīl had a rather simplified technical language. See ibid., 1:34–40.

Although Khalīl attempted to write a univocal work, he did not believe that all jurists within the school were of the lowest level and had no rights of interpretation.[130] Rather, his *Mukhtaṣar* served to create a sharp distinction between what was the position of the school, i.e., the rule (*ḥukm*) of the school, and what was the opinion (*qawl*) of an individual jurist. This is manifested in Khalīl's use of the term *aqwāl*, "opinions." Khalīl noted in his introduction that he used this term only in those areas of the law where he was unable to find an explicit reference attributed to one of the master-jurists of the Mālikī school [226] declaring one of these conflicting opinions to be stronger.[131] Khalīl himself often held an opinion regarding which of the conflicting opinions was stronger. Because it was only his opinion, it found no place within the *Mukhtaṣar*, which was restricted to legal rules; however, his position regarding which opinion was stronger found a legitimate outlet in the genre of commentary. Therefore, Khalīl included his own opinions in *al-Tawḍīḥ*, his commentary on Ibn Ḥājib's *Mukhtaṣar*, where, in vivid contrast to his practice in the *Mukhtaṣar*, he would declare which of the conflicting positions was stronger, relying on his own evaluation of the merit of the various opinions. Moreover, in all cases in which he reported his own opinion, he openly attributed that interpretive act to himself, using his first initial, *khā'*.[132]

Khalīl's *Mukhtaṣar* strove for the univocality that seems to be the most important characteristic of codes of law. For this reason it seems justified to consider his work to be, at the very least, code-like. On the other hand, as we have already seen, Khalīl was not able to achieve a perfectly univocal text for the reason that in many areas of the law, the school had succeeded only in producing opinions, not rules. Thus, in addition to his use of the term "*aqwāl*" to refer to these problematic contexts within the law, he also used the terms "*khilāf*" (controversy) and "*taraddud*" (hesitation).[133]

TAQLĪD AND THE RULE OF LAW

Surprisingly, Western historians of Islamic law have not identified the spirit informing *mukhtaṣars* as one striving toward the creation of uniform legal doctrine. Schacht noted that these works "are not in the nature of codes; Islamic law is not a corpus of legislation but the living result of legal science."[134] Without denying that Islamic law continued to evolve even after the genre of *mukhtaṣars* came to dominate Islamic legal writing, I find Schacht's observation problematic for it fails to explain why, in the case of the Mālikī school for

130. Indeed, al-Ḥaṭṭāb asserted that when a rule was followed by the expression "*ustuḥsina,*" that was to indicate that that was the position supported by Khalīl. Ibid., 1:38.

131. Ibid., 1:36.

132. Ibid.

133. Ibid., 1:36 and 1:38.

134. Schacht, *Introduction, 71.*

example, no new *mukhtaṣars* of any importance were produced after Khalīl.[135] One [227] suspects that the same was true for the other schools of Islamic law: each produced a *mukhtaṣar* that represented the base line doctrine of the school, and whose text (*matn*) was not subsequently revised from generation to generation.[136] Most importantly, however, Schacht fails to explain why this genre of legal writing is "not in the nature of" a code. Although Coulson was aware of the different gradations of opinions within schools of law, i.e., *mashhūr*, *rājiḥ* (strong) and *ḍaʿīf* (weak),[137] he argued that because Islamic law was religious, the determination of the law was ultimately a matter of the judge's conscience whenever he was faced with a question for which revelation failed to provide an explicit answer. Because of this feature of Islamic law, the creation of uniform legal doctrine could not be one of its goals, and therefore, Islamic law had no need for the institution of judicial review whose only function was to achieve uniformity in law:

> The Sharīʿa is an attempt to define the will of Allāh, and since the unequivocal texts of divine revelation were comparatively limited, the deliberations of the jurists produced many conflicting opinions and views which represent merely probable rules of law. While one *qāḍī* may base his judgment on one opinion, an exactly similar case may subsequently be decided according to the contrary opinion, *for in each case the onus of the determination of the rule applicable falls upon the conscience of the individual qāḍī concerned. This attitude runs directly counter to the notions of uniformity and certainty in the law which are at once the object and result of a case-law system. In short, it may be argued, this conflict reflects one of the fundamental distinctions between a secular and religious legal system.*[138] (emphasis added)

Coulson's statement would hold true only in a context where the judge was practicing *ijtihād*; however, where the judge was a *muqallid*, his activities were regulated by a non-subjective "rule of recognition" whose explicit goal was to ensure that judges and *muftīs* applied the same rule to similar cases.[139] Likewise, we have also adduced much [228]

135. One could argue that the work of the Egyptian Mālikī jurist al-Dārdir, *al-Sharḥ al-ṣaghīr*, became a very popular *mukhtaṣar* at least for Egyptian Mālikīs. However, it never replaced *Mukhtaṣar Khalīl*; instead, it served as an introductory text that was studied prior to the law student's study of *Mukhtaṣar Khalīl* at a more advanced stage of study. See Aḥmad b. Muḥammad b. Aḥmad al-Dārdir, *al-Sharḥ al-ṣaghīr*, ed. Kamāl Waṣfī, 4 vols. (Cairo: Dār al-Maʿārif, 1986).

136. The authoritative Shāfiʿī text *(matn)*, for example, was the 7th/13th century *Minhāj* of al-Nawawī. The stress, however, should be placed on "text," for commentaries of course could, and did, change from generation to generation. See Hallaq, "From *Fatwās* to *Furūʿ*." The study of the different commentaries on works such as *Jāmiʿ al-ummahāt* and *Mukhtaṣar Khalīl is* an important subject that has yet to be explored.

137. Coulson, *History*, 145.

138. Coulson, "Muslim Custom and Case-Law," 20–21.

139. Coulson conceded in another work that "[t]heory, of course, required that in cases of conflict the *qāḍī* should normally follow the dominant doctrine of his school. But in the interests of justice it was often a 'preferable' or even a 'weak' opinion which found favor with the courts." It is hard to say to

evidence demonstrating that judges and *muftīs*, particularly those in the lower ranks of the legal establishment, were bound to explicit rules, and their powers of interpretation were severely circumscribed, if they were given any at all.

The last piece of our argument on this point will focus on the problem raised by Coulson—judicial review.[140] If one agrees with Coulson that Muslim judges were accountable to none other than God, one would have to conclude that Islamic law had no need for judicial review. The question before us, however, is whether or not Muslim jurists held judges accountable for their decisions, and if so, how? Answering such a broad question for a legal tradition as diverse and ancient as that of Islamic law is difficult. In the context of post-8th/14th century Mālikism, however, the relevant texts from *Mukhtaṣar Khalīl* would certainly be the best place from which to begin the search for an answer to this question. In discussing the grounds on which judgment may be overturned, Khalīl stated the following:

> The ruling of an unjust [judge] is null as is [the ruling of] an ignorant [judge] who does not consult. Otherwise, it [viz., the judgment of the ignorant judge who consults] is reviewed (*tuʿuqqiba*) and the correct [rulings] are enforced. The judgments of the knowledgeable just judge are not reviewed (*lā yutaʿaqqab*). Whatever contradicts a certain [text of revelation] or an a fortiori analogy is overturned and the grounds [for its repeal] must be clarified . . . as well as rulings against an enemy or [a ruling] based on [the judge's] knowledge [gained] prior to the case ... or that he intended such-and-such [a rule] but made a mistake [wherever there are witnesses to the judge's mistake] ... and only he can repeal it [viz., his ruling] if another rule [subsequently] appears to him as more correct or if he [unintentionally] departed from his opinion or the opinion of his Imām.[141]

In the opening sentence of this passage, Khalīl referred to the rulings of three kinds of judges: the unjust judge (both ignorant and knowledgeable), the just and knowledgeable judge, and the ignorant judge who consults, and, by implication, is just. The judgments of the first [229] group are by definition null, those of the second are by definition valid and binding, and those of third, i.e., the ignorant judge who consults, do not become

what extent this represents a revision of his previous position on this question—or did he believe that determination of "the interests of justice" was a question left to the individual judge? If the latter is true, it is not much of a revision at all. Coulson, *History*, 146.

140. Compare Coulson's position with that of David Powers, "On Judicial Review in Islamic Law," *Law and Society Review*, 26, 2 (1992), 315–41, where the author confirmed the existence of a power of judicial review in the Mālikī school which he terms "successor review."

141. Muḥammad b. Yūsuf al-ʿAbdarī al-Mawwāq, *al-Tāj wa-al-iklīl* on the margin of *Mawāhib al-jalīl*, 6 vols. (3d ed., Beirut: Dār al-Fikr, 1412/1992), 6:135–38.

valid and binding before being reviewed. Obviously, Khalīl at least imagined the potential for the systematic review of judicial decisions for this category of judges.

Khalīl further complicated his discussion of which judgments were liable to being overturned by making a broad distinction between objective errors—meaning errors that could be corrected by any Muslim judge—and subjective errors—meaning errors that only the presiding judge himself could correct. The objective category included obvious errors of law, i.e., contradicting an explicit text of revelation, errors in following procedural rules, i.e., a judge ruling against a personal enemy, and errors in following rules of evidence, i.e., the judge ruling based on knowledge gained outside of the courtroom.

Those errors which were subjective in nature—and could only be repealed by the presiding judge—were of three types. The first was where the judge, after ruling, found a more appropriate rule, and wished to revise his first ruling in light of his subsequent reasoning. The second was where the judge mistakenly applied the wrong rule to the case before him. According to al-Ḥaṭṭāb these two cases applied only in situations in which the judge was ruling based on his own *ijtihād*.[142] Likewise, al-Kharshī noted that these two rules applied only to a *mujtahid*, or to a *muqallid* who was of sufficient rank in the school to weigh the strength of the school's various doctrines.[143] Al-Zurqānī (d. 1099/1687) interpreted this clause similarly to al-Kharshī.[144]

The third type of subjective error mentioned by Khalīl was that of a *muqallid* who failed to apply the rule of his Imām. An example of this kind of error, according to al-ʿAdawī (d. 1189/1775), would be if a judge intended to rule based on the opinion of Ibn al-Qāsim, but mistakenly applied the opinion of Ashhab. In this situation, since none other than the judge could know that he had mistakenly applied an incorrect opinion, only he was able to correct it. However, this clause applied only if the judge who made the mistake had the jurisdictional freedom to rule based on opinions of more than one jurist. If he had been appointed to rule according to the opinion of one scholar (*ʿālim*), however, a judgment rendered according to the opinion of another [230] scholar (*ʿālim*) would be null and void.[145] Al-Zurqānī offered the same qualification to this clause, adding that such a judge "has no jurisdictional authority to rule based on something other than it [viz., the opinion of the scholar whose opinion he was required to follow] (*li-annahu maʿzūl ʿan al-ḥukm bihi*)."[146] Al-Bunānī (d. 1194/1780), meanwhile, argued that the first two cases, i.e., where a judge wished to reverse a previous ruling in the light of his subsequent opinion,

142. Al-Ḥaṭṭāb, 6:138.

143. Al-Kharshī, *Sharḥ al-Kharshī ʿalā mukhtaṣar sīdī Khalīl*, 4 vols. (Beirut: Dār al-Fikr, n.d.), 4:7:177.

144. ʿAbd al-Bāqī al-Zurqānī, *Sharḥ al-Zurqānī ʿalā mukhtaṣar sīdī Khalīl*, 4 vols. (Beirut: Dār al-Fikr, n.d.), 4:7:147.

145. ʿAlī al-ʿAdawī, *Ḥāshiyat al-ʿAdawī*, on the margin of *Sharḥ al-Kharshī ʿalā mukhtaṣar Sīdī Khalīl*, 4:7:166.

146. Al-Zurqānī, 4:7:147.

and where he mistakenly applied the incorrect rule, applied exclusively to a judge who was a *mujtahid*, while the last one, i.e., the failure of the judge who was a *muqallid* to apply his Imām's rule, was specific to the *muqallid* of the upper echelons of the school. If he was not of this stature, his rulings were null if they did not conform to the *mashhūr*. In support of this opinion, al-Bunānī quoted Ibn ʿArafa as saying, "The only rulings of contemporary judges considered to be valid are those that do not contradict the *mashhūr* and the position of the *Mudawwana*."[147] Likewise, al-Bunānī quoted al-Burzulī (d. 841/1437) to demonstrate that not only was this the doctrinal position of the school, but also that the rulings of judges in the past had been overturned for their failure to apply the *mashhūr*.[148]

Therefore, while it seems that Khalīl imagined a situation in which the decisions of a *muqallid*-judge would not have been subject to outside review, his commentators only exempted the rulings of a *muqallid* judge from review if he was of sufficient rank to select among the varying positions of the school. If not, the *muqallid*-judge was limited to the *mashhūr*; if he used a non-*mashhūr* doctrine, his ruling was null. Likewise, both al-Zurqānī and al-Kharshī had already made the point expressed by al-Bunānī in an earlier section in the *Mukhtaṣar*.[149]

In conclusion, later Mālikī jurists held that a judge's authority to use non-*mashhūr* positions was restricted by two conditions: the first was the legal credentials of the judge in question, and the second was the terms of the judge's appointment. Al-Bunānī, who was from the Maghrib, insisted that the validity of the judge's ruling was a pure question of law, and therefore, the terms of appointment had nothing to do with a judge's lack of authority to use non-*mashhūr* positions. Under his [231] reading of Khalīl, any judge could overturn a ruling by a *muqallid* of the lowest rank that was not based on the *mashhūr*. The Egyptian jurists, al-Zurqānī and al-Kharshī, restricted the right of correcting a mistake of this type to the *muqallid* himself, unless his appointment stipulated that he could only rule based on certain opinions. Therefore, both positions would allow for the possibility of review as long as the judge was neither a jurist of the highest rank, nor appointed to rule based only on certain opinions.

Finally, it is important to consider the attributes "knowledgeable" and "ignorant" as used by Khalīl. The preceding discussion established that the judicial decisions of an ignorant judge were valid only if he "consulted." Even if such a judge consulted, however, his rulings were still to be supervised systematically. This means that if a *muqallid* was considered to be knowledgeable, his decisions would not be supervised. Thus, many of his mistakes or abuses of discretion could potentially escape undetected. The definition of "knowledgeable" and "ignorant," however, is implicit in what has already been men-

---

147. Al-Bunānī, on the margin of *Sharḥ al-Zurqānī ʿalā mukhtaṣar sīdī Khalīl* (Beirut: Dār al-Fikr, n.d.), 4:7:147–48.

148. Ibid., 4:7:148.

149. Ibid., 4:7:124; al-Kharshī, 4:7:140.

tioned: *ʿālim* was understood by Khalīl's commentators to be a *mujtahid* or a *mujtahid* within a school of law. This was expressed explicitly by Ibn ʿAbd al-Salām (d. 1258/1842 or 1259/1843), who noted that the ancient authorities of the school used *jāhil* in the same way that later jurists used the term *muqallid*. He also quoted al-Wansharīsī, (d. 914/ 1508) as saying, "There is no controversy regarding the permissibility of reviewing, meaning inspection, of the rulings of the *muqallid*, and he is the one who is described in the books of our Imāms as ignorant."[150] Likewise, al-Burzulī was cited by al-Tusūlī as noting that among early Mālikī authorities, "*al-muqallid*, the ignorant and the commoner are synonymous terms."[151] Thus, according to this last author, Khalīl's statement "*jāhil lam yushāwir*" is a *muqallid*, meaning that before the rulings of a *muqallid*-judge could be enforced, they had to be reviewed. The purpose of consultation was to ensure that the judge used only the rules recognized by the *madhhab*. Its effect was to place the judge under the supervision of a *muftī* more learned than he in the law. On the other hand, the only judge whose decisions escaped systematic review was the *mujtahid*, whether independent of any school, or within the domains of a particular schoo1.[152]

[232] Therefore, it is clear that legal theory created the potential for systematic review of legal decisions so as to ensure that the school's rules were being applied by the courts. Whether this was carried out or not is another issue,[153] but to claim that Muslim jurists, or at the very least Mālikī jurists, because they were guardians of a religious law, had no interest in insuring that a uniform, objectively knowable body of rules was applied by the courts, is to make a claim that renders the positions of these jurists unintelligible.[154]

CONCLUSION

Islamic legal theory began by allowing the judge complete freedom to rule in areas of the law that had not been governed by an explicit text of revelation using his own reasoning.

150. Abū al-Ḥasan ʿAlī b. ʿAbd al-Salām al-Tusūlī, *al-Bahja fī sharḥ al-tuḥfa ʿalā urjūzat tuḥfat al-ḥukkām li-Ibn ʿĀṣim*, 2 vols. (Cairo: al-Maṭbaʿa al-Khayriyya, 1304/1886), 1:21.

151. Ibid.

152. Al-Tusūlī notes that the rulings of figures like Ibn Rushd and al-Lakhmī, as well as other late jurists, because they were considered to be *mujtahids* within the *madhhab*, were not subject to review. Instead, they fell under Khalīl's statement that the rulings of a knowledgeable just judge are not reviewed. On the other hand, the decisions of a judge who was not a *mujtahid* within the *madhhab* had to be reviewed to ensure compliance with the rule of the school. Ibid.

153. For evidence that these rules were indeed followed, see Powers, 329–36.

154. The kind of review process outlined by Khalīl is dissimilar to that in case-law, where the appellate court decisions are recognized as sources of law. The function of the review process recognized by Khalīl is simply to eliminate errors in the law. Therefore, because Islamic law does not recognize the doctrine of *stare decisis*, its process of review does not constitute proper case-law.

Slowly, this freedom came to be challenged as the need for uniform rules began to be felt. Since jurists could not produce uniform legal doctrine using the legal methodology governing *ijtihād*, they turned to the doctrine of *taqlīd*, whose purpose was to bind the vast majority of legal officials to the opinion of one *mujtahid*. *Taqlīd*, however, never extended to all jurists, and those jurists who ascended to the summit of their legal schools retained the right to create new doctrine in the absence of an established rule, as well as revising old doctrine, but only after showing why the school's prevailing rule could not be applied for the case at hand.[155]

In order to make *taqlīd* more effective, the genre of the *mukhtaṣar* was popularized, beginning in the 7th/13th century with the *Jāmiᶜ al-ummahāt* of Ibn al-Ḥājib, followed in the 8th/14th century by *Mukhtaṣar Khalīl*. The basic aim of these two works was to present the rules of the school as well as representative cases illustrating their application. But the production of *mukhtaṣars* could not proceed without attempting to resolve the problem of contradictory opinions within [233] the school. The Mālikī school of the post-7th/13th century attempted to solve this problem through an application of the theory of abrogation to the different opinions attributed to the Imām Mālik. Thus, "Mālik's last opinion," *qawl Mālik al-marjūᶜ ilayhi*, became the authoritative rule of the school. Parallel to the rise of this concept, the term *mashhūr*, which previously had been used generically to identify the prevailing rule of the school, became almost synonymous with the notion of "Mālik's last opinion." Thus, the *mashhūr* evolved from an interpretive category to one of pure authority which relied solely on the alleged transmission-history of the school's opinions. Khalīl, who limited his *Mukhtaṣar* to the *mashhūr* doctrines of the school, was able to construct a text which in many ways resembled a legal code that claimed to present an authoritative account of the law. Because his work did not bind all jurists, however, it cannot be considered a full-fledged code. Nevertheless, it would be accurate to describe Islamic law, if the Mālikī school is taken as representative, as having undergone a long-term evolution from one resembling a case-law system to one resembling civil law, with the exception that upper-level jurists always succeeded in retaining their right to override rules of the school in situations that demanded it. Thus, Islamic law in the age of *mukhtaṣars* came to occupy a position between the two extremes of judge-made law and code-law, a position that may be called a codified Common Law.

155. For a clear example illustrating this issue, see Wael Hallaq, "Murder in Cordoba: *Ijtihād, Iftā'* and the Evolution of Substantive Law in Medieval Islam," *Acta Orientalia*, 40 (1994, 95), 1–29.

5

"*ISTAFTI QALBAKA WA IN AFTĀKA AL-NĀSU WA AFTŪKA*"*: THE ETHICAL OBLIGATIONS OF THE *MUQALLID* BETWEEN AUTONOMY AND TRUST

Mohammad Fadel

[105] In the theological tradition of *kalām*, epistemology and dogma are fused. The fusion between epistemology and dogma is evidenced by the claim of Muslim theologians that theological dogma must be based on knowledge (*ʿilm*), which by definition is accessible to all rational persons.[1] This emphasis on epistemology is also evidenced in the many works of Sunnī jurisprudence (*uṣūl al-fiqh*), whether Ashʿarī or Muʿtazilī, which adopt the distinction between knowledge and considered opinion (*ẓann*). In contrast to *kalām*, for example, which demands certainty for its conclusions,[2] *uṣūl al-fiqh* was generally satisfied if the conclusions its methods supported were merely probable (*rājiḥ*).[3]

One can also distinguish *kalām* from *uṣūl al-fiqh* in another important respect: all individuals, in their individual capacities, are required to have knowledge of the truth of

This article was originally published in *Islamic Law in Theory: Studies on Jurisprudence in Honor of Bernard Weiss*, edited by A. Kevin Reinhart and Robert Gleave (Leiden: Brill, 2014), pp. 105–126.

I would like to thank the participants in the ALTA II conference held between September 26–29, 2008 for the valuable comments I received on a draft version of this paper.

* Part of a hadith in which the Prophet Muḥammad, when asked about the meaning of righteousness (*al-birr*), replied by saying: "Seek the opinion of your heart, even if the people give you opinions to the contrary."

1. See, e.g., 9 *Nafāʾis al-uṣūl fī sharḥ al-maḥṣūl*, Shihāb al-Dīn Aḥmad b. Idrīs al-Qarāfī, ed. by ʿĀdil Aḥmad ʿAbd al-Mawjūd and ʿAlī Muḥammad Muʿawwaḍ 4026 (Maktabat Nizār Muṣṭafā al-Bāz: Riyāḍ, 1997) (quoting Fakhr al-Dīn al-Rāzī as saying, with regard to the fundamentals of religion (*al-uṣūl*), that "God, may He be glorified, has laid out for these [foundational] requirements certain proofs (*adilla qāṭiʿa*), and He enabled rational persons to know them"); see also, Abū Ḥāmid Muḥammad b. Muḥammad al-Ghazālī, *al-Mustaṣfā* 347–348 (Dar al-kutub al-ʿilmiyya, Beirut: 1993) (linking the possibility of sin to the possibility of knowledge); and Aron Zysow, "The Economy of Certainty" 1 (unpub. Ph.D. Diss., Harvard University, 1984).

2. Mohammad Fadel, "The True, the Good and the Reasonable: the Theological and Ethical Roots of Public Reason in Islamic law," *21 Can. J. Law&Juris.* 1, 21–23 (2008).

3. Zysow, *supra* n. 1 at 4.

kalām's theological propositions,[4] while in the domain of jurisprudence individuals are generally not obliged to reach a substantive conclusion regarding the judgments produced in jurisprudence.

[106] Instead, most individual Muslims were non-specialists (*muqallid*) who were obliged to identify an appropriate scholar-specialist—one who has mastered the tools of jurisprudence (*mujtahid* or *muftī*)—and to follow the jurisprudential opinions of that scholar-specialist without affirming or rejecting that scholar-specialist's reasoning (*ijtihād*) in support of that opinion (*taqlīd*). As Professor Weiss has suggested, this task is itself a type of *ijtihād*, but unlike the *mujtahid-muftī* who sought a probative opinion regarding a rule of conduct, the *mujtahid-muqallid* "was trying to arrive at a sound opinion as to who might be truly qualified to interpret the law for him."[5] This task, however, was complicated by the range of views expressed by *mujtahid-muftīs*, thus giving rise to the problem of how a *muqallid* could determine his ethical obligations in the face of divergent, even contradictory opinions of *muftīs*.[6]

In this chapter, I will survey the views and arguments of various pre-modern scholars of *uṣūl al-fiqh* on the ethical dilemma facing *muqallids* as a result of the ethical pluralism generated by *uṣūl al-fiqh*'s individualist ethical paradigm. I will begin with a general discussion of the epistemological context (or the domain) in which *taqlīd* is operative and its relationship to moral obligation. I will then take up the different views expressed on the question of how the ethical obligation of an individual is to be determined in a context of moral controversy. I will then argue that the pre-modern solutions to this problem, because of their focus on epistemology, are highly unsatisfactory. I instead suggest that a better way to understand *taqlīd* is as a relationship of trust in which an otherwise autonomous individual gives up aspects of his own autonomy for rational self-regarding reasons, but only because that other is morally worthy of receiving that trust. On the account of *taqlīd* I propose, the *muqallid* plays a central role in maintaining the integrity of Islamic law by monitoring would-be *mujtahids* to ensure that they conform to Islamic ethical ideals.

A. INDIVIDUAL OBLIGATIONS AND THE DOMAIN OF *TAQLĪD*

Islamic theology and ethics adopted an epistemological approach rooted in theoretical reason's ability to discover the truth of God's commands (the basis of moral obligations according to the Ashʿarīs), or the ethical [107] content of good and evil (the basis of moral obligations according to the Muʿtazilīs) in contrast, for example, to a Kantian approach

4. See, e.g., al-Faḍālī, *Kifāyat al-ʿawāmm min ʿilm al-kalām*, trans. Duncan b. Macdonald in *Development of Muslim theology, Jurisprudence, and Constitutional History* (Unit Printing House, Lahore: 1964) 323–324.

5. Bernard Weiss, *The Spirit of Islamic Law* 128 (University of Georgia Press, Athens: 1998).

6. Id. at 129.

to ethics which is grounded in the practical reason of autonomous persons.[7] Indeed, al-Ghāzalī goes so far as to say that a *mujtahid* can commit sin only in those areas where it is possible to attain epistemological certainty.[8] The theological propositions to which one must subscribe are claimed to be rational and therefore individuals may know them to be true, in the same manner they can know other rational propositions, e.g. that an object cannot be in two places at once, or that parallel lines never meet, are also true. Accordingly, despite the fact that theologians oblige non-*mujtahids* to follow the legal opinions of *mujtahids* in matters of substantive law (*furūᶜ*), they prohibit *taqlīd* with respect to theological dogma, *uṣūl al-dīn*.[9] This seems to suggest that all Muslims must be *mutakallimūn*, and indeed, the theologian al-Faḍālī states that theology must be the first object of study, for without an understanding of this subject, one could not even make a judgment as to whether one's prayers were valid.[10]

But is it really the case that all Muslims must become *mutakallimūn* in order for their faith to be valid? It turns out that for many, if not most theologians, the answer is clearly not: it is sufficient if a person has a general proof (*ijmālī*) as to the truth of Islamic dogma, rather than the detailed (*tafṣīlī*) proofs of *kalām*. This distinction was popular for at least two reasons: first, it answered the palpable skepticism that was expressed by opponents of *kalām* when theologians claimed that rational understanding of the Islamic creed was a condition for the validity of faith; and second, it also provided a counter to dissidents within the theological tradition, e.g. the Baghdadi Muᶜtazilites, who rejected *taqlīd* in its entirety, whether in theology or in law.[11]

For opponents of *kalām*, the claim that rational proof was required for faith to be valid was not only contrary to the experience of the Muslim community, it was also absurd on its face, insofar as it inevitably led to [108] the conclusion that the vast majority of professing Muslims—given the undeniable fact that most Muslims did not understand theological argument and probably never could—were in fact unbelievers.[12] The notion

7. For an introduction to Kantian ethics, see J.B. Schneewind, "Autonomy, Obligation, and Virtue: An Overview of Kant's Moral Philosophy," in *The Cambridge Companion to Kant*, ed. by Paul Geyer (Cambridge University Press: New York, 1992), 309–341.

8. Al-Ghazālī, *supra* n. 1 at 347–348.

9. For a summary of various theologians' views on the necessity of individuals' holding a rational belief in God, see Fadel, *supra* n. 2 at 31–33 (2008).

10. Al-Faḍālī, *supra* n. 4 at 327.

11. See, e.g., Abū al- Ḥusayn Muḥammad b. ᶜAlī al-Baṣrī, 2 *al-Muᶜtamad fi uṣūl al-fiqh* 360 (Dar al-kutub al-ᶜilmiyya, Beirut: 1983) and Sayf al-Dīn ᶜAlī b. Abī ᶜAlī al-Āmidī, 4 *al-Iḥkām fi uṣūl al-aḥkām* 306 (Beirut, Dar al-kutub al-ᶜilmiyya: 1983).

12. Indeed, during the Saljuk era, this led to the scandalous issue known as *takfīr al-ᶜawāmm*, which was used to discredit Ashᶜarī theologians before the Saljuk sultans. See Wilferd Madelung, "The Spread of Maturidism and the Turks," in *Actas IV Congresso de estudos árabes e islāmicos* 109, 129 n. 52 (describing persecution of Ashᶜarites by Tughrulbeg as a consequence, in part, of the Ashᶜarī doctrine of *takfīr al-ᶜawāmm*) (1968).

of a general proof responded to both of these objections: while it was no doubt true that the early community did not develop sophisticated theological proofs of God's unity, for example, there was ample evidence that they had general proofs for the existence of God, and that even the rude Bedouin were capable of apprehending such proofs.[13]

The notion of a general proof also answered the Baghdadi Muᶜtazilites who criticized the doctrine of *taqlīd* in substantive law as being inconsistent with the notion that knowledge was required in theological matters: a prohibition of *taqlīd* in matters of substantive law is tantamount to one of two things, either *muqallids* are not subject to moral obligation, or *muqallids* are obliged to undertake *ijtihād* when faced with a situation not covered by an express rule. While all agree that *muqallids* are subject to moral obligation even when there is no express text of revelation, nonetheless forcing *muqallids* to become *mujtahids* would be absurd because it would lead to the end of civilization—all productive activities would grind to a halt because people would become preoccupied with learning the tools of *ijtihād* rather than, for example, cultivating the soil. Theological matters, however, are relatively easy to grasp, because they are rational propositions, especially if all that is needed is a general proof. Accordingly, for the Basran Muᶜtazilites and the Ashᶜarites generally, it appears that *taqlīd* in matters of substantive law is akin to a special dispensation—a kind of *rukhṣa*—that is necessitated by the deleterious consequences to collective human life should everyone attempt to be a *mujtahid* in matters of substantive law.

The distinction between a general proof—which is assumed to be within the reasonable grasp of all rational individuals—and the detailed proofs of theology does not solve the problem, however, so much as dissolve it. Fakhr al-Dīn al-Rāzī criticized this distinction as meaningless because it misconstrues the nature of a proof: a proof must include only those propositions that are necessary to demonstrate the truth of the [109] proposition being asserted. If, in the course of the proof, a proposition is added, or is deleted, or is accepted without proof, the proof is not a simplified version of the "real" proof: it is simply no longer a proof and can only be accepted on the basis of *taqlīd*.[14] And in fact, this is the case of general proofs in al-Rāzī's opinion: they are insufficient to save the generality of Muslims from the charge that their religious faith is simply the result of opinion and not based on knowledge.[15]

Al-Rāzī also pointed out that the conventional anti-*ijtihād* argument used by both the Basran Muᶜtazilites and the Ashᶜarites to refute the Baghdadi Muᶜtazilites—that it is

13. Fadel, *supra* n. 2 at 33 (quoting al-Jurjānī's *Sharḥ al-mawāqif* for the proposition that the early Muslim community, including the Bedouin, had general proofs of divine unity).

14. Fakhr al-Dīn al-Rāzī, 2 *al-Maḥṣūl fī ᶜilm uṣūl al-fiqh* (Dar al-kutub al-ᶜilmiyya, Beirut: 1988) 529–530.

15. In an apparent criticism of al-Ghazālī, al-Rāzī rejected the argument put forth by al-Ghazālī that knowledge of the truth of the Prophet—by virtue of his miracles—is sufficient to absolve a Muslim of the charge of *taqlīd*. According to al-Rāzī, knowledge of the Prophet's miracles does not necessitate by itself that Muḥammad was a prophet who was truthful in his claims unless a host of other propositions are also demonstrated to be true. Id. at 530–531.

a social impossibility for everyone to be a *mujtahid*—is only true if one accepts other controversial epistemological premises, specifically, the obligation to act in accordance with the requirements of solitary reports (*khabar al-wāḥid*) and analogy (*qiyās*). Otherwise, if one rejects the authority of solitary traditions and analogy, ethical reasoning would not require years of specialized training because in areas of life where revelation is either silent or ambiguous, individuals would be left to the judgment of reason, which is accessible to all without great effort, and in cases where an individual is unable to discern what reason requires, it would be a relatively simple matter for the *mujtahid* to point out to the *muqallid* what the rational principles governing the issue are.[16]

Given Islamic theology's epistemological preference for knowledge, and its general condemnation of *taqlīd*, it is unsurprising that the obligation to perform *taqlīd* was somewhat of an embarrassment. All things being equal, a *mujtahid* could not, for example, rely on the conclusions of another *mujtahid*, but instead had to engage in his own *ijtihād* when faced with an issue that he had heretofore not considered. Indeed, it was a controversial matter as to whether a *mujtahid*, having once pondered a question of law, was then required to reconsider his earlier reasoning if the issue came up later or whether he could simply rely on his previous [110] reasoning.[17] There was no general agreement on this point, however. Al-Qarāfī, for example, argued that the passage of time is relevant to the reasoning of a *mujtahid*—presumably because of new learning and new experience—and accordingly, in most cases, it would be erroneous to assume that the *mujtahid* would give the same opinion at the end of his life that he gave in its beginning, as evidenced by the multiple opinions attributed to the historical *mujtahids*. Accordingly, a *mujtahid* is obliged to reconsider issues even when he recalls his original analysis of the question.[18]

The disrepute of *taqlīd* also led to a line of argument that denied that the obligation of a *muqallid* to defer to the judgment of a *mujtahid* counted as *taqlīd* at all. According to this argument, *taqlīd* is accepting the opinion of another without proof, but the kind of *taqlīd* that Sunnī theologians countenanced did not suffer from this defect: the legitimacy of the Sunnī institution of *taqlīd* was grounded in objective proof (or so it was claimed). This argument goes back at least as far as al-Ghazālī who stated that, unlike the *taqlīd* of the *ḥashwiyya* and the *Taʿlīmiyya*, his call for *muqallids* to adhere to the opinions of *mujtahids* is grounded in certain proof. Because it is not self-evident that the authority whom a person takes as a source of moral instruction is truthful, a rational person demands proof

16. Id. at 528–529.

17. See, for example, al-Qarāfī, *supra* n. 1 at pp. 4098–4099 (quoting Fakhr al-Dīn al-Rāzī as permitting a *mujtahid* to rely on his previous analysis of a legal issue only to the extent that he recalls his previous reasoning, but if he has forgotten his previous reasoning, he is obliged to reconsider the issue). See also, Bernard Weiss, *The Search for God's Law* (University of Utah Press: Salt Lake City, 1992) 723 (noting that al-Āmidī described this issue as controversial among *uṣūlīs*).

18. al-Qarāfī, *supra* n. 1 at p. 4101 (arguing in favor of an absolute obligation to engage in *ijtihād* each time the issue comes up, even when the *mujtahid* recalls his previous reasoning).

from such an authority that he is truthful before he would agree to defer to his teachings. In the case of the Prophet Muḥammad, that proof lies in the various miracles he wrought. Because we know that the Prophet Muḥammad is truthful, al-Ghazālī argued, we know that what he reports about God is also truthful. We also know that the consensus of the Muslim community is truthful because the Prophet informed us that the consensus of the Muslim community is immune from error. Accordingly, following the command of the consensus of the Muslim community does not constitute *taqlīd* because it is justified by our knowledge that consensus is an infallible source of moral truth.

[111] The institution of *taqlīd*, according to al-Ghazālī, can be analogized to judicial procedure which requires a judge to accept the testimony of upright witnesses, despite the possibility that they may be lying. In this case, the judge cannot be accused of having engaged in *taqlīd* because he is giving effect to a rule derived from consensus, and is thus acting on proof. The same principle applies to the *muqallid*: when he follows the opinion of the *mujtahid*, he is acting in accordance with the command of an infallible source, in this case, consensus. This infallible source obliges him to follow the opinion of the *mujtahid*, whether or not the *mujtahid* is truthful, just as consensus obliges the judge to rule in accordance with the testimony of upright witnesses despite the possibility that they may be lying. *Taqlīd*, on al-Ghazālī's account, is therefore a procedure for satisfying the ethical obligations of a *muqallid*; the legitimacy of this procedure is established with certainty, even if its results may be erroneous in particular circumstances. The Sunnī practice of *taqlīd* cannot, therefore, be compared to the *Taᶜlīmiyya*'s version of *taqlīd* because the latter cannot provide a rational justification for why individuals should submit to the teachings of their Imam.[19]

Taqlīd, therefore, for the Ashᶜarites and Basran Muᶜtazilites, was limited to rules of conduct (*fiqhiyyāt*) (provided of course that the issue was not covered by an express text, e.g. the prohibition of *khamr* (grape wine), or fornication). It did not apply to dogma or even the rational matters of *uṣūl al-fiqh* (*al-ᶜaqliyyāt*), such as whether a solitary tradition or analogy constitutes proofs of a divine rule, or whether every *mujtahid* is correct or only one. *Taqlīd* in matters of conduct was tolerable in part not only because of the epistemological uncertainty that characterized *ijtihād*, but also because, from a theological perspective, not much was at stake: while theological error involved blasphemy insofar as it entailed affirming statements about God that were false, controversies regarding matters of conduct all revolved around affirming or denying the positive commands or prohibitions of God, any of which, from a rational perspective, God might conceivably have decreed.[20] Because errors in rules of conduct do not carry the risk of blasphemy, there is no harm in deferring to the views of others. [112]

19. al-Ghazālī, *supra* n. 1 at 371.
20. al-Qarāfī, *supra* n. 118 at 4136.

B. *TAQLĪD* AND MORAL CONTROVERSY: THE *MUQALLID*'S VIEW

According to the *uṣūlīs*, the *muqallid* is as much a moral agent (*mukallaf*) as the *mujtahid*. Both are subject to the same obligation of having true knowledge of God. Both are required to affirm the truth of the prophets when confronted by evidence that they are truthful in their claims. Both are required to conform their conduct according to prophetic teachings to the extent such teachings are indisputable (the so-called *mā ʿulima min al-dīn bi-l-ḍarūra*).[21] Their obligations only differ when it comes to determining the scope of moral obligation for acts that are not subject to an express rule of revelation. When faced with such a circumstance, the *mujtahid* reasons to a rule using the texts of revelation as a basis for forming his rule. The *muqallid*, however, is subject to another duty: to find a *mujtahid* and ask him what to do.[22]

It is important to keep in mind that the obligation to perform *taqlīd* is contingent upon the inability of the *muqallid* to investigate the texts of revelation himself to arrive at an answer. More importantly, the *muqallid*, given his theological knowledge, knows that he is not in a position to resolve any ethical dilemmas that might arise as a result of events not subject to an express revelatory rule. He also knows that he could escape the obligation of *taqlīd* were he to devote himself to becoming a *mujtahid*. On the other hand, while he has no ethical obligation to become a *mujtahid*, he does have the choice to devote himself to learning and become a *mujtahid* or continue living a life unconnected with learning and scholarship. For a person uninterested in religious scholarship, then, *taqlīd* offers a practical solution to the general problem that ethical knowledge—other than the basic ethical obligations that are a necessary part of revelation—is specialized knowledge. *Taqlīd* seems to offer the *muqallid* the opportunity to have his cake and eat it too: the chance to live an ethical life without having to master the various obscure sciences required of a *mujtahid*.

But, if something is too good to be true, we may have reason to be skeptical. *Taqlīd* is no exception. Less dramatically, *taqlīd* is really only [113] helpful to a *muqallid* when he is lucky enough to know the views of only one *mujtahid*. In this case, his ethical life is greatly simplified: whenever he has a question, he simply asks the *mujtahid* and acts in conformity with what the *mujtahid* tells him.[23] But how does a *muqallid* know that someone is a *mujtahid*, i.e. possesses that combination of learning and moral integrity that permits

21. This follows simply from the fact that such rules are established with certainty so there is no room for disagreement with respect to such an obligation.

22. See, e.g., al-Āmidī, *supra* n. 11 at 275–276 (a *mujtahid* always engages in independent *ijtihād* when faced with a novel question) and at 299 (a *muqallid* is obliged to follow the opinion of a *mujtahid* with respect to matters of *ijtihād*); see also, al-Ghazālī, *supra* n. 1 at 368–369 (same with respect to the *mujtahid*) and at 362–363 (same with respect to the *muqallid*).

23. See, for example, Abū al-Walīd Sulaymān b. Khalaf al-Bājī, *Iḥkām al-fuṣūl fi aḥkām al-uṣūl*, ed. ʿAbdallāh Muḥammad al-Jabūrī (Muʾassasat al-risāla: Beirut, 1989) 644; al-Ghazālī, *supra* n. 1 at 373.

him to serve as a source of ethical knowledge for the *muqallid*? For most *uṣūlīs*, a *muqallid* can ascertain whether someone is a *mujtahid* by consideration of certain objective social facts. For example, if the person in question gives *fatwas* publicly, the public accepts him as an authority (as evidenced by the fact that they seek out his *fatwas*), the public generally accepts that person's *fatwas*, and no one challenges his credentials, then a *muqallid* in that case has a sufficient basis to believe that such person is in fact a *mujtahid*.[24]

If he comes to know about more than one *mujtahid*, his ethical life becomes more complicated, but only slightly: so long as he is ignorant of any disagreements between or among the *mujtahids* that he knows, he is free to question any of the *mujtahids* he knows for advice.[25] When the *muqallid* comes to know that *mujtahids* disagree, however, matters become complex. The solution to this problem, moreover, does not turn on one's stand with respect to the fallibility of *mujtahids*: in the absence of an institutional mechanism whereby one of the many proposed solutions to an ethical problem could be declared to be correct and the others mistaken, the fact that one *mujtahid* is correct and the others are mistaken is irrelevant from the perspective of a *muqallid*. Because Islamic ethical theory does not provide an objective perspective from which anyone (whether a *mujtahid* or *muqallid*) could conclude which of the competing opinions is the one that ought to be implemented, all opinions of *mujtahids* from the perspective of the *muqallid* seem to have a *prima facie* claim to validity. In short, when faced with ethical controversy, it is not at all clear what the *muqallid* should do, or even whether it makes sense to speak of the *muqallid* in this context as having an ethical obligation at all.[26]

[114] Disagreement among *mujtahids* creates numerous potential ethical problems for the *uṣūlī* tradition.[27] To be clear, this uncertainty also had the potential to undermine the efficacy and integrity of the entire legal system derived from Islamic jurisprudence.[28] As I have argued elsewhere, the institutionalization of *taqlīd* in courts and public-*fatwa* giving served to mitigate substantially the political problems arising out of indeterminacy.[29] Here, however, I wish to focus on another problem: the ethical obligations of the *muqallid* when faced with conflicting opinions of *mujtahids*, and whether the *uṣūlīs* proposed a workable solution for a *muqallid* who is assumed to be acting with moral integrity (*ʿadl*).

---

24. See, e.g., al-Baṣrī, *supra* n. 11 at 363; Abū Isḥāq Ibrāhīm b. Musā al-Shāṭibī, 4 *al-Muwāfaqāt fī uṣūl al-Sharīʿa* 262 (Dār al-maʿrifa, Beirut: n.d.); al-Āmidī, *supra* n. 11 at 311.

25. See, e.g., al-Ghazālī, *supra* n. 1 at 373; 4 al-Shāṭibī, *supra* n. 24 at 132–133.

26. See *infra* n. 41.

27. For a summary of these problems, see Zysow, *supra* n. 1 at 479–483.

28. See, e.g., al-Shāṭibī, *supra* n. 24 at 135–136 (discussing the deleterious impact of *takhyīr* upon the integrity of the legal system).

29. See Mohammad Fadel, "The Social Logic of Taqlīd and the Rise of the Mukhtaṣar," 3,2 *Islamic Law & Society* 193 (1996).

Looming large in the discussions of the *uṣūlīs* was whether an irresolvable dispute among *mujtahids* meant that the *muqallid* was free to choose among any of the positions advanced by a qualified *mujtahid*, a position known as *takhyīr*. It would be tempting to suppose that those who advocated *takhyīr* also endorsed the doctrine of the infallibility of *mujtahids* with regard to their moral reasoning. While this was the case for the infallibilist Abū Bakr al-Bāqillānī,[30] not all *uṣūlīs*' views on *takhyīr* were derivative of their position on infallibilism. Some *uṣūlīs* who endorsed infallibilism, al-Ghazālī, for example, nevertheless rejected *takhyīr* in favor of imposing an obligation on the *muqallid* to engage in a process of *tarjīḥ*, weighing the competing opinions, although as we shall see below, no jurist who advocated *tarjīḥ* suggested that *muqallids* could weigh the substantive merits of the different views expressed.[31] Likewise, some *uṣūlīs* who rejected infallibilism, al-Āmidī, for example, nevertheless endorsed *takhyīr*,[32] albeit on the grounds of consensus rather than rational ones.[33]

[115] Despite the association of infallibilism with subjectivism, and fallibilism with objectivism,[34] jurists such as al-Ghazālī and al-Shāṭibī, despite their differences on fallibilism,[35] each endorsed an obligation of *tarjīḥ* for *muqallids* in controversial matters rather than *takhyīr* because of what was, essentially, a subjectivist view of moral obligation. The advocates of *takhyīr*, for example al-Qarāfī and al-ʿIzz b. ʿAbdassalām, by contrast, took an ethical position that was indifferent to the subjective views of the *muqallid*; accordingly, they judged the conduct of that person solely from the objective perspective of whether it conformed to a valid opinion of any *mujtahid*.[36] For al-Ghazālī and al-Shāṭibī, *takhyīr* was immoral precisely because it was indifferent to the subjective motivation of the individual *muqallid*. This indifference subverted what to them was one of the highest purposes of revelation: to subject human beings to law. *Takhyīr* was inconsistent with this goal because it functioned as a *de facto* means of broadening the category of the permissible to all things that were in dispute among the jurists. Al-Shāṭibī, for example, com-

30. Zysow, *supra* n. 1 at 464.

31. Al-Ghazālī, *supra* n. 1 at 352 (endorsing infallibilism) and at 374 (rejecting the doctrine of *takhyīr*).

32. Al-Āmidī, *supra* n. 11 at 247 (rejecting infallibilism) and at 318 (endorsing *takhyīr*); Weiss, *Search*, supra n. 17 at 728.

33. Id. at 318 (stating that but for the consensus of the companions on this point, the position rejecting *takhyīr* would be the better argument). The Mālikī jurist al-Bājī shared al-Āmidī's views, endorsing *takhyīr* on historical grounds even as he rejected infallibilism. al-Bājī, *supra* n. 23 at 623 (rejecting infallibilism) and at 644–645 (endorsing *takhyīr*).

34. See Zysow, *supra* n. 1 at 466–467 ("fallibilism in its various versions holds that the result of *ijtihād* can be tested against an objective measure.") and at 469 ("essentially, infallibilism is a doctrine of solipsism.").

35. Al-Shāṭibī, *supra* n. 24 at 118–131.

36. Al-Qarāfī, *supra* n. 1 at 4134 (quoting with approval Ibn ʿAbdassalām's position that it was permissible to follow any opinion so long as it was a valid rule, meaning, were a judge to rule on the basis of that rule, his ruling would not be overturned).

plained that jurists of his time had gone so far as to take the existence of a controversy among jurists as evidence that the conduct at issue was morally indifferent (*ibāḥa*).[37]

In making his case, al-Shāṭibī argued that there was a categorical difference, on the one hand, between the right of a *muqallid* to follow the view of one among the many *mujtahids* he happened upon without ascertaining which was the most qualified, and on the other hand, arbitrarily following one among the many opinions expressed by various *mujtahids* after the *muqallid* became aware of their disagreement.[38] The failure to distinguish these two scenarios led many to make the erroneous analogy between the practice of the early Muslim community—which allowed *muqallids* to ask the opinion of any of the companions who were *mujtahids* without requiring them to identify which of them was the most reliable in his reasoning—and the practice of *takhyīr* which gives the *muqallid* the right to choose arbitrarily among the various *mujtahids*' opinions.

[116] The reason these two scenarios are different is that in the first case—where the *muqallid* is ignorant of the controversy—he is giving effect to the reasoning of the *mujtahid*, and by hypothesis, the *mujtahid* has engaged in a good faith effort to understand what God wants in this particular situation. Accordingly, the *muqallid* is acting in concert with some good faith understanding of God's will. In the second case—where the *muqallid* is given the freedom to choose which opinion he will follow—the *muqallid* is not giving effect to the relevant revelatory text which the *mujtahid* had relied upon, but is rather giving effect simply to his own ends. As a consequence, he is acting out of desire (*hawā*) rather than in compliance with the teachings of revelation. *Takhyīr* in al-Shāṭibī's view severs the nexus between subjective apprehension of probability born out of good faith interpretation of revelation and moral obligation, and therefore subverts one of the primary goals of revelation: to replace desire as the motive for human behavior with obedience to God.[39]

While al-Ghazālī suggests a weak epistemological argument in favor of *tarjīḥ* (that there is a chance that a *mujtahid* made an error by failing to identify an express text that applies to the case), his primary objection to *takhyīr* is ethical, not epistemological. Like al-Shāṭibī, he complained that *takhyīr* has the effect of relieving *muqallids* of the burdens of moral obligation. Indeed, he identified the asymmetry between the ethical obligations of the *mujtahid*—who is subject to a categorical obligation to exercise his judgment in matters for which there is no express revelatory text and to follow his probable judgment that results from the exercise of that duty in virtually all cases—and the obligations of the *muqallid* under a rule of *takhyīr*—in which the requirement of having a probable judgment is abandoned—as being fatal to *takhyīr*. The principle of *takhyīr*, moreover, contains within it the threat that it would subvert the need for *ijtihād*: in all cases where there is

37. Al-Shāṭibī, *supra* n. 24 at 141. 38.
38. Id. at 132–133.
39. Id. at 132–135.

no explicit revelatory text, a *mujtahid* could conclude that he can do whatever he wants because whatever he chooses will conform with the view of one *mujtahid*, and therefore will be permissible. In short, *takhyīr* not only freed the vast majority of Muslims from firm ethical obligations, it also had the potential to subvert the incentives of *mujtahids* and thereby threaten the continuing viability of the activity of *ijtihād* itself.[40]

[117] That the advocates of *tarjīḥ* were more concerned with the moral integrity of the individual Muslim, whether a *mujtahid* or a *muqallid*, than the objective coherence of the ethical system, is evidenced by their discussion of what happens when it is impossible for a *muqallid* to determine which of the competing *mujtahids*' views is weightier. In theory, the *muqallid* was to treat the different opinions of the *mujtahids* in the same manner a *mujtahid* would treat conflicting texts of revelation. While a *mujtahid* would apply substantive criteria to determine which text ought to be given greater weight in such a circumstance, the task of the *muqallid* was limited to determine which *mujtahid* was more virtuous, virtue being measured along an index of two variables: piety and learning. Accordingly, the *muqallid* should adopt the opinion of that *mujtahid* whom he believes to be the most learned and most pious. The numerous possible combinations of piety and learning, and whether piety is weightier than learning, are not important in this context except to the extent that they reveal the difficulty of discharging such a task. Nevertheless, the point for those *uṣūlī*s who demanded *tarjīḥ* was that the *muqallid* make this attempt, and if he reaches a conclusion, then he is bound to accept the opinions of that *mujtahid* without engaging in "*fatwa*-shopping." If, however, after having engaged in this process, he is unable to reach a probable judgment regarding which *mujtahid* is more virtuous, he is relieved of moral obligation with respect to that particular issue, at least with respect to God, *in toto*.[41]

Al-Qarāfī, and his teacher al-Izz b. ʿAbdassalām, by contrast, are indifferent to the nexus between the conduct of the actor and the actor's subjective understanding of his action in light of revelation. Because of al-Qarāfī's commitment to the notion that legal obligation is tied to some benefit to the actor (*maṣlaḥa*), he rejected the argument that imposition of *taklīf*—simply for the sake of imposing obligation—was a goal of revelation. Indeed, he dismissed this argument on the grounds that it imposed hardship (*mashaqqa*) upon individuals simply for the purpose of hardship [118] rather than furthering their

40. Al-Ghazālī, *supra* n. 1 at 373–374.

41. Al-Shāṭibī, *supra* n. 24 at 291 (stating that where a *muqallid* is unable to know what his obligation is, the *muqallid* is in a position akin to that which exists prior to the advent of revelation and were the *muqallid* to be subject to some obligation in such circumstances, it would be impossible for him to discharge it); Abū al-Maʿālī ʿAbdalmalik b. ʿAbdallāh al-Juwaynī, 2 *al-Burhān fī uṣūl al-fiqh* 884 (stating that when a *muqallid* cannot determine which *mujtahid* is more virtuous, he is like someone on a deserted island who only knows the foundations of Islam, and accordingly, has no obligations toward God with respect to that issue). Al-Ghazālī, however, in this circumstance permitted *takhyīr*. Al-Ghazālī, *supra* n. 1 at 16.

own good, a principle that he believed the Sharīʿa denied. Accordingly, al-Qarāfī understood ethical controversy as creating a kind of "freedom for the actor (*tawsiʿa ʿalā al-mukallaf*)." Al-Qarāfī limited this qualified ethical freedom in two respects: first, the *muqallid* must not choose among the various *mujtahids*' positions in such a manner as would produce a violation of consensus; and second, he must not follow an opinion which, if it were the basis of a judicial ruling, could be overturned by a subsequent judge (a "pseudo-rule").[42] Both of these limitations, moreover, are objective, meaning they do not depend upon the *muqallid*'s subjective appreciation that he violated consensus or acted on the basis of a pseudo-rule.

Al-Qarāfī gave the following example (apparently from his own experience) of how the first limitation could become relevant. A follower of al-Shāfiʿī asked him whether it would be permissible for him to follow Mālik's view regarding the purity of clothes stitched with pig hair. Al-Qarāfī replied in the affirmative, but cautioned that if the questioner intended to follow Mālik's view on the purity of his garment as opposed to the rule of al-Shāfiʿī, then he had to take care to follow Mālik's views on the requirements of valid ablutions, paying particular attention to those rules in which Mālik differed from al-Shāfiʿī. Accordingly, if the Shāfiʿī followed Mālik regarding the purity of his garment, but followed al-Shāfiʿī with respect to the permissibility of rubbing only a portion of the head during ablutions, both Imām Mālik and Imām al-Shāfiʿī would declare that man's prayer to be invalid. Thus, *takhyīr* poses a risk to the *muqallid* that following the doctrine of one school does not: inadvertently nullifying the validity of one's acts of devotion, and for that reason, al-Qarāfī suggested to his Shāfiʿī questioner that he might be better off sticking to the teachings of his own school.[43]

As for the second limitation on *takhyīr*, a pseudo-rule is one that is contrary to consensus (*ijmāʿ*), a legal principle (*al-qawāʿid*), an explicit text (*al-naṣṣ alladhī lā yaḥtamil al-taʾwīl*) or an a fortiori analogy (*al-qiyās al-jalī*). An example of such a pseudo-rule is the Ḥanafī rule giving neighbors a right of first refusal (*shufʿat al-jiwār*) in connection with the sale of adjoining real property. Because a judge who ruled in accordance with that rule would have his ruling overturned (at least according to the Mālikīs), *a fortiori* it is impermissible for a *muqallid* to act upon that rule [119] in his private life.[44] Other than these two objective limitations, however, al-Qarāfī is unconcerned about the consequences of *takhyīr* on the moral life of *muqallids*. In fact, he denied that it is impermissible for *muqallids* to seek out, consciously, the dispensations (*rukhaṣ*) of the various *mujtahids*, on the condition that in so doing the *muqallid* takes care not to violate consensus or follow a pseudo-rule.[45] Unlike al-Ghazālī and al-Shāṭibī, who viewed imposing moral obligation

42. Al-Qarāfī, *supra* n. 18 at 4148. 43 Id. at 4149.
43. Id. at 4149.
44. Id. at 4148.
45. Id. at 4149.

on human beings as one of the most important functions of revelation, al-Qarāfī denied that revelation came simply to impose obligations on people willy-nilly; rather, he understood the purpose of revelation as being to assist individuals to achieve various beneficial ends.[46] Unlike al-Ghazālī and al-Shāṭibī, then, al-Qarāfī's strand of soft infallibilism, combined with *takhyīr*, operated to produce an objective method by which a *muqallid*, presumably in consultation with a scholar, could know whether his conduct was consistent with the demands of Islamic normativity. This objective account of the *muqallid*'s ethical obligations, however, resulted in a fundamentally different standard of behavior for a *muqallid* relative to a *mujtahid*: while the latter was obligated to conduct his life in accordance with his understanding of revelatory evidence (*al-adilla al-sharʿiyya*), the *muqallid* was free to pursue the ends of his life without considering the implications of revelatory evidence, directly or indirectly, except insofar as they produced incontrovertible rules.

C. TRUST AND AUTONOMY

The *mujtahid*, at least with respect to those areas of life which are unregulated by an express revelatory norm, appears to be a law unto himself: answerable only to God, his ethical life is governed only by universal norms that are either true in themselves, i.e. such rules that constitute the *maʿlūm min al-dīn bi-l-ḍarūra*, or particular rules that he has formulated for himself based on his considered opinion using the interpretive techniques of *uṣūl al-fiqh*. The *muqallid*'s ethical life, as we saw from the previous section, is more (e.g. under al-Ghazālī's or al-Shāṭibī's reasoning) or less (e.g. under al-Qarāfī's or Ibn ʿAbdassalām's reasoning) derivative of [120] the *mujtahid*'s ethical reasoning. The *muqallid* does not, as discussed previously, defer to the *mujtahid* because he lacks the capacity for independent moral reasoning. Presumably, he chooses to be a *muqallid* because, given the various options available to him in his life, he would rather spend his time doing something, e.g. farming or trading, other than becoming a theological/ethical/legal specialist, a task that could very well be quite burdensome.[47]

To choose the option of *taqlīd*, however, a *muqallid* must have some basis on which he can distinguish a genuine *mujtahid* from a mere pretender. In other words, a *muqallid* must have a basis to trust the judgment of the would-be *mujtahid*. In this context the term trust is probably a more accurate translation of the term *ẓann* than probable belief, despite the fact that the *uṣūlī*s claim that the *muqallid* is responsible to confirm that he has a reasonable belief that the person whom he is asking for a *fatwa* is in fact a qualified *mujtahid*. *Ẓann*, of course, is literally different from trust insofar as it denotes a particular

46. Id. (*al-sharīʿa lam tarid li-maqṣid ilzām al-ʿibād al-mashāqq bal bi-taḥṣīl al-maṣāliḥ al-khāṣṣa* [sic: read *al-khāliṣa*] *aw al-rājiḥa*).

47. For a discussion of the topics someone must master in order to qualify as a *mujtahid*, see, e.g., al-Ghazālī, *supra* n. 1 at 242–244 (noting in particular the difficulties of mastering knowledge of the *sunna*).

subjective state of mind that entails the belief that A, for example, is more likely to be true than B.

Trust, as some contemporary moral philosophers have argued, cannot be reduced simply to a determination that some particular fact has a more likely existence than not. It involves a relationship between one party, A, and another party, B, in which A reaches some subjective assessment as to the likelihood that B will act in a certain way, but in circumstances where A cannot directly observe B's conduct. In addition, in a relationship of trust the manner by which B conducts himself will have an important effect on A.[48] There is also an important asymmetry in trust: "it cannot be given except by those who have only limited knowledge, and usually even less control, over those to whom it is given,"[49] and while there may be an accounting of sorts, the accounting is usually deferred sometime into the future.[50] Trust also connotes something different than merely obeying commands; instead, it is "to take instruction or counsel, to take advice, to be patient and defer satisfying one's reasonable desire to understand what is going on, to learn some valuable discipline, or to conform to authoritative laws which others have made."[51] As a consequence, a trust [121] relationship can be viewed as an investment by A whose returns, if successful, will increase with time, thus benefitting A, but if B turns out to be untrustworthy, the relationship will prove detrimental to A. Trust accordingly always involves risk to A that B will abuse the relationship to A's loss.[52]

In my view, the relationship of the *muqallid* to the *mujtahid* is better understood as a relationship of trust rather than one of epistemological dependence. Weiss has suggested that the enterprise of *ijtihād* is, in an important sense, a cooperative relationship, at least in the sense that the *mujtahid* depends upon a steady stream of questions from *muqallids* to provide him with the opportunity to develop legal rules.[53] I would suggest, however, that the cooperative nature of the enterprise of *ijtihād*, and hence the development of Islamic ethics and law through the interpretation of revelation, requires a much thicker notion of cooperation and trust than that which would be required if the only function

48. Annette Baier, "Trusting People," 6 *Philosophical Perspectives, Ethics* 137–153, 138.

49. Id. at 139.

50. Id. at 140.

51. Id. at 144.

52. Id. at 147. Note that one might raise the objection that the relationship between the *mujtahid* and the *muqallid* does not need trust because the *muqallid* does not suffer any moral injury if he mistakenly, but in good faith, relies on someone who is not a genuine *mujtahid*, or if the *mujtahid* fails to carry out his duty in investigating the *muqallid*'s question. Even though the *muqallid* does not bear the risk of sin arising out of misplaced trust, he does face the risk that he will suffer worldly injury in terms of regret with respect to choices made vis-à-vis others. In certain cases, he might also suffer a tangible economic loss if he relies on the advice of an incompetent *mujtahid*. The profitable side of the ledger is easier to grasp: the *muqallid* is able to obtain valid opinions on God's law if he successfully identifies a *mujtahid*.

53. Weiss, *supra* n. 5 at 128.

of the *muqallid* were to provide the questions necessary for the development of the *mujtahid*'s thought. Indeed, such a conception of the rôle of the *muqallid* reduces him to a mere instrument of the *mujtahid*: the *muqallid* would be at once the occasion for the development of the law and its object, but would have no role whatsoever in its development.

If the *muqallid-mujtahid* relationship were understood to be a relationship of trust, on the other hand, it may be the case that the *muqallid* necessarily would play a more active role in the development of Islamic law than that accorded to them by *uṣūlīs*. This is especially so for *uṣūlīs* such as al-Ghazālī, al-Shāṭibī and al-Juwaynī who reject *takhyīr* in favor of *tarjīḥ*. *Tarjīḥ* is only possible on the assumption that *muqalllids* are responsible to choose their moral advisors carefully, by monitoring their objective characteristics—such as learning and (outward) piety—to confirm that they are persons of moral integrity. Indeed, even for those *uṣūlīs* who accept *takhyīr*—whether with diffidence in the example of al-Āmidī, [122] or embrace it in the example of al-Qarāfī—the concept of the moral integrity (*ʿadāla*) of the *mujtahid* is central to the functioning of the system.[54]

The judgment that a particular person possesses moral integrity, of course, is an ongoing one: unlike a judicial determination ruling that the property in dispute belongs to A and not B, a judgment of moral integrity is always provisional and thus is always subject to revision based on future experience. The responsibility to monitor prospective *mujtahids*' moral integrity is a burden that falls on everyone, not simply *mujtahids*. Tellingly, virtually all of the *uṣūlīs* surveyed for this essay agree that a *muqallid* can rely on the collective judgment of his contemporaries regarding the moral credibility of a prospective *mujtahid* as evidenced by the fact that this person is in fact engaged in public *fatwa*-giving without censure. While these authors did not explain why this is sufficient evidence, one could justify this assumption if one believes that individual members of society have had sufficiently lengthy and ethically significant interactions with that figure to have allowed them to conclude, independently of one another, that he is a person of moral integrity. Here, the logic of *tawātur* seems to be implicit in the justification of this kind of evidence for moral integrity. In the absence of an assumption of active independent monitoring by large numbers of persons of those who publicly give *fatwas*, the right to rely on such a fact could not justify a *muqallid* placing his trust in that person.

Indeed, the one dissenter on this point—al-Juwaynī—confirms the argument developed here that the *mujtahid-muqallid* relationship is one of trust rather than knowledge. For al-Juwaynī, collective judgments regarding the qualifications of a person who engages in public *fatwa*-giving cannot justify a *muqallid*'s conclusion that such a person is in fact a *mujtahid*. Al-Juwaynī denied the probative force of this collective report on the grounds that the determination of whether a person is, or is not, a *mujtahid*—and hence

54. Moral integrity, while not strictly speaking a condition of *ijtihād*, is a condition for the validity of a *fatwa*. see, e.g., al-Ghazālī, *supra* n. 1 at 342.

qualified to give *fatwas*—cannot be resolved by reputation evidence, no matter the number of witnesses.

But, al-Juwaynī's solution to this problem is even more radical in exposing the trust that is at the core of this relationship: he proposed that the only way for a *muqallid* to reach a probative judgment as to whether someone is a *mujtahid* is simply to ask the would-be *mujtahid*.

[123] Al-Juwaynī's argument cuts to the heart of the matter: we have no way of knowing that a person is in fact a *mujtahid* because the most critical element of the vocation—moral integrity—is not amenable to outside verification, but is only something that can be discovered over time. At the beginning of the relationship, all a *muqallid* can do is ask, and hope that the person answering is trustworthy. At its beginning, however, the *muqallid* would lack any basis upon which he could objectively justify his relationship with the *mujtahid* at issue. It is only over time, as a result of repeated interactions between him and the *mujtahid* (and perhaps other encounters between other *muqallid*s known to him and that *mujtahid* as well) that the *muqallid* can determine whether the trust he had reposed in the *mujtahid* was justifiable. Given this, asking seems like an obvious way to begin.

But, does the *uṣūlī* discourse on the *muqallid* justify the belief that a *muqallid* is in a position to engage in the monitoring activity that is arguably necessary in order to generate the trust required for the relationship between *mujtahid*s and *muqallid*s to succeed? Indeed, one of the principal objections to the *tarjīḥ* position was that *muqallid*s are incapable of determining which *mujtahid* is "the more learned and the more pious" with any competence. Indeed, one could take as further evidence of *muqallid*s' incompetence the fact that advocates of *tarjīḥ* refused to permit *muqallid*s to engage in *tarjīḥ* based on the substance of the different opinions. Al-Ghazālī and al-Rāzī, for example, dismiss the possibility that *muqallid*s could engage in substantive *tarjīḥ* on the grounds that it would constitute moral negligence: just as a parent would be held negligent and liable if he medicated his sick child using his own judgment, even after consulting with doctors, so too a *muqallid* would be negligent and morally culpable if he took it upon himself to judge which of the two contradictory positions is substantively stronger.[55] In both cases, he simply lacks the competency to engage in the judgment. Al-Juwaynī was even more blunt in rejecting this possibility, which he described as "giving reign to intuition and idiocy (*ittibāʿ al-hawājis wa al-ḥamāqāt*).[56]

Al-Shāṭibī, unlike al-Juwaynī, al-Ghazālī and al-Rāzī, did not even raise the possibility of the *muqallid* engaging in his own substantive *tarjīḥ*. While he accepted the notion of *tarjīḥ* based on piety and learning—which al-Shāṭibī called referred to as "general weighing (*tarjīḥ ʿāmm*)"—he [124] introduced another technique for giving precedence to one

55. Al-Ghazālī, *supra* n. 1 at 374; al-Rāzī, *supra* n. 14 at 534.
56. Al-Juwaynī, *supra* n. 41 at 883.

mujtahid over another which he called "particular weighing (*tarjīḥ khāṣṣ*)." This method of selection explicitly incorporates the notion of the *mujtahid* as a moral exemplar, someone whose life—and not just his learning or outward piety—represents an outstanding model of moral excellence (*qudwa*). The most important feature of such a *mujtahid* is his moral integrity as evidenced by the consistency between his private actions and his public pronouncements.[57]

That *muqallids* are incompetent to judge the substantive reasoning of a *mujtahid* is somewhat of a puzzle, however, at least to the extent that *muqallids* are endowed with the attributes given to them in *uṣūl al-fiqh*. After all, the *uṣūlīs*' conception of *taqlīd* assumes that the *muqallid* has full rational capacity, something that allows him to recognize the theological and ethical truths of Islam. One might have expected that, given this reservoir of true theological and moral knowledge, *muqallids* might have a legitimate basis upon which they could evaluate the substance of different *fatwas*. Indeed, one of the hadiths included in al-Nawawī's popular 40 hadiths suggests that even the most ordinary individuals carry within them the capacity for moral discrimination between virtue and vice. According to that hadith, Wābiṣa, a companion of the Prophet Muḥammad asked him about righteousness (*al-birr*), to which the Prophet was said to have replied, saying: "ask the opinion of your soul! ask the opinion of your heart," repeating that three times. Then, the Prophet continued, saying: "Righteousness is that in which the soul and heart find tranquility and sin is that which pricks the soul and bounces back and forth in the breast, even though the people may you give opinions [to the contrary]."[58]

For al-Shāṭibī, and perhaps al-Ghazālī, the implicit answer seems to be that even if the *muqallid* has substantial theological and moral knowledge, when it comes to matters of moral controversy, he is too self-interested to behave morally: he will consistently choose that which pleases him and serves his interest (*hawā*) rather than engaging in an objective moral analysis of what God requires of him. It could therefore be argued that it is precisely because a *muqallid* has theological and ethical knowledge that he comes to be conscious of how his ethical decision making can be tainted by his self-interest, and therefore that he ought to defer to the [125] views of a trustworthy third-party, the *mujtahid*, who can judge the ethical consequences of the situation objectively. Accordingly, the fact that the moral knowledge of a *muqallid* is inoperative when it comes to his own conduct does not negate the fact that he is in fact a bearer of moral knowledge; it could be that it is the problematic element of self-interest that precludes him from relying on that self-knowledge in morally controversial matters. Conversely, he would be capable of serving as a monitor of *mujtahids* because in that case there would not be a conflict between judgment and desire. It is the *muqallid*'s capacity for disinterested moral judgment

57. Al-Shāṭibī, *supra* n. 24 at 270–271.

58. See ʿAbdarraḥmān b. Aḥmad Ibn Rajab, *Jāmiʿ al-ʿulūm wa-l-ḥikam* 272 (Dar al-jīl, Beirut: 1987).

that allows for the relationship of trust that is at the heart of the *mujtahid-muqallid* relationship to form and be sustained over time.

CONCLUSION

The relationship of epistemology to obligation in Islamic theology and ethics ultimately led to the recognition of a limited kind of moral pluralism. This fact in turn generated political as well as ethical problems. With respect to the problem of how to maintain a sense of ethical obligation in morally controversial areas of life, Sunnī Muslim theologians split into two camps, those advocating *takhyīr* and those advocating *tarjīḥ*. While both sides of this debate understood that *muqallids*' moral obligations in controversial areas were derived from *mujtahids*' reasoning, each camp had a fundamentally different view of what moral obligation entailed in the case of a *muqallid*. For at least some of those who advocated *takhyīr* like al-Qarāfī and his teacher al-ʿIzz b. ʿAbdassalām, moral obligation was objective: as long as a *mukallaf* did not violate the objective boundaries of Islamic ethical norms, his conduct was both legal and moral. For at least some of those who advocated *tarjīḥ*, moral obligation was much thicker: it required the *muqallid* to justify his conduct by reference to some revelatory source (*dalīl*). It was the role of the *mujtahid* to provide the nexus between a *mukallaf*'s conduct and revelation. For them, it ultimately did not matter what the conduct was, so much that it was grounded in a good faith interpretation of revelation. For either system to work, however, *muqallids* need to have sufficient moral judgment to identify trustworthy authorities. The theological tradition of *uṣūl al-fiqh* surveyed in this article, however, under-theorizes this problem by failing to explain how a *muqallid* may be able to identify trustworthy authorities. I suggest that the answer (if there is one) must lie in the notion that *muqallids* do in fact possess a robust—even if incomplete—set of moral data provided by [126] the moral truths of Islam which is sufficient to permit them to distinguish between genuine *mujtahids* and mere pretenders. A fully determined theory of *taqlīd* would require an explanation of how the moral truths in the possession of the *muqallid* enable him to process, critically, the performance of would-be *mujtahids* as a condition for the trust implicit in the relationship to arise. Such a theory, however, at least as far as I know, has yet to be developed.

BIBLIOGRAPHY

al-Āmidī, Sayf al-Dīn ʿAlī b. Abi ʿAlī. *al-Iḥkām fī uṣūl al-aḥkām*, 4 vols. (Beirut: Dār al-kutub al-ʿilmiyya: 1983).

Baier, Annette. "Trusting People." *Philosophical Perspectives* 6 (1992): 137–153.

al-Bājī, Abū al-Walīd Sulaymān b. Khalaf. *Iḥkām al-fuṣūl fī aḥkām al-uṣūl*. Ed. ʿAbdallāh Muḥammad al-Jabūrī. (Beirut: Muʾassassat al-risāla, 1989).

al-Baṣrī, Abū al-Ḥusayn Muḥammad b. ʿAlī. *al-Muʿtamad fī uṣūl al-fiqh*, 2 vols. Ed. Khalīl al-Mays. (Beirut: Dār al-kutub al-ʿilmiyya, 1983).

al-Faḍālī, Muḥammad b. Shāfiʿī. *Kifāyat al-ʿawāmm min ʿilm al-kalām*. Trans. Duncan B. Macdonald, in *Development of Muslim theology, Jurisprudence, and Constitutional Theory* (Lahore: Unit Printing House, 1964).

Fadel, Mohammad H. "The True, the Good and the Reasonable." *The Canadian Journal of law and Jurisprudence* 21, 1 (January 2008): 5–69.

——. "The Social Logic of *Taqlīd* and the Rise of the *Mukhtaṣar*." *Islamic Law and Society* 3, 2 (1996): 193–233.

al-Ghazālī, Abū Ḥāmid Muḥammad b. Muḥammad. *al-Mustaṣfā fī ʿilm al-uṣūl*. (Beirut: Dār al-kutub al-ʿilmiyya, 1993).

Ibn Rajab, ʿAbdarraḥmān b. Aḥmad. *Jāmiʿ al-ʿulūm wa'l-ḥikam*. (Beirut: Dār al-jīl, 1987).

al-Juwaynī, Abū al-Maʿālī ʿAbdalmalik b. ʿAbdallāh. *al-Burhān fī uṣūl al-fiqh*. Ed. ʿAbd al-ʿaẓīm Maḥmūd al-Dīb. (Mansura, Egypt: 1992).

Madelung, Wilferd. "The Spread of Maturidism and the Turks." *Actas IV Congresso de estudos arabes e islamicos*. (Leiden: Brill, 1968).

al-Qarāfī, Shihābaddīn Aḥmad b. Idrīs. *Nafāʾis al-uṣūl fī sharḥ al-maḥṣūl*, 9 vols. ed. ʿĀdil ʿAbdalmawjūd and ʿAlī Maḥmud Muʿawwaḍ. (Riyadh: Maktabat Nizār Muṣṭafā al-Bāz, 1997).

al-Rāzī, Fakhr al-Dīn Muḥammad b. ʿUmar. *al-Maḥṣūl fī ʿilm uṣūl al-fiqh*, 2 vols. (Beirut, Dar al-kutub al-ʿilmiyya, 1988).

al-Shāṭibī, Abū Isḥāq Ibrāhīm b. Mūsā. *al-Muwāfaqāt fī uṣūl al-sharīʿa*, 4 vols. (Beirut: Dār al-maʿrifah, n.d.).

Weiss, Bernard. *The Spirit of Islamic Law*. (Athens, GA: University of Georgia Press, 1998).

——. *The Search for God's Law*. (Salt Lake City, UT: University of Utah Press, 1992).

Zysow, Aron. *The Economy of Certainty* (unpublished Ph.D. dissertation, Harvard University, 1984).

6

"*ISTIḤSĀN* IS NINE-TENTHS OF THE LAW": THE PUZZLING RELATIONSHIP OF *UṢŪL* TO *FURŪᶜ* IN THE MĀLIKĪ *MADHHAB*

Mohammad Fadel

[161] The " conventional wisdom" in the study of Islamic legal history goes something like this: for approximately the first two centuries following the death of the Prophet Muhammad, the nascent Islamic community had yet to develop a self-consciously Islamic jurisprudence that was conceptually distinct from the customs of the early Arab Muslims themselves.[1] This formative period of Islamic jurisprudence was characterized by direct appeals to informal practical reason, i.e., *raʾy,* as well as to custom. The latter was generically termed *sunna.* What this proto-Islamic jurisprudence lacked in self-conscious theoretization and universality, however, it made up for in flexibility, adaptability and pragmatism.

The arrival of al-Shāfiᶜī in the last quarter of the second Hijrī century, however, put this all to an end: Unlike the members of the "ancient schools" of law whose concerns were relatively parochial, al-Shāfiᶜī attempted a great synthesis, to wed the proto-rationalism of ᶜIraqi jurisprudence with the conservative "sunnah-centered" approach of the Ḥijāzīs. The product of this great synthesis was al-Shāfiᶜī's *Risāla,* a work that is commonly considered the first in *Uṣūl al-fiqh.* The breakthrough of al- Shāfiᶜī, the conventional account tells us, is that legal reasoning, viz., the logic that was to guide a jurist in explicating rules for unprecedented situations, no longer was to depend upon the seemingly arbitrary justifications of the "ancient schools," namely, "*raʾy*" and "*sunna,*" but rather, would rest on the more objective formal grounds of a hierarchy of material legal sources, beginning first with the Qurʾān, then the Sunna of the Prophet, but only if authoritatively documented, consensus *(ijmāᶜ)* and finally, [162] analogy (*qiyās*). Furthermore, the Qurʾān and Sunna, being textual, had to be understood

This article was originally published as a chapter in *Studies in Islamic Law and Society*, edited by Bernard Weiss (Boston: Brill, 2002), pp. 161–176.

1. See, for example, N.J. Coulson, *A History of Islamic Law* (Edinburgh: Edinburgh University Press, 1964); Joseph Schacht, *An Introduction to Islamic Law* (Oxford: Oxford University Press, 1964).

according to the objective rules of interpretation derived from a scientific study of the Arabic language.[2]

Presumably, al-Shāfiʿī's objective method would render legal reasoning more transparent and hence, more public, universal and therefore, accountable. Although the "ancient schools" did not abandon their particular doctrines, their informal—and in comparison to al Shāfiʿī—almost naive approach to legal problems, gave way to his more rigorous method. Henceforth, all jurists would be forced to use either al-Shāfiʿī's method, or some variation thereof, or risk being castigated as one who followed mere habit *(muqallid)* or, worse, capricious desire *(hawā).* In the opinion of the conventional wisdom, then, al-Shāfiʿī is fundamental because he defined, or helped define, the structure of what counts as an argument within Islamic law—one that is based on evidence drawn from an authoritative source and is consistent with the logical implications of the hierarchy of legal sources—and at the same time what is not an Islamic argument at all, but rather is something else, e.g., blind adherence to unsubstantiated "custom" *(sunna)* or pursuit of "capricious desire" *(hawā).* At first blush, this account of the structure of legal argument seems irrefutable: More and more of the great minds of Islamic jurisprudence indubitably became pre-occupied with questions of method and ascertaining the formal structure of a proper Islamic legal argument. Even the Mālikī school, which has been accused of being relatively indifferent to the discipline of *uṣūl al-fiqh,* produced important works of *uṣūl al-fiqh* that seem to owe more to al-Shāfiʿī than they do to Mālik b. Anas. These authors include such notable Mālikīs as Ibn al-Ḥājib (d. 646/1248),[3] author of the famous *mukhtaṣar* in *uṣūl al-fiqh;* al-Bājī (d. 474/1081), author of *Iḥkām al-Fuṣūl fī Aḥkām al-Uṣūl*[4] and, al Qarāfī's (d. 684/1285) *Tanqīḥ al-fuṣūl.*[5] Structurally, these works do [163] not seem to differ significantly from the works of their Shāfiʿī colleagues. Pride of place is given to the textual sources of revelation, and much of the work is devoted to hermeneutical questions.[6] Mālikī works of *uṣūl* seem to share the fundamental

2. In recognition of al-Shāfiʿī's critical role in the development of Islamic jurisprudence, he is often dubbed the "Master Architect" of Islamic jurisprudence. This view of al-Shāfiʿī's role, however, has not gone unchallenged in recent scholarship. See Wael Hallaq "Was al-Shāfiʿī the Master Architect of Islamic Jurisprudence?" *International Journal of Middle East Studies,* 25 (1993), 587–605.

3. Jamāl al-Dīn ʿUthmān b. ʿAmr b. Abī Bakr.

4. Abū al-Walīd Sulaymān b. Khalaf al-Bājī, *Iḥkām al-Fuṣūl fī Aḥkām al-Uṣūl,* ed. ʿAbd Allāh Muḥammad al-Jabūrī (Beirut: Mu'assasat al-Risāla, 1409/1989).

5. Abū al-ʿAbbās Shihāb al-Dīn Aḥmad b. Idrīs al-Qārāfī, *Sharḥ Tanqīḥ al-fuṣūl fī ikhtiṣār al-maḥṣūl fī al-uṣūl,* ed. Ṭāhā ʿAbd al-Raʾūf Saʿd (Cairo: Maktabat al-Kulliyyāt al-Azhariyya, 1414/1993).

6. Compare the previous Mālikī works to those authored by the Shāfiʿī authors Abū Ḥāmid Muḥammad b. Muḥammad b. Muḥammad al-Ghazālī, *al-Mustaṣfā fī ʿilm al-uṣūl* (Beirut: Dar al-Kutub al-ʿIlmīyya, 1414/1993); Abū al-Ḥasan Sayf al-Dīn ʿAlī b. Abī ʿAlī b. Muḥammad al-Āmidī, *al-Iḥkām fī uṣūl al-aḥkām* (Beirut: Dār al-Kutub al-ʿIlmīyya, 1403/1983), 4 vols.; Fakhr al-Dīn Muḥammad b. ʿUmar b. al-Ḥasan al-Rāzī, *al-Maḥṣūl fī ʿilm uṣūl al-fiqh* (Beirut: Muʿassat al-Risāla, 1312/1992), 6 vols. I do not wish it

premise of al-Shāfiʿī, namely, that Islamic law in the first instance means rules derived from revelation. Thus, the pedigree of a rule depends on its affiliation to revelation. This leads to a natural hierarchy of sources (s. *dalīl*/pl. *adilla*) into those that are strictly revelatory, i.e., Qurʾān, Sunna and Ijmāʿ, and those that are derivative, e.g., *qiyās, istiḥsān, maṣlaḥa* and *istiṣḥāb al-ḥāl*.[7] Despite substantial disagreements on the details of what constitutes Sunna and Ijmāʿ, or whether *maṣlaḥa* and *istiḥṣān* constitute valid alternatives to analogy, Mālikī works of *uṣūl al-fiqh* apparently agree with Shāfiʿī works that the rules of Islamic law need to be derived from authentic historical sources in a manner consistent with the ontological priority of revelatory sources to ancillary ones.

This bias toward textual sources manifests itself in some *khilāf* works, such as Ibn Rushd the Grandson's (d. 595/1198) *Bidāyat al-Mujtahid wa Nihāyat al-Muqtaṣid* (hereafter, *Bidāya*).[8] Ibn Rushd himself [164] is aware of the limited scope of his book, and in his (very brief) introduction he reminds his readers that the purpose of his book is limited to "cases having a textual basis in revelation or are closely related thereto" (*wa hādhihi al-masāʾil fī al-akthar hiya al-masāʾil al-manṭūq bihā fī al-sharʿ aw tataʿallaq bi al-manṭūq bihi taʿalluqan qarīban*) (*Bidāya*, 1:325). While not surprising, his failure to explain rules that are not "closely related" to revelatory sources is disappointing because it certainly must be the case that, at least in purely quantitative terms, rules derived from non-revelatory sources make up the vast majority of actual Islamic law, viz., the rulings found in the *furūʿ* manuals, at least in the Mālikī school. Indeed, Mālik is reported as having said, "*Istiḥsān* is nine-tenths of [legal] knowledge (*al-istiḥsān tisʿat aʿshār al-ʿilm*)."[9]

---

to be understood that the works of these various authors are indistinguishable. Obviously, they are. The point I wish to make, however, is simply that affiliation to a particular school of fiqh did not "translate" into a particular approach to *uṣūl al-fiqh*. Instead, authors in the *uṣūl al-fiqh* tradition appear to analyze a discrete set of problems as problems of *uṣūl al-fiqh*, rather than analyzing problems particular to the rules of their madhhab. The generic independence of *uṣūl al-fiqh* from the particular rulings of a school of positive law is perhaps best demonstrated by the fact that al-Qarāfī, a Mālikī, chose the *uṣūl*-work of a Shāfiʿī, Fakhr al-Dīn al-Rāzī, as the text which he would first summarize, and then, upon which he would compose a commentary, as is evident from the title of his *Tanqīḥ*. Conversely, many Shāfiʿīs wrote commentaries on the text of Ibn al-Ḥājib's *Mukhtaṣar*.

7. Thus, al-Bājī, for example, divides the proofs of the revelation into three categories. The first he terms *aṣl*, the second he terms *maʿqūl al-aṣl* and the third he terms *istiṣḥāb al-ḥāl*. *Aṣl*, in turn, includes the Qurʾān, the Sunna and Ijmāʿ. *Maʿqūl al-aṣl* refers to certain hermeneutic techniques, e.g., *faḥwā al-khiṭāb*, and includes *qiyās*, referred to obliquely in the introduction as *maʿnā al-khiṭāb*. *Al-Iḥkām*, p. 69, 456.

8. Abū al-Walīd Muḥammad b. Aḥmad b. Muḥammad Ibn Rushd al-Ḥafīd, *Bidāyat al-Mujtahid wa Nihāyat al-Muqtaṣid*, ed. ʿAlī Muḥammad Muʿawwaḍ and ʿĀdil Aḥmad ʿAbd al-Mawjūd (Beirut: Dār al-Kutub al-ʿIlmiyya, 1416/1996), 6 vols. Citations to *Bidāya* will be made in the text.

9. Aḥmad b. Muḥammad al-Ṣāwī, *Bulghat al-sālik li-aqrab al-masālik* (hereafter, *al-Bulgha*), on the margin of Abū al-Barakāt Aḥmad b. Muḥammad b. Aḥmad al-Dardīr, *al-Sharḥ al-ṣaghīr* (hereafter, *Sharḥ*), ed. Muṣṭafā Kamāl Waṣfī (Cairo: Dār al-Maʿārif, n.d.), 4 vols. 3:638.

Interestingly, the Mālikī uṣūlīs such as al-Qarāfī, al-Bājī and Ibn al-Ḥājib were also masters of Mālikī *furūᶜ*, each one having authored an important work on Mālikī *furūᶜ*: Ibn al-Ḥājib authored his *mukhtaṣar* in *fiqh*, *Jāmiᶜ al-ummahāt*, which served as the basic *matn* of Mālikī fiqh until the *mukhtaṣar* of Khalīl;[10] al-Bājī authored the *Muntaqā*, which is really a work of Mālikī *furūᶜ* in the guise of a commentary on the *Muwaṭṭaʾ*; and, al-Qarāfī published the monumental *al-Dhakhīra*. The persistent interest of Mālikī *uṣūlīs* in *furūᶜ* appears in stark contrast to the careers of two of their prominent Shāfiᶜī *uṣūlī* colleagues, Fakhr al-Dīn al-Rāzī (d. 606/1209) and Sayf al-Dīn al-Āmidī (d. 631/ 1233). I do not mean to suggest that Shāfiᶜīs were more "theoretical" than Mālikīs or that the Mālikīs were more "practical" than the Shāfiᶜīs. The contrast is useful, however, to the extent that it reveals that a scholar could be a master of *uṣūl al-fiqh* without being a recognized expert in *furūᶜ*. Likewise, one could also be recognized as a master of *furūᶜ* without gaining such recognition in *uṣūl al-fiqh*. Of course, as the three Mālikī authors demonstrate, it was possible to be accomplished in both, but it was by no means necessary.

Yet, [165] if there is no necessary relationship between mastery of *uṣūl al-fiqh* and mastery of *furūᶜ*, one is tempted to question whether al-Shāfiᶜī's insistence on adherence to a rigorous method had the impact on legal argument that is commonly supposed. What if legal reasoning within the "ancient" schools continued by developing their own criteria for legitimate argumentation, but one whose validity did not transcend the limits of a particular school?

This essay raises, but does not seek to answer that question. Instead, it desires to explore the impact of *uṣūl*-based legal argumentation on the *furūᶜ* doctrine of the Mālikī school through Ibn Rushd the Grandson's famous *khilāf* work, *Bidāyat al-mujtahid*. Specifically, I will focus on an innocuous topic, that of pledges (*ruhūn*). The goal is to show that an *uṣūl*-inspired work such as that of Ibn Rushd not only is incapable of explaining the actual corpus of what constitutes the law of pledges, but also that the portion of the corpus that it does explain can only be described as marginal.

Ibn Rushd begins his discussion of this topic by noting its revelatory source, namely, Baqarah 283, which states, "If you are on a journey and find not a scribe [to record the debt], then pledges, possessed" (*Bidāya*, 5:236). Leaving aside the fact that the pledges referred to in this verse seem to refer exclusively to evidentiary problems arising from contracting far away from urban centers, the verse is utterly silent on the rights and obligations of the pledgor (*al-rāhin*) and the pledgee (*al-murtahin*).[11] It is also silent as to what types of property can be pledged by a debtor as collateral.

---

10. See Mohammad Fadel, "Adjudication in the Mālikī Madhhab: A Study of Legal Process in Medieval Islamic Law" (Ph.D. diss., University of Chicago, 1995), 237–42. Ibnal-Ḥājib's important work has recently been published. Jamāl al-Dīn ᶜUthmān b. ᶜAmr b. Abī Bakr, *Jāmiᶜ al-ummahāt*, ed. Abū ᶜAbd al-Raḥmān al-Akhḍar al-Akhḍarī (Beirut: Dār al-Yamāma, 1418/1998).

11. Part of the difficulty of this area of the law is the ambiguity of the terms used, especially in the

Nonetheless, Ibn Rushd notes that the principal right the pledgee obtains by virtue of his agreement with the pledgor is the right to retain possession of the pledge until the pledgor repays his debt to the pledgee. Furthermore, when the pledgor fails to repay his debt in a timely fashion, the pledgee has the right, with the pledgor's permission, to sell the collateral and satisfy his debt from the proceeds of that sale. If the pledgor refuses to permit the sale of the collateral, the pledgee has the right to seek a judicial sale of the collateral. The [166] issue of the pledgor's permission to foreclose on the collateral can be avoided if the pledgor agrees to make the pledgee his agent for purposes of sale of the collateral, although Ibn Rushd reports that Mālik discouraged (*kariha*) that arrangement (*Bidāya*, 5:241).

Interestingly, Ibn Rushd cites no revelatory authority for these propositions. He explicitly refutes the possibility that consensus can be a revelatory *aṣl* in the absence of a specific revelatory text or valid analogy based on such a text: "As for consensus, it rests on one of these four[12] means [of establishing a legal ruling]. When a rule is established by means of one of [these four], however, and that ruling is not conclusive, consensus will elevate it from a probable [judgment] to a conclusive one. Consensus is not an independent source in itself, but rather necessarily depends on other sources, for were it otherwise, that would necessitate admitting revelation subsequent to the Prophet (S)" (*Bidāya*, 1:328–29). We can thus exclude *Ijmāʿ* as the legal source for these propositions.

Another important right of a pledgee is only implicit in Ibn Rushd's treatment of pledges: A pledgee has prior claim to the value of the collateral—as against the pledgor's other creditors—in the event of bankruptcy. One can deduce this rule from Ibn Rushd's discussion of possession of the collateral in conjunction with the right of the pledgee to foreclose on the collateral in the event of the debtor's default. Thus, he states that according to Mālik, possession of the collateral is only a condition of perfection (*sharṭ al-tamām*), not a condition of contractual validity (*sharṭ al-ṣiḥḥa*) (*Bidāya*, 5:239).[13] Essentially, the position he ascribes to Mālik is this: As between the pledgor and the pledgee, the pledge is a valid contract binding the two regardless of possession. The pledge contract, however, becomes void if the pledgee fails to take possession (*ḥiyāza, qabḍ*) of the collateral prior to the death, mortal illness or bankruptcy of the pledgor. If the pledgee

early sources. Later sources consistently use *rāhin* to mean pledgor and *murtahin* to mean the pledgee. Early sources, however, might use the terms interchangeably, viz., *rāhin* and *murtahin* may mean either pledgor or pledgee. For that reason, one has to be very sensitive to the linguistic context in the early sources to determine whether the text is discussing a pledgor or a pledgee.

12. In other words, either a spoken utterance (*lafẓ*) of the Lawgiver, an act (*fiʿl*) of the Lawgiver or the tacit approval (*iqrār*) of the Lawgiver. The fourth means is analogy (*qiyās*), but it is controversial, and it is restricted to those areas for which the Lawgiver was silent (*Bidāya*, 1:325).

13. I have chosen to translate *tamām* in this context as "perfection" rather than "completion" to emphasize its precise equivalence to the term "perfection" in Anglo-American jurisprudence, as that term is used in secured transactions, which includes pledges.

has failed to "perfect" her pledge by possession in any of these three contingencies, her only recourse is a claim based on the [167] debt (*dayn*) owed to her by the pledgor; her claim to the particular asset pledged by the pledgor disappears.[14]

The term of art used by the Mālikīs for the pledgee's priority with respect to the collateral is *ikhtiṣāṣ*, viz., the priority of the creditor's claim over that of other creditors to the value of the asset. The effect of *ikhtiṣāṣ* is dramatic. In its absence, the value of the pledged collateral is shared proportionately by all the creditors of the pledgor (*uswat al-ghuramāʾ*).

Ibn Rushd again refers to *Baqara* 283 as the revelatory source for the "requirement" of possession, whether for purposes of validity or for perfection (*Bidāya*, 5:239–40). At the risk of sounding overly critical, however, I wish to note that the verse does not speak at all to the issue of a pledgee's priority in the pledged collateral. Furthermore, the verse seems to be addressing the use of pledges to solve an evidentiary problem that arises as a consequence of the parties' inability to record their contract. In other words, while the Qurʾān expressly contemplates the parties' use of collateral in lieu of a writing evidencing the debtor's obligation, it does not appear that the plain language of the verse has any relevance to the question of whether the pledgee also enjoys priority to the value of the pledged asset in the event his debtor is unable to pay his debt, whether because of death or bankruptcy. Thus, Ibn Rushd's treatment of pledges fails to provide a ground in revelation for the central property right created by the pledge: Perfection of the pledge by possession gives the pledgee priority against the entire world in the pledged asset.

To the extent that Ibn Rushd provides texts from the Sunna, they are inconclusive and deal with secondary issues. The first such issue is whether accretions (*namāʾ*) to the collateral are considered part of the collateral, or belong outright to the pledgor, e.g., whether the fruit of a tree pledged as collateral is part of the collateral, or whether it is a separate item of property such that the pledgee has no rights in it (*Bidāya*, 5:243–49). The Shāfiʿīs took the position that accretions belonged to the pledgor whereas the Ḥanafīs argued that accretions became part of the collateral. Mālik's position was more nuanced, depending upon the nature of the collateral at issue. Thus, he held that the offspring of humans and livestock were an [168] extension of the mother that was the collateral and hence were part of the collateral, whereas the output of trees, the rents of property and the earnings of a slave were independent of the collateral and thus belonged to the pledgor. The criterion Ibn Rushd claims Mālik used to distinguish one class from the other is the following: When the accretion is separate, but its appearance resembles the collateral, it is treated as though it is part of the collateral (*mā kāna min namāʾ al-rahn al-munfaṣil ʿalā khilqatihi wa ṣūratihi fa-innahu dākhil fī al-rahn*); where the accretion differs in form from the collateral, whether it is a natural product of the collateral or not, it is not part of the collateral, but rather forms an entirely distinct item of property (*mā lam yakun*

14. *Sharḥ*, 3:306.

ʿalā khilqatihi fa-innahu lā yadkhul fī al-rahn kāna mutawallidan ʿanhu ka-thamar al-nakhl aw ghayr mutawallid ka-kirāʾ al-dār wa kharāj al-ghulām) (*Bidāya*, 5:245).[15]

Mālik, Ibn Rushd explains, distinguished between the offspring of humans and livestock, on the one hand, and agricultural products, on the other, because the law of sales distinguishes between them (*Bidāya*, 5:249: *wa-farraqa bayna al-thamar wa al-walad fī dhālika bi al-sunna al-mufarriqa fī dhālika*). Mālik reported in the *Muwaṭṭaʾ* that the Prophet (S) said "Whoever sells date-palms that have been pollinated is entitled to their fruit unless the purchaser stipulates otherwise."[16] Mālik also reported subsequent to that *hadith* that "There is no difference among us [in Madīna] that whoever sells a pregnant slave-girl or livestock that is pregnant, he has also sold the fetus to the purchaser whether or not the [purchaser] stipulates it." If we assume that Mālik's logic is driven by the rigor of *uṣūl al-fiqh,* his rule distinguishing what types of accretions naturally belong to the collateral and what does not appears to be a generalization based on the *hadith* he cited in the *Muwaṭṭaʾ*. Yet, Mālik concludes his discussion of this question in the *Muwaṭṭaʾ* with the observation that "What clarifies [169] this is that people customarily pledge the dates of their palm trees without pledging the trees [themselves], but no one pledges a fetus in the belly of its mother, whether a slave or livestock."[17]

The Shāfiʿīs, according to Ibn Rushd, also based their position on a *hadith* which attributes to the Prophet (S) the saying that "Pledges are milked and ridden (*al-rahn maḥlūb wa markūb*)" (*Bidāya*, 5:245–46). The Shāfiʿīs read this to mean that in the absence of a stipulation providing otherwise, accretions belong to the pledgor. They also cite the *hadith* in which the Prophet says "[Destruction] of the collateral is [borne] by the one pledging it as collateral. To him belongs its profit and he suffers its loss (*al-rahn mimman rahanahu lahu ghunmuhu wa ʿalayhi ghurmuhu*)" in order to strengthen their position (*Bidāya*, 5:246).[18] The Ḥanafīs argue for their position, ac-

---

15. While the distinction in Ibn Rushd appears at first glance to explain Malik's rulings, the explanation is not very convincing, especially with regard to accretions that are "natural," for in their case, whether the "accretion" resembles the collateral is a function of the time at which one chooses to make the comparison. Thus, fruits will eventually "resemble" the trees that bore them, just as a fetus will eventually become a human being if born alive. With regard to this rule's applicability to a human fetus, the more likely explanation is the prohibition of separating a slave woman from her minor offspring, whether that is by sale or by pledge.

16. Mālik b. Anas, *Muwaṭṭaʾ al-Imām Mālik*, with the commentary of Jalāl al-Dīn al-Suyūṭī, *Tanwīr al-ḥawālik* (Cairo: Maktabat Muṣṭafā al-Bābī al-Ḥalabī, 1369/1950), 2 vols., 2:112–13.

17. This apparent reticence of the Medinese to pledge a fetus cannot be attributed to the prohibition on *gharar*, for the Mālikīs allowed other contingent property interests, such as a runaway slave, or fruit that had yet to ripen, to serve as collateral, despite the *gharar* inhering in the ultimate existence of the collateral at the time the debt matured. *Sharḥ*, 3:305.

18. According to the editors of *Bidāya*, this *hadith* was attributed in one version to the Prophet by the companion Abū Hurayra (*mawṣūl*), and in another, although it is attributed to the Prophet, its chain

cording to Ibn Rushd, based on what appears to be a common sense principle: just as the "branch" is a derivative of the "root" (*al-furūʿ tābiʿa li'l-uṣūl*), so the accretion of the collateral is also a part thereof (*Bidāya*, 5:248). Thus, any increase in the collateral is part of the collateral and therefore goes to the benefit of the pledgee unless the pledge is redeemed by payment of the debt.

A casual glance at these three different positions might lead to the conclusion that the differences among the three legal schools are significant. Such a conclusion, however, would be premature, for the schools have a deeper agreement that renders their particular position on this question relatively unimportant—whatever the rule of each school might be, they all agree it is only a default rule that applies in the absence of an agreement between the pledgor and the pledgee.

The Mālikīs, Shāfiʿīs and Ḥanafīs also dispute who bears the risk of loss (*ḍamān*) in the event of the destruction of the collateral while in the possession of the pledgee in much the same manner that they dispute whether accretions belong, as an initial matter, to the pledgee or to the pledgor. Thus, the Shāfiʿīs place the risk of loss on the [170] pledgor, on the theory that the contract between the pledgor and the pledgee creates a bailment (*Bidāya*, 5:250).[19] The Ḥanafīs, on the other hand, treat the collateral as though it were the property of the pledgee, and accordingly, force the pledgee to bear the risk of its loss. Mālik, just as he did regarding the question of who benefits from "accretions" to the collateral, refused to adopt a categorical rule, and instead adopted a rule that looked to the nature of the collateral to determine which party bore the risk of its loss. Thus, where the collateral was personal property that could be easily hidden (*mā yughāb ʿalayhi*), e.g., gold, clothing, or other fungible commodities, Mālik placed the risk of loss on the pledgee, but where the collateral was non-moveable real property (*mā lā yughāb ʿalayhi*) or property whose destruction would be obvious (*mā lā yakhfā halākuhu*), e.g., land, homes, or animals, the risk of loss remained on the pledgor (*Bidāya*, 5:251).

The Shāfiʿīs relied for their proof-text, according to Ibn Rushd, on the same *hadith* they cited for the proposition that accretions belong to the pledgor, namely, "[Destruction] of the collateral is [borne] by the one pledging it as collateral. To him belongs its profit and he suffers its loss" (*al-rahn mimman rahanahu lahu ghunmuhu wa ʿalayhi ghurmuhu*) (*Bidāyah*, 5:250). Ibn Rushd provides two arguments for the Ḥanafīs, one derived from analogy, and the other based on a proof-text. As for the analogy, the Ḥanafīs take as the principal case (*al-aṣl*) the rule governing who bears the risk of loss when the seller retains possession of a sold item (*al-mabīʿ*) until the

of transmission ceases at the successor, Saʿīd b. al-Musayyab (*mursal*). For the details of this text's transmission, see *Bidāya*, 5:246, n. 1063.

19. Ibn Rushd also attributes this position to Aḥmad b. Ḥanbal, Abū Thawr and the majority of the scholars of *hadith*.

purchaser pays its purchase price in full. Here, the majority of scholars agree that the seller bears the risk of loss, because he is maintaining possession for his own benefit. Likewise, the pledgee is holding the pledge for his own benefit, and therefore, he should bear the risk of loss in this case just as he does in the principal case (*Bidāya*, 5:251). Their proof text consists of a *mursal*-report where a man pledged a horse as collateral. That horse subsequently perished while in the possession of the pledgee. When the Prophet was made aware of the situation, he is said to have stated to the pledgee "Your right has departed [with the departure of the pledge]" (*dhahaba ḥaqquka*) (*Bidāya*, 5:251).

[171] Mālik, according to Ibn Rushd, reached his conclusion by means of *istiḥsān*, which Ibn Rushd defines as "the harmonization of contradictory [revelatory] proofs" (*jamᶜ bayna al-adilla al-mutaᶜāriḍa*) (*Bidāya*, 5:251). Mālik's "harmonization," however, does not attempt to reconcile the language of the contradictory reports alternatively cited by the Shāfiᶜīs and the Ḥanafīs; instead, the basis of Mālik's distinction between collateral that may be secreted away (*mā yughāb ᶜalayhi*) and that which cannot (*mā lā yughāb ᶜalayhi*) is the notion of "suspicion (*tuhma*)."[20] Thus, Ibn Rushd states that destruction of collateral that may be squirreled away (*mā yughāb ᶜalayhi*) raises suspicion (*al-tuhma talḥaq*) as to whether in fact it was destroyed or simply misappropriated, while the destruction of collateral that cannot be so easily hidden (*mā la yughāb ᶜalayhi*) raises no such suspicion (*Bidāya*, 5:251).[21]

Two general observations are in order with regard to the competing rules governing the allocation of property rights to the accretions of collateral and which party bears the risk of the collateral's destruction. First, it does not appear that the controversies among the *fuqahāʾ* regarding these two questions, while real enough, could have had any appreciable impact upon the debtor-creditor relationship. This "irrelevancy" hypothesis is not based on the cliche that Islamic law is "idealistic" and therefore irrelevant to social practice. Rather, it is based on the observation

20. *Tuhma* is a term of art in Islamic law. In this context, it closely corresponds to the notion of "moral hazard" used by contemporary economists.

21. Ibn Rushd the Grandfather's analysis of Mālik's reasoning is especially lucid. He states expressly that the basis of Mālik's distinction is that in the case of collateral that is easily hidden, the truth of what happened can be obtained *only* from the pledgee. Because the pledgee is in exclusive possession of the evidence necessary to resolve the question of how the pledge perished, a moral hazard exists, viz., the temptation on the part of the pledgee to claim the destruction of the collateral while keeping it for himself or selling it and keeping its price. Accordingly, it is necessary to hold him liable for its destruction unless he can produce objective evidence (*bayyina*) that he was not responsible for its destruction. On the other hand, where the collateral is property that cannot be easily hidden, e.g., a home, land, or an animal (*mā lā yakhfā halākuhu*), no moral hazard exists because the obvious nature of the property allows a judge to ascertain what happened to the collateral independently of the pledgee's potentially self-serving statements. Abū al-Walīd Muḥammad b. Aḥmad Ibn Rushd al-Jadd, *al-Muqaddimmāt al-mumahhidāt*, ed. Saᶜīd Aḥmad Aᶜrāb (Beirut: Dār al-Gharb al-Islāmī, 1408/1988), 3 vols., 2:397–98.

that, with respect to determining the property rights of the parties to the collateral's accretions, the *fuqahāʾ* apparently agreed that the pledgor and pledgee [172] could stipulate by agreement which party would benefit in the appreciation of the collateral. In other words the *fuqahāʾ* were arguing about a default rule that applied only in the absence of the parties' agreement. Assuming that contracting parties are well-informed of their legal rights, and there are no unusual obstacles preventing them from bargaining over which of the parties will benefit from the appreciation of the collateral, one can assume that they will bargain to the result that is most consistent with their interests. The same point applies with respect to the various rules regarding which party bears the risk of the collateral's loss: So long as the pledge is to secure contractual indebtedness,[22] the price of the debt will reflect which party bears the risk of the collateral's loss. In these contexts, where a legal system has an option of adopting one of several plausible rules, the most important function of law is to specify which of the plausible rules will be the applicable rule in the absence of an agreement, thereby creating a basis from which the parties' bargaining may proceed.[23]

The second point is that even if one believes that these disputes were of major doctrinal significance, it is significant that Ibn Rushd is unable to produce any conclusive evidence—from the viewpoint of the *uṣūl al-fiqh* paradigm at least—for the positions of any of the parties. It is not only the relative paucity of revelatory material that poses a problem for the effective functioning of the *uṣūl al-fiqh* paradigm; rather, it is the ambiguity of the reported proof-texts themselves that ultimately render the formalistic method of *uṣūl al-fiqh* of scant utility in deriving rules in this area of the law.[24]

[173] Much more significant than these two issues, however, is first, what type of property the law recognizes as being amenable to collateralization; and, second, what acts of the creditor are necessary to satisfy the requirement of possession.[25]

22. Of course, the applicable liability rule would carry more significance where the pledge is given as security for a debt arising from a tort (*jināya*), because in this case the creditor would not have the freedom to vary the credit terms to reflect the costs associated with bearing the risk of loss. On the general relationship of legal rules to social behavior, see Ronald H. Coase, "The Problem of Social Cost," *Journal of Law and Economics*, 3 (1960).

23. This is another justification for *taqlīd*: where parties can bargain to their own solution, it is less important that the legal rule be correct, than it is for it to be precise. Ambiguity in such circumstances decreases the possibility that the parties will be able to reach their own agreement.

24. Take, for example, the *hadith* text cited repeatedly by the Shāfiʿīs: *al-rahn mimman rahanahu lahu ghurmuhu wa ʿalayhi ghurmuhu*. While in the usage of later jurists the verb *rahana* and its cognates denote the pledgor and the verb *irtahana* and its cognates denote the pledgee, earlier texts use the two verbs and their cognates interchangeably. Thus, one could also cite that *hadith* for precisely the opposite meaning advanced by the Shāfiʿīs.

25. Accordingly, the jurists are not differing over a default rule in this context, and thus, the choice

Ibn Rushd mentions, briefly, the profound difference of opinion between the Mālikīs and the Shāfiʿīs in this regard, but fails to explain either position in detail, or the "proof" either party held out in favor of its opinion. The main point of contention separating the Mālikīs from the Shāfiʿīs with regard to the first question is whether the restrictions on the consideration (*ʿiwaḍ*) in a contract of sale also apply to the collateral in a contract of pledge. Mālikīs argued that they did not. Accordingly, they allowed contingent property rights to be pledged as collateral. Shāfiʿīs on the other hand argued that collateral is akin to consideration in a contract of sale. Therefore, collateral must not run afoul of the legal restrictions applicable to consideration, thereby effectively foreclosing the collateralization of contingent property rights.

Some Mālikīs distinguished a contract of pledge from a contract of sale on the purely formal grounds that, in contrast to a sale, which transfers title to the property exchanged, a pledge contract does not.[26] On this basis they concluded that the conditions regulating a contract of sale that effects an immediate transfer of title should not apply to a pledge contract that does not. Nonetheless, they required that collateral must satisfy the minimal conditions of property, viz., it must have monetary value (*mutamawwal*).[27] Furthermore, it must act as security for a lawful debt. Thus, al-Dardīr defines a pledge as "[Something] having monetary value taken [from its owner] in order to gain security thereby for a binding debt or for [one] maturing into a binding [debt]" (*al-rahn mutamawwal ukhidha tawaththuqan bihi fī dayn lāzim aw ṣāʾir ilā al-luzūm*).[28] Because the debt is already in legal existence prior to the pledge contract, al-Dardīr can take the position that any *gharar*[29] involving the collateral is irrelevant[174] because "The pledge of collateral [suffering from] *gharar* is valid because it is permissible not to have a pledge at all; therefore, having some security is better than nothing" (*fa-innahu yaṣiḥḥu rahnuhu li-jawāz tark al-rahn min aṣlihi fa-shayʾ yutawaththaq bihi khayr min ʿadamihi*).[30]

While later Mālikīs seemed to have no problem with accepting the validity of a contingent property right serving as collateral—despite the fact that such a contin-

of rule will have an impact on social behavior because the options of parties will be constrained by the legal regime's choice of rule.

26. Al-Dardīr, 3:304; al-Ṣāwī, 3:304.

27. Al-Dardīr, 3:305. This is a perplexing requirement in light of the prohibition on the sale of contingent property rights. It is hard to conceive that such a right could be viewed as having any value such as to constitute property (*mutamawwal*) because it could not be sold and thus no value could be realized from it.

28. Id., 304.

29. While the concept of *gharar* is complex and highly-nuanced, in this context, it is helpful to consider *gharar* as the equivalent of a contingency affecting the existence or non-existence of some item of property.

30. Id., 305.

gent right could not be the object of a valid contract of sale—earlier Mālikīs were troubled by the notion. Al-Ḥaṭṭāb (d. 954/1547) reported that while all Mālikīs agreed that such a pledge would be permissible if it were independent of and subsequent to the contract creating the debt, if the pledge were part and parcel of the debt agreement, some Mālikīs objected for the cogent reason that in this latter case, part of the purchase price is for collateral, an outright sale of which would be invalid.[31] Despite the economic soundness of this criticism, the Mālikī school nevertheless adopted the position that contingent property rights could serve as collateral.

More importantly for our purposes, however, Ibn Rushd does not explain why this rule was adopted instead of the one proposed by the dissenters. Nor does Ibn Rushd attempt to ground the Mālikī's distinction between the requirements of lawful consideration and lawful collateral in any revelatory source. Instead, he just reports the difference of opinion regarding the issue without any reference at all to sources that would be considered authoritative within the *uṣūl al-fiqh* paradigm (*Bidāya*, 5:237).

Just as the Mālikīs allow contingent property rights to serve as collateral, they also allow intangible property rights to serve as [175] collateral, a position that is, again, diametrically opposed to the position of the Shāfiʿīs, but for which no revelatory justification is given (*Bidāya*, 5:236–37). One could argue that the positions of the Mālikīs and the Shāfiʿīs are simply extensions of their respective positions on the permissibility of the sale of a debt—the Shāfiʿī position being one of prohibition while the Mālikīs took the position of its permissibility, at least under limited circumstances. This explanation, however, ignores the truly dramatic implications the Mālikī position holds for the law of pledges.

The bedrock principle around which the entire system of pledges is organized is that the pledgee does not enjoy a property right in the collateral unless she has possession of the collateral. Only this principle claimed a consensus among Muslim jurists. The basis for this universal consensus, Ibn Rushd claimed, is the verse in *Baqara* which refers to "collateral, possessed" (*rihān maqbūḍa*). Note, however, that once it

31. Muḥammad b. Muḥammad al-Ḥaṭṭāb, *Mawāhib al-jalīl*. 6 vols. (Beirut: Dār al-Fikr, 1412/1992), 5:3. When a seller sells on credit, and in the same contract of sale obtains a pledge consisting of a contingent property right from the purchaser—fruit that has yet to ripen, for example—the purchase price is a function of the value of the actual property that is the object of the contract of sale less the value of the contingent property right the debtor gives the seller to secure the debt. In other words, when a seller sells on credit to Purchaser 1 and receives from her collateral in the form of a contingent property right, and also sells to Purchaser 2 on credit but receives no collateral, the seller—all things being equal—will charge Purchaser 2 more for the sale than he will charge Purchaser 1. For this reason the Mālikī dissenters argued that to allow a contingent property interest to serve as collateral in these circumstances was tantamount to allowing the sale of a contingent property interest, something that was strictly prohibited on the grounds of *gharar*.

is admitted that intangible property can validly be offered as collateral a problem arises: How does one possess intangible property?[32] Given the centrality of possession to the doctrine of pledges in all the madhhabs, one would perhaps assume that a rule implying that a pledge can exist despite the physical impossibility of possession might give Ibn Rushd reason to pause to explain how the Mālikīs justified such a ruling. Instead, it does not appear to have caused him any embarrassment, much less have driven him to produce a justification rooted in *uṣūl al-fiqh* in support of the Mālikī position. Mālik's reported solution to this problem is reported in the *Mudawwana.* It is simple, elegant and, one might add, not lacking in irony. Saḥnūn reports that he asked Ibn al-Qāsim whether, in the opinion of Mālik, one could offer a debt that is owed to him by another as collateral for a debt he owes to another creditor. Ibn al-Qāsim replied that Malik believed this was permissible. The pledgee in this case, Mālik says, takes possession of the collateral by taking possession of the writing evidencing the debt that is owed to the pledgor.[33]

[176] Modern narratives of Islamic legal history have generally assumed that around the beginning of the third Islamic century, or maybe shortly thereafter, the structure of Islamic legal arguments took a radical new turn, largely as the result of the independent development of *uṣūl al-fiqh*. The purpose of this essay, however, is to raise the question whether the impact of this new science on legal argumentation was necessarily as dramatic has been supposed. Accordingly, I have attempted a case-study of *uṣūl al-fiqh*'s impact by analyzing Ibn Rushd's treatment of pledges in his famous *khilāf*-work, *Bidāyat al-mujtahid*, which is self-consciously an applied *uṣūl al-fiqh* work. Ibn Rushd, for whatever reason, dealt with only a few of the issues otherwise discussed in the positive-law manuals. Moreover, *uṣūl al-fiqh* failed to provide any clear solution for those issues, such as who owns accretions to the collateral, which he discussed. Most importantly, however, Ibn Rushd was completely silent on the revelatory justification for the pledgee's priority to the collateral vis-a-vis the debtor's other creditors, despite the fact that the Qurʾān appears to authorize the use of pledges only for the purpose of evidencing an obligation when it is impracticable for contracting parties to memorialize the debt. Instead of relying on the

32. Indeed, for this same reason, the Ḥanafīs did not permit the collateralization of real property held as a tenancy in common (*mushāʿ*).

33. *Qāla Mālik: naʿam lahu an yartahina dhālika fa-yaqbiḍ dhukr al-ḥaqq wa yushhid. Al-Mudawwana al-kubrā*, 4:176 (Beirut: Dār al-Fikr, n.d.). The irony lies in the fact that the one rule in the law of pledge which enjoys a plausible claim to revelatory authority is the requirement that the collateral be possessed for the purpose of evidencing an indebtedness in lieu of a writing. In this case, Mālik is allowing possession of the writing evidencing the obligation to substitute for the collateral itself, not for an evidentiary purpose, but rather to give the holder of the writing priority to payments under a debt owed to his debtor. One cannot overstate the interpretive distance traveled between *Baqara* 2:283 and Mālik's opinion in the *Mudawwana.*

arguments considered conclusive in *uṣūl al-fiqh*, however, Ibn Rushd's discussion of Mālikī doctrine reveals the continued vitality and centrality of *istiḥsān*—a doctrine relegated to the status of a "subsidiary source of law"[34] within the paradigm of *uṣūl al-fiqh*. Nonetheless, Mālikīs, it appeared, remained faithful to the principle of their eponym, namely, that "*istiḥsān* is nine-tenths of [legal] knowledge" to justify the centrality of empirical analysis to their analysis of revelatory texts, thereby lessening the impact of *uṣūl al-fiqh*'s linguistic formalism on the development of Mālikī legal doctrine. Further work must be done before this hypothesis can be confirmed. At any event, it should not be assumed that the development of *uṣūl al-fiqh* as a major field of legal production necessarily revolutionized legal argument or the subsequent development of legal doctrine, at least in the Mālikī school.

34. Ahmad Hasan, *Analogical Reasoning in Islamic Jurisprudence* (Islamabad: Islamic Research Institute, 1986), p. 409.

7

IS HISTORICISM A VIABLE STRATEGY FOR ISLAMIC LAW REFORM? THE CASE OF 'NEVER SHALL A FOLK PROSPER WHO HAVE APPOINTED A WOMAN TO RULE THEM'

Mohammad Fadel

1. INTRODUCTION: ISLAM, GENDER AND ISLAMIC REFORM

[132] Issues of gender equality have been contentious in the Muslim world since the 19th century;[1] they have also served as a flashpoint in an assumed clash of civilizations. The combination of Orientalism and colonialism, with the former often giving the latter normative justification for intervention in, and conquest and transformation of, the Islamic world in the name of defending oppressed Muslim women, moreover, has complicated internal Muslim debates on normative questions related to issues of gender equality.[2] As a result, Muslims with commitments to gender equality ("progressive Muslims") often find themselves fighting a two-front war: one against Orientalist and colonialist discourses that seek to justify western domination of Muslim societies using a trope grounded in Islam's oppression of woman, and the other against hierarchical, and even misogynistic, interpretations of gender relations in historically Muslim societies.[3] One self-identified progressive Muslim, Ebrahim Moosa, identifies "text fundamentalism"—the belief in the

---

This article was originally published in *Islamic Law and Society* 18, 2011, pp. 131–176

This article is based on a presentation given at the American Society of Legal History, Ottawa, Canada, Nov. 15, 2008. I would like to thank my co-panelists, Sherman Jackson, Lena Salaymeh, Intisar Rabb and Mitra Sharafi, for helpful comments on my presentation. I also would like to thank Audrey Macklin, Ebrahim Moosa, Laury Silvers, Joseph Lowry, Haider Hamoudi, Karen Bauer and Kerry Rittich for helpful comments on previous drafts of this article; Ahmed Saleh for his valuable research assistance; and the editors of ILS and the anonymous reviewers for helpful comments. All errors are my own.

1. See Karen Bauer, "The Male Is Not Like the Female (Q 3:36): The Question of Gender Egalitarianism in the Qurʾan," *Religion Compass* 3:4 (2009) 637.

2. Saʿdiyya Shaikh, "Transforming Feminisms: Islam, Women and Gender Justice," in *Progressive Mulsims on Justice, Gender and Pluralism*, ed. Omid Safi (Oxford: Oneworld Publications, 2003), 147–162.

3. Ibid., 155–156.

absolute sovereignty of the revealed text, to the exclusion of history and the experience of the Muslim community—as an important obstacle facing Muslim reformers in their struggle to promote progressive Islamic conceptions.[4] Ironically, "text fundamentalism," according to Moosa, tempts even progressive Muslims. One way they are tempted is to argue that the Qur'an plainly advocates a norm of gender egalitarianism without giving a satisfactory account of those revelatory texts that are inconsistent [133] with their view.[5] Moosa instead advocates a historicist approach to Islamic religious texts, including those aspects of scripture that deal with legal matters.[6] Conversely, progressive Muslims can sometimes find themselves paralyzed when confronted with certain texts that apparently teach that women are inferior to men, at least in certain contexts. This article will analyze one such text, the *hadith* stating that "No folk who has entrusted their affairs to a woman shall prosper," with the express goal of demonstrating that it is possible for progressive Muslims, at least in certain cases, to engage such texts without either succumbing to paralysis or engaging in "hermeneutical acrobatics" by exploiting the historical and interpretive resources of the Islamic legal tradition.[7]

Although Moosa expressed the view that historicism was an antidote to the text fundamentalism described above, he did not provide a clear sense of what he meant by historicism. It may very well be that a certain kind of historicism—one that pays greater attention to the historical context of revelatory texts, a method which I will call "hermeneutical historicism"—has an important role to play in progressive Muslims' call for Islamic legal reform. It could potentially play this positive role by destabilizing common sense, univocal interpretations of a text in favor of a more open-ended method of reading which discloses the multivalent possibilities of the text, some of which may be consistent with a progressive political agenda, in this case, gender egalitarianism. Such a method may even find some resonance within traditionalist Muslim circles, especially when compared to attempts by progressive Muslims (including Muslim feminists) to argue that Islamic revelatory texts, *properly read*, express an unequivocal commitment to gender [134] egalitarianism.[8] An important reason why traditionalist religious scholars

---

4. Ebrahim Moosa, "The Debts and Burdens of Critical Islam," in *Progressive Muslims on Justice, Gender and Pluralism*, ed. Omid Safi (Oxford: Oneworld Publications, 2003) at 123–125 [*hereinafter*, "*Debts*"].

5. Ibid., 125. See also Kecia Ali, *Sexual Ethics & Islam: Feminist Reflections on Qur'an, Hadith, and Jurisprudence* (Oxford: Oneworld Publications, 2006), 132–133 (progressive interpreters make a mistake in failing to acknowledge the interpretive legitimacy of hierarchical readings of the Qur'an).

6. Ibid., 121 and 125. See also Ebrahim Moosa, "The Poetics and Politics of Law after Empire: Reading Women's Rights in the Contestations of Law," *UCLA J. Islamic & Near E. L.* 1:1 (2001–2002): 1–46, at 45 [*hereinafter*, "*Poetics*"].

7. Fatima Mernissi, "A Feminist Interpretation of Women's Rights in Islam," in *Liberal Islam: A Sourcebook*, ed. Charles Kurzman (New York: Oxford University Press, 1998) 112–113 (describing her own feeling of being "[s]ilenced, defeated and furious" when confronted with this *hadith*).

8. Ali, *supra* n. 5 at 132 (criticizing a Muslim feminist for failing to "acknowledge the possibility that a

have been generally dismissive of feminist interpretations of the Qur'an is the implication that the tradition has, with respect to women, acted in bad faith, even consciously suppressing true Islamic teachings on gender.[9] Hermeneutical historicism, then, is responsive to what Andrew March has called the "Reformer's Dilemma": because it is discursively less "costly" in terms of moral capital to make revisions to applied doctrine than to methodological or foundational doctrines, an effective reformer is likely to exhaust the former before repairing to the ground of the latter.[10] Given that progressive Islam is an explicitly political project, it would seem appropriate for progressive Muslims to heed the Reformer's Dilemma, and to that extent, hermeneutical historicism would appear to be a valuable tool in their rhetorical strategies. Such a method could justify departures from the plain sense of a revealed text while avoiding "hermeneutical acrobatics." Progressive Muslims should pay special attention to what I am calling "hermeneutical historicism" given its affinity to discussions within traditional jurisprudence (*uṣūl al-fiqh*) regarding the circumstances in which it is appropriate for an interpreter to assume that a general term was intended to apply more restrictively than its literal sense would suggest. These discussions are treated under the rubric of *takhṣīṣ al-ʿāmm* (specification of the general term). As Moosa shows, even traditionalist scholars took historical circumstances into account in interpreting the legal consequences of revelation.[11] Indeed, the use of extrinsic evidence to interpret legal texts is a well-established, albeit controversial interpretive technique, in non-Islamic legal systems such as that of the United States.[12] [135] Hermeneutical historicism should be contrasted to what would be, from the perspective of historical orthodox Sunni Islam, a more controversial version of historicism, one, for example, which assumes that history moves progressively toward a specific telos, whether the classless society posited by Karl Marx, or perhaps liberal democracy in the eyes of Francis Fukuyama. I refer broadly to this class of historicist arguments as "progressive historicism." Progressive historicism uses history to relativize the moral significance of a particular legal text found in the Islamic revelatory sources. A progressive Muslim reformer applying progressive historicism might argue, for example, that although revelation communicates a clear rule without expressly including any kind of temporal restriction, Muslims today are nevertheless justified in restricting it to a dis-

---

reading of the Qurʾan that arrives at different conclusions [than those of feminists] could be a legitimate reading or a faithful explication of 'the Qurʾan's teachings.'").

9. Moosa, *Poetics* at 44

10. Andrew F. March, *Law as a Vanishing Mediator in the Theological Ethics of Tariq Ramadan* (available at http://papers.ssrn.com/sol3/papers.cfm?abstract_id=1478910, forthcoming in the *European Journal of Political Theory*), 32.

11. Moosa, *Debts*, at 126.

12. W. Eskridge, P. Frickey and E. Garrett, *Legislation and Statutory Interpretation* (New York: Foundation Press, 2000), 223–236 (discussing the role of extrinsic historical evidence in the interpretation of statutes in United States jurisprudence).

tant (or perhaps not so distant) past on the grounds that its moral significance is rightly constrained by what were the inherent practical limitations on achieving perfect justice (typically understood as consistent with the particular conception of justice adhered to by the interpreter) prevailing at the time of the Islamic dispensation in early seventh century Arabia. Progressive historicism might be used to generate readings of revelation that render rules reinforcing a system of gender subordination obsolete by, for example, limiting their application to the unique circumstances of pre-modern societies on the ground that they lacked the economic and institutional means to support a system of gender egalitarianism. Progressive historicist readings might also claim that revelation's universal and abstract texts point to an ideal transcending the practical limitations that inevitably arose out of the fact that revelation also addressed the very particular problems of seventh century Arabia. This is essentially the approach to the Qur'an taken by the modernist Pakistani-American theologian Fazlur Rahman.[13]

[136] That progressive historicism is not altogether alien even to traditionalist religious scholars is evidenced in the justification given for the abolition of slavery.[14] Traditionalist religious scholars often make the argument that the Qur'an aimed, first of all, to restrict the scope of slavery and raise the status of slaves in society, with the aim of its complete abolition. On this account, the fact that the Qur'an did not itself demand absolute abolition is not an obstacle to Islamic support for abolition. Progressive historicism, however, remains controversial in traditionalist and fundamentalist circles as a general interpretive strategy, probably because its theory that moral progress is a reason to suspend the effectiveness of various Qurʾanic legal provisions may suggest that revelation is imperfect.

Hermeneutical historicism, on the other hand, is only an additional interpretive tool in the hands of a jurist that allows her to use history to arrive at a better understanding of the Lawgiver's admittedly indeterminate intent by investigating the circumstances of the text. Hermeneutical historicism also has the advantage of historical Islamic legitimacy: Islamic scholarship of the Qurʾan generally,[15] and Islamic jurisprudence, through

13. See Mohammad Fadel, "Public Reason as a Strategy for Principled Reconciliation: the Case of Islamic Law and International Human Rights Law," *Chicago J. Int'l L.* 8:1 (Winter 2007): 1–20, at 14 (giving an example of how Rahman used progressive historicist arguments in connection with advocating gender egalitarianism in the Islamic context). For other modern Muslims who use this interpretive strategy, see Amina Wadud-Muhsin's work *Quran and Woman* (Kuala Lumpur: Penerbit Fajar Bakti Sdn. Bhd., 1994), 81, and some arguments of Fatima Mernissi, Ali, *supra* n. 5 at 54.

14. William Clarence-Smith, *Islam and the Abolition of Slavery* (Oxford: Oxford University Press, 2006), 195–218 (dividing Muslim abolitionists between "radicals" and "gradualists"); Fazlur Rahman, *Islam and Modernity* (Chicago: University of Chicago Press, 1984), 19 (arguing that the goal of the Qur'an was abolition, even if it is not an expressly abolitionist document).

15. A sub-field of Qurʾanic exegesis is known as *asbāb al-nuzūl* or "the occasions of revelation." Because the Qurʾan was revealed gradually over twenty-three years, this science seeks to document the

the concept of *takhṣīṣ al-ʿāmm* (specification of the general term) specifically,[16] both attempted to account for the unique circumstances in which religious or legal texts were communicated, and the relationship of those circumstances to a proper understanding of the text. Hermeneutical historicism, because of the potential it has for excavating alternative readings of the text, may have the potential of generating new (and relatively more progressive) interpretations while avoiding potentially controversial (and usually irrelevant) theological controversy. Progressive Muslim reformers should of course not abandon progressive historicism entirely; rather, it would [137] appear that the more politically prudent course for reformers would be first to exhaust the progressive possibilities inherent in conventional methods of interpretation, including hermeneutical historicism, before adverting to more controversial justifications, such as progressive historicism.

The concern with historical context in Islamic hermeneutics manifests itself in connection with Muslim jurists' discussion of the semantics of the "general term" (*al-lafẓ al-ʿāmm*).[17] While the formalist bent of traditional Muslim jurisprudence certainly might be an ally of text fundamentalism,[18] traditional Muslim legal interpretation also recognized the importance of context to interpretation.[19] To that extent, jurisprudential controversies regarding how to interpret the general term, as well as the larger question of the role of context in determining meaning, might play an important role in subverting unexamined, univocal readings of texts supporting various kinds of social hierarchies. Such a strategy might be particularly worthy for Muslim reformers to consider because it is peculiarly responsive to the difficult political circumstances facing them. These circumstances, as Saʿdiyya Shaikh emphasized, require progressive Muslims, simultaneously, to defend the Islamic tradition against hostile hegemonic western discourses while at the same time maintaining a posture of internal criticism in order to achieve the political goal of a more just and egalitarian society.[20] [138] In this article I take up Moosa's

---

particular historical circumstances in which the constituent texts of the Qurʾan were believed to have been revealed.

16. See discussion in Part 3.d, *infra*.

17. For a detailed discussion of the general term, see Bernard Weiss, *The Search for God's Law: Islamic Jurisprudence in the Writings of Sayf al-Dīn al-Āmidī* (Salt Lake City: University of Utah Press, 1992), 389–446.

18. Sherman Jackson, "Literalism, Empiricism and Induction: Apprehending and Concretizing Islamic Law's *Maqāṣid al-Sharīʿa* in the Modern World," *Mich. St. L. Rev.* (2006) 1469–1486, at 1471–1473 (noting the pre-modern commitment of Muslim jurists to a formalist theory of law that relied heavily on the efficacy of literal understanding of legal texts).

19. Sherman Jackson, "Fiction and Formalism: Toward a Functional Analysis of *Uṣūl al-fiqh*," in *Studies in Islamic Legal Theory*, ed. Bernard G. Weiss (Leiden: Brill, 2002), 192–193 (discussing the important role of "contextual indicators" in the determination of the intended meaning of legal language in Islamic jurisprudence).

20. Shaikh, *supra* n. 2 at 155:

"Muslim women and men with feminist commitments need to navigate the terrain between

invitation to apply a historicist method to revelatory texts as a reform strategy but from the perspective of hermeneutical historicism rather than progressive historicism. There may very well be instances where an advocate of legal reform concludes that the traditional reading of a text is the correct reading, with the result that he will have to apply a theologically controversial method of interpretation, e.g., progressive historicism, in order to carry her argument.[21] As I will show, however, the issue of female political participation appears amenable to resolution in a manner broadly consistent with progressive politics without resorting to the Islamically more controversial method of progressive historicism.[22]

I will test the practicability of this strategy by analyzing the *hadith* "Never shall a folk prosper who appoint a woman to rule them," or in a different version, "No people has prospered who has appointed a woman to lead them." Many pre-modern Sunni Muslims invoked this [139] text to justify the complete exclusion of women from various public offices. It also appears that, at least in certain contemporary Muslims societies, this *hadith* continues to be commonly used to justify exclusion of women from public office.[23] Given the general desire of even Muslim traditionalists in the modern period to exonerate the

being critical of sexist interpretations of Islam and patriarchy in their religious communities while simultaneously criticizing neo-colonial feminist discourses on Islam."

21. See, for example, Amina Wadud, *Inside the Gender Jihad: Women's Reform in Islam* (Oxford: Oneworld, 2006), 192 (describing circumstances in the Qurʾanic text where reinterpretation is insufficient and she must instead say "no" to the text based on some other value).

22. It goes without saying that the interpretive strategy proposed here (use of the concept of *takhṣīṣ al-ʿāmm* or specification of the general term) does not provide a magical solution to all questions of gender hierarchy in the Islamic legal tradition. Nor am I suggesting that the exclusion of women from the public sphere in contemporary Muslim societies can be remedied simply by re-reading the *hadith* in question in a manner acceptable to both progressives and traditionalists. Nevertheless, the *hadith* in question plays an important symbolic role in legitimating the exclusion of women from political life, something that justifies the greater attention Muslim progressives have given to this *hadith* relative to the more technical rules of substantive law (*fiqh*), e.g., the obligation of women to stay at home, even though such rules also pose substantial practical problems for female participation in the public sphere, and even though it is sometimes claimed that such rules are the subject of consensus (*ijmāʿ*). Because these technical rules are generally understood to be the product of juridical reflection rather than the words of God or the Prophet Muḥammad, they have less "sanctity" and thus reduced symbolic power in justifying relations of gender subordination in the modern world. For a detailed discussion of some pre-modern substantive rules in the Shāfiʿī school that justified gender subordination, see Scott Lucas, "Justifying Gender Inequality in the Shāfiʿī School," *Journal of the American Oriental Society* 129:2 (2009): 237–258. For a more comprehensive defense of the right of women to participate in the public affairs of the Muslim community that includes a revisionist interpretation of this *hadith* but goes well beyond it, see Yūsuf al-Qaraḍāwī, *Min Fiqh al-Dawla fī al-Islām* (Cairo: Dār al-Shurūq, 1997), 161–176, and ʿAbd al-Ḥalīm Maḥmūd Abū Shuqqa, *Taḥrīr al-Marʾa fī ʿAṣr al-Risāla*, 4 vols. (Dār al-Qalam: Kuwait, 1990).

23. Mernissi, *supra* note 7, 112–113 (describing the use of this *hadith* in Moroccan culture to exclude women from political life).

Islamic tradition of openly misogynistic views, however, contemporary Muslim understanding of this Prophetic report, as well as the question of female participation in public affairs, has undergone substantial revision.[24]

Unsurprisingly, this *hadith* has earned the particular scorn of Muslim feminists, at least one of whom has written an extensive refutation of its normative status.[25] Another well-known progressive Muslim author, Khaled Abou el Fadl, has also challenged the normativity of this report.[26] Unlike many misogynistic reports attributed to the Prophet Muḥammad that are universally deemed to be of dubious historical authenticity, the report at issue here is included in sources that Muslims deem to represent the most historically authoritative collections of the Prophet's words. Accordingly, denial of the text's authenticity is not a readily available option, at least without raising the kinds of foundational questions that the Reformer's Dilemma suggests should be avoided unless necessary.[27]

Accordingly, the analysis of this text could serve as a test case of whether hermeneutical historicism can offer results that are both substantively satisfactory from a progressive perspective and politically [140] superior to other progressive methods of reinterpretation because of the potential it offers in winning the support of a broader Muslim public. Finally, because this *hadith* uses a general expression—the negation of an indefinite noun[28]—a historical analysis of this text might also serve as a test case for determining the extent to which progressive interpretations of revelatory texts can emerge through a more critical use of traditional hermeneutical tools such as *takhṣīṣ al-ʿāmm* (specification of the general term) which allows an interpreter, in theory, at least, to take into account particular historical circumstances in an effort to establish the intended meaning of a particular legal text.[29]

---

24. Conservative scholars such as Yūsuf al-Qaraḍāwī have attempted to reinterpret the meaning of this report. See, for example, *al-Marʾa wa-l-ʿAmal al-Siyāsī* (Part IV) ("Women and Political Activism"), Ana TV Channel, available at http://www.youtube.com/watch?v=ei9LVMaEaBY (last visited September 19, 2009) (Qaraḍāwī explaining that the Prophetic report at issue must be read in light of the Qur'an's story of Bilqīs, the Queen of Sheba, whom the Qurʾan depicts as a wise and upright ruler). More generally, scholars such as al-Qaraḍāwī have advocated positions in support of women's political participation that are substantially at odds with the ethos of the pre-modern tradition. See al-Qaraḍāwī, *supra* n. 22, 161–176

25. See, for example, Mernissi, *supra* n. 7, 113–120.

26. Khaled Abou el Fadl, *Speaking in God's Name: Islamic Law, Authority and Women* (Oxford: Oneworld Publications, 2001), 111–114.

27. Mernissi, however, has challenged its authenticity. Ibid. See also, Shaikh, *supra* n. 2 at 158.

28. Weiss, *supra* n. 17 at 397–398; Sherman Jackson, "*Taqlīd*, Legal Scaffolding and the Scope of Legal Injunctions in Post-Formative Theory: *Muṭlaq* and *ʿĀmm* in the Jurisprudence of Shihāb al-Dīn al-Qarāfī," *Islamic Law & Society* 3:2 (1996): 165–192, at166.

29. See Ali, *supra* n. 5 at p. xx (arguing that a constructive and critical engagement with the pre-

2. THE *HADITH* SOURCES

Versions of this *hadith* appear in four major Sunni collections from the 9th and 10th centuries: the *Musnad* of Aḥmad b. Ḥanbal (d. 855/240);[30] the *Ṣaḥīḥ* of al-Bukhārī (d. 869/255);[31] the *Sunan* of al-Tirmidhī (d. 892/279);[32] and the *Sunan* of al-Nasāʾī (d. 915/302).[33] It also appears in the *Muṣannaf* of Ibn Abī Shayba (d. 849/234).[34] It subsequently appears in various (and substantially truncated) forms in late medieval/ [141] early modern *hadith* encyclopedias such as *Majmaʿ al-Zawāʾid* of Nūr al-Dīn ʿAlī b. Abī Bakr (d. 1405/807),[35] *al-Jāmiʿ al-Ṣaghīr* of Jalāl al-Dīn al-Suyūṭī (d. 1505/910),[36] *Kanz al-ʿUmmāl* of ʿAlī b. ʿAbd al-Malik al-Muttaqī (d. 1567/974),[37] and *Kashf al-Khafāʾ* of Ismāʿīl b. Muḥammad al-Jarrāḥ (d. 1748/1161).[38] All sources trace this report to one contemporary of the Prophet Muḥammad: Abū Bakra Nufayʿ b. al-Ḥārith (d. 671 or 672/51 or 52).[39] Likewise, all historical sources agree that this tradition was narrated exclusively by Baṣrans. This fact is especially significant because many Baṣrans fought on the losing side of the first civil war in Islamic history, a memory which was to provide a significant frame for some of this *hadith*'s subsequent narrations.

The *Muṣannaf* includes one version of this *hadith* in its lengthy chapter on the first civil war. There, Ibn Abī Shayba quoted Abū Bakra as saying "Never shall a folk prosper who delegate their affairs to a woman."[40] The *Musnad* includes eight versions of this *had-*

---

modern Islamic legal tradition has an important role to play in the renewal of modern Muslim ethical and legal thought).

30. Aḥmad b. Muḥammad Ibn Ḥanbal, *Musnad al-Imām Aḥmad Ibn Ḥanbal*, ed. ʿĀdil Murshid and Shuʿayb Arnaʾūṭ, 52 vols. (Beirut: Muʾassasat al-Risāla, 1993) [hereinafter "the *Musnad* "].

31. Muḥammad b. Ismāʿīl al-Bukhārī, *al-Jāmiʿ al-Musnad al-Ṣaḥīḥ al-Mukhtaṣar min Umūr Rasul Allāh wa-sunanihi wa-ayyāmih*, 5 vols. (Beirut: Dar al-Fikr, 2006).

32. Muḥammad b. ʿĪsā al-Tirmidhī, *Sunan al-Tirmidhī: Wa-Huwa al-Jāmiʿ al-Ṣaḥīḥ*, ed. Muḥammad ʿAbd al-Rahman b. ʿAbd al-Raḥīm Mubārakfūrī, et al. 3rd ed., 5 vols. (Dār al-Fikr, 1978).

33. Aḥmad b. Shuʿayb al-Nasāʾī, *Sunan al-Nasāʾī*, 8 vols. (Egypt: Muṣṭafā al-Bābī al-Ḥalabī, 1964–65).

34. ʿAbd Allāh b. Muḥammad Ibn Abī Shayba, *Al-Kitāb al-Muṣannaf Fī al-Aḥādīth wa'l-Āthār*, ed. Muḥammad ʿAbd al-Salām Shāhīn, 9 vols., 1st ed. (Beirut: Dār al-Kutub al-ʿIlmiyya, 1995), 7:538 [*hereinafter* "the *Muṣannaf* "]. I would like to thank Lena Saleymeh for suggesting this source to me.

35. Nūr al-Dīn ʿAlī b. Abī Bakr Haythamī, *Bughyat al-Rāʾid fī Taḥqīq Majmaʿ al-Zawāʾid wa-Manbaʿ al-Fawāʾid*, ed. ʿAbd Allāh Muḥammad Darwīsh, 10 vols. (Beirut: Dār al-Fikr, 1991), 5:378.

36. ʿAbd al-Raʾūf b. Tāj al-ʿĀrifīn Munāwī, *Fayḍ al-Qadīr: Sharḥ al-Jāmiʿ al-Ṣaghīr min Aḥādīth al-Bashīr al-Nadhīr*, ed. Aḥmad ʿAbd al-Salām, 6 vols. (Beirut: Dār al-Kutub al-ʿIlmiyya, 2001), 5:386.

37. ʿAlī b. ʿAbd al-Malik Muttaqī, *Kanz al-ʿUmmāl fī Sunan al-Aqwāl wa'l-Afʿāl*, ed. Isḥāq Ṭībī, 2 vols. (Bridgeview, Il: Bayt al-Afkār al-Dawliyya, 1999), 1:580.

38. Ismāʿīl b. Muḥammad Jarrāḥ ʿAjlūnī, *Kashf al-Khafā' wa-Muzīl al-Ilbās*, ed. Muḥammad b. ʿAbd al-Raḥmān Sakhāwī, 2nd ed. (Beirut: Dār Iḥyāʾ al-Turāth al-ʿArabī, 1968), 150.

39. ʿIzz al-Dīn Ibn al-Athīr, *Usd al-Ghāba fī Maʿrifat al-Ṣaḥāba*, 5 vols. (Beirut: Dār al-Maʿrifa, 1997), 4:392 (reporting his death date as either 51 or 52 AH).

40. Ibn Abī Shayba, *supra* n. 34

ith. One states that the Prophet said "Never shall a folk prosper who have entrusted their affairs to a woman."[41] Another states: "A Persian came to the Prophet and [the Prophet] said [to the Persian]: 'My Lord has killed your lord.' i.e. Chosroe, and it was said to him, i.e. the Prophet, 'He appointed his daughter to succeed him.' He said, 'No folk who is ruled by a woman shall prosper.'"[42] Yet another version states that "Abū Bakra witnessed a messenger come to the Prophet while he was reclining in ʿĀʾisha's bt. [142] Abī Bakr al-Ṣiddīq (d. 677 or 694/57 or 75)] lap and reported to him that they had been victorious over their enemy, so he stood and prostrated in thanks. Then, he began to ask the messenger various questions, and the messenger answered them. Among the things he told the Prophet was that a woman now ruled them. The Prophet then said, 'Now, the men have perished when they obey women,' three times."[43] The last version quotes Abū Bakra as stating "The Prophet said, 'Who governs Persia?' They replied 'A woman.' He said, 'No folk that a woman governs has prospered.'"[44]

Al-Bukhārī included two versions of this *hadith*. The first appears in *Kitāb al-Maghāzī, Bāb Kitāb al-Nabī ilā Kisrā wa Qayṣar* (The Book of Campaigns, Chapter: The Prophet's Diplomatic Correspondence with Chosroe and Caesar).[45] In this version Abū Bakra states, "God permitted me to benefit on the Day of the Camel from some words of the Prophet that I had heard, after I had almost joined the forces of the Camel to fight with them." He said, "When the Prophet was told that the Persians had appointed Chosroe's daughter as their ruler, he said, 'Never shall a folk prosper who have appointed a woman to rule them.'" Al-Bukhārī also included another version in *Kitāb al-Fitan* (The Book of Civil Strife).[46] In this version, Abū Bakra states, "God permitted me to benefit from some words on the Day of the Camel. When the Prophet was told that the Persians had made Chosroe's daughter their ruler, he said, "Never shall a folk prosper who have appointed a woman to rule them."

Al-Tirmidhī included only one version of the *hadith* in *Kitāb al-Fitan*.[47] In that version Abū Bakra said, "God protected me with something that I had heard from the Messenger of God: When Chosroe died, he said 'Whom have they appointed as his successor?' They replied, 'His daughter,' upon which the Prophet commented, 'Never shall a folk prosper who have appointed a woman to rule them.' So [143] when ʿĀʾisha came, [i.e. to Baṣra,] I remembered the Prophet's statement. Thus, God protected me through it.'"

41. The *Musnad* includes five versions of this *hadith* that are substantially similar to this version. Aḥmad b. Ḥanbal, *supra* n. 30, 34:43, 120, 121–122, 149

42. Ibid., at 85–86

43. Ibid., at 106–108

44. Ibid., at 144.

45. Aḥmad b. ʿAlī al-ʿAsqalānī, *Fatḥ al-bārī sharḥ ṣaḥīḥ al-Bukhārī*, ed. ʿAbd al-ʿAzīz b. Bāz, 16 vols. (Beirut: Dār al-Kutub al-ʿilmiyya, 1989), 8:159–160.

46. Ibid., 13:67.

47. Al-Tirmidhī, *supra* n. 32, at 3:360

Al-Nasāʾī included this *hadith* in *Kitāb Ādāb al-Quḍāt* (The Chapter of the Rules [Applicable to] Judges)[48] in a form that is virtually the same as that included in al-Tirmidhī's collection, except that al-Nasāʾī omitted Abū Bakra's concluding comment in which he stated that he remembered this statement at the time of ʿĀʾisha's arrival in Baṣra. Part 4 will explain in greater detail the interpretive significance of these different framings.

3. THE HERMENEUTICS OF THE GENERAL TERM IN ISLAMIC JURISPRUDENCE (*UṢŪL AL-FIQH*)

The linguistic category of the "general term" (*al-lafẓ al-ʿāmm*), and exceptions thereto or specifications thereof (*al-takhṣīṣ*), were important and controversial topics in Islamic jurisprudence (*uṣūl al-fiqh*) during the fifth-eighth/eleventh-fourteenth centuries.[49] It is unremarkable that the scope of the general term would be contentious in jurisprudential theory given the fact "that the range of application of the law is determined by general terms."[50] Moreover, the very fact of a term's generality means that it can come into conflict with other provisions of the law, a problem that justifies the hermeneutical preoccupation with setting out intelligible standards for its interpretation.[51]

One of the linguistic guises in which the general term appears is the negation of an indefinite noun; therefore, Abū Bakra's *hadith*—in its various versions—clearly engages jurisprudential debates on the [144] semantic scope of the general term. Before considering Muslim jurists' theory of the general term, however, a brief introduction to their theory of language is first needed.

A. An Overview of Pre-Modern Islamic Legal Hermeneutics

For most Muslim scholars of jurisprudence of this era, a speaker conveyed meaning through the deliberate use of specific utterances (*alfāẓ*). At some primordial moment, meaning was assigned by convention (*waḍʿ*) to all the words in a language. Because this primordial assignment was intended to further the interests of the speech-community using that language, Muslim jurists argued that a word's original, primordial meaning also constitutes that word's *proper* or *literal* usage, a sense they referred to as its *ḥaqīqa*.

48. Al-Nasāʾī, *supra* n. 33, at 8:200.

49. Jackson, *supra* n. 28 at 174 (noting the centrality of discussions of the scope of the general term to *medieval* Islamic jurisprudence). While Anglo-American jurisprudence has its own tradition of formalist statutory interpretation, including a formidable array of "canons of construction," see W. Eskridge, P. Frickey and E. Garrett, *Legislation and Statutory Interpretation* (New York: Foundation Press, 2000), 251–276, Anglo-American jurisprudence had not traditionally given a rigorous theoretical account of exceptions and their role in legal language. See Fredrick Schauer, "Exceptions" *U. Chi. L. Rev.* 58 (1991): 871–899.

50. Aron Zysow, *The Economy of Certainty* (unpublished Ph.D. diss., Harvard University, 1984) at 128.

51. Ibid.

Speakers, however, frequently use words in a non-literal or figurative sense. Such usage is called *majāz*, an Arabic noun indicating that the speaker literally "crosses" the proper boundaries of the word's original meaning.

Muslim jurists assume that speakers know both the primordial meanings of the words constituting their language and the relevant linguistic conventions of their language. They also assume that speakers, above all the Lawgiver (whether God directly in the Qur'an or indirectly through the Prophet Muḥammad's *sunna*), choose their words rationally to express their intended meanings. Muslim jurists therefore begin with the presumption that speakers ordinarily intend the plain or literal sense of the words they use. Only if there is evidence to the contrary, for example some extrinsic circumstance (*qarīna*) suggesting that the speaker intends a non-literal sense, would the listener be justified in interpreting the utterance figuratively.[52] Because the listener may fail to take into account relevant circumstantial evidence, however, the literal sense of an utterance, taken by itself, is only presumptive (*ẓāhir*) but not dispositive (*qaṭʿī*) evidence of the speaker's intent. Legal conclusions derived from the plain sense of revelatory texts, therefore, generally yield only probable judgment (*ẓann*) rather than certain knowledge [145] (*ʿilm*).[53] Mainstream Sunni jurisprudence, therefore, may be characterized as having adopted what the American legal scholar William Eskridge calls a "soft plain meaning rule,"[54] meaning that the object of jurisprudential inquiry into the words of the Lawgiver is to discover the Lawgiver's intent, and that plain meaning is an important, but not dispositive, means for discovering that intent.

B. The Controversial Hermeneutics of the General Term

When faced with linguistic forms that suggest generality (*ṣiyagh al-ʿumūm*), Muslim jurists must determine whether the literal sense of such forms applies to all instances of the relevant concept. The majority of Muslim scholars of jurisprudence concluded that the literal sense of such terms is indeed general. They also conclude that one of the means by which a speaker communicates generality is to negate an indefinite singular noun, as in the sentence "*laysa fī al-dār rajul*" ("There is not a man in the house."). This majority, the so-called *arbāb al-ʿumūm* ("the partisans of general expression"), construe general terms as providing presumptive evidence that the Lawgiver intends their application to

52. For a general introduction to the use of circumstantial evidence in Islamic legal theory, see Wael Hallaq, "Notes on the term *Qarīna* in Islamic Legal Discourse," *J. Am. Oriental Soc.* 108:3 (1988), 475–480.

53. The primary dissenters with respect to this view, at least as applied to the semantics of the general term, were the Ḥanafīs. Zysow, *supra* n. 50 at 129. The most important dissenter from this formalist theory of language was the Andalusian jurist Abū Isḥāq al-Shāṭibī who instead proposed a pragmatic theory of language grounded in the universal ends of religion (*al-maqāṣid al-kulliyya*). Ibrāhīm b. Mūsā al-Shāṭibī, *al-Muwāfaqāt*, 4 vols. (al-Khubar: Dār Ibn ʿAffān, 1997), 4:7–49.

54. Eskridge et al., *supra* n. 49 at 224–225.

all instances of the relevant class.[55] This presumption could, and was, regularly defeated by other evidence suggesting that the Lawgiver intended a more specific meaning, a phenomenon known as *takhṣīṣ al-ʿāmm* (specification of the general term).[56]

A not insubstantial minority, the so-called *arbāb al-khuṣūṣ* ("the partisans of specific reference"), rejected this analysis. Relying on the frequency with which speakers use general terms while intending a more specific meaning, they argued that, when faced with a general term, a [146] jurist is only entitled to presume that the rule applied to some, but not all, of the members of the relevant class. The third (and smallest) group of jurists (*al-wāqifiyya*) held that it is impossible to justify any kind of presumption as to the scope of a general term in the absence of additional evidence of the Lawgiver's intent.

Each of the three positions, then, is open to further interpretation of a general term; indeed, even the majority believed that a jurist, before applying a general term, is under an obligation to search for circumstantial evidence that may clarify whether the Lawgiver had used the general term in a non-literal fashion.[57] As a practical matter the real issue separating Muslim jurists was the scope of rules communicated using general terms for which the Lawgiver did *not* provide any circumstantial evidence relevant to determining the Lawgiver's intent. For the majority, the Lawgiver's use of a general term justifies the conclusion that the rule should be applied generally; the minority, meanwhile, hold that the rule may be applied only to the particular members of the class to which it is known to apply, a position that is practically indistinguishable from those jurists who view general texts as inherently ambiguous and thus are in need of clarification before any legal rule may be derived from them.[58] Applying these principles to Abū Bakra's *hadith*, the majority of Muslim jurists would conclude, in the absence of any other evidence, that its literal sense establishes that women are not fit to rule.

i. Specification of the General Term

Evidence that the Lawgiver used a general term while intending a more specific meaning may come from multiple sources. In some non-controversial cases, the evidence is explicit and part of the same utterance (*al-dalīl al-muttaṣil*), an express exception to the general term being the most obvious, as in the Islamic declaration of faith, "*lā ilāha*

55. Weiss, *supra* n. 17 at 404–5.

56. The frequency by which general terms were in fact subject to specification by jurists gave rise to common juristic saying that "there is no general term that has not been subject to specification (*mā min ʿāmm illā khuṣṣa*)." Zysow, *supra* n. 50 at 129.

57. A minority of the partisans of general expression rejected such an obligation on the theory that it would make it practically impossible to apply any general rule. Sulaymān b. Khalaf al-Bājī, *Iḥkām al-fuṣūl fī aḥkām al-uṣūl*, ed. ʿAbd Allāh Muḥammad al-Jabūrī (Beirut: Muʾassasat al-risāla, 1989), 143–144.

58. Weiss, *supra* n. 17 at 405.

illā allāh" (There is no god except for God). It is the so-called "disconnected [147] indicant of specification" (*al-dalīl al-munfaṣil*), however, that generates the greatest controversy.

Jurists identify three kinds of disconnected indicants of specification: rational, empirical and textual. The first two are narrow and generally understood to be implicated only when the plain sense of general term would render the statement logically or empirically absurd. Accordingly, rational considerations lead to specification of phrases in the Qurʾan like "God is the creator of all things" so as to exclude God from membership in the class of "things." Similarly, empirical considerations require specification of the Qurʾanic verse in which God describes a wind as "destroying everything," because empirically we know that it did not destroy the heavens or the earth. Finally, other texts of revelation can specify general terms. For example, the *hadith* attributed to the Prophet Muḥammad in which he was reported to have said that "There is no amputation for a thief who steals property having value of less than one-fourth of a gold dinar," was taken to limit the seemingly general Qurʾanic verse whose terms impose amputation of the thief 's hand.[59]

A minority of scholars of jurisprudence held that the specific circumstances surrounding the communication of a legal text may serve as circumstantial evidence of the Lawgiver's intent that the text's scope is specific rather than general.[60] The majority instead affirmed the principle that "consideration is given to the generality of the words, not the specificity of their occasion" (*al-ʿibra fī ʿumūm al-lafẓ lā khuṣūṣ al-sabab*). As will be shown in greater detail below, whether the particular circumstances surrounding the communication of a legal text are relevant to the proper interpretation of the text is an important consideration in interpreting Abū Bakra's *hadith*. Accordingly, I will conclude this section with a brief discussion of this issue.

ii. Can the Specific Circumstances of a Legal Text Specify the Scope of a General Term?

[148] Abū Ḥāmid al-Ghazālī (d. 1111/505) displays the ambivalence characteristic of Muslim jurisprudence with respect to the tension between its commitment to objectivism in hermeneutics and the inescapable need to give effect to context, even non-linguistic context. Thus, al-Ghazālī affirmed the majority's position that the circumstances of a text's communication are generally ineffective to specify the general term while at the same time admitting that such extra-textual circumstances may make it more likely that a more specific intent was intended, thus permitting specification with even a relatively

59. Ibid., at 424.

60. Hallaq, *supra* n. 52 at 475 (noting the importance of circumstantial evidence to determinations of whether the scope of a text should be narrowed). This intra-Muslim debate regarding the relevance of non-verbal circumstances in construing the words of the Lawgiver is in important respects analogous to the debate in American jurisprudence regarding the legitimacy of using extrinsic evidence, such as legislative history, to interpret a statute. Eskridge et al., *supra* n. 49 at 223–236.

weak indicant (*dalīl akhaff wa-aḍʿaf*).[61] Indeed, in some cases, despite the general rule, it is simply impossible to resist the conclusion that the relevant circumstances require specification of the general term, as in the case in which one man tells another, "Speak with so-and-so about such-and-such," and the other man then swears an oath, saying, "By God, I shall never talk to him." Here, al-Ghazālī said, the oath is understood to apply only to conversations with that third person regarding that particular event, not absolutely.[62]

Al-Āmidī (d. 1233/630) related that whether or not the circumstances of a legal text are taken into account depends both on the specific circumstances that prompted the communication and the nature of the legal text. Accordingly, if the Lawgiver is asked about a specific act, but provides a response broader than the question asked, many jurists who otherwise affirm the general expression would, in this circumstance, restrict that text's application to the circumstances of the question.[63] On the other hand, if the Lawgiver is asked a question, and [149] the answer is broader than the specific circumstances that gave rise to the question, and the answer is logically independent of the question, then the partisans of the general expression unanimously apply the text generally.[64] A fortiori, for partisans of the general expression, if the Lawgiver uses a general term without prompting by the questioner, the general term applies generally according to its presumptive sense.[65]

It was reported, however, that foundational figures in Islamic jurisprudence accepted the minority position, including Mālik b. Anas (d. 796/179), Abū Thawr (d. 240/854), al-Muzanī (d. 877/263) and al-Shāfiʿī (d. 820/204), at least in some of the views attributed to him.[66] This controversy, moreover, generated differences in legal rules. For example,

61. Abū Ḥāmid Muḥammad b. Muḥammad al-Ghazālī, *al-Mustaṣfā*, ed. Muḥammad ʿAbd al-Salām ʿAbd al-Shāfī (Beirut: Dār al-kutub al-ʿilmiyya, 1993) at 236.

62. Ibid.

63. Sayf al-Dīn Al-Āmidī, *al-Iḥkām fī uṣūl al-aḥkām*, 4 vols. (Beirut: Dār al-Kutub al-ʿIlmiyya, 1983), 2:346–347. A standard example involves the case of a well and whether its water was ritually pure. The Prophet Muḥammad was asked about the water of a particular well and was told that wild animals drink from it as do humans. His reply was that "Water has been created pure; nothing pollutes it unless its taste, odor or color is changed." Most jurists took this report, despite its general language, as applying specifically to that particular well, given what was known about the vastness of its water supply.

64. Ibid. The example used to illustrate this principle involved a group of people who asked the Prophet whether they could perform ritual ablution using sea water while they are out at sea. The Prophet Muḥammad replied saying, "Its water is purifying, and its dead [creatures] are lawful to eat." Because the question did not raise the issue of whether such animals could be eaten, Muslim jurists concluded that this general expression was intended to communicate a general rule that eating such animals was permissible.

65. Ibid.

66. Taqī al-Dīn ʿAlī b. ʿAbd al-Kāfī al-Subkī, *al-Ibhāj fī Sharḥ al-Minhāj: ʿAlā Minhāj al-Wuṣūl ilā ʿIlm al-Uṣūl lil-Qāḍī al-Bayḍāwī*, ed. Shaʿbān Muḥammad Ismāʿīl, 3 vols. (Cairo: Maktabat al-kulliyyāt al-azhariyya, 1981–1982), 2:1004–1005.

Shāfiʿīs disagreed regarding the scope of the dispensation (*rukhṣa*) concerning the *ʿarāyā* sale. The *ʿarāyā* is a transaction pursuant to which a person uses dried dates to purchase fresh dates in an apparent violation of the Islamic doctrine of *ribā* (usury).[67] The disagreement is whether this dispensation is available to all persons without regard to their personal wealth, or is limited to needy persons on the grounds that the text giving this permission was prompted by questions from the poor. The majority of Shāfiʿī jurists concluded that the dispensation is universal while a minority limit it to the needy.[68] Another example involves interpretation of the Qurʾanic verse which states, "Say (O Muḥammad)!: I find nothing in that which has been revealed to me proscribing what one may eat other than [the flesh of] carrion or the blood [of slaughtered animals]." Al-Shāfiʿī, who took this [150] verse as arising out of a polemic against pre-Islamic Arab pagans rather than a text setting out dietary rules for Muslims, ignored it when he formulated Islamic dietary restrictions.[69] Mālik, however, applied the text generally with the result that, for him, other texts, e.g. Prophetic *hadiths*, the plain meaning of which appear to prohibit eating the flesh of carnivorous animals, were taken to signify disapproval (*karāha*), not prohibition (*taḥrīm*).[70] Al-Zarkashī (d. 1392/794) provided another example of al-Shāfiʿī using circumstances to circumscribe a text's applicability: contrary to the Ḥanafīs, who held that female apostates may not be executed, al-Shāfiʿī held that their treatment was no different from male apostates, despite the Prophet's prohibition against killing women. Al-Shāfiʿī, however, argued that the *hadith* prohibiting the killing of women refers to the women of hostile non-Muslim tribes, not Muslim women who apostatized.[71] This dispute was also characterized by at least some Muslim jurisprudents as part of a larger problem: does a rule that no longer serves its original purpose continue to apply by its terms or does it lapse by virtue of the legal cause's disappearance (*ʿilla*)?[72]

As these examples make clear, even among the partisans of the general term, willingness existed to take into account substantive context in an attempt to produce an interpretation of the Lawgiver's intent that appeared sensible to the interpreter. This general sensitivity to context, however, did not seem to play a role in jurists' understanding of Abū Bakra's *hadith*, even though, as Part 4 will show, it would not have been difficult to argue that a more specific meaning was in fact intended. Part Six will make the case that Muslim jurists did not attempt to justify a more-narrow reading of the

67. For a detailed overview of the complex and various doctrines falling under the legal category of *ribā*, see Mohammad Fadel, "*Ribā*, Efficiency and Prudential Regulation: Preliminary Thoughts," *Wis. Int'l L.J.* 25 (2008), 655–702

68. Al-Subkī, *supra* n. 66 at 1004–1005.

69. Muḥammad b. Bahādur al-Zarkashī, *al-Baḥr al-Muḥīt fī Uṣūl al-Fiqh*, ed. Muḥammad Muḥammad Tāmir, 4 vols. (Beirut: Manshūrāt Muḥammad ʿAlī Bayḍūn, Dār al-Kutub al-ʿIlmiyya, 2000), 2:359–61.

70. Yasin Dutton, *Original Islam: Mālik and the* Madhhab *of Madina* (New York: Routledge, 2007), at 87.

71. Al-Zarkashi, *supra* n. 69 at 60–61.

72. Ibid., 363, 385.

hadith for the simple reason that, because of a generally prevailing androcentric (if not misogynistic) culture, they were insufficiently motivated to apply the critical tools [151] otherwise available to them in interpreting this *hadith*, something that would change in the modern era.

4. *HADITH* GENRE, INTERPRETATION AND NARRATIVE FRAME

For Sunni Muslims, the scholar-compilers active in the ninth and tenth centuries of what would later become the "canonical" collections of Prophetic *hadiths* are generally most esteemed for their attempts to authenticate the historical material attributed to the Prophet Muḥammad.[73] Rigorous historical authentication of the Prophet Muḥammad's teachings was not, however, their exclusive goal. The generic structure of *hadith* works, the scholar-compiler's decision where to place a *hadith* within his compilation, and sometimes subtle editorial comments or changes (e.g., with respect to the omission or inclusion of certain background facts) combine to provide evidence that some compiler-scholars were also engaged in their own interpretive projects and *wanted* their texts to be read in a particular way.

To appreciate how literary context can shape perceptions of a *hadith*'s meaning, a brief introduction to the various genres of *hadith* collections is helpful. The collections which record various original versions of this incident fall into three different genres. The first genre, known as *muṣannaf*, of which Ibn Abī Shayba's *Muṣannaf* is an outstanding example, emerged in the second half of the eighth century. This work includes material on theology, history of the early Muslim community and law. Ibn Abī Shayba arranged his material topically. Unlike later *hadith* works, Prophetic *hadiths* are only a small part of its materials. Moreover, the concern to include only historically sound material, as evidenced by a reliable chain of transmitters (*isnād*), is absent.[74] The second genre, known as the *musnad*, emerged in the late eighth and early ninth centuries and was responsive to the perceived need to authenticate more rigorously the material attributed to the Prophet [152] Muḥammad. Unlike *muṣannafs*, material in a *musnad* was arranged alphabetically by the name of the report's first transmitter. This genre was especially popular with *hadith* critics, for whom study of the chain of transmitters was a critical tool in assessing the authenticity of a historical text.[75] The *Musnad* stands as an exemplar of this genre. The third genre of early *hadith* scholarship can be described as the *ṣaḥīḥ/sunan* genre. This type of *hadith* scholarship represented a synthesis of the older *muṣannaf*

73. For an introduction to the history of the study of *hadith* in Sunni Islam and to the various genres of *hadith* works, see Jonathan Brown, *Hadith: Muhammad's Legacy in the Medieval and Modern World* (Oxford: One World, 2009), esp. Chapter 2 "The Transmission and Collection of Prophetic Traditions," 15–66.

74. Ibid., 25–28.

75. Ibid., 28–31.

genre with the rigorous historical standards of the *hadith* critics to produce works organized by topic but restricted largely to Prophetic *hadiths* that were deemed to be reliable based on the historical-critical methods of the *hadith* scholars.[76] The collections of al-Bukhārī, al-Tirmidhī and al-Nasāʾī are exemplars of this genre. Finally, encyclopedic collections of *hadith* whose primary function appears to have been as reference books for non-specialists, were produced between the fifteenth and eighteenth centuries. Works such as *Kanz al-ʿUmmāl, Majmaʿ al-Zawāʾid, Kashf al-Khafāʾ* and *al-Jāmiʿ al-Ṣaghīr* are representative of this genre.[77]

When close attention is paid to the narrative context in which this incident appears, one can speak meaningfully of the reports having materially different implications. As will be shown below, only one of these early *hadith* collections, that of al-Nasāʾī, made an explicit connection between Abū Bakra's *hadith* and qualifications for political office.[78] Al-Bukhārī's placements of the *hadith*, however, suggests a reading of the text that functions more to vindicate the Prophet Muḥammad's claims of prophecy[79] and the need to remain neutral in times of civil war,[80] while al-Tirmidhī's report suggests that the text's main lesson is to maintain neutrality in the context of civil war.[81] Ibn Abī Shayba's version,[82] meanwhile, parallels the prophetic dimension al-Bukhārī gave to the text, but in a substantially different manner: while al-Bukhārī's [153] placement points to a specific incident in Persia as the referent of the Prophet's statement, Ibn Abī Shayba's placement suggests that it was a prophecy of the doomed intervention of ʿĀʾisha on the losing side of the first Muslim civil war.[83]

To make this point clear, I now turn to the various versions of this incident as reported in the collections cited in Part 2 above. The *musnads* and the *hadith* encyclopedias are superficially similar in that both minimize authorial voice in interpretation of the text, and in so doing, may have the effect of reinforcing a formalist approach to their interpretation. This feature, while apparently intentional in the *hadith* encyclopedias (their compilers stripped out background facts so as to include only what was deemed to be normatively relevant, i.e., the Prophet's words, acts or omissions), is only incidental in

---

76. Ibid., 31–34.

77. Ibid., 59.

78. See al-Nasāʾī, *supra* n. 33.

79. See Ibn Ḥajar, *supra* n. 45.

80. See Ibn Ḥajar, *supra* n. 46.

81. See al-Tirmidhī, *supra* n. 32.

82. See Ibn Abī Shayba, *supra* n. 34.

83. In his discussion of this *hadith*, Abou el Fadl argues that it is necessary to raise the question of Abū Bakra's "authorial voice" relative to the "authorial voice" of the Prophet Muḥammad. Unlike Abou el Fadl, I draw attention to the "authorial voice" of the compilers of *hadith* works who included this text in their compilations, a task which, in my opinion, is far more achievable than recovering the "authorial voice" of either Abū Bakra or the Prophet Muḥammad.

musnads like that of Ibn Ḥanbal, which preserve the contextual integrity of each report, at least to the extent that the original narrators of the reports thought relevant. This feature of the *hadith* encyclopedias is consistent both with the formalism of post-formative Islamic jurisprudence and with the practice of jurists to cite Prophetic *hadiths* that were reported in connection with specific events in the form of legal maxims that ignore the specificity of the Prophet's statement, e.g. "the child belongs to the marriage-bed (*al-walad li'l-firāsh*),"[84] and "profit follows risk of loss (*al-kharāj bi'l-ḍamān*)."[85]

The *hadith* encyclopedias were compiled specifically to make the work of jurists easier by compiling all legally relevant *hadiths* in one convenient source. And while these encyclopedias then provided relevant citation information for the reader which would permit him, if he so desired, to read the full version of the reports in the original collections, he certainly did not need to do so, especially since this abbreviated [154] method of citing *hadiths* was consistent with the legal formalism that dominated Islamic jurisprudence in the post-formative period.

The *ṣaḥīḥ/sunan* works of al-Bukhārī, al-Tirmidhī and al-Nasāʾī, by contrast, are arranged topically. The author's placement of a *hadith* in these works reveals how the author wanted his readers to understand the text. This aspect of al-Bukhārī's collection is especially complex and has been the subject of a tradition of learned commentary by Muslim scholarship. Unlike the compilers of the *musnads*, al-Bukhārī's interpretive voice stands at the center of his work: he included his materials under various chapter headings that in many cases take explicitly normative positions, virtually instructing the reader as to the conclusion that should be drawn from the material he transmits.[86]

Al-Tirmidhī's and al-Nasāʾī's collections in contrast occupy an intermediate position between the two extremes of the *Musnad*, which disclaims any interpretive stance with respect to its material, and al-Bukhārī's, which takes interpretive questions as central to its structure. While al-Tirmidhī and al-Nasāʾī both organize their materials thematically, they are not engaged in (overt) polemical argumentation in the fashion of al-Bukhārī. At the same time, the manner by which they organize their materials reveals their subjective understanding of the material presented. When al-Bukhārī's placement of this text is compared with that of al-Tirmidhī and al-Nasāʾī, important differences emerge. Al-Bukhārī included it in two different chapters of his book, "The Chapter of [Military] Campaigns, Section: The Prophet's Diplomatic Correspondence with Chosroe and Caesar," and "The Chapter of Civil Strife." Al-Tirmidhī, however, included it solely in his "Chapter

84. See Ibn Ḥajar, *supra* n. 45, 12:36.

85. Muḥammad b. Yazīd b. Māja, *Sunan Ibn Māja*, ed. Bashshār ʿAwwād Maʿrūf, 6 vols., 1st ed. (Beirut: Dār al-Jīl, 1998), 3:576.

86. Mohammad Fadel, "Ibn al-Ḥajar's Hady al-Sārī: A Medieval Theory of the Structure of al-Bukhārī's *al-Jāmiʿ al-Ṣaḥīḥ*, Introduction and Translation," *Journal of Near Eastern Studies* 54:3 (1995): 161–197, at 164.

of Civil Strife," and al-Nasāʾī included it solely in "The Chapter of the Rules [Applicable to] Judges."

Based on al-Bukhārī's placement of this text, it appears that he viewed it primarily in the context of the Prophet's diplomatic contacts with the neighboring powers of Byzantium and Persia, and secondarily as a guide to how one should conduct one's self at a time of civil strife. The *hadith* that precedes Abū Bakra's report in al-Bukhārī's collection is [155] consistent with this reading. That report tells us that the Prophet Muḥammad had sent a diplomatic letter to the ruler of Persia who, after reading it, tore it up dismissively. Al-Bukhārī reported that when the Prophet learned what happened to his diplomatic initiative, he called on God to destroy the Persian state (*fa daʿā ʿalayhim rasūl allahu an yumazzaqū kulla mumazzaq*).[87] This would suggest that the report at issue, at least in al-Bukhārī's view, functions to vindicate the Prophet's claim of prophecy insofar as it represents a prophecy that the Persian state would soon collapse, something that would take place shortly after the Prophet died.[88]

Two fifteenth-century *hadith* commentators, Ibn Ḥajar al-ʿAsqalānī (d. 1449/853) and Badr al-Dīn al-ʿAynī (d. 1451/855),[89] emphasized the Persian context of this text in their respective commentaries on this text in al-Bukhārī's *ṣaḥīḥ*. Ibn Ḥajar explained that al-Bukhārī included Abū Bakra's *hadith* in the section dealing with the Prophet's diplomatic activities, because "it is the conclusion of the story of Chosroe who had ripped up the Prophet's letter. As a result, God set Chosroe's son against his father, murdering him. He [i.e. the son] then killed his brothers, with the result that they were forced to appoint a woman as their ruler. That led to the destruction of their dynasty, and they were destroyed, just as the Prophet had asked God to do."

Ibn Ḥajar provides a detailed account of the internal strife that brought down the Persian state: Shīrawayhi, the son who had murdered his father Pervez in order to become king, died within six months of his parricide and regicide, ironically, at the hands of his father. In Ibn Ḥajar's account of the incident, after discovering that his son was [156] responsible for taking his life, Pervez plotted revenge against his son. To that end Pervez, presumably as he lay dying, prepared a poison which he placed in a jar in the royal treasury, labeling it an aphrodisiac, confident that his son would consume it. Sure enough, Shīrawayhi subsequently discovered the jar, drank its contents, and died. Prior

87. Ibn Ḥajar, *supra* n. 45, at 8:161.

88. Al-Bukhārī, unlike either al-Tirmidhī or al-Nasāʾī, frequently repeated *hadiths* in various chapters of his work in order to draw out what he believed were the full normative implications of the report. Fadel, *supra* n. 86 at 183. Because he included in his work a lengthy chapter devoted exclusively to issues of governance, *Kitāb al-Aḥkām* ("The Book of Legal Judgments"), Ibn Ḥajar, *supra* n. 45, at 13:139–268, his failure to include Abū Bakra's *hadith* in that chapter provides a reasonable basis for concluding that he did not believe it had political significance. The same conclusion cannot be as confidently asserted with respect to al-Tirmidhī given the fact that he did not generally repeat the same *hadith* in his book.

89. Badr al-Dīn Maḥmūd b. Aḥmad al-ʿAynī, *Umdat al-Qārī* (Beirut: Idārat al-Ṭibāʿa al-Munīriyya, 1970).

to his consumption of the poison, however, Shīrawayhi had killed all his brothers in an attempt to secure his own rule, but because of his father's actions, he did not live long enough to produce a male heir. As a result, the Persians were forced to appoint Būrān, Shīrawayhi's daughter, as their new ruler.[90] Al-ʿAynī provides additional detail in support of al-Bukhārī's contention that the Persian ruler's arrogance was the cause of his downfall, reporting that Chosroe not only tore up the letter, but arrogantly exclaimed, "Does he dare to address me in such a manner, even though he [i.e. the Prophet Muḥammad] is a slave?"[91]

Al-Tirmidhī's version preserves the notion that the Prophet made this statement in connection with political developments in Persia. Unlike al-Bukhārī, however, he did not include any information relating to the Prophet's diplomatic exchanges with Persia. Accordingly, the Prophet's general statement upon being informed that a woman had been recently appointed their leader—"Never shall a folk prosper who have appointed a woman to rule them"—in al-Tirmidhī's *Sunan* takes the appearance of the objective comment of a disinterested observer rather than a prophecy of imminent doom. Al-Tirmidhī's inclusion of the *hadith* in the Book of Civil Strife, meanwhile, suggests that he saw the *hadith* primarily as a lesson on the importance of neutrality in the context of civil strife, something that is emphasized by the slightly changed wording in Abū Bakra's *hadith* in which he is reported to have used the word "protect" rather than "benefit."[92]

[157] Like al-Bukhārī, Ibn Abī Shayba also placed this *hadith* in a prophetic context, but one related to ʿĀʾisha's ill-fated role in the first Muslim civil war. He included this report in his chapter dealing with the events of the first civil war (*Kitāb al-Jamal*), where it is immediately preceded by two reports that attribute to the Prophet Muḥammad foreknowledge of the civil war. Ibn Abī Shayba quoted the Prophet Muḥammad as saying, presumably to his wives, "Oh, which of you shall be the master of the camel ... around whom shall be great slaughter, but she shall survive?" Ibn Abī Shayba also quotes Abū Bakra as saying that, when asked why he did not join the Baṣran forces at the time of the civil war, he had heard the Prophet Muḥammad say, "A group shall rebel, and they will perish and shall not succeed. Their leader will be a woman, but they are people of Paradise." Ibn Abī Shayba, immediately after these two reports, then includes Abū Bakra's

---

90. Ibn Ḥajar, *supra* n. 45 at 162.

91. Al-ʿAynī, *supra* n. 89 at 18:58.

92. "The Chapter of Civil Strife [*fitan*]" deals with civil war and events said to occur during "the last days." For this reason, one might take the view that the inclusion of this *hadith* under this heading by both al-Bukhārī and al-Tirmidhī implies their position that one of the signs of "the last days" is the assumption of positions of political leadership by women. While this possibility cannot be excluded, the subtlety of the implication was lost on Ibn Ḥajar, who makes no connection between the report and "the last days." In his commentary on this *hadith* in the Chapter of Civil Strife, he notes that while Abū Bakra agreed with ʿĀʾisha's substantive position during the first civil war, i.e., the need to avenge the killers of ʿUthmān, he held a pacifist position with respect to intra-Muslim warfare. Ibn Ḥajar, *supra* n. 46, at 70–71.

hadith. He quotes Abū Bakra as saying that he had heard the Prophet Muḥammad say, "No folk who has entrusted their affairs to a woman shall prosper." In Ibn Abī Shayba's narrative, the *hadith* is the climax to the Prophet's prediction of ʿĀʾisha's crushing defeat. Ibn Abī Shayba thus explains to his readers why Abū Bakra felt fortunate: he escaped the fate of his Baṣran comrades who joined ʿĀʾisha's army solely because he had heard from the Prophet Muḥammad himself prophecies that led him to conclude that ʿĀʾisha's campaign would end up disastrously.

Finally, al-Nasāʾī, uniquely among the compilers of the *ṣaḥīḥ/sunan* genre, includes Abū Bakra's *hadith* in a chapter titled "The Book of the Rules [Applicable to] Judges." The report itself is prefaced with the short statement, "Section: The Prohibition Against Appointing Women to Rule (*bāb al-nahy ʿan istiʿmāl al-nisāʾ fīʾl ḥukm*)." This suggests that al-Nasāʾi viewed the *hadith* as establishing maleness as one of the conditions necessary to serve in public office. This may explain why al-Nasāʾī omits Abū Bakra's statement "When ʿĀʾisha came to Baṣra, I remembered the Prophet's statement," even though al-Tirmidhī's version includes it and al-Nasāʾī's informants are the same as al-Tirmidhī's. While each of these authors—Ibn Abī Shayba, al-Bukhārī, al-Tirmidhī and al-Nasāʾī—narrate substantially the same text from substantially [158] the same sources, their placement of the text within their broader works differs in important respects, each one suggesting a different interpretation of the text. The interpretive challenges posed by the placement of this *hadith* in the *ṣaḥīḥ/sunan* genre, however, was largely dissolved by the compilers of the *hadith* encyclopedias between the 15th and 18th centuries. Those works, apparently influenced by the formalist doctrines of jurisprudence, limited themselves to the formally dispositive elements of the Prophet's teachings—his words, his acts and his omissions. The result was to make the contextual frames of the authors of the *ṣaḥīḥ/sunan* genre irrelevant.

5. ABŪ BAKRA'S *HADITH* IN SUBSTANTIVE LAW

Part 4 demonstrated how the same *hadith* could be, and in fact was, understood differently depending on the narrative context in which it appears. This Part will further explore the relationship of text, context and interpreter by looking at how this *hadith* was used in substantive law by considering how jurists interpreted this text in connection with their rules governing qualifications for public office.

Islamic substantive law generally requires the holders of public offices to be male. Accordingly, only men may serve as the head of the Islamic state (*imām* or *khalīfa*). The same requirement applies to judges of Islamic courts as well, with only a minority of Muslim jurists permitting the appointment of female judges.[93] Discrimination against

93. Mohammad Fadel, "Two Women, One Man: Knowledge, Power and Gender in Medieval Sunni Legal Thought," *Int't J. Middle East Studies* 29 (1997): 185–204, at 196 (noting minority views permitting

women is not unique to the pre-19th century Islamic legal system, and to that extent is unexceptional.[94] A more complex question is determining the [159] precise role played by this *hadith* in producing these discriminatory doctrines, or justifying them once they were in place. Surviving works of substantive law from the first 300 years of Islamic history, for example, do not appear to have cited it to justify the exclusion of women from public offices, a fact that suggests that this *hadith* played only an ex post justificatory role rather than a "but for" cause of the discrimination evidenced in the legal rules.[95]

It is almost certainly the case that the increasing formalization of legal education, along with the incorporation of legal debate (*munāẓara*) and the formal study of legal controversy (*ikhtilāf* or *khilāf*), was the catalyst for the ever-increasing reference to this *hadith* in legal treatises. Al-Māwardī (d. 1058/450), a prominent Shāfiʿī jurist, cited it to justify the Shāfiʿī rule that only men may serve as judges,[96] explicitly refuting the views of dissenters such as Muḥammad b. Jarīr al-Ṭabarī (d. 923/310), who permitted women to serve as judges in all types of cases, and the Ḥanafīs, who permitted women to serve as judges, but only in non-capital cases.[97] The 12th-century Andalusian Mālikī jurist and Ashʿarī theologian al-Qāḍī Abū Bakr Ibn al-ʿArabī (d. 1148/543) took up this issue in connection with his comments on the Qurʾanic story of Bilqīs. There, he relied on the *hadith* as conclusive evidence that women not only cannot serve as head of the Islamic state (caliph), but also for the proposition that women cannot be judges. Indeed, Ibn al-ʿArabī went so far as to deny that al-Ṭabarī, whom he describes as "the Imam of religion," could ever have held the view ascribed to him regarding women judges, a position that Ibn al-ʿArabī obviously [160] considered scandalous. He also expressed doubts that Abū Ḥanīfa had actually permitted women to serve as judges, even in non-capital cases. He instead

women to be Islamic law judges). For a more comprehensive treatment of women as judges under medieval Islamic law, see Karen Bauer, "The Gender Hierarchy and the Question of Women as Judges and Witnesses in Pre-Modern Islamic Law" (forthcoming in *The Journal of the American Oriental Society*). For an overview of women as judges in the legal systems of modern Arab states, see Monique C. Cardinal, "Why Aren't Women Sharīʿa Court Judges? Se Case of Syria," *Islamic Law and Society* 17:2 (2010), 185–214.

94. See, for example, Rachel Dulitz, "A King ... and Not a Queen," *JOFA* (Jewish Orthodox Feminist Alliance) *Journal* (2004), at 7–9 (describing pre-modern Jewish prohibitions against women exercising leadership positions over men, whether in the capacity of a ruler, judge or witness, and modern transformations of that doctrine). I would like to thank Raquel Ukeles for this reference.

95. In reaching this conclusion, I searched using the phrase "*lan yufliḥ*" and "*mā aflaḥ*" on the electronic collection of Arabic texts called *al-Maktaba al-Shāmila* which includes among its sources major early works such as the *Mudawwana al-Kubrā*, *Kitāb al-Umm*, and *al-Mabsūṭ*. For a survey of later jurists' use of this *hadith* to justify the exclusion of women from political office, see Bauer, *supra* n. 93.

96. ʿAlī b. Muḥammad al-Māwardī, *al-Ḥāwī al-Kabīr fī Fiqh Madhhab al-Imām al-Shāfiʿī*, ed. ʿAlī Muḥammad Muʿawwaḍ et al., 19 vols. (Beirut: Dār al-Kutub al-ʿIlmiyya, 1999), 16 :156; Abū Isḥāq Ibrāhīm b. ʿAlī b. Yūsuf al-Fīrūzābādī al-Shīrāzī, *al-Muhadhdhab fī Fiqh al-Imām al-Shāfiʿī*, ed. Muḥammad Muṣṭafā Zuḥaylī, 6 vols. (Damascus: Dār al-Qalam, 1992), 5:471–472.

97. Ibid., 156.

interprets Abū Ḥanīfa's view as permitting women to serve only as arbitrators in private cases in which female testimony is admissible, e.g. contract disputes or cases involving a claim for monetary compensation, or perhaps that women may be appointed for specific cases, but not that they may exercise general jurisdiction. He also dismissed historical reports stating that ʿUmar b. al-Khaṭṭāb, the second caliph, had appointed a woman as a market inspector in Madina as the work of "deviant forgers" (*min dasāʾis al-mubtadiʿa*).[98] Certainly by the 13th century, references to this *hadith* had already became common in Mālikī and Ḥanbalī legal treatises.[99] It became a regular feature of post-13th century legal treatises in all the schools of Islamic law, but especially of the Shāfiʿīs.[100]

If Ibn al-ʿArabī is to be believed, the controversy over women's capacity for political office was so heated that it became the subject of a formal public debate in the court of the Buwayhid amir of Baghdad, ʿAḍud al-Dawla (d. 982), in which Abū al-Faraj b. Ṭarār (d. 1000/390)—leader of Baghdad's Shāfiʿī jurists at the time according to Ibn [161] ʿArabī—debated this question with the famous Mālikī jurist and Ashʿarī theologian Abū Bakr al-Bāqillānī (d. 1013/403). Al-Ṭarār, who as a Shāfiʿī rejected al-Ṭabarī's reasoning (at least according to Ibn ʿArabī),[101] was nevertheless charged with defending al-Ṭabarī's view while al-Bāqillānī defended the majority view.

Al-Ṭarār made the following points in support of the validity of a woman's appointment as a judge: the goal of law is to have the judge enforce the rules, to hear evidence relevant to those rules, and to resolve the disputes of litigants, and a woman is as capable as a man in the performance of these things (*wa dhālika yumkin min al-marʾa ka-imkānihi*

98. Muḥammad b. ʿAbd Allāh Ibn al-ʿArabī, *Aḥkām al-Qurʾān*, ed. Muḥammad Bakr Ismāʿīl, 4 vols. (Cairo: Dar al-Manār, 2002), 3:457.

99. See, for example, Muwaffaq al-Dīn ʿAbd Allāh b. Aḥmad Ibn Qudāma, *al-Mughnī*, ed. ʿAbd Allāh b. ʿAbd al-Muḥsin Turkī et al., 15 vols. (Cairo: Hajr, 1986) (Ḥanbalī), 14:12–13 and Aḥmad b. Idrīs al-Qarāfī, *al-Dhakhīra*, ed. Muḥammad Ḥajjī, 14 vols. (Beirut: Dār al-Gharb al-Islāmī, 1994), 10:21 (Mālikī).

100. See, for example, Zakariyyā b. Muḥammad Anṣārī, *Asnā al-Maṭālib Sharḥ Rawḍ al-Ṭālib*, ed. Ismāʿīl b. Abī Bakr Ibn al-Muqriʾ and Aḥmad b. Aḥmad Ramlī, 4 vols. (al-Maktabah al-Islāmiyya, 1978), 1:217 and 4:108 and 4:278 (Shāfiʿī); Muḥammad b. Aḥmad al-Shirbīnī, *Mughnī al-Muḥtāj ilā Maʿrifat Maʿānī Alfāẓ al-Minhāj*, ed. ʿAlī Muḥammad Muʿawwaḍ et al., 6 vols. (Beirut: Dār al-Kutub al-ʿIlmiyya, 1994), 1:482 (Shāfiʿī); and, Aḥmad b. Muḥammad Ibn Ḥajar al-Haytamī, *Tuḥfat al-Muḥtāj*, 9 vols. (Bombay: Muḥammad ʿAbd al-ʿAzīz al-Surah, 1970), 9:75 (Shāfiʿī); Muḥammad b. Aḥmad al-Fāsī, *Sharḥ Mayyāra al-Fāsī Abī ʿAbd Allāh Muḥammad Ibn Aḥmad ʿala Tuḥfat al-Ḥukkām fī Nukat al-ʿuqūd wa-al-Aḥkām*, ed. Ḥasan ibn Raḥḥal al-Maydānī and ʿAbd al-Laṭīf Ḥasan ʿAbd al-Raḥmān, 2 vols. (Beirut: Dār al-Kutub al-ʿIlmiyya, 2000), 1:20 (Mālikī); and ʿAlī b. ʿAbd al-Salām al-Tusūlī, *Al-Bahja Fī Sharḥ al-Tuḥfa*, ed. Muḥammad ʿAbd al-Qādir Shāhīn and Muḥammad Tāwudī, 2 vols. (Beirut: Dār al-Kutub al-ʿIlmiyya, 1998), 1: 36 (Mālikī) and Muwaffaq al-Dīn ʿAbd Allāh b. Aḥmad Ibn Qudāma, *al-Kāfī fī Fiqh al-Imām Aḥmad Ibn Ḥanbal*, ed. Muḥammad Fāris and Masʿad ʿAbd al-Ḥamīd Saʿdānī, 4 vols., 1st ed. (Beirut: Dār al-Kutub al-ʿIlmiyya, 1994), 4:222 (Ḥanbalī).

101. Ibn Khallikān reported his name as Ṭarārā, or Ṭarāra, not Ṭarār, and he reports his full name as al-Muʿāfā b. Zakariyyā al-Nahrawānī. He also described him as a follower of al-Ṭabarī, not a Shāfiʿī jurist. Ibn Khallikān, *Wafiyyāt al-Aʿyān*, ed. Iḥsān ʿAbbās, 8 vols. (Beirut: Dār Ṣādir, 1973–74), 5:221–224.

min al-rajul). Al-Bāqillānī's response appears to have been based on the consensus (*ijmāʿ*) that women may not be caliph, despite the fact that a woman is capable of fulfilling all the ends for which the caliphate was established (*inna al-gharaḍ minhā [al-imāma al-kubrā] ḥifẓ al-thughūr wa tadbīr al-umūr wa ḥimāyat al-bayḍa wa qabḍ al-kharāj wa radduhu ʿalā mustaḥiqqīhi wa dhālika yataʾattā min al-marʾa ka-taʾattīhi min al-rajul*). Ibn al-ʿArabī dismissed the arguments of both, saying that a woman may not be either a judge or a caliph because, among other things, she is not permitted to mix with men.[102]

The debate between al-Ṭarār and al-Bāqillānī foreshadows the modern dilemma of Islamic law: how to resolve a commitment to law as a rational system that is functionally related to the realization of substantive ends, such as those set out in the law of the caliphate, but that are justified by an appeal to historical texts whose plain meaning may contradict the rationality for which the law strives, such as the consensus prohibiting women from serving as caliph? Significantly, while both al-Ṭarār and al-Bāqillānī concede that, as a rational matter, females may [162] be as qualified as men for all public offices, including that of caliph, al-Bāqillānī's argument implies that the existence of a consensus prohibiting the appointment of a woman as caliph proves conclusively that rational possibility, by itself, is insufficient to resolve the debate.

In the pre-modern period, when there was probably a dearth of women trained in the law and thus capable of serving as judges, it would have been relatively costless for al-Bāqillānī and other jurists to invoke a notion of substantive irrationality in the context of a debate which, in 10th-century Baghdad, was almost certainly only of theoretical interest. In the modern age, however, because capable women are found in substantial numbers, and many of these capable women are part of a religious scholar's constituency, it becomes quite costly, perhaps prohibitively so, for a religious scholar to adopt al-Bāqillānī's line of reasoning.[103] It is therefore not surprising to see that at least some modern Muslim jurists have abandoned this view altogether, a topic which Parts 6 and 7 of this Article will take up in greater detail.

By the 14th century at the latest, the Sunni law schools, with the exception of the Ḥanafīs, had come to justify their exclusion of women from political offices on the basis of revelatory grounds in general, and Abū Bakra's *hadith* in particular. This in turn generated a Ḥanafī response, one that was predicated on distinguishing between the moral

---

102. Ibn al-ʿArabī, *supra* n. 98, 3:457. Modern democratic sensibilities are, surprisingly, not so far removed from Ibn ʿArabī's reasoning. For example, Thomas Jefferson himself is reported to have stated that "Were our state a pure democracy, there would still be excluded from our deliberations ... women, who, to prevent depravation of morals and ambiguity of issues, should not mix promiscuously in gatherings of men." Ruth Bader Ginsburg, "Sexual Equality Under the Fourteenth and Equal Rights Amendments," *Washington University Law Quarterly* (Winter 1979): 161–178, at 172.

103. Cf. al-Qaraḍāwī, *supra* n. 24 at 169 (attributing the paucity of women in positions of authority historically to their relative lack of education, a fact that no longer holds true in the modern age where there are "millions of educated women" with capabilities similar, equal or surpassing that of men).

and the legal, and making an appeal to the purposes of the law along the lines suggested by al-Ṭarār. The earliest Ḥanafī authority I found making these arguments is Kamāl al-Dīn Muḥammad Ibn al-Humām (d. 1457/861). Relying on what by now had become a standard Ḥanafī argument,[104] Ibn al-Humām explained that judgeship, like giving testimony before a judge, is a manifestation of public power (*min bāb al-wilāya*). Because the law grants women the capacity to testify in court, she has the analogous capacity to act as a judge in all cases which admit female testimony. [105] Abū Bakra's *hadith* does not invalidate this [163] principle because, according to Ibn al-Humām, its prohibition is addressed only to appointing powers, not the women who are appointed judges. Nothing in the *hadith* suggests that the rulings of a woman who has been appointed judge and whose judgments are otherwise in conformity with the law are invalid simply because she is a woman.[106] Zayn al-Dīn Ibn Nujaym (d. 1562/969), who quotes Ibn al-Humām, develops this line of argument further.[107] He argues that although a woman has the capacity to serve as a judge, "the party appointing a woman incurs a sin because of the *hadith*, 'Never shall a folk prosper who have appointed a woman to rule them.'" Even though he affirms sin on the part of the appointing party, Ibn Nujaym goes *further* than Ibn al-Humām in recognizing the legitimacy of women as political actors, stating, "as for a woman acting as ruler (*salṭanatuhā*), it is valid and a woman named Shajarat al-Durr (d. 1257/655), the slave-girl of al-Malik al-Ṣāliḥ b. Ayyūb (d. 1249/647), served as ruler of Egypt."[108] Thereafter, Ḥanafī jurists interpreted this *hadith* as creating a moral prohibition against the appointment of women to public offices, but not as creating a legal bar to the validity of a woman's legal judgments.[109]

Ibn al-Humām laid the groundwork for this arguably counterintuitive result. He argued that revelation provides no basis for concluding that a substantively correct legal decision by a woman should be denied enforcement, nor is there anything in revelation that implies that qualified women lack capacity to serve in political office. Although revelation does affirm that women are deficient in comparison to men, that deficiency is not so grave as to strip women of political capacity entirely. Thus, women have the capacity to serve as a witness in a court of law, to administer a trust, and to serve as a guardian of

104. Fadel, *supra* n. 93 at 196.

105. Muḥammad b. ʿAbd al-Wāḥid Ibn al-Humām, *Sharḥ Fatḥ al-Qadīr li'l-ʿĀjiz al-Faqīr*, 8 vols., 1st ed. (Beirut: Dār Sādir, 197), 5:485–486.

106. Ibid.

107. ʿAbd Allāh b. Ahmad al-Nasafī, *al-Baḥr al-Rāʾiq, Sharḥ Kanz al-Daqāʾiq*, 9 vols. (Beirut: Dār al-Kutub al-ʿIlmiyya, 1997). 7:8–9.

108. Ibid.

109. See, for example, Muḥammad Amīn b. ʿUmar Ibn ʿĀbidīn, *Radd al-Muḥtār ʿalā al-Durr al-Mukhtār Sharḥ Tanwīr al-Abṣār*, ed. 'Ādil Aḥmad 'Abd al-Mawjūd and 'Alī Muḥammad Muʿawwaḍ, 14 vols. (Beirut: Dār al-Kutub al-ʿIlmiyya, 1994), 8:142–143, and ʿAbd al-Raḥmān b. Muḥammad Shaykh Zādah, *Majmaʿ al-Anhur fī Sharḥ Multaqā al-Abḥur*, 2 vols. (Istanbul: Būsnawī al-Ḥājj Muḥarram Afandī, 1310), 2:168.

an orphan. Whatever deficiency women suffer from, it is relative, not absolute, and more importantly, it is attributed to women as a *class*, not as individuals [164] Accordingly, some women may be more capable than some or even many men. Therefore, when it comes to assessing the capacity of a woman to be a judge, the only issue is whether her decisions are in accordance with the law, not whether she is disqualified on account of her gender. Ibn al-Humām, in effect, turns the rules of formalism on itself: if Abū Bakra's *hadith* is general with respect to all women, then it is the case that it applies to all women only in a presumptive sense (*al-ẓāhir*), with the consequence that it does not apply to women who are in fact capable of discharging the offices to which they were appointed.

In the modern period this commitment to the functional rationality of the law, combined with new social experiences, led reformist Muslim jurists to argue for substantial revisions to historical Islamic legal doctrines restricting the capacities of women. In order to appreciate these developments, however, one must first appreciate the depth (and breadth) of the view prevailing prior to the 20th century that women lack these capacities.

6. MUSLIM ANDROCENTRISM, THE NORMATIVE EXCLUSION OF WOMEN FROM POLITICAL LIFE AND MODERN REVISIONISM

Both *hadith* scholarship of the ninth and tenth centuries, and subsequent scholarly commentary on that literature as evidenced by Ibn Ḥajar and Badr al-Dīn al-ʿAynī in the 15th century, as well as some versions of Islamic substantive law during this period, suggested greater possibilities for the inclusion of women in the exercise of political power than was effectively realized in Muslim societies prior to the 20th century. Given the existence of a robust minoritarian[110] opinion that was relatively open to the possibility of female participation in the public political life of the Muslim community, it becomes less plausible to attribute the de jure and de facto marginalization of women from the public political life of the Muslim community to Islamic legal theory.[111]

[165] Why, then, did no Muslim jurist (Ḥanafī or non-Ḥanafī) argue, contrary to the hegemonic position apparently introduced around the time of al-Māwardī, that the circumstances of Abū Bakra's *hadith* permit the inference that a more specific meaning was intended? Al-Bukhārī himself placed this report in the context of the Prophet's diplomatic correspondence with Persia, not in The Chapter of Judgments. Even Abū Bakra's statement that he benefited (or in the variant transmission "was protected") by his

---

110. In the Arab Middle East (with the exclusion of Morocco), Central Asia and the Indian subcontinent, the Ḥanafīs, while only one of the four Sunni schools of law, became, in the late medieval and early modern periods, the dominant school of law, both in terms of the numbers of its followers as well as effective political power.

111. See Part 3, *supra*.

recollection of this *hadith* is ambiguous: after all, if he realized that the party of ʿĀʾisha was bound to lose because a female (ʿĀʾisha) led them, it would seem that the reasonable course of action would have been to join the forces of ʿAlī, rather than remaining neutral. Moreover, if Abū Bakra had really believed that this *hadith* prohibits delegation of political power to a woman, one would have expected him to have reprimanded ʿĀʾisha and her allies, rather than maintaining a posture of neutrality.[112] According to Ibn Abī Shayba, moreover, ʿAlī never criticized ʿĀʾisha's allies for forming an alliance with a woman against him; instead, he criticized them for breaking their previously given pledge of loyalty (*bayʿa*).[113]

As Sherman Jackson has noted, however, Islamic jurisprudence provides no guidance as to how hard (or even where) an interpreter might look for circumstantial evidence that evinces an intent to specify the range of the general term, or even how to determine whether that obligation had been satisfactorily discharged.[114] Instead, he suggested that it is impossible to understand juristic attempts to limit the scope of a revelatory text, or conversely, their failure to do so, without taking into account their subjective motivations and concerns.[115] Jackson's hypothesis regarding the importance of subjective motivations is confirmed by modern Muslim jurists' revisionist treatment of this *hadith*. The well-known contemporary Egyptian-Qatari jurist, Yūsuf al-Qaraḍāwī, for example, takes the Qurʾanic story of Bilqīs as a textual indicant qualifying Abū Bakra's *hadith*, effectively inverting the [166] traditional understanding of the relationship of these two texts.[116] For al-Qaraḍāwī, Bilqīs is a model ruler who relies on deliberation and reason (*imraʾa shūrawiyya*) and justice (*ḥākima ʿādila*) in her political decision-making, not arbitrary and autocratic opinion, therefore weakening—even if not eliminating entirely—the force of this *hadith* as justification for the exclusion of women from public office.[117] Another modern Egyptian scholar, Muḥammad al-Ghazālī, dismisses the relevance of Abū Bakra's *hadith*, stating that it applies exclusively to the internal turmoil then prevailing in the Persian state, and that the Prophet had meant only that the Persian state was doomed to fall, not that Muslim woman were unfit for political office.[118]

---

112. See Abou el Fadl, *supra* n. 26 at 112–114 (discussing the interpretive difficulties relating to Abū Bakra's *hadith*).

113. Ibn Abī Shayba, *supra* n. 34 at 7:536–537.

114. Jackson, *supra* n. 19 at 193.

115. Ibid., at 194.

116. See *infra* n. 129.

117. Al-Qaraḍāwī thus concludes that while women remain ineligible to be the leaders of the entire Muslim community, they can serve as presidents of Islamic states, with the qualification that it would be preferable for men to fill this position. See https://www.youtube.com/watch?v=ei9LVMaEaBY. See also, al-Qaraḍāwī, *supra* n. 24 at 176.

118. Brown, *supra* n. 73 at 163. See also al-Qaraḍāwī, *supra* n. 24 at 174–175.

Modern conservative scholars have managed to put forth revisionist interpretations of this *hadith* despite the fact that the weight of the tradition is against them. Why then did Muslim jurists prior to the 20th century not produce similar accounts of this *hadith*? The simple answer appears to be the question of motive: because of a normalized ideology of gender hierarchy that sometimes degenerated into misogyny, they simply lacked sufficient motivation to challenge the prevailing formalist reading of the *hadith*, especially when nothing practical seemed to turn on that interpretation, and in circumstances in which the formalist reading confirmed all their social and cultural biases against women. Despite the fact that it is impossible to make categorical characterizations about Islamic law and gender equality prior to the 20th century, jurists' accounts "of male authority, women's deficiencies, and gendered public space represent a coherent picture of a 'natural' social hierarchy and gender roles"[119] which privileged men; and, that this cultural and social reality substantially explains why, prior to the 20th century, jurists failed to deploy the critical resources of the legal tradition in an effort to understand this *hadith*.

[167] While assumptions that misogyny was a universal Islamic norm are clearly erroneous,[120] evidence of an entrenched androcentrism that at times bordered on misogyny was certainly a part of the general cultural and social ambience of the religious intellectuals whose writings are surveyed here.[121] Indeed, openly androcentric and misogynistic statements were tolerated within public discourse, as evidenced by various Muslim authors' use of demeaning language to describe women and their capabilities. The late thirteenth-century Egyptian theologian and Mālikī jurist Shihāb al-Dīn al-Qarāfī (d. 1285/684), for example, described women as having intellectual powers not far above animals,[122] notwithstanding his position that as a general rule, women are equally sub-

119. Bauer, *supra* n. 93 at 1–2.

120. See, for example, Fadel, *Two Women, One Man*, *supra* n. 93 (describing how pre-modern Sunni Islamic law contemplated the equal participation of women in the production of knowledge, including legal knowledge, even as it formulated discriminatory rules of evidence to be applied by courts which were in turn justified by sociological or political, rather than natural, reasons).

121. One of the sections of a celebrated early anthology of pre-Islamic and early Islamic poetry, for example, was titled "Excoriation of Women" (*Bāb madhammat al-nisāʾ*). Suzanne Stetkevych, *Abū Tammām and the Poetics of the ʿAbbasid Age* (New York: Brill, 1991), 239. For a good overview of the impact of misogyny on the development of secular Islamic political culture in the middle ages see D.A. Spellberg, *Politics, Gender, and the Islamic Past: The Legacy of ʿAʾisha bint Abi Bakr* (New York: Columbia University Press, 1994), 140–149 (discussing misogyny in the political writings of Niẓām al-Mulk, the celebrated 11th-century vizier of the Seljuk dynasty). Muslims hardly invented the notion that women were ill-suited to politics and perhaps even destructive when given the opportunity to be politically active. Such a view dates back at least as far as the ancient Greeks and was also articulated by pre-Islamic Christian authors. Ibid. at 142.

122. Shihāb al-Dīn Aḥmad b. Idrīs al-Qarāfī, *Nafāʾis al-Usūl fī Sharḥ al-Maḥṣūl*, ed. ʿĀdil Aḥmad ʿAbd al-Mawjūd and ʿAlī Muḥammad Muʿawwaḍ, 9 vols. (Riyad: Maktabat Nizār Muṣṭafā al-Bāz, 1997), 9:4051 ("*al-niswān qarīb min al-bahāʾim*").

ject to the rules of Islamic morality as men.[123] It is unsurprising that this background culture, combined with the social reality of female dependency on men, affected the interpretation of revelation. A few examples should make this clear.

Fakhr al-Dīn al-Rāzī (d. 1210/606), a Transoxanian theologian and Shāfiʿī jurist, who wrote a celebrated theological-cum-philosophical commentary on the Qurʾan called *Mafātīḥ al-Ghayb* ("The Keys to the Unseen") is a good example of how cultural and social androcentrism/ [168] misogyny influenced interpretation of the Qurʾan. In commenting on the verse which states, "And among His signs is that He created for you mates from yourselves that you may find tranquility in them and He formed love and mercy between you [as a result],"[124] al-Rāzī argued not only that the phrase, "He created for you," is proof that God created women for the convenience of men (a not uncommon position at that time), but he also went so far as to argue that women, unlike men, were not the intended subjects of the law's moral commands (*taklīf*). For al-Rāzī, God subjected women to the law's discipline only for the convenience of men.[125]

His introduction of gender hierarchy into a verse that is facially gender neutral stands in stark contrast to his *erasure* of the female entirely when faced with the express use of gendered language in a context suggesting that both men and women have independently valuable moral lives in the sight of God.[126] While it would have been possible for him to affirm the spiritual equality of men and women while also affirming a gender-based social hierarchy, al-Rāzī appears oblivious to the contradiction that arises out of his claim that women were not given moral obligation for any reason other than the benefit of men, on the one hand, and the language of these and other verses that suggest women have a moral life equal in dignity to that of men, on the other. When one looks at verse 34 of *al-Nisāʾ* (4:34) or verse 228 of *al-Baqara* (2:228), both of which seem to endorse (or at least take for granted) a gender hierarchy, however, many pre-19th century Mus-

123. Mohammad Fadel, "Public Reason as a Strategy for Principled Reconciliation: The Case of Islamic Law and International Human Rights Law," Fadel, *supra* n. 13, at 14 (2007).

124. *Al-Rūm*, 30:21.

125. Fakhr al-Dīn Muḥammad b. ʿUmar al-Rāzī, *Mafātīḥ al-Ghayb*, 6 vols. (Cairo: al-Maṭbaʿa al-Miṣriyya al-ʿĀmiriyya, 1862) 5:185. Despite the attribution of the entirety of this work of exegesis to Fakhr al-Din al-Rāzī, Sohaib Saeed (trans., *The Great Exegesis*, vol. I [Cambridge: The Royal Aal al-Bayt Institute for Islamic Thought, 2018], pp. xii–xiii) remarks that there is reason to believe that al-Rāzī did not complete this work before he died. Furthermore, Rāzī scholars believe that it is likely that al-Rāzī was not responsible for the portion of the commentary in which this passage appears. See ʿAbd al-Raḥmān al-Muʿallimī, *al-Majmūʿ*, ed. Mājid al-Ziyadī, Mecca: al-Maktaba al-Makkiyya, 1996, pp. 118, 134.

126. See, for example, his commentary on *al-Tawba*, 9:71–72, ibid., at 3:486–488, whose plain language affirms that "the believing men" (*al-muʾminūn*) and "the believing women" (*al-muʾmināt*) are, using gender-neutral language, "guardians of one another" (*baʿḍuhum awliyāʾ baʿḍ*); that they (both believing men and women) "command the good and forbid the evil"; establish prayer; give alms; are obedient to God and His messenger; that God will show "them" mercy; and that God promised both "the believing men" and "the believing women" eternal bliss in Paradise.

lim exegetes simply affirmed the superiority of men to women as though nothing could be more obvious. In his commentary on 2:228, for example, Abū Bakr b. al-ʿArabī, stated with complete self-assurance that "the superiority of men to women is not something that is hidden to[169] [anyone with] good sense" (*wa lā yakhfā ʿalā labīb faḍl al-rijāl ʿalā al-nisāʾ*).[127] Similarly, Ibn Kathīr (d. 1373/774), in explaining why Q. 4:34 gives men power over women, states simply that "men are more virtuous than women and a man is better than a woman" (*al-rijāl afḍal min al-nisāʾ wa'l-rajul khayrun min al-marʾa*).[128]

Given a broad cultural understanding of men's *obvious* natural superiority, it is not surprising that the story of Bilqīs was viewed as anomalous and had to be neutralized by references to male superiority. Abū Bakra's *hadith* was especially useful in achieving this goal.[129] Abū Ḥayyān Muḥammad b. Yūsuf al-Andalusī (d. 1344/745), author of the Qurʾan commentary *al-Baḥr al-Muḥīṭ*, recognized the subversive implications of Bilqīs' story, and therefore explicitly dismissed the notion that it has any normative significance for Muslims. He states: "[Making Bilqīs ruler] was the action of her people, and they were non-believers so it cannot serve as a proof" (*dhālika min fiʿl qawm bilqīs wa hum kuffār fa-lā ḥujjata fī dhālika*). The normative Islamic rule, according to Abū Ḥayyān, is supplied by Abū Bakra's *hadith*.[130]

Given this cultural and social background, the extent to which Muslim jurists within the domain of substantive law were willing to contemplate the possibility that women could serve in public offices at all, despite both normative and cultural opposition to such an idea, is in itself surprising. Substantive law's ability to generate the idea that women were equally capable as men to serve in public office (as articulated in the public debate between al-Ṭarār and al-Bāqillānī) is, in some [170] ways, even more surprising given the historical fact that no woman had been appointed a judge of a Muslim city. Indeed, for some jurists who denied women's capacity to serve in public office, the historical practice of the Muslim community on this score was dispositive.[131]

---

127. Ibn al-ʿArabī, *supra* n. 98, 1:230.

128. Ismāʿīl b. Umar b. Kathīr, *Tafsīr Ibn Kathīr*, ed. Sāmī b. Muḥammad al-Salāma, 8 vols. (Riyadh: Dār Tība, 1997), 2:292.

129. Some commentaries that introduce Abū Bakra's *hadith* in connection with the story of Bilqīs are: Al-Ḥusayn b. Masʿūd Baghawī, *Tafsīr al-Baghawī* ed. Khālid ʿAbd al-Raḥmān ʿAkk and Marwān Sawār, 5 vols. (Beirut: Dār Iḥyāʾ al-Turāth al-ʿArabī, 2002), 3:499; Muḥammad b. Aḥmad Qurṭubī, *al-Jāmiʿ li-Aḥkām al-Qurʾān*, ed. ʿAbd Allāh b. ʿAbd al-Muḥsin Turkī and Muḥammad Riḍwān ʿIrqsūsī, 24 vols. (Beirut: Muʾassasat al-Risāla, 2006), 16:183; ʿAlī b. Muḥammad al-Māwardī, *al-Nukat wa'l-ʿUyūn: Tafsīr al-Māwardī*, ed. Al-Sayyid b. ʿAbd al-Maqṣūd b. ʿAbd al-Raḥīm, 6 vols. (Beirut, 1992), 4:208; Abū Ḥayyān Muḥammad b. Yūsuf, *Tafsīr al-Baḥr al-Muḥīt*, ed. ʿAbd al-Razzāq Mahdī, 8 vols. (Beirut: Dār Iḥyāʾ al-Turāth al-ʿArabī, 2002), 7:87; and, Muḥammad b. Aḥmad Shirbīnī, *Tafsīr al-Khaṭīb al-Shirbīnī: al-Musammā al-Sirāj al-Munīr*, ed. Ibrāhīm Shams al-Dīn, 4 vols. (Beirut: Dār al-Kutub al-ʿIlmiyya, 2004), 3:99.

130. Abū Ḥayyān at 7:87.

131. Ibn Qudāma, *supra* n. 99.

Moreover, when the extent of the pre-19th century tradition's androcentrism (as well as its occasional misogyny) is taken into account, modern views of scholars such as Muḥammad al-Ghazālī and Yūsuf al-Qaraḍāwī can be better appreciated for their relatively egalitarian positions: while pre-19th century Muslim jurists understood the exclusion of women from political office to be an obvious consequence of their natural deficiencies in terms of judgment, reasoning and virtue, al-Qaraḍāwī, for example, does not attribute any political limitations placed on women to their nature. Instead, to the extent that he contemplates limitations on women's participation in the political sphere, it is on account of *conflicting* moral obligations that individual women might have rather than any inherent natural or moral deficiency.[132]

7. CONCLUSION

In this article, we have seen how a text that was traditionally deployed to reinforce a prevailing culture of androcentrism may very well be read differently, even according to the canons of interpretation developed by the historical tradition itself. Equally important, this study shows how a particularly formalist method of reading legal texts can reinforce already dominant androcentric attitudes by clothing bias in the garb of objective interpretation. On the other hand, the very same hermeneutical theory that reinforced, and gave legitimacy to, a misogynistic reading of Abū Bakra's *hadith* can also undermine that reading: by taking seriously the principle that general terms must not be applied generally until care has been taken to exclude the possibility that circumstantial evidence indicates a more specific intent, it would be entirely credible for a contemporary reader of this *hadith* to follow al-Bukhārī's or Ibn Abī Shayba's lead to conclude that this *hadith* is irrelevant to the question of whether women have the capacity to govern. Indeed, that is [171] precisely what two modern 20th-century reform-minded jurists, Yūsuf al-Qaraḍāwī and Muḥammad al-Ghazālī, have done.

At the same time, the Ḥanafī reaction to the growing appeal to this *hadith* to refute their doctrine, which permits women to serve as judges in non-capital cases, shows that the commitment to the rational ideals of the law can also lead to conceptual legal change, which, even if it did not result in any legal change prior to the 20th century, suggests possibilities for modern Muslims. For the Ḥanafīs, the relevant question (at least in the context of whether women can be judges), is whether anything in Islamic law precludes the enforcement of *otherwise* valid judgments simply because of the judge's gender, and here the answer to *that* question is no. Note that the reasoning of this argument can easily be extended to the office of caliph: given the willingness of jurists, dating at least to the time of al-Ghazālī, to accept the notion that the caliph can discharge all the office's legal obli-

132. Al-Qaraḍāwī, *supra* n. 24 at 170.

gations through the appointment of competent delegates, it seems that a female caliph might remedy whatever natural "deficiencies" she might have, i.e. a physical inability to participate in combat directly, through appointment of competent generals, provided, of course, that she has the capacity to make wise political decisions.

A careful study of androcentrism, as well as misogyny, along with the texts and assumptions used to justify them within the Islamic tradition, is a critical step in understanding how such biases have conditioned the interpretive activities of various Muslim intellectuals throughout history, and undertaking such studies along the lines outlined here can serve a useful function in subverting the "text fundamentalism" of which Moosa complains. Abū Bakra's *hadith* is a good example of how the framing of a text can play an important, even if subtle, role in determining how it is read and understood. Al-Bukhārī's decision to include this *hadith* in the chapter of the Prophet's diplomatic correspondence, for example, or Ibn Abī Shayba's inclusion of it as part of the events of the first civil war, casts the *hadith* in a substantially different light than al-Nasāʾī's decision to include it in the materials dealing with judges, to say nothing of the later *hadith* encyclopedias in which all (or most) contextual facts were edited out entirely.

To be clear, the method of hermeneutical historicism deployed here does not claim to establish a "correct" frame for the text; its goal is [172] simply to subvert the commonsense reception of a text that has been used to justify exclusion of women from the Muslim public by demonstrating the historically multivalent nature of that text. The efficacy of this strategy thus depends on the assumption that once a hierarchical reading of an exclusionary text is exposed as a choice rather than a necessity, substantively egalitarian positions will find a more receptive audience. What I am calling "hermeneutical historicism" is a particularly useful interpretive strategy in this regard, given its close affinity to the traditional jurisprudential concept of *takhṣīṣ al-ʿāmm*, specification of the general term.

Reform-minded Muslim intellectuals may therefore find that laying out a detailed genealogy of the particulars of historical instances of Muslim patriarchy, androcentrism and misogyny—along the lines suggested in this article—is a more effective strategy for realizing effective reform in the area of gender than, for example, the strategy adopted by either Fatima Mernissi or Khaled Abou el Fadl. Both Abou el Fadl and Mernissi attack the historical reliability of this *hadith* on the grounds that Abū Bakra, for many reasons, had various incentives to forge it, including perhaps a deep hatred for women; his conviction for slander (*qadhf*) should have stripped him of the requisite moral integrity (*ʿadāla*) to be an accepted narrator of Prophetic *hadith*; and, in any case, he was too marginal a figure in the early Islamic community to be relied upon for such an important teaching.

If the purpose of reformist criticism is to generate a new *Islamic* position (rather than a post-Islamic position), however, it is important to use arguments that are capable of winning over a critical mass of Muslim support. From this perspective, it is unlikely that the arguments advanced by Abou El Fadl and Mernissi—to the extent they challenge the integrity of Abū Bakra—can succeed. The integrity of the Prophet Muḥammad's Companions (Abū Bakra being a companion)—at least with respect to the question of their reports of what the Prophet said, did or permitted—is one of the theological *foundations* of Sunni Islam, in contrast to Shiᶜism and the Khawārij, both of which, to different extents, rejected this proposition.[133] The integrity of the Companions [173] for Sunnis, however, does not entail their infallibility, and thus, it would be perfectly unexceptional if they had criticized Abū Bakra for his interpretation of the *hadith*, assuming that he understood it in the same manner as later generations of Muslims.[134] By attacking Abū Bakra's credibility, however, Mernissi transforms what is essentially a legal question, i.e. whether women, from an Islamic perspective, have legal capacity to participate in the political domain and hold public office, into a theological one (and one that is, to that extent, ultimately irresolvable) in which she inadvertently appears to take the side of sectarians (at least from the Sunni perspective).[135] By questioning the authenticity of the text rather than its historical interpretation, Mernissi further reinforces, even if inadvertently, the role that univocal understandings of texts play in constructing modern conceptions of Islamic normativity.

The attack on Abū Bakra and the implication that this *hadith* is inauthentic also obscures the depth of the historical conviction that women's natural deficiencies require that they play a minimal role in public affairs. Given the depth (and breadth) of the historical tradition's opposition to women in public roles, it is remarkable that otherwise conservative jurists such as al-Qaraḍāwī have openly endorsed the right, and perhaps even the obligation, of Muslim women to participate in political affairs. While al-Qaraḍāwī can in no way be confused for a principled gender egalitarian,[136] his views on

---

133. See, e.g., Abū Jaᶜfar Aḥmad b. Muḥammad al-Ṭaḥāwī, *The Creed of Imam al-Ṭaḥāwī*, trans. Hamza Yusuf (n.p.: Zaytuna Institute, 2007), 76 § 118 (stating that love of the Companions is part of true faith, and to speak ill of any of them is sinful); al-Āmidī, *supra* n. 63, 2:128–130 (all of the Prophet Muḥammad's Companions are deemed to possess integrity for purposes of accepting their reports of the Prophet's words); Scott Lucas, *Constructive Critics, Hadith Literature, and the Articulation of Sunnī Islam* (Brill: Boston, 2004), 221 ("the collective probity" of the Prophet Muḥammad's companions is a "pillar" of Sunni Islam).

134. Abou el Fadl raises the possibility that Abū Bakra may have made a mistake in reporting the Prophet's words. He postulates that the Prophet may have said something along the lines that "*This* people [i.e., the Persians] will not succeed under the leadership of *this* woman [i.e., Būrān]," but that Abū Bakra mistakenly reported it using general language, perhaps as a result of his bias against women. Abou el Fadl, *supra* n. 26 at 113.

135. G.F. Haddad, in his criticism of Muslim feminists' attacks on Abu Bakra, limited his analysis to the defense of Abū Bakra's moral integrity and did not even address the substantive issue of women's capacity to hold political office. *Abū Bakrah and the Feminists*, G.F. Haddad (Jan. 14, 2005) http://www.abc.se/~m9783/o/abfm_e.html (last visited October 9, 2009).

136. See, for example, al-Qaraḍāwī's defense of traditional Islamic rules of evidence which discriminate against the admissibility of female testimony, available at: https://web.archive.org/web/20070318030045/http://www.islamonline.net/servlet/Satellite?cid=1119503544348&pagename=IslamOnline-English-Ask_Scholar/FatwaE/FatwaEAskTheScholar (link updated May 28, 2023).

the capacity of women to [174] engage meaningfully in politics can rightfully be characterized, from the perspective of the Islamic tradition, as revolutionary. Gone are any arguments about natural deficiencies in women that render them incapable of playing a positive role in politics or dooming them to the cunning use of guile that is the contrary of political wisdom. Al-Qaraḍāwī simply takes for granted the fact that women have the same capacity as men to exercise good and bad political judgment. Accordingly, the only limitations on the participation of Muslim women in politics are that of conflicting *moral* obligation rather than capacity, an issue that is to be resolved on individual grounds not generic ones.[137] In the case of female political participation, at least, the experience of seeing women engage successfully in public life, along with the perceived Islamic need to respond positively to critics of Islam, has generated the desire to rethink commitments that one might reasonably have believed to be unshakeable, based on the nearly universal agreement among Muslim jurists prior to the 20th century that women not only have nothing positive to contribute to the public life of their communities, but also that their participation in governance is usually destructive.

This shift in juristic opinion points to a broader observation about the relationship of Islamic law as a historical tradition to developments in modern Islamic law: what may appear from the perspective of the historical tradition to be an absolute commitment often takes on the appearance of a contingent rule based only superficially, if at all, on Islamic revealed sources from the perspective of modern Muslims who have had the benefit of experiences that materially differ from their predecessors. Hermeneutical historicism fits quite comfortably within even a conservative reformist trend because it uses historical experience to propose interpretations of revelatory sources that appear to the modern reader as having greater hermeneutical integrity than historically-entrenched readings. In the case of Abū Bakra's *hadith*, the revisionist reading appears to explain more convincingly both the data of revelation and the data of historical experience and can thus displace the [175] pre-modern reading without substantial resistance. It should not be particularly surprising, moreover, that the discourse of Islamic law is particularly amenable, perhaps more so than Qurʾanic exegesis, to this kind of doctrinal change: Islamic jurisprudence, despite its textual grounding, is also committed to a functional rationality that is supposed to make sense of the empirical world in light of the universal goals of Islamic law.[138] This gives rise to a dialectic between doctrine and experience that continually results in slow, but very real, doctrinal change.

On the other hand, there persist legal commitments that seem to survive the social changes wrought by modernity. Such commitments are not amenable to revisionist

137. Al-Qaraḍāwī, *supra* n. 24 at 164, 170.

138. The most sophisticated theoretical expression of this functional rationality is the theory of the "universal purposes of Islamic law" (*al-maqāṣid al-kulliyya*). See Mohammad Fadel, "The True, the Good and the Reasonable," *Can. J. L. & Jur.* 21 (January 2008): 5–69, at 54–57.

interpretation using the methods of hermeneutical historicism. A case in point is the continued salience of the *ḥudūd* penalties, or in the context of Islamic family law, the continued centrality of 4:34 (*al-Nisāʾ*).[139] To go beyond the rules of these verses, a more radical historicism, perhaps along the lines of what I have called progressive historicism, is required. Such an approach must be willing to go beyond specific textual commands by saying in effect that we do not deny the moral integrity of the traditional interpretations of the *ḥudūd* verses or that of Q. 4:34; rather, we instead deny their moral relevance to us at this time.[140]

It is not quite clear what kind of historicism Moosa had in mind in his article "The Debts and Burdens of Critical Islam."[141] In this article, I have explored the possibilities of hermeneutical historicism rather than progressive historicism. Because invocation of progressive historicism [176] to justify legal reform requires the introduction of theologically controversial propositions, I have argued that it is wiser to make use of less controversial strategies when they are reasonably available. In the case of the *hadith* discussed here, the traditional jurisprudential concept of *takhṣīṣ al-ʿāmm*, specification of the general term, has proven to be a useful tool for subverting historically entrenched readings of this text. This concept could be successfully deployed because of the rich historical detail preserved by the tradition itself regarding this report. These historical details provide a reasonable basis for an interpreter to argue that a non-literal meaning was in fact originally intended. The traditional hermeneutic methods of Muslim jurists, which include but are not limited to, *takhṣīṣ al-ʿāmm*, remain a flexible yet principled method of interpreting textual meaning that has the potential to be deployed for progressive change. Before attempting to effect theological revolutions by implication, then, progressive Muslims ought first to take more seriously the recognized interpretive tools within the tradition of substantive law.[142]

139. Qurʾan 4:34 vests men with moral authority husbands over wives, requiring wives to be obedient to their husbands and authorizing husbands to discipline rebellious views using admonition (*waʿẓ*), by temporarily abandoning the marriage bed (*hajr*), and finally, by physical discipline (*ḍarb*).

140. For an example of a theologically sophisticated reading of 4:34 by a Muslim feminist, see Laury Silvers, "ʿIn the Book We Have Left Out Nothing': The Ethical Problem of the Existence of 4:34 in the Qurʾan," *Comparative Islamic Studies* 2:2 (2006): 171–180. See also Wadud, *supra* n. 21, 192, for an example of an approach to understanding the Qurʾan that goes beyond textual interpretation.

141. *Debts, supra* n. 4 at 122.

142. See, for example, Ali, *supra* n. 5 at p. xx.

Islamic Law, Gender, and the Family

8
TWO WOMEN, ONE MAN: KNOWLEDGE, POWER, AND GENDER IN MEDIEVAL SUNNI LEGAL THOUGHT

Mohammad Fadel

[185] Many Muslim feminists have argued that at the core of Islam lies a gender-neutral belief system that has been obscured by a centuries-long tradition of male-dominated interpretation.[1] Although this gender-neutral system of belief had been almost entirely suppressed by the ruling Islamic discourses, according to Leila Ahmed marginalized discourses such as Sufism and the antinomian Carmathians were able to preserve Islam's message of the ethical equality of men and women.[2] Amina Wadud-Muhsin argues that the traditional verse-by-verse method of Qur'anic exegesis, along with its domination by male practitioners, marginalized female experiences in understanding revelation. In her view, these two factors ultimately led to the suppression of the Qur'an's message of gender equality.[3] Fatima Mernissi, in *The Veil and the Male Elite,* instead argues that the religious scholars of Islam, because of their fear of subjectivity, were content with a purely empirical science of religion—a methodology that left the door wide open to the manipulation of revelation through interpretation.[4] Unlike Ahmed, however, she recognizes that even within

This article was originally published in *International Journal of Middle East Studies*, vol. 29, 1997, pp. 185–204.

1. See, for example, Leila Ahmed, *Women and Gender in Islam* (New Haven: Yale University Press, 1992), 65–66; Amina Wadud-Muhsin, *Quran and Woman* (Kuala Lumpur: Penerbit Fajar Bakti Sdn. Bhd., 1994); Fatima Mernissi, *The Veil and the Male Elite* (New York: Addison-Wesley, 1987), 75, 126; Ghada Talhami, "The Human Rights of Women in Islam," *Journal of Social Philosophy* 16 (Winter 1985): 1–7.

2. Ahmed, *Women and Gender*, 66–67. She also argues, however, that the gender-neutral message of Islam mitigated the misogynistic practices that prevailed in Near Eastern societies.

3. Wadud-Muhsin, *Quran*, 1–2.

4. What Mernissi means by empirical is that the task of a religious scholar was to collect positive facts, whether these were in the form of sayings attributed to the Prophet or his companions or the opinions of other scholars. According to Mernissi, religious scholarship did not attempt to "transcend" these facts by extracting from them general universal rules that could serve as a check against both arbitrary, subjective interpretation and errors in the facts themselves. Mernissi, *The Veil*, 128.

the dominant discourse of the Sunni scholars, not all spoke of women in the same monotonously misogynistic voice.[5]

Whether or not one finds these arguments convincing, they raise a fundamental problem relating to the viability of any ethical discourse in the context of social inequality. If social inequality, whether it is grounded in gender, race, or class, is so powerful that it can sometimes obscure an ethical truth, and at other times suppress it entirely, one is left to wonder whether ethical discourse can ever be efficacious in realizing social change. These arguments also raise an important hermeneutical question: to what extent is interpretation simply an objective process of extracting meaning from a text, and to what extent is it fundamentally subjective, in reality being no more than a reflection of the reader's particular circumstances and tastes?

To differing extents, these authors share a view of reading that suggests that the understanding of a text has more to do with the circumstances surrounding the activity of interpretation than with the text itself. If this is the case, however, arguing that Islam contains a message of gender equality verges on the absurd, because "Islam" would [186] have as many teachings on gender as the different social circumstances in which it is interpreted. Perhaps for this reason Wadud-Muhsin has rightly pointed out that the question of Islam and gender as posed may simply be an anachronism.[6] Instead of focusing on the meaning of revelation, then, it may be more fruitful to examine texts and discourses for a specific period to see what light they can shed on issues of gender for that period. Although one is rightly skeptical of any interpretation that claims for its results universal validity, this skepticism should not lead to the assumption that *all* reading is simply a reflection of the reader's particular circumstances. Thus, the possibility that an interpretation of a text such as the Qur'an could emerge that moves beyond an existing sociological reality should not be precluded a priori. This is especially true if the interpretation uses a methodology that interrogates the text instead of just using it to confirm pre-existing social beliefs. This view also seems to be shared by Mernissi, whose criticisms of the religious scholars are not so much that they found their own misogynism confirmed by God in revelation, but rather that they failed in creating "principles, laws, or axioms that would allow the reader to distinguish the structural from the circumstantial."[7] In concluding that the religious sciences were all empirical, however, Mernissi may have been guilty of generalizing based on the nature of the sources she used—exege-

5. Ibid., 75, 77.

6. Wadud-Muhsin implies this when she notes in her preface that "the question of the concept of woman in the Qurʾān did not arise-perhaps because the concept of gendered man did not arise" (Wadud-Muhsin, *Quran*, v).

7. Mernissi, *The Veil*, 127.

sis *(tafsīr)* and Prophetic reports *(hadith)*.[8] Jurisprudence *(fiqh)*, by contrast, was an interpretive science whose very meaning, "understanding," connoted an ability to transform the countless "facts" of revelation into "principles, laws, or axioms."

To claim, as do these Muslim feminists, that Islam advocates a message of gender equality implies, however, that there is an objective core of meaning in revelation accessible to any fair-minded reader, male or female. If this is the case, the claim that Islam proclaims a message of gender equality ought to have manifested itself in the consciousness of at least some of the male readers who are recognized as being central in the formation of the Muslim canon. And if the characterization of jurisprudence as being that Islamic science which, to use Mernissi's terminology, transcended the empirical in order to distinguish the structural from the accidental is correct, then it is the most likely domain wherein issues that bear upon gender equality could have been discussed in a critical manner. Because the issue of gender equality in Islam is too large a topic to discuss in one paper, this paper will discuss the issue of gender equality as it arises in a complex of related issues: the production, reproduction, and application of medieval Islamic law as it appears in the works of Sunni jurists from the post-Ayyubid period. I will, moreover, contrast the treatment of this issue in the separate domains of exegesis and jurisprudence. I will argue that jurisprudence, precisely because it takes a broader interpretive perspective, allows for the possibility of a gender-neutral interpretation of female participation in the law to emerge. Exegesis, on the other hand—which was dominated by the atomistic methodology of verse-by-verse interpretation—allowed the misogynistic assumptions of the reader to dominate the text. Equally important, this paper also demonstrates that legal interpretation cannot be understood simply as a "reflection" of social beliefs. What is most striking about the medieval Sunni legal discourse on this complex of issues is the extent to which it exists in tension with popular notions of gender roles.

TWO WOMEN EQUAL ONE MAN : QUR'AN 2:282 IN EXEGESIS

[187] The best-known example of discrimination against women in the law and its application is the relative weight given to women's testimony as witnesses in comparison to men's. The origin of this discrimination seems to lie squarely in the Qur'an's treatment of testimony, where God commands the believers to bring two male witnesses, or in the absence of two males, a male and two females, to witness certain types of contracts:

8. This is doubly true in the case of exegesis, where her main source was Muḥammad ibn Jarīr al-Ṭabarī's encyclopedic work *Jāmiʿ al-bayān fī taʾwīl āy al-qurʾān*, in which he sought to gather every opinion expressed by a recognized scholar.

> Oh believers, when you contract a debt one upon another for a stated term, write it down... And call in to witness two witnesses, men; or, if they be not men, then one man and two women, such witnesses as you approve of, lest one of the two [women] err, then the other will remind her.

That the possibility of error is explicitly attributed to the female witnesses and not the males allows for the interpretation that women are more prone to error than men, and for that reason a female witness needs a second woman to remind her. In other words, the Qur'an seems to be saying, at least by way of implication, that the testimony of a woman is less credible than that of a man. This common-sense reading, moreover, was adopted by various exegetes throughout Islamic history. The fact that women were more prone to error, they explained, was a result of their "nature." Whereas the theologian Fakhr al-Dīn al-Rāzī (d. 1210) explained that the woman's different biological nature made her more prone to forget than a man, the 20th-century Egyptian Sayyid Quṭb argued that it was the woman's psychology–specifically her motherly instincts–that prevented her from possessing the objectivity necessary for a witness.[9]

It seems that the first exegete to challenge this notion was the celebrated Egyptian modernist and reformer Muḥammad ʿAbduh, when he denied that the requirement of two female witnesses was based on the different natures of men and women; instead, he argued that both men and women have the same capacity for remembering and forgetting, the sole difference being that the different economic roles of men and women in society made each vulnerable to forgetting those things which were not part of his or her daily experience.[10] Thus, while a woman was more prone than a man to make a mistake regarding a commercial transaction, she would be more likely to be correct concerning a household matter. Muslim modernists have taken

9. Fakhr al-Dīn al-Rāzī, *al-Tafsīr al-kabīr*, 32 vols. (Cairo: Al-Maṭbaʿa al-Bahāʾiyya al-Miṣriyya, 1357/1938), 7:122; Sayyid Quṭb, *Fī Ẓilāl al-qurʾān*, 6 vols. (Cairo: Dār al-Shurūq, n.d.), 1:336. It is worth noting, moreover, that both Quṭb and al-Rāzī rely on sciences external to the discourse of revelation–the former, psychology, and the latter, Aristotelian biology–to interpret the verse and reach their conclusion that women were inherently less veracious than men. Al-Qurṭubī does not give an explanation of why a woman's testimony is worth half of a man's, although he accepts that as the meaning of the verse. See Muḥammad ibn Aḥmad al-Qurṭubī, *al-Jāmiʿ li-aḥkām al-qurʿān*, ed. Aḥmad ʿAbd al-ʿAlīm al-Bardūnī, 20 vols. (Cairo: Dār al-kātib al-ʿarabī, 1387/1967), 3:389–98. It is possible that his belief that women are intellectually inferior is such an obvious fact that he does not even need to mention it explicitly. See his explanation of the sentence "*al-rijāl qawwāmūn ʿalā al-nisāʾ*" in *al-Nisāʾ*, 4:34, where he explains that the husband's right to discipline his wife, command her obedience, manage her affairs, prevent her from leaving her home, and so on, all based solely on his discretion, is at least partially a consequence of his possession of *ʿaql*: Al-Qurṭubī, *al-Jāmiʿ li-aḥkām al-qurʾān*, 5:169.

10. ʿAbduh's commentary on the Qur'an is known to us principally through the work of his student and disciple Rashīd Riḍā, who published his teacher's views in *Tafsīr al-manār*. Rashīd Riḍā, *Tafsīr al-manār*, 12 vols. (Beirut: Dār al-Maʿrifa, n.d.), 3:124–25.

ʿAbduh's lead in interpreting this verse as being the result of a temporal division of labor between the sexes. According to them, the apparent rule established by this verse was neither universally applicable across time nor generally applicable to all cases tried by a court.[11]

THE POLITICS OF TESTIMONY: RIWĀYA/FATWĀ VERSUS SHAHĀDA/ḤUKM

For the different exegetes whose opinions I have surveyed, Qur'an 2:282 was taken as having established epistemological criteria regarding the relative credibility of male and female witnesses based on their respective stature as repositories and transmitters of knowledge. For post-11th-century jurists *(fuqahāʾ)*, the acceptance of testimony or its rejection by a judge was not an issue simply of credibility; it was also intimately [188] connected to issues of social status, such as the witness's religion and whether the witness was free or slave. Witnesses, however, are only one of several human elements who participate in the judicial process, others being the plaintiff, the defendant, and the judge. In principle, it is only the disputing plaintiff and defendant who have interests at stake in the process. However, the witnesses and the judge possess power. The witnesses provide, for purposes of the judicial proceedings, a "truthful" account of what actually transpired between the plaintiff and the defendant. The judge imposes his own version of legal reality on the two contesting parties. For these reasons, both the defendant and the plaintiff have an interest in insuring that witnesses and judges exercise their power responsibly. Although judges and witnesses are distinguished from other participants in the legal process by virtue of their possession of specialized knowledge without which the process could not move forward, the fact that they possess the political power to impose this knowledge on others who might have different answers to the same questions transforms the judicial process from a neutral process of discovery of truth to one that is laden with partisan interests—the plaintiff seeking the vindication of his claim, the defendant seeking to prove the falsity of the charge entered against him, and both the plaintiff and the defendant trying to prevent an arbitrary use of power by the judge and the witnesses that would lessen each's chance of winning the case, not to mention that the judge and the witnesses might have hidden interests in the outcome of the case. In brief, although the judicial process requires the specialized knowledge of the judge and the witnesses for its operation, it is also an intersection of knowledge and power. Because of the presence of power, the legitimacy of the judicial process is always subject to challenge. Therefore, the role of the witness and the judge can be understood only when the political context of their functions within the judicial process is afforded the same attention that has traditionally been given to their roles as "objective" providers of specialized information to

11. Wadud-Muhsin, *Quran*, 85–86.

that process.[12] Precisely because Islamic procedural law assigns to gender an important role in determining who can participate in the judicial process, to what extent, and in what capacity, it also provides a rich site for the exploration of the relationships governing knowledge, power, and gender in medieval Muslim legal thought.

Any adequate understanding of the obstacles limiting the admission of female testimony in Islamic law must first come to terms with the manner in which legal discourse attempted to differentiate what I call "political" discourse from "normative" discourse. The former was embodied in those statements which, if admitted, would lead to some immediate, binding consequence, usually in favor of one party and against another. Moreover, the beneficiary of this statement could seek to have it imposed on the losing party in the event of the latter's non-compliance. A witness's testimony and a judge's verdict are both political because the consequences of each are immediate, tangible, and binding, irrespective of the consent of the party who contests either the facts presented by the witnesses or the rule of law applied by the judge. Normative discourse, on the other hand, if admitted, establishes a universal norm or fact, but only *potentially* affects tangible interests. Muslim jurists used the terms *shahāda* (testimony) and *ḥukm* (verdict) to distinguish discourse that had political consequences from the normative discourse that was described with the terms *riwāya* (narration) and *fatwā* (non-binding legal opinion).[13]

[189] Interestingly, Islamic law established different criteria to evaluate the truth of political and normative speech. A disputed fact, in the context of a lawsuit, could generally be established by the testimony of two men. On the other hand, normative statements used by an independent interpreter of the law (*mujtahid*) as material sources for the derivation of the law need only have been narrated by one person. The narration of normative statements, unlike testimony, was explicitly gender neutral. Thus, Fāṭima's narration of a Prophetic saying or precedent would be as probative as ʿAlī's, assuming that both narrators were credible (*ʿadl*).[14] Negatively, statements such as legal claims (*daʿāwā*) were prima facie so laden with self-interest that they were always in need of independent corroboration, no matter how truthful the

12. For a very insightful discussion of the relationship of judicial legitimacy to the actual rules of procedure used by courts, see Martin Shapiro, *Courts: A Comparative and Political Analysis* (Chicago: University of Chicago Press, 1981), 2–3.

13. For more information regarding the manner in which law regulated statements of legal significance, see Tāj al-Dīn ʿAbd al-Wahhāb ibn ʿAlī al-Subkī, *al-Ashbāh wa-l-naẓāʾir*, 2 vols., ed. ʿĀdil Aḥmad ʿAbd al-Mawjūd and ʿAlī Muḥammad ʿAwaḍ (Beirut: Dār al-Kutub al-ʿIlmiyya, 1991), 2:162; Shihāb al-Dīn al-Qarāfī, *al-Furūq*, 4 vols. (Beirut: ʿĀlam al-Kutub, n.d.), 1:6–7. Also, see Mohammad Fadel, "Adjudication in the Mālikī Madhhab: A Study of Legal Process in Medieval Islamic Law" (Ph.D. diss., University of Chicago, 1995), 127–36.

14. Al-Qarāfī, *al-Furūq*, 1:4–5.

claimant was thought to be. Like narration, moreover, a claim's truth or falsehood had no relationship to the gender of the claimant.[15]

Because the truth or falsity of political and normative statements are judged according to *muṭābaqa*—that is, a correspondence theory of truth—one suspects that considerations other than epistemological ones lay at the heart of the distinction between *shahāda* and *riwāya*. In other words, something other than a woman's general ability to gain, preserve, and communicate knowledge to others must have been behind the decision to reject her uncorroborated statements in the particular context of testimony before a judge. This suspicion is confirmed by the analysis of these two terms provided by the 13th-century Egyptian jurist al-Qarāfī (d. 1285), who argued that the law distinguishes between these two types of statements because of their different contexts. Al-Qarāfī observed that in cases of *riwāya*, the narrator (*rāwī*) is himself affected by the report. Therefore, he has little interest in lying. Conversely, because the witness suffers no harm should he lie or make a mistake, he has little interest in ensuring the accuracy of his testimony. Paradoxically, it is the very disinterestedness of the witness that gives rise to suspicion about the reliability of his testimony. For this reason, the law required a second witness to corroborate the first witness's testimony.

Equally important are the differing degrees to which *riwāya* and *shahāda* are socially regulated: because the topics of narration have universal applicability, society itself has a universal and continuing interest in investigating the truth of these reports. Thus, al-Qarāfī argues that in the case of narration, there is a natural social mechanism of corroboration that will usually root out any lies or mistakes made by individual narrators. Even if a mistake or lie should occur, humanity has until the end of time to discover it. In testimony, however, it is only the party against whom the false testimony is entered who has an interest in discovering the lie or the mistake. Furthermore, the consequences of false testimony are immediate and severe, possibly leading to the loss of property or life and limb. The chances that the wronged individual will be able to prove the falsity of the testimony in a timely fashion is almost nil. Therefore, the law requires two witnesses to establish a fact in a court of law in an attempt to create a formal system of corroboration in the absence of a natural, social method of corroboration.[16]

---

15. Thus, in disputes between a husband and a wife, each party's claim is evaluated solely as a function of its inherent plausibility or lack thereof. In the Mālikī school, for example, the wife will be taken on her word that her marriage was consummated based simply on the evidence of the couple's having had an opportunity to consummate the marriage, even if the husband denies the occurrence of intercourse. See Aḥmad al-Dardīr, *al-Sharḥ al-Ṣaghīr*, 4 vols., ed. Kamāl Waṣfī (Cairo: Dār al-Maʿārif, 1986), 2:438–39. Similarly, the gender of the litigants was not an issue in determining which party to a lawsuit had the right to take the oath and whether that oath would be effective in winning the claim.

16. Al-Qarāfī, *al-Furūq*, 1:6–7.

Just as the narration of Prophetic reports was part of the normative domain, and therefore was not subject to the gendered rules of testimony, the process by which legal norms were derived from those reports was also considered normative. Interpretation of revelation, then, was also free of gender restrictions. Therefore, a woman's [190] opinion *(fatwā)* in law was just as valid and morally binding as the legal opinion of a man. Thus, a woman could legitimately be a *muftī*, a legal expert whose task it was to communicate legal rules to non-specialists, including at times judges and other holders of political power. Ibn al-Ṣalāḥ's (d. 1245) treatment of this issue is typical of the Sunni jurists of the post-Ayyubid period. He noted in his work *Adab al-muftī wa-l-mustaftī* that:

Maleness and freedom are not required of the *muftī*, just as is the case for the narrator ... because the *muftī* is taken to be one reporting the law in a manner non-specific to a person, and in this respect, he is like a narrator, not a witness. Moreover, his *fatwā* is non-binding, in contrast to a judge's [verdict].[17]

JUSTIFYING THE GENDERED NATURE OF TESTIMONY (SHAHĀDA), PART 1: WOMEN AS PARTICIPANTS IN SCHOLARLY DISCOURSE

If a woman's transmissions of Prophetic reports, her legal opinions, and her legal claims were treated in the same manner as those of men, how did the law structure courtroom testimony so as to weaken the testimony of women in certain cases, even excluding it entirely in some? Modern scholarship, lay Muslim opinion, and even the opinion of the majority of exegetes have been united in assuming that this marginalization of women's testimony was premised on a gendered epistemology. For this reason, Leila Ahmed mistakenly writes that had the medieval law of testimony prevailed in the early centuries of Islamic history, the reports of women regarding the life of the Prophet would not have been incorporated into normative religious doctrine.[18] What she presents as a seeming contradiction is resolved by the fact, as we have seen, that testimony and transmission were regulated differently.

Although jurists must have been tempted to, and in fact did, argue that women were inherently less reliable than men, especially in nonlegal discourses, leading jurists could not so easily endorse general discrimination against the testimony of women on epistemological grounds. Had there been a natural quality inherent in women rendering their statements more unreliable than those of men, the law should have consistently dis-

---

17. *Lā yushtaraṭ fī al-muftī al-ḥurriyya wa al-dhukūriyya ka-mā fī al-rāwī ... li-anna al-muftī fī ḥukm man yukhbir ʿan al-sharʿ bi-mā lā ikhtiṣāṣ lahu bi-shakhṣ wa kāna fī dhālika ka-l-rāwī lā ka-l-shāhid wa fatwāhu lā yartabiṭ bihi ilzām bi-khilāf al-qāḍī* (Abū ʿAmr ʿAbd al-Raḥmān Ibn al-Ṣalāḥ, *Fatāwā wa masāʾil Ibn al-Ṣalāḥ*, 2 vols., ed. ʿAbd al-Muʿṭī Amīn Qalʿajī (Beirut: Dār al-Maʿrifa, 1406/1986), 1:42).

18. Ahmed, *Women and Gender*, 74.

criminated against the statements of women, whether in the normative or in the political domain.

Furthermore, if the law deemed a woman's rationality to be so defective that even in the recollection of facts she was not to be trusted, it would seem that the law should a fortiori reject her interpretations of revelation as being necessarily defective. In fact, however, we have seen that a woman's legal opinion (*fatwā*) was considered to be on par with that of a man. The equality, moreover, that women's reports enjoyed with men's in other areas of the law was not just a theoretical possibility; indeed, the fact that many women, to differing extents, participated in the production and reproduction of the theoretical sciences that were the backbone of religious learning no doubt also played an important role in circumscribing the types of arguments that could be marshaled to justify this discrimination. Among the first generation of Muslims, there were several women who were involved in both the transmission of the new religion as well as the development of its legal doctrine.[19] The most prominent of these women was ʿĀʾisha bint Abī Bakr, the youngest wife of the Prophet Muhammad. She was not only an important transmitter of religious doctrine, but she was also recognized as an independent legal authority by [191] both her contemporaries and succeeding generations of Muslim religious scholars.[20] She practiced this freedom as an interpreter of the law to issue legal opinions on controversial legal matters. Often, later jurists would bolster their positions with her opinions. The fact that ʿĀʾisha was a wife of the Prophet gave her privileged status as a transmitter of religious doctrine. It was her own qualities as an individual, however, that afforded her the authority to interpret law.[21]

Female participation in the production and reproduction of the religious sciences did not cease, however, with the demise of the first generation of Muslims. The domain most widely recognized by modern scholarship in which women continued to participate alongside men was the public transmission of the *hadith*, the normative reports containing the history of the Prophet and the earliest Muslim community. Evidence of female participation in this realm can be found in the many diplomas (*ijāzas*) containing women's names and in the colophons of manuscripts that mention women as teachers and as students. Further evidence of the recognized role of women's scholarship is the fact that many of these female scholars were even given academic titles, such as *al-musnida*, which

19. Ibn Qayyim al-Jawziyya, while mentioning which companions of the Prophet also served as *muftīs*, records the names of several women. See Ibn Qayyim al-Jawziyya, *Iʿlām al-muwaqqiʿīn ʿan rabb al-ʿālamīn*, 4 vols., ed. ʿAbd al-Raḥmān al-Wakīl (Cairo: Dār al-Kutub al-Ḥadītha, 1969), 1:12–15.

20. For example, the 14th-century jurist al-Zarkashī wrote a book that gathered ʿĀʾisha's legal opinions, *al-Iṣāba fī mā istadrakathu ʿĀʾisha ʿalā al-Ṣaḥāba*, wherein she challenged the accuracy of the opinions of her male colleagues.

21. For more on the controversial nature of ʿĀʾisha bint Abī Bakr, see D. A. Spellberg, *Politics, Gender, and the Islamic Past, the Legacy of ʿĀʾisha bint Abī Bakr* (New York: Columbia University Press, 1994).

can be translated roughly as "the authority."[22] Jonathan Berkey, in his important study of the educational system in medieval Cairo, suggests that women's participation in the intellectual life of Cairo was largely limited to the purely historical science of *hadith.*[23] However, there is some evidence that women also participated openly and legitimately in the more speculative branches of the religious sciences, such as positive law and speculative legal philosophy. Al-Ḥaṭṭāb, a North African jurist of the 16th century, carefully mentions in the introduction of one of his works the names of his teachers, his teachers' teachers, and the chain of authorities *(isnād)* that linked him to the authors of the various books that he had studied in his legal career. Two women appear in these chains of authorities. The first woman, Zaynab bint al-Kamāl al-Maqdisiyya *al-musnida* (d. 1339), seems to have been involved only in the transmission of *hadith.* The second woman, however, Umm al-Ḥasan Fāṭima bint Khalīl al-Kattānī (or al-Kinānī), transmitted to al-Ḥaṭṭāb the works of the great Mālikī jurist Shihāb al-Dīn al-Qarāfī. Through the transmission of this woman, then, al-Ḥaṭṭāb received al-Qarāfī's encyclopedic work on Mālikī positive law, the *Dhakhīra;* three works on speculative legal philosophy, *Tanqīḥ al-fuṣūl, Sharḥ tanqiḥ al-fuṣūl,* and *Sharḥ al-maḥṣūl;* a work on the legal principles of the Mālikī school, *al-Qawāʿid;* and *al-Umniyya fī idrāk al-niyya,* a work discussing the notion of intention and intentionality in the law.[24]

Although the number of men who studied the religious sciences far exceeded that of women, it is sufficient to note that the participation of women in the production and reproduction of religious knowledge was of a sufficient pedigree and skill that female authorities were recognized to be the intellectual equals of men by the institutions of learning within certain medieval Muslim societies, even in the context of law.[25] This of-

22. For details of women's participation in the science of hadith, see Muhammad Zubayr Siddiqi, *Hadith Literature: Its Origin, Development, and Special Features* (Cambridge: Islamic Texts Society, 1993), 117–23.

23. Jonathan Berkey, *The Transmission of Knowledge in Medieval Cairo* (Princeton, N.J.: Princeton University Press, 1992), 190.

24. Muḥammad ibn Muḥammad al-Ḥaṭṭāb, *Mawāhib al-jalīl,* 6 vols. (Beirut: Dār al-Fikr, 1412/1992), 1:9. It should also be noted, however, that some of the works on hadith that al-Ḥaṭṭāb mentions as having been transmitted through Zaynab dealt with the theoretical science of hadith and, therefore, involved more than the simple recollection of a text. For more information on this woman, see Ibn al-Ḥajar al-ʿAsqālanī, *Al-Durar al-kāmina fī aʿyān al-miʾa al-thāmina,* 5 vols., ed. Muḥammad Sayyid Jād al-Ḥaqq (Cairo: Dār al-Kutub al-Ḥadītha, 1966), 2:209–10. For the biography of Umm al-Ḥasan, see Muḥammad ibn ʿAbd al-Raḥmān al-Sakhāwī, *Al-Ḍawʾ al-lāmiʿ li-ahl al-qarn al-tāsiʿ,* 12 vols. (Beirut: Dār Maktabat al-Ḥayāt, 1966), 12:91.

25. The twelfth volume of al-Sakhāwī's *Ḍawʾ* focuses exclusively on the prominent women of the 9th Islamic century. Some of these women whom he explicitly mentioned as having studied legal works include Amat al-Khāliq bint ʿAbd al-Laṭīf ibn Ṣadaqa, 12:9; Amat al-Qāhir bint Qāsim ibn Muḥammad, 12:10; Bayram bint Aḥmad ibn Muḥammad al-Mālikiyya, 12:15; Khadīja bint ʿAbd al-Raḥmān, 12:28; and ʿĀʾisha bint ʿAlī, 12:78–79. It should be added that Sakhāwī's information can hardly be considered

ficial recognition is implicit in the fact that a woman's transmission of a book, a *hadith*, or a legal opinion did nothing to lessen the legitimacy of the text being transmitted or the validity of the norm being enunciated. This fact of women's recognized participation as intellectuals created awareness of the contradiction between the epistemological equality women enjoyed in the production and transmission of knowledge and her marginalized position in political contexts, whether as a witness or as a judge in a court of law. Furthermore, it lessened the plausibility of [192] any argument that sought to ground discrimination against women's testimony in the nature of the female.

JUSTIFYING THE GENDERED NATURE OF TESTIMONY (SHAHĀDA), PART II: WOMEN AS POLITICALLY MARGINALIZED SOCIAL ACTORS

I have located two post-12th-century arguments that attempt to defend the gender-based distinctions established in the medieval Islamic law of testimony. These arguments are important because they agree with the modernist position that ultimately locates the source of this discrimination not within the woman and her proclivity to telling the truth or lack thereof, but rather to specific social circumstances and the role that women played within those social circumstances.

The first argument is made by al-Qarāfī. His presentation displays much of the same ambivalence, if not to say outright confusion, that jurists faced in attempting to understand Islamic law's evidentiary discrimination against women. He begins by noting the difficulty courts have in enforcing their decisions. This institutional argument is compounded by the fact that men (including himself) in his 13th-century Egyptian society viewed women as being generally inferior to men. These two premises intersect in the person of the witness whose testimony before a judge has the effect of creating a "true" account of a past event. As a result of this "true" narrative, the losing party becomes obliged to act in a manner contrary to his wishes. Al-Qarāfī argues that losing parties bear a grudge toward the witnesses who testified against them in court. In the eyes of the losing party, the witnesses exercised authority and dominion (*sulṭān wa ghalaba wa qahr wa istīlā*ʾ) over them and were therefore responsible for their loss of the lawsuit. This resentment against the witnesses is greatly compounded when the losing party knows that his loss was a result of a woman's testimony. Subsequently, there is a greater likelihood that the losing party (whom al-Qarāfī assumes is a man) will not respect the court's decision. Two women were required by the law in order to lessen the blow to the losing

---

conclusive or complete. For example, in his biography of Umm al-Ḥasan (see n. 24) he failed to mention that she had transmitted works of positive law and legal methodology. Ibn Ḥajar also described some of the women in his work as having both studied the law and understood it well. See Ibn Ḥajar, *Al-Durar*, 3:307–8, 5:167–68.

party's already wounded male pride, thereby increasing the chance that he would voluntarily comply with the court's decision.

Al-Qarāfī adds as a second justification for this evidentiary discrimination a remark that displays the same reasoning used by Sayyid Quṭb and al-Rāzī: that women are inherently deficient in reason and religion (*al-nisāʾ nāqiṣāt ʿaql wa dīn*). Therefore, it is appropriate that two women should be required in order to lessen the harm that occurs from their deficient memories. Al-Qarāfī's commentator, Ibn al-Shāṭṭ (d. 1323), describes this argument as weak because if one accepts that female witnesses are deficient in reason and religion, this deficiency must also be present when a woman acts as a narrator of hadith. In that case, harm would still occur as a result of her deficient reason and character. However, he adds the narration of a woman—unlike her testimony—does not need to be corroborated before it is accepted. Therefore, by default, we are left with only the first of al-Qarāfī's two arguments as a plausible account for the basis of the discrimination.[26]

The second argument is advanced by the 15th-century Syrian Ḥanafī jurist al-Ṭarābulusī. He begins his analysis by explicitly noting that the reports of men and women are equally probative. Despite this, the law refused to consider an individual [193] woman's statement a proof (*ḥujja*) because the law, in order to avoid social corruption and disorder, obliged her to stay at home. He remarks that:

> Our opinion is valid because a woman is equal to a man in that [characteristic] upon which the qualifications of testimony are based, and these are the ability to see, to be precise, to memorize, and to rehearse testimony because of the existence of the implement of this power, and it is reason, [that faculty] which distinguishes things and comprehends them and a speaking tongue. Thus, the testimony of women gives rise to overwhelming likelihood [of truth] and to certainty in the heart about the truth of the witnesses. This is in contrast to the testimony of women by themselves, which is not accepted. Although their statements result in probability, the law did not take it into account as a proof because they are forbidden to go out because that leads to disorder and corruption, and the cause of corruption must be removed. Thus, a male was required as one of the two witnesses to prevent decisively the occurrence of corruption to the extent possible.[27]

---

26. Al-Qarāfī, al-Furūq, 1:6–7; Qāsim ibn ʿAbd Allāh ibn Muḥammad, known as Ibn al-Shāṭṭ, *Tahdhīb al-furūq* on the margin of *al-Furūq* (Beirut: ʿĀlam al-Kutub, n.d.), 1:6–7

27. *Wa ṣaḥīḥ qawlunā li-anna al-marʾa sāwat al-rajula fīmā yabtanī ʿalayhi ahliyyat al-shahāda wa huwa al-qudra ʿalā al-mushāhada wa al-ḍabṭ wa al-ḥifẓ wa al-adāʾ li-wujūd ālat al-qudra wa huwa al-ʿaql al-mumayyiz al-mudrik li-l-ashyāʾ wa al-lisān al-nāṭiq fa-tufīd shahādat al-nisāʾ ḥuṣūl ghalabat al-ẓann wa ṭumaʾnīnat al-qalb bi-ṣidq al-shuhūd bi-khilāf shahādat al-nisāʾ waḥdahunna lā tuqbal li-anna ghalabat al-ẓann taḥṣul bi-khabarihinna wa lakinna al-sharʿ lam yaʿtabirhā ḥujja li-annahunna manhiyyāt ʿan al-khurūj wa dhālika sabab al-fitna wa al-fasād wa sabab al-fasād yajib nafyuhu fa-rūʿiyat al-dhukūra fī aḥad al-sharṭayn ḥasman li-māddat al-fasād*

His argument seems to be that while the truth value of testimony is independent of the speaker's gender, women are required to stay at home to prevent the inevitable social corruption that results from the casual mingling of the sexes. The law discriminates against the testimony of women in order to discourage the use of female witnesses. By increasing the costs associated with female witnesses, the law ensures that individuals will be more likely to ask men to witness their civil transactions, thus reducing the need for women to leave their homes. In this manner, the law of testimony helps preserve the sexual boundaries of society by reducing the need for women to mingle with strange men.

Al-Qarāfī's first argument, as well as al-Ṭarābulusī's, both justify discrimination against women's testimony on grounds other than epistemological ones. After all, neither of their arguments calls into question the credibility of women's testimony as such; instead, the two arguments point to the social costs of treating a woman's testimony as the equivalent of a man's: for al-Qarāfī, this would have been a reduction in voluntary compliance with the decisions of the court, while for al-Ṭarābulusī the cost would have been an increase in sexual licentiousness. For both these men, these social costs were too high to be paid.

These arguments, then, should be considered political because they are based on an attempt to balance the competing interests of society and individuals. Based on these arguments, if it were possible to have a society in which men would voluntarily comply with verdicts regardless of the gender of the witnesses who presented the damaging evidence, or in which the casual mingling of the sexes did not lead to an increase in sexual licentiousness, the legal rule regulating female witnesses would presumably need revision.

Finally, the arguments of al-Qarāfī and al-Ṭarābulusī about the rules regarding the statements of women in medieval Islamic law are important for what they say, how they say it, and what they do not say. One would expect that any discussion of women's testimony in medieval Islamic law would be centered on Qur'an 2:282. In fact, neither al-Qarāfī nor al-Ṭarābulusī refers to it. Instead, their chief concern is to rationalize a legal doctrine that seems to take a slightly schizophrenic stance in its assessments of the reliability of women's statements. This fact in and of itself is significant in demonstrating the maturity of Muslim jurisprudence in the Ayyubid period—while Islamic law may have been derived ultimately from revelation, it was no longer being [194] interpreted solely with reference to revelation. Rather, it was being interpreted from the internal perspective of jurisprudence itself, one of whose ultimate goals was the creation of systematic legal rules that were internally coherent. In light of jurists' desire to create internally coherent legal doctrine, the fact that no Sunni jurist suggested purchasing doctrinal coher-

bi-l-qadr al-mumkin (ʿAlāʾ al-Dīn al-Ḥasan ibn ʿAlī ibn Khalīl ibn al-Ṭarābulusī, *Muʿīn al-ḥukkām fī mā yataraddadu bayn al-khaṣmayn min al-aḥkām* [Cairo: Muṣṭafā al-Bābī al-Ḥalabī, 1393/1973], 91–92).

ence at the price of extending the discriminatory rules of testimony to the field of narration stands as strong circumstantial evidence that these medieval jurists realized that attributing a general intellectual inferiority to women was, within the existing structure of Islamic law, an untenable position.

PUBLIC AND PRIVATE SPACE, NORMATIVE AND POLITICAL DISCOURSE, AND GENDER

The political nature of testimony is also reflected rather clearly in the different evidentiary standards required for a claimant to prove her case. Islamic procedural law generally divides claims into those which are financial and those which deal with the body. A woman's testimony has to be corroborated by a man's, according to jurists, but it is admissible in the first place only if the dispute is financial. Therefore, the testimony of women is not only excluded entirely from all capital cases, but it is also excluded from claims of marriage and divorce, because those cases encompass issues dealing primarily with the human body and its status.[28] On the other hand, in issues of fact dealing exclusively with the female body, the testimony of two female witnesses uncorroborated by a male witness is enough to win the claim.[29] Significantly, the testimony of women is admitted in these cases because they involve facts to which men are not privy (*mā lā yaẓhar li-l-rijāl*).

Instead of the cliche that in Islamic law, a woman's word is worth half of a man's, a more meaningful characterization of Islamic evidentiary discrimination against women would be that medieval Islamic law imagines legal disputes taking place across a public-private continuum. Because public space is regarded as men's space, the admissibility of women's testimony gradually decreases as the nature of the claim acquires more and more of a public quality. Thus, in a dispute regarding whether a baby was stillborn or died after birth, for example, the testimony of two women is sufficient, despite the fact that the dispute is both financial, in that the fact in question establishes rights of inheritance, and bodily, in that it establishes nonmonetary legal obligations. The private nature of the event precludes a male (public) presence, and therefore the law admitted the testimony of women uncorroborated by the testimony of men.[30] It should be noted that this

28. Ḥanafīs, however, will admit women's testimony in all cases, with the exception of capital cases and crimes of blood vengeance: al-Ṭarābulusī, *Muʿīn al-ḥukkām*, 91–92.

29. Muḥammad ibn Yūsuf al-ʿAbdarī al-Mawwāq, *al-Tāj wa al-iklīl*, on the margin of *Mawāhib al-jalīl*, 6 vols. (Beirut: Dar al-Fikr, 1412/1992), 6:182.

30. Ibn al-Shāṭṭ noted that "the law made the [testimony of a] woman like [that of a] man in cases where his presence is absolutely impossible and it made her [testimony] like his where his absence is simply coincidental with the stipulation of another [woman's] corroboration (*inna al-sharʿ jaʿala al-marʾa ka-l-rajul fī maḥall taʿadhdhur iṭṭilāʿihi al-iṭlāqī wa jaʿalahā mithlahu bi-sharṭ al-istiẓhār bi-ukhrā fī maḥall taʿadhdhur iṭṭilāʿihi al-ittifāqī*, Ibn al-Shāṭṭ, *Tahdhīb al-furūq*, 1:6).

is the case in spite of the fact that men's interests—indeed, often the interests of the state itself—were affected by these cases. Financial transactions, being essentially private matters, likewise admit the testimony of women. Because they are generally witnessed by men, however, they are quasi-public, and therefore the role of women is reduced. At the other, fully public end of the continuum, cases such as assault and robbery, because they occur in the public domain, excluded the testimony of women entirely. This is also the case with marriage and divorce: although they are private relations, they must meet standards of public recognition much more rigorous than that involving a mere financial transaction.[31]

On the other hand, though, we have seen that something so public as the transmission of Prophetic hadiths and the enunciation of legal norms transcended gender boundaries altogether, a fact that causes us to reconsider the whole notion of "public." [195] It seems that in the exclusion of women's reports, two factors are actually involved: whether the content of that report is public or private, and whether the context of that report is political or normative. Al-Qarāfī had already made use of this notion when he noted that because witnesses exercise power over the parties to a lawsuit, a plurality of witnesses was required. Interestingly, though, the transmission of learning, whether it was in the form of hadith or in the form of law, was never recognized as a political act. In contrast to testimony that bound a particular third party, the transmission of a hadith or of a legal ruling, because it contained a normative standard, bound all human beings, including the reporter, to the end of time. The very universality of the fact or the norm being reported removed it from the domain of political speech, where extra safeguards are provided to protect the particular interests involved, and placed it in the domain of narration, where all humans, free and slave, male and female, are equal. Most important, the existence of such a normative domain gave women the legal right to participate in court procedures that seem, at first glance, to fall squarely within the public domain and for that reason should have precluded the possibility of women's participation outright.

That the intrusion of the normative domain upon the political could open up further space for women's participation in the legal system is evidenced by al-Ṭarābulusī's discussion of the procedure used by judges in certifying the reliability of witnesses (*taʿdīl*). According to him, because this process is a religious affair (*min umūr al-dīn*), the opinions of men and women regarding the credibility of witnesses are equal, just as is the case in their transmission of reports (*riwāyat al-akhbār*)—that is, hadiths. Because this function is now understood to be an instance of transmission and not testimony, the Ḥanafīs allow

31. The public's interest in maintaining the integrity of marriages is reflected in the fact that individuals have a responsibility to report to judges men who have divorced their wives but continue cohabiting with them, even when their wives are unwilling to file for divorce. Financial claims, on the other hand, can be entered only by the aggrieved party himself.

a judge to certify a witness based on a woman's statement as long as she "is *barza*, one who mixes with the people and engages them [in commerce and other affairs], because she has experience in their affairs [in this case], thus making the [judge's] question [of her] meaningful (*idhā kānat imraʾatan barzatan tukhāliṭ al-nās wa tuʿāmiluhum li-anna lahā khibratan bi-umūrihim fa yufīd al-suʾāl*)." This is a paradoxical result, because al-Ṭarābulusī, in the same work, will later say in defense of the law's evidentiary discrimination against women that the law forbids them to leave their homes![32]

Similarly, because *fatwās* are normative speech, gender plays no part in the construction of a valid legal opinion. Perhaps even more remarkable, however, is that expert testimony was also considered normative for the same reason that legal opinions were normative: court-appointed experts, it was believed, simply reported facts about the external world that were universally valid, just as a *muftī* reported facts about the law that were universally valid. If one man was wounded by another, for example, the gravity of that wound was purely a medical question independent of the parties involved in the lawsuit; therefore, the testimony of the court-appointed doctor investigating the wound lacked the partisan nature that was the distinguishing characteristic of testimony. Mālikī jurists, for example, were so committed to the notion that expert testimony was objective that they did not subject it, unlike ordinary testimony, to rebuttal. For this reason, Ibn Hishām (d. 1209) noted that:

> There is no rebuttal of them (i.e., their expert opinions), because they were not asked to testify. Indeed, the judge only asked them for information, so they provided him with it. Rebuttal is only allowed in [cases of] doubt and suspicion of the witnesses, and this has been the basis of [legal] practice according to the master jurists.[33]

[196] Because this type of information was understood to be "objective," women in theory could, and in practice actually did, serve as court-appointed expert witnesses. When the court did appoint a female expert witness, the court would accept her assessment of the facts without seeking a corroborating statement from another expert, female or male.[34]

Berkey explained the relative paucity of women who studied jurisprudence in contrast to their more active participation in the transmission of hadith by noting that:

---

32. Al-Ṭarābulusī, *Muʿīn al-ḥukkām*, 87. Mālikīs, however, do not admit a woman's statement in this case even though they agree with the Ḥanafīs that this is an instance of narration and not testimony. In this case, the Mālikī rule contradicts the basic logic that distinguishes between narration and testimony.

33. *Lam yakun fīhim iʿdhār li-annahum lam yusʾalū al-shahāda wa innamā al-qāḍī [istakhbarahum] fa-akhbarūhu wa al-iʿdhār innamā huwa ʿalā al-ẓunūn wa al-tuhma li-l-shuhūd wa bi-hādhihi jarā al-ʿamal ʿinda al-shuyūkh* (Ibn Hishām, *al-Mufīd li-l-ḥukkām fī mā yaʿriḍ lahum min nawāzil al-aḥkām*, Cairo, Arab League Manuscript Institute, Fiqh Mālikī, no. 35, 54a).

34. Burhān al-Dīn Ibrāhīm ibn ʿAlī ibn Muḥammad ibn Farḥūn, *Tabṣirat al-ḥukkām fī uṣūl al-aqḍiya wa manāhij al-aḥkām*, 2 vols. (Cairo: al-Qāhira al-ḥadītha li-l-ṭibāʿa, 1406/1986), 2:82.

> Women were systematically excluded from holding judicial posts that would position them to resolve disputes among men. A similar concern may have lurked subconsciously behind their apparent exclusion from the intensive study of subjects such as jurisprudence, where the assertion of a woman's analytical and forensic skills could have threatened to place her, intellectually at least, in a position of authority over men.[35]

While the assertion that women were excluded, at least by custom if not by law, from positions in which they could exercise power over men is almost certainly true, Berkey's statement must be read in light of what medieval Muslims understood to be acts of power. Muslim jurists, for reasons already mentioned, were unanimous in permitting women to interpret the law and issue legal opinions.

What is most surprising, though, is even those functions that Muslim jurists took to be overtly political, such as testimony and judgeship, were never entirely closed to the possibility of women's participation. To the extent that women participated in these tasks, of course, they would have been recognized as exercising actual power over men. In financial affairs, for example, the testimony of women, although relatively weaker than that of men, could prove decisive. Nor is it true that there was a consensus among jurists that women could not be judges.[36] Rather, it is precisely because the majority of Muslim jurists understood testimony to be political that the Ḥanafī legal school allowed women to serve as judges for all cases admitting female testimony.[37] Al-Ṭabarī (d. 923),

---

35. Berkey, *Transmission of Knowledge*, 180–81.

36. Emile Tyan, *Histoire de l'organisation judiciaire en pays d'Islam*, 2nd ed. (Leiden: E.J. Brill, 1960), 163. Although the Ḥanafīs were the only Sunni school to allow women to be judges, several prominent individual jurists also permitted it. Among them was the celebrated Muḥammad ibn Jarīr al-Ṭabarī. Muhammad ibn al-Ḥasan al-Shaybānī who, although a disciple of Abū Ḥanīfa, agreed with al-Ṭabarī in permitting women to be judges in all areas of the law, unlike the rest of Abū Ḥanīfa's followers, who restricted women's judicial competence to cases that admitted their testimony. See Abū al-Walīd Sulaymān ibn Khalaf al-Bājī, *al-Muntaqā*, 7 vols. (Cairo: Dār al-Fikr al-ʿArabī), 5:182; Abū al-Walīd Muḥammad ibn Aḥmad Ibn Rushd (Averroes), *Bidāyat al-mujtahid*, 2 vols. (Beirut: Dār al-Fikr, n.d.), 2:344; Muwaffaq al-Dīn ʿAbd Allāh ibn Aḥmad Ibn Qudāma, *al-Mughnī*, 14 vols., ed. ʿAbd al-Fattāḥ Muḥammad al-Ḥulw and ʿAbd Allāh ʿAbd al-Munʿim al-Turkī (Cairo: Dār Hajr, 1986), 14:12; Abū al-Walīd Muḥammad ibn Aḥmad Ibn Rushd (the Grandfather), *Kitāb al-muqaddimāt*, 3 vols., ed. Saʿīd Aḥmad Aʿrāb (Beirut: Dār al-Gharb al-Islāmī, 1988), 2:258. Likewise, al-Ḥaṭṭāb reported that Ibn al-Qāsim is also said to have considered the appointment of women to the bench to be permissible, although later Mālikīs were unsure whether he held the same opinion on this issue as al-Ṭabarī and al-Shaybānī, or agreed with the majority of the Ḥanafī school, who would restrict women to those cases where their testimony was admissible (al-Ḥaṭṭāb, *Mawāhib al-jalīl*, 6:87–88).

37. The gist of the Ḥanafī argument was that witnesses are similar to judges in that both exercise power over the litigants. Because a woman when testifying against a litigant exercises power over that litigant, there is no reason to believe she cannot exercise power over that same litigant in the capacity of a judge. See Tyan, *Histoire*, 162. For more on the analogy between judges and witnesses in Islamic law,

meanwhile, permitted women to be judges in all areas of the law, arguing that if their *fatwās* were legitimate in all areas of the law, then a fortiori their rulings as judges must also be valid.[38]

TRANSCENDING THE POLITICAL/NORMATIVE DICHOTOMY: IBN TAYMIYYA AND IBN QAYYIM AL-JAWZIYYA

The dominant juridical discourse, as represented above, was premised on the existence of a normative realm and a political realm. The former was characterized as a domain of human life regulated by universal norms, as a result of which harmony existed between the interests of credible individuals (*ʿudūl*) and the truth. Although this does not guarantee that all statements of credible individuals will prove to be true, it allows us to be reasonably sure that their statements in this context are made in good faith and are not the result of deliberate deception and manipulation.[39] The political realm, in contrast to the normative realm, is that domain of life dominated by selfish, particular interests. The hold of these particular interests on even credible individuals is so strong that the statements of normally veracious individuals in this context cannot be taken at face value. In other words, when particular interests are involved, a higher degree of skepticism is required due to the presence of tangible interests.[197] Although we might find the idea of the existence of such a normative domain to be naive, belief in its existence nonetheless offered women greater space for participating in the legal system than would otherwise have been the case. On the other hand, we also find a few but important jurists—namely, the Syrian Ḥanbalites lbn Taymiyya (d. 1327) and Ibn Qayyim al-Jawziyya (d. 1350) who rejected this distinction between political speech (*shahāda*) and normative speech (*riwāya*) altogether. While arguing that the testimony of a slave should be treated in the same manner as that of a free person, the latter said:

> It should not be argued that transmission is less stringent [in its stipulations] than testimony, and therefore more precautions should be taken in the latter in

see Fadel, "Adjudication," 76–77. In general, it seems that the Ḥanafī *madhhab* was the most liberal of the Sunni schools of law regarding the question of the legitimacy of women's political power. See, for example, Ibn al-Humām, who notes that "when a woman is ruler, her command establishing the Friday prayer is valid, although her actual leading of it is not" (*wa al-marʾa idhā kānat sulṭāna yajūz amruhā bi-l-iqāma lā iqāmatuhā*). Muḥammad ibn ʿAbd al-Wāḥid lbn al-Humām, *Sharḥ fatḥ al-qadīr*, 10 vols. [Cairo: Muṣṭafā al-Bābī al-Ḥalabī, 1970], 2:55).

38. Abu al Ḥasan ʿAlī ibn Muḥammad ibn Ḥabīb al-Māwardī, *al-Ḥāwī al-kabīr*, 19 vols., ed. ʿAlī Muḥammad Muʿawwaḍ and ʿĀdil Aḥmad ʿAbd al-Mawjūd (Beirut: Dār al-Kutub al-ʿIlmiyya, 1994), 16:156.

39. For this reason, al-Qarāfī notes that if a slave were to transmit a hadith whose meaning would require that he be granted his freedom, he would nevertheless still be believed despite the fact that he has a particular interest in the truth of his report because "narration is far removed from suspicion" (*bāb al riwāya baʿīd ʿan al-tuham jiddan*). Al-Qarāfī, *al-Furūq*, 1:16.

> contrast to transmission [of Prophetic reports]. Although many have adopted this doctrine, it has neither been proved nor is it correct. Indeed, the most important thing for which precautions should be taken and precision required is testimony about the Prophet, may God bless him and grant him peace, for a lie [or mistake] about him is not like a lie [or mistake] about someone else.... The reason for which his [viz., the slave's] transmission [of Prophetic reports] was accepted is the same reason his testimony [before a judge] should be accepted.[40]

Obviously, this argument for the admissibility of a slave's testimony, based as it is on the fact that the slave's transmission of Prophetic reports was admissible, held implications for the wider acceptance of women's testimony, a fact that was not lost on Ibn al-Qayyim. In developing his argument for increasing the admissibility of women's testimony, he argued that the purpose of testimony was to gain truth about a past event. Therefore, if a woman was believed to be reliable in her testimony regarding financial dealings, she must be assumed, all things being equal, also to be reliable in other areas of life.[41] Limiting her testimony to financial claims, therefore, was arbitrary.

The second part of Ibn al-Qayyim's argument dealt directly with the issue of whether gender was a material factor in determining the relative credibility of a witness. For Ibn al-Qayyim and Ibn Taymiyya, the answer was simple: a judge should be allowed to rule based on the testimony of men or women, *as long as that evidence was likely to be true.* The gender of the witness, then, was made secondary to the issue of whether the witness's testimony was credible in itself. For this reason, both Ibn Taymiyya and Ibn al-Qayyim rejected the two-women-equal-one-man rule that lay at the heart of discrimination against women's testimony. They argued that this rule resulted from ignoring the difference between recording testimony for the purpose of protecting a right in the event of a future dispute, known as *taḥammul al-shahāda*, and testifying before a judge, known as *adāʾ al-shahāda*. Thus,

> There is no doubt that the reason for a plurality [of women in the Qur'anic verse] is [only] in recording testimony. However, *when a woman is intelligent and remembers and is trustworthy in her religion*, then the purpose [of testimony] is

40. Ibn Qayyim al-Jawziyya, *al-Ṭuruq al-ḥukmiyya*, ed. Muḥammad Jamīl Ghāzī (Cairo: Maṭbaʿat al-Madanī, 1977), 245. Others defended the exclusion of slaves' testimony by arguing that testimony is a type of political jurisdiction (*wilāya*) and, therefore, any witness must by definition be free. Ibn al-Qayyim described this argument as being particularly weak (Ibn al-Qayyim, *al-Ṭuruq*, 248).

41. *Al-maqṣūd bi-l-shahāda an yuʿlama bihā thubūt al-mashhūd bihi wa annahu ḥaqq wa ṣidq fa-innahā khabar ʿanhu wa hādhā lā yakhtalif bi-kawn al-mashhūd bihi mālan aw ṭalāqan aw ʿitqan aw waṣiyya bal man ṣuddiqa fī hādhā ṣuddiqa fī hādhā* (Ibn Qayyim al-Jawziyya, *Iʿlām al-muwaqqiʿīn bi-rabb al-ʿālamīn*, 3 vols., ed. Ṭāhā ʿAbd al-Raʾūf Saʿd [Beirut: Dār al-Jīl, n.d.], I :95).

> attained through her statement just as it is in her transmissions [in] religious [contexts] (emphasis mine).[42]

Although this seems to be a prima facie reasonable interpretation of the verse in question, Ibn Taymiyya also felt compelled to demonstrate the weakness of interpreting Qur'an 2:282 to justify evidentiary discrimination against women in general. He begins by noting that the plain meaning of the verse is not directed toward judges but, rather, toward individuals who are involved in a transaction. Thus, the verse's [198] significance, if it has any relevance at all to courtroom proceedings, is only implicit. The implicit meaning of this verse, if taken to address judges, would be, "Rule with two male witnesses. And if not two male witnesses, then one male and two female witnesses." He points out astutely, however, that no school of Muslim law has actually restricted a judge to using only two male witnesses, or in their absence one male and two female witnesses. Instead, Muslim jurists agree that a judge is also allowed to rule based on various combinations of witnesses, oaths (*yamīn*), and the refusal to swear (*al-nukūl*). It is therefore known with certainty that the implicit meaning of the verse was not intended by the Lawgiver. He concluded the argument by noting that "the command to ask two women to testify at the time of recording [the testimony] does not necessitate that judgment cannot be rendered with a number less than this. The means by which a judge rules are broader than the means by which God advised the possessor of a right to protect it."[43] Ibn Taymiyya and Ibn al-Qayyim, then, reach the conclusion that the admissibility of testimony is not determined by gender but, rather, by credibility. When a woman offers credible testimony, therefore, the judge must admit it, just as he would admit the credible testimony of a man. One should not infer from their analysis, however, that Ibn al-Qayyim and Ibn Taymiyya believed there was no difference in the probative value of men's and women's testimony. Indeed, Ibn al-Qayyim maintains that although Qur'an 2:282 does not prejudice the admission of female testimony qua testimony before a judge, it does establish that two male witnesses are usually the best guarantee that one's rights will be respected in the event of a future challenge. Interestingly, his explanation of why this is so turns on sociological as well as epistemological arguments. Thus, he says that "the testimony

---

42. *Wa lā rayba anna hādhihi al-ḥikma fī al-taʿaddud hiya fī al-taḥammul fa-ammā idhā ʿaqalat al-marʾa wa ḥafiẓat wa kānat mimman yūthaq bi-dīnihā fa-inna al-maqṣūd ḥāṣil bi-khabarihā ka-mā yaḥṣul bi-akhbār al-diyānāt* (ibid.).

43. *Lā yalzam min al-amr bi-istishhād al-marʾatayn waqt al-taḥammul allā yuḥkama bi-aqalla minhumā ... fa-l-ṭuruq allatī yaḥkum bihā al-ḥākim awsaʿ min al-ṭuruq allatī arshada allāhu ṣāḥib al-ḥaqq ilā an yaḥfaẓa ḥaqqahu bihā* (ibid., 95–96). Al-Qurṭubī made a similar argument in arguing for the legitimacy of a judge's verdict based on the testimony of one witness and the oath of the claimant: Al-Qurṭubī, *al-Jāmiʿ li-aḥkām al-qurʾān*, 3:392. Ibn Taymiyya also made the remarkable claim that a verdict based upon the testimony of single woman along with the oath of the claimant would be valid: *wa law qīla yuḥkam bi-shahādat imraʾa wa yamīn al-ṭālib la-kāna mutawajjihan* (Ibn al-Qayyim, *Iʿlām al-muwaqqiʿīn*, ed. Ṭāhā, 95).

of one man is superior to [that of] two women because it is *usually impossible* for women to attend court sessions, and their memory and precision is less than that of males [emphasis added]."[44] What he means here, obviously, is that an individual who is seeking the most effective means of preserving his rights will prefer male witnesses, as they will be more likely than female witnesses to be able to testify before a judge in the event of a dispute.

Of the two reasons raised by Ibn al-Qayyim, however, it is the relative lack of freedom of movement that would most likely prejudice an individual against using female witnesses. After all, Ibn al-Qayyim is willing to grant the equality of a woman's testimony to a man's as long as the individual woman is "intelligent and remembers and is trustworthy in her religion." Presumably, when one seeks witnesses to one's transactions, one would seek those who are recognized as trustworthy, regardless of their gender. It is the fact that a female witness lacks the same access as a man to court that renders her substantially less useful in preserving one's rights and, therefore, less desirable as a witness.

As if to confirm that this is the actual reason that it is preferable to use men as witnesses, Ibn al-Qayyim argues that the admission of the testimony of one man and two women is a valid basis for judgment, *even in the presence of two male witnesses.* Because the female witness shares with a male witness the qualities of honesty, trustworthiness, and religiosity, when her testimony is corroborated by another woman, her testimony may actually become stronger than the uncorroborated testimony of the male witness. Moreover, the probative value of the testimony of certain exceptional women, such as Umm al-Dardāʾ[45] and Umm ʿAṭiyya,[46] is without doubt greater than that of a single man of lesser stature.[47]

[199] The clear thrust of Ibn al-Qayyim's analysis of women's testimony is that it must be treated individually. Although he does believe that women are generally more prone to committing errors than men, this does not in itself justify blanket discrimination against the testimony of women, the result of which would be the rejection of

44. *Fa-inna shahādat al-rajul al-wāḥid aqwā min shahādat al-marʾatayn li-anna al-nisāʾ yataʿadhdhar ghāliban ḥuḍūruhunna majālis al-ḥukkām wa ḥifẓuhunna wa ḍabṭuhunna dūna ḥifẓ al-rijāl wa ḍabṭihim* (Ibn al-Qayyim, *al-Ṭuruq*, 219).

45. Umm al-Dardāʾ Khayra bint Abī Hadrad. She was a famous Anṣārī companion of the Prophet. She died in Syria during the caliphate of ʿUthmān ibn ʿAffān. Ibn ʿAbd al-Barr described her as being virtuous, intelligent, and possessing good judgment, in addition to having great piety. A large group of successors transmitted different hadiths on her authority. See Ibn Ḥajar al-ʿAsqalānī, *al-Iṣāba fī tamyīz al-ṣaḥāba*, 13 vols., ed. Ṭāhā Muḥammad al-Zaynī (Cairo: Maktabat al-Kulliyyāt al-Azhariyya, 1297/1917), 12:241–42.

46. Umm ʿAṭiyya Nusayba bint al-Ḥārith was also an Anṣārī companion of the Prophet. Several of her hadiths have been included in the works of al-Bukhārī and Muslim: ibid., 13:253–54.

47. *Wa lā rayba anna al-ẓann al-mustafād min shahādat mithl umm al-dardāʾ wa umm ʿaṭiyya aqwā min al-ẓann al-mustafād min rajul wāḥid dūnahumā wa dūna amthālihimā* (ibid., 236).

truthful evidence. Indeed, whenever a woman has shown herself to be credible, her evidence should be admitted. Moreover, it would not be wildly speculative to suggest that he would have agreed to the proposition, had it been suggested to him, that any perceived deficiencies in women's reason and memory were more likely a result of sociological factors than of biological ones.[48]

CONCLUSION

I began this essay with the observation of many Muslim feminists that historical Muslim societies have experienced a tension between an Islam that is ethically egalitarian and bears a message that is explicitly gender-neutral and an Islam that is historically determined, with certain pragmatic regulations that tend to obviate that ethical message. Ahmed advanced this thesis forcefully, saying:

> There appears, therefore, to be two distinct voices within Islam, and two competing understandings of gender, one expressed in the pragmatic regulations for society..., the other in the articulation of an ethical vision.... While the first voice has been extensively elaborated into a body of political and legal thought, which constitutes the technical understanding of Islam, the second—the voice to which ordinary believing Muslims, who are essentially ignorant of the details of Islam's technical legacy, give their assent—has left little trace on the political and legal heritage of Islam.[49]

The detailed analysis in this essay of the manner in which post Ayyubid Sunni jurists treated the various issues related to women's participation in the production, transmission, and application of the law, however, we discovered that the ethical voice certainly *did* leave a trace on the medieval doctrine. Perhaps the conclusions reached by these jurists are not what we would have wanted them to be, but that does not detract from the fact that they realized that Islamic law's evidentiary discrimination against women constituted a *legal* problem—that is, something that was problematic even within the parameters of Islamic law. Even al-Qarāfī, who attempted to ground this discrimination

48. This conclusion is also consistent with the sense of the root *ʿa-qa-la* in classical Arabic and in the usage of the term *ʿaql* by the jurists and the scholars of hadith. Thus, Riḍwān al-Sayyid argues that in "the opinion of the scholars of hadith and the jurists, the [intellectual] inequality among people is not a result of [differences in] instinctive reason, but rather [a result] of their judgment or practical reason. Reason develops in an individual just as his body develops, just as his other instincts develop. It is the experiences of the environment or the surroundings which produce the [capacity for] practical reason (i.e., judgment), wherein people are unequal." He also quotes al-Māwardī as saying that "everything needs reason, but reason is in need of experience." See Riḍwān al-Sayyid, *al-Umma wa al-sulṭa wa al-jamāʿa* (Beirut: Dār Iqra', 1404/1984), 195–96.

49. Ahmed, *Women and Gender*, 65–66.

in the nature of women, was forced to develop a sociological argument that, although hardly palatable to modern sensibilities, plausibly argues that this discrimination had as much to do with male chauvinism as it did with female witness's presumptive lack of credibility. Al-Ṭarābulusī's defense of the law, meanwhile, seems to have taken into account the weakness of any argument claiming that this discrimination was a result of the inferior probative value of a woman's testimony. Like al-Qarāfī, then, al-Ṭarābulusī proposed a sociological argument in defense of this rule, which, according to him, helped preserve the sexual mores of his society.

For both of these authors, the difficulty of the established law regarding women's testimony was not so much that it discriminated against women but, rather, that it was contradictory, at times treating women's statements in the same manner that it treated men's, while at other times discriminating against it. This contradiction had been resolved by the creation of two distinct arenas for speech-one normative, where [200] gender was not an issue in evaluating the probative value of a statement, and the other political, where it was. For Ibn Taymiyya and Ibn al-Qayyim, though, the only issue was the probative value of the statement, regardless of the normative or political context of the statement. Thus, both of these jurists urged that judges be allowed to treat a woman's testimony in the same manner as a man's as long as the judge found the woman's testimony to be probative.

The importance of the categories of normative and political speech, however, is not limited to the narrow issue of women's testimony before a judge. Because testimony was considered to be political speech, it was not difficult to argue, as the Ḥanafī school did, that women could be judges in all cases that admitted women's testimony. Conversely, because the communication of legal opinions was considered to lie in the normative domain, there was complete agreement among Sunni jurists that women could be *muftīs*. It was as a result of the law's acceptance of women as *muftīs*, moreover, that led al-Ṭabarī to argue that a woman could be a judge in all areas of the law.

To conclude, then, one must agree with Ahmed that there *are* two voices within Islam regarding gender: one ethical and one pragmatic. But, it also cannot be denied that their relationship was in constant tension, if not in an outright dialectic. The rules of positive law, *fiqh*, treating women express their relationship rather clearly. It is especially obvious in the law's treatment of women's statements, as we have shown above. This also reveals the nature of jurisprudence as a discourse, in contrast to that of exegesis—the task of the latter is simply to explain the meaning of the verse at hand; the jurist, however, must take into account a much wider set of data before reaching his judgment. Because jurists necessarily had to take into account all the legal rules regulating women's statements, they were forced to reconsider the basis of evidentiary discrimination against women's testimony. When they did this, it became obvious that impeaching the probative value of women's statements based on their gender was not a satisfactory explanation of the law. It was this realization that led them, or at least some of them, to offer sociological explanations. The jurists' treatment of this issue should be contrasted with that of the exegetes, none of whom, as far as I was able to ascertain, even attempted to explain why the normative statements of women were granted the same moral and scientific weight as those made by men, while women's testimony was deemed to be less weighty than that of men. In light of the preceding evidence, moreover, one can no longer simply assume that modernist interpretations of Qur'an 2:282 represent a radical break from Islamic law; indeed, from the perspective of *fiqh*, the sociological interpretation, not the natural or the psychological one, is the only plausible reading of the verse. Furthermore, this suggests that Muslim modernism in general, and Muslim feminism in particular, might profit from exploiting problems and tensions that have long been recognized to exist within Islamic law. In the long run, this strategy may be more successful than claiming the need for a "new" jurisprudence that is to be derived *ex nihilo* from the original sources of Islamic law. This assumes that many of the issues that make up the modernist agenda have potential solutions waiting to be derived from already existing principles of Islamic law. Although this may or may not actually turn out to be the case, the evidence presented regarding women's testimony suggests that the battle between the "two voices" of Islam manifested itself more dramatically in positive law than it did in other arenas of religious discourse. [201] Therefore, any study of gender in the Islamic middle periods that ignores *fiqh* is not only dangerously incomplete, but it will also probably miss the most interesting medieval discussions of gender.

9

REINTERPRETING THE GUARDIAN'S ROLE IN THE ISLAMIC CONTRACT OF MARRIAGE: THE CASE OF THE MĀLIKĪ SCHOOL

Mohammad Fadel

I. INTRODUCTION

[1] It is not unusual to hear said in the popular media that Islamic law disadvantages women. Indeed, the behavior of many Muslim societies, and their interpretations of Islamic law, seem to provide clear support to this popular perception.[1] I do not wish to counter this popular perception in this brief essay. Rather, my goal is merely to [2] take a critical look at a doctrine that is often cited—by Muslims and non-Muslims alike—as indicative of Islamic law's systematic gender discrimination: the legal requirement that a Muslim woman, prior to her marriage, must gain the permission of her father, or another male relative. This is in contrast to a Muslim male, who, it is said, may marry without the permission of his father, or any other relative.

A proper understanding of this legal requirement is critical for modern Muslims in the United States, given the centrality of notions of personal autonomy and gender equality in modern American life—notions that Muslims in the United States generally accept as normative, and believe are compatible with Islam, at least at an abstract level. The challenge is whether we can reconcile our modern notions of individual autonomy and gender equality with a body of legal doctrines—as well as boisterous claims by obscurantist Muslims—that apparently fly in the face of these concepts. In particular, the popular understanding that Islamic law requires a woman to garner her father's approval to marry, or the approval of another male relative, smacks of patriarchy—a vestige of a system in which males had quasi-property interests in the female members of the family.

This article was originally published in *The Journal of Islamic Law Addressing Issues of Law, Religion, and Culture*, vol. 3, no. 1, Spring/Summer 1998, pp. 1–26

1. The most stark example of course is the Taliban's so-called Islamic regime in Afghanistan. Unfortunately, I do not believe the record of Saudi Arabia in this regard is much better.

In fact, medieval Islamic law[2] poses many conundrums of the sort raised by the apparently differential treatment of men and women vis-à-vis the requirement of the guardian prior to marriage. It is simply because most of us will marry that we become aware of the rules regarding the guardian in marriage, and its seemingly discriminatory nature. When the problem is so acute, self-serving repetition of slogans about the dignity of women in Islam are not sufficient to answer the troubling question of whether Islamic law awards males a property interest[3] in their female relatives.

[3] This essay will not attempt a detailed analysis of all the rules regarding the role of the guardian in the marriage contract. That in itself would require a monograph. Instead, I attempt to provide a broad overview of the competing interpretations that have been given to the guardian's role in one school of Islamic law, the Mālikī school. The Mālikī school is named after Mālik b. Anas, the great legist of Madīna who died in the second century of the Hijra. It subsequently came to predominate in Northern, Western and sub-Saharan Africa. My choice of the Mālikī school is merely one of convenience since it is the body of fiqh which I have studied in most detail. It is possible that other schools of jurisprudence offer entirely different readings of the guardian's role.

Based on a close reading of Mālikī doctrines[4] on the guardian, I have reached the following conclusions. The first and most important conclusion is a negative one—while Muslims might have good faith disputes regarding the positive role that a guardian is to play in a marriage, there is no basis to the belief that Islamic law requires a male guardian because the guardian has a private interest in the marriage of his female relative that Islamic law protects by stipulating the guardian's assent to the contract. In other words, there is no basis to conclude that Islamic law, at least as interpreted by the Mālikīs, subordinates female autonomy to the private interests of her male relatives. Therefore, Islamic law categorically rejects the notion that men have a property interest in their female relatives.

2. When I use the term "medieval Islamic law," I am referring to the post-formative period of Islamic law, when the schools of law had become firmly established and each had produced an authoritative body of legal doctrine and legal texts, roughly from the 13th century to the 18th century of the Christian Era.

3. This alleged property right, however, is only partial—it is limited to the power to exclude. It would not include other incidents of property, e.g., the right to alienate, the right to enjoy, etc. As I will argue, the nature of the guardian's relationship to the woman cannot be analogized to a form of private property.

4. The Mālikī school, like other schools of jurisprudence, was characterized by a great deal of internal dispute regarding what the "right" rule for a given issue should be. Nonetheless, the school did have a dominant opinion whose technical label was the *mashhūr,* i.e., the "famous" opinion. All things being equal, which often was not the case, courts are supposed to apply the *mashhūr* opinion.

The second conclusion is more in the nature of an observation: Mālikī doctrine is characterized by a deep split regarding the role of the public authority in the marriage contract.[5] Although prevailing [4] Mālikī doctrine sought to involve the public in the contract whenever possible, later Mālikīs, especially in Egypt, sought to minimize the role of public authorities in the supervision of marriages, preferring to keep marriage entirely within the private sphere of the natural family.

Third, as a matter of legal doctrine, the importance of the guardian's role is exclusively a function of the majority, or lack thereof, of the ward, not the gender of the ward. Thus, the guardian of a minor, assuming he is the biological father, has almost absolute powers to compel the marriage of both his minor sons and daughters. At the other extreme, the biological father has no power to compel the marriage of either his adult son or daughter. The problem for Muslim women however, was that the Mālikī school established discriminatory standards of emancipation (*tarshīd*), namely, that while a male was presumptively emancipated from his father's control upon reaching the age of majority, a woman had to prove that she was capable of managing her own affairs to win emancipation. Otherwise, she remained subject to her father's control as though she were a minor until her first marriage.[6]

Fourth, where the woman has been emancipated, although the law stipulates the permission of a guardian, in fact, the woman is free to ignore the wishes of her male relatives and instead ask for permission to marry from the public authority. This suggests, based on the general structure of Islamic constitutional law, that the authority [5] exercised by a guardian, understood as the closest male relative of the female in the marriage of an adult woman, is not by virtue of a vested private right. but rather as a delegation from the public authority. In other words, Islamic law created, as a default rule, that a male relative of the bride would act as the public's representative in each marriage. Because the guardian is acting pursuant to a delegation of power, it is within

5. Muslim jurists would generally refer to the public authority, interchangeably, as the "Imām," or the "sulṭān," or the "ḥākim." Thus, when jurists say something like "It is a matter for the Imām," it should not be taken literally. In other words, they are saying it is merely a question for the public authority, not literally that the person with the title of "Imām" is empowered to resolve it. It should be noted that use of the term "qāḍī" or judge also qualifies as a generic representative of the public authority because the judge is a creature of the public.

6. I argue, however, that even assuming the Mālikīs' distinction between males and females in regard to emancipation was legally justified, their continued treatment of an adult female incapable of managing her own affairs as a minor was an error because in this case the cause of her legal incapacity is no longer minority, but rather the legal cause of her alleged incompetence is managing her property. A father did not have power to compel the marriage of an adult male whose legal incompetence was a consequence of his inability to manage his own financial affairs. Therefore, the proper treatment of an adult, unemancipated woman should have been the same as a male who was incapable of managing his own financial affairs, i.e., while the father has the power to veto such an incompetent's marriage, he does not have the power to compel her to marry contrary to her will.

the prerogative of the public authority to change the default entitlement, withdraw it from the family of the bride, and exercise it directly through the public's agents. Were this suggestion to be followed, and if the public's agents routinely served as guardians of marriages, rather than exceptionally as is presently the case, the perception that Islam's requirement of a guardian is rooted in gender discrimination would be replaced with the more accurate, and to moderns at least, the more appealing notion that Islam requires a guardian to ensure that the public's interest in the marriage is being protected.

II. BACKGROUND

Mālikī works of positive law *(furūʿ)* such as *al-Sharḥ al-Ṣaghīr* do not discuss why a guardian is required in all marriage contracts but rather take the requirement for granted.[7] These works proceed by dividing guardians into two types, those that have the power to compel the marriage of their wards, and those that do not.[8] In general, the Mālikīs award a father the power to compel the first marriage of his daughter.[9] A father also retains the power to compel [6] the marriage of his previously married (*thayyib*) minor daughter who became a widow prior to puberty.[10] Finally, the father enjoys the power to compel the marriage of a daughter who suffers from a permanent state of mental disability.[11] The only limitation on the father's right to exercise this power is that the daughter suffers no legally cognizable harm from the marriage.[12] In the absence of the father, the general

7. Cf. Ibn Rushd the Grandson, 2 *Bidāyat al-Mujtahid wa Nihāyat al-Muqtaṣid* 7–9 (Beirut: Dār al-fikr, n.d.) (arguing that the scriptural basis for the stipulation of a guardian in the marriage contract for a mature woman is conjectural at best).

8. The power to compel the ward to marry is called *jabr*. A guardian possessed of such power is called a *mujbir*. The ward, depending on whether he is a male or a female, is called *mujbar* and *mujbara*, respectively.

9. In other words, the father has the right to compel his virgin daughter's marriage. However, virginity is a term of art, meaning never having been married, not physical virginity. Thus, al-Dardīr states in colorful language that as far as the law is concerned, a girl who has never been married, but nonetheless has repeatedly engaged in unlawful sexual intercourse such that the "cloak of modesty has left her face," is nevertheless a virgin for purposes of this rule.

10. In the pre-modern era, marriage of minors was a common practice although consummation was not to occur until the onset of puberty. This rule simply states that a minor girl who is married but whose marriage is never legally consummated retains the legal status of a virgin for the question of the father's power to compel her subsequent marriage.

11. In other words, a father could not compel the marriage of his schizophrenic daughter, assuming she suffered only periodic attacks of schizophrenia, on grounds of her insanity. Of course, he could still compel her marriage on either of the two previously mentioned grounds.

12. Abū al-Barakāt Aḥmad b. al-Dardīr, 2 *al-Sharḥ al-Ṣaghīr*, 355 ("*wa maḥall jabr alab fī al-thalātha idh lam yalzam ʿalā tazwījihā ḍarar ʿāda ... mimma yuraddu al-zawj bihi sharʿan*" = 'The father enjoys the power to compel in the three mentioned cases] so long as no harm by which the husband would be considered legally unfit results to her from the [compelled] marriage'). [Editor's note: The essence of the principles

rule is that no successor guardian by relation, e.g., brother, paternal uncle, etc., possesses the power to compel marriage.[13] The deceased father, however, can choose to convey this power to his daughter's designated guardian (*waṣī*) by testament. In the absence of an express grant of this authority, however, the father's testamentary successor in guardianship does not enjoy the power to compel marriage.[14] It would seem that [7] where the father dies or disappears, and he fails to appoint a guardian for his minor daughter or fails to convey to that guardian the power to compel her marriage, the orphaned daughter could not marry prior to reaching the age of majority and then only with her consent.[15] In fact, however, the power to compel her marriage upon the father's demise, according to the Mālikīs, devolves to the state. Thus, a judge can permit her guardian by relation to contract her marriage if the orphan daughter has reached marriageable age, and there is evidence that failure to marry will lead to either her moral corruption or economic ruin.[16] Putting these rules together, what emerges is a private power in the father to compel his minor daughter's marriage that does not pass by inheritance, although it can be conveyed by designation (*waṣiyya*). In the absence of the father, and his designated successor (*waṣī*), the private power to compel marriage disappears. In its place the public assumes this power through its agent, the state, which usually delegates this power to the judge. Finally, in the absence of the state, this power devolves to the community of Muslims.[17] [8] It would be easy for a casual observer to assume that the power to compel

---

from the Arabic language authorities upon which the author of this article relied are treated within the body of the text. Transliterated quotations of those principles, accompanied by English translations, are set out in the footnotes of the article, as demonstrated here.]

13. Id. p. 356 ("*thumma baʿda al-ab wa waṣiyyihi fī al-bikr wa al-ṣaghīra wa al-majnūna lā jabra li-aḥad min al-awliyāʾ ʿala unthā ṣaghīra aw kabīra*" = "Other than the father, and the guardian by testamentary designation, with respect to a virgin, an orphan, or mentally disabled female, no guardian has the power to compel the marriage of a female, be she an adult or a minor").

14. 14 Id. p. 355 ("*fa-waṣiyyuhu ... in ʿayyana lahu ... al-zawja ... aw amarahu .. bihi [al-jabr] aw bi-l-nikāḥ.*" = "Then the guardian by testamentary ... if the father designated for him the husband, ... or [the father] commanded him to compel [her marriage] ... or marriage.").

15. Id. pp. 356–57 ("*wa idhā lam yakun li-aḥad minhum jabr fa-innamā tuzawwaj bāligh ... bi-idhnihā wa riḍāhā sawāʾ kānat al-bāligh bikran aw thayyiban.*" = "Since none of them can compel [the marriage], she may only be married as an adult ... with her permission and consent, whether she has or has not been previously married").

16. Id. p. 357 ("*illā ... yatīma ... khīfa ʿalayhā immā li-fasādihā fī al-dīn wa immā li-ḍayāʿihā fī al-dunyā li faqrihā wa qillat al-infāq ʿalayhā aw li-khawf ḍayāʿ māliha*" = "unless ... she is an orphan whose moral corruption is feared ... or that she will suffer economic ruin due to her poverty and lack of resources or fear that her property will be dissipated").

17. Aḥmad b. Muḥammad al-Ṣāwī, 2 *Bulghat al-sālik ilā aqrab al-masālik* 358 ("*fa in-lam yūjad qāḍin yushāwar li-ʿadamihi aw li-kawnihi ẓāliman kafā jamāʿat al-muslimīn.*" = "If there is no judge to be consulted, due either to his actual absence or because he is unjust, the community of Muslims is sufficient").

Interestingly, the Egyptian Mālikīs of the late Ottoman period, from which both al-Dardīr and al-Ṣāwī hailed, rejected this rule, and stated that the male guardian by relation could compel the marriage of

the marriage of a minor girl is simply a function of a patriarchal system of family relations characterized by the subordination of females to males. Such a conclusion, however, would be hasty since Mālikī doctrine explicitly provided that a father enjoyed the same power over his minor sons. In the father's absence, this power could be exercised either by the minor's designated guardian (*waṣī*), or the state through the judge.[18] In an important respect, however, the law was less protective of a male's autonomy than a female's—whereas the designated guardian (*waṣī*) could only compel a female's marriage if the father had expressly conveyed that [9] power to him, *supra*, the designated guardian's power to compel an orphan boy's marriage was part of his default powers.[19]

---

his orphan ward without the permission of the public authorities, so long as the guardian had evidence that failure to marry would harm her either morally or materially. Thus, al-Dardīr states that if her guardian compels her to marry, failure to consult the judge will not render the marriage invalid so long as the other legal requirements have been met. However, he does state that it is "better" to consult the judge to insure the validity of the marriage ("*naʿam tustaḥsan al-mushāwara li-thubūt al-wājibāt wa rafʿ al-munāzaʿāt*" = "yes, consultation (of the judge) is preferable in order to ascertain [the fulfillment] of legal obligations, and resolving disputes"). Al-Dardīr, 358. Al-Ṣāwī goes further in granting the successor guardian the same powers of the father by removing the requirement that she at least reach marriageable age, concluding that the guardian can compel the marriage of his minor female ward whenever he fears for her moral or material welfare ("*qawluhu* [al-Dardīr]) "*aw lam tablugh ʿashran*" *ẓāhiruhu annahā idhā lam tablugh ʿashran wa zuwwijat maʿ khawf al-fasād yufsakh qabl al-dukhūl wa al-ṭūl wa laysa ka-dhālika bal huwa ṣaḥīḥ ibtidāʾan ... illā idhā zuwwijat min ghayri khawfi fasād*." = "As for his [al-Dardir] saying 'or she has not reached ten,' it would appear that if she has not reached ten, and she was married off due to fear of ruin, it would be invalidated, unless she dwelt for a lengthy period with him [i.e., with her husband], but that is not the case; rather the marriage is valid at the time of contracting unless she was married [for a reason] other than fear of ruin"). Al-Ṣāwī, 358. The probable explanation for their rejection of the Mālikī school's basic distinction between the powers of a guardian who is a father, and all other private guardians is the relative decline in prestige of the Egyptian state in the late 18th and early 19th centuries.

18. 2 Al-Dardīr 396 ("*wa jabara ab wa waṣī wa ḥākim lā ghayruhum dhakaran ... ṣaghīran li-maṣlaḥa*"= 'A father, a guardian by testamentary designation, and a judge—no one else—can compel the marriage of a male orphan for his benefit.').

19. 2 Al-Ṣāwī 396 ("*li-l waṣī jabr al-dhakar li-l-maṣlaḥa wa law lam yakun lahu jabr al-unthā kamā idhā qāla [al-ab] lahu: anta waṣiyyī ʿalā waladī*" = "The guardian by testamentary designation can compel the marriage of a male for his benefit, even though he [the guardian by testamentary designation] does not have (the power) to compel [the marriage] of a female, as is the case, for example, when the father tells him, 'You are my designated successor over my children'"). It should be noted, however, that the jurists' tone in discussing the exercise of this power is substantially different in the case of a male than a female: A guardian compels the marriage of his male ward to gain an advantage for his ward, whereas the guardian compels the marriage of his female ward out of fear for her moral or material well-being. 3 Al-Ḥaṭṭāb, *Mawāhib al-jalīl* 458 ("*lā khilāf fī jawāz inkāḥ ibnihi al-ṣaghīr ... idhā kāna fīh al-ghibṭa wa al-raghba ka-nikāḥihi min al marʾa al-mūsara*" = "There is no dispute regarding the permissibility of compelling the marriage of a minor boy... so long as it [the marriage] is desirable and advantageous, as is the case, for example, in his marriage to a wealthy woman").

The most important difference between male and female children with respect to freedom to marry was a consequence of the rules of emancipation. Whereas a male child was automatically emancipated from his father's jurisdiction upon reaching biological and social maturity, a female was not emancipated from her father's jurisdiction until two additional requirements were satisfied—entry into her marital home and the testimony of reliable witnesses that she could successfully manage her property.[20] Alternatively, a female could be emancipated if her father or her guardian as designated by her father, declared her to be mature in front of a court.[21] In both cases, a female could only become emancipated after the intervention of legal process.

[10] This different treatment of males and females by the law of emancipation was justified—at least in the sight of later Mālikīs—by a factual stereotype of women as profligate.[22] In effect, then, the law of emancipation presumed—subject to rebuttal in court—that a biologically mature woman was unable to manage her financial affairs independently. Thus, although a physically and socially mature male could not be subject to the guardianship of a third person unless his inability to manage his own affairs was proven in court, women had to demonstrate their social maturity prior to enjoying their legal rights as autonomous individuals. Analytically, then, a female's legal incapacity can be divided into two stages: First, she is legally incapacitated because of youth; second, upon reaching physical maturity, she is treated as legally incapacitated because of presumed inability to manage her property (*safah*).[23] While identifying the precise ground upon which the female's incapacity rested seems irrelevant, it is in fact critical in determining the limits of the guardian's power over his ward. While, as we have seen above, the father and his designated guardian enjoyed the power to compel the marriage of minors, that power does not seem to be afforded to the guardian of a ward who suffers from legal incapacity arising from an inability to manage property reasonably (*safah*). While I have not found an explicit rule stating that the guardian of a profligate male lacks the power to compel his marriage, that is impliedly the rule provided by al-Dardīr, who states that the

---

20. 3 Al-Dardīr 382–383 ("*wa al-ṣabī maḥjūr ʿalayhi ... li-bulūghihi rashīdan wa zīda ... fī al-unthā dukhūl zawj bihā ... wa shahādat al-ʿudūl bi-ḥifẓihā mālaha.*" = "A minor male is legally incapacitated until he attains puberty, in a sound state of mind ... It is also required in the case of a woman that she enter her marital home ... and the testimony of upright witnesses that she can manage her property").

21. 5 Al-Ḥaṭṭāb 69 ("*wa li-l ab tarshīduhā qabla dukhūlihā... ka-l'waṣī.*" = "The father, like the guardian by designation, may emancipate her prior to her taking up residence in her marital home.").

22. Al-Dardīr 383 ("*wa innamā iḥtīja li-l-ishhād li-anna shaʾna al-nisāʾ al-iṣrāf fa-madār al-rushd ʿindanā ʿalā ṣawn al-māl faqaṭ.*" = 'The reason testimony [prior to her emancipation] is needed is because women are generally profligate, and for us, [social] maturity is solely a question of the [ability] to preserve property').

23. Id. Al-Dardīr 381 (the five grounds for the legal incapacity are bankruptcy, insanity, youth, profligacy (*tabdhīr*), and slavery).

only free males whose marriages can be compelled are those of the insane and minors.[24] Instead, the male profligate [*al-safīh*] enjoys a right to marriage that is contingent on the approval of his guardian. Thus, a guardian, upon [11] learning that his profligate ward has married, is given the option of annulling the marriage or leaving it be.[25] Indeed, if the profligate was found to have reformed in the time between he contracted his marriage and the moment his guardian discovered it, the guardian is deprived of all authority over the marriage.[26] This is in sharp contrast to the marriage of a female subject to a guardian's power to compel her marriage—the marriage contract is considered invalid from its origin, and therefore, whenever this defect is discovered, it is subject to mandatory annulment under all the circumstances.[27]

Thus, the argument presented here is that there is a fundamental mistake of law in the Mālikī treatment of a guardian's powers over a female ward who has attained physical maturity: Since the proffered reason for her continued legal incapacity is an inability to manage her affairs independently, she is a profligate *(safīha)*, and therefore should no longer be subject to the guardian's power to compel her marriage. Thus, even within the strict parameters of the Mālikī school, a physically mature woman's marriage cannot be compelled. The fact that Mālikīs allowed such a woman to be married against her will, insofar as they considered her to lack complete legal capacity, can only be described as a major error in legal reasoning.[28]

[12] III. THE *WALĪ* AS AGENT OF THE WOMAN/COMMUNITY

In the absence of a guardian possessing the power to compel the marriage of his ward, a female can only be married with her consent.[29] Despite an adult woman's apparent freedom to reject marriage, Mālikī law nevertheless conditioned the validity of her marriage upon the approval of her guardian. In trying to understand the

24. Id. pp. 395–96 (mentioning that only the father, his designated successor. and the judge may compel the marriage of the insane and minor males).

25. Id. p. 394 ("*wa li-walī safīh tazawwaja bi-ghayri idhn waliyyihi radd nikāḥihi ... in lam yarshud.*" = 'the guardian of a profligate male, who has married without the permission of his guardian, may void the marriage ... so long as [the profligate male] does not attain [social] maturity.').

26. Id. ("*fa-in rashada fa-lā kalāma li-waliyyihi.*" = 'But, if he attains social maturity, then the guardian has no standing [to void the marriage]').

27. Id. pp. 363–64 ("*wa ṣaḥḥa al nikāḥ bi-abʿad ... maʿ wujūd aqrab lā yujbir ... wa illā bi-an kāna al-walī mujbiran ... fa-lā yaṣiḥḥ ... wa fusikha abadan.*"= "A marriage is valid when contracted by a distant [guardian] ... although a more closely related guardian was present, so long as he did not have the power to compel [marriage]. Otherwise, when the close guardian has the power to compel, the marriage is invalid and it is null [no matter how long the couple lives together]."

28. In some sense, it is charitable to describe this as a "mistake" and not attribute it to some other, less benign, explanations.

29. Id. p. 356.

possible functions of such a rule, as a preliminary matter two questions need to be answered. The first is who exercises jurisdiction over her power to marry; the second is what is the function of this guardian under a regime that avowedly denies the guardian any rights to compel his female ward to accept any proposed marriage?

Interestingly, the Mālikīs did not assign the father priority in this respect; rather, the woman's son was the law's first choice to be her guardian in such a case. Her grandson was its second choice, and her father was its third choice.[30] Of course, in many cases, perhaps even most, the father would be the first choice to serve as her guardian because she would have no children of her own. Nonetheless, the priority given to the son is significant insofar as it signifies that the role of guardian in the marriage contract cannot be explained simply as a means for the patriarchal family to control its female members.

More importantly, the role of the guardian in validating the marriage of an adult woman is greatly diluted when compared to his role in the marriage of a minor. Thus, although the law may specify a specific male relative as her guardian, she is in fact free to have any of her male relatives serve as her guardian in the marriage, even though the proper guardian is present and opposes the marriage, in which case the marriage would be valid *so long as she consented.*[31] Indeed, the [13] woman need not use a male relative as her guardian—she is free to ask the judge to serve as her guardian even though her male relatives are present and object to the marriage.[32] The fact that an adult woman has the right to use any male relative as her guardian, or even the judge when she is unable to find a cooperative male relative, implies that she is entitled to marry the groom of her choice, and indeed, it is the rule of the Mālikī school that the guardian of an adult woman

---

30. Id. p. 359–360.

31. Id. ("*wa-ṣaḥḥa al-nikāḥ bi-abʿada min al-awliyāʾ ka-ʿamm wa ibnihi maʿ wujūd aqraba lā yujbir ka-ab wa ibn fī sharīfa wa ghayrihā fa-lā yufsakh bi-ḥāl*" = "The marriage is valid with a distant guardian, e.g., a paternal uncle and his son, even though a closer, non-compelling guardian, e.g., a father and son, is present; so [such a marriage] is not to be annulled under any circumstances."), pp. 363–64; see also, 3 Al-Mawwāq 432 (providing citations to ancient Mālikī sources who recognize the validity of such a marriage contract so long as the woman consents).

32. 2 Al-Ṣāwī 363 ("*wa law kāna al-abʿad al-ḥākim maʿ wujūd akhaṣṣ al-awliyāʾ fa-idhā lam tarḍa al-marʾa bi-ḥuḍūr aḥad min aqāribihā wa zawwajahā al-ḥākim kāna al-nikāḥ ṣaḥīḥan*"= "If the more distant [guardian] is the ruler, and the closest [natural] guardian is also present, but the woman does not consent to the presence of anyone of her relatives, and the ruler marries her off, the marriage is valid"); 3 Al-Ḥaṭṭāb 432 ("*al-nikāḥ yaṣiḥḥ idhā ʿaqadahu al-abʿad maʿ wujūd al-aqrab idhā lam yakun mujbiran wa law kāna al-abʿad huwa al-ḥākim*" = "The marriage is valid when the more distant guardian contracts it despite the nearer guardian's presence, so long as the near cannot compel marriage, even if the more distant guardian [approving the marriage] is the ruler"). According to al-Ṣāwī the requirement of a guardian, at least in the order of priority recognized in the Mālikī school, is either supererogatory *(nadb)*, or obligatory (*wājib*), but not a condition for the validity of the marriage. 2 Al-Ṣāwī 363.

is duty bound to marry her to any free, male Muslim whom she wishes to marry.[33] The fact that an adult woman need not obtain the permission of her actual guardian to marry makes her right to sue her guardian to compel performance of his legal duties almost superfluous.[34] In conclusion, then, an adult woman's right to marry [14] whom she wishes, even if her wish contradicts that of her legal guardian, was protected by two rules: the first allowed her to use any of her male relatives or the judge as her guardian, and the second allowed her to sue her own guardian for what amounts to a remedy of specific performance of his duties as guardian.

The fact that legal doctrine creates two mechanisms whereby an adult woman can circumvent the opposition of her guardian to her marriage suggests that the requirement of a guardian does not function to subject the woman to the guardian's physical control.[35] If the guardian has no legal power to block her marriage, then, what function does the guardian play in the marriage of an adult woman? Al-Mawwāq quotes the Andalusian jurist, Ibn Lubb, as saying "The requirement of a guardian is only to assure that the [requirement of] *kafāʾa* is met, [which is accomplished] by means of the guardian's judgment."[36] *Kafāʾa* is a term of art in Islamic law that refers to the social and religious

---

33. 2 Al-Dardīr 375 ("*wa ʿalā al-walī wujūban al-ijāba li-kufʾ raḍiyat bihi al-zawja al-ghayr al-mujbara*"= "When the woman cannot be compelled to marry, the guardian is legally obliged to consent to a groom whom she desires, so long as the groom is her peer."); 3 Al-Mawwāq 439 ("*wa kufʾuhā awlā fīhā [al-mudawwana] idhā raḍiyat thayyib bi-kufʾ fī dīnihi wa huwa dūnaha fī al-nasab wa raddahu ab aw walī zawwajahā minhu al-imām*" = "It is better for her [to marry] the peer of her [choice]; in it [the *Mudawwana*] 'when a previously married woman desires [to marry a man] who is her equal in religion, but beneath her in ancestry, so the father or [another] guardian rejects him [on that account] the Imam can contract the marriage between the man and the woman.")

34. The rule of the Mālikī school is that when a guardian of an adult woman refuses to marry her to a husband whom she wishes to marry, she has the right to initiate a complaint in court, and upon a judicial finding that the husband is a free, male Muslim (*kufʾ*), the guardian is declared to be *ʿāḍil*, an active participle derived from a verb whose meaning is to cause another person trouble, and the judge orders the guardian to marry her to the husband of her choice. If he persists in his refusal, the judge will then act as her guardian unless the guardian shows good cause for his refusal to accede to her desire to marry. 2 Al-Dardīr 376 ("*wa illā yuzawwijhā min kufʾihā bi-an imtanaʿa min kufʾ raḍiyat al-zawja bihi kāna ʿāḍilan bi-mujarrad al-imtināʿ fa-yaʾmuruhu al-ḥākim in rafaʿat lahu bi-tazwījihā thumma in imtanaʿa zawwaja al-ḥākim*" = "If he does not [let her marry whom she wishes] by rejecting a suitor whom she desires, he becomes *ʿāḍil* simply by the act of refusal, in which case, the judge orders him, if she files a claim, to consent to marriage. If he continues to refuse, the judge can contract the marriage.")

35. Of course, one cannot speculate about the efficacy of these remedies. It is conceivable that social attitudes, political considerations, etc., would conspire to deprive an adult woman of any real remedy to her guardian's refusal to allow her to marry the husband of her choice. What is important to note in this context, however, is simply that legal doctrine provides two strong remedies for an adult woman who finds herself in this undesirable situation.

36. 3 al-Mawwāq, *al-Tāj wa-l-iklīl*, 432 (n.d.) ("*ṭalab al-walī innamā huwa li-taḥṣula al-kafāʾa bi-naẓar al-walī*" = "The requirement of a guardian is stipulated only to guarantee *kafāʾa* through the vehicle of the guardian.").

status of the bride and groom. In the Mālikī school, however, it is limited to simply religion and physical condition. Thus, it is defined as piety, i.e., in the sense of possessing religious consciousness (*tadayyun*), and an absence of physical [15] defects that by law give the other party an option to annul the marriage (*al-salāma min al-ʿuyūb al-mūjiba li-l-radd*).[37]

Moreover, *kafāʾa* is only optional; both the wife and the guardian are free to accept a groom that is not the social "peer" of the wife.[38] If the legal function of the guardian is to insure the existence of an attribute, *kafāʾa,* that is not very stringent, and at any rate, is subject to waiver, it is not surprising that Mālikī doctrine should make it relatively easy for an adult woman to circumvent her guardian's refusal to agree to her marriage. Does this mean that the requirement of a guardian in the marriage of an adult woman is nearly an empty form? Not necessarily, although the real answer may have more to do with the dynamics of contracting than with the legal role played by the guardian.

The principal role of the guardian, where the woman is an adult, is not to determine whom she will marry but rather the terms on which she will marry. In other words, although the law describes this person as a guardian, *walī*, in fact his role is more akin to an agent, *wakīl*. Normally, however, a principal is always free to contract for himself without the intermediation of an agent. What needs explanation, then, is why medieval Islamic law would require female principals to conduct marriage contracts exclusively through an agent.

I think the answer to this question lies in the nature of the marriage contract as occupying an intermediate position between a purely private relationship, and a publicly regulated relationship. The ambiguous role of the guardian reflects this tension. On the one hand, the fact that an adult woman needs the permission of a guardian to marry restricts her power to marry.[39]

On the other hand, a woman [16] will normally have a series of guardians to whom she can turn in the event that her closest guardian refuses to allow her to marry. Finally, the state exists as a guardian of last resort for a woman who is unable to find a male relative willing to permit her marriage. The fact that a woman is not subject to an absolute "veto" necessarily lessens the ability of a guardian to exercise his authority arbitrarily.

If the guardian is conscientious, and performs according to the requirements of law, i.e., he approves any marriage that his principal agrees to so long as the minimal require-

37. 2 al-Dardīr 399–400.

38. Id. ("*wa lahā ... wa li-l-walī tarkuhā ay: al-kafāʾa wa al-riḍā bi-ʿadamihā wa al-tazwīj bi-fāsiq aw ma'yūb* [sic] *aw ʿabd*" = "Both the wife and the guardian can waive it, i.e., *kafāʾa* and they may consent, despite its absence, to marriage to a dissolute groom, a physically disabled groom, or a slave").

39. Incidentally, this also necessarily restricts the right of men to marry as well. Were the government to play the role of guardian in the marriages of all adults, the guardian's role as protector of public interests would be seen more clearly, and the requirement of the guardian would be less closely linked with the interests of the woman's male relatives. See the discussion of this point in greater detail, *infra*.

ments of *kafāʾa* have been met, does it make any sense to require the woman to contract her marriage through the agency of her guardian rather than directly? Such a requirement could make sense if one assumes that the guardian will strike a better "bargain" for his principal than the principal could strike for herself. Such a justification need not be based on a paternalistic assumption regarding female negotiating abilities.[40] Rather, it might be a recognition that parties to a marriage, because of the nature of the relationship, are poorly situated to reach the bargain that both parties would presumably want to reach. In other words, if the prospective bride were to bargain directly with the prospective groom over the terms of the contract, the transaction costs[41] would be sufficiently high so that either agreement would not be reached, or one or both parties will agree to "unreasonable" terms [17] because of a fear that "tough bargaining" would risk the agreement entirely.

The requirement of a guardian may be a function of the need to lessen the transaction costs that prevent the prospective betrotheds from reaching the optimal set of contractual terms. When the guardian is the state, moreover, there is the added benefit that the parties' agreement will reflect society's interests in the success of the relationship, something that may be ignored if the marriage contract is treated purely as a private relationship between the man and the woman. On the other hand, one would expect—given the obviously large number of marriages that would be contracted under this bargaining arrangement—that a set of "optimal" default contract terms reflecting a majoritarian understanding of the "optimal" terms would be reached rather quickly.[42] In this case the guardian's role would be little more than ministerial. Nonetheless, preservation of the requirement of a guardian may be justified when we realize majoritarian contract terms are "optimal" only on the average; particular couples may always desire to deviate from the majoritarian model. I believe it is particularly in these circumstances, viz., when contracting parties wish to depart from majoritarian default rules, that the guardian's role as an independent bargainer may be the most useful. Because the transaction costs

40. For example, women were not required to act in the marketplace through an agent.

41. By transaction costs I refer to the costs required to reach an agreement. In certain situations, even though an agreement would benefit both parties, transaction costs may prevent the parties from reaching agreement. In the context of the marriage contract, for example, a consequence of direct bargaining over the terms might be a reduction in the feelings of affection between the prospective betrotheds. If the "costs" associated with bargaining over the terms exceed the benefit of the marriage itself, the parties will not marry. Therefore, reduction of transaction costs is a salutary goal of law because it enables more beneficial exchanges to occur. Although the term transaction costs is an economic term, it corresponds roughly to the concept of "*rafʿ al-ḥaraj*," i.e., removal of difficulty, in Islamic law. The importance of this concept in Islamic law is too great to do it justice other than in an independent article.

42. Indeed, this seems to be what in fact occurred historically, as one can find the terms of "model" marriage contracts that were developed by notaries (*al-muwaththiqīn*) in "form" books from the Middle Ages. I have translated such a model marriage contract for the appendix of this essay.

present in any attempt by one or both of the parties to alter majoritarian default rules are obviously high, the guardian, in consultation with the parties, may be in a better position to individualize the terms of the contract than the parties themselves.

Arguably, then, the mandatory use of a guardian, although in some sense paternalistic, nonetheless can be justified on efficiency grounds because the presence of a third-party guardian allows idiosyncratic parties to reach individualized agreements that would *not* otherwise have been reached in the guardian's absence. Even were we to assume that parties with idiosyncratic preferences would [18] eventually marry anyway, their inability to individualize the terms of their agreement would probably lessen to some degree the likelihood of the success of their relationship. Therefore, to the extent that we believe that individualized contract terms reflecting parties' *ex ante* expectations are positively linked with the success of their marriage, requiring a guardian as a facilitator of individualized contractual terms is a rule promoting efficient outcomes, i.e., successful marriages. The previous analysis of the role of the guardian in the formation of the marriage contract leads to the following inescapable conclusion—whatever the "correct" rule may be regarding the identity of the guardian or his powers, the requirement of a guardian is not intended to protect a private right of the guardian. In other words, it is a mistake to consider the requirement of a guardian as a vestige of a system characterized by families having property interests in their women. This raises an important question: if the guardian is not acting to protect his own interests, whose interests is he representing? I believe the only answer can be that the guardian promotes the interests of the Muslim community by ensuring that the contract is an equitable arrangement between the husband and the wife. This is at once both a more attractive and more accurate interpretation than one that claims that his role is to protect the woman's interests in the marriage. After all, the requirement of a guardian also burdens a man's right to marry. The fact that the guardian is usually from the wife's family, however, gives the impression that his role is exclusively to "protect" the woman's interest. As mentioned above, however, if we assume that the woman is an adult, she is always free to have the state function as her guardian rather than one of her male kin.

Indeed, if it were the case that the state, rather than the wife's family, routinely served as the guardian for the contract, the nexus between the requirement of a guardian and gender would be cut out by its roots. This is precisely the solution which I advocate—the requirement of a guardian should be understood to mean that a marriage under Islamic law requires the recognition of some public authority. To the extent that Islamic law authorized private persons, viz., the family of the woman, to exercise this power, they did so only [19] pursuant to a grant of power from the public authority; they were not exercising a vested private right outside the legitimate review of the community's political authorities. Thus, it is always the right of a Muslim government to refuse to delegate this authority to the family of the woman and instead exercise it itself.

That the role of the guardian in marriage should be interpreted as though the guardian was exercising a delegated power from the state is implicit in the jurisdictional structure of Islamic law. As far as I know, it is a fundamental premise of Islamic constitutional law that all jurisdictional authority of limited authority (*wilāya khāṣṣa*) is exercised pursuant to a delegation (*tafwīḍ*) from the Imam, who is the fountainhead of all lesser jurisdictions in the Islamic constitutional order.[43] Therefore, under Islamic constitutional law, the state is both the guardian of those who lack a natural guardian, and those with natural guardians. Although jurists routinely justify [20] the state's intervention in otherwise private relationships on the grounds that the state is the guardian of those who do not have a natural guardian, they did not accept the negative pregnant (*mafhūm al-khilāf*) of this statement. Thus, a Mālikī authority noted that "its negative pregnant, viz., the state [i.e., the judge is not a guardian for whomsoever has a guardian], is not correct. Rather, the judge [i.e., the state] is the guardian of every person."[44]

Likewise, although medieval jurists assumed that the guardian would usually be a male member of the woman's family, it is not clear whether they thought this was a vested right or simply a custom-based default rule. What is true is that jurists assumed that the normal legal requirements of integrity (*ʿadāla*) were required of "natural" guardians, just as it was a requirement for other holders of public office. Thus, Ibn Qayyim al-Jawziyya reported that some jurists wanted to strip "natural" guardians of their authority over marriage contracts on the grounds that they lacked the integrity necessary for that office in favor, presumably, of the guardianship of an official of the state. While Ibn al-Qayyim disagreed with this position, his argument is revealing—while he admitted "natural" guardians might lack the integrity required under the strict standards of the law, it was not clear to him that (1) public officials were necessarily any more upright; and, (2) he believed that "natural" guardians were generally superior to public guardians because of the feelings of kinship. When it comes to a choice between public and private guardians, Ibn al-Qayyim prefers the private guardian not because of a vested, God-given right the private guardian is presumed to enjoy, but rather because of the perception that the "natural" guardian is better situated to perform the role intended by the law for the guardian. In other words, the private guardian, according to Ibn [21] al-Qayyim, bears a strong family resemblance to that well-known figure of American tort law—the Best Problem Solver.[45]

---

43. Al-Māwardī, *al-Aḥkām al-sulṭāniyya*. (n.d.)

44. 3 Al-Ḥaṭṭāb 432 ("*qawluhu walī man lā waliyya lahu mafhūmuhu man lahā walī fa-laysa bi-walī lahā wa laysa ka-dhālika bal al-qāḍī walī kulli wāḥid*" = "The statement, 'Guardian for those who have no [natural] guardian,' its negative pregnant is 'The judge is not the guardian of any woman having a natural guardian,' but that is not the case; indeed, the judge is the guardian of every person.").

45. Ibn Qayyim al-Jawziyya, *al-Ṭuruq al-ḥukmiyya* 256 (1978).

IV. CONCLUSION

All this might be interesting, but the reader must surely be wondering whether any of the preceding discussion has any relevance to the conduct of marriages pursuant to Islamic law in the United States. I assure you that it does, and in the remaining few pages, I will try to make that relationship clear. It goes without saying that the power of a guardian to compel the marriage of his minor children, whether male or female, although it was understood to be a natural outgrowth of the father's duty to take care of his children, has no place in the practice of the modern Muslim community in North America. Just as the guardian's power to contract marriages for his minor children was limited by situations that were deemed by the law to be harmful for the child, surely the vast majority of Muslims living in North America would recognize the marriage of children to be categorically harmful to their interests and therefore unlawful under Islamic law. More importantly, and more controversially, I propose that Muslim communities play the role of guardian in the marriages of American Muslims rather than the "natural" family of the woman. [22] There are several reasons for this suggestion. As a matter of legal doctrine, the Muslim community, when it is not living under the authority of a Muslim state, enjoys the legal prerogatives of the Muslim state.[46]

Thus, Muslim communities in North America have the legal right to recognize only those marriage contracts that meet their standards. Obviously, they also have the right to delegate this authority to the "natural" guardians of the wife, or to any other Muslim, male or female. In my opinion, however, there are advantages to keeping this authority in the hands of the community. Unless marriage contracts are made with the active participation of the community, the community will be deprived of the critical information necessary to determine what are the equitable "default" terms of a marriage contract between Muslim men and women in North America. Moreover, when both parties know that the community intervenes as a matter of course in the matter of the marriage contract, it is more likely the parties will be more willing to share their concerns about their future relationship since the moral authority of the community can be used to help fashion the final agreement between the parties.

Furthermore, the regular use of the community as the marriage guardian will help to ensure that each party's legal rights are being respected, and that the interests of the Muslim community in the success of the marriage are adequately protected. If the role of guardian is fulfilled by the Muslim community rather than a male relative of the wife, the perception that the legal capacity of a woman is less than a man's will be removed, and needless to say, fighting this perception is extremely important. Indeed, while I have

---

46. Al-Mawwāq quotes al-Qābisī as saying that "the action of the community [of Muslims], in the absence of an Imam [viz., an organized political state], is like the ruling of the Imam." 4 *al-Tāj wa-al-iklīl* 156.

only anecdotal evidence supporting this proposition, it seems that many Muslim women, especially the more highly educated of them, are reluctant to marry out of a perception that the "rules" are stacked against them. Of course, if my suggestion were enforced, but the "community" was not represented in a democratic fashion such that the views of Muslim men and women [23] were not taken into account in fashioning the community's view on what constitutes an equitable marriage contract, this reform could conceivably make things worse for those women whose "natural" guardians would have routinely carried out their preferences. Finally, by reasserting that marriage is not simply a private relationship between the husband, wife, and to a lesser extent their families, but also one that affects the interests of the community as a whole, the community will be in a better position to help work with couples after marriage to help resolve differences between spouses amicably, and failing that, to minimize the damage that can occur as a result of a failed marriage.

[24] (Model Marriage Contract)
A Father's Marriage of His Virgin Daughter Who Is Under His Authority
by Muḥammad b. Aḥmad al-Umawī, d. 399/1009

This is what So-and-so, son of So-and-so, gave to his wife, So-and-so, the daughter of So-and-so, as a dowry. He gave her such-and-such gold coins of the prevailing currency in Cordoba at the time of this writing, [some in] cash and [some as] a debt. The cash portion of the dowry was such-and-such gold coins. So-and-so, her father, took possession of them from her husband, as she is a virgin under his authority and subject to his direction. He took possession [of the cash dowry] so that he could prepare her trousseau and other accoutrements for marriage. He [the father] declared that he [the groom] satisfied [the cash obligation of payment of the dowry]; therefore, he [the groom] is free of that obligation.

The debt portion of the dowry is such-and-such gold pieces of the same quality, the husband's payment of which is deferred, due in payments upon such-and-such years, the first of which is such-and-such month in such-and-such year.

So-and-so, son of So-and-so, has undertaken the following obligations to his wife, willingly and freely, in order to win her affection and to seek her utmost happiness:

Never to take another wife while married to her nor to take a concubine nor an *umm walad.*[47] If he does any of these things, she becomes master of her own affair [i.e., she can

47. *Umm walad* is a term that literally means the mother of a child. It refers to a slave woman that has borne her master a child. An *umm walad* enjoys certain privileges that other slaves do not. It is not clear to me what the difference is between a promise not to take a concubine, viz., *la yatasarrā maʿahā*, and a promise not to take an *umm walad*, since it would seem that the former would necessarily encompass the latter.

divorce him], the [25] second wife is divorced, the *umm walad* is emancipated for the sake of God the Great, and control of the concubine is in her hands: if she wishes, she can sell her; if she wishes, she can [permit him] to retain her; and, if she wishes, she can emancipate her from his ownership.

[He also has promised:] Never to desert her, whether [the journey is] near or far, for more than six months unless he is undertaking the duty of Pilgrimage, in which case he may be apart from her for up to three years, on condition that he announces this intention when he departs on his journey, setting out toward [*Makka*], leaving her sufficient funds for her maintenance, clothing, and housing. If his absence should exceed both limits, or either of them, she is free to do as she wishes; and, she is to be believed, upon [her claim of] the passing of either of the two time limits, after she swears in her home, in the presence of two reliable witnesses, who warn her of God [i.e., the consequences of a false oath], that he [i.e., her husband] has been absent for longer than the stipulated period. Then, she is free to do as she wishes [i.e., she can divorce herself], or she may wait for his return, but her waiting shall not nullify her stipulation [i.e., her right to divorce herself].

[He also promised]: Never to take her from her home that is in such-and-such city without her permission and her consent; and if he removes her against her will, she is free to do as she wishes. If she departs with him willingly, and then she requests to return, but he does not return her within thirty days of her request, she is free to do as she wishes, and he is obliged to compensate her for the expense of the journey, both going and returning. [He also promised]: Never to prevent her from visiting all her female relatives and her closest male relatives whom she is forbidden to marry [*maḥārim*], nor to prevent them from visiting her in the manner that is customary among family and relatives. If he does this, she is free to do as she wishes.

He is obliged to be a good companion for her and use his best efforts to live with her harmoniously, as God, may He be sanctified and glorified, has commanded him; and he has the right to the same good companionship and best efforts from her, just as God has said, "And husbands have over them [i.e., their wives] a degree."

[26] So-and-so, the son of So-and-so, knows that his wife, So-and-so, is not one who serves herself, but that, because of her social position and condition, she is in need of servants; he declares that he is able to provide her servants and that his property is sufficient for that, and he has willingly obliged himself to serve her. He married her according to the word of God, may He be glorified and elevated, and according to the practice of His prophet Muḥammad, may God grant him blessings and peace, so that she will be with him as a trust from God [*amānat Allāh*], may He be sanctified and glorified, and [he married her] knowing that God gave wives rights over their husbands, namely, that they live together with the kindness required by custom, or they separate on generous terms.

Her father, So-and-so, the son of So-and-so, gave her to him in marriage as a never before married girl, under his authority and control, in good health, pursuant to the authority God, may He be glorified and elevated, gave him over her person and over her marriage contract. There witnessed the declarations of the husband So-and-so, the son of So-and-so, and the father [*al-munkiḥ*] So-and-so, son of So-and-so, who were mentioned in this writing, against themselves according to what was mentioned about them in it [the writing] those who heard that from them and knew them, and [that their statements occurred] while they were of sound mind and body and of full legal capacity, on the month of such-and-such of the year such-and-such.

10
POLITICAL LIBERALISM, ISLAMIC FAMILY LAW, AND FAMILY LAW PLURALISM

Mohammad H. Fadel

[164] Western democracies in recent years have witnessed dramatic (and often highly charged) debates regarding Islamic law, women, and the limits of pluralism in a liberal polity. Perhaps the most relevant of these for the issue of family law pluralism was the "Sharīʿa Arbitration controversy" of Ontario, Canada, of 2004–2005. Although Jewish, Christian, and Ismāʿīlī Muslim (a relatively small sect of Shīʿa Muslims who follow the Agha Khan) residents of Ontario had long made use of private arbitration for the resolution of intracommunal family disputes, when a group of Sunni Muslims announced their intent to establish a mechanism to allow orthodox Muslims to arbitrate their family law disputes in accordance with their understanding of Islamic law, a transatlantic controversy erupted that was resolved only when Ontario took the drastic step of prohibiting the arbitration of all family law disputes in which the arbitrator purported to apply non-Canadian law.[1] Great Britain, too, experienced its own moment of Islamic law anxiety when the Archbishop of Canterbury suggested that British commitments to pluralism might require the English legal system to recognize certain aspects of Islamic law.[2] That

This article was originally published as a chapter in the book *Marriage and Divorce in a Multi-Cultural Context*, edited by Joel Nichols (New York: Cambridge University Press, 2011), pp. 164–98.

1. Numerous academic articles in response to the Sharīʿa Arbitration controversy have been published. See, e.g., Jean-Francois Gaudreault-DesBiens, "The Limits of Private Justice? The Problems of the State Recognition of Arbitral Awards in Family and Personal Status Disputes in Ontario," *Perspectives* 16:1 (Jan. 2005): 18–31; Natasha Bakht, "Family Arbitration Using Sharia Law: Examining Ontario's Arbitration Act and Its Impact on Women," *Muslim World Journal of Human Rights* 1:1 (2004); Ayelet Shachar, "Privatizing Diversity: A Cautionary Tale from Religious Arbitration in Family Law," *Theoretical Inquiries in Law* 9:2 (July 2008): 573–607; Anver Emon, "Islamic Law and the Canadian Mosaic: Politics, Jurisprudence, and Multicultural Accommodation," *Canadian Bar Review* 87:2 (February 2009): 391–425; and Melissa Williams, "The Politics of Fear and the Decline of Multiculturalism," in *The Ties that Bind*, eds. John Erik Fossum, Johanne Poirier, and Paul Magnette (Brussels: P.I.E. Peter Lang, 2009), 53–77. For a critical overview of the reaction to the controversy related to Islamic arbitration, see Natasha Bakht, "Were Muslim Barbarians Really Knocking on the Gates of Ontario?: The Religious Arbitration Controversy—Another Perspective," *Ottawa Law Review* 40 (2006): 67–82.

2. See, e.g., John F. Burns, "Top Anglicans Rally to Besieged Archbishop," *New York Times*, Feb. 12, 2008

controversy was subsequently heightened when it was revealed that British [165] Muslims had already set up judicial councils that engaged in legally binding arbitration of family law disputes pursuant to British law permitting binding arbitration.[3]

Given the general anxiety surrounding Islamic law in Western democracies, the fact that fear of Islamic law should be a substantial stumbling block to increasing legal pluralism in the domain of family law is ironic given the pluralistic nature of Islamic law's regulation of the family. At the same time, legal recognition of family law pluralism is not without its genuine risks: The rules of Islamic family law, as well as the rules and traditions of other subcommunities within a liberal polity, are not substantively equivalent to the generally applicable rules of civil law. Any system of family law pluralism within a liberal polity, therefore, must establish institutional mechanisms to ensure that legal pluralism does not become a tool to deprive individuals of their rights as citizens.[4]

This chapter will attempt to explain how the Islamic religious and legal commitments of "orthodox"[5] Muslims can reinforce and promote Islamic conceptions of the family within the general legal background provided by a liberal system of family law. Indeed, this chapter will make the perhaps surprising case that for orthodox Muslims, a liberal family law—at least in the context of a religiously heterogeneous polity—represents the preferred means for the recognition of family law pluralism, in contrast to other arguments in support of family law pluralism that would give greater power directly to religious bodies in the administration of family law.[6] Orthodox Muslims have their own profound disagreements on the nature of marriage and its legal and religious consequences, a fact that gives them strong Islamic reasons to support family law pluralism. Orthodox Islam also has a well-established historical commitment to the recog-

(discussing the controversy that erupted in Britain as a result of Archbishop Rowan Williams' comments that recognizing certain elements of Islamic law would be consistent with British law). A copy of the speech is available at http://www.archbishopofcanterbury.org/1575.

3. Abul Taher, "Revealed: UK's First Official Shari'a Courts," *The Sunday Times* , Sept. 15, 2008. For more information on the operation in the United Kingdom of the Muslim Arbitration Tribunal, see http://www.matribunal.com.

4. See Linda C. McClain, "Marriage Pluralism in the United States: On Civil and Religious Jurisdiction and the Demands of Equal Citizenship," in *Marriage and Divorce in a Multi-Cultural Context*, edited by Joel Nichols (New York: Cambridge University Press, 2011), pp. 309–340.

5. Any reference to "orthodox" Muslims in this chapter should not be taken to refer to any specific group of Muslims living in any contemporary society, but rather refers to a theoretical category intended to capture individuals who affirm the truth of the historically accepted theological doctrines of Sunni Islam and grant at least prima facie authority to historically accepted Sunni ethical and legal doctrines.

6. For one argument as to why democratic states should be willing to cede regulatory authority over marriages to religious authorities, see Joel A. Nichols, "Multi-Tiered Marriage: Ideas and Influences from New York and Louisiana to the International Community," *Vanderbilt Journal of Transnational Law* 40 (January 2007): 135–196.

nition of non-Islamic conceptions of marriages, a fact that also contributes to Muslim comfort with family law pluralism. At the same [166] time liberal family law, because of its commitments to autonomy, contemplates the legitimate use of private ordering within the family subject to certain limits. The space liberalism creates for private ordering within the family is sufficient for robust manifestations of Islamic family life that are also consistent with the minimum requirements of liberalism. Accordingly, there is no need, from an Islamic perspective at least, for a system of family law pluralism beyond that already implicit within liberalism itself.

In exploring the interaction of Islamic religious and legal conceptions of the family with liberal family law, this chapter accepts as normative a version of liberal family law derived from Rawls's conception of political liberalism (focusing in particular on Rawls's remarks on the family in "The Idea of Public Reason Revisited") rather than on other versions of family law that might adopt a more comprehensive form of liberalism.[7] This chapter will argue that despite orthodox Muslims' religiously grounded understanding of marriage, a politically liberal family law along the lines espoused by Rawls—because of its neutrality with respect to metaphysical conceptions of the family and its commitment to provide a qualified form of autonomy for the family—is entitled to the support of orthodox Muslims even if it would exclude as impermissible certain norms of the family that orthodox Muslims would deem morally permissible or even just.

The chapter begins with a brief account of the role of the family in political liberalism and the limits political liberalism places on both the public regulation of the family and the family's internal autonomy within those limits (Section I). To determine whether Islamic conceptions of the family can satisfy political liberalism's limitations on the family's autonomy, Section II provides a general description of how orthodox Islam understands the relationship between the legal and moral spheres and the role of individual conscience in that relationship. Section III explains why the difference between objective law and subjective moral obligation generates pluralism in Islam, a fact that in the context of family law generates competing legal doctrines of the family, relatively broad contractual freedom within the marriage contract, and competing religious visions of the family. Not all manifestations of Islamic conceptions of the family will be consistent with the requirements of political liberalism, however, and for that reason it is appropriate that any system of legal pluralism that permits Muslim citizens to use Islamic law to adjudicate their family law disputes be conducted pursuant to institutional [167] arrangements that can confirm that the results of such adjudication are in conformity with

---

7. For the significance of the differences between a comprehensive liberal's approach to matters of family law and gender equality and their relationship to religion, and the approach of a political liberal, see Susan Moller Okin, *Is Multiculturalism Bad for Women?*, eds. Joshua Cohen, Matthew Howard, and Martha C. Nussbaum (Princeton, NJ: Princeton University Press, 1999), 7–26, and Martha C. Nussbaum's reply, "A Plea for Difficulty," in *Is Multiculturalism Bad for Women?* , 105–114.

the minimum requirements of a liberal legal order. Section IV gives examples of some salient historical differences in Muslim understandings of family law and their relationship to Islamic religious conceptions of marriage. Then Section V turns to why, from an Islamic perspective, a politically liberal family law could very well be attractive to orthodox Muslims; it further investigates whether the use of Islamic law to conduct family law arbitration, from the perspective of political liberalism, could be consistent with political liberalism's approach to regulating the family. Section VI discusses cases from New York involving family law arbitration in the context of Orthodox Jewish law to demonstrate that, as a practical matter, courts in a liberal jurisdiction have the institutional capacity to give effect to the autonomy of nonliberal citizens as evidenced by their desire to abide by their own family laws while simultaneously protecting successfully those aspects of family law that are mandatory from the intrusion of nonliberal norms. This suggests, as Section VII concludes, that courts in liberal jurisdictions could do the same in the case of Muslim family law arbitrations, despite the contrary outcome in Ontario.[8]

I. FAMILY LAW PLURALISM AND POLITICAL LIBERALISM

One of the central objections to the legal recognition of Islamic family law arbitrations raised at the time of the Sharīʿa Arbitration controversy in Ontario was that Islamic law would conflict with Canadian commitments to gender equality within the family.[9] The meaning of equality within the family, however, remains deeply contested, even among liberals. And even religions that are commonly viewed as endorsing a patriarchal family structure have their own conceptions of gender equality: Islam, for example, teaches the equal moral worth of men and women, and the New Testament states that men and women are "all one in Christ Jesus."[10]

Equality, therefore, can mean radically different things, especially in connection with its application to particular disputes. Numerous plausible (though incompatible) theories could be advanced regarding the family that are consistent with [168] some theory of liberal equality. For example, one could take the view that gender equality in marriage should be viewed as a matter of distributive justice, in which case equality means that men and women should receive an equal share of the benefits of married

---

8. Compare Daniel Cere, "Canadian Conjugal Mosaic: From Multiculturalism to Multi-Conjugalism?," in *Marriage and Divorce in a Multi-Cultural Context*, edited by Joel Nichols (New York: Cambridge University Press, 2011), pp. 284–308. (suggesting that Canadian family law has, in recent years, taken a decided turn toward comprehensive rather than political liberalism).

9. See, e.g., Anna C. Korteweg, "The Sharia Debate in Ontario," *ISIM Review* 18 (Autumn 2006): 50–51.

10. Qur'an, *Āl ʿImrān*, 3:195 ("And so their Lord answered their prayers, saying 'I suffer not the loss of the deeds of any of you, whether male or female; you are of one another.'") and *Al-Nisāʾ*, 4:124 ("Whosoever does a righteous deed, whether male or female, and is a believer, they shall enter Paradise."); Galatians 3:28 (New International Version).

life. One potential drawback of such a conception, however, is that it would not exclude marriages organized around a gendered division of labor, if such a marriage resulted in fact in an equal (or relatively equal) sharing of the burdens and benefits of marriage.[11] Alternatively, equality within the family could produce a conception of marriage as "an egalitarian liberal community" that "resists individual accounting" of desert.[12] Such a conception would preclude traditional homemakers from receiving any tangible rewards for nonmarket services they perform in the household. Some feminists, however, argue that marriage should be treated in a manner analogous to a partnership, in which case equality would require valuing the individual contributions of each spouse to the family, including the nonmonetary contributions historically provided by wives in the form of child rearing and housework.[13] If "care work" is monetized, however, it might encourage women to continue to specialize in household rather than market production.[14] This would have the (unintentional) effect of reinforcing the gendered division of labor that many feminists have traditionally sought to eliminate.

Political liberalism does not attempt to determine which of these liberal (or nonliberal) conceptions of equality is correct. It instead regulates the family from the perspective of what is required "to reproduce political society over time" in a manner consistent with its ideal of treating all citizens as "free and equal."[15] Because the family is part of political society's basic structure, labor inside the family is "socially necessary labor."[16] On Rawls's account, however, the family is an association[17] and therefore "the principles of justice—including principles of distributive justice—[do not] apply directly to the internal life of the family."[18] They are relevant only in a [169] negative sense, meaning that the basic rights of women as citizens place limits on permissible forms of family

---

11. Empirical evidence in fact suggests that traditional marriages are more likely to produce this result than most two-wage earner couples. Amy L. Wax, "Bargaining in the Shadow of the Market: Is There a Future for Egalitarian Marriage?" *Virginia Law Review* 84 (May 1998): 509–672, 519.

12. Carolyn J. Frantz and Hanoch Dagan, "Properties of Marriage," *Columbia Law Review* 104 (January 2004): 75–133, 77–78.

13. Cynthia Lee Starnes, "Mothers, Myths, and the Law of Divorce: One More Feminist Case for Partnership," *William and Mary Journal of Women and the Law* 13 (Fall 2006): 203–233, 232–233.

14. Philomila Tsoukala, "Gary Becker, Legal Feminism, and the Costs of Moralizing Care," *Columbia Journal of Gender and Law* 16 (2007): 357–428, 421–422, 425.

15. John Rawls, "The Idea of Public Reason Revisited," *University of Chicago Law Review* 64 (Summer 1997): 765–807, 779–780.

16. Ibid., 788.

17. John Rawls, *Political Liberalism* (New York: Columbia University Press, expanded ed. 2005), 40–43 (describing "association" as a kind of voluntary ordering within political society that, because of its voluntary nature, is entitled, among other things, to offer different terms to different persons in the association).

18. Rawls, "The Idea of Public Reason Revisited," 790.

organization.[19] The public constraints of justice on matters of internal associational life must not be so severe, however, as to constrain "a free and flourishing internal life [of the association]."[20]

Rawls's analysis of the family effectively places it in a median position between public institutions (to which the principles of justice apply directly) and associations (to which the principles of justice require only a right of exit). On the one hand, the family, because of its essential role in the reproduction of political society over time, is part of the basic structure of society; on the other hand, it is a voluntary association and thus the principles of justice do not apply to it in the same way that the principles of justice constrain a wholly public institution such as the legislature or courts. Rawls's analysis of the family within political liberalism has important implications for equality within a system of family law that is politically liberal: It tolerates the continued existence of inequality within the family, but on the condition that such inequality "is fully voluntary."[21] Religiously justified hierarchies of the family, therefore, are consistent with the principles of justice if the background conditions of political justice are met.

The only gender-based inequality that must be abolished as a matter of the principles of justice is that which is involuntary.[22] Religiously justified inequality satisfies the voluntariness requirement because adherence to religion in a politically liberal regime is, by definition, voluntary. Although Rawls appears indifferent as to whether the burdens of labor in the family should be shared equally between men and women or whether it is enough for women to be fairly compensated for taking on a disproportionate share of such labor, he insists that justice requires that one of these two possibilities be satisfied.[23]

Family law, therefore, plays a secondary role for Rawls in guaranteeing gender equality because women enjoy all the basic rights of citizens and also have access to the material means necessary to allow them to make effective use of their liberties and opportunities.[24] In such circumstances, any residual gender-based inequality can be assumed to be voluntary. From a Rawlsian perspective, therefore, as long as women are being fairly compensated for any additional work they take on with respect to reproductive labor (measured against a hypothetical baseline of [170] reproductive labor that reflects a gender-neutral division of labor) and the background political conditions are otherwise just,

19. Ibid., 789–790
20. Ibid., 790
21. Ibid., 792 (stating that a liberal conception of justice "may have to allow for some traditional gendered division of labor within families"). Rawls further explains that an action is only "voluntary" if it is rational from the perspective of the actor and "all the surrounding conditions are also fair." Ibid. n. 68.
22. Ibid.
23. Ibid., 792–793.
24. Rawls, *Political Liberalism*, 469–471.

political liberalism has nothing to say about the internal organization of the family, even one explicitly endorsing a gendered division of labor.[25]

II. THE RELATIONSHIP OF ISLAMIC LAW TO ISLAMIC ETHICS

Despite the oft-repeated claim that Islamic law is a "religious" law, Islamic law in fact regularly distinguishes between the moral or ethical consequences of human actions and their legal consequences.[26] As a general matter, Islamic ethics is scripturalist in orientation: It claims to derive its moral judgments from an examination of Islamic revelatory sources that are believed, in principle, to provide morally conclusive knowledge.[27] The goal of Islamic ethical inquiry is to classify all human acts into one of five ethical categories: forbidden, obligatory, indifferent, disfavored, or supererogatory. Because these categories represent God's judgment of human acts, they are primarily theological categories and are not necessarily rules of law.[28] Muslim theologians refer to these categories as "the rules of obligation" because they apply to the conduct of a morally responsible person and represent ethical judgments regarding the conduct of such a person.[29]

Revelation itself yields conclusive answers for only a limited set of moral questions, thus giving rise to the need for good-faith interpretation of revelation. Interpretation is an equivocal enterprise, and consequently Islamic ethics, despite its scripturalist commitments, recognizes that Muslims acting in good faith will have different views of the contents of God's commands. In the absence of a temporal authority that can conclusively resolve these ethical and theological disputes, individual Muslims [171] satisfy their moral obligations to God by adhering to that rule that they in good faith believe best represents the divine will as evidenced by Islamic revelatory sources.[30] Ethical conduct

25. One might object to this conception of the family on the grounds that it does not sufficiently take into account the effect on children of growing up in a family organized around principles of gender hierarchy. Presumably Rawls's reply would be that children, too, are exposed to the principles of justice through mandatory public education, and therefore a family organized around principles of gender hierarchy would not be free to insulate their children from the egalitarian norms of public reason. Rawls, *Political Liberalism*, 199–200.

26. For example, the Ḥanafī school of Islamic law provides that a mother has a religious obligation (*diyānatan*) to nurse her infant child, but that such an obligation cannot be enforced by a court (*qaḍāʾan*). 2 ʿUmar b. Ibrahim Ibn Nujaym, *Al-Nahr al-Fāʾiq Sharḥ Kanz al-Daqāʾiq* (Beirut: Dār al-Kutub al-ʿIlmiyya, 2002), 518–519. For a more detailed description of the relationship of Islamic ethics to Islamic law, see Mohammad H. Fadel, "The True, the Good and the Reasonable: The Theological and Ethical Roots of Public Reason in Islamic Law," *Canadian Journal of Law and Jurisprudence* 21:1 (January 2008): 5–69, 19–29.

27. The three revelatory sources are the Quran, Islam's holy book; the *sunna*—the normative statements and practices of the Prophet Muḥammad; and consensus.

28. See Bernard G. Weiss, *The Spirit of Islamic Law* (Athens, GA: University of Georgia Press, 1998), 20.

29. Fadel, "The True, the Good and the Reasonable," 68.

30. Ibid., 41–43.

requires also that a human must direct his actions for the purpose of pleasing God rather than self-interest.[31] Islamic ethics, therefore, consists of a combination of theoretical knowledge regarding the status of one's action in the eyes of God, conformity of one's conduct to that theoretical judgment, and the intention by an individual to perform the act in question for the sake of God. For example, the valid discharge of the obligation to pray prescribed Islamic prayers five times daily requires (1) knowledge that to do so is obligatory, (2) knowledge of the manner by which the prayer is to be performed, (3) performance of the prescribed ritual acts in accordance with the rules for ritual prayer, and (4) an intention to perform the prayer solely for the sake of God. Whereas all ritual acts require a religious intention, secular acts—such as entering into contracts, including a contract for marriage—are valid without the requirement of a religious intention.[32]

Islamic law, in contrast to Islamic ethics, is concerned solely with determining the secular consequences of human conduct within a system of temporal justice that, although certainly related to the ethical norms of Islamic revelation, is never wholly determined by it.[33] Moreover, Islamic law, as a secular system of justice, does not attempt to determine the subjective states of human actors, even though in the absence of such data it is impossible to know the true moral status of any act.[34] Because of rule indeterminacy and fact indeterminacy,[35] the judgments of courts, viewed from a moral perspective, can only produce valid (*ẓāhir*) judgments rather than morally true (*bāṭin*) judgments. Whereas a judge's verdict is sufficient to terminate the dispute that gave rise to the litigation in the secular world, it is not enough [172]to discharge the conscience of the prevailing litigant unless she acted in good faith. Good faith means two things: first, that the successful

31. This principle is set forth in a statement attributed to the Prophet Muḥammad in which he is alleged to have said, "Actions [are judged] solely by intentions, and each individual shall only receive what he intends. Therefore, whoever immigrated [to Medina] for the sake of God and His prophet, then his immigration was for the sake of God and His messenger. As for the one who immigrated for the sake of a worldly gain or to marry a woman, then his immigration was for that [and not God]." "Hadith Number One: Actions are but by Intentions," *Ibn Rajab's Commentary on Imam Nawawi's Forty Hadith,* trans. Mohammed Fadel, available at https://sunnah.org/2010/08/28/explaination-of-the-hadith-actions-are-but-by-intentions/.

32. Shihāb al-Dīn al-Qarāfī, *al-Umniyya fī Idrāk al-Niyya*, ed. Musāʿid b. Qāsim al-Fāliḥ (Riyad: Maktabat al-Ḥaramayn, 1988), 112.

33. A more accurate conception of the relationship of Islamic ethics to Islamic law is that the latter exists within certain boundaries established by the former. Fadel, "The Good, the True and the Reasonable," 23–29, 48–49.

34. Baber Johansen, "Truth and Validity of the Qadi's Judgment. A Legal Debate among Muslim Sunnite Jurists from the 9th to the 13th centuries," *Recht van de Islam* 14 (1997): 1–26.

35. "Rule indeterminacy" arises from the impossibility of knowing whether the judge has applied the "correct" rule of law to the case (correct in the sense of corresponding with God's rule for the case); "fact indeterminacy" refers to the risk that the evidence provided by the litigants to the court may not correspond to the actual facts of the case.

litigant did not deceive the court as to the facts of the case;[36] and second, that the successful litigant did not advance a rule of law that he or she subjectively rejects.[37] If these two conditions are met, the judge's ruling grants the prevailing party not only a legal entitlement but also a moral entitlement to that which had been previously in dispute, and it categorically moots the prior moral controversy with respect to that particular case.[38]

However, legal rules cannot be viewed as entirely separate from a Muslim's moral obligations. For example, an invalid contract of sale may result in a defective transfer of title, with the result that the recipient of the property is deemed to be holding the object of the sale not as an owner but rather as a trustee with corresponding moral and legal obligations to return the item to its true owner without making any use of it for himself.[39] Or, in the case of family law, "if a man and a woman enter into a marriage in a manner that does not conform to the basic requirements of a marriage contract, the couple may not be considered to be truly married, and sexual intercourse between them will be illicit."[40] Moreover, legal rules do not derive exclusively from jurists' interpretations of revelation: State officials may promulgate legally binding rules under a doctrine known as *siyāsa sharʿiyya* on the condition that such rules do not contradict Islamic norms, that is, that they do not command an act that would be religiously forbidden or prohibit an act that would be religiously obligatory.[41]

Two sets of regulations, therefore, are relevant to the ethical decisions of an orthodox Muslim: his subjective perception of his religious obligations and the legal system's objective regulation of his conduct.[42] Where a discrepancy exists between the two sets of norms, an individual Muslim faces the moral problem of determining [173] whether he will abide by the legal rule in question or his own moral opinion. If the legal rule in ques-

---

36. Johansen, "Truth and Validity of the Qadi's Judgment," 12–13; Mohammad Fadel, "Adjudication in the Maliki Madhhab: A Study of Legal Process in Medieval Islamic Law," 114–116 (unpublished Ph.D.dissertation, University of Chicago, 1995).

37. An example would be one in which a defendant asserts the validity of his marriage to a woman despite the fact that it was contracted without the approval of the wife's father, who was alive and present, in reliance on a Ḥanafī rule recognizing the validity of such marriages, even though the defendant is a Mālikī and subjectively believes that a marriage in such circumstances is invalid in the absence of the father's consent. Fadel, "Adjudication in the Maliki Madhhab," 115 n. 223.

38. Ibid., 116.

39. Weiss, *Spirit of Islamic Law*, 21; 2 Aḥmad b. Muḥammad b. Aḥmad al-Dardīr, *al-Sharḥ al-Ṣaghir*, ed. Muṣṭafā Kamāl Waṣfī (Cairo: Dar al-Maʿārif, 1986), 110.

40. Weiss, *Spirit of Islamic Law*, 21.

41. Fadel, "The True, the Good and the Reasonable," 58 n. 234.

42. The problems arising from the duality of ethical/legal regulation that an orthodox Muslim faces would exist even if this Muslim lived in a perfectionist Islamic state. See Johansen, "Truth and Validity of the Qadi's Judgment." See also Haider Ala Hamoudi, "Baghdad Booksellers, Basra Carpet Merchants, and the Law of God and Man: Legal Pluralism and the Contemporary Muslim Experience," *Berkeley Journal of Middle Eastern and Islamic Law* 1 (2008): 1.

tion is a mandatory rule of law, that is, either commanding an act or an omission, Muslim jurists are of the view that a Muslim can, in good faith, comply with a legal rule that he rejects as unjust provided that compliance with that rule does not entail disobedience to God. In other words, mere moral disagreement with the inherent rightness of a legal rule does not excuse compliance—only a true conflict between fidelity to the rule of law and fidelity to God could excuse compliance with a mandatory law.[43] A Muslim's obedience in such a context does not imply his or her moral agreement with the command in question or that it is just, only that he or she can comply with it without committing a sin.

The distinction between the moral and the legal in the context of permissive rules creates for observant Muslims what can only be described as a moral quandary: The person may be objectively entitled under prevailing law to press a certain claim or raise a certain defense, but unless he or she subjectively assents, as a moral matter, to that right or defense, that person is not religiously entitled to avail himself or herself of that particular rule because to do so would be to act in a manner that he or she subjectively understands to be unjust.[44] This moral problem is especially pressing in the case of certain rules of family law regarding a Muslim woman's right to remarry and rules regarding the distribution of marital property on termination of a marriage.

III. THE SCOPE OF ISLAMIC FAMILY LAW AND ITS RELATIONSHIP TO ISLAMIC ETHICS[45]

To understand the dynamics of Islamic family law[46] and the interaction of ethical and legal claims in the life of an orthodox Muslim, one must keep in mind that Islamic [174]

43. For this reason, a government agent that unlawfully killed another could not raise as a defense that he was merely acting on the instructions of his superior on the theory that he has a moral duty to resist an immoral command. See, e.g., 5 Muḥammad b. Muḥammad al-Khaṭīb al-Shirbīnī, *Mughnī al-Muḥtāj ilā Maʿrifat Maʿāni Alfāẓ al-Minhāj*, eds. ʿAlī Muḥammad Muʿawwaḍ and ʿĀdil Aḥmad ʿAbd al-Mawjūd (Beirut: Dār al-Kutub al-ʿIlmiyya, 1994) (holding an executioner personally liable if he knows that the victim was unjustly executed and jointly liable with his superior if he pleads duress).

44. Mālikīs, for example, routinely cite the example of the Ḥanafī principle giving neighbors a legal right of first refusal in the event of a sale of land as a rule for which it would be immoral for a Mālikī to act on, given their belief that a legal right of first refusal only accrues to partners in land, not neighbors.

45. References to Islamic law in this chapter do not refer to any system of positive law enacted or given effect by a state, but rather to the doctrines of Islamic family law in pre-nineteenth-century legal treatises by Muslim jurists. Although many of these rules are no longer politically salient because they have been replaced or modified by positive legislation in states that have incorporated Islamic family law as part of their legal system, their authority is independent of any state command, and therefore they remain highly relevant to orthodox Muslims' understandings of their rights and obligations, especially in liberal jurisdictions where there is no state-established system of Islamic law adjudication.

46. For overviews of classical and contemporary interpretations of Islamic family law, see John L. Esposito with Natana J. Delong-Bas, *Women in Muslim Family Law* (Syracuse, NY: Syracuse University Press,

family law operates principally at two different levels. First, Islamic law regulates sexual intimacy and the lawful reproduction of children, where the most important rule is that sexual intimacy (including intimate contact not involving intercourse) is illicit in the absence of a valid marriage; it in fact constitutes a mortal sin and, in certain cases, a capital crime.[47] Only children conceived pursuant to a recognized marriage contract are considered legitimate.[48] The legal validity of marriage contracts is generally a matter of strict liability: Even good-faith mistakes can result in the contract being defective, in which case the parties are generally required to separate, at least until a valid contract is concluded.[49] The Islamic law of divorce also regulates sexual intimacy by rendering sexual intimacy between the former spouses illicit, immoral, and potentially subject to criminal sanction.[50] Divorce does not affect the relationship of the parent to the child, however; a legitimate child remains permanently part of each parent's kin group even after dissolution of the marriage.

Second, Islamic law introduces a broad new set of economic relationships, primarily within the nuclear family but also within the extended family. A valid marriage contract creates new economic relationships within the family requiring, for example, periodic transfers of property from the husband to his wife; from the father to any minor children; and from adult children to their parents, if the parents become indigent. Such transfers are mandated both during the lifetimes of the individuals concerned (in the form of mandatory maintenance obligations) and after death (in the form of a manda-

---

2d ed. 2001); Dawoud S. El Alami, *The Marriage Contract in Islamic Law in the Shariʿah and Personal Status Laws of Egypt and Morocco* (London: Graham and Trotman, 1992); Jamal J. Nasir, *The Status of Women Under Islamic Law and Under Modern Islamic Legislation* (London: Graham and Trotman, 2d ed. 1994).

47. Illicit intercourse constitutes the crime of *zinā*, which, according to traditional doctrines of Islamic law, is the subject of a mandatory penalty (one of the so-called *ḥudūd* [sing. *ḥadd*] penalties). The penalty set forth in the Qur'an for adultery is 100 lashes. *Al-Nūr*, 24:2. Muslim jurists, however, limited this punishment to illicit intercourse between persons who were legally virgins (*bikr*) that is, had not experienced marital intercourse. The punishment for individuals who had the experience of marital intercourse (*muḥṣan*) was stoning to death, which, although not mentioned in the Qur'an, was believed to have been practiced by the Prophet Muḥammad.

48. Children born outside of a lawful relationship are lawful descendants of the mother but can never be lawful descendants of the father, even where the biological father admits paternity or subsequently marries the mother. Daniel Pollack et al., "Classical Religious Perspectives of Adoption Law," *Notre Dame Law Review* 79 (February 2004): 693–753, 734–735.

49. 2 al-Dardīr, *al-Sharḥ al-Ṣaghīr*, 384 (stating that the general rule is that invalid marriages must be annulled); 2 Ibn Nujaym, *al-Nahr al-Fā'iq Sharḥ Kanz al-Daqā'iq*, 252 (stating that it is obligatory to annul an invalid marriage contract). Children born of an invalid marriage, however, are nevertheless deemed to be legitimate. Ibid., 254. Other incidents of a lawful marriage, for example, the right to inherit, are present until the marriage is annulled. 2 al-Dardīr, *al-Sharḥ al-Ṣaghīr*, 388.

50. David S. Powers, "From Almohadism to Malikism: The Case of al-Haskuri, the Mocking Jurist, *ca* . 712–716/1312–1316," in *Law, Society and Culture in the Maghrib, 1300–1500* (Cambridge: Cambridge University Press, 2009), 53–94.

tory scheme of inheritance). Maintenance obligations [175] between parents and legitimate children are mandatory by virtue of the relationship itself.[51] A husband's obligation to support the wife is contingent on the continued existence of the marriage. Once the marriage is dissolved by divorce or death, any ongoing maintenance obligation terminates after a limited time.[52]

Although universal agreement exists with respect to certain aspects of family law, such as the impermissibility of sexual intimacy in the absence of a valid marriage contract, for example, not all Islamic ethical or legal rules regulating family life enjoy such universal recognition. In particular, because the background rules governing property relations are more permissive than those involving sexual intimacy, there is substantially wider scope within Islamic ethics and law for the organization of a household's economic relations than would be contemplated for the organization of sexual relations. The next section will discuss the practical consequences of intra-Muslim differences of opinion regarding both the ethical and legal rules governing family life and how such differences, as a historical matter, helped sustain an Islamic version of family law pluralism.

IV. ISLAM AND FAMILY LAW PLURALISM

Four factors lie behind pluralism of family regulation in societies governed by Islamic law. First, intra-Islamic pluralism arises by virtue of the role of human interpretation in the law-finding process and the impossibility of resolving resulting differences of opinion. Second, Islamic family law is a mix of mandatory and permissive rules, resulting in potential departures of Islamic marriage contracts from the default terms of Islamic law (and at times in a manner that appears to subvert the religiously normative "ideals" of marriage). Third, there is nonjudicial religious and moral regulation of the family. Fourth, Islamic law is willing to give partial recognition to non-Islamic systems of family law.

A. Intra-Islamic Legal Pluralism and Islamic Family Law

As a result of the relationships between and among Islamic ethical theory, moral epistemology, and law, four distinct systems of substantive law (commonly referred to as "schools of law") arose among Sunni Muslims: the Ḥanafī, the Mālikī, the Shāfiʿī, and the Ḥanbalī. Although each system of law is considered equally "orthodox" from an ethical perspective, they nevertheless often have material differences in [176] their substantive

51. Pollack et al., "Classical Religious Perspectives of Adoption Law," 733–735.

52. Maintenance is required until the divorce becomes final upon expiration of the applicable waiting period (ʿ*idda*, which in the case of a woman who is not pregnant, is approximately three months). *Al-Baqara*, 2:228. For a pregnant divorcée, the husband's maintenance obligation continues until she delivers. *Al-Ṭalāq*, 65:6. The widow's waiting period is four months and ten days. *Al-Baqara*, 2:234.

legal doctrines, including their approaches to the regulation of the family. To illustrate the range of substantive disagreement, consider a few salient differences between the Ḥanafī and Mālikī schools.[53]

Whereas both the Ḥanafī and the Mālikī schools of law recognize the right of an adult woman to marry without the consent of her father (or her father's male relatives in the absence of the father),[54] the Ḥanafīs give the father (or the father's male relatives) the right to annul a daughter's marriage if it was contracted without his consent and if the bridegroom was not the wife's social equal (*kufʾ*).[55] Although the Mālikīs also recognize the doctrine of social equality (*kafāʾa*) in marriage, they restrict it to religion and freedom, and, accordingly, the father (or a male relative of the father) has no right to annul the marriage of his adult daughter if contracted without his consent (or even in defiance of his will) on the grounds that her husband is not her social equal. Significantly, the relatively greater independence Mālikī law gives women to contract their own marriages results in a correspondingly *weaker* claim to maintenance against their extended kin group relative to the Ḥanafī rule. Whereas the Ḥanafī law of maintenance obliges the father or the father's male kin to maintain even adult unmarried or divorced daughters (or daughters whose husbands fail to provide for them), the Mālikī law of maintenance does not recognize intrafamilial maintenance obligations other than those between a parent and a child.[56]

Another important difference between the two schools of law pertains to the law of spousal maintenance. Whereas both agree that it is the husband's duty to support the wife, the Ḥanafīs understand the maintenance obligation to be more akin to a gift rather than a contractual undertaking. Accordingly, the failure of a husband to honor this obligation does not give rise to an enforceable legal claim for money on the part of the wife.[57] Only after the wife complains to the judge and the judge reduces the maintenance obligation to a sum certain (whether payable as a lump sum, monthly, or yearly), or after the wife enters into a specific contractual agreement with her husband regarding the

53. Historically, both the Ḥanafī and the Mālikī schools of law have been closely associated with dynasties in the Islamic world. In the modern era, Ḥanafī doctrines largely prevail in the field of family law in much of the Arab world with the exception of North Africa, where Mālikī influence on modern family law codes is greater. For a discussion of some of the differences between the Mālikīs, the Ḥanafīs, and modern Arab family law codes, see Lama Abu-Odeh, "Modernizing Muslim Family Law: The Case of Egypt," *Vanderbilt Journal of Transnational Law* 37 (October 2004): 1043–1146.

54. Mohammad Fadel, "Reinterpreting the Guardian's Role in the Islamic Contract of Marriage: The Case of the Maliki School," *Journal of Islamic Law* 3 (1998): 1–26, 12–14.

55. Farhat J. Ziadeh, "Equality (*Kafāʾa*) in the Muslim Law of Marriage," *American Journal of Comparative Law* 6 (1957): 503–517, 510.

56. 2 al-Dardīr, *al-Sharḥ al-Ṣaghīr*, 750–751; 2 Ibn Nujaym, *al-Nahr al-Fāʾiq Sharḥ Kanz al-Daqāʾiq* , 510.

57. 2 Ibn Nujaym, *al-Nahr al-Fāʾiq Sharḥ Kanz al-Daqāʾiq*, 512 (unpaid maintenance is not enforceable by a judge because it is in the nature of a gift, not a debt).

amount of her maintenance, does the wife [177] have an enforceable claim against the husband.[58] Moreover, repeated failures of a husband to meet his maintenance obligation do not give rise to a right of divorce; instead, the wife may borrow money on the credit of the husband in order to satisfy her needs,[59] or the judge may imprison the recalcitrant husband as he would imprison any other recalcitrant debtor in order to induce him to perform his financial obligations.[60] For the Mālikīs, however, the maintenance obligation is a debt owed by the husband to the wife that she is free to enforce legally at any time.[61] In addition, the Mālikīs deem a husband's failure to maintain his wife a fundamental breach of the marriage contract, giving her a right to divorce as a result.[62]

The Ḥanafīs and the Mālikīs also differ on the law governing consensual divorce (*khulʿ*). Both schools agree that if the husband is at fault, that is, the wife is not in a state of disobedience (*nushūz*) to the husband, then a husband is prohibited from receiving any consideration from his wife in exchange for divorce.[63] The Ḥanafīs characterize this prohibition as only a religious and not a legal obligation. Thus, an innocent wife's agreement to pay her husband consideration in exchange for a divorce is legally binding and she has no right to seek repayment of that amount.[64] The Mālikīs, however, treat this prohibition as creating both religious and legal obligations. They therefore grant a divorced woman a cause of action for the recovery of any sum wrongfully paid to her ex-husband if she can prove that she had been entitled to a divorce from her husband (if, for example, he had been abusing her).[65] Indeed, even a cuckolded husband is not permitted by the Mālikīs to harass his wife into accepting a separation by *khulʿ*.[66] The contrasting positions of the Ḥanafīs and Mālikīs on this issue reflect, in turn, a deeper disagreement on judicial divorce: The Ḥanafīs only grant a judicial divorce on extremely limited grounds whereas the Mālikīs permit the judge to divorce a wife whenever she proves harm.

Finally, the Ḥanafīs and the Mālikīs have substantially different understandings of the financial consequences of a wife's disobedience. For the Ḥanafīs, the wife loses her right to maintenance simply by virtue of her disobedience, and it is not restored until she

58. Ibid.

59. Ibid., 510.

60. Muḥammad b.ʿAlī al-Ḥaddād, *al-Jawhara al-Nayyira*, 246.

61. 2 al-Dardīr, *al-Sharḥ al-Ṣaghīr*, 754.

62. Ibid., 745–746.

63. 2 Ibn Nujaym, *al-Nahr al-Fā'iq Sharḥ Kanz al-Daqāʾiq* , 436.

64. 3 ʿAlaʾ al-Dīn Abū Bakr b. Masʿūd al-Kāsānī, *Badāʾiʿ al-Ṣanāʾiʿ fī Tartib al-Sharāʾiʿ* (Beirut: Dār al-Kutub al-ʿIlmiyya), 150.

65. The husband's return of property unlawfully received from his wife in exchange for the divorce does not vitiate the divorce's effectiveness. 2 al-Dardīr, *al-Sharḥ al-Ṣaghīr*, 530.

66. 3 Muḥmmad b. Yūsuf al-Mawwāq, *al-Tāj wa al-Iklīl li-Mukhtaṣar Khalīl* 3 (Beirut: Dār al-Fikr, 1992), 491.

submits again to her husband's authority.[67] For the Mālikīs, however, a [178] husband's maintenance obligation persists until the husband exhausts all legal avenues to secure the submission of the rebellious wife to his authority.[68]

The schools' abstract and general agreements on certain fundamental points[69] should not obscure the often-profound differences regarding how to give concrete effect to such principles within a general system of rights and remedies. Although none of the historical schools of Islamic law directly provides grounds for a liberal conception of marriage (such as a partnership of equals), some are more consistent with a politically liberal family law than others. As the preceding examples indicate, Mālikī rules appear substantially more favorable to women, both from the perspective of distributive justice and protecting a woman's right to exit an undesirable marriage. Accordingly, the default rules of Mālikī family law may provide greater doctrinal resources for fashioning Islamic marriage contracts that satisfy the minimum substantive requirements of political liberalism relative to the default rules of Ḥanafī family law.

B. The Contractual Nature of Islamic Family Law

Islamic marriage law permits tailor-made agreements (if drafted using the proper contractual formula) that may deviate, within specific bounds, from the legally provided terms of the marriage contract. Parties are not free, however, to include terms that are "repugnant" to the Islamic conception of marriage, that is, terms that purport to alter fundamentals of the Islamic marriage contract. If such a term is sufficiently "repugnant," it could render the contract void in its entirety. An example of such a repugnant term, from the Sunni perspective, is a marriage contracted for a specific period of time (*mutʿa*). The Mālikī school also considers "repugnant" an agreement to marry on condition that the parties will keep the marriage a secret or an agreement that the husband will not spend the night with the wife or will visit her only during certain specified times (e.g., the day time).[70] Other terms, although not repugnant to the marriage contract, may not be judicially enforceable by specific performance, such as a promise by a husband to refrain from marrying another woman or from causing her to settle in another town. The non-enforceability of such a term does not, however, vitiate the validity [179] of the

---

67. 2 Ibn Nujaym, *Al-Nahr al-Fāʾiq Sharḥ Kanz al-Daqāʾiq*, 507.

68. 2 al-Dardīr, *al-Sharḥ al-Ṣaghīr*, 740.

69. Lama Abu-Odeh has observed that the historical schools "tend to pull toward a particular position" in certain basic questions regarding the family. For example, they generally endorse a family structure that is both gendered and hierarchical and that accrues "to the benefit of the husband ... but with a strong underlying element of transactional reciprocity of obligations ... in which husbands provide money, in the form of maintenance, and women provide conjugal society in return." Abu-Odeh, "Modernizing Muslim Family Law," 1070, 1073.

70. 2 al-Dardīr, *al-Sharḥ al-Ṣaghīr*, 382–384.

marriage[71] nor does it imply that the husband is morally free to ignore it.[72] The enforceability of other terms, for example, a marriage on the condition that the wife possesses a unilateral right to divorce at any time, is controversial: the Mālikīs do not recognize it, but the Ḥanafīs do.[73]

The breach of a contractual term may give rise to monetary damages even if it is not enforceable through specific performance. The Ḥanafīs, for example, hold that if a woman agrees to a reduction in her dowry in consideration for the groom's promise to perform or to refrain from an act that is beneficial to her or another and is otherwise lawful (e.g., a husband's promise not to take another wife), then a subsequent breach by the husband entitles her to receive compensation. Damages would be calculated as the difference between the dowry she would have ordinarily received (*mahr al-mithl*) but for the husband's promise and the dowry she actually received pursuant to the contract.[74]

More important than the availability of damages, however, is the ability of parties to transform what would be a non-enforceable term into one that is enforceable by including an express remedy for breach. For example, a contractual clause granting the wife a unilateral right to divorce in the event that her husband marries a second wife is enforceable, even if a general promise by the husband not to take a second wife is not. Because Islamic law views such a provision as an oath or a conditional divorce, the right to divorce becomes available to the wife simply by virtue of the occurrence of the specified contingency without regard to whether the wife offered a financial concession in exchange for that contingency. The conditional structure of this device allows it to protect the wife from all sorts of contingencies for which the law does not provide a remedy, for example, a prolonged absence of the husband from the marital home. Accordingly, even the Ḥanafī school, which is the most restrictive in terms of allowing judicial divorces to women, provides women greater access to divorce as a matter of the spouses' contract than the school's default rules would otherwise permit.

As a matter of both social and legal history, we know that Islamic marriage contracts routinely departed from the legally provided default rules; examples of standard [180] form marriage contracts with terms that depart from legal default rules appear as early as the late tenth and early eleventh centuries. One such model from Andalusia includes provi-

71. Such conditions are viewed as legally unenforceable promises that ought to be kept as a matter of morality.

72. Abū al-Walīd Muḥammad b. Aḥmad Ibn Rushd (the Grandfather), *al-Bayān wa-l-Tāḥṣīl* (Beirut: Dār al-Gharb al-Islāmī, 1984), 377 (explaining that a husband is morally but not legally bound to fulfill a promise to his wife not to prevent her from attending the mosque).

73. 2 al-Dardīr, *al-Sharḥ al-Ṣaghīr*, 386; 2 Ibn Nujaym, *al-Nahr al-Fa'iq Sharḥ Kanz al-Daqā'iq* , 371–372.

74. 2 Ibn Nujaym, *al-Nahr al-Fa'iq Sharḥ Kanz al-Daqā'iq* , 245–246. See also Lucy Carroll Stout, "Muslim Marriage Contracts in South Asia: Possibilities and Limitations," in Harvard Law School, Islamic Legal Studies Program: Conference on the Islamic Marriage Contract, January 1999 (unpublished manuscript on file with the author).

sions providing the wife the option of divorce in the event her husband took a second wife, left the marital home beyond a contractually defined period of time, or demanded that the wife leave her hometown for another.[75] Such provisions were enforced in courts.[76]

Likewise, in the urban centers of fourteenth- and fifteenth-century Mamluk Egypt and Syria, monetization of the marriage contract had become sufficiently widespread as to undermine the "patriarchal ideal of conjugal harmony ... [pursuant to which] a household should constitute one indivisible economic unit ... [un]contaminated by the monetary transactions taking place outside the household."[77] Far from condemning these contractual innovations, Islamic law gave them legitimacy through the development of new contractual clauses[78] that came to be inserted routinely in marriage contracts even though some religious authorities condemned such clauses as contrary to normative Islamic conceptions of the family.[79]

Islamic law thus furthered an internal system of family law pluralism by promoting the use of nonstandard contractual terms to replace default legal terms, with the result that Islamic family law is best understood as a mixed system of mandatory public rules and contractual private rules.

C. Religious Regulation of the Family in Islam

At the same time that Islamic contractual legal principles provide parties with significant opportunities to depart from the default terms of Islamic law, so too religion [181] and religious rhetoric impact the regulation of Muslims' marital life,[80] especially in light

75. Muḥammad b. Aḥmad al-Umawī, "A Father's Marriage of His Virgin Daughter Who is Under His Authority," appendix in Fadel, "Reinterpreting the Guardian's Role in the Islamic Contract of Marriage," 24–25.

76. David S. Powers, "Women and Divorce in the Islamic West: Three Cases,"*Hawwa* 1:1 (2003): 29–45, 39.

77. Yossef Rapoport, *Marriage, Money and Divorce in Medieval Islamic Society* (Cambridge: Cambridge University Press, 2005), 52.

78. Two new clauses were particularly important in these developments. The first transformed the husband's maintenance obligation from one payable in kind—food, clothing, and shelter—to one payable only in cash at regular intervals. The second transformed the husband's obligation to pay a dowry from an obligation payable only upon a fixed schedule or upon death or divorce to an obligation payable at the demand of the wife. Ibid., 52–53, 56.

79. Ibid., 57 (quoting Ibn Qayyim al-Jawziyya, a famous Syrian jurist from the fourteenth century, as complaining that "[i]f a husband scolds his wife for her housekeeping or prevents her from stepping out or leaving his house, or does not let her go wherever she wishes, the wife then demands her marriage gift. The husband is sent to prison, while she goes wherever she wants.").

80. Reform of the pre-Islamic Arabian family (both at a moral level and at a legal level) was an express goal of numerous verses of the Quran. See, e.g., Quran, *al-Takwīr*, 81:8–9 (condemning the pre-Islamic Arabian practice of female infanticide); *al-Nisāʾ*, 4:19 (prohibiting the pre-Islamic practice of "inheriting" women for remarriage, prohibiting men from harassing women in order to extort property from

of strains of (especially historical) religious rhetoric that value an ethic of female sacrifice[81]—sometimes to the point of self-abnegation[82]—over individual rights. Different religious conceptions of marriage may account for the different approaches taken by the Mālikīs and the Ḥanafīs here.[83] Whereas both the Ḥanafīs [182] and the Mālikīs treat marriage as a contract that is supererogatory, the Ḥanafīs give marriage greater devotional

---

them, and admonishing them to live with women in kindness); *al-Baqara*, 2:229 (calling on men to live with their wives in kindness or to divorce them in a spirit of generosity); *al-Baqara*, 2:233 ("The mothers shall nurse their children for two years, if the father desires to complete the term. But he shall bear the cost of their food and clothing on equitable terms. No soul shall have a burden laid on it greater than it can bear. No mother shall suffer an injury on account of her child, nor [shall the] father on account of his child [suffer an injury].... If they mutually agree to wean the child and after they consult with one another, there is no blame on them. If ye decide on a foster-mother for your offspring, there is no blame on you, provided ye pay (the mother) what ye offered, on equitable terms. But fear Allah and know that Allah sees well what ye do.").

81. Abū Ḥāmid Muḥammad b. Muḥammad al-Ghazālī, *The Proper Conduct of Marriage in Islam*, trans. Muhtar Holland (Al-Baz Publishing, 1998), 61 (attributing to the Prophet Muḥammad the statement that a woman who endures a bad husband will receive heavenly reward); and Aḥmad b. Muḥammad Ibn Ḥajar al-Haytamī, *al-Ifṣāḥ ʿan Aḥādīth al-Nikāḥ* (Baghdad: al-Maktaba al-ʿAlamiyya, 1988), 87 n.3 (attributing to the Prophet Muḥammad the statement that a woman, even if her husband is oppressive, should not disobey him) and 93 (attributing to the Prophet Muḥammad the statement that a woman who demands a divorce from her husband without just cause will be deprived from even the "scent of Paradise"). For an example of a modern manifestation of this ethic among Turkish Muslims in Thrace, Greece, see Robin Fretwell Wilson, "The Perils of Privatized Marriage," in *Marriage and Divorce in a Multi-Cultural Context*, edited by Joel Nichols (New York: Cambridge University Press, 2011), pp. 253–283.

82. The expectation that a wife should completely subordinate her individual desires to the service of her husband was periodically expressed by medieval Muslim (male) writers on marriage. For example, the well-known medieval Muslim theologian, jurist, and philosopher al-Ghazālī described the virtuous wife in the following terms:

> "She should stay inside her house, and stick to her spinning wheel. She should not go up too often to the roof and look around. She should talk little with the neighbors, and visit them only when it is really necessary to do so. She should look after the interests of her spouse in his absence and in his presence, seeking to please him in all that she does. She must be loyal to him in respect of herself and of her property. She should not go out of her house without his permission. When she does go out with his permission, she should be disguised in shabby attire, keeping to out-of-the-way places far from the main streets and markets. She should be careful not to disclose her identity to her husband's friends; indeed, she should avoid recognition by anyone who thinks he knows her, or whom she recognizes. Her only concern should be to keep things right and to manage her household."

Al-Ghazālī, *Proper Conduct of Marriage in Islam*, 92–93.

83. Hina Azam argues that the different legal approaches taken by the Ḥanafīs and the Mālikīs reflect a deeper disagreement on the nature of human sexuality and ownership of the body, with the Ḥanafīs adopting a "theocentric" view of the body and sexuality whereas the Mālikīs took a more "proprietary" view of the body and sexuality. Hina Azam, "Identifying the Victim: God vs. the Woman in Islamic Rape Law," lecture delivered at *the 2008 Annual Meeting of the Middle East Studies Association* (unpublished manuscript on file with the author).

weight than the Mālikīs. One later Ḥanafī author, for example, states that aside from faith in God, marriage is the only religious obligation that began with Adam and Eve, persists for the entirety of human history, and continues into the afterlife.[84] This kind of religious rhetoric surrounding marriage is largely absent from Mālikī sources, which are simply content to state that all things being equal, marriage is a religiously meritorious act on account of the secular benefits it provides.[85]

This does not mean, however, that religious ideals do not inform Mālikī family law. For example, Mālik, the eponymous founder of the Mālikī school, reportedly discouraged contractual stipulations in marriage contracts on the theory that their inclusion is inconsistent with the relationship of trust at the heart of marriage.[86] Further, religious conceptions of marriage manifest themselves even in strictly legal matters. Islamic law treats marriage contracts differently from commercial ones. To illustrate, the norms of arm's-length bargaining permit each party to seek its maximum advantage (*mushāḥḥa* or *mukāyasa*) in commercial contracts. Marriage contracts, however, are construed according to the principal of mutual generosity (*musāmaḥa* or *mukārama*), pursuant to which the norms of magnanimity and sharing prevail over individual welfare-maximizing interpretations of the contract.[87] For that reason, the Mālikīs do not permit a husband to annul his marriage in the event that certain contractual representations, for example, actual virginity, were breached, even if such representations were explicitly demanded by the husband.[88] This interpretive principle also meant, however, that a woman's economic contribution to the household can easily be recharacterized as a gift to the husband rather than as a loan that the husband must repay.[89] In short, tension exists between the values of Islamic law [183] as a legal system and traditionalist Islamic religious discourse: The former protects and vindicates the individual rights of the parties to the marriage

84. 3 Ibn ʿĀbidīn, *Ḥāshiyat Radd al-Muḥtār* (Cairo: Muṣṭafā al-Bābī al-Ḥalabī, 1966), 4.

85. 2 al-Dardīr, *al-Sharḥ al-Ṣaghīr*, 330.

86. Abū al-Walīd Muḥammad b. Aḥmad Ibn Rushd (the Grandfather), 4 *al-Bayān wa-l-Taḥṣīl* 3 (Beirut: Dār al-Gharb al-Islāmī, 1984), 311–312. According to Ibn Rushd the Grandfather (twelfth century), however, Mālik disliked such conditions, not for religious reasons as such, but because they are bad deals for women: In most instances a woman will never have an opportunity to exercise her contingent rights, yet she agrees in advance to a reduced dowry in consideration for these additional stipulations.

87. Ibid., 263.

88. 3 al-Mawwāq, *al-Tāj wa al-Iklīl*, 491.

89. Mālikī law required a wife to swear an oath that she intended to treat her contributions to the household as a debt payable in the future in order for her to receive compensation for such contributions in the future. 4 al-Mawwāq, *al-Tāj wa al-Iklīl*, 193; see also Ibn Rushd, 4 *al-Bayān wa-l-Taḥṣīl*, 345–346. Moreover, a wife's failure to timely claim amounts that her husband owes her would result in a dismissal of her claim. *Al-Ḥadīqa al-Mustaqilla al-Naḍra fī al-Fatāwā al-Ṣādira ʿan ʿUlamāʾ al-Ḥaḍra* 24b (unpublished manuscript, containing legal opinions from fourteenth- to fifteenth-century Granada, on file with the author).

contract (even rights that go beyond those proscribed by law), whereas the latter promotes an ethic of sacrifice, trust, love, and female subordination to their husbands.

To the extent that individual Muslims internalize the traditional religious discourse regarding marriage, the prospect that they will use their ability to opt out of the default terms of Islamic law would seem, necessarily, to be diminished, and to that extent giving effect to family law arbitrations that reflected such a discourse would be inconsistent with political liberalism. Traditional religious discourse, however, does not exercise a monopoly over Islamic religious conceptions of marriage and gender relations.[90] Islamic discourse on gender and the family over the last one hundred and fifty years has generally stressed egalitarian religious themes at the expense of the traditionalist doctrines described earlier in this chapter.[91] To the extent contemporary Muslims internalize this discourse, one would expect that they would be more willing to take advantage of the contractual structure of Islamic law to opt out of its default terms in favor of a more egalitarian marriage contract that could in principle be consistent with the requirements of political liberalism.

In short, religious beliefs, at least in the contemporary context, operate as a wild card in determining the behavior of individual Muslims: Some religious Muslims may be traditionalist in their views of marriage, whereas other religious Muslims may adopt a much more egalitarian view of the family. The prevalence of divergent subjective religious beliefs among Muslim citizens further exacerbates the problem [184] of family law pluralism within the Muslim community because it reinforces the gap between the norms of an objective legal system (whether or not nominally Islamic) and the subjective moral norms of individual Muslims.

90. Even among conservative groups that are typically labeled "Islamist," important in the religious discourse toward a more egalitarian understanding of marriage and gender relations have taken place. See Gudrun Krämer, "Justice in Modern Islamic Thought," in *Shariʿa: Islamic Law in the Contemporary Context*, eds. Abbas Amanat and Frank Griffel (Stanford, CA: Stanford University Press, 2007), 20–37, 33. Indeed, the translator of al-Ghazālī's *The Proper Conduct of Marriage In Islam* described the difficulties he had in finding an Islamic publishing house willing to publish the entire translation, presumably because they found some of Ghazālī's statements regarding women's role in marriage to be an obsolete relic of the middle ages, if not an outright embarrassment.

91. See, e.g., Qasim Amin, "The Emancipation of Woman and the New Woman," in *Modernist Islam 1840 1940: A Sourcebook*, ed. Charles Kurzman (Oxford: Oxford University Press, 2002), 61–69; Nazira Zein-ed-Din, "Unveiling and Veiling," in *Liberal Islam: A Sourcebook*, ed. Charles Kurzman (Oxford: Oxford University Press, 1998), 101–106; Fatima Mernissi, "A Feminist Interpretation of Women's Rights in Islam," in Kurzman, *Liberal Islam* , 112–126; Amina Wadud-Muhsin, "Qur'an and Woman," in Kurzman, *Liberal Islam* , 127–138; Muhammad Shahrour, "Islam and the 1995 Beijing World Conference on Women," in Kurzman, *Liberal Islam*, 139–144; Khaled Abou el Fadl, *Speaking in God's Name: Islamic Law, Authority and Women* (Oxford: One World Publications, 2001); Kecia Ali, *Sexual Ethics & Islam: Feminist Reflections on Qur'an, Hadith and Jurisprudence* (Oxford: One World Publications, 2006).

D. Marriages of Non-Muslims and Islamic Family Law

Another important historical cause of family law pluralism is Islamic law's historical willingness to afford limited recognition to marriages conducted under non-Islamic law, pursuant to the principle that non-Muslims enjoyed autonomy over their religious affairs.[92] Islamic law did not view such recognition as an endorsement of the specific moral conceptions underlying non-Islamic marriages; rather, it was a function of the political agreement between the Islamic state and the particular group of non-Muslims permanently residing in an Islamic state (*dhimmīs*). Thus, Islamic law was willing to tolerate marriages that it would condemn as incestuous if the marriage at issue was believed to be permissible according to the parties' own religion.[93] Non-Muslims, according to the Ḥanafīs (but not the Mālikīs), could avail themselves of Islamic family law, but only if both parties agreed to submit their dispute to an Islamic court.[94]

Whereas Islamic law took a strong hands-off position respecting the standards that governed the formation and dissolution of non-Muslim marriages, Muslim jurists did not feel such restraint regarding intrahousehold transfers of wealth. Accordingly, a non-Muslim husband was subject to the same legal duty to maintain his wife as was a Muslim husband. If that husband breached or could not fulfill those duties, the extended family had to take on those maintenance obligations to the same extent a Muslim family would have.[95] Similarly, whereas Islamic law gave non-Muslim parents the right to raise their own children (including teaching them a non-Islamic religion),[96] they could not take actions that would endanger the *secular* well-being of their children (such as agreeing to send them to enemy territory where they could be enslaved).[97] Thus, to the extent that a family law dispute appeared to implicate a norm that Muslims believed was nonreligious, sectarian identity did not shield non-Muslims from the jurisdiction of an Islamic court. [185]

E. Conclusion

Islam, as a religious and a legal system, systematically contributes both to the social fact of family law pluralism (by sustaining numerous ways in which families can live) and a

92. The Ḥanafī principle was expressed in the rule that "they are to be left alone in matters that pertain to their religion (*yutrakūn wa mā yadinūn*)."

93. Fadel, "The True, the Good and the Reasonable," 58–59.

94. 2 Ibn Nujaym, *al-Nahr al-Fāʾiq Sharḥ Kanz al-Daqāʾiq*, 285.

95. 3 Ibn ʿĀbidīn, *Ḥāshiyat Radd al-Muḥtār*, 159; 2 Ibn Nujaym, *al-Nahr al-Fāʾiq Sharḥ Kanz al-Daqāʾiq*, 266 (both noting that rules governing maintenance, descent, inheritance, and the option of a minor to annul his or her marriage upon puberty all apply to non-Muslims).

96. Pollack et al., "Classical Religious Perspectives of Adoption Law," 746–747.

97. 5 Muḥammad b. Aḥmad al-Sarakhsī , ed. Muḥammad Ḥasan Muḥammad Ḥasan Ismāʿīl al-Shāfiʿī, *Sharḥ Kitāb al-Siyar al-Kabīr* (Beirut: Dār al-kutub al-ʿilmiyya, 1997), 46.

normative system of family law pluralism (by legally recognizing the existence of different legal rules that can apply to issues of family and by allowing individuals to create their own "rules" via inclusion of express contractual terms in their marriage contracts that depart from legally provided default rules). As a matter of religious doctrine, traditional Islamic religious teachings endorse a hierarchical relationship with a strong emphasis on female subordination and sacrifice. The rules of Islamic law, which permit women to insert favorable provisions into the marriage contract that strengthen their positions with respect to their husbands and which emphasize a rights-based approach to marriage, have mitigated this ethic. Even the Ḥanafī school, which has produced legal doctrine substantially increasing the vulnerability of married women to domestic abuse, has recognized the legal validity of these contractual provisions. Moreover, in the modern period, even traditional Islamic religious rhetoric has itself taken a turn toward egalitarianism, even if it has not embraced gender blindness as a norm within the family.

Islamic religious and legal tradition thus gives broad support to a robust system of family law pluralism. The dynamic aspect of religious understandings of marriage and gender, as well as Islamic law's support for individualized marriage contracts, further support the notion that orthodox Muslims have sufficient Islamic resources to generate both religious and legal norms of family law that are consistent with politically liberal limits on family law pluralism. The next section discusses why orthodox Muslims may find a politically liberal system of family law to be normatively attractive, even if it might foreclose some kinds of legitimately Islamic families.

V. THE ATTRACTIVENESS OF A POLITICALLY LIBERAL FAMILY LAW TO MUSLIMS

Because of Islamic law's distinction between a legitimate rule of law and moral truth, an orthodox Muslim's decision as to whether she can comply in good faith with non-Islamic norms will entail two judgments: First, whether the conduct demanded of her would require her to act in a manner that is sinful, and second, whether she is required to endorse a doctrine that she believes to be false.[98] This Islamic reticence [186] to endorse false metaphysical reasoning suggests that political liberalism's agnosticism with respect to the truth of various non-political metaphysical doctrines makes it more palatable to orthodox Muslims than a "Christian" or "Jewish" or a "Judaeo-Christian" state (or even a state based on a comprehensive secular philosophy for that matter), despite the many shared practical norms that Judaism or Christianity have with Islam but some

98. Fadel, "The True, the Good and the Reasonable," 58 n.234; Andrew F. March, "Islamic Foundations for a Social Contract in Non-Muslim Liberal Democracies," *American Political Science Review* 101:2 (May 2007): 235–252, 251 (stating that for Muslims, "the *rhetoric* employed by a state ... is crucial—are Muslims being asked to *profess* something contrary to Islam or even to endure quietly the glorification of a contrary truth?" [italics in original]).

of whose metaphysical foundations Muslims find objectionable. Because political liberalism only requires Muslims to endorse non-Islamic conceptions on political rather than metaphysical grounds, nothing more is at stake from the perspective of an orthodox Muslim than the political recognition of non-Muslim marriages, something not fundamentally different from premodern Islamic law's recognition of non-Islamic marriages on political but not moral grounds.[99] Political liberalism's refusal to endorse any specific metaphysical foundation for the family, provided it continues to do so, has the potential of solving many Islamic objections to features of contemporary family law in the United States and Canada.

A few examples may clarify why orthodox Muslims could find the metaphysical neutrality of a politically liberal family law attractive. Consider the historical prohibition on polygamy in common law jurisdictions.[100] Numerous reasons have been advanced to justify the historical ban on polygamy in common law jurisdictions, some of which could be viewed as implicitly racist.[101] Some common law courts asserted that polygamy is socially dangerous as evidenced by its draconian punishment in common law,[102] is politically incompatible with democracy,[103] and is contrary to the norm of "Christendom."[104] Given the strong historical connection between the teachings of Christianity and the common law's regulation of the family,[105] it ought to be no surprise that Muslims may consider the prohibition [187] of polygamy to be a reflection more of religious policy than the views of a neutral lawmaker. Orthodox Muslims could hardly be expected to endorse a ban on polygamy on the historical grounds articulated by these common law courts because to

99. 2 Ibn Nujaym, *al-Nahr al-Fāʾiq Sharḥ Kanz al-Daqāʾiq*, 283–284.

100. The anti-polygamy provisions of the common law took an especially extreme form in South Africa, where the legal system refuses to recognize the validity of any marriage that is "potentially polygamous" even if the marriage is in fact monogamous. Rashida Manjoo, "Legislative Recognition of Muslim Marriages in South Africa," *International Journal of Legal Information* 32 (Summer 2004): 271–282, 276. See also Johan D. van der Vyver, "Multi-Tiered Marriages in South Africa," in *Marriage and Divorce in a Multi-Cultural Context*, edited by Joel Nichols (New York: Cambridge University Press, 2011), pp. 200–218

101. *Reynolds v. United States*, 98 U.S. 145, 164 (1878) (describing polygamy as a practice that is "odious among the northern and western nations of Europe" and that is "almost exclusively a feature of the life of Asiatic and of African people").

102. Ibid., 165 (stating that English law, and later the laws of her American colonies, including Virginia, punished bigamy and polygamy with death).

103. Ibid., 165–166 (quoting an expert for the proposition that polygamy leads to "stationary despotism," whereas monogamy prevents it).

104. *Hyde v. Hyde and Woodmansee*, L.R. 1 P&D 130, 133 (HL) (1866) (stating that "marriage, as understood in Christendom, may for this purpose be defined as the voluntary union of life of one man and one woman, to the exclusion of all others").

105. *Reynolds*, 98 US at 165 (stating that "ecclesiastical [courts] were supposed to be the most appropriate for the trial of matrimonial causes and offences against the rights of marriage"); see also Nichols, "Multi-Tiered Marriage," 142–147 (discussing influence of Roman Catholic and Anglican churches in the substance of American family law).

do so would require them to abandon their belief that the Quran is an inerrant source of moral truth.[106] Muslims could, however, endorse legal regulation or even prohibition of polygamy if the justification for such a ban was morally "neutral," that is, it did not condemn polygamy as morally odious or inherently degrading to women but instead justified the regulation or prohibition of polygamy on the grounds that it unjustifiably injured the interests of children, that the ex-ante availability of polygamy inefficiently raised barriers to marriage, or that it prevented women in polygamous marriages from enjoying equal rights as a citizen.[107]

Another problematic example from the perspective of an orthodox Muslim would be the definition of marriage included in "covenant marriage" legislation appearing in certain U.S. jurisdictions. In Louisiana, for example, a couple who desires to choose covenant marriage must "solemnly declare that marriage is a covenant between a man and a woman who agree to live together as husband and wife for so long as they both may live."[108] This conception of marriage, to the ears of an orthodox Muslim, smacks of a legislative endorsement of a peculiarly *Christian* ideal of marriage as a lifelong commitment between one man and one woman.[109] If the [188] justification of covenant marriage, however, were more along the lines suggested by Professors Robert and Elizabeth Scott—a

---

106. According to orthodox interpreters, the Quran expressly allows a qualified form of polygamy. Quran, *Al-Nisāʾ*, 4:3 ("So marry women as you please, two, three or four, but if you fear that you will not be just [among them] then [marry only] one.").

107. See Mohammad H. Fadel, "Public Reason as a Strategy for Principled Reconciliation: The Case of Islamic Law and International Human Rights Law," *Chicago Journal of International Law* 8 (Summer 2007): 1–20. See also Rawls, "The Idea of Public Reason Revisited," 779 (stating that the prohibition of polygamy must be justified solely in terms of women's rights as citizens and not in terms of the value of monogamy as such). The fact that such arguments are consistent with public reason does not necessarily mean that they are persuasive. For an argument that a liberal political order can tolerate polygamy, see Andrew F. March, "Is There a Right to Polygamy? Marriage, Equality and Subsidizing Families in Liberal Public Justification," *Journal of Moral Philosophy* 8(2) (2011): 244–270.

108. La. Rev. Stat. Ann. § 9:273(A)(1) (2006). On the relationship of religion to covenant marriage, see Nichols, "Multi-Tiered Marriage," 147–152. See Katherine Shaw Spaht, "Covenant Marriage Laws: A Model for Compromise," in *Marriage and Divorce in a Multi-Cultural Context*, edited by Joel Nichols (New York: Cambridge University Press, 2011), pp. 120–137.

109. Since the middle ages, Muslims have identified the conception of marriage as a lifelong relationship as a specifically Christian conception of marriage as distinguished from that of Sunni Islam, which characterized the relationship as one of indefinite duration. See, e.g., 2 Abu Isḥāq al-Shāṭibī, *al-Muwāfaqāt fī Uṣūl al-Sharīʿa* (Cairo: al-Maktaba al-Tijāriyya al-Kubrā, 1975), 389 (stating that permanence, even if it is one of the legal goals of marriage, is not a necessary element of a lawful marriage in Islam; and rejecting the requirement of permanence in marriage as an unreasonable restraint [*taḍyīq*]). See also ibid., 398–399. D.S. D'Avray provides a compelling historical account of the relationship between Christian metaphysical conceptions of the relationship of the Church to Jesus Christ and the historical origins of the legal doctrine of marriage indissolubility in the Latin middle ages in *Medieval Marriage: Symbolism and Society* (Oxford: Oxford University Press, 2005).

means to allow couples to opt out of the no-fault regime in order to encourage greater marital-specific investments by prospective spouses—then no theological norms from an Islamic perspective would be implicated.[110]

The implicit norm of marital permanence that still infuses much of current family law does not simply amount to an expressive injury to Muslims that can be dismissed as lacking practical consequence;[111] the historical ideal of marital permanence, despite its clear sectarian roots in Christian theology and despite lip service to the ideal of the "clean break" following the adoption of no-fault divorce, continues to have a profound impact on the law of spousal support as evidenced by the continued salience of "need" in fashioning spousal support awards.[112] Need-based spousal support awards broadly conflict with Islamic conceptions of maintenance obligations in numerous respects. The most significant area of conflict is the gender-blind approach to the law of spousal support, for a wife never has an obligation to support her husband in Islamic law—and if she does support him, she has the right to treat such support as a debt for which she can demand repayment.[113] Moreover, although a wife could agree to forego her present right to maintenance in favor of supporting herself from her own property, or to forgive accrued maintenance debts,[114] she cannot prospectively waive her right to maintenance because Islamic law deems such a condition repugnant to an essential term [189] of the marriage contract—the husband's duty to provide support.[115] In the secular law of the United States and Canada, however, a Muslim wife can find herself saddled with both her

110. Elizabeth S. Scott and Robert E. Scott, "Marriage as a Relational Contract," *Virginia Law Review* 84 (October 1998): 1225–1334, 1331–1332.

111. In cases involving religious sentiment, sometimes expressive injury simpliciter is the greatest injury imaginable. See, e.g., Martha C. Nussbaum, "India: Implementing Sex Equality Through Law," *Chicago Journal of International Law* 2 (Spring 2001): 35–58, 44–45 (describing the tone in the opinion of the Shah Bano case as "contemptuous" of Islam, with the result that large segments of the Indian Muslim community abandoned previous openness to greater gender egalitarianism).

112. See, e.g., Carol Rogerson, "The Canadian Law of Spousal Support," *Family Law Quarterly* 38 (Spring 2004): 69–110, 71–73 (describing persistence of "need" as basis for spousal support orders in Canada decades after the no-fault divorce revolution rendered traditional justifications of alimony obsolete); *Divorce Act*, R.S.C. 1985 c. 3 (2nd Supp.), § 15.2(4) (requiring Canadian courts, in fashioning a spousal support order, to take into account the "needs ... of each spouse"); *Uniform Marriage and Divorce Act* § 308, 9A U.L.A. (West 2008) (permitting court to grant an order for maintenance to either spouse based on the spouse's need). The sectarian roots of marital permanence as an ideal receives further circumstantial support in the historical split between European and Middle Eastern Jewry's approaches to family law. See Michael J. Broyde, "New York's Regulation of Jewish Marriage: Covenant, Contract, or Statute?," in *Marriage and Divorce in a Multi-Cultural Context*, edited by Joel Nichols (New York: Cambridge University Press, 2011), pp. 138–163.

113. See 4 al-Mawwāq, *al-Tāj wa al-iklīl*, 193.

114. 2 Aḥmad b. Muḥammad al-Ṣāwī, *Bulghat al-Sālik* (on the margin of 2 al-Dardīr, *al-Sharḥ al-Ṣaghīr*), 385–386.

115. Ibid., 386.

equitable share of the marital household's debts at divorce and also a prospective obligation to provide financial support to her ex-husband in circumstances where she is better prepared for life post-divorce than her husband.[116]

These contradictory outcomes in spousal support (between the default civil law of an equitable distribution or a community property scheme and the default rules under Islamic family law) create an opportunity for strategic forum shopping on the part of both Muslim spouses. Such post hoc strategic behavior, relative to a Muslim couple's ex ante expectations regarding their economic rights and obligations by virtue of their marriage under Islamic law, is most acute in circumstances where the wife is saddled with household liabilities, prospective support obligations, or both. It is also present, however, when the Muslim wife is the beneficiary of the jurisdiction's default laws, particularly with respect to a claim for prospective support on the basis of need.

The basic norm of gender blindness with respect to distribution of the economic burdens and benefits of the marriage derives from the liberal conception of marriage as a community based on sharing.[117] Such a norm of spousal sharing in an intact marriage is consistent with Islamic law and Islamic religious teaching, but Islamic law does not apply the same norms at dissolution. Instead, Islamic law assumes that the divorcing parties maintain separate "accounts" for their property, and it is the task of the court to determine precisely the "contents" of each spouse's account at dissolution, with no right of redistribution of those assets between the spouses. To illustrate, consider Islamic Law's treatment of the bride's dowry (*mahr* or *ṣadāq*) and her trousseau (*jihāz* or *shuwār*). The former is a gift from the husband to the wife at the time the parties agree to marry, whereas the latter is a gift from the bride's parents to the bride at the time of her marriage. Both are legally the bride's property,[118] but while the marriage remains intact, Islamic law states that her individual ownership right to both the dowry and the trousseau is qualified. For example, a bride is customarily obligated to bring to the marital home a trousseau commensurate with the size of the dowry she received from her husband.[119] This is because the groom has the right to use the bride's trousseau in an intact marriage, even though it is nominally her exclusive property.[120] Only upon the dissolution of the marriage does the wife receive unfettered control of her dowry and trousseau.

[190] The fact that Islamic law has its own conception of the requirements of distributive justice at dissolution does not in itself explain why orthodox Muslims should object to the application of a different civil norm, given that Islamic law generally does not object to positive legislation unless it commands disobedience to God. The issue, rather,

116. American Law Institute, *Principles of the Law of Family Dissolution* § 4.09(1) (2002).
117. See Frantz and Dagan, "Properties of Marriage."
118. Rapoport, *Marriage, Money and Divorce*, 14–15.
119. 2 al-Dardīr, *al-Sharḥ al-Ṣaghīr*, 382–384
120. Ibid., 735.

is that although compliance with the secular command to redistribute assets from one spouse to another may not be morally problematic for the spouse from whom assets are being redistributed (because it does not command disobedience to God), the recipient spouse may not be morally entitled to bring such a claim based on her subjective Islamic conception of justice. Orthodox Muslim spouses will thus recognize that there are potential conflicts at divorce between the default civil laws regarding marital assets and their private Islamic conceptions of what constitutes a just distribution. They will individually need to consider whether these material differences are consistent with their Islamic conceptions of justice. There are three possible responses from the recipient spouse: (1) *No Conflict*: The recipient spouse believes in good faith that the jurisdiction's default norms are consistent with Islamic norms of justice and thus can present his or her legal claims consistent with his or her subjective Islamic ethical commitments; (2) *Conflict with Opt-Out* : The recipient spouse believes that the jurisdiction's default rules are inconsistent with his or her Islamic conception of justice, and thus he or she does not make a claim to his or her full "legal" entitlement, resulting in such a Muslim spouse opting into an Islamic distributive scheme, even though it makes him or her economically worse off than he or she would have been under the jurisdiction's rules; and (3) *Strategic Opt-In*: The recipient spouse believes that the jurisdiction's default rules are inconsistent with his or her Islamic conception of justice, but because the jurisdiction's default laws would make him or her better off, he or she chooses to apply the jurisdiction's rules in contradiction to his or her own conception of what justice requires out of self-interest.

These last two cases illustrate that because of the potential conflict between a jurisdiction's default norms and those of Islamic law, orthodox Muslims have an important ethical stake in the debate on family law pluralism. However, orthodox Muslims can resolve the conflict by endorsing a form of family law pluralism that allows an opt-out of generally applicable civil norms and a precommitment to an Islamic conception of distributive justice. A more general delegation of powers to religious authorities, even if such authorities could be conclusively identified would be both unnecessary and undesirable—both from an Islamic perspective (because such authorities could impose their own subjective understandings of Islamic norms on the parties) and from a politically liberal perspective (because it would make citizens' rights contingent on their religious community). As a further rationale for this position, historical experience suggests that when Muslims find themselves as a minority and are governed by a mandatory system of Islamic family law, the integrity [191] of Islamic family law becomes fused with the minority's Islamic identity, making it more difficult to achieve internal reform of Islamic family law.

Binding arbitration agreements executed in advance of marital breakdown are perhaps the most and maybe even the only effective means of giving orthodox Muslims who worry about the possibility of strategic behavior a way to solve this problem. Binding arbitration agreements also have the potential to solve the particular problems facing Muslim women who obtain a civil divorce but are unable to procure an Islamic divorce from their husbands.[121] In such a case, an orthodox Muslim woman might not believe she is eligible for remarriage, especially if her Muslim husband openly denies having divorced her Islamically. Or, even if she believes she is eligible to remarry, some consequential proportion of her religious community may not recognize her divorce as valid, therefore creating a substantial obstacle to her ability to remarry. Unlike Jewish law, Islamic law (except for the Ḥanafīs) provides a remedy for women whose husbands refuse to divorce them: a judicial divorce. Because an Islamic court is theologically empowered to resolve morally controversial cases, a judgment from an Islamic court that a woman is divorced conclusively establishes her legal and moral entitlements within the Muslim community. In the absence of the establishment of Islamic courts in liberal jurisdictions, only arbitration conducted pursuant to Islamic law can fulfill this important function of generating moral certainty. Indeed, from a purely religious perspective, it is critical that the law assures specific performance of a Muslim couples' obligation to appear at arbitration even if the jurisdiction is unwilling to respect the results of the arbitration.[122]

Contemporary family law in Canada and the United States already largely provides a structure that should enable orthodox Muslims to opt out of conflicting family law provisions,[123] including affording them the right to arbitrate their family [192] law disputes (with the exception of Ontario and Quebec).[124] Given the flexibility of Islamic family law in both legal doctrine and its recognition of parties' right to depart from the default terms of the marriage contract, one cannot assume that orthodox Muslims would not contract Islamic marriages and regulate the legal incidents of their dissolution (using

121. Compare the situation in Jewish law with obtaining a *get*, described in Broyde, "New York's Regulation."

122. See, e.g., 4 al-Dardīr, *al-Sharḥ al-Ṣaghīr*, 199 (stating that an arbitrator cannot rule against an absent party).

123. See, e.g., ALI *Principles of the Law of Family Dissolution* § 7.04 (permitting parties to use premarital agreements to opt out of default state law marital property distribution principles if procedural requirements are met); ibid., § 7.09(2) (separation agreements); *Uniform Premarital Agreement Act* § 6 (2001) (providing for the enforcement of premarital agreements subject to certain requirements); *Canadian Divorce Act* § 9(2) (1968) (encouraging parties to "negotiate[e] ... the matters that may be the subject of a support order"); *Family Law Act*, R.S.O. 1990, c. F.3, § 2(10) (2006) (making provisions of Ontario Family Law Act subject to parties' agreement "unless this Act provides otherwise") and § 52(1) (permitting marital parties to contractually regulate "their respective rights and obligations under the marriage or on separation"); and Carol Rogerson, "Case Comment: *Miglin v. Miglin* 2003 SCC 24 'They Are Agreements Nonetheless,'" *Canadian Journal of Family Law* 20 (2003): 197–228. Compare the chapters by Brian H. Bix, "Pluralism and Decentralization in Marriage Regulation," in *Marriage and Divorce in a Multi-Cultural Context*, edited by Joel Nichols (New York: Cambridge University Press, 2011), pp. 60–77 and Ann Laquer Estin, "Unofficial Family Law," in *Marriage and Divorce in a Multi-Cultural Context*, edited by Joel Nichols (New York: Cambridge University Press, 2011), pp. 92–119.

124. But see Bakht, "Were Muslim Barbarians Really Knocking on the Gates of Ontario?," 80–81 (suggesting that arbitration of family law disputes pursuant to religious norms is still permitted in Ontario despite the *Family Law Amendment Act* of 2005 that purported to prohibit such arbitrations).

binding arbitration) in a manner that would inevitably violate the limits of a politically liberal regime's mandatory law. In other words, state enforcement of binding family law arbitration agreements (subject to the state's right to confirm that such arbitration agreements were validly entered into and that the results of such arbitrations do not violate public policy) should be sufficient to meet orthodox Muslims' religious commitments with respect to family law within a politically liberal polity. A liberal regime should also be satisfied that its public policy boundaries are sufficient to police such arbitral awards.

This does not mean that orthodox Muslims might not have legitimate complaints regarding certain details of the actual rules in particular jurisdictions (rather than the rules of an idealized politically liberal family law). For example, given the role the state has assigned to intact couples for the distribution of various public benefits, the state may be justified in refusing to recognize polygamous unions for these distributive purposes.[125] This would not, however, at least in circumstances where there has been a broad deregulation of consensual sexual relations between adults, justify the continued criminalization of polygamy or punishment of an officiant of such a marriage.[126] Similarly, Muslims can legitimately criticize the continued incorporation of need in spousal support determinations, despite its theoretical inconsistency with no-fault divorce, as a tacit endorsement of a sectarian view of marriage as a lifelong commitment.[127]

[193] As the outcome of the Sharīᶜa Arbitration controversy in Ontario and the continued controversy regarding Islamic family law arbitration in the United Kingdom[128]

---

125. Mary Anne Case, "Marriage Licenses," *Minnesota Law Review* 89 (June 2005): 1758–1797, 1783.

126. Polygamy is prohibited by statute in both the United States and Canada. See, e.g., N.Y. Penal Law § 255.15 (2008) (criminalizing bigamy and classifying it as a class E felony); R.S.C. 1985, c. C-46, § 290 (criminalizing bigamy). Canada also punishes any person who "celebrates, assists or is a party to a rite, ceremony, contract or consent that purports to sanction a [polygamous] relationship." R.S.C. 1985, c. C-46, § 293(1). Aiding and abetting liability might apply to reach a similar result in U.S. jurisdictions, at least according to some nineteenth-century cases. See, e.g., *Boggus v. State*, 34 Ga. 275 (1866). Other features of Canadian law, however, are quite permissive with respect to polygamous unions, such as recognizing the validity of polygamous marriages if they were contracted in a jurisdiction that recognizes polygamous marriages. R.S.O. 1990 c. F3, § 1(2). Likewise, the Family Law Act's definition of "spouse" can result in a person having numerous spouses for support purposes. See Marion Boyd, *Dispute Resolution in Family Law: Protecting Choice, Promoting Inclusion* (December 2004), 24, available at https://web.archive.org/web/20050917203820/http://www.attorneygeneral.jus.gov.on.ca/english/about/pubs/boyd/fullreport.pdf (link updated May 28, 2023).

127. Recognizing the anomalous nature of need-based spousal support orders, the ALI's proposed *Principles of the Law of Family Dissolution* expressly seeks to substitute "*compensation for loss* rather than *relief of need*" (italics in original) as the justification for post-divorce spousal support orders. ALI Principles of the Law of Family Dissolution, § 5.02, comment a. Unlike need, "compensation for loss" is broadly consistent with Islamic conceptions of distributive justice, and for that reason their adoption as law in the United States would result in a law of spousal support that would be more consistent with both public reason and Islamic law.

128. See Ayelet Shachar, "Faith in Law? Diffusing Tensions Between Diversity and Equality," in *Mar-*

reveal, the recognition of Islamic family law arbitration remains extremely contentious. The next section will use the example of New York and how its courts have monitored family law arbitrations conducted pursuant to orthodox Jewish law to demonstrate the practical ability of courts in a liberal jurisdiction to ensure that the results of religious arbitrations are consistent with public policy and individuals' rights as citizens. The success of New York in this regard ought to dispel much of the reasonable (and not irrational) concern that family law arbitration conducted pursuant to Islamic law could systematically deprive individuals of their rights.

VI. FAMILY LAW ARBITRATION, RELIGIOUS LAW, AND PUBLIC POLICY: THE CASE OF NEW YORK

As stated previously, arbitration of family law disputes is conceptually consistent with the structure of a politically liberal family law. Because liberal family law must allow parties the right to opt out of at least some legal provisions out of respect for the parties' autonomy,[129] it is difficult to understand why arbitration of disputes within family law that are governed by permissive rather than mandatory law (e.g., division of marital assets and post-divorce support agreements) should be forbidden as a normative matter. If, however, there are practical reasons (e.g., the fear that the judicial system is incapable of ensuring that arbitrations are conducted in accordance with mandatory law, or that individuals who would make use of family law arbitration are ignorant of their rights), then these are defects in the background conditions of justice that should be, from a Rawlsian perspective, addressed directly rather than used as reasons to restrict an otherwise permissible liberty.

As a practical matter, arbitration also appears to be the most promising institutional tool for reconciling liberal and nonliberal conceptions of the family.[130] From [194] a liberal perspective, the permission to use arbitration to resolve family law disputes can only

---

riage and Divorce in a Multi-Cultural Context, edited by Joel Nichols (New York: Cambridge University Press, 2011), pp. 341–356.

129. The recent Canadian Supreme Court decision of *Bruker v. Marcovitz* , [2007] 3. S.C.R. 607, 2007 SCC 54, gives support to the notion that religiously motivated contracts, to the extent that they are valid contracts, are equally amenable to enforcement under Canadian law as a contract entered into with a secular motive.

130. The procedures governing the enforceability of an arbitrator's orders provide a practical mechanism for creating a dialogue between the mandatory norms of a liberal regime and the internal norms of a nonliberal community. See Patrick Macklem, "Militant Democracy, Legal Pluralism and the Paradox of Self-Determination," *International Journal of Constitutional Law* 4 (July 2006): 488–516, 512–513 (arguing for the need to initiate a "jurisprudential dialogue between [liberal] and Islamic legal orders, where the individual tenets of one system are tested against those of the other" rather than dismissing a commitment to the values of Islamic law as indicative of the wholesale rejection of democratic values).

be tolerated if it is not used to shield parties from the reach of family law's mandatory elements.[131] However, adherence to liberal principles of autonomy would seem to require a reviewing court to enforce an arbitrator's decision in permissive areas of family law to the same extent a reviewing court would enforce a private agreement between those parties covering the same issues.[132]

This is the path family law arbitration has taken in numerous decisions of New York courts involving disputes between Jewish couples who had submitted or agreed to submit some or all of their family law disputes to Jewish religious courts for resolution. The New York case law is clear that, as a threshold matter, a court is to determine whether the dispute is amenable to arbitration, that is, that the dispute does not involve some matter of mandatory public law.[133] Because matters such as division of marital assets and post-divorce spousal support are not, as a general matter, subject to public policy restraints, they are presumptively amenable to arbitration (provided the procedural requirements for a valid arbitration are met)[134] and an arbitrator's decision in these matters must be enforced.[135] Decisions regarding child custody are not amenable to arbitration, because that would violate mandatory public policy, which in New York requires a court to determine custody arrangements in the "best interests of the child."[136] New York courts also specifically enforce the obligation to arbitrate the dispute, even if the arbitration agreement provides for [195] religious norms to govern the arbitration.[137] More controversially, perhaps, they have refused to find that an agreement to arbitrate could be set

131. Gaudreault-DesBiens, "Limits of Private Justice," 18.

132. This is consistent with the Supreme Court of Canada's reasoning in *Miglin v. Miglin*, 1 S.C.R. 303, 2003 SCC 24 (2003), which upheld a spousal support agreement against a challenge that it was inconsistent with the terms of the Divorce Act by holding that vindicating the spouses' autonomy as reflected in their agreement takes precedence over the Divorce Act's provisions regarding spousal support.

133. *Glauber v. Glauber*, 192 A.D.2d 94, 96–97 (N.Y. App. Div. 1993).

134. *Stein v. Stein*, 707 N.Y.S.2d 754, 759 (N.Y. Sup. Ct. 1999) (declining to confirm arbitrator's order where there was no evidence that procedural requirements of the arbitration statute were satisfied); *Golding v. Golding*, 176 A.D.2d 20 (N.Y. App. Div. 1992) (refusing to enforce an arbitrator's award where the court found that the wife was compelled to participate as a result of the husband's threat to refuse to grant her a Jewish divorce).

135. *Hirsch v. Hirsch*, 37 N.Y.2d 312 (N.Y. 1975) (upholding agreement to arbitrate spousal support claims); *Hampton v. Hampton*, 261 A.D.2d 362, 363 (N.Y. App. Div. 1999); *Lieberman v. Lieberman* , 566 N.Y.S.2d 490 (N.Y. Sup. Ct. 1991).

136. *Glauber*, 192 A.D.2d at 97–98. New York courts, moreover, follow a principle of severance in the event that an arbitrator's decision included both permissible objects of arbitration and nonpermissible objects of arbitration. *Lieberman*, 566 N.Y.S.2d 490 (upholding decision of rabbinical tribunal granting a religious divorce, dividing marital assets, and awarding child support, but vacating order for joint parental custody).

137. *Avitzur v. Avitzur* , 446 N.E.2d 136 (N.Y. 1983) (upholding order compelling husband to appear before a rabbinic tribunal pursuant to an agreement contained in his *ketubah*, a Jewish religious marriage contract).

aside on the grounds of duress where a woman was subjected to the threat of "shame, scorn, ridicule and public ostracism" by the members of her religious community if she did not agree to participate in the arbitration.[138] In short, the jurisprudence of New York courts with respect to family law arbitration seems to be to enforce agreements to arbitrate and to enforce the results of such proceedings to the same extent that the court would enforce the parties' own private agreements.

This approach of New York courts (policing arbitral results on a case-by-case basis for conformity with public policy and only striking down those elements of an order that actually violate public policy) is consistent with Rawls's conception of a politically liberal family law: This approach understands that the function of public law in the context of the family is to ensure that the internal governance of the family does not deprive any of its members of their fundamental rights as citizens, and as long as that condition is satisfied a family should enjoy autonomy. The approach contrasts with the categorical approach taken by Ontario, which simply states that an arbitrator's decision, if it is based on non-Canadian law, violates public policy *simpliciter*, without a need to determine any actual substantive conflict between the arbitrator's decision and Ontarian law.[139]

Ontario law in this regard mimics the suggestion of Professor Gaudreault-DesBiens, who argues against a policy of legal recognition of arbitrators' awards in the context of family law while at the same time allowing believers to continue to submit their disputes to arbitrations.[140] Although he cites many reasons why he believes that legal recognition of arbitral decisions in the family law context is misguided and perhaps even dangerous,[141] Professor Gaudreault-DesBiens's primary argument is that because family law affects the status of the person, it raises "the potential application of constitutional values such as dignity and equality, over which the State may still legitimately insist upon retaining some normative monopoly."[142] Even though he recognizes that recognition of faith-based arbitration—whether based on Islam or [196] another religion—will not inevitably result in "outcomes that undermine the dignity or the equality of the individuals involved,"[143] he nevertheless concludes that nonrecognition is the best policy choice because it minimizes the risk that " fundamental constitutional values could be undermined."[144]

---

138. *Lieberman*, 566 N.Y.S.2d at 494.

139. *Family Law Act*, R.S.O. 1990, c. F.3, § 59.2(1)(b).

140. Gaudreault-DesBiens, "Limits of Private Justice," 23.

141. Ibid., 21 (recognition of faith-based arbitration in family law disputes could lead a minority group to demand "the creation of separate institutions exercising some form of *imperium* over a segment of the population" [italics in original]).

142. Ibid., 20. Compare McClain, "Marriage Pluralism in the United States," and Wilson, "The Perils of Privatized Marriage," concerning equality and the potential for negative outcomes in faith-based arbitration.

143. Gaudreult-DesBiens, "Limits of Private Justice," 20.

144. Ibid., 22.

Gaudreault-DesBiens's approach can best be described as a comprehensive liberal approach in which the boundaries of mandatory law—here the Canadian Charter of Rights and Freedoms—are applied to matters of family governance directly, rather than in the indirect fashion that Rawls endorsed. To the extent that Gaudreault-DesBiens justifies this approach on a controversial normative conception of equality, however, he is advocating the use of state power to impose a comprehensive rather than a political doctrine, and thus on Rawlsian terms, his proposal is unreasonable.[145] To the extent that his objections are prudential,[146] it is not clear why those prudential concerns should not be addressed directly instead of taking the drastic step of eliminating a normatively justified method for the resolution of family law disputes.[147]

VII. CONCLUSION

Muslims have a keen interest in preserving and even enhancing a pluralistic system of family law. Muslims are interested in maintaining a political system (and a family law) that is neutral with respect to both religious and secular comprehensive doctrines. Some kinds of family law pluralism, such as that implicit in the covenant marriage statutes, appear to endorse a sectarian religious understanding of marriage rather than foster a family law pluralism that is consistent with a metaphysically neutral family law. At the same time, a politically liberal family law along the lines Rawls describes is sufficiently respectful of family autonomy to permit orthodox Muslims to structure their family life within some (but not all) Islamic conceptions of the family. The current regime of family law in the United [197] States and Canada is broadly consistent with Rawls's conception that principles of justice apply to the family indirectly, especially to the extent that faith-based arbitration is permitted. Accordingly, within the bounds required by these principles, orthodox Muslims should have adequate resources to adjust their doctrines in a manner that is faithful to their own ethical commitments while also respecting the public values of a liberal democracy.

---

145. Rawls, *Political Liberalism*, 37 (stating that society cannot remain united on a version of liberalism without "the sanctions of state power," something he refers to as "the fact of oppression"). See also Cere, "Canadian Conjugal Mosaic" and Shachar, "Faith in Law?"

146. That is, based on the empirical conditions, whether there are particular defects in the Canadian legal system that make it implausible for Canadian courts to regulate arbitrations in the manner undertaken by New York courts or whether there are unique sociological circumstances involving the Canadian Muslim community that render its members particularly vulnerable to the involuntary loss of their rights in the context of arbitration.

147. Indeed, a former attorney general of Ontario, Marion Boyd, suggested a reform of the Arbitration Act that would preserve the right of religious arbitration while including greater procedural protections to ensure that the results of arbitrations would be consistent with Canadian law. See Boyd, *Dispute Resolution in Family Law*. See also Shachar, "Faith in Law?"

For these reasons, orthodox Muslims' interests in family law pluralism are better served through marginal reforms to the current family law regime (such as decriminalization of polygamy and replacement of spousal need with compensation for loss as a basis for post-divorce spousal awards) that render it closer to the Rawlsian ideal of neutrality in contrast to more robust proposals that would award religious institutions greater jurisdiction over family life. Even if the state were to cede such jurisdiction equally to all religious groups and thus ameliorate Muslims' concerns about the state endorsing a sectarian conception of marriage, orthodox Muslims in a liberal state would still worry about the state ceding power over family law to a Muslim religious institution. Because orthodox Islam is inherently pluralistic, the state would inevitably have to privilege one group of Muslims and their interpretation of Islam over another group, with the result that some otherwise permissible conceptions of family life (both from the perspective of political liberalism and Islam) could be excluded. Accordingly, arbitration of family law disputes, at least for Muslims, is an ideal institution. Because arbitration is essentially contractual and therefore voluntary from a political standpoint, it respects the autonomy of individual Muslims both as religious believers (against the views of other believers) and as citizens (by allowing them to opt out of general default rules). Arbitration does not, as its critics often assume, amount to a kind of delegation of state power to an imagined Muslim collectivity.

The most substantial fear in applying the New York model of state supervision of religiously motivated family law arbitration to Muslim communities may be that U.S. courts lack sufficient capacity regarding Islamic law to perform this task effectively.[148] As evidenced by the U.S. cases discussed by Linda McClain, American courts have reached wildly divergent interpretations of the meaning of the *mahr* (a sum paid or payable from the husband to the wife, which is included in the Islamic marriage contract).[149] More sinisterly, there is the risk that anti-Islam bias could infect judicial interpretations of Islamic law in a fashion that exacerbates [198] rather than reduces Muslim alienation from public law.[150] Arbitration reduces both of these problems. To the extent that disputes arising from Muslim marriages are resolved through arbitration rather than civil court proceedings, civil courts will avoid thorny issues arising out of the interpretation

---

148. Compare Estin, "Unofficial Family Law."

149. Different interpretations of the *mahr* reflect, in part, the strategic behavior of parties once they are involved in litigation. They are also a reflection of parties' conflation of cultural norms, Islamic law norms, and even legal confusion resulting from the fusion of Islamic and common law conceptions of divorce. See McClain, "Marriage Pluralism in the United States."

150. See, e.g., Mohammad Fadel, "German Judge and Legal Orientalism," March 29, 2007, [available at http://shanfaraa.com/2011/07/german-judge-and-legal-orientalism-originally-posted-march-29-2007/] formerly available at http://www.progressiveislam.org/german_judge_and_legal_orientalism (discussing the tendency of judges in Western jurisdictions to ascribe exotic positions to Islamic law based on its assumed "otherness").

of Islamic law. Questions that currently bedevil civil courts, such as the "true" meaning of *mahr*, whether *mahr* is a religious or legal obligation, or whether a woman who initiates divorce is entitled to retain her *mahr*, would simply be moot in a proceeding for the enforcement of an arbitral award.

Although Muslim communities in the United States and Canada have much work to do if they wish to transform the premodern Islamic legal tradition into a workable body of rules that satisfies the requirements of political liberalism, some of the structural features of Islamic family law will be especially helpful in this regard. The first is the contractual nature of the marital relationship. Orthodox Muslim communities could prepare standard premarital agreements, for example, that are drafted to conform to both the requirements of the local jurisdiction and Islamic law.[151] The second is more doctrinal: Building on the notion that a woman is generally not obligated to contribute to the economic welfare of the household, Islamic law could take the view that contributions by the wife to the household remain debts unless the husband proves that she intended them to be gifts. This change, even though doctrinally marginal (essentially consisting of only a shift in the burden of proof), would substantially enhance a traditional wife's economic position within the family while also respecting Islamic law's policy of treating intrahousehold transfers within an intact marriage as undertaken in a spirit of liberality rather than expectation of profit.

At the same time, one should not underestimate the possibility that large numbers of Muslims—even religiously committed Muslims—will accept the default norms of applicable family law as consistent with their religious values. Given the relative flexibility of liberal family law, as well as Islamic family law's general willingness to respect parties' agreements and its respect for intra-Muslim pluralism, it should not be surprising that even orthodox Muslims might not feel the need for substantial changes to the present family law regime. Viewed in this light, incidents such as the Sharīʿa Arbitration controversy overstate the tension between Islamic family law and that of a liberal regime. With hindsight, they may very well appear to have been little more than tempests in the proverbial teapot. Although it is of course possible that bad-faith religious fanaticism and deeply held anti-Muslim sentiments (or some [199] combination thereof) will come together again in the future to produce an even more noxious brew than was served in Ontario during the Sharīʿa Arbitration controversy, the example of New York shows quite clearly that liberal jurisdictions have sufficient resources to manage the interaction between religious and public norms. Hopefully, this lesson will be remembered the next time the issue of Islamic family law becomes a political football in a liberal jurisdiction.

151. Compare the discussion of Jewish agreements in Broyde, "New York's Regulation."

11
ADOPTION IN ISLAMIC LAW

Mohammad Fadel

[138] To speak of an Islamic law of adoption may strike some as an oddity or a radical doctrinal innovation. After all, it is well known that Islamic law prohibits adoption, at least insofar as it would entail a notion of fictive kinship. In this case, however, popular perceptions simplify, mask and distort a complex and subtle body of legal doctrine that deals with children of unknown parentage. By analyzing the legal rules articulated during the pre-Modern period which govern foundlings (s. *laqīṭ* / pl. *luqaṭā'*), this Part will (1) show that the Islamic law of foundlings functions as a near substitute for adoption and (2) point the way to a more robust set of rules that would be more friendly to quasi-adoptive relationships. It will proceed by describing in broad outline the principal doctrinal features governing [139] foundlings. This Part will then attempt to explain the doctrine as a result of a series of compromises among competing substantive values within the pre-modern legal system, not all of which could be simultaneously vindicated. Finally, it will conclude with a reassessment of the pre-modern jurists' interpretation of the foundational revelatory texts upon which they built their doctrines, thus pointing the way for a reformulation of Islamic law's prohibition of adoption.

A. BASIC DOCTRINE

Certain well-known facts within the Islamic legal tradition buttress the notion that Islam categorically prohibits adoption. First, the revelatory sources of Islamic law, the Qur'ān and the Prophetic traditions, seem to reject the notion that a person other than the biological parent of the child can be a parent to that child. Thus, in the case of mothers, the Qur'ān states "[t]heir mothers are only those who have given birth to them,"[261] and in the case of fathers, it states,

> "God did not make those whom you call your sons your sons [in reality]. That is no more than an expression from your mouths and God speaks the truth and He

This excerpt is Part III (pp. 732–752) of the article entitled "Classical Religious Perspectives of Adoption Law," *Notre Dame Law Review* vol. 79, no. 2, 2003–2004, pp. 138–158.

261. *Al-Mujādila* 58:2.

> guides to the [correct] way. Attribute them to their fathers: That is more just in the eyes of God, but if you know not the names of their fathers, then they are your brothers in faith and your dependents."[262]

In commenting upon this verse, exegetes were in agreement that the verse prohibits a man from adopting a child, at least where adoption is understood to entail the introduction of a fictive relationship of descent between the child and the adoptive father.[263]

Indeed, the verse's prohibition was first applied to the adopted son of the Prophet Muḥammad. The Prophet Muḥammad had a freed slave by the name of Zayd b. Ḥāritha, whom he chose to "adopt" (*tabannā*) prior to the advent of Islam.[264] As was the Arab custom of the pre-Islamic era, Muḥammad declared to his fellow tribesmen that he had adopted Zayd, and from that moment until this verse was revealed, he became known as Zayd, the son of Muḥammad, instead of Zayd, the son of Ḥāritha.[265] Adoption [140] according to pre-Islamic usage meant that, for all practical purposes, the adopted child and the adoptive father acceded to all the rights and obligations that were incident to a parent-child relationship, including rights of inheritance as well as obligations of mutual defense.[266] Upon the revelation of the verse that rejected this pre-Islamic practice, Zayd's name was restored to Zayd, son of Ḥāritha, but he remained a dependent (*mawlā*) of Muḥammad.[267] And, with the dissolution of the adoptive relationship between the two men, their mutual rights of inheritance also dissolved, as confirmed by the Qur'ān which states, "[with respect to] close relatives, some are more deserving than others under the command of God than the believers and the emigrants, except that you may choose to do good to your dependents."[268]

The verses in Qur'ān 33:4–5 could suggest on one reading that as between a stranger and the biological father, the biological father will always have a superior claim to being the legal father of the child. Islamic jurists, however, did not adopt this reading, for the legal designation of father in Islamic law was not solely a biological matter. Instead, fatherhood derived from the concept of legitimate sexual intercourse—a man could not become the "father" of a child unless the child was the product of lawful intercourse—and thus combined a presumption of biological descent with the requirement of a legal

---

262. *Al-Aḥzāb* 33:4–5.

263. See, e.g., 14 Muḥammad b. Aḥmad al-Qurṭubī, *al-Jāmi' li-aḥākm al-Qur'ān* 118–19 (1967); 3 Abū al-Qāsim Maḥmūd b. 'Umar al-Zamakhsharī, *al-Kashshāf 'an ḥaqā'iq al-tanzīl wa 'uyūn al-aqāwīl wa wujūh al-ta'wīl* 225–26 (n.d.).

264. 14 al-Qurṭubī, *supra* note 263, at 118–19; 3 al-Zamakhsharī, *supra* note 263, at 225–26.

265. 14 al-Qurṭubī, *supra* note 263, at 118–19; 3 al-Zamakhsharī, *supra* note 263, at 225–226.

266. 14 al-Qurṭubī, *supra* note 263, at 119.

267. 3 al-Zamakhsharī, *supra* note 263, at 227.

268. *Al-Aḥzāb* 33:6.

marriage.[269] This rule was based on a report attributed to the Prophet where two men came to him, disputing the custody of an orphaned child.[270] One claimed as the brother of the deceased biological father, while the other claimed the child in his capacity as the heir of the master who owned the child's mother. The Prophet is reported to have ruled in this case that "[t]he child belongs to the bed, and the male adulterer gets nothing."[271] Muslim jurists applied this principal—that the male adulterer gets nothing—to prohibit adulterous males from subsequently gaining status as the legal "father" of the child.[272] Thus, even if an adulterous male married the mother of his child, he would [141] not become the legal father of a child illicitly conceived.[273] Accordingly, the Islamic "prohibition" on adoption is a result of the interaction of two principles: first, that a male adulterer has no rights in a child born of an illicit relationship,[274] and second, that a stranger to the child cannot, by mere social convention, accede to the legal rights and responsibilities of the child's legal father.[275]

B. THE LAW OF FOUNDLINGS AS A SUBSTITUTE LAW OF ADOPTION

Given the social stigma of illegitimacy in medieval Muslim societies, it is not an unreasonable assumption that most children who were conceived outside of wedlock were aban-

---

269. See infra notes 270–75 and accompanying text.

270. 12 Aḥmad b. ʿAlī b. Ḥajar al-ʿAsqalānī, *Fatḥ al-bārī Sharḥ ṣaḥīḥ al-Bukhārī* 36 (1989).

271. 12 id. Although in this case the mother was a slave girl, and the child was ultimately awarded to the master's son, the same rule was also applied to marriages, with the legal husband being entitled to the child, even if the child was in fact a result of an adulterous relationship.

272. See *infra* note 273.

273. This principle was embodied in the maxim that "the sperm of adultery is of no standing" (*mā' al-zinā muhdar*). Other rules reinforced this prohibition. For example, adulterous couples were required to wait three months (*istibrā' al-zinā*) from the last day in which they had intercourse prior to marrying to ensure that any child born to them was conceived as a result of lawful intercourse. Mālikīs and Ḥanafīs, for example, interpreted revelation as prohibiting any relationship of descent between the adulterous father and his illegitimate offspring (*al-sharʿ qaṭaʿa nasabahu ʿan al-zānī*). 3 Muḥammad al-Kharshī, *Sharḥ mukhtaṣar Khalīl li-l-Kharshī* pt. 2, at 101 (n.d.); see also 17 Muḥammad b. Aḥmad al-Sarakhsī, *al-Mabsūṭ* 154 (1993) ("When a man commits adultery with a woman who gives birth as a result thereof, and the male adulterer claims [paternity of] the child, no parent-child relationship is established because of the absence of a licit relationship.").

274. In contrast to the rule depriving the adulterous male of any rights in the child, the adulterous female is given the status of legal mother of any child born of an adulterous relationship. See 17 al-Sarakhsī, *supra* note 273, at 154–55.

275. These could be significant, including, inter alia, the right to receive financial support from the child upon the father's incapacity and need as well as the right to inherit from the child if she predeceased the father. Conversely, paternity was also a source of monetary liability, as the father was responsible to provide for his children during their minority, and was required to answer monetarily for their torts, even after their emancipation.

doned at birth. Indeed ancient Mālikī texts explicitly differentiated between a child who is abandoned at birth, presumably as a result of the stigma associated from adultery, and one abandoned by his lawful parents as a result of straitened circumstances in the hope that others better able to provide for her would find her and take care of her.[276] These ancient authorities, therefore, reserved the term *manbūdh* for the former category, whereas they limited the term *laqīṭ* to the [142] latter.[277] Whether the foundling was illegitimate or legitimate, however, was immaterial from the perspective of Islamic law, and to a significant extent, there was broad agreement among the various Sunnī schools of law regarding the mutual relationships of the foundling, the rescuer (*al-multaqiṭ*), and the state.[278]

In this respect, three doctrinal principles were virtually universally recognized by Muslim jurists in the Middle Ages. First, caring for foundlings was legally obligatory (*wājib*), but the obligation was societal (*farḍ kifāya*), not individual, unless (1) the child was found in a life-threatening situation, or (2) a person voluntarily took custody of the foundling. In the first case, the person so finding her becomes individually obliged to take custody of the child and care for her. In the second case, the caregiver remains individually obliged to tend to the child's needs until: (1) another caregiver (*kāfil*) is found; (2) the child reaches the age of majority and is able to fend for himself; or (3) in the case of a female, the foundling marries.[279] Second, the rescuer, while he could become the caregiver of the child, could not become the legal parent of the foundling simply by virtue of caring for the child. Accordingly, the financial rights, e.g., inheritance (*irth*), and obligations, e.g., maintenance (*nafaqa*) and insurance (*'aql*), that are incident to parenthood in the case of the foundling devolve upon the state.[280] Third, a foundling was free, and in the absence of compelling evidence, could not be enslaved.[281] A closer look at these three doctrines is in order.

C. DEFINITION OF THE FOUNDLING AND THE OBLIGATION TO CARE FOR FOUNDLINGS

The various schools of Muslim jurisprudence[282] were in general [143] agreement regarding the definition of the foundling. The Mālikīs defined the foundling as "a lost child of

276. See 6 Muḥammad b. Muḥammad al-Ḥaṭṭāb, *Mawāhib al-jalīl li-sharḥ mukhtaṣar Khalīl* 299 (n.d.).

277. 6 id.

278. See *infra* notes 283–301 and accompanying text.

279. See, e.g., 4 al-Kharshī, *supra* note 273, pt. 1, at 130 ("Caring for the abandoned child and maintaining her are legal obligations of her rescuer until she reaches the age of majority and becomes independent.").

280. See *infra* notes 302–19 and accompanying text.

281. See *infra* note 320 and accompanying text.

282. Islamic law has been cited as a classic example of a "jurists' law." Prior to the nineteenth century, Muslim legal scholars developed a vast legal literature that set forth applicable rules of ritual law,

unknown parentage."[283] The Ḥanbalīs defined the foundling as "a child, up to the age of discernment, whose paternity (*nasab*) and [status as] slave [or free] are unknown, who has been abandoned, or is lost."[284] The Shāfi'īs' definition included all abandoned children who have not reached the age of majority and have no caregiver.[285] The Ḥanafī definition states that "the foundling is a name for a baby, born alive, whose family has cast her aside, either out of fear of poverty or suspicion of adultery."[286] While not explicitly stated by all the jurists, abandonment of the child is a sinful act, while taking custody of the foundling is deemed an act of piety.[287]

Interestingly, the different schools of jurisprudence relied on different proof-texts in the Qur'ān to support the obligation to care for foundlings. The Ḥanbalīs and the Shāfi'īs

---

private law, constitutional law, and to a lesser extent, criminal law. One of the consequences of the centrality of scholarship in the development of Islamic law was the rise of "legal schools" that arose out of the teachings of particularly learned early authorities, all of whom died in the second and third Islamic centuries. Historically, four such schools came to dominate legal doctrine for Sunni Muslims: (1) the Ḥanafī school, named after Abū Ḥanīfa al-Nu'mān b. Thābit; (2) the Mālikī school, named after Mālik b. Anas; (3) the Shāfi'ī school, named after Muḥammad b. Idrīs al-Shāfi'ī; and (4) the Ḥanbalī school, named after Aḥmad b. Ḥanbal. Abū Ḥanīfa lived in Iraq and subsequently his teachings became the dominant legal school for Muslims living in Iraq, Eastern Europe, Central Asia, and the Indian subcontinent. Mālik b. Anas lived in the sacred city of Madīna, in the western Arabian province known as the Ḥijāz. His teachings became the dominant legal school throughout North and Sub-Saharan Africa, Islamic Spain, and Upper Egypt. Al-Shāfi'ī was born in Gaza, Palestine, and studied with the leading authorities of Madīna, including Mālik b. Anas, and Iraq, including the leading students of Abū Ḥanīfa. He finally settled and died in Egypt. His doctrines prevailed in Lower Egypt (including Cairo), much of Syria, Yemen, and in contemporary times, Southeast Asia and East Africa. Aḥmad b. Ḥanbal lived and taught in Baghdad, and his followers were limited primarily to that city as well as some Syrian cities. Followers of this school are numerically the least significant of the four Sunni schools of law, but it is the official school of law applied in the Kingdom of Saudi Arabia. For a general history of the formation of Muslim schools of law, see Christopher Melchert, *The Formation of the Sunni Schools of Law, 9th–10th Centuries C.E.* (1997).

283. 4 al-Kharshī, *supra* note 273, pt. 1, at 130. One commentator noted that whether or not the child's lineage is known is irrelevant to his status as a foundling. 'Alī al-'Adawī, *Ḥāshiyat al-'Adawī*, in 4 al-Kharshī, *supra* note 273, pt. 1, at 130 (margin comment).

284. 4 Manṣūr b. Yūnus b. Idrīs al-Buhūtī, *Kashshāf al-qinā' 'an matn al-iqnā'* 226 (1982) [hereinafter *al-Kashshāf*]. Many in the Ḥanbalī school permit a child to be treated as a foundling until she reaches the age of majority.

285. 5 Zakariyyā b. Muḥammad al-Anṣārī, *Asnā al-maṭālib sharḥ rawḍ al-ṭālib* 612 (Muḥammad Tāmir ed., 2001) [hereinafter *Asnā al-maṭālib*].

286. 5 Muḥammad b. Maḥmūd al-Bābartī, *al-'Ināya sharḥ al-hidāya*, in *Fatḥ al-Qadīr* 342 (1970) (margin comment).

287. See, e.g., 4 'Uthmān b. 'Alī al-Zayla'ī, *Tabyīn al-ḥaqā'iq sharḥ kanz al-daqā'iq* 200 (Aḥmad 'Ināya ed., 2000) ("[T]he one who takes custody of the foundling is rewarded, while the one who abandons him is a sinner.").

quote the general obligation to "cooperate [in all things] good and pious."[288] Similarly, the Qur'ān later states that [144] "whosoever saves a human life, it is as though he has saved humanity in its entirety," which was also cited as authority for the merits of caring for foundlings.[289] The Ḥanafīs also point to a report that during the reign of 'Alī b. Abī Ṭālib, the fourth Caliph and the Prophet Muḥammad's son-in-law, a man came to him with a foundling, and 'Alī said to him: "He is free, and I would rather have participated in his affairs to the same degree that you [have participated] than this, this, and this [i.e., a laundry list of pious acts]," thus demonstrating the great religious merit of caring for foundlings.[290] The Ḥanafīs also cited a tradition of the Prophet Muḥammad, in which he was reported to have excluded those who are cruel to children from the ranks of the Muslim community.[291]

The principal policy imperative giving rise to the obligation to rescue abandoned children was to save life. Thus, Ibn Rushd, an Andalusian Mālikī jurist, stated that "taking [custody] of a foundling is obligatory because were he to be left [in his condition], he would be lost and die."[292] Similarly, the Ḥanafī author of the *Tabyīn* notes that rescuing the foundling becomes an individual obligation of anyone who discovers the foundling in life-threatening circumstances.[293] The Shāfi'īs cite the same principal, e.g., saving life,[294] in support of the rule that rescuing a foundling who has been abandoned in life-threatening circumstances is obligatory. This is in contrast to their ruling that taking possession of lost property, while meritorious, is not a legal obligation. The two cases are distinguishable in that the law already provides individuals with sufficient incentives to take possession of lost or abandoned property, since in due course, finders might become the lawful owners of such property. In the case of abandoned children, however, no economic benefit will accrue to a rescuer, and thus introducing the threat of legal liability is appropriate.[295]

---

288. *Al-Mā'ida* 5:2. See, e.g., 6 Zakariyyā b. Muḥammad al-Anṣārī, *al-Ghurar al-bahiyya fī sharḥ manẓūmat al-bahja al-wardiyya* 508 (Muḥammad 'Aṭā ed., 1997) [hereinafter *al-Ghurar*]; 4 *al-Kashshāf*, *supra* note 284, at 226.

289. *Al-Mā'ida* 5:32. See, e.g., 6 *al-Ghurar*, *supra* note 288, at 508; 4 al-Zayla'ī, *supra* note 287, at 200.

290. See *infra* note 291.

291. 4 al-Zayla'ī, *supra* note 287, at 200 (quoting the Prophet Muḥammad as saying, "Whosoever does not show mercy to our children ... is not one of us.").

292. 6 Muḥammad b. Yūsuf al-Mawwāq, *al-Tāj wa-al-iklīl* 71 (n.d.).

293. 4 al-Zayla'ī, *supra* note 287, at 200–01. The Ḥanafī author explained:

> "[Taking custody of the foundling] is commendable if the [foundling] is discovered in circumstances in which it is unlikely that she would die, as is the case were she to be found in a city ... but [taking custody of the foundling] becomes obligatory if it is likely the foundling will perish [if she is not immediately rescued], as is the case were she to be discovered in the desert or some other dangerous location, in order to protect her from death."

294. 6 al-Ghurar, *supra* note 288, at 508.

295. See 3 Aḥmad b. Aḥmad al-Qalyūbī, *Hāshiyatā Qalyūbī wa 'Umayra* 188 (1997) ("[The foundling]

[145] Upon taking custody of a foundling, whether or not legally obligatory, the majority of Muslim jurists concluded that the rescuer became obliged to care for the foundling until such time as another caregiver could be found (including a judge as representative of the state) or the child reached the age of majority.[296] The Mālikīs' position is unique. They permit the rescuer to return the foundling to the place where he was found if (1) the rescuer took custody of the foundling for the sole purpose of delivering him to the judge, i.e., the responsible public authority; (2) the responsible public authority refused to accept the foundling; and (3) the foundling will not be abandoned in a location in which his life would be threatened.[297] Although the rescuer is obliged to care for the foundling, this obligation does not entail more than providing physical protection and educational direction.[298] The rescuer is always free, but is not obliged, to provide for the financial needs of the foundling. If he does so provide, he generally acts as a volunteer[299] with no recourse against the foundling or the foundling's [146] father, if and when he is identified, to recover amounts advanced to maintain the foundling.

---

differs from lost property insofar as taking custody of the latter is not obligatory ... because profit is the primary motive [with respect] to [taking custody of] it and human nature is disposed to [taking custody] of it, so it was unnecessary to make it obligatory.").

296. See, e.g., 5 *Asnā al-maṭālib*, *supra* note 285, at 614.

> "[I]f he [the rescuer] is unable to care for him [i.e., the foundling] ... then ... he delivers him to the judge. Indeed, he can turn him over [to] the judge solely because he has grown tired of caring for him or for any other reason, even if he is still able to care for him ... but it is illegal for him to abandon him or to return him to where he was [found]."

297. See, e.g., 6 al-Mawwāq, *supra* note 292, at 82.

> "[H]e [i.e., the rescuer] shall not return him [i.e., the foundling] after taking custody of him unless he took custody of him solely to deliver him to the state, which did not accept him, and the place [where he leaves the foundling] is well-traveled... The judge Abū al-Walīd said, 'This means in my opinion that the place must be one where there is no fear that he [i.e., the foundling] would perish because of the throngs of people therein and that he [i.e., the rescuer] is certain that people will hasten to take custody of him [i.e., the foundling]."

298. See, e.g., 5 *Asnā al-maṭālib*, *supra* note 285, at 614.

> "The rescuer is obliged to protect the foundling and oversee his development, i.e., raise him, because those are the purposes of taking custody of him, not to provide for his financial needs or to provide him with a nurse [in his infancy] ... for those are a tremendous burden and great expense."

299. 3 Mālik b. Anas, *Al-Mudawwana al-kubrā* 382 (n.d.) [hereinafter Mālik].

> "I said, 'What is the rule if a person rescues a foundling, takes him to the public authorities, and they order him to care for him and provide for him financially?' Mālik said, 'The foundling, amounts spent on him are for the sake of God, and the one who maintains him does so only expecting divine reward.'"

3 id.; see also 10 al-Sarakhsī, *supra* note 273, at 210 ("[I]f the rescuer supports [the foundling] financially, he is a volunteer with respect to such support."); 4 al-Zaylaʿī, *supra* note 287, at 201 ("[I]f the rescuer were to support [the foundling] from his own property, it is a gift, for he has no authority to compel.").

However, recourse against the child's father is permitted if (1) the rescuer, at the time he advanced the funds, had subjectively intended to seek repayment from the foundling's father for those expenses, and (2) the father, at the time the rescuer advanced the funds, was solvent.[300] The Ḥanafīs also contemplated recourse against the foundling if funds advanced by the rescuer for the benefit of the foundling were approved by a court.[301]

D. SUPPORTING THE FOUNDLING: WHO IS RESPONSIBLE?

If Muslim jurists were in general agreement that the rescuer was not legally obliged to maintain the foundling out of his own funds, how were the health, welfare and education of the foundling to be financed? In the first instance, any property of the foundling, including property found on or near his person, was to be spent upon his upkeep.[302] Likewise, any gifts that were given to the foundling, or any funds received from trusts established for the benefit of foundlings, could be applied by the foundling's caregiver toward the foundling's expenses.[303] The general rule was that the rescuer could accept such charitable sums given to the foundling on her behalf, but the Shāfiʿīs obliged the rescuer to notify the court of any such property and to seek the judge's permission prior to spending the foundling's property.[304] The rescuer could also spend reasonably from his own funds for the maintenance of the foundling, with the expectation of recovering from the foundling in the future with the permission of a judge. However, in these circumstances, the foundling could not, upon reaching majority, expect an accounting from the rescuer, or sue to recover from the rescuer amounts unreasonably spent in the absence of evidence of the rescuer's negligence.[305]

[147] If the foundling's private resources, as supplemented from time to time by private charity, were not sufficient to maintain him, the jurists obliged the state to provide sufficient funds to meet the foundling's financial needs.[306] In support of this proposition, the jurists of all schools relied upon a precedent established during the reign of the Ca-

300. See 6 al-Ḥaṭṭāb, *supra* note 276, at 193–94.

301. 6 Abū Bakr b. Masʿūd al-Kāsānī, *Badāʾiʿ al-ṣanāʾiʿ fī tartīb al-sharāʾiʿ* 199 (1974) ("If [the rescuer] maintains [the foundling] out of his own property, he has recourse against him if he did so with the permission of the judge, but if he did so without his permission, then he has no recourse against him because he is a volunteer.").

302. See 3 Manṣūr b. Yūnus al-Buhūtī, *Sharḥ muntahā al-irādāt* 482 (1979) ("[H]e is to be maintained from that which is [found] with him."); 6 *al-Ghurar, supra* note 288, at 518; 6 al-Kāsānī, *supra* note 301, at 199 (explaining that there is no public obligation to support the foundling if she has her own property); 4 al-Kharshī, *supra* note 273, pt. 1, at 131.

303. 4 al-Kharshī, *supra* note 273, pt. 1, at 131.

304. 6 *al-Ghurar, supra* note 288, at 518.

305. See 4 *al-Kashshāf, supra* note 284, at 228.

306. See infra notes 310–13 and accompanying text.

liph ʻUmar b. al-Khaṭṭāb, the second Caliph of Islam. Imam Mālik b. Anas, the eponym of the Mālikī legal school, reported that a man found an abandoned child during the reign of ʻUmar b. al-Khaṭṭāb.[307] He appeared before ʻUmar who asked him why he had taken custody of that child. He replied that the child was lost, so he took him.[308] At this point, the man's commanding officer cried out, "Oh Commander of the Faithful, he is a virtuous man!" ʻUmar asked him whether this was so, and when he replied yes, ʻUmar said, "Go! He [i.e., the foundling] is free, and you are in charge of his upbringing, and we are obliged to provide for him."[309]

Islamic law therefore provided that the expenses associated with raising foundlings was an obligation that belonged to the entire community,[310] and accordingly, a portion of the resources of the public fisc were to be dedicated to that task. The jurists differed, however, in what to do when the fisc *lacked* adequate resources to maintain a foundling. For the Ḥanbalīs and the Shāfiʻīs, the public fisc, if it lacked funds, was obliged to borrow money from the public in order to meet its obligation to foundlings.[311] Indeed, the Shāfiʻīs went so far as to suggest that, in the event the public fisc could not find someone who would voluntarily lend money to the state for this purpose, the government could compel, on a per capita basis, wealthy individuals—including the ruler in his personal capacity—to lend money to the state to fund the financial needs of a foundling.[312] Mālikī doctrine, however, did not contemplate public borrowing to fund the needs of foundlings. Instead, the jurists of this school obliged the rescuer in these circumstances to provide for the financial needs of the foundling in his custody.[313]

[148] The public was not only responsible in the first instance for providing for the foundlings' material needs, the Muslim jurists also held that it was monetarily responsible for torts committed by the foundling while in the custody of his rescuer.[314] Additionally, the public was the foundling's legal heir until such time as the foundling became

307. 7 Walīd b. Sulaymān al-Bājī, *al-Muntaqā sharḥ al-muwaṭṭa'* 328 (1999).

308. 7 id.

309. 7 id.

310. See 6 *al-Ghurar*, *supra* note 288, at 510 (protecting and raising the foundling, after she has been rescued, is also a societal obligation).

311. See, e.g., 5 *Asnā al-maṭālib*, *supra* note 285, at 617; 6 ʻAlī b. Sulaymān al-Mardawī, *al-Inṣāf fī maʻrifat al-rājiḥ min al-khilāf ʻalā madhhab al-imām al-mubajjal Aḥmad b. Ḥanbal* 433 (Muḥammad al-Fiqī ed., 1980).

312. 5 *Asnā al-maṭālib*, *supra* note 285, at 617 ("If the fisc lacks funds ... the ruler borrows [from those willing to lend] but if that fails, he divides the obligation among the wealthy (to be treated as a loan to the fisc), including himself, or among those whom he selects in his good-faith discretion, if they are numerous....").

313. 4 al-Kharshī, *supra* note 273, pt. 1, at 130 (stating that taking care of the foundling and maintaining her financially are obligatory upon her rescuer, if funds are not provided from the public fisc).

314. See, e.g., 6 *al-Gharar*, *supra* note 288, at 532 ("compensation of the foundling's torts (negligent and reckless) are an obligation of the public fisc"); 6 al-Kāsānī, *supra* note 301, at 199 (noting that unless the foundling establishes a relationship of dependency (*walā'*) with a specific person, the public treasury

an adult and produced heirs of her own.[315] The Ḥanafīs, however, treated this rule as a default rule, and thus provided the foundling with an option to opt out of her status as a ward of the state by entering into a contractual relationship of guardianship (*walā'*) with an individual member of the Muslim community.[316] So long as this relationship was created prior to a time when the public was called upon to answer for the foundling's torts, the contract was valid.[317] In this case, the foundling's private contract displaced the public from its twin roles as insurer of the foundling's torts and its legal heir. The party with whom the foundling contracted then became answerable monetarily for the foundling's torts, and became the foundling's legal heir if the foundling died without another heir.[318]

It should be understood, however, that the duty of providing for the foundling was ultimately derivate of the father's obligation to provide for his children. For that reason, if and when the foundling's father was found, the foundling was returned to him and the father resumed his duty of providing for the foundling's material and emotional well being. The jurists disagreed, however, on what kind of proof was needed to establish the paternity of a foundling. The Mālikīs were the strictest, requiring third party witnesses to testify to the fact that the foundling was the legitimate child of the claimant; however, the other schools were more accommodating, and would simply accept an admission of paternity from the claimant, in light of the foundling's need for a legal father who would become legally obligated to provide for him.

E. THE FREEDOM OF THE FOUNDLING

[149] A fundamental feature of the doctrine of foundlings in Islamic jurisprudence was that the foundling was free.[319] The fear that an abandoned child might become enslaved clearly haunted the thoughts of Muslim jurists. Indeed, this fear—in addition to the possibility that the child could die—was one of the concerns that drove the jurists to describe the duty of rescuing foundlings as obligatory. Because there were no legitimate domestic

---

is liable for his torts); 6 al-Mawwāq, *supra* note 292, at 81 (attributing to 'Umar b. al-Khaṭṭāb the view that the public fisc is liable for the torts of foundlings).

315. See 3 al-Buhūtī, *supra* note 302, at 485 (stating that the public is the foundling's heir); 6 al-Kāsānī, *supra* note 301, at 199 (stating that the government is the foundling's successor).

316. 6 al-Kāsānī, *supra* note 301, at 199.

317. 6 id.

318. In effect, the contractual guardian would be guaranteed to inherit something from the foundling unless the foundling died with legitimate male offspring.

319. See, e.g., 2 Mālik, *supra* note 299, at 398 ("Mālik said: 'The foundling is free'"); 4 Muḥammad b. Mufliḥ al-Maqdisī, *Kitāb al-furū'* 574 ('Abd al-Laṭīf al-Subkī ed., 1982) ("He [i.e., the foundling] ... is free."); 8 Al-Sarakhsī, *supra* note 273, at 113 ("The foundling is free, the public is his heir and it is liable for his torts."); 4 Muḥammad b. Idrīs al-Shāfi'ī, *al-Umm* 70 (stating that the foundling is free) (n.d.).

sources of slaves other than the offspring of slaves,[320] the legal assumption with respect to all births within the territories in which Islamic law reigned supreme was that persons were free.[321] Accordingly, distinguishing between foundlings and enslaved children was an evidentiary problem of the first order, a problem that was perhaps never adequately resolved. Also, because slaves could be lawfully imported into Islamic territory, a moral hazard existed with respect to foundlings: instead of taking custody of a foundling to save her life, the would-be rescuer might be tempted instead to claim the child as a slave.

Muslim jurists attempted to prevent the enslavement of foundlings by their rescuers through the use of legal presumptions of freedom, differing only in regard to the strength of such presumptions.[322] To buttress the presumptions of freedom, rescuers of foundlings were either encouraged or required to appear before a court in order to memorialize the identity of the foundling, thereby establishing binding evidence of the foundling's freedom.[323]

The Shāfiʿīs' position in this respect was the most protective of the [150] freedom of foundlings. Not only did the Shāfiʿīs presume that all minors were free, they would also reject evidence to the contrary unless the witnesses could testify in detail as to the manner by which such minor became a slave.[324] The Shāfiʿīs also required rescuers to appear before a court with the foundling in order to receive any of the legal benefits of a rescuer.[325] Likewise, if a rescuer failed to appear before a judge in this manner, the judge was entitled to remove the child from the rescuer's custody.[326] At the opposite end of the

---

320. If the father of the child was also the master of the slave who gave birth to the child, the child was deemed free.

321. Slaves under Islamic law must originate outside the territory of the Islamic state, for enslavement of a free person within Islamic territories was strictly forbidden. See 10 al-Sarakhsī, *supra* note 273, at 209 ("[T]he foundling is presumptively free in light of the [legal] presumption [of freedom] and [the law of Islamic] territories [in which he was born]."). A free person residing outside of the domains of the Islamic state, however, could be legitimately enslaved if he were not a Muslim. The person could then be imported into the territories of an Islamic state as a slave, just as any other property acquired outside of the borders of an Islamic state could be imported by its owner to an Islamic state.

322. See infra notes 325–28 and accompanying text.

323. See 3 al-Buhūtī, *supra* note 302, at 478 (noting that it is desirable for the foundling's rescuer to notify the court that he discovered the foundling so that he does not enslave her in the future).

324. See al-Muzanī, *Mukhtaṣar al-Muzanī*, in 8 al-Shāfiʿī, *supra* note 319, at 137. The author, al-Muzanī, quotes al-Shāfiʿī as saying:

> "If a man claims that a foundling is his slave, I do not accept his witnesses unless they testify that they saw the slave-girl of so-and-so give birth to him .... I am reluctant to accept the testimony of witnesses [who testify simply that he is his slave] because [the child] might be seen in the man's possession, and the witnesses might testify on that basis [alone]."

Id. Note, however, that al-Muzanī also quotes al-Shāfiʿī as holding a contrary opinion, which al-Muzanī described as the stronger position. Id.

325. See 5 *Asnā al-maṭālib*, *supra* note 285, at 611; 6 *al-Ghurar*, *supra* note 288, at 509–10.

326. 5 *Asnā al-maṭālib*, *supra* note 285, at 611 ("When [the foundling] is rescued ... giving notice to the

spectrum were the Ḥanafīs, who were more indulgent of claims of slavery than were the Shāfiʿīs. Thus, while the Ḥanafīs agreed that all foundlings were free, if the possessor of a child claimed the existence of a master-slave relationship rather than a rescuer-foundling relationship, the Ḥanafīs were inclined to accept the claim.[327]

F. TENSIONS WITHIN THE LEGAL DOCTRINE

Despite the broad agreement they enjoyed among medieval Muslim jurists, the legal doctrines governing the foundling were characterized by a profound tension between two competing paradigms—a tension that is reflected more broadly in Islamic family law generally. The first approach [151] treats legal questions dealing with the foundling from the perspective of the best interests of the foundling. The second places greater emphasis on the unknown parents of the foundling and is best characterized as a parental rights paradigm rooted in concepts of property law.

Principles of property law permeate the jurists' discussions of issues relating to the financial needs of the foundling and the allocation of the various rights and duties between the rescuer, on the one hand, and the "public" as represented by the state, on the other. For example, in reiterating the notion that the public fisc is the heir of the foundling, as well as the insurer of his torts, some jurists appealed to a well-known principal of property law, *al-kharāj bi-l-ḍamān* (profit is only with risk of loss).[328]

Once it is assumed that the rescuer cannot become a legal parent by virtue of his custodial relationship with the foundling, this principle becomes the key to understanding many details of the legal doctrine. Because the rescuer is not a legal parent, he is not entitled to inherit from the foundling, nor is he entitled to receive financial support from the foundling in the rescuer's old age.[329] Conversely, because the rescuer, unlike a legal parent, has no claims to the financial assets of the foundling, he cannot be held

court of the foundling ... and of any property [found] with him, is obligatory ... and if [the rescuer] does not give such notice, the court may remove the child and whatever property is with him from such rescuer"); 6 *al-Ghurar*, *supra* note 288, at 509–10.

327. 7 Al-Sarakhsī, *supra* note 273, at 172.

> "A small boy, who lacks capacity, is in the custody of a man, who says 'This is my slave'; it is as he says, so long as the contrary is not known, for the boy has no possession over himself, and therefore there is no claim to the contrary [before the court], so the claim of the man holding him is established [by default] against [the boy]. What is in the man's custody is his property by all appearances, so if he claims what is corroborated by appearances, his claim is given credence just as would be the case if he held in his possession a beast of burden or a dress, and said, 'This belongs to me.'" 7 id.

328. See 6 al-Kāsānī, *supra* note 301, at 199.

329. See *supra* note 315 and accompanying text.

monetarily liable for the torts of the foundling.[330] Another example of the dominance of the parental-property-rights paradigm is the rule regarding the financial liability of the foundling's father. Under Islamic law, a father cannot renounce financial liability for his children.[331] Thus, if the rescuer can show that the father was solvent at the time the rescuer maintained the foundling, then he can potentially recover such funds from the father on the theory that under the circumstances, the rescuer's advance of funds on behalf of the foundling was merely a discharge of the father's indebtedness.[332] Accordingly, those doctrines of the law of foundlings which allocate economic responsibilities seem to be straightforward applications of fundamental concepts of property law.

On the other hand, the property paradigm also appears in contexts that would seem distant from economic matters. For example, a particularly thorny question that the law of foundlings had to deal with was the foundling's religion. In principle, the foundling took the religion of his parents, a principle that lies comfortably within a vision of the family [152] where children are the quasi-property of the parents.[333] But, because the identity of the foundling's parents was unknown, other techniques had to be used to assign a religion to the foundling. One such technique was to consider the place where the foundling was discovered: If she was found in a church, she would be deemed a Christian, or if in a synagogue, a Jew, but otherwise she would be deemed a Muslim.[334] Others took a probabilistic approach: If the majority of a town or village where the foundling was discovered was of a particular religion, then the parents of the foundling would be assumed to have come from the majority religious group.[335] But in a significant departure from the focus on the parents of the foundling, other jurists insisted that a foundling should be deemed a

330. See *supra* note 314 and accompanying text.

331. 4 *al-Kashshāf*, *supra* note 284, at 227 (noting that the government has recourse against the foundling's father, if and when he is discovered, for amounts spent in rearing the foundling, assuming the father was solvent, because in that case, he was obliged to provide for the needs of his child).

332. 4 id.

333. See 10 al-Sarakhsī, *supra* note 273, at 62 (quoting the Prophet Muḥammad as saying, "Every child is born subject to the natural [faith of primitive monotheism], and his parents make him a Jew, a Christian or a Magian, until such time as he can speak for himself, either giving thanks to God or rejecting Him," in support of the legal presumption that children take the religion of their parents).

334. Muḥammad b. ʿAbd al-Wāḥid Ibn al-Humām, *Sharḥ fatḥ al-qadīr* 345 (1970) ("If he [i.e., the foundling] is discovered in a village of non-Muslims, or in a synagogue or a church, he is a non-Muslim.").

335. 3 Mālik, *supra* note 299, at 384–85.

> "I believe that if [the foundling] was in a town or city of Islam, or where [Muslims] live, I deem him a Muslim, but if he was discovered in the cities of non-Muslims or those of the protected [non-Muslim] peoples, I deem him to be a non-Muslim, and he should be left alone. If [the rescuer], found him in a village wherein there are both Muslims and Christians, it must be taken into consideration whether there are only one or two Muslims with the Christians ... in which case he belongs to the Christians and should be left alone."

3 id.

Muslim if there is any theoretical possibility that one of the child's parents was a Muslim, viz., if even one person in the village was a Muslim.[336] This rule, they said, was necessary to assure that the foundling's interests were fully protected, including his interest in avoiding enslavement.[337] While there is no doubt that this rule also incorporated elements of belief in the religious superiority of Islam to Christianity and Judaism, it would be incorrect to assume that Islamic law systematically privileged Muslims over Christians and Jews. In fact, in many circumstances, the law, at least with respect to foundlings, treated Muslims, Christians and Jews equally.[338]

Thus, it [153] seems that for those jurists who advocated what was a virtual legal presumption of Muslim descent for foundlings, the determinative consideration, so long as there was no proof of the identity of the true parent, was the perceived best interest of the child. This was not the only circumstance in which the interests of the child were given greater weight than the putative rights of the missing parents, or the caregiver who was temporarily in charge of the child. In disputes concerning who should be the custodian of the foundling, the first in time principle generally was outcome determinative, so long as that custodian was deemed fit.[339] If it was impossible to determine which of the claimants first took custody of the child, or if the first to take custody was not fit, the court would award custody based on its perception of the child's interests.[340] The foundling could also be removed from the care of an immoral caregiver or one prone to squander property.[341] Similarly, it was prohibited for the rescuer, if he was a Bedouin, for example, to take the child from a city or village to the desert, or even from a city to a village.[342] The justification given for this rule was straightforward: In addition to the great hardship and deprivation that is attendant to a life in the desert among nomadic people or among villagers, life in a city would assure moral, educational and economic opportunities for the child that could

336. 5 *Asnā al-maṭālib*, *supra* note 285, at 620 ("If the foundling is discovered in territory subject to the laws of Islam ... and there is a single Muslim living there who could be the parent, even if he denies it, ... the foundling is deemed a Muslim.").

337. See 5 id.; 7 al-Bājī, *supra* note 307, at 331 (quoting an early Mālikī as holding that, in a dispute between a Muslim and a non-Muslim over who should have custody of a foundling, custody should be given to the Muslim "so as to ensure that he does not make him a Christian, or that [the foundling's] affairs become forgotten and he becomes enslaved"); 6 *al-Ghurar*, *supra* note 288, at 522–24.

338. See, e.g., 6 *al-Ghurar*, *supra* note 288, at 512 (stating that priority is not given to a Muslim claimant over a non-Muslim claimant unless the child is deemed to be a Muslim); 3 Mālik, *supra* note 299, at 60 (holding that if a non-Muslim claims paternity of a child in the custody of a Muslim, he is awarded the child if he can prove paternity).

339. 5 *Asnā al-maṭālib*, *supra* note 285, at 613.

340. 5 id.

341. See, e.g., 6 *al-Ghurar*, *supra* note 288, at 510–11 (stating that the caregiver must neither be immoral nor a spendthrift); 4 al-Maqdisī, *supra* note 320, at 576–77 (noting that the foundling is not to be left in the custody of a caregiver who is immoral, untrustworthy or a spendthrift).

342. See 4 *al-Kashshāf*, *supra* note 284, at 229; 6 al-Mardawī, *supra* note 311, at 441.

not be found either in the desert or small villages.[343] And in cases where the judge could neither determine that the rescuer was of good character or bad character, the Shāfiʿīs, while awarding him custody of the child, imposed a duty on the government to surreptitiously monitor the conduct of the caregiver (but under court supervision) to insure that the caregiver did not harm the child.[344]

Another area of the law of foundlings in which the best interests of the child is the dominant theme concerns the rules dealing with admissions of paternity (*al-iqrār bi-l-nasab*). The Ḥanbalīs and the Ḥanafīs gave force to admissions of paternity without asking for any proof.[345] In defense of this [154] rule, the Ḥanafīs made an express appeal to the best interests of the child.[346] While admitting that rigorous application of legal principles would demand that the party claiming to be the foundling's father produce proof for his claim, al-Kāsānī argued that compelling policy considerations, in favor of both the child and the putative parent, justified giving force to an admission of paternity unsupported by objective evidence.[347] The relative laxity in this regard of the Ḥanafīs and the Ḥanbalīs is to be contrasted with the rigor of the Mālikīs, who would not admit claims of paternity absent proof that the child was the legal child of the person claiming her.[348] Shāfiʿī doctrine seems ambiguous on this point, with the same authority implying that admissions of paternity, with respect to foundlings,[349]

343. 6 *al-Ghurar*, *supra* note 288, at 516.

344. 6 id. at 510; see also 5 *Asnā al-maṭālib*, *supra* note 285, at 613.

345. See, e.g., 6 al-Mardawī, *supra* note 311, at 452 ("[I]f a person acknowledges that [the foundling] is his child, paternity is established, whether the claimant is a Muslim or a non-Muslim, man or woman, and whether the foundling is dead or alive."); 4 al-Zaylaʿī, *supra* note 287, at 202–03 (explaining that the paternity of the foundling can be established equally by the admission of either the rescuer or a third party).

346. 10 al-Sarakhsī, *supra* note 273, at 214 (arguing that a claim of paternity benefits the foundling).

347. 6 al-Kāsānī, *supra* note 301, at 199.

> "Policy justifies [accepting an admission of paternity in this context] because [it] is a report regarding something that may be true and it is obligatory to accept reports that may be true, if only to give [the speaker] the benefit of the doubt, unless accepting the report's truth harms a third party. Here, however, accepting the report and establishing a relationship of paternity is beneficial to both: [It is beneficial for] the foundling by providing him with the dignity of paternity, education and protection from death and injury as well as other benefits. [It is beneficial for] the putative parent by providing him with a child who can assist him in satisfying his religious and secular needs." 6 id.

348. 6 al-Mawwāq, *supra* note 292, at 82 (stating that the foundling is not deemed the child of his rescuer or anyone else without adequate proof of paternity).

349. 5 *Asnā al-maṭālib*, *supra* note 285, at 626.

> "Whosoever claims the foundling becomes his parent without the testimony of witnesses or expert testimony because he has admitted an obligation so it resembles [the case of] one who admits a debt, and because requiring witnesses in order to prove paternity is difficult

are valid without any proof of paternity, and in another context excluding the possibility that such an admission could be legally effective if the child was illegitimate.[350]

The express commitment to the best interest of the child is clearest in Ḥanafī doctrine.[351] The Ḥanafīs, for example, will take at face value the [155] claim by any man that he is the father of the foundling, but only to the extent that such a claim benefits the foundling.[352] Thus, if a non-Muslim or a slave were to claim paternity of the child, the Ḥanafīs would recognize the claimant's paternity (*nasab*) for purposes of establishing the parent-child relationship, but would not enforce all the normal incidents of parenthood.[353] If the child is claimed by a non-Muslim, but the child has already been deemed a Muslim by virtue of the location in which he was found, he would continue to be raised as a Muslim. Similarly, if the person acknowledging the foundling as his child is a slave, the child would not be enslaved based on that admission, but he would enjoy the benefits of a parent-child relationship.[354]

G. CONCLUSIONS ON ISLAMIC LAW AND ADOPTION

Although traditional Islamic law prohibits adoption, at least insofar as it creates a fictive relationship of descent between the adoptive parent and the child, it was not indifferent to the plight of abandoned children. The law of foundlings was the principal area of Islamic jurisprudence that dealt with the social problems created by the two main causes of child abandonment: illegitimacy and poverty. Unfortunately, the law's ability to confront these problems directly was hampered by the unresolved tension between a paradigm of parental rights which relied on concepts of property law and a paradigm that put as a priority the best interests of the child. Once this tension is made clear, one can re-read the foundational texts of Islamic law with a view to resolving these tensions

---

> and were the mere claim of paternity [in these circumstances] not sufficient to establish paternity, the paternity of many would be lost."

350. 5 id. at 171 (stating that a child conceived as a result of illicit sexual intercourse cannot be attributed to the father).

351. 4 al-Zaylaʿī, *supra* note 287, at 203.

> "[T]he admission [of paternity] of the child is beneficial to him, because he is ennobled by the [recognition of] paternity while he is harmed by the absence [of such a relationship], as he will be stigmatized as a result [of being of unknown parentage]. He also gains one who will be responsible to care for him and to provide for his needs out of desire, not [one who is] holding over him his favors."

4 id. Thus, the Ḥanafīs will accept the rescuer's claim of paternity even though it contradicts his earlier claim that the child was a foundling. 4 id.

352. See 17 al-Sarakhsī, *supra* note 273, at 128–29.

353. See 17 id

354. See 17 id. at 129.

and creating new legal doctrine that would be more sympathetic to quasi-adoptive relationships.

The first step in reinterpreting inherited legal doctrine would be a reconsideration of the Prophetic dictum, "the child belongs to the bed, and the male adulterer gets nothing."[355] First, one could distinguish this precedent from adoption on its own facts, insofar as this dictum was a ruling in the context of a custody dispute. The precedent then, instead of standing for the proposition that no relationship exists between an adulterous father and his offspring, could be viewed to stand for the [156] proposition that notwithstanding adultery, a child born in a legally recognized family is a part of that family, unless the legal father takes steps to disavow paternity.[356] One could also point out that the Prophetic ruling speaks only of the rights of the adulterous father, but is silent as to his obligations. If one were to take a "best interest of the child" approach to this precedent, one could argue that the ruling stands for the proposition that the adulterous father enjoys none of the benefits of paternity, but remains accountable for the obligations of paternity, to the extent no legitimate father exists.

It appears that this reading was not countenanced because of the interplay between parental rights and the principles of property law. The medieval jurists must have reasoned that, to the extent the adulterous father gets none of the benefits of the parent-child relationship, it would be unfair to hold him liable for the obligations of the child. But this is a concept of property law, and is ultimately irrelevant to the welfare of the child. Indeed, one could argue that if one of the purposes of the Prophetic ruling was to deter male adulterers by precluding them from benefiting from their illicit sexual relationship, this purpose would be further served by imposing upon the adulterous father the same obligations toward the illegitimate child as would have been the case had the child been the issue of lawful intercourse.

The same approach could be taken with respect to the Qur'ānic verse, which seems to prohibit adoption. If the example of the Prophet Muḥammad and his adopted son Zayd is taken as paradigmatic, the Prophet Muḥammad adopted Zayd after he had already become a young man, and despite the fact that Zayd had a known father. In these circumstances, the best interests of the child are not being vindicated; instead, the goal is the preservation of an already existing father-child relationship. Furthermore, the adoption practiced by the pre-Islamic Arabs and condemned by the Qur'ān, was effectively a consensual relationship between the adoptive father and the adopted child that negated an already existing father-child relationship. To the extent an adult child could adopt a new father, as Zayd did with Muḥammad, a father's ability to rely on his

355. See *supra* notes 271–75 and accompanying text.

356. This is the purpose of the Qur'ānic procedure of *li'ān*, whereby a husband, who witnesses the adultery of his wife, can simultaneously terminate the marriage and disavow the paternity of any child resulting from that illicit relationship. *Al-Nūr* 24:6–10.

children in his old age would be lessened, and therefore a father's incentive to look after his children when they were young would be reduced. Thus, not only was the pre-Islamic practice not inspired by a concern for children, it also weakened the bonds between fathers and children, and was a custom that was probably detrimental to children. Accordingly, if a best interest of the child approach is taken to interpreting this verse, the prohibition against [157] adoption would be restricted to circumstances where the adopted child is already an adult with a known father, or more generally, to situations where the adopted child has a known father, whether legitimate or not.

In light of Islamic law's historical concern for the best interest of the child, one can argue for a principled inclusion of at least a quasi-adoptive relationship within Islamic family law. Space does not allow for the complete elaboration of the details of this relationship, but its main features are clear—an adoptive father would be obliged to perform all the economic obligations that would normally be the duty of the actual father and would correspondingly receive the parental rights of the child's theoretical father. Inheritance could be provided via mandatory testamentary disposition, but fictive kinship need not be recognized. Such a synthesis would be faithful to the revelatory norms of Islam, to the Islamic legal tradition, and to the wellbeing of children.

Islamic Law and the Market

12

RIBĀ, EFFICIENCY, AND PRUDENTIAL REGULATION: PRELIMINARY THOUGHTS

Mohammad H. Fadel

I. INTRODUCTION

[655] The last decade has witnessed the birth and remarkable expansion of a specialized niche within the world of global finance known as "Islamic finance." While no precise figures exist with respect to the aggregate size of this sector, it has grown sufficiently to attract the attention of conventional commercial and investment banking institutions, many of which have set up Islamic finance divisions within their firms.[1] The ostensible justification for the existence of this niche is that Muslims—because of religious proscriptions set forth in the *sharīʿa* (Islamic law)—are unable to use conventional financial products, and accordingly, Islamic finance responds to this need by creating products that are claimed to comply with the requirements of Islamic law.[2] The most important rule of Islamic law that is said to justify the existence of Islamic finance is the prohibition against paying or receiving *ribā*, which is often, although inaccurately, translated as interest.[3] The irony, of course, is that Islamic finance largely consists of designing instruments that can be deemed to comply with the formal requirements of Islamic law while, at the same time, bearing all the economic attributes of the conventional financial

This article was originally published in *Wisconsin Journal of International Law* 25 no. 4 (2008), pp. 655–702.

1. See, e.g., Will McSheehy & Shanthy Nambiar, *Islamic Bond Fatwas Surge on Million-Dollar Scholars*, Bloomberg, May 1, 2007, https://www.livemint.com/Money/QXvD7Wi7imDNLFIlWMnpKO/Islamic-bond-fatwas-surge-on-milliondollar-scholars.html (suggesting that amount of wealth managed according to Islamic law is approximately $1 trillion and projecting it to reach $2.8 trillion by 2015).

2. Mahmoud A. El-Gamal, *Islamic Finance*, 11–12 (2006).

3. Id. at 2 (describing how "Islamic" products mimic the features of conventional ones, with one series of "Islamic" bonds claiming to pay "4 percent annual profit" rather than "interest"). Given the breadth of the doctrine of *ribā*, a more accurate translation of *ribā* might be "unjust enrichment." See Frank E. Vogel & Samuel L. Hayes, III, *Islamic Law and Finance* 84 (1998) (suggesting that unjust enrichment is one theory underlying the doctrine of *ribā*). Cf. Nabil A. Saleh, *Unlawful Gain and Legitimate Profit in Islamic Law: Ribā, Gharar and Islamic Banking* 13 (1986) (defining *ribā* as "unlawful advantage by way of excess or deferment").

instruments, including bearing interest, that are criticized for being inconsistent with Islamic law.[4]

[656] Many scholars have attacked the schizophrenic relationship of Islamic finance vis-à-vis conventional finance as little more than crass exploitation of religious sentiment. One leading scholar coined the term "*sharīʿa* arbitrage" to describe Islamic finance as little more than the extraction of fees simply for transforming a conventional product into one that seems to comply with the formal requirements of Islamic law, while retaining all the economic features of that conventional product.[5] This paper has nothing to say directly regarding the social desirability of the rise of or the continued existence of Islamic finance; instead, its goal is to address, from the perspective of Islamic law, the jurisprudential puzzle that allows for *sharīʿa* arbitrage to exist in the first place. It is now generally recognized, at least among scholars, that Islamic law permits numerous transactions which at the very least incorporate implicit interest in their structure.[6] At the same time, Islamic law also prohibits several transactions on grounds that they contain *ribā*, even though the transactions in question, because they are consummated in the spot market, lack an element of economic interest. To further complicate the meaning of this term, *ribā* literally means "increase," but there is universal agreement that not all increases resulting from trade are subject [657] to the restrictions of *ribā*. This paper argues that the rules of *ribā* should be analyzed as consisting of ex-ante and ex-post restrictions on contractual freedom. When viewed from this perspective, the historical

4. See El-Gamal, *supra* note 2, at 2. Whether a specific instrument is deemed to be sufficiently in compliance with the norms of Islamic law so as to permit a Muslim in good-faith to avail herself of the product is generally determined by the opinion of one or more Islamic law experts. These experts work closely with bankers in structuring the terms of instruments (on an instrument-by-instrument basis) in order to permit them to give an affirmative opinion regarding the permissibility of an investment from an Islamic perspective in the instrument in question. See McSheehy & Nambiar, *supra* note 1.

5. Haider Ala Hamoudi, *Jurisprudential Schizophrenia: On Form and Function in Islamic Finance* 7 CHI. J. INT'L L. 605, 606 (2007) (claiming that "something akin to schizophrenia [exists] in the Islamic financial community, where formalist means have led to formalist ends, which proponents describe as functional"); El-Gamal, *supra* note 2, at 1 (comparing the practice of *sharīʿa* experts giving opinions on the compliance of particular financial instruments with the *sharīʿa* to the pre-Reformation practice of selling indulgences by the Catholic Church). To the extent Islamic financial products merely replicate already existing financial instruments, the costs generated by Islamic finance are simply dead-weight losses from a social perspective. To the extent that Muslim investors or end-users of financial products are unwilling to avail themselves of conventional financial products, however, the existence of an Islamic financial sector could nevertheless be socially efficient, even if suboptimal. For this to be true, one would have to assume that social gains in the form of increased savings and investment arising out of the existence of Islamic investment and credit alternatives exceed the dead-weight losses arising out of *sharīʿa* arbitrage.

6. El-Gamal, *supra* note 2, at 51–52 (explaining that *ribā* is not synonymous with "interest," and that "even the most conservative contemporary [Muslim] jurists do not consider all forms of what economists and regulators call interest to be forbidden *ribā*").

doctrine of *ribā* might be understood as part of a prudential scheme of regulation adopted to reinforce a wider system of rationing basic commodities under general conditions of scarcity; therefore, the rules at issue sacrificed individual efficiency gains in order to serve socially desirable distributive goals. This paper takes no position, however, as to whether the doctrine of *ribā*, even if it prohibited some Pareto superior trades, may have nevertheless been Kaldor-Hicks efficient.

This paper will consist of four parts. Part II is an overview of the historical rules associated with the prohibition against *ribā*. Part III is a jurisprudential digression into whether it is legitimate, from the internal perspective of Islamic law, to consider the welfare-effects of the rules of Islamic law. Part IV provides an overview of historical and contemporary justifications of Muslim jurists for the historical doctrines of *ribā*, including as applied to the permissibility of conventional banking practices, as well as revisionist accounts providing alternative justifications for these doctrines. Part IV also attempts to place the historical doctrine of *ribā* within a wider context of prudential and categorical regulations in Islamic law concerned with maintaining an equitable distribution of basic commodities. This paper concludes with the argument that *ribā* restrictions are best understood as a type of price-setting regime designed to reinforce a public guarantee of a minimum distribution of basic goods.

II. OVERVIEW OF THE HISTORICAL DOCTRINE OF *RIBĀ*

The proscriptions against *ribā* can be broadly broken down into two types of contractual restrictions, ex-ante and ex-post.[7] I will begin with a description of ex-post restrictions and then proceed to discuss ex-ante restrictions. Ex-ante restrictions, in turn, can be further broken down into restrictions on contracts in the spot market and restrictions on contracts in credit transactions.
[658]

A. Ex-Post Ribā-Based Restrictions on Contracts in Islamic Law

Ex-post restrictions on the settlement of obligations represent the core of the doctrine of *ribā* as this prohibition was set forth expressly in the Qur'an.[8] According to early jurists and exegetes of the Qur'an, the transaction referenced in the Qur'an occurred in connection with a debtor's failure to pay a debt upon its maturity date.[9] In this case, the

7. Saleh, *supra* note 3, at 13 (describing three basic kinds of *ribā*).

8. See *al-Baqara* 2:275–76, 2:278; *Āl ʿImran* 3:130; *al-Nisāʾ* 4:161; *al-Rūm* 30:39; 1 Wahbah al-Zuḥaylī, *Financial Transactions in Islamic Jurisprudence* 311 (Mahmoud A. El-Gamal trans., Dār al-fikr, 2003).

9. See 3 Muḥammad Al-Zurqānī, *Sharḥ Al-Zurqānī ʿAlā Muwaṭṭaʾ Al-Imām Mālik* 324 (Dār al-maʿrifa 1987) (17th Century).

creditor would agree with the debtor to defer the debt's maturity date in exchange for an increase in the amount owed.[10] Although the pre-Islamic practice of the settlement of debts in this fashion was defended as being similar to the ex-ante mark-ups customarily charged by merchants at the time of the original sale—the legitimacy of which the Qur'an did not contest[11]—the Qur'an categorically condemned the ex-post agreement as constituting *ribā*, threatening creditors with damnation[12] [659] and a "war from God and His messenger"[13] if they did not desist from this practice. Instead, the Qur'an counseled creditors of bankrupt debtors to defer their debts gratis until the debtor's solvency, or to forgive such debts altogether.[14] Because of this transaction's association with the

---

In the days before Islam, *ribā* would occur in cases where one man owed another a debt maturing in the future, and when that debt matured, the creditor would ask his debtor 'Shall you pay or shall you increase?' If the debtor paid, he would take [his debt], but if the debtor did not pay, he would defer the maturity date and increase the debt.

3 Muḥammad b. Jarīr al-Ṭabarī, *Jāmiʿ al-Bayān ʿan Taʾwīl al-Qurʾān* 101 (Maktabat Muṣṭafā al-Bābī al-Ḥalabī, 3rd ed. 1968) (9th Century) (quoting an early authority as saying that, "[t]he *ribā* of the people before Islam would occur when a seller sold on credit, with the debt maturing on a specific date in the future. When the debt matured, but the debtor had no means to discharge the debt, the creditor would defer payment and increase the debt."); 1 Abū Bakr Muḥammad b. ʿAbdallāh ibn al-ʿArabī, *Aḥkām al-Qurʾān* 241 (ʿAlī Muḥammad al-Bijāwī ed., Dār al-Maʿrifa n.d.) ("*Ribā* was known to them [and consisted of] one selling to another [with payment due] in the future, and when the debt matured, [the seller] would say 'Shall you pay or shall you increase?' meaning 'Shall you increase the amount you owe me and I wait an additional term?'").

10. See *supra* note 9 and accompanying text.

11. See al-Ṭabarī, *supra* note 9, at 103–4 (stating that the mark-up charged by the seller at the origin of a contract is licit profit, in contrast to the increase charged in exchange for a deferral of the maturity date); Ibn al-ʿArabī, supra note 9, at 242:

> [The people before Islam] would say that "selling is like *ribā*," meaning that the increase [agreed to] at the time of the debt's maturity [in exchange for] a subsequent maturity date is like the original price [agreed to] at the time of the [original] contract, but God, may He be glorified, rejected their statement.

Al-Zuḥaylī, *supra* note 8, at 310 n.3.

12. *al-Baqara* 2:275:

> Those who devour *ribā* walk not save as one possessed by the devil: that is because they say "Indeed, is not trade the equivalent of *ribā*?" But God has made trade lawful and forbidden *ribā*. So, whosoever desists, having received admonition from his Lord, may retain what he has previously taken [as *ribā*] and his affair shall be [settled by] God. But whosoever resumes [taking *ribā*], they are the denizens of Hell wherein they shall dwell forever.

13. *al-Baqara* 2:279:

> If you desist not [from taking *ribā*], then take notice of a war from God and His Messenger. But if you repent, you are entitled to your capital amounts, neither being treated unfairly nor treating [others] unfairly.

14. *al-Baqara* 2:280:

> And if [the debtor] is insolvent, then [grant him] a deferral until [such time as he is] solvent and to [forgive the debt] as an act of charity would be better for you.

period in Arab history prior to Islam, the jurists called it *ribā al-jāhiliyya*, the *ribā* of the pre-Islamic days.[15] It was also referred to as *ribā al-Qur'ān*, the *ribā* of the Qur'an, since it was expressly prohibited by the Qur'an,[16] in contrast to other transactions that were also prohibited on the grounds of *ribā*, but whose prohibitions lacked a basis in the Qur'an's text.[17] Although the Qur'anic prohibition is closely associated with the treatment of bankrupt debtors, and many early authorities expressly associated this transaction as one involving insolvent debtors, the rule eventually formulated by Muslim jurists simply prohibited settlement of one debt with a future debt on terms different than that of the original debt, without regard to whether the debtor was insolvent.[18]

In addition to the prohibition of pre-Islamic *ribā*, the majority of Muslim jurists also prohibited agreements between a creditor and his debtor which purported to settle the debt by allowing the debtor to pre-pay his obligation in exchange for a discount on the amount owed.[19] According to Ibn Rushd the Grandson, known to the West as Averroes, this latter rule was derived analogically from the prohibition of the pre-[660]Islamic *ribā*.[20] According to this analysis, the only benefit the creditor receives from pre-payment is time, just as the only benefit the debtor receives in the case of pre-Islamic *ribā* deferral, is time.[21]

B. Ex-Ante Ribā-Based Restrictions in Contracts in Islamic Law

In addition to restricting the freedom of contracting parties in connection with the settlement of existing debts, Islamic law also placed restrictions in the name of *ribā* on the formation of contracts. These restrictions existed for contracts involving both spot transactions and credit transactions, and were not based on the Qur'an; they instead derived from a set of statements attributed to the Prophet Muhammad.[22]

See Ibn al-ʿArabī, *supra* note 9, at 242:

> God made clear that, if the debt matures, and the debtor does not have the means to pay the debt, he should be given a deferral until he is solvent in order to lighten [his burden].

15. See, e.g., 3 Aḥmad Ibn Muḥammad al-Dardīr, *al-Sharḥ al-Ṣaghīr* 96 (Muṣṭafā Kamāl Waṣfī, ed., Dār al-Maʿārif 1972).

16. Muḥammad Abū Zahra, *Buḥūth fī al-ribā* 33 (Dār al-Buḥūth al-ʿIlmiyya 1970).

17. Id. at 78–79.

18. Al-Dardīr, *supra* note 15, at 96.

19. See, e.g., id. at 69 (not allowing a creditor to accept as repayment a quantity of food less than the contractually specified amount prior to the maturity of the debt).

20. 4 Abū al-Walīd Muḥammad b. Aḥmad Ibn Rushd the Grandson (*known as* Averroes), *Bidāyat al-mujtahid wa nihāyat al-muqtaṣid* 525 (ʿAlī Muḥammad Muʿawwaḍ & ʿĀdil Aḥmad ʿAbd al-Mawjūd, eds., Dār al-Kutub al-ʿIlmiyya 1996) (12th century).

21. Id.; al-Zuḥaylī, *supra* note 8, at 329 ("a reduction of liability based on prepayment is very similar to increasing it based on deferment").

22. Abū Zahra, *supra* note 16, at 78–79. Muslims generally accord the statements of the Prophet

Unlike the rules that restricted ex-post agreements on the settlement of debts, this category of rules proved to be much more controversial among Muslim jurists; while all Muslim jurists accepted the legitimacy of at least some of these restrictions, they disagreed on the reasons for these restrictions.[23] As a result, some schools of jurisprudence—principally the Ẓāhirīs[24]—refused to extend the application of these restrictions to transactions other than those specified in the relevant statements of the Prophet.[25] The three schools of Sunni jurisprudence that have been historically dominant, however, agreed that the transactions prohibited by the Prophet were only examples of a [661] broader class of prohibited transactions, not a conclusive enumeration of the restricted transactions.

In the next section, the restrictions on spot transactions will be analyzed first, followed by a description of the restrictions on credit transactions.[26]

1. The Prohibition against the *Ribā* of "Excess"

The basic prohibition against the *ribā* of "excess," known as *ribā al-faḍl*, derives from a statement attributed to the Prophet Muhammad in which he:

> prohibit[ed] the sale of gold for gold, silver for silver, wheat for wheat, barley for barley, dates for dates, salt for salt, unless it is the same [quantity] for the same [quantity] or the thing [itself] for the thing [itself], and that whosoever gives an increase or receives an increase, has committed *ribā* [of excess].[27]

Each of the three Sunni schools of law offered different explanations for identifying which commodities should be subject to the regime of the *ribā* of excess, sometimes

---

Muhammad normative weight in determining the content of Islamic law to the extent such statements can be attributed to him with reasonable likelihood.

23. See Ibn Rushd, *supra* note 20, at 497–506 (describing various theories justifying *ribā*-based prohibitions); Saleh, *supra* note 3, at 14–18.

24. The Ẓāhirīs were a school of Islamic jurisprudence that rejected the use of analogy for the derivation of law in favor of strict adherence to the plain meaning of revelation. Saleh, *supra* note 3, at 15.

25. Ibn Rushd, *supra* note 20, at 503; Saleh, *supra* note 3, at 15 (mentioning the limited scope of *ribā* according to the Ẓāhirīs). Some prominent Sunni jurists also expressed skepticism toward the historical doctrines of *ribā*. See, e.g., 1 ʿIzz al-Dīn b. ʿAbd al-Salām, *Qawāʿid al-Aḥkām fī Maṣāliḥ al-Anām* 164–65 (Dār al-Maʿrifa n.d.) (13th century) (discerning no purpose justifying the rules of *ribā*).

26. It is common to refer to four schools of Sunni jurisprudence: the Ḥanafīs, the Mālikīs, the Shāfiʿīs, and the Ḥanbalīs. The Ḥanbalīs, however, were generally of minor historical importance prior to the twentieth century. Their prominence in the modern era is the result of two factors: (1) the Kingdom of Saudi Arabia follows the Ḥanbalī school; and (2) oil was discovered in Saudi Arabia during the twentieth century. Accordingly, this paper will focus generally on the theories of the three historically dominant schools of Islamic law.

27. Ibn Rushd, *supra* note 20, at 497–98.

with dramatic differences for the scope of the prohibition. The Ḥanafī approach was the broadest, holding that any item sold by weight or volume was subject to the rules of the *ribā* of excess.[28] The Shāfiʿīs, while they did not apply this prohibition to metals other than gold or silver, concluded that it applied to all kinds of food.[29] The Mālikīs put forth the narrowest interpretation of the *ribā* of excess; like the Shāfiʿīs, they excluded all metals other than gold or silver from its scope.[30] With respect to food, the Mālikīs limited the prohibition to non-perishable staple foods.[31] The rules prohibiting [662] trading in genera which are subject to the rules of the *ribā* of excess, however, contained a significant loophole: if the counter-values in a proposed trade involved different genera, all jurists agreed that the contracting parties could make the trade on whatever terms they desired, on the condition that the trade was immediately settled.[32]

Thus, the combination of the prohibition against trades within a genus, with permission to trade goods of different genera, permits a trader to exchange one measure of high-quality dates for one hundred measures of wheat, or one measure of gold for fifty measures of silver, even if both rates are well in excess of the going market price; however, it prohibits trading one measure of high-quality dates for two measures of low-quality dates, even if that is the market value of the high-quality dates relative to low-quality dates. In this case, where someone holding high-quality dates wishes to exchange them for lower-quality dates, she will be forced to enter into two trades. First, she must exchange her high-quality dates for goods from another genus, for example, barley; and second, she must trade the barley she obtained in exchange for her high-quality dates for the lower-quality dates she desires. Muslim jurists, far from being disturbed by this transaction as a circumvention of the prohibition against the *ribā* of excess, expressly encouraged traders to enter into such back-to-back trades.[33] They also seemed uncon-

---

28. Saleh, *supra* note 3, at 19; Ibn Rushd, *supra* note 20, at 500.

29. Saleh, *supra* note 3, at 21; Ibn Rushd, *supra* note 20, at 500. The Shāfiʿīs defined *ribā* as "a contract for a specified consideration (i) whose equivalence is not known according to the [relevant] legal measure at the time of the contract or (ii) with a deferral [in the delivery] of one or both of the considerations." 2 Muḥammad b. Muḥammad al-Khaṭīb al-Shirbīnī, *Mughnī al-Muḥtāj ilā Maʿrifat Maʿānī Alfāẓ Al-Minhāj* 363 (ʿAlī Muḥammad Muʿawwaḍ & ʿĀdil Aḥmad ʿAbd al-Mawjūd, eds., Dār al-Kutub al-ʿIlmiyya 1994).

30. Saleh, *supra* note 3, at 16.

31. Id. at 24; Ibn Rushd, *supra* note 20, at 499.

32. In some versions of the aforementioned statement of the Prophet, there is additional language that states, "you may sell gold for silver as you wish so long as delivery is mutual and immediate, and wheat for barley as you wish so long as delivery is mutual and immediate." Ibn Rushd, *supra* note 20, at 498–99.

33. The legitimacy of back-to-back sales is attested to in a statement attributed to the Prophet Muhammad in which he counseled his followers to sell their low-quality dates and use the proceeds from the sale to purchase the higher quality dates which they desired, instead of trading two measures of low-quality dates for one measure of high-quality dates. Id., at 504, hadith no. 954; see also El-Gamal, *supra* note 2, at 53; Saleh, *supra* note 3, at 19.

cerned that traders might enter into such trades at a price that was far in excess of the prevailing market rate.[34] Therefore, in effect, the rules of the *ribā* of excess are a prohibition against trading within a genus of goods based on differences in quality. Moreover, because the restrictions against the *ribā* of excess apply only to spot transactions, the purported prohibition of interest is irrelevant to understanding this category of trading restrictions.[35]

[663] 2. The Prohibition Against the *Ribā* of "Delay"

Just as Islamic law established commodity-specific restrictions on spot transactions, it also placed limitations on the terms on which certain commodities could be traded on a deferred basis. This set of prohibitions is also based on a statement attributed to the Prophet Muhammad in which he is reported to have said:

> [Trading] gold for gold is *ribā* unless [delivery is] hand-to-hand;
> [trading] wheat for wheat is *ribā* unless [delivery is] hand-to-hand;
> [trading] dates for dates is *ribā* unless [delivery is] hand-to-hand;
> [trading] barley for barley is *ribā* unless [delivery is] hand-to-hand.[36]

Accordingly, although the restrictions of the *ribā* of excess did not prohibit trades involving the specified commodities of the same genus so long as the counter-values were equal and delivery was immediate, the doctrine of the *ribā* of delay prohibited trading these commodities on a deferred basis, even if the counter-values were equivalent.[37] While Ḥanafī, Mālikī, and Shāfiʿī jurists agreed that this prohibition applied to the six commodities enumerated in the report establishing the doctrine of the *ribā* of excess—gold, silver, barley, wheat, dates, and salt—and agreed that the prohibition extended to other deferred trades as well, they differed as to the scope of the prohibition against deferred trades.[38] For the Mālikīs, the reason for the prohibition against the deferred trade of wheat, barley, dates, and salt was simply their quality of being food, and accordingly, all deferred trades involving counter-values which were both food, were prohibited by the doctrine of the *ribā* of delay.[39] In such cases it did not matter whether the counter-

34. Al-Dardīr, *supra* note 15, at 48. Aḥmad al-Ṣāwī expressly notes that mispriced exchanges of gold and silver are nevertheless binding. Aḥmad b. al-Ṣāwī, *Bulghat al-Sālik*, printed on the margin of 3 Aḥmad Ibn Muḥammad al-Dardīr, *al-Sharḥ al-Ṣaghīr* 48 (Muṣṭafā Kamāl Waṣfī, ed., Dār al-Maʿārif 1972) (stating that off-market spot trades of gold for silver are binding).

35. See El-Gamal, *supra* note 2, at 52.

36. Ibn Rushd, *supra* note 20, at 498. The prohibition against deferred trades in specified commodities is also supported by the additional phrase included in some of the versions of the Prophet's statement prohibiting trading within the same genus of certain commodities. See *supra* note 32.

37. Saleh, *supra* note 3, at 19–21, 25.

38. Id.

39. Id. at 25.

value was a staple or capable of being stored, whether the genera of the counter-values differed, or whether they were being traded in like quantities—the deferred trade of foodstuffs was categorically prohibited.[40] The Shāfiᶜīs applied the same theory as the Mālikīs with respect to the deferred trade of food.[41] The Shāfiᶜīs and the Mālikīs both agreed that gold and silver were subject to the rules of the *ribā* of excess [664] and delay because they served as prices for private contracting (*al-thamaniyya*) and for the compensation of injuries to persons and property.[42]

[664] With respect to commodities that were not subject to the rules of *ribā* of excess and were not food (e.g., cloth), the Mālikīs permitted deferred trades in these commodities unless (1) the counter-values were of the same genus,[43] and (2) the counter-values were not equivalent.[44] The Shāfiᶜīs, however, permitted all deferred trades so long as the counter-values were not food and the proposed trade would otherwise be permitted under the rules of the *ribā* of excess, with the exception of deferred exchanges of gold and silver, which were categorically prohibited.[45] For the Ḥanafīs, all trades involving commodities sold by weight or volume could not be settled on a deferred basis unless one of the counter-values was gold, silver, or copper coins, or a good not sold by weight or volume (e.g., cloth).[46] In addition, deferred trades involving the same commodity, even if such commodity was not sold on the basis of weight or volume and thus not subject to the rules of the *ribā* of excess, were also prohibited, even if the counter-values were equivalent.[47]

---

40. Ibn Rushd, *supra* note 20, at 499–500; Saleh, *supra* note 3, at 25.

41. Ibn Rushd, *supra* note 20, at 500; Saleh, *supra* note 3, at 21.

42. Ibn Rushd, *supra* note 20, at 500. Gold and silver are unique in serving this pricing function according to the Mālikīs and the Shāfiᶜīs and for that reason, the prohibitions applying to trading in gold and silver do not extend to anything else. Id. at 499. Thus, the Shāfiᶜīs do not apply the rules of *ribā* to the exchange of copper coins. Al-Shirbīnī, *supra* note 29, at 369.

> [T]he reason gold and silver are subject to the rules of *ribā* is they are the usual method of pricing and this quality is absent from copper coins and other goods .... and the reference to 'usual' is necessary to exclude copper coins that are in general circulation, for *ribā* does not apply to them.

43. "Genus" for this purpose was defined loosely—accordingly, a sheep which is traded to be slaughtered for its meat is considered "different" than a sheep which is traded for its potential to produce milk. Ibn Rushd, *supra* note 20, at 508.

44. Id. at 507; see also Saleh, *supra* note 3, at 25–26 (summarizing the Mālikī prohibitions with respect to spot and deferred trades).

45. Saleh, *supra* note 3, at 21–22 (summarizing the Shāfiᶜīs' prohibitions with respect to spot and deferred trades).

46. Id. at 20–21.

47. Id. at 20 (summarizing the Ḥanafī prohibitions with respect to spot and deferred trades). The Ḥanafīs defined *ribā* as "the [uncompensated] excess to which one of the contracting parties is entitled by a contractual stipulation in a trade." 7 Muḥammad b. ᶜAbd al-Wāḥid (known as Ibn al-Humām), *Sharḥ Fatḥ al-Qadīr* 8 (Maktabat wa Maṭbaᶜat Muṣṭafā al-Bābī al-Ḥalabī 1970), reprinted in Encyclopedia

[665] Accordingly, the Shāfiʿīs took the narrowest view of the *ribā* of delay: so long as the counter-values were not subject to the rules of the *ribā* of excess, the rules regarding the *ribā* of delay simply were inapplicable to the trade.[48] The Ḥanafīs gave the broadest scope to the doctrine, with the Mālikīs taking a position in between these two extremes. Thus, the Shāfiʿīs unconditionally permitted the trade of one sheep in exchange for two sheep to be delivered in the future, while the Mālikīs would permit this trade only if the exchanged sheep had different use values, e.g., one was for meat, and the other two sheep for milk. The Ḥanafīs, however, prohibited the deferred trade of one sheep for one sheep, or one sheep for two sheep, even if the uses of the sheep in the two trades were different.[49]

All three schools of law, however, permitted deferred trades if one of the two counter-values was gold or silver, or even copper coins, and the other counter-value was food or any other commodity.[50] Likewise, they all permitted the deferred trade of food or other fungibles for non-fungibles (e.g., the trade of wheat for cloth).[51] In any case, so long as the trade in question did not violate the formal rules of the *ribā* of delay (or for that matter the rules of the *ribā* of excess), the jurists were largely unconcerned with the pricing terms agreed to by the parties.[52]

---

of Islamic Jurisprudence CD-ROM, Kuwaiti Ministry of Endowments, the Islamic Development Bank & Harf Info. Tech. 2004. For purposes of applying this definition, receiving a good immediately against a future delivery obligation constitutes a preference that results in an uncompensated excess, thereby explaining the requirement of simultaneous delivery in the case of the trade of goods of the same genus. Muḥammad b. Maḥmūd al-Bābartī, *Sharḥ al-ʿInāya ʿalā al-Hidāya*, printed on the margin of 7 Ibn al-Humām, *Sharḥ Fatḥ al-Qadīr* 7, reprinted in *Encyclopedia of Islamic Jurisprudence* CD-ROM, Kuwaiti Ministry of Endowments, the Islamic Development Bank & Harf Info. Tech. 2004. See also, Ibn Rushd, *supra* note 20, at 507. Ibn Rushd also reports that the Mālikīs, as a result of their prohibition of self-interested loans (*salaf jarra nafʿan*), would also prohibit deferred trades of goods from the same genus. Id. at 508. There is a dispute within the Mālikī school as to whether the prohibition against self-interested loans is a self-standing principle of law (*aṣl*) or is merely a prophylactic measure (*sadd al-dharīʿa*). Id. at 510–11.

48. Saleh, *supra* note 3, at 21.

49. Ibn Rushd, *supra* note 20, at 508.

50. Saleh, *supra* note 3, at 19–22, 25–26.

51. Id.

52. As a general rule, if the price was determined by arm's length bargaining (*mukāyasa*), the fact that the contract price was off-market (*ghabn fāḥish*) would not invalidate the contract. See 4 Muḥammad b. Muḥammad b. ʿAbd al-Raḥmān al-Ḥaṭṭāb, *Mawāhib al-Jalīl li-Sharḥ Mukhtaṣar Khalīl* 468 (Dār al-fikr 1992) (16th century). Al-Ḥaṭṭāb quotes Ibn Rushd the Grandfather as saying that mispricing, even if material, does not give the purchaser an option to rescind the sale, as long as the sale was an arm's length transaction and the purchaser had full contractual capacity. Id. at 469. Indeed, Ibn Rushd the Grandfather cites the ruling of an early Mālikī jurist, who concluded that the contract of a merchant who sold a good valued at 150 dinars for 1000 dinars on credit, and took a pledge from the purchaser as security for that obligation was binding, as evidence for the general rule that pricing errors do not effect the validity of a contract negotiated at arm's length. Id.; cf. Al-ʿArabī, *supra* note 9, at 242 (mentioning

[666] 3. Excursus on *Ribā* and Loans

As described above, the doctrine of *ribā* was primarily concerned with the terms of sales and the settlement of debts. In addition, the label *ribā* was also sometimes attached to any increase (or even more broadly, any benefit, whether or not monetary) that was obtained in connection with a loan, the legal term for which is *qarḍ*.[53] (Because its definition among Muslim jurists is different from contemporary usage, I will refer to it using its Arabic name.) The most important feature of a *qarḍ* was its charitable nature (*tabarruᶜ*).[54] Accordingly, the person extending the *qarḍ* had to have the legal capacity to engage in charity (*ahliyyat al-tabarruᶜ*).[55] Consistent with its charitable nature, no date for repayment was required for the *qarḍ* to be valid according to the Mālikīs,[56] and neither the Ḥanafīs nor the Shāfiᶜīs would enforce a stipulated date for repayment.[57]

Because of its charitable nature, if a condition was stipulated in the contract that gave a benefit to the person making the *qarḍ*, the transaction was invalid.[58] Because of the deferred repayment obligation involved in a *qarḍ*, it might appear to be prohibited by the

---

a minority opinion within the Mālikī school that would permit a trader to rescind up to a third of a contract whose terms are substantially off-market).

53. See, e.g., al-Shirbīnī, *supra* note 29, at 363 (identifying one type of *ribā* as the "*ribā* of a *qarḍ* in which a benefit is stipulated"). A loan could also be referred to using the term *salaf.*

54. 3 Muḥammad b. Muḥammad al-Khāṭib al-Shirbīnī, *Mughnī al-Muḥtāj ilā Maᶜrifat Maᶜānī Alfāẓ al-Minhāj* 31 (ᶜAlī Muḥammad Muᶜawwaḍ & ᶜĀdil Aḥmad ᶜAbd al-Mawjūd, eds., Dār al-Kutub al-ᶜIlmiyya 1994) (16th century); 10 Abū Bakr b. Masᶜūd al-Kāsānī, *Badāʾiᶜ al-Ṣanāʾiᶜ fī Tartīb al-Sharāʾiᶜ* 4981 (Maṭbaᶜat al-Imām n.d.) (12th century); al-Dardīr, *supra* note 15, at 292 (stating that a *qarḍ* is a morally meritorious (*mandūb*) act because it is a form of "cooperation in piety and kindness").

55. 4 Abū Zakariyyā Yaḥyā b. Sharaf al-Nawawī, *Rawḍat al-Ṭālibīn* 32 (al-Maktab al-Islāmī li-l-ṭibāᶜa wa-l-nashr n.d.) (13th century); al-Kāsānī, *supra* note 54, at 4981. For that reason, guardians of minors could not use their property to make a *qarḍ* according to the Shāfiᶜīs. See, e.g., al-Shirbīnī, *supra* note 54, at 31. Ḥanafīs held guardians personally liable to their wards in the event they used the wards' property for a *qarḍ* which was not repaid. Ibn al-Humām, *supra* note 47.

56. The Mālikīs would enforce a repayment term if it was specified in the contract. Al-Dardīr, *supra* note 15, at 295–96.

57. Al-Kāsānī, *supra* note 54, at 4983 (stating that a repayment date for a *qarḍ*, unlike other debts, is not binding, whether or not stipulated at the time of the contract or subsequently); al-Nawawī, *supra* note 55, at 34 (stating that the stipulation of a repayment date in connection with a *qarḍ* is neither permissible nor enforceable).

58. Al-Shirbīnī, *supra* note 54, at 34 ("the purpose of this contract is to provide relief [*irfāq*], so if [the creditor] stipulates a condition that gives him a right, it is no longer consistent with that purpose, so it becomes invalid"); al-Nawawī, *supra* note 55, at 34; al-Kāsānī, *supra* note 54, at 4983; al-Dardīr, *supra* note 15, at 295. Al-Dardīr's definition of *qarḍ* made clear that it had to be for the exclusive benefit of its recipient. Id. at 291 ("[A] *qarḍ* is the giving of property against a similar consideration payable in the future solely for the recipient's benefit").

rules of the *ribā* of delay; however, [667] it is excluded from the prohibitions of the *ribā* of delay because of the exchange's explicitly charitable nature.[59]

C. Economic Objections to the Doctrine of Ribā

The primary economic objection to the doctrines of *ribā*, in all their various forms, is that by restricting contractual freedom, they prohibit what otherwise would appear to be Pareto superior trades, and accordingly appear to be inefficient.[60] Despite the fact that the doctrines of *ribā* may appear to be either paternalistic or inefficient insofar as they reduce parties ex-ante and ex-post contractual freedom (and thus by hypothesis, the individual welfare of traders), economists recognize that in some circumstances, particularly where welfare is maximized only through mutual cooperation, restrictions on the "freedom" of individuals to "defect" (e.g., prohibitions on their ability to enter into side agreements) are often necessary to achieve the *Pareto* optimal result.[61] El-Gamal suggests that the doctrines of *ribā* can be understood as a type of divine command, i.e., a moral injunction, not to defect from a scheme of social cooperation that has the potential to increase the welfare of all, but only if all (or substantially all) are committed to its rules.[62]

Based on this interpretation, the doctrines of *ribā* would, at least in certain circumstances, be efficiency enhancing. More importantly, if this interpretation of the historical doctrines is correct, it suggests that the doctrines themselves are simply pre-commitment devices necessary to secure the level of cooperation necessary to achieve social efficiency in certain states of the world; accordingly, these rules ought to be subject to revision in light of overall systematic considerations of efficiency.[63] Some may question whether considerations of efficiency, however, are [668] even relevant. Islamic law is said to be a "religious" law, so consideration of the welfare effects of legal rules may simply be illegitimate, or even if welfare concerns are a historically plausible explanation for the origins of the rules, Islamic jurisprudence may simply render such analysis irrelevant to

59. El-Gamal, *supra* note 2, at 57 (citing a medieval jurist for the proposition that *qarḍ* "is exempted from the rules of *ribā* because of its charitable nature"); Abū Zahra, *supra* note 16, at 89 (stating that some jurists described a loan contract as "an act that originates as charity and concludes as compensatory").

60. See El-Gamal, *supra* note 2, at 8–9 (noting that law and economics scholars describe limits on contractual freedom, including laws against interest-based lending and borrowing, as inefficient and paternalistic).

61. Id. at 10 (describing two person prisoners' dilemma in which if both parties pursued their own interests they would each be worse off than if they agreed to adopt a cooperative strategy).

62. Id.

63. Id. at 11 (noting that attempts to apply the doctrines of *ribā* in connection with the rise of "Islamic finance" has resulted in dead-weight losses relative to conventional financial products). This contrasts with earlier periods of Islamic history when the prohibitions of *ribā*, according to El-Gamal, were more likely to have been consistent with social welfare.

the prospective articulation of its rules. Whether efficiency is a relevant factor in Islamic jurisprudence and contract law will be taken up in the next part.

III. THE RELATIONSHIP OF WELFARE TO ISLAMIC LAW

Noel Coulson, a leading twentieth-century English scholar of Islamic law, notes that, "[i]t is a trite assertion that Islamic law is a God-given and religious legal system as opposed to the secular man-made legal systems of the West."[64] Because of this religious orientation, Professor Coulson argues, "equitable considerations of the individual conscience in matters of profit and loss override the technicalities of commercial dealings,"[65] in contrast to "[c]ommercial law ... in the West [which] is oriented towards the intrinsic needs of sound economics, such as stability of obligation and certitude of promised performance."[66] Whether the sharp differences Professor Coulson suggests exist between "Western" commercial law and Islamic law are as profound as he claims, or even assuming that such differences exist, whether those differences can reasonably be attributed to the "religious" nature of Islamic law in contrast to the "secular" nature of Western law is questionable.[67]

Rather than debating the proper characterization of Islamic law as "religious" or "secular," it is sufficient for the purposes of this paper to ask whether Muslim jurists, in the course of formulating their various legal doctrines, exhibited concern for and sensitivity to the economic impact of their rules.[68] Viewed from this perspective, it is hardly [669] debatable that pre-nineteenth century Muslim jurists were concerned with the impact of their rules on the secular well-being of individuals, and that they largely—even if erroneously—assumed that the rules they formulated for the regulation of the economic realm were broadly consistent with society's need to preserve wealth and encourage its useful exploitation.

As a general matter, Muslim jurists understood Islamic law's rules to be made up of rules that could be rationally justified and those which were devotional; however, this

---

64. Saleh, *supra* note 3, at xi-xii.

65. Id. at xii.

66. Id.

67. See, e.g., Oussama Arabi, *Al-Sanhuri's Reconstruction of the Islamic Law of Contract Defects: Error and Real Intent,* in Studies in Modern Islamic Law and Jurisprudence 63 (2001) (noting that Islamic law's doctrines of error in contracts concerned with protecting the stability of market transactions and respect for the real intent of contracting parties).

68. But note that the Muslim jurisprudence explicitly recognized the Prophet Muhammad to have acted in the dual capacities of a prophet and a secular lawgiver, with important consequences arising from this distinction. See Sherman A. Jackson, *From Prophetic Actions to Constitutional Theory* 25, Int'l. J. of Middle E. Stud. 71, 74 (1993) (discussing the important legal differences that arise as a consequence of whether the Prophet Muhammad was acting as a prophet or a secular ruler).

latter category was largely limited to devotional acts (i.e., ritual law).[69] As for those rules of Islamic law that dealt with secular human existence, the conclusions reached by reason, in principle, should be consistent with the rules that are derived from revelation.[70] Indeed, the general congruence between the revealed law and the secular welfare of human beings had become the jurisprudential solution to the theological problem arising out of the simultaneous commitments to a revealed law and the use of reason in ordering human affairs.[71] The notion that revealed law was consistent with reason led to the theory of the five "universals" which revelation aimed to protect: religion, life, reason, progeny, and property.[72] The fact that Islamic jurisprudence recognized the protection of property as one of its universal ends, and that its rules should do so in a rationally cognizable manner, forecloses the possibility that Muslim jurists were, in [670] principle, opposed to the substantive analysis of the economic consequences of their rules.

Muslim jurists also stated their belief that rules regulating trade were specifically intended to further human welfare; thus, al-Ḥaṭṭāb, a sixteenth century Muslim jurist, explained that trade is permitted "for the purpose of easing the condition of people and [to assist them] in cooperating to obtain [the means of their] livelihood."[73] Similarly, Ibn Farḥūn, a fifteenth century jurist, after explaining that God's revealed law was based on substantive ends which were intended to secure the various needs of mankind, identified one class of such rules as those intended to provide for the necessities of human life: "the law of sales, lease, silent partnership, and partnership in cultivation of the earth, because of the need humans have for items possessed by others, and their need to use others to satisfy their own needs."[74] Islamic law also recognized exceptions to the doctrine of *ribā*

---

69. ʿAbd al-Salām, *supra* note 25, at 4. Indeed, Ibn ʿAbd al-Salām also states that while revelation is indispensable for knowledge of the hereafter, and the means by which one attains eternal happiness:

> [T]he benefits and the harms of the profane world and the causes thereof are known via necessity, experience, custom and considered opinion, and if something is ambiguous, inquiry is made [using] its evidence [viz., necessity, experience, etc.]. And, whoever wishes to understand the substantive reasons [for revelatory rules regulating the profane world], the costs and benefits [of certain conduct], and the weightier of these considerations, he should present these [questions] to his mind, imagining that revelation was silent on these matters, and then he should derive rules. In this case, hardly will a rule [imposed by revelation] differ from the conclusions reached, save for such devotional rules as God has imposed upon His servants with respect to which He did not reveal to them either its benefit or its harm. Id.

70. Id.

71. Felicitas Opwis, *Maṣlaḥa in Contemporary Islamic Legal Theory*, 12 Islamic L. & Soc'y 182, 189–190 (2005).

72. Id. at 188.

73. Al-Ḥaṭṭāb, *supra* note 52, at 227.

74. 2 Burhān al-Dīn Ibrāhīm B. Muḥammad b. Farḥūn (*known as* Ibn Farḥūn), *Tabṣirat al-Ḥukkām fī Uṣūl al-Aqḍiya wa-Manāhij al-Aḥkām* 105 (Dār al-Kutub al-ʿIlmiyya 1995) (14th century).

where it was believed strict application of the rules would be harmful.[75] Likewise, muftis also recognized exceptions to the prohibitions against *ribā*[76] and other restrictions[77] where doing so would further an individual's welfare, thereby increasing the scope of permissible economic cooperation.

One particularly interesting example can be found in an opinion given by Abū Isḥāq al-Shāṭibī, a Spanish Muslim jurist.[78] He was asked about partnerships for the manufacture of cheese in which individuals [671] would contribute milk and divide the cheese in proportion to their contributions of milk.[79] Although he noted that, strictly speaking, this arrangement was a violation of the rules of *ribā* of delay and excess,[80] he believed that such partnerships were nevertheless permissible.[81] First, al-Shāṭibī noted that humans engage in many cooperative ventures that are essentially not-for-profit (e.g., sharing food in the context of journeys or as part of neighborly relations).[82] Because individu-

75. One such example is the *ʿariyya* sale, pursuant to which the owner of a fruit tree could enter into a contract to purchase dried fruit immediately against his future obligation to deliver the same kind of fresh fruit at the time of harvest. The amount of the fruit to be sold was determined by the estimated amount that the seller's tree would yield. Al-Dardīr, *supra* note 15 at 238.

76. Muḥammad b. Yūsuf al-Mawwāq, *al-Tāj wa al-Iklīl li-Mukhtaṣar Khalīl*, printed on the margin of 4 Muḥammad b. Muḥammad b. ʿAbd al-Raḥmān al-Ḥaṭṭāb, *Mawāhib al-Jalīl li-Sharḥ Mukhtaṣar Khalīl* 317–18 (Dār al-fikr, 1992) (permitting individuals to press their olives jointly, with the oil being distributed proportionally to each person's contribution of olives, even though different olives yield different amounts of oil, thus resulting in the unequal and the deferred exchange of olives for oil in violation of the rules of the *ribā* of excess and delay because "people must have what benefits them").

77. Later jurists, for example, permitted the use of copper coins as the capital of a silent partnership (*commenda*) in lieu of gold or silver, on the grounds that gold and silver are not desired in themselves, but only for their potential to be invested profitably. Al-Ṣāwī, *supra* note 35 at 684; see also Abraham L. Udovitch, *Partnership and Profit in Medieval Islam* 177–83 (1970) (explaining controversy and development of doctrine regarding what constituted permissible capital for a *commenda* partnership).

78. 5 Aḥmad b. Yaḥyā al-Wansharīsī, *al-Miʿyar al-Muʿrib* 215 (Muḥammad Ḥajjī, ed. Dār al-Gharb al-Islāmī 1990).

79. Id.

80. See, e.g., al-Dardīr, *supra* note 15, at 462 (stating that partnerships whose capital consisted of food are invalid).

81. Id. The partnerships at issue facially violated the restrictions against the *ribā* of delay and the *ribā* of excess for two reasons. First, because the partnership's capital consisted of milk, and its output was cheese, it was the equivalent of trading food for food on a deferred basis, thus running afoul of the prohibition against delay in trading food. Second, because the amount of cheese produced by a certain amount of milk varied depending on the quality of the milk, there was no guarantee that the partners, when they distributed the output, could do so consistently with the requirement that trades in milk, since it was subject to the rules of *ribā* of excess according to the Mālikīs, be conducted on a basis of strict equivalence. Accordingly, if the partners distributed the output based on their pro rata contribution of milk to the enterprise, they would almost certainly violate the rule of equivalence which governs trades of milk for milk.

82. Id.

als lack a profit motive in these cases, such exchanges have been exempted from the rules of *ribā*. Second, he noted that because most individuals only have small amounts of milk, it would be impracticable for them to produce cheese using solely their own milk.[83] Were the law to prohibit individuals from entering into these partnerships, it would create hardship.[84] The scope of hardship that would be imposed through the strict application of the rules of *ribā* to partnerships for the manufacture of cheese also manifested itself in another Andalusian practice which al-Shāṭibī endorsed in this opinion.[85] Most shepherds oversee flocks consisting of livestock belonging to numerous individuals. Because the shepherds take these flocks to distant pastures, it would be impracticable for the shepherds to separate the milk of each person who contributed livestock to the flock, much less require the shepherd to manufacture cheese separately for each individual.[86] Significantly, the joint-venture between the shepherds and the owners of the livestock for the production of cheese is a profit-making venture, but al-Shāṭibī nevertheless resorts [672] to the principle of "removal of hardship (*rafʿ al-ḥaraj*)" as a justification for the arrangement.[87]

Accordingly, whether or not Islamic law is described as "religious," it is clear that both at the level of Islamic jurisprudence and Islamic substantive law, Islamic law historically seemed to be concerned with justifying its rules in relation to secular outcomes, particularly in relation to the secular welfare of individuals. Likewise, modern authorities have denied that the prohibitions against *ribā* are of a devotional character.[88] We will now turn our attention to the justifications Muslim jurists have given for the doctrines of *ribā*.

83. Id.

84. Id. at 216.

85. Id.

86. Id.

87. Id.

> The difficulty in this case facing shepherds and the owners of livestock exceeds the [hardship involved in the] previous example of the orphan's property [where the orphan's guardian was permitted to commingle his assets with that of the orphan provided he acted faithfully because of the difficulty of separating the orphan's property from that of the guardian], and accordingly, this principle [i.e. removal of hardship] requires permitting partners to commingle milk for that purpose.

The legal principle of "removal of hardship" has its origins in various verses of the Qur'an which deny the notion that God imposes hardships as a part of religion. See, e.g., *al-Baqara* 2:220 ("Had God wished, He would have burdened you"); *al-Ḥajj* 22:78 ("He has made no hardship for you in religion").

88. Abū Zahra, *supra* note 16, at 81 ("There is no doubt that the majority of jurists do not consider a text prohibiting a type of sale to be devotional, because devotional rules, i.e. those rules whose legal causes are not sought, are limited to rituals, not to financial transactions that occur among people.").

IV. THEORIES IN SUPPORT OF THE HISTORICAL PROHIBITIONS OF *RIBĀ*

Given the jurisprudential assumption that the rules of Islamic law are rationally related to the secular welfare of human beings, it is not surprising that Muslim jurists offered theories in support of the prohibitions against *ribā*. I will begin with a discussion of the pre-modern justifications offered by Muslim jurists, then proceed to justifications offered by modern Muslim jurists, and conclude with a discussion of revisionist justifications offered by non-jurists.

[673] *A. Historical Justifications for the Prohibition Against* Ribā

Ibn Rushd, in his discussion of the doctrine of *ribā*, noted that the controversial nature of *ribā* was due to the nature of the analogical enterprise itself as applied to the prohibitions found in Prophetic teachings.[89] Leaving aside the objections of the Ẓāhirīs, a school of Islamic law that for principled reasons rejected analogy as a valid method of interpreting revelation, Ibn Rushd noted that even some Muslim jurists who accepted analogy nevertheless rejected the doctrines of *ribā* which were developed by the three principal Sunni schools of jurisprudence.[90] To such critics, the attempt to apply the doctrine of *ribā* to transactions other than those specified in the texts was unconvincing since it was based on an analogy known as "the analogy of resemblance" (*qiyās al-shabah*). In contrast to an "analogy of principle" (*qiyās al-maʿnā*), the "analogy of resemblance" was considered jurisprudentially weak by many jurists. Accordingly, these critics rejected the majority's extension of these prohibitions.[91] For Ibn Rushd, it was the problematic nature of the analogies used by the Sunni schools of law which created the substantially different interpretations of the scope of the *ribā* prohibitions.[92]

Despite Ibn Rushd's apparent sympathies for those Muslim scholars who were skeptical of the reasoning that led to the expansion of the *ribā* prohibitions, he argued for the Ḥanafī position as the most sensible interpretation of *ribā*, although he, himself, was a Mālikī.[93] Ibn Rushd believed that the Ḥanafī approach, which applied the prohibition to all commodities that were traded by weight or volume, to be sensible. To the extent that traders engaged in intra-generic trading of fungible goods, there was a high risk of mispricing (*ghabn*) due to the similarity of the counter-values.[94] This risk militated against the possibility that the terms of any agreement would be fair. In addition, because the

89. See Ibn Rushd, *supra* note 20, at 525.
90. Id. at 503.
91. Id.
92. Id.
93. Id. at 505 (describing the Ḥanafī theory of *ribā* as the best explanation).
94. Id.

utilities associated with each of the counter-values were substantially similar, such trades only made sense to the extent that they took advantage of differences in quality within goods of the same genus. Accordingly, [674] such trades did not further any fundamental needs (*ḥāja ḍarūriyya*) of the traders, but rather only served to help them obtain advantages that Ibn Rushd dismissed as a type of "extravagance" (*ṣaraf*).[95] In other words, Ibn Rushd believed that the purpose of the *ribā* of excess prohibitions was to foreclose mis-priced trades in connection with the exchange of fungible goods, where the only rational benefit to be obtained from such a trade represented a kind of "extravagance," rather than a genuine need. Accordingly, applying the rules of *ribā* to all fungible goods would thus further the ultimate goal of establishing fair terms of exchange without sacrificing the fundamental interests of traders.[96]

Ibn Rushd also reports other justifications of *ribā* that he thinks plausible. He states that an early Muslim jurist limited *ribā* to food that was sold by weight or volume, thus combining the Ḥanafīs' concern with fair pricing of similar products with the intuition of the Shāfiᶜīs and the Mālikīs that the law should be more concerned about fairness when it came to trades that dealt with the necessities of human life.[97] In addition, Ibn Rushd reports the opinion that limited the application of *ribā* to those commodities that were also subject to *zakāt*, a kind of tax levied on property which was intended for relief of the poor.[98] Finally, Ibn Rushd reports that an early Mālikī authority, Ibn al-Mājishūn, proposed that the rules of *ribā* should apply to all types of property because it was intended to protect property by preventing mis-pricing (*manᶜ al-ghabn*).[99]

If the Ḥanafīs are concerned about mis-pricing, one might wonder why they restricted the scope of *ribā* to goods that are sold by weight or volume rather than applying the rules of *ribā* to all goods, especially since they believe that implicit in the notion of trade is that each person receives something substantially equivalent to what she gives up.[100] Al-Bābartī explains the limited scope of *ribā*'s application on the grounds that only when goods of the same genus are traded does it become clear whether there is inequality in the terms of the trade;[101] [675] accordingly the trade remains permitted in accordance

95. Id. at 506.

96. Id.

97. Id.

98. Id.

99. Id.

100. Ibn al-Humām, *supra* note 47 ("[The hadith] imposed the obligation of equivalence as a condition in the sale ... since it [i.e., "sale"] implies correspondence which is satisfied when [each of the exchanged considerations] is equivalent.").

101. Al-Bābartī, *supra* note 47, at 7

> [W]hen [a good] is exchanged for [another good] of its genus, all of its parts correspond to all of the parts [of the good for which it is exchanged]. So, if there is an excess in one of the two [goods], that excess is a loss to its owner. In order to protect people from such losses,

with the basic rule of permission that governs contracts involving the trade of cross-generic goods subject to *ribā*.[102]

The other puzzle posed by the Ḥanafī doctrine is why, if equivalence is the touchstone of a lawful sale, are only quantity and genus taken into account, and not quality? Ibn al-Humām gives three possible explanations, two of which may be described as based in legal reasoning and one which is, for lack of a better term, "faith-based." The faith-based reason is simply that the Prophet is reported to have said, in connection with trades involving goods of the same genus, that "high-quality [goods] and low-quality [goods] are equivalent."[103] The legal reasons are either that: (1) traders do not customarily take into account quality differences; or (2) were the law to permit traders to take into account differences in quality, it would reduce the volume of trade.[104] His commentator al-Bābartī, expressed skepticism regarding the claim that quality differences are irrelevant to traders, but found the second to be more plausible.[105] For Ibn Rushd, however, the whole point of the rules of the *ribā* of excess was to prevent intra-genus trades, since the only conceivable reason for such trades was to exploit differences in quality, a goal which he had dismissed as "extravagance."[106]

The Ḥanafīs, in the course of refuting the Shāfiʿī doctrines regarding *ribā*, also report why the Shāfiʿīs limited *ribā* to foodstuff and gold and silver. As reported by the Ḥanafīs, the Shāfiʿīs took a somewhat literal approach to the language of the Prophetic injunction, and concluded that trades in food and gold and silver are presumptively prohibited.[107] Accordingly, the requirement of equivalence and [676] simultaneous delivery is a condition to the permissibility of trades involving these commodities. The presumptive prohibition against intra-generic trades in food and gold and silver, which can only be overcome by the equivalence and mutual-delivery of the considerations, implies that food and gold and silver involve matters of grave importance (*khaṭar*) and scarcity (*ʿizza*), and accordingly, any justification offered for the rules of *ribā* must be consistent with this notion. Based on this analysis, the Shāfiʿīs argue that it is appropriate (*munāsib*) that the

---

equivalence is an obligation [in the case of such trades], in contrast to an exchange of a good for [another good] not of its genus. In this case, it is impossible to ascertain non-equivalence and thus impossible to ascertain a loss.

102. Id. ("Permission is the legal presumption regarding the exchange of one good subject to the rules of *ribā* for another good also subject to the rules of *ribā*.").

103. Ibn al-Humām, *supra* note 47, at 8.

104. Id. ("Quality is not taken into account because it is not customarily considered [to result in] a difference or because taking it into account [results] in an obstacle to trade").

105. Al-Bābartī, *supra* note 47, at 8.

106. Ibn Rushd, *supra* note 20, at 506 ("The prohibition of non-equivalence in these items necessitates the cessation of such trades since the utilities [of the counter-values] do not differ. The need to trade arises only when the utilities [of the exchanged counter-values] differ.").

107. See Maḥmūd b. Aḥmad al-Zanjānī, *Takhrīj al-Furūʿ ʿalā al-Uṣūl* 143 (Muḥammad Adīb al-Ṣāliḥ ed., Maktabat ʿUbaykān 1999) (13th century).

rules of *ribā* be limited to food and gold and silver because food and gold and silver are, respectively, necessary for the preservation of human life and property; the latter only being preserved to the extent property is subject to a pricing mechanism.[108] The Ḥanafīs response is that while the Shāfiʿīs may be correct in identifying the necessity of food and gold and silver for human existence, they are mistaken in their inference from these facts of social life that God would make dealings in these necessities more difficult than other goods.[109] Indeed, to the contrary, "divine wisdom with respect to humanity has been to permit broadly all things for which [human] need is greater as is the case with water and pasture for livestock."[110]

B. Modern Justifications for the Prohibition Against Ribā

In this subsection, I will discuss two modern approaches to the traditional doctrines of *ribā*. The first approach represents the dominant view which equates the modern practice of lending at interest with *ribā* and forms the theoretical basis for the existence of Islamic finance. The second approach, which I call the dissenting view, takes the view that the modern practice of lending at interest may qualify as *ribā* in a technical sense, but it does not constitute the *ribā* condemned in the Qur'an, nor is it categorically prohibited by other proscriptions of Islamic law.

[677] 1. The Dominant View

For modern Muslim jurists who believe that lending at interest is unlawful, the doctrines of *ribā* are viewed as a means to achieve economic justice. For al-Zuḥaylī, the *ribā* of excess "was prohibited to avoid injustice and financial losses."[111] He adds that, "the general reason for the prohibition of [the *ribā* of delay] is that it is conducive to exploitation of the poor by the rich, and putting undue financial pressures on the needy,"[112] and when

108. Ibn al-Humām, *supra* note 47, at 6; see also al-Bābartī, *supra* note 47, at 6 (attributing to the Shāfiʿīs the same position described by Ibn al-Humām but adding the Shāfiʿī criticism of the Ḥanafī justification of *ribā* as failing to take into account the special importance of food and specie in the life of humans).

109. Al-Bābartī, *supra* note 47, at 8 ("the path [of the divine law] in such [matters] is freedom [from restrictions] to the greatest extent because of the extreme need for [such things], not restricting [access] to [such things]").

110. Id.

111. Al-Zuḥaylī, *supra* note 8, at 317. He also asserts that permitting deferred trades in foodstuffs could result in shortages of food in the markets. Id. at 321.

112. Id. at 321. Of course, the doctrine of the *ribā* of delay does not categorically prohibit credit sales of food; only deferred trades where both countervalues are food are prohibited. See, e.g., id. at 320 n. 32 (stating that deferred barters of food are "suspected to be exploitative" but deferred payment of food for cash "is permitted since such deferred payments meet people's needs").

the deferred trade involves food, it poses the risk of creating artificial shortages by merchants who would prefer to sell food on credit so as to increase their return.[113] Al-Zuḥaylī points out, however, that despite Islamic law's intent to prevent economic injustice, "*ribā* is not restricted to exploitative transactions," suggesting that Islamic law is willing to tolerate efficiency losses in the form of over-broad rules in order to prevent exploitation.[114]

Abū Zahra blames lending at interest for a host of social and economic ills, and concludes that it is a "destructive convention rejection of which is obligatory," regardless of its status under revelation.[115] [678] Indeed, it was the moral criticism of lending at interest by religious scholars such as Abū Zahra that gave rise to the birth of Islamic finance in the latter-half of the twentieth century.[116]

Lending at interest, regardless of its impact on social welfare, was only marginally related to the pre-modern doctrines of *ribā*. Instead of coming directly under the framework of *ribā*, self-interested loans were simply prohibited as being contrary to the charitable nature of a *qarḍ*.[117] Indeed, one Ḥanafī authority expressly distinguished self-interested loans from *ribā*, arguing that although such loans are not *ribā*, they are prohibited because of their resemblance thereto.[118] A Shāfiʿī authority argued that self-interested

113. Id.

114. Id. at 317.

115. Abū Zahra, *supra* note 16, at 21. Among the social and economic ills he attributes to lending at interest are: excessive greed and sloth, id. at 21–22 (money-lenders are greedy insofar as their income comes solely from the effort of others without any equitable sharing of the risk of loss and results in slothfulness since they can earn returns without any personal effort); excessive risk-taking, id. at 22 (availability of credit leads merchants to take on too much risk that destroys their businesses when the economy subsequently contracts); excessive consumption and suboptimal savings ("the proliferation of lending at interest has encouraged many to become extravagant and neglect to save"); oppression of the working class by the moneyed-classes, id. at 19 ("the spread of lending at interest is nothing other than the severe tyranny of capital over labor and all other means of production"); and general economic instability, id. at 22–23:

> It has been established that the crises that effect the world economy are caused by debts which are owed by companies. When they are unable to discharge those debts because of a recession, they are forced to sell their goods at reduced prices, if they are able to find anyone to buy at all. As a result, these [economic] crises are treated by reducing debts by various means, such as increasing the money supply in order to depreciate the value of the currency [in which the debt is denominated], thereby reducing the debt, as the United States did in 1934.

Indeed, he also claims that lending at interest leads to psychiatric disorders from the stress created by debt. Id. at 24 ("[I]n addition to the economic dislocation [lending at interest causes], it also produces constant anxiety for both parties" whose source is covetousness.).

116. See generally Hamoudi, *supra* note 5, at 615–616 (noting the importance of social justice and fairness in the rhetoric of those who advocate an Islamic financial system).

117. See *supra* Part II.B.2.a.

118. Al-Kāsānī, *supra* note 54, at 4983 ("[A] contractually required increase [in a loan contract] resembles *ribā* because [the stipulated increase] is an uncompensated benefit.").

loans are simply an instance of the *ribā* of excess,[119] a doctrine that has generally been treated as simply prophylactic, even by modern authorities who are staunch opponents of lending at interest.[120] Likewise, although the Mālikīs also prohibited self-interested loans, it is not clear whether this is an independent principle or merely a prophylactic rule.[121] More generally, however, authorities such as al-Zuḥaylī and Abū Zahra who condemn lending at interest have assimilated, without any discussion, the practice of commercial lending to the *ribā* of the pre-Islamic days,[122] even though [679] the latter involved an ex-post agreement between debtors and creditors occurring after the original debt had matured,[123] and the former relates to an obligation that arises simultaneously with the ex-ante origination of the debt. Therefore, it would seem that if lending at interest is prohibited, it would be prohibited by the rules of the *ribā* of delay, and not the prohibition of the *ribā* of the pre-Islamic days.[124] Both of these authors also justify the

---

119. Al-Shirbīnī, *supra* note 29, at 363 (attributing to al-Zarkashī the view that self-interested loans are simply an instance of the *ribā* of excess); see also Al-Zuḥaylī, *supra* note 8, at 315.

120. See, e.g., Al-Zuḥaylī, *supra* note 8, at 342–43 (describing the rules of the *ribā* of excess as a prophylactic measure to prevent circumvention of the law, but nevertheless condemning lending at interest as categorically forbidden).

121. See *supra* note 47 and accompanying text.

122. See, e.g., Abū Zahra, *supra* note 16, at 37 ("[T]he *ribā* set forth in the Qur'an is precisely the *ribā* that banks deal in, and the basis of the people's commercial dealings. Accordingly, there is no doubt that it is prohibited."); Al-Zuḥaylī, *supra* note 8, at 342:

> There are two types of the forbidden *ribā* in Islam. The first is *ribā al-nasī'a* [sic, i.e. the *ribā* of the pre-Islamic days], which is effected through an increase in the debt amount in compensation for deferment of its maturity.... Commercial bank interest is a form of *ribā al-nasī'a*, whether it is simple or compounded.

At the same time, however, both authorities continue to describe the pre-Islamic transaction of *ribā* (which the express language of the Qur'an condemns) as involving a pre-existing debt which is settled by a new debt whose principal amount is increased in exchange for a deferral of the term. See, e.g., Abū Zahra, *supra* note 16, at 34 (Quoting an early authority for the proposition that "the *ribā* for which there is no doubt occurs when a creditor asks his debtor 'Shall you pay or shall you increase?' If [the debtor] does not pay, [the debtor] increases the [principal] amount owed to the [creditor], and [the creditor] defers the maturity date."); Al-Zuḥaylī, *supra* note 8, at 311 ("*Ribā al-nasī'a*, which is the only type known to pre-Islamic Arabia ... is the *ribā* collected in compensation for deferring a due debt to a new term of deferment.").

123. See *supra*, Part I.A.

124. Al-Zuḥaylī, *supra* note 8, at 343. Al-Zuḥaylī notes that the prohibition against self-interested loans is not based on strong textual evidence, but is instead based on the fact that a number of the Prophet Muhammad's companions prohibited interest-bearing loans by analogy to the Prophet's prohibition against the bundling of a loan with other transactions, such as a sale. Id. Were commercial loan transactions to be analyzed under the rules of the *ribā* of delay, there is at least a facially valid (even if purely formal) argument that the Shāfiʿī and Mālikī doctrines would permit such loans, at least so long as the loan involves fiat currency. See id. at 324–25. Al-Zuḥaylī, recognizing the potential force of this argument, attempts to pre-empt it by acknowledging that in this case, he departed "from the

prohibition against lending at interest on the grounds that permitting interest-bearing loans amounts to turning currency into an object of commerce, when it is intended only to be a measure of value of goods.[125]

[680] 2. The Dissenting View

a. Rashīd Riḍā

Perhaps the most important religious scholar who rejected the claim that an interest-bearing loan from its inception is forbidden is Rashīd Riḍā, the early twentieth century Muslim legal reformer.[126] Responding to a series of questions presented to him regarding *ribā* in 1907, Riḍā concluded that the rules of the *ribā* of excess are entirely prophylactic,[127] and the only kind of *ribā* that is morally condemned by the Qur'an is the *ribā* of the pre-Islamic era.[128] Moreover, Riḍā makes clear that in his view, the initial increase in the principal amount of a debt at its origination is an instance of the *ribā* of

traditional Shāfiʿī position [in favor of the Ḥanafī position]" so that "all modern monies, including paper currency, [are subject to] *ribā*." Id. at 325. Al-Zuḥaylī also dismissed the views of those who would exempt transactions involving fiat currencies from the rules of *ribā* by analogy to the pre-modern exclusion of copper coins because in prior periods, transactions involving copper currency represented only a de minimis amount of aggregate economic activity. See id. at 347. Shaykh ʿAlī Jumuʿa, official mufti of the Arab Republic of Egypt, recently opined that bank interest was permissible, in part because Egyptian currency has no relationship to gold or silver and that banks and their depositors do not engage in lending as understood by Islamic law. https://www.youtube.com/watch?v=1DHsurAm1RY.

125. See, e.g., Abū Zahra, *supra* note 16, at 40 (quoting Aristotle approvingly for the proposition that profit from lending at interest is contrary to nature because the presumption is that the value of money does not change as a result of time or place in contrast to other types of property); id. at 59 (stating that selling a good at a markup is permissible because the prices of goods change with time, but "currencies are the means of valuation, so time by hypothesis does not effect them. They should always maintain the same value because they are not an article of commerce whose value increases and decreases"); id. at 88 (stating that gold and silver are subject to the rules of *ribā* so that they do not become commercial goods); Al-Zuḥaylī, *supra* note 8, at 321 ("[Permitting] *ribā al-nasī'a* would lead to dire economic consequences, since the resulting commodification of money and trading it in different quantities, would cause an imbalance by preventing money from serving the role of stable numeraire.").

126. *Fatāwā al-Imām Muḥammad Rashīd Riḍā*, 603–9 (Ṣalāḥ al-Dīn al-Munajjid & Yūsuf Khūrī eds., Dār al-Kitāb al-Jadīd 1970).

127. Id. at 606 ("[T]he *ribā* of excess was not prohibited for its own sake, but rather was prohibited to prevent a means to circumvent the law").

128. Id. ("Accordingly, the *ribā* which the Qur'an condemned is limited to the *ribā* of delay as was customary in the days before Islam ... ."); id. at 608–9

> The *ribā* of delay that was customary [in the days prior to Islam] was the [*ribā*] that occurred after the debt had matured as a result of a [second] delay [in repayment] and if that occurred repeatedly, it would result in a doubling [of the principal amount] as they used to do in the days before Islam.

excess, even though the creditor insists on the increase as a result of accepting payment in the future.[129]

It was the prophylactic nature of this prohibition, Riḍā argued, that led both the Ḥanafī and the Shāfiʿī jurists to authorize transactions that were designed to evade the technical doctrines of *ribā*.[130] One such device that became well-known in the Ottoman Empire was the *muʿāmala*, pursuant to which the creditor, after lending a sum of money (e.g., $900) to the borrower, would then sell the borrower on credit a handkerchief (or any other low-priced good) at a price that was well in excess of its market value (e.g., $100), thereby giving the creditor the desired return on the loan.[131] According to Riḍā, the Ḥanafīs and the Shāfiʿīs permitted this evasion of the rules of *ribā* in reliance on the statement attributed to the Prophet where he instructed his followers who wished to trade two measures of low-quality dates for one-measure of high-quality dates to sell the low-quality dates and use the proceeds to [681] purchase the high-quality dates.[132] Because they rejected the use of such devices, Mālikīs instead accept the argument that prophylactic rules may be revised or abandoned where it would be beneficial to do so.[133]

Riḍā argued that the only way to understand the prohibitions against the *ribā* of excess was as a prophylactic device, "because there is no point in requiring that the exchange of currency or food for its like be simultaneous and in equivalent quantities for its own sake, because no rational person would ever do that, because [such a trade] lacks any benefit."[134] The only reason people trade is to obtain "an increase, either in quantity or quality, and neither is prohibited for its own sake, since obtaining a gain is the very ... goal of commerce."[135] Since that is the case, the prohibitions of the *ribā* of excess can be overridden whenever there is a legitimate need to do so. Among the examples that Riḍā gives as justifying a relaxation in the rules of *ribā* are: (1) the need to invest the property of an orphan or a widow; or (2) a student, who would otherwise be unable to invest his property for income, with the undesirable result that he could not continue his studies.[136] Although lending at interest is justified by the need of either the creditor to invest her money or the debtor to borrow, the law must be careful not to allow such transactions

129. Id. at 608.
130. Id. at 607.
131. Id.
132. See *supra* note 33 and accompanying text.
133. *Fatāwā al-Imām Muḥammad Rashīd Riḍā*, *supra* note 126, at 607–8.
134. Id. at 608.
135. Id.
136. Id.

to result in the "doubling"[137] of debts, something explicitly condemned by the Qur'an.[138] For that reason, Riḍā praised the Ottoman-era rule that placed a maximum interest rate on lending transactions as consistent with "the definitive [Qur'anic] rule prohibiting the doubling of debts while at the same time taking into account the well-being [of people] or [necessity]."[139]

b. ʿAbd al-Razzaq al-Sanhūrī

ʿAbd al-Razzāq al-Sanhūrī, drafter of the Egyptian Civil Code as well as the civil codes of numerous other Arab countries, discussed the doctrines of *ribā* at length in his work, *Maṣādir al-Ḥaqq fī al-Fiqh al-Islāmī* [The Sources of Obligation in Islamic Law].[140] [682] Consistent with his training as a scholar of comparative law,[141] Sanhūrī, after giving a broad survey of the positions of Muslim jurists on the doctrine of *ribā*,[142] places Islamic legislation on this subject within a comparative perspective of the regulation of lending at interest.[143] For Sanhūrī, Islamic law's approach to *ribā* is characterized by two opposing trends. The first takes a broad view of *ribā* and expands its scope until it covers broad areas of trade. The second attempts to narrow the application of *ribā* to a more or less limited set of transactions, or in the alternative, permits parties to circumvent the prohibitions of *ribā* by using legal fictions.[144] One such fiction was the back-to-back sale, pursuant to which the prospective debtor would agree to "sell" a commodity (e.g., ten bushels of grain) for the desired principal amount in cash (e.g., $100); then agree to purchase from the first purchaser another commodity (e.g., ten bushes of grain) at a price equal to the original sale price plus a mark-up to be paid in the future (e.g., $110 in one year).

---

137. Id. at 609 ("If this results in a doubling of the debt owed by the borrower, it is contrary to the wisdom of the Lawgiver, and no one with any piety would deem it lawful."); see also *supra* note 128 and accompanying text.

138. Āl ʿImrān, 3:130 ("O you who believe! Do not devour *ribā*, doubled and doubled").

139. *Fatāwā al-Imām Muḥammad Rashīd Riḍā*, *supra* note 126, at 608.

140. See generally ʿAbd al-Razzāq al-Sanhūrī, *Maṣādir al-Ḥaqq fī al-Fiqh al-Islāmī* (Dār al-Fikr 1953–1954) (3 volumes).

141. Several commentators have discussed the role of comparative law in Sanhūrī's project to create a modernized Islamic law. See Enid Hill, *Al-Sanhuri and Islamic Law*, 3 Arab L.Q. 33 (1988); 'Amr Shalakany, *Between Identity and Distribution: Sanhuri, Genealogy and the Will to Islamize*, 8 Islamic L. & Soc. 201 (2001); 'Amr Shalakany, *Sanhuri, and the Historical Origins of Comparative Law in the Arab World*, in *Rethinking the Masters of Comparative Law* 152 (Annelise Riles ed., 2001).

142. ʿAbd al-Razzāq al-Sanhūrī, 3 *Maṣādir al-Ḥaqq fī al-Fiqh al-Islāmī* 176–94 (Dār al-Fikr 1953–1954).

143. Id. at 194–98 (discussing restrictions on lending at interest in ancient Egypt, the broader prohibitions in Judaism and Christianity, and the legalization of lending at interest in Europe as a consequence of the French Revolution and the introduction of the Napoleonic Code).

144. Id. at 199 ("Originally, the scope of *ribā* in [Islamic law] was quite broad ... then it began to narrow as a result of economic pressures. This latter development was preceded by the recognition of numerous legal fictions which were used to legitimate otherwise illicit profits.").

As a result of the two sales, the first seller/debtor receives one hundred dollars in cash against an obligation to pay one hundred and ten dollars in a year.[145] Another legal fiction involved a loan and a sale, as in the case where a person wishes to borrow one hundred dollars for a year, and the creditor wishes to receive one hundred and ten dollars a year later. In this case, a simple agreement to lend one hundred dollars against an obligation to repay one hundred and ten dollars would be unlawful because it involved a loan with a stipulated benefit. Here, the lender could sell the borrower an item of trivial value for a price equal to ten dollars due in a year (the interest component) and then lend him the [683] principal amount, resulting in a net obligation on the borrower to repay the lender the desired return.[146] Indeed, this latter fiction had become so entrenched in the Ottoman Empire that the state authorities placed a limit on the maximum interest which was permissible in such transactions.[147]

In contrast to the legal trend which expanded the scope of *ribā* (subsequently leading to the recognition of legal fictions to allow parties to circumvent those rules), al-Sanhūrī identifies a minority of early jurists led by Ibn ʿAbbās, a religious scholar who was the Prophet Muhammad's cousin, who attempted to restrict the application of *ribā* only to the *ribā* of the pre-Islamic days; however, their position was overwhelmed by the majority of jurists who favored the broad approach.[148] Finally, al-Sanhūrī identifies a third group of Muslim jurists who put forth two intermediate positions regarding *ribā*. The first of these two interpretations distinguishes the *ribā* of excess, on the one hand, from

145. Id.

146. Id. In this case, if the sale precedes the loan, the Ḥanafīs deemed the contract to be permissible (*jā'iz*), but if the loan preceded the sale, the transaction was deemed to be disfavored (*makrūh*). Id.

147. Id. at 200 n.1 (reporting that the statutory maximum was 5 percent at one time and 15 percent at others); see also Muḥammad Amīn b. ʿUmar (known as Ibn ʿĀbidīn), *Radd al-Muḥtār ʿalā al-Durr al-Mukhtār, Bāb al-Murābaha,* (13th Century) reprinted in *Encyclopedia of Islamic Jurisprudence* CD-ROM, Kuwaiti Ministry of Endowments, the Islamic Development Bank & Harf Info. Tech. 2004 (discussing remedy in the event lender imposed an interest rate in excess of the legal maximum). The Shāfiʿīs also permitted loans in which it was understood—but not expressly stipulated—that the debtor would voluntarily repay his creditor in excess of the principal amount. Al-Sanhūrī, *supra* note 142, at 239–40

> [I]f it is known that a man, when he borrows, customarily repays an amount in excess of the principal, there are two positions [within the Shāfiʿī school regarding the permissibility] of lending to him. The first is that it is impermissible to make a loan to him unless it is stipulated that he will return only what is owed, because what is known by custom is akin to that which is contractually stipulated and, had the excess been expressly stipulated, it would not have been permissible, so the same [rule] should apply if [the impermissible stipulation] is established by custom. The second is that it is permissible, and that is the rule [that is followed] because it is [religiously] commendable to return an amount in excess [of that which was borrowed based on a saying of the Prophet that "the best of you is the most generous in the discharge of his obligations"], so it is impermissible to deny the validity of this contract based on that [consideration].

148. Al-Sanhūrī, *supra* note 142, at 201.

the *ribā* of delay, on the other hand, concluding that the former was a type of "subtle" *ribā* that was not prohibited for its own sake, but only because it could lead to "obvious" *ribā* (the *ribā* of delay), which this group of jurists concluded had been prohibited for its own sake.[149] The second group of jurists identified both the *ribā* of excess [684] and the *ribā* of delay as prophylactic prohibitions, i.e., they represented a "subtle" form of *ribā*, with only the *ribā* of the pre-Islamic era being categorically prohibited.[150] The legal implications of this middle position was that "subtle" *ribā*, whether defined as the *ribā* of excess or as both the *ribā* of excess and the *ribā* of delay, continued to apply, but only to the extent that a legitimate countervailing need could not justify an exception from the applications of these doctrines.[151]

Al-Sanhūrī himself adopts the second of the two middle positions.[152] He identifies three policy goals behind the doctrines of *ribā* which presumably justify the contin-

---

149. Id. at 202. According to al-Sanhūrī, the principal representative of this position is Ibn Qayyim al-Jawziyya, although Ibn Rushd comes close to Ibn al-Qayyim's position. Id. at 203.

150. Id. at 202. This second position differs from that of Ibn ʿAbbās to the extent that it continues to respect—at least presumptively—the prohibitions against the *ribā* of excess and delay, whereas Ibn 'Abbas did not recognize them at all. Al-Sanhūrī, however, attributed the second position to Rashīd Riḍā rather than to any pre-modern jurists. Id. at 219. At the same time, he criticized as arbitrary Ibn al-Qayyim's implicit assimilation of the *ribā* of delay into the "obvious" *ribā*. Id. at 218–19. To the extent that neither the *ribā* of delay nor the *ribā* of excess is set forth in the Qur'an (unlike the condemnation of the *ribā* of the pre-Islamic era), al-Sanhūrī argued that they should receive similar treatment, i.e. each prohibition should be treated as prophylactic, not categorical. Id.

151. Id. at 206

> There is an important consequence to distinguishing the *ribā* of excess from the *ribā* of delay and that is: because [in the view of Ibn al-Qayyim] the *ribā* of delay is prohibited for itself while the *ribā* of excess is prohibited only to the extent that it is a means to something illegal, [but is] not illegal in itself, the illegality of the *ribā* of delay is more severe than the illegality of the *ribā* of excess. Accordingly, no exceptions are allowed from the *ribā* of delay unless a pressing legal necessity exists, such as that which would permit consumption of carrion or blood, whereas in the case of the *ribā* of excess, exceptions may be recognized for a need. It is obvious that a need is less [demanding] than a necessity. Accordingly, whenever there is a need for a transaction that involves the *ribā* of excess, it is permitted.

Al-Sanhūrī cites numerous examples of such exceptions to the prohibition against the *ribā* of excess. See id. at 209 (permitting the exchange of an estimated quantity of ripe dates prior to their harvest against a known quantity of dried dates); id. at 211–13 (excluding the sale of gold or silver jewelry for gold or silver from the scope of the *ribā* of excess to take into account the value of the labor in the jewelry); id. at 214–15 (excluding the trade of any type of property which is ordinarily subject to the prohibition against the *ribā* of excess from its scope where that property has been transformed by human art, e.g. bread for bread); id. at 215–17 (excluding the exchange of coins for bullion from the prohibition against the *ribā* of excess where the difference is the implicit cost of the mint's work and the need for cash is time-sensitive, e.g. a merchant who is departing on a trading venture).

152. Id. at 237 (concluding that while the *ribā* of the pre-Islamic era is prohibited for its own sake—and thus exceptions to it can only be made in cases of pressing necessity—the prohibitions against

ued application of the rules of the *ribā* of excess and delay, even if only on a prudential grounds.[153] The [685] first is to prevent the hoarding of food.[154] The second is to prevent manipulation of currency which could result in instability of prices as a consequence of currency becoming an object rather than measure of commerce.[155] The third is to prevent mis-pricing in the case of barter transactions involving goods of the same genus.[156] Finally, al-Sanhūrī concludes that interest-bearing loans are not, properly speaking, subject to the doctrine of *ribā* at all, but instead involve only *quasi-ribā* and should be treated as a species of either the *ribā* of excess or the *ribā* of delay. Under this analysis, interest-bearing loans would presumptively be unlawful, subject to exceptions based on need.[157] Al-Sanhūrī then concludes his discussion by addressing the question of whether a need exists for interest-bearing loans. Unsurprisingly, he concludes that the need of modern enterprises in a market economy for large amounts of capital in excess of what could be practicably raised via equity offerings represents precisely the kind of need under Islamic law that renders interest-bearing loans legitimate.[158]

c. Mahmoud el-Gamal

Mahmoud el-Gamal has applied the methods of law and economics to the problem of *ribā*. El-Gamal argues that the doctrines associated with *ribā* should be understood functionally, i.e., as a species of benefits analysis, rather than as an exercise in formal adher-

---

the *ribā* of increase and delay are only prophylactic and thus may be overridden whenever there is a legitimate need). Later, Al-Sanhūrī notes that it is inconceivable that a legal excuse could ever exist that would permit a creditor to violate the prohibition against the *ribā* of the pre-Islamic era. Id. at 242.

153. Id. at 236.

154. Id.

155. Id.

156. Id.

157. Id. at 241

> Because interest in respect of a loan is not in reality *ribā*, but only something that resembles *ribā*, it must be deemed to be either a type of the *ribā* of delay or the *ribā* of excess, and although these kinds of *ribā* are all prohibited, the prohibition is prophylactic, not for itself, and accordingly, the prohibition lapses when a need arises.

158. Id. at 243–44. Consistent with his analysis of the types of *ribā*, however, he condemns compound interest as constituting the *ribā* of the pre-Islamic era, and consistent with his view that the rules regarding the *ribā* of delay are intended to prevent the occurrence of the *ribā* of the pre-Islamic era, he argues that the state should set maximum interest rates. Id. at 244. In fact, al-Sanhūrī explains that the Egyptian civil code, which he largely drafted, included many provisions intended to protect debtors, and these provisions were inspired by Islamic law's prohibitions against *ribā*. Id. at 244–46 (discussing provisions in Egypt's civil law including its prohibition against compound interest, its provision of a maximum interest rate, its prohibition against a creditor collecting interest in an amount in excess of the principal except in cases of long-term loans used for investment, and the right of debtors to pre-pay their debts after giving creditors six-month notice without any penalties other than payment of the principal and six-months' interest).

ence to [686] bright-line rules, the very structure of which invites easy circumvention.[159] In the case of the prohibitions involved in the *ribā* of excess and the *ribā* of delay, the primary benefit which is to be attained is trade on equitable terms by insuring the use of transparent market pricing mechanisms.[160] Because it would be impossible to enforce such a policy in all trades, the doctrine of *ribā* was limited to those trades (intra-generic trades exploiting differences in quality) that raise particularly obvious problems in pricing, and have the effect of forcing the prospective traders, before they can complete their trade, to first sell their goods in the market and then buy, using the proceeds from that first trade, the ultimate goods they desire. According to El-Gamal, the rules of the *ribā* of excess function:

> [A]s a mechanism that pre-commits [individuals] to collection of information about market conditions, and marking terms of trade to market prices. This protects individuals against engaging in disadvantageous trades and enhances overall exchange efficiency.... Hence, justice and efficiency both dictate following this mark-to-market approach to establishing trading ratios.[161]

The same price discovery justification applies to the restrictions of the *ribā* of delay by requiring that credit be extended in connection with the purchase of a specific asset, e.g., a deferred sale of a car—the prohibition against the *ribā* of delay functions to force traders to establish the appropriate interest rate in light of the future value of the asset being financed. Presumably, this rule results in a more accurate interest rate than would have been the case if the transaction were simply a loan of money, with respect to which the creditor either was ignorant regarding how the debtor would use the proceeds, or could not satisfactorily bind the debtor to use the proceeds from the loan in a specified manner.[162] By tying the price of credit to the specific asset that the debtor seeks to finance, the rules of the *ribā* of delay contribute to the equitable pricing of credit, and may contribute to reducing the risks of asset bubbles in, for [687] example, housing markets.[163] Accordingly, El-Gamal suggests that the prohibition of the *ribā* of delay

---

159. El-Gamal, *supra* note 2, at 30 (agreeing with the view of ʿAbd al-Wahhāb Khallāf, a 20th century Islamic jurist from Egypt who argued that, in the context of financial transactions, "benefits analysis should be the final arbiter").

160. Id. at 53.

161. Id.

162. Id. at 53–54. This also suggests that an implicit interest rate in an otherwise formally compliant transaction that exceeds the market interest-rate should be considered to violate the spirit of the *ribā* prohibitions. Id. at 54.

163. Id. at 56–57 (suggesting that in structuring an Islamic lease to finance the purchase of a home, the purchaser/borrower would be able to compare the contractual rent against the prevailing market rent, and to the extent that the former exceeds the latter, she would be on notice that the there is a high likelihood that the asset is overpriced).

be understood as a prohibition of "the unbundled sale of credit, wherein it is difficult to mark the interest rate to market."[164] Viewed from this perspective, the prohibition against the *ribā* of delay is simply a special instance of *gharar*, a doctrine which invalidated contracts that included contingent pay-offs or other material uncertainties in the contract's terms.[165] Moreover, El-Gamal is relatively optimistic that unsecured credit is not, for the most part, necessary for the functioning of even a modern economy, as "all the financial ends that can be served through commercial lending can be equally if not better served through other forms of commutative contracts (such as sales, leases, and the like)."[166] Finally, the paternalism inherent in the prohibitions against *ribā* is justified, even in contemporary circumstances, for two reasons. The first is the documented human irrationality with respect to time preference which results in individuals taking on excessive debt and eventually, in some cases, leading to the bankruptcy of those individuals.[167] The second is that although the financial system is monitored by paternalistic regulators who impose restrictions to protect against excessive risk taking, they do so either from the perspective of protecting the health of the financial system in the aggregate, in the case of bank regulators, or the health of the bank, in the case of bank credit departments that oversee the extension of loans.[168] [688] Neither set of regulators, however, is focused on the welfare of the bank's customers; thus, bank regulators may allow banks to engage in risky transactions without regard to individual customers' welfare, so long as the soundness of the banking system is not threatened thereby. Similarly, a bank's loan officers may permit the bank to extend credit to individuals who are otherwise not creditworthy if the loans are made to a large enough number of borrowers so that the profits made from the pool of loans exceed the losses incurred from defaulting credits. The paternalistic regulations set forth in the prohibitions against *ribā* thus fill a regula-

---

164. Id. at 57. This observation might be especially salient in a society that lacks developed credit markets but has established markets for the future delivery of commodities such as food or livestock.

165. Mahmoud A. El-Gamal, *A Simple Fiqh-and-Economics Rationale for Mutualization in Islamic Financial Intermediation* 5 (2006), http://www.ruf.rice.edu/~elgamal/files/mutualize.pdf.

> If we accept those two economic definitions of *ribā* and *gharar* [i.e. the unbundled sale of credit and risk, respectively], then we recognize that *ribā* is also an extreme form of *gharar*: The sale or extension of unbundled credit (e.g. in an unsecured loan) is a counter purchase of credit risk (which is a negatively-priced bad, the risk of debtor default, the price of which would be one of the main components of the interest charged). Credit risk includes substantial uncertainty, because the probability of default may be difficult to estimate, and the resulting losses in case of default (esp. due to bankruptcy) can be quite substantial.

166. El-Gamal, *supra* note 2, at 57.

167. Id. at 55–56 (citing empirical evidence of "time preference anomalies" that lead to dynamic inconsistency in human patterns of savings, spending and borrowing).

168. Id. at 55.

tory gap, so to speak, by putting prudential limitations on individuals, just as there are already prudential limitations imposed on banks.[169]

In substance then, El-Gamal agrees with Riḍā and al-Sanhūrī that *ribā* is primarily a prophylactic doctrine; however, he differs from them insofar as he adopts the Ḥanafī view that *ribā* essentially applies to all trades in order to prevent mis-pricing. While he would not condemn transactions that are not formally in compliance with the requirements of Islamic law where there is little to no actual risk of mis-pricing, he condemns those who confer Islamic legitimacy to a trade simply on account of the transaction's formal adherence to the requirements of Islamic law without respecting the goal of promoting fair pricing, a practice he calls "*sharīʿa* arbitrage."[170]

C. Difficulties with the Proposed Justifications of the Rules of Ribā

Sunni jurists have long believed that Islamic transactional law, including the prohibitions associated with the various doctrines of *ribā*, exist to further the secular welfare of human beings.[171] Accordingly, it is not surprising that the juristic literature attempted to provide rational [689] justifications for the doctrines of *ribā*. Nevertheless, despite the various theories of *ribā* that have been proposed throughout Islamic history, none of them seem to explain adequately the historical rules.[172] Even if one is prepared to accept the notion that some *ribā*-based prohibitions are in fact prudential and not categorical, it is often difficult to see what concerns gave rise to these "prudential" doctrines in the first place.[173] Consider the traditional Ḥanafīs explanation of *ribā*. In its generality, it purports

169. Id. ("Thus, restrictions imposed by regulators and financial professionals require supplementary protections for individuals against their own irrational behavior—a function that can be fulfilled by religious law."). It is not clear what the institutional implications of El-Gamal's analysis are, other than that religiously-motivated, paternalistic regulation might complement legal regulation of the financial sector by reducing the tendency of individuals to engage in irrational behavior that may be profitably exploited by the financial sector.

170. Id. at 11 (noting that many secular legal constraints have substantially eliminated the ills addressed by the juristic doctrine of *ribā* but that formal adherence to "Islamic" contractual forms sometimes not only add dead-weight costs in the form of higher transaction costs, but also fail to mitigate the underlying substantive risks that were the basis of the Islamic prohibition in the first place).

171. See *supra* note 88.

172. Vogel & Hayes, *supra* note 3 at 78–87 (reviewing various theories justifying the doctrines of *ribā*, but concluding that "none of the ....explanations is wholly satisfactory," even if they "offer something towards comprehending [the] results").

173. Al-Zuḥaylī, for example, states that the *ribā* of excess is prohibited in order "to prevent the means of circumventing the prohibition of" the *ribā* of delay, but he does not explain the connection between the two. Al-Zuḥaylī, *supra* note 8 at 317. One could argue more convincingly perhaps that the trades prohibited by the doctrine of *ribā* of excess were common means of evading the prohibition against the *ribā* of the pre-Islamic era. A creditor of an insolvent debtor could "sell" his debtor one

to apply to every transaction in which there is a contractually-fixed but uncompensated consideration that accrues to one of the parties to the trade.[174] Leaving aside the question of what circumstances would lead rational traders to agree to such a one-sided trade, the Ḥanafī account of *ribā* at least has the virtue of being related to a general problem of how to guarantee that private trades will occur on fair terms. Unfortunately, the concern for fair pricing, while it might explain the rules of *ribā*, is completely contrary to the notion that the parties are bound to even bad bargains, so long as the law deemed the terms to have been set pursuant to arm's length bargaining and the absence of fraud.[175] Indeed, one Mālikī jurist stated that exploiting differences in subjective valuations of goods was deemed by early Mālikī scholars to be part of the "art of commerce."[176]

More generally, however, given the doctrinal importance of the *ribā* restrictions, why should the rules be so easy to evade simply by trading goods across genera rather than within the same genus? Likewise, why should one be able to trade goods of different genera which are subject to the *ribā* restrictions in unequal quantities (e.g., one [690] measure of wheat for two measures of dates), but only if delivery of both counter-values is simultaneous? In other words, why would the *ribā* of delay prohibit a trade on a deferred basis that the doctrine of *ribā* of excess would permit on an immediate basis? Clearly, it could not be that the creditor is exploiting the debtor in this circumstance, because (assuming that the debtor has a positive discount rate) the debtor is receiving his consideration at a lower price in the credit transaction than he would have in the cash transaction. Perhaps then, it is the opposite—it is the debtor in the credit transaction who is exploiting the creditor by enjoying the immediate delivery of a good against an obligation to deliver a consideration in the future whose value, even assuming performance, may be substantially less than what the price on the delivery would have been.[177] This would suggest a general suspicion of credit transactions based on the notion that they are too amenable to mis-pricing. If that is the concern, however, why permit credit sales

---

measure of dates for two measures, for example, resulting in a net transfer from the debtor to the creditor of one measure of dates. The two for one transaction, then, amounts to a fictitious sale that results in compensation to the creditor for deferring collection of his debt. This risk, however, would appear to be more efficiently policed by bankruptcy law, which denies a bankrupt debtor the capacity to enter into new contracts without adequate consideration. See Al-Dardīr, *supra* note 15 at 345 ("[A]n insolvent debtor, prior to the initiation of bankruptcy proceedings, is prohibited from dealing in his property except for [adequate] consideration, and [any such transactions] are not binding.").

174. See *supra* note 47 and accompanying text.

175. See *supra* note 52 and accompanying text.

176. Ibn al-ʿArabī, *supra* note 9 at 242.

177. Indeed, the Ḥanafīs justify the prohibition against the deferred trade of goods subject to *ribā*, even in equal quantities, on the grounds that immediate delivery is more valuable than a deferred delivery, thus resulting in an uncompensated benefit for the debtor. See, e.g., Al-Zuḥaylī, *supra* note 8, at 336 ("(i) an identified object is better than one described as a liability and (ii) an immediately available object is preferred to the same object deferred.").

of food if the consideration paid is either cash or goods that are not food (e.g., cloth)? It seems difficult to make the case that whatever risk of mis-pricing exists in connection with credit sales, that risk is substantially mitigated (at least where food is the object of sale) by forcing the purchaser to pay in either money or goods that are not food.

Similarly, the classical rules pertaining to *qarḍ* and how the doctrine of *ribā* applies to it are equally confusing. Because a *qarḍ* is meant to be charitable, if the lender stipulates a benefit for himself (or even another) it becomes invalid. In this case, however, it would appear that a self-interested loan is simply a sale, an analysis which is confirmed by the thirteenth century Egyptian jurist, Shihāb al-Dīn al-Qarāfī.[178] If this is true, the legal treatment of the transaction should turn on whether it violates the restrictions of the *ribā* of delay. Accordingly, while a self-interested *qarḍ* granted in gold or silver would run afoul of the rules of the *ribā* of delay, presumably a self-interested *qarḍ* of copper coins or cloth would not (since neither commodity is subject to the rules of the *ribā* of delay, at least according to the Shāfiʿīs and the Mālikīs). There is evidence, however, that such a loan was deemed to include *ribā* by at [691] least some authorities.[179] Moreover, although it was unlawful to bundle a sale and a *qarḍ*, (e.g., conditioning the extension of the *qarḍ* on using it to purchase a good), a merchant could simply sell the good to the purchaser on credit at a markup to the cash price, a transaction which was not deemed to be exceptional despite its inclusion of an implicit interest-bearing loan.[180]

Modern authorities opposed to lending at interest claim to base their position on the grounds of traditional Islamic legal doctrine; however, more realistically, their condemnation of commercial banking is based on a combination of intuitions regarding social justice and social costs that arise from the sale of credit.[181] Instead of interest-based financing, which they condemn as unfair because it guarantees a profit to the lender even as the entrepreneur bears the risk that the venture will lose money, they propose profit-loss sharing finance.[182] Even if one ignores for a moment the fact that pre-modern

178. 4 Shihāb al-Dīn Aḥmad b. Idrīs al-Qarāfī, *Al-Furūq* 2 (ʿĀlam al-Kutub n.d.) (13th century).

179. See Al-Nawawī, supra note 55, at 34; Al-Dardīr, *supra* note 18 at 291 (condemning self-interested *qarḍ* as involving *ribā* without conducting an analysis under the rules governing sales).

180. See El-Gamal, *supra* note 2, at 50 (discussing the fact that jurists took for granted that the markup in credit sales relative to cash prices reflected the time-value of money).

181. See, e.g., Al-Sanhūrī, *supra* note 142, at 229 (quoting al-Darrāz, a 20th century Egyptian religious scholar, for the proposition that lending at interest privileges capital at the expense of the working class and reinforces class differences); Al-Zuḥaylī, *supra* note 8, at 347 (arguing that the harms arising out of lending at interest—even if only to finance production and not consumption—exceed whatever benefits that may arise from such a practice and even suggesting that lending at interest "may produce bad distortionary effects, and may even force an inflationary spiral that harms all economic agents in the long run").

182. Al-Sanhūrī, *supra* note 142, at 230 (quoting al-Darrāz for the proposition that instead of interest-based lending, which is unfair, investments should be financed using partnership where losses and profits are divided equitably); Abū Zahra, *supra* note 16, at 74 (condemning interest-based lending for

Islamic law displays no aversion to fixed-price contracts, (so long as they are compliant with the rules of *ribā*) and thus, there is no basis to conclude that Islamic law has a bias toward equity-financing rather than debt-financing, the preferred mode of financing put forth by modern religious scholars, *muḍāraba* (also called *qirāḍ* and known as *commenda* in Europe), is inconsistent with the very profit-loss sharing model they urge as being paradigmatically "Islamic." In a *muḍāraba*, the investor delivers capital to an entrepreneur who then invests it in return for a share of the venture's profits. Significantly, the entrepreneur is not entitled to any [692] returns until all of the investor's capital has been returned. Accordingly, in the event of a loss of capital, the entrepreneur's labor is valued at zero. If a *muḍāraba* was truly a partnership between the investor and the entrepreneur, the entrepreneur would be deemed to own a share of the firm's capital, in which case upon dissolution of the firm, so long as some equity remained, the entrepreneur would receive some of the firm's remaining value. In fact, Islamic partnership law (*sharika*) expressly provided that a partnership could not be formed where one partner contributed financial capital and the other partner contributed labor.[183] The refusal to permit capital and labor to co-exist as partners seems to be derived from the notion that labor works in exchange for a wage, which must be fixed as a condition for the validity of the labor contract.[184] Accordingly, traditional jurisprudence deemed *muḍāraba* to be an exceptional contract (*rukhṣa*), insofar as the compensation provided for the entrepreneur's labor is contingent, something that is ordinarily impermissible.[185] Therefore, the general rule of Islamic law is that labor should not be expected to bear business risk, a result that is consistent with the non-diversifiable (and therefore riskier) nature of human capital relative to financial capital.[186]

---

not sharing the risk of loss with the entrepreneur and proposing equity investments as an alternative means to finance investments); Al-Zuḥaylī, *supra* note 8, at 349–350 (describing Islamic banks as making their profits from partnerships with entrepreneurs and thus being exposed to the risk of loss arising from commercial ventures as well as the possibility of profit).

183. Al-Dardīr, *supra* note 15, at 455–456 (dividing partnerships into "commercial partnerships" to which each partner contributes financial capital and "labor partnerships" to which each partner contributes labor). The most important exception to this rule was a sharecropping contract (*muzāraʿa*), where the cultivator's labor was deemed to be part of the joint venture's capital. See id. at 492–500 (explaining rules of sharecropping).

184. 4 Aḥmad Ibn Muḥammad al-Dardīr, *al-Sharḥ al-Ṣaghīr* 81 (Muṣṭafā Kamāl Waṣfī, ed., Dār al-Maʿārif 1972) (stating that among other requirements for validity, a wage must be fixed at the time of the contract with respect to its nature, amount, and time of payment).

185. Al-Ṣāwī, *supra* note 34, at 681 (noting the exceptional nature of the employment contract described by al-Dardīr).

186. See generally David Levhari & Yoram Weiss, *The Effect of Risk on the Investment in Human Capital*, 64 Am. Econ. Rev. 950 (1974) (noting the especially risky nature of human capital relative to other forms of capital). Note, however, that Islamic law provides for a unilateral contract of hire that operates as an option in the favor of the laborer. Pursuant to this contract, a worker, upon acceptance of the offer, has

1. *Ribā* as Price-Setting

It is perhaps too ambitious to aspire to a single, unified theory of *ribā*, but I will nevertheless suggest that the various doctrines of *ribā* are designed to prevent the occurrence of unjust enrichment. Accordingly, [693] *ribā* occurs whenever one party to a trade receives a stipulated benefit for which she did not compensate her counterparty. What distinguishes the Islamic concept of *ribā* from the common law concept of unjust enrichment is that certain transactions are conclusively, in the case of the *ribā* of the pre-Islamic era, and presumptively, in the case of the *ribā* of excess and delay, deemed by law to involve unjust enrichment regardless of the parties' consent, sophistication, or knowledge. In other words, a certain class of transactions is simply excluded from the universe of permissible market transactions, even though some traders view such trades favorably.[187]

Another way of describing the rules of the *ribā* of excess is that Islamic law sets the price of quality differences with respect to goods subject to the *ribā* of excess at zero, but only when such goods are traded intra-generically. In the same vein, one can understand the rules of the *ribā* of delay as simple prohibitions on the deferred trading of food for food, or gold or silver for gold or silver. Accordingly, the rules of the *ribā* of excess and the *ribā* of delay can be understood to be a type of self-executing price-setting regulation that applies whenever a market includes only limited types (perhaps even only one) of goods, something which presumably occurs only in circumstances of extreme scarcity.[188]

---

the right, but not the obligation, to perform a specified task in consideration of payment that is earned only upon successful completion of that task. Upon acceptance of the offer by initiating performance, the offeror loses the right to withdraw the offer until the offeree ceases performance. See Al-Dardīr, *supra* note 184, at 79–85 (describing rules of unilateral hire contract).

187. Ibn Rushd, *supra* note 20, at 506 (observing that the rules of the *ribā* of excess, insofar as they operate to "forbid the trade of unequal amounts in these items results in the absence of such trades on account of the fact that the benefits [of such items] do not differ but trade is necessary only where differing utilities are to be obtained"). Ibn al-ʿArabī makes a similar point when he argues that although *ribā* is defined as "every increase received without a corresponding consideration (*kullu ziyāda lam yuqābilhā ʿiwaḍ*)," the existence of *ribā* can only be determined in respect of the considerations proposed in any particular trade. Ibn al-ʿArabī, *supra* note 9, at 242. Considerations that are offered in contracts, he argues, are divided into two classes: a class of considerations for which revelation has determined their values and a class of considerations whose values are determined not by the law, but by the contracting parties themselves. Id. With respect to this latter class, the only issue raised is whether the price terms of an agreement may be set aside if they are materially off-market. Id. Ibn al-'Arabi concludes that even in this case, the contract should not be set aside—in the absence of fraud—because both parties presumably are or were in need of the considerations at the time they contracted, thus explaining why they entered into the trade. Id.

188. 2 Muḥammad b. Muḥammad b. ʿAbd al-Rahman al-Ḥaṭṭāb, *Mawāhib al-Jalīl li-Sharḥ Mukhtaṣar Khalīl* 368 (Dār al-Fikr 1992) (16th century) (quoting Mālik for the proposition that the staple of the Medinese diet was largely dates).

That would be consistent with its primary effect, which is to prohibit certain trades from occurring despite the fact that certain traders would wish to make those trades; however, in circumstances where the market is well-supplied with numerous types of goods, such price-restraints become irrelevant because prices could be set freely through inter-[694] generic trading. In that case, it is unlikely that traders would prefer to trade intra-generically based on quality differences when a differentiated product market, with its greater trading opportunities, exists.

The prohibition against the *ribā* of the pre-Islamic era can also be understood as a type of price-setting, insofar as Islamic law sets the price of deferral of a debt's repayment at zero once the debtor's default has occurred, while at the same time permitting the contracting parties to determine the price of deferral on an ex-ante basis so long as the trade complies with the ex-ante restrictions of the *ribā* of delay.[189] Accordingly, the parties could freely trade wheat for gold on a deferred basis with a price that implicitly accords a value to the delay in the debtor's delivery of his consideration, but they could not set a positive price for delay after the debtor defaulted.[190]

If the rules of *ribā* are a type of price-setting, several questions arise. For example, with respect to the rules of the *ribā* of excess and delay, what are the justifications for this policy of price-setting in these specific commodities, especially in light of the strong legal norm of respecting parties' bargains and the ability of parties to escape the ex-ante prohibitions simply by engaging in two trades instead of one? Another important question that arises with respect to the ex-ante *ribā* restrictions is the matter of compliance: is it plausible to believe that traders would have complied with the rules of *ribā*, and if so, under what circumstances? In contrast to the prohibition against the *ribā* of the pre-Islamic era, which is substantially similar to modern restrictions on [695] creditors'

---

189. See, e.g., Ibn al-ʿArabī, *supra* note 9, at 242

> [The people prior to Islam] would do this ... by charging an increase for which no consideration was paid, and they would say "But selling is like *ribā*," meaning that the increase charged upon the maturity of the debt ex post is like the original price [which implicitly included an increase] of the contract ex ante, but God rejected their claim and made what they believed to be lawful sinful to them and He made clear that upon the maturity date [of a debt,] if the debtor lacks the means to discharge [it], he is to be deferred until [the debtor] is again solvent, in order to lighten [the debtor's burden].

190. Although the Qur'an's treatment of *ribā* appears only to require that free deferrals be granted to bankrupt debtors, Islamic law simply prohibited ex post mark ups of a debt in exchange for a deferral, without regard to the solvency of the debtor. It may be the case, however, that the overwhelming majority of such defaulting debtors were in fact bankrupt, even if the rule did not stipulate the debtor's insolvency as a condition for the invalidation of an ex post agreement to defer payment of a debt in consideration for increasing the principal amount owed. See, e.g., Al-Wansharīsī, *supra* note 78, at 229–30 (discussing the case of an insolvent Bedouin whose creditor was not allowed to accept food from his debtor in lieu of a debt owed since it would have the effect of a deferred trade of food in violation of the prohibition against the *ribā* of delay).

rights with respect to bankrupt debtors,[191] the ex-ante *ribā* restrictions remain puzzling. In the next section, I will address the questions arising out of the *ribā* of excess and delay in light of broader pro-consumer regulation in Islamic law, with a special focus on their application to food.

2. *Ribā* in the Broader Context of Islamic Prudential Regulation of the Market and Guarantees of Minimum Entitlements

As has been explained above, Islamic law generally recognizes as binding the price terms that result from arm's length bargains, even in circumstances where it turns out that the contract price deviated materially from fair market value. The primary exceptions to this laissez-faire attitude toward trade are the rules of *ribā* and *gharar*, respectively; however, in addition to those two doctrines, lesser-known doctrines exist which also limit the ability of certain parties to trade freely. Three examples of such doctrines are: (1) the rule against city-dwellers acting as selling agents on behalf of Bedouin producers,[192] (2) the rule prohibiting city-based retail merchants from purchasing goods of a caravan prior to its arrival in the city's markets,[193] and (3) the rule permitting the government to set the prices at which retail merchants (but not producers or wholesale importers) sell staple foods.[194] Each one of these rules functions to increase the urban consumer's share of the surplus arising from trade. In the case of the first rule, the presumption is clearly that the Bedouin, being relatively ignorant of local prices, is willing to sell to the urban consumer at a price less than the equilibrium [696] price prevailing in the town but for the intermediation of an urban agent.[195] The second rule is also intended to prevent a group of urban merchants from diverting to themselves the consumer surplus arising from the

191. The prohibition against the *ribā* of the pre-Islamic era is substantially similar to the general rule that an unsecured creditor is not entitled to claim post-petition interest against the bankrupt debtor. See 11 U.S.C. § 502(b) (2006) (providing that interest ceases to accrue as of the date the bankruptcy petition is filed); id. § 506(b) (allowing post-petition interest in respect of a secured claim only to the extent that the value of the security interest exceeds the value of the claim). It is also consistent with the sharing norm of bankruptcy law which prohibits a debtor from favoring one creditor over another, which would be the result if a bankrupt were permitted to enter into an agreement with a creditor deferring his obligation in consideration for a markup in the principal amount owed to that creditor. Both Islamic law and contemporary Chapter 11 prohibit a bankrupt from entering into new contracts without the approval of the court.

192. See, e.g., ʿAbdallāh b. Aḥmad al-Nasafī, *Al-Baḥr al-Rāʾiq Sharḥ Kanz al-Daqāʾiq*, reprinted in, *Encyclopedia of Islamic Jurisprudence* CD-ROM, Kuwaiti Ministry of Endowments, the Islamic Development Bank & Harf Info. Tech. 2004; Al-Ḥaṭṭāb, *supra* note 52, at 378.

193. Al-Ḥaṭṭāb, *supra* note 52, at 378–79.

194. Id. at 227–28.

195. Id. at 378 ("[This rule applies] when the urban agent takes charge of negotiating the contract or accompanies the good's owner in order to discourage him from selling by telling him that the bid is less than its [market] price").

willingness of the caravan's merchants, due to their relative ignorance of local prices, to sell the caravan's goods at a price less than that prevailing in the city.[196] The third rule decreases retail merchants' share of consumer surplus generated by trade in food by not permitting them to sell above a government set maximum which by hypothesis is below the market-clearing rate.[197] Interestingly, Muslim jurists took each one of these rules as creating prudential standards of regulation, and accordingly they limited the application of the first two rules to situations where failure to apply the rule would harm the residents of the town.[198] In the case of the third rule, despite an express report attributed to the Prophet Muhammad in which he was purportedly asked to set prices and pointedly refused on the grounds that he was reticent to interfere in the prices that were set by the market,[199] they permitted governmental price-setting on the grounds that price-setting, despite the Prophetic injunction, [697] is permissible where necessary to prevent harm to the city's population that may occur as a result of "hoarding."[200]

---

196. Al-Nasafī, *supra* note 192 (stating that prohibition applies on its fact to cases where the urban merchants intend to purchase the goods from the caravan and then hope to re-sell it at an increase in the city on account of the need of the towns' folk for the goods or where they buy it from the caravan at a discount to the prevailing price due to the caravan's ignorance of the local price).

197. See, e.g., ʿUthmān b. ʿAlī al-Zaylaʿī, *Tabyīn al-Ḥaqāʾiq Sharḥ Kanz al-Daqāʾiq, faṣl fī al-bayʿ*, reprinted in *Encyclopedia of Islamic Jurisprudence* CD-ROM, Kuwaiti Ministry of Endowments, the Islamic Development Bank & Harf Info. Tech. 2004; Sulaymān b. Khalaf al-Bājī, *Al-Muntaqā Sharḥ al-Muwaṭṭaʾ*, reprinted in Encyclopedia of Islamic Jurisprudence CD-ROM, Kuwaiti Ministry of Endowments, the Islamic Development Bank & Harf Info. Tech.; Al-Ḥaṭṭāb, *supra* note 52, at 227–28.

198. See, e.g., Al-Nasafī, *supra* note 192 (stating that the prohibition against urban merchants purchasing from a caravan outside the city limits and the prohibition against a city dweller acting as a selling agent for a Bedouin both apply only where doing so causes harm to the town's residents).

199. Al-Zaylaʿī, *supra* note 197 (quoting the Prophet Muhammad as saying "do not set prices, for God sets prices; He constricts and grants provision, and He is the provider"); Muwaffaq al-Dīn ʿAbdallāh b. Aḥmad b. Muḥammad (known as Ibn Qudāma), *Al-Mughnī, faṣl fī al-tasʿīr*, reprinted in *Encyclopedia of Islamic Jurisprudence* CD-ROM, Kuwaiti Ministry of Endowments, the Islamic Development Bank & Harf Info. Tech.

> [P]rices had risen in Madina during the time of the Prophet Muhammad so [the people] said "O Messenger of God! Prices have risen, so set a price for us." He replied "God sets prices; He constricts and grants provision, and He is the provider. Indeed, I earnestly hope to meet God with no claims brought against me involving blood or property..."

200. See, e.g., Al-Zaylaʿī, *supra* note 197 (permitting the government to set prices for food when they rise far above their normal price resulting in harm to the public); Al-Bājī, supra note 197 (permitting government to set prices for fungibles to protect public interest); *Al-Fatawā al-Hindiyya, faṣl fī al-iḥtikār*, reprinted in Encyclopedia of Islamic Jurisprudence CD-ROM, Kuwaiti Ministry of Endowments, the Islamic Development Bank & Harf Info. Tech. (permitting the government to force merchants to sell at a specific price where there is reason to fear for the well-being of the populace). But see Ibn Qudāma, *supra* note 199 (concluding that government price-setting is responsible for increases in prices because it causes goods to disappear from the market). See generally Keith Sharfman, *The Law and Economics of*

Viewed from this perspective, it may very well be the case that the rules prohibiting the *ribā* of excess and delay are related to the same general policy: maintaining an adequate minimum supply of food for all people in the community by setting prices in critical staples.[201] Economists generally look askance at price controls, arguing that they generally promote surpluses, if the price restraint is set at a minimum, or shortages, if the price restraint is set at a maximum, and as a result, only justify them as a short-term response to emergencies.[202] In addition to normative arguments against price-restraints, the history of price controls "appears to be one of unrelieved botchery and failure."[203] This raises the question of whether, assuming the ex-ante rules of *ribā* are akin to price [698] restraints, they were in fact observed in times when it was impossible to trade around their restrictions due to an economic crisis, or whether these rules would have been systematically circumvented through the equivalent of "black-market" trading.

Before one can answer this question, one must consider the impact of the institution of *zakāt*, a tax on agricultural produce[204] in excess of a year's provision whose pro-

---

Hoarding, 19 Loy. Consumer L. Rev. 179 (2007) (conducting an economic analysis of anti-hoarding rules in the Talmud).

201. For purposes of this article, I am assuming that the ex ante *ribā* restrictions arise out of a concern related to the regulation of the money supply. Muslim jurists recognized the power of the state to regulate the value of currency by issuing new series of currencies, and in the case of copper currencies, by setting the exchange rate of the copper. See, e.g., Aḥmad b. Muḥammad Ibn Ḥajar al-Haytamī, *al-Fatāwā al-Fiqhiyya al-Kubrā, al-faṣl al-thānī fī mā yunqad fīhi qaḍā' al-qāḍī*, reprinted in Encyclopedia of Islamic Jurisprudence CD-ROM, Kuwaiti Ministry of Endowments, the Islamic Development Bank & Harf Info. Tech. (describing rule applicable to contract denominated in copper when the exchange rate of that currency for silver is increased after the date of the contract). Alternatively, rules prohibiting deferred trades in gold and silver, but allowing deferred trades of gold and silver for food, might be consistent with the rationing/price-restraint scheme that I am speculating existed in the early Islamic state of Madina. On this theory, while a person with excess gold or silver was permitted to use it to import food or other goods to be delivered in the future, he could not attempt to profit from trading in these two commodities. Thus, a person with savings in gold and silver could either use them to purchase goods in the spot or the credit market, or he could lend them gratis. Such a policy would also be consistent with theoretical work explaining prohibitions against interest-bearing loans as a type of social insurance in societies with high and impermanent income equalities and with low growth rates, circumstances which certainly applied to seventh-century Madina. See Edward L. Glaeser & Jose Scheinkman, *Neither a Borrower nor a Lender Be: An Economic Analysis of Interest Restrictions and Usury Laws*, 41 J. LAW & ECON. 1 (1998).

202. See, e.g., Hugh Rockoff, Price Controls, in *The Concise Encyclopedia of Economics*, http://www.econlib.org/LIBRARY/Enc/PriceControls.html (last visited Feb. 14, 2008).

203. John Kenneth Galbraith, *A Theory of Price Control* 3 (1952).

204. Savings held in gold and silver were also subject to this tax, but in contrast to the rules applicable to crops, the government could collect the tax from cultivators, whereas taxes on savings were subject to a self-reporting regime. Baber Johansen, *Amwal Zahira and Amwal Batina: Town and Countryside as Reflected in the Tax System of the Hanafite School*, in *Studia Arabica et Islamica* 247, 252–53 (Wadad al-Qadi ed., 1981).

ceeds are dedicated to the poor.[205] This institution provided (or attempted to provide) a minimum amount of food for all. Moreover, there is considerable overlap between the commodities that are subject to *zakāt* and those that were subject to the ex-ante rules of *ribā*.[206] In addition, the rules governing the sale of the *ʿariyya*, one of the contracts that was expressly permitted despite its being a violation of the rules of the *ribā* of excess, limited it to amounts less than five *awsuq*, the quantity that was understood to represent the minimum amount of food necessary to feed one person for a year.[207]

The fact that Islamic law established that each person had a minimum entitlement to one year's worth of food suggests that *zakāt* was a type of rationing program. The existence of this rationing system, if successfully implemented, would have made the likelihood of compliance with the ex-ante *ribā* restraints much higher, at least in theory.[208] Moreover, to the extent that *zakāt* is a rationing system, it appears that the ex-ante *ribā* restraints are simply a means of enforcing that initial distribution against the risk that recipients will dissipate their ration through trade and be in need of an additional allowance [699] subsequently.[209] This explanation of the function of the ex-ante *ribā*-restraints also casts in a more favorable light Ibn Rushd's criticism of intra-generic trading as a kind of "extravagance"—his moral criticism is based on the intuition that whatever private gains in utility accrue to the trader are offset by the social costs of that trade. It also explains why such trades could be viewed as a type of unjust enrichment—whatever gains are obtained by the parties from intra-generic trading come at the expense of undermining the publicly supported distributive outcome established by *zakāt*. Finally, the fact that the ex-ante *ribā*-based restraints reinforce the distribution of minimum-

205. A person was defined as "poor," and therefore entitled to receive *zakāt* if she owned less than a year's worth of food.

206. Indeed, Ibn Rushd mentions the view of one early authority who attempted to make the connection between *zakāt* and *ribā* by arguing that only those commodities which were subject to the *zakāt* obligation were subject to the restraints of *ribā*. See *supra* note 98 and accompanying text.

207. Al-Dardīr, *supra* note 15, at 239.

208. See generally Galbraith, *supra* note 203, at 10.

> There has never been any doubt, in theory, of the ability of a price control authority to maintain a fixed price in a particular market if the price-fixing is supplemented by rationing. Rationing, if properly administered, has the well-understood effect of limiting demand to what is available at the fixed price and thus establishing a special market equilibrium that is wholly stable.

209. Consider the case of a person who receives a food ration, but, unsatisfied with the quality of the food, desires to "trade up" for higher quality food by exchanging two measures of her lower quality food for one measure of higher quality food. If that trade were allowed, she would increase her own short-term welfare, but at the risk that the public will have to make up the shortfall later. Cf. Eric Posner, *Contract Law in the Welfare State: A Defense of the Unconscionability Doctrine, Usury Laws, and Related Limitations on the Freedom of Contract*, 24 J. Legal Stud. 283 (1995) (arguing that the existence of a welfare state creates perverse incentives for individuals to take excessive risks).

entitlements guaranteed by *zakāt* also casts light on verses in the Qur'an which portray *ribā* as the opposite of charity.[210]

The persuasiveness of this interpretation of *ribā* largely depends on whether the assumptions it makes regarding the economic conditions prevailing in western Arabia in the seventh century are consistent with what we know about early Islamic social and economic history. While little can be said regarding this period with certainty, it is fairly uncontroversial to describe the people of western Arabia as being quite poor.[211] The town of Madina, the first capital of the Islamic state following the immigration of the Prophet and his followers there, was an agricultural oasis, but was unlikely to have been producing a large enough agricultural surplus to sustain a population that would have been expanding dramatically as a result of the growth in the number of Muslims.[212] Moreover, until the eighth year after his migration to Madina, when the Prophet returned triumphantly to Makka, his home town, it was his conscious policy to encourage new converts to [700] immigrate to Madina.[213] Accordingly, it is plausible to believe that even as Islam was winning new adherents, the economic strains on Madina would have been growing. This intuition is supported by express language of the Qur'an which praises the residents of Madina for "loving those who immigrated to them, not harboring any grudges on account of what was given to the [immigrants], and preferring them [to themselves with respect to the resources of the city] although they themselves are needy."[214] Accordingly, it seems reasonable that the Prophet Muhammad would have been very concerned to maintain an equitable distribution of food in light of the general poverty of his followers and the fact that the increasing number of Muslims in Madina would have strained the ability of Madina to feed everyone.

---

210. See, e.g., *al-Rūm*, 30:39; *al-Baqara*, 2:278.

211. Cf. Glaeser & Scheinkman, *supra* note 201, at 19–21 (noting the chronic poverty in Hebrew society as the background of the Old Testament's prohibition of lending at interest).

212. In the years between the Prophet's migration to Madina and his return to Makka in year 8, new Muslims were strongly encouraged to immigrate to Madina, and often did. "*Hidjra*," in *The Encyclopaedia of Islam* 366, 366–67 (B. Lewis, V. L. Menage, Ch. Pellat, & J. Schacht eds., 1971).

213. See generally Carl W. Ernst, *Following Muḥammad: Rethinking Islam in the Contemporary World* 88–91 (2003). The Prophet Muhammad was also reported to have announced, after his return to Makka, that "There is no migration after the conquest [of Makka]." 6 Aḥmad b. ʿAlī (*known as* Ibn Ḥajar al-ʿAsqalānī), *Fatḥ al-Bārī Sharḥ Ṣaḥīḥ al-Bukhārī* 48 (ʿAbd al-ʿAzīz b. Bāz & Muḥammad ʿAbd al-Bāqī eds., Dār al-Kutub a-ʿIlmiyya 1989) (9th Century) (explaining that until the defeat of Makka, persons who converted to Islam were under a religious obligation to immigrate to Madina).

214. *Al-Ḥashr*, 59:9.

V. CONCLUSION

The doctrines of *ribā* are a fundamental part of Islamic contract law that have received new attention in light of the rise of Islamic finance. Although often reduced to a prohibition of interest, the doctrines of *ribā* apply even to spot transactions in which no interest is involved. At the same time, the doctrines of *ribā* do not apply to numerous credit transactions despite the inclusion of an implicit interest rate in their terms. The core of the prohibition consists of protecting bankrupt debtors against creditors who seek to increase the principal amount owed by the debtor subsequent to default in exchange for deferring the time of repayment. While this rule is largely consistent with modern bankruptcy policies, ex-ante restrictions on contracts involving the sale of specified goods, largely staple foods and gold and silver, were also referred to using the term *ribā*.

I have argued in this paper that Islamic law has generally been unable to offer a convincing account for the basis of these rules as evidenced by the numerous differences of opinions among Muslim jurists, both historically and in the last one hundred and fifty years, [701] regarding the nature and application of these rules. I argue instead that the ex-ante *ribā* restrictions are best understood as a type of price restraint designed to protect the distribution of entitlements guaranteed under the Islamic wealth-redistribution mechanism of *zakāt*. The particular feature of *ribā* as a regulator of market prices is that, because it is focused on intra-generic trades in the spot market, and credit trades of food or credit trades of gold and silver, it only becomes relevant in times of crisis where it becomes impossible to trade around the rules due to shortages in these commodities. Accordingly, it is a simple price setting mechanism that by its own terms operates only in emergency or near emergency situations and loses its relevance once that crisis has passed. This interpretation of *ribā* is consistent with other short-term regulatory strategies adopted by Muslim jurists in times of economic strain intended to protect the interests of urban consumers against a broader policy of laissez-faire with respect to private bargains.

This analysis can be criticized for its dependence on an economic history of the Islamic state in Madina under the Prophet Muhammad that is speculative; however, it seems clear that without some historical perspective about the economic context in which these rules were initially introduced, it will be impossible to offer a rational interpretation of these rules. Moreover, because the majority of Muslim jurists have assumed that the doctrines of *ribā* can be justified rationally, it seems relatively unproblematic to make reasonable assumptions regarding the economic characteristics of the society in which these rules were first formulated. Accordingly, this analysis is consistent with, though different from, the trend within Islamic law that has treated the ex-ante *ribā*-restrictions as prudential rather than mandatory. And accordingly, it stands firmly on the side of those Muslim jurists who believe that Islamic transactional law must be primarily understood functionally, rather than as an exercise in fidelity to religiously normative texts.

The unsettled state of Islamic law with respect to *ribā*, combined with classical Islamic law's willingness to respect contractual bargains, even those that include credit terms with implicit interest rates in excess of the prevailing market rate, and unwillingness to subject the economic terms of any formally valid contract to substantive tests such as fairness, equity, or efficiency provide the legal context in which *sharīʿa* arbitrage can flourish. To go beyond *sharīʿa* arbitrage, Islamic law must offer an alternative explanation of the historical doctrines of *ribā*. After all, if the doctrines of *ribā* are, at bottom, faith-based claims, then *sharīʿa* arbitrage is not a problem. If, on the other hand, Muslims believe that Islamic law, especially in the area of commerce, is intended to further secular human welfare, then they should find the incoherence of pre-modern Islamic law regarding *ribā* to be troubling. The legal strategies underlying Islamic finance, far from contributing to a resolution of this doctrinal incoherence, exploit them for the gain of the private financial sector, which may even have an interest in perpetuating this incoherence. If this Article can succeed in giving a plausible functional account for the historical doctrines of *ribā*, it may prove helpful in combating the trend in Islamic finance to exalt form over substance with the attendant risk of accomplishing nothing other than imposing dead weight costs in the form of increased transaction costs.

13

ETHICS AND FINANCE: AN ISLAMIC PERSPECTIVE IN THE LIGHT OF THE PURPOSES OF ISLAMIC *SHARĪʿA*

Mohammad Fadel

INTRODUCTION

[16] I have written this paper in response to an invitation from the Research Center for Islamic Legislation and Ethics in Doha, Qatar, to participate in a seminar innocuously titled "Ethics and Economics." The organizers of the seminar asked me to address the following question: "From an Islamic perspective, what are the main objectives of 'Islamic Finance' in relation to the individual, society, state, and global economy?" They also asked me to address the following sub-questions: "What is your assessment of the Islamic finance journey so far (e.g. Islamic banks, Islamic Development Bank, Islamic Dow Jones)?" and "To what extent has Islamic finance introduced an alternative paradigm, or does it function within the boundaries of the current neo-liberal economic system?" All seminar participants circulated their papers in advance of the three-day meeting; and while this paper is, in broad outlines at least, unchanged from the pre-seminar version, I have revised it in the light of the questions and issues raised during the course of the often-lively exchanges that took place during the seminar and added additional detailed citations from the *fiqh* and hadith literature for the benefit of the reader.

The paper will proceed as follows. I will begin with a discussion of what it means, from a methodological perspective [17] to adopt a purposive approach (*maqāṣidī*) to understanding Islamic law (*Sharīʿa*). After this methodological introduction, I will proceed to discuss my understanding of what a purposive approach to finance grounded in the norms of Islamic *Sharīʿa* would mean. My analysis begins by identifying the extent to which the explicit textual sources of the *Sharīʿa* broadly recognize the legitimacy of finance, and identifies the different kinds of finance that the *Sharīʿa* explicitly recognizes, including, a for-profit financial sector and a charitable (or not-for-profit financial sector) and public finance. I then provide a substantive analysis of each sector, arguing that each sector is governed by its own particular purposes (*maqāṣid*), and that it would be inap-

This article was originally published in *Islam and Applied Ethics*, edited by Fethi B. Jomaa Ahmed (Doha: Al Jazeera Printing, 2017), pp. 16–65.

propriate to import the concerns of one sector, for example, the for-profit sector, into analysis of another sector, for example, the not-for-profit sector, but that all sectors are united by a meta-Islamic ethic of a commitment to efficiency, or from an operational perspective, an anti-waste principle. I will then discuss specific problems related to contemporary Islamic finance: the failure of Islamic banks to guarantee the money of depositors by virtue of their use of the two-tiered *muḍāraba* structure to finance their dealings; the difficulties raised by the current approach of Islamic equity indices, such as the Dow Jones Islamic Index; how to transform *zakāt* into an effective tool for distributive justice by overcoming the historical legacy of legal formalism in the jurisprudence of *zakāt*; and, the role of general taxation in public finance in Islam and the achievement of social justice. The paper will then conclude on the state of the art in the theory and practice of Islamic finance across the various dimensions discussed in this paper.

A. THE METHODOLOGY OF PURPOSIVISM IN ISLAMIC JURISPRUDENCE (*AL-FIQH AL-MAQĀṢIDĪ*)

[18] Before one can develop a purposive understanding of finance in the light of the *Sharīʿa*, one must first begin with an understanding of the jurisprudential assumptions of purposivism (*al-fiqh al-maqāṣidī*) and how this method is to be applied for the purpose of deriving rules of Islamic law.

Purposivism is often understood to find its first explicit articulation in the writings of the great Shāfiʿī jurist and Ashʿarī theologian, Abū Ḥāmid al-Ghazālī. Al-Ghazālī argued in his *al-Mustaṣfā fī uṣūl al-fiqh* that the *Sharīʿa* existed to serve five universal ends (*maqāṣid kulliyya*) of the preservation of religion (*dīn*), life (*ḥayāt*), property (*māl*), progeny (*nasl*), and capacity/rationality (*ʿaql*). All rules of the *Sharīʿa*, in turn, furthered one of these ends, but along three different levels of importance, which al-Ghazālī identified as primary/necessary (*ḍarūrī*), secondary/convenient (*ḥājī*) and tertiary/decorative (*tazyīnī*). Post-Ghazalian jurists further developed his theory of the *maqāṣid*, with such jurists as ʿAbd al-ʿAzīz b. ʿAbd al-Salām, author of *Qawāʿid al-aḥkām fī maṣāliḥ al-anām*, and Abū Isḥāq al-Shāṭibī, author of *al-Muwāfaqāt fī uṣūl al-Sharīʿa*, giving pride of place to *maqāṣid* in their jurisprudential theories of the *Sharīʿa*.

It would be a mistake, however, to think that the purposive approach to understanding the *Sharīʿa* was a relatively late development in the history of Islamic law. While the explicit formulation of the theory of the *maqāṣid* may have come at a later date, purposive interpretation characterized Sunni juristic activity from its earliest history. While traditional accounts of Islamic legal history tend to recognize Imam Mālik as the early jurist who gave pride of place to *maṣāliḥ mursala* (the [19] textually unattested public welfare) in his juristic system while his younger contemporary and critic, Imam al-Shāfiʿī, is said to have rejected such analysis in favor of a stricter textualism, careful analysis of al-Shāfiʿī's interpretation of revealed texts confirms his assumption that correct interpretation requires knowledge of the purposes of the revealed rule. This is clear in his treatment of the verse "and test the orphans when they reach the age of marriage, and if you find them to be of sound mind, deliver to them their property" (4:6, *al-Nisāʾ*), where he relied on the social distinctions in how minor boys and girls were raised to justify the different evidentiary presumptions that were to be used to determine when minor boys and girls, respectively, should obtain full ownership of their properties.[1]

Even before the explicit introduction of *maqāṣid al-sharīʿa* as a technical jurisprudential concept, the general acceptance by Sunni jurists of analogy was dependent on the assumption that the rules of the *Sharīʿa* existed to promote certain ends or goals (*maqāṣid*), and that human reason could reasonably infer what those goals were from the explicit rules of revelation. Accordingly, we could understand that revelation prohibited grape wine (*khamr*) not because of its color, taste, or texture, but because of its particular capacity to undermine the rational capacity (*izālat al-ʿaql*) of those who drank it. Of course, to be able to identify wine's capacity to cause inebriation as the legal cause (*ʿilla*) of its prohibition while excluding its other characteristics as the basis for the prohibition assumes that God's rules are purposive. The implicit assumption that God's revelation is purposive formed the basis for the *Ẓāhirī* critique of analogy as an unwarranted assumption by human beings that they could understand divine purposes.

Although acceptance of the purposiveness of revelation is deep-rooted in Sunni jurisprudence, it is also a controversial [20] position, as evidenced not only by the *Ẓāhirī* rejection of the entire justification of analogical reasoning, but also by the skepticism numerous jurists have expressed with regard to the capacity of human beings to discern the *true* purpose intended by divine revelation. More conservative jurists, such as the late Shaykh al-Būṭī, for example, have expressed doubts about our ability to apprehend the correct goal of revelation, and that instead, we should assume that the goal of the Lawgiver is perfectly assimilated into the textual rule itself, in which case, the best means to achieving the goal of the Lawgiver is through complete obedience to the rule without regard for the empirical consequences that result from conforming to the rule.[2]

I reject this approach, not because it is methodologically indefensible, but because as a practical matter it does violence to the entire enterprise of jurisprudence (*fiqh*), not only at the level of particular rules, but also at the level of the structure of jurisprudence, which implicitly assumes our capacity to understand the purposes of revelation as viewed from a *human* perspective, and thus apply the

1. Muḥammad b. Idrīs al-Shāfiʿī, 3 *al-Umm* (Dār al-maʿrifa: Beirut, 1990), p. 224.
2. Felicitas Opwis, "*Maṣlaḥa* in Contemporary Islamic Legal Theory," 12,2 *Islamic Law and Society* (2005), pp. 215–20.

norms of revelation to an infinite set of *human* problems.[3] As Ibn Rushd the Grandson stated in defense of the obligation of *ijtihād*: texts are finite, but cases are infinite, and it is impossible for the finite to encompass the infinite.[4] Accordingly, the proper *maqāṣidī* approach to revelation is to begin with the texts of revelation; proceed to the empirical circumstances in which that rule originally operated; then propose the goal, that is, the *maqṣūd* or the *maṣlaḥa* which the rule furthers; and, finally, apply the textual rule to new circumstances while taking into account (*murāʿāt*) what the jurist theorizes to be the original purpose of the rule. In other words, an interpretive dialectic, grounded largely in practical reason, must take place among our linguistic understanding of the texts of revelation, our own understanding of our empirical [21] (immanent) good in the light of our best understanding of the world at the time of the interpretation (*al-sunan al-ʿādiyya*), and our best understanding of the circumstances in which the rule will be applied. Finally, the *maqāṣidī* approach I adopt does not limit itself to regarding the texts of revelation discretely, but rather requires reading them together in an inductive fashion (*istiqrāʾ*), along with the interpretations historically provided by the jurists, in order to best determine the Lawgiver's goal. This is essentially the method that the great Mālikī jurist and scholar of *uṣūl al-fiqh* Abū Isḥāq al-Shāṭibī proposed in his magisterial work on *maqāṣid* and its relationship to theoretical jurisprudence, *al-Muwāfaqāt fī uṣūl al-fiqh*.

B. FINANCE, THE FOUNDATIONAL TEXTS OF REVELATION AND FINANCE'S STATUS AS AN ESSENTIAL GOOD (*MAṢLAḤA ḌARŪRIYYA*)

To answer the principal question posed by this seminar—"what are the main objectives of 'Islamic Finance' in relation to the individual, society, state and global economy?"—we must begin with an inductive survey of the texts of revelation to identify the extent to which revelation addresses questions that are directly relevant to finance, whether in a legislative mode, that is, through direct commands, or in a confirmatory mode, that is, confirming social practices that are essentially financial. But we cannot begin the Islamic inquiry without first answering the question, "What is finance?" By finance, we mean the process by which surplus funds in the hands of savers—whether individuals, firms, or governments—are transferred to individuals and entities in need of those funds, whether for investment or for consumption. A financial system can be described as more or less efficient by measuring its success in transferring surplus, unused funds from savers to consumers and investors.

3. Indeed, at its extreme, the textualist approach to *maqāṣid* would obliterate the vital distinction between rules of devotion (*al-ʿibādāt*) and transactional rules (*muʿāmalāt*).

4. Ibn Rushd *Bidāyat al-mujtahid*, ed. ʿAlī Muḥammad Muʿawwaḍ and ʿĀdil Aḥmad ʿAbd al-Mawjūd (Dār al-kutub al-ʿilmiyya: Beirut, 1996), p. 326.

[22] The need for a financial system stems not only from the fact of an unequal distribution of income and opportunities, but also from the reality of an unequal distribution of talent and desire: even if we imagined a world in which property was distributed in a perfectly equal fashion, so long as individuals have different desires in terms of consumption and saving, and talents with respect to how they wish to deploy their resources, there will exist a need to transfer property which is idle in the hands of its owner to another person who can make more productive use of it.

There is also a pressing need to transfer savings to debtors because of the reality of consumption patterns over a single lifetime: individuals' expenses and incomes vary depending on their age, for example, children and the aged, because they lack income, must draw on the surpluses generated by the working population, while persons in the prime of their career will generally generate income in excess of their present needs, which they need to save for future expenses. Accordingly, consumption patterns need to be adjusted to the natural rise and decline of actual incomes over a person's lifetime. Finance, therefore, entails more than the present transfer of surplus property from those who do not need it to those who need it immediately, something which could be accomplished simply by means of a present gift. It also refers to intertemporal exchange, whereby the person or entity with the surplus transfers it conditionally in the expectation of receiving its like in the future, oftentimes with an expectation of an increase, so that the saver will be able to meet their *future* needs, whether personal, for example, the cost of a child's wedding, or social, for example, the pensions of retired workers.

The only way to envision a society that lacks a financial system is to imagine one in which trade is absolutely prohibited [23] or to imagine a society in which all individuals have the same initial endowments and have the same tastes, in which case there would be no need for them to trade and in which current income is always sufficient to satisfy its members' current needs, regardless of age or circumstance. Because such a society has never existed, and as a matter of experience, is extremely unlikely (*mutaʿaddhir*) to exist, we can safely conclude that that existence of a financial system in human society is a fundamental interest (*maṣlaḥa ḍarūriyya*) insofar as it is inconceivable for *any* human society to exist without some system for transferring surplus property to those who are in a deficit.

There is little doubt that the Qur'an and *Sunna*, as a general matter, recognize the role of finance, that is, the transfer of surpluses to those in deficit, in human society by encouraging the circulation of wealth. In so doing, the Qur'an recognizes both commercial (profit-seeking) and non-commercial (altruistic) means to effect these transfers of property. The following list includes some—but by no means all—texts of revelation that relate to finance:

(a) the Qur'an condemns those who hoard wealth ("Those who hoard gold and silver and spend it not on the path of God ...," *al-Tawba*, 34–5);

(b) it instructs that public property (*fay*) is to be spent on the needy so that "its circulation is not limited to the wealthy among you" (*al-Ḥashr*, 7);

(c) it repeatedly commands the believers with means to pay a portion of their property as *zakāt* in favor of the needy, as an obligation and not an act of charity (e.g. *al-Tawba*, 103, and *al-Maʿārij*, 24–5);

(d) the Qur'an repeatedly encourages believers to extend "godly loans" (*qarḍan ḥasanan*) for the sake of God, (e.g. *Baqara*, 245);

(e) the Qur'an not only recognized the permissibility of trade in the spot market (*tijāra ḥāḍira*), it also recognized the validity of credit sales (*al-bayʿ ilā ajal*), [24] as manifested by the fact that the single longest verse of the Qur'an, *Baqara*, 282, lays out the rules for documenting credit sales;

(f) the *Sunna* recognized the permissibility of commercial contracts (profit-seeking contracts) that include a credit term, such as *salam* (forward sale), *muzāraʿa* (share-cropping), and *musāqāt* (a special kind of share-cropping arrangement);

(g) the *Sunna* recognized the validity of guaranty contracts (*ʿaqd al-ḍamān* or *kafāla*) as well as social insurance (*al-diya ʿalā al-ʿāqila*);

(h) the *Sunna* recognized equity finance (*sharika*) with pure profit-and-loss sharing, and preferred equity finance (*qirāḍ* or *muḍāraba*) where only profits are shared; and

(i) the *Sunna* also recognized public borrowing, as set out in the *Sunan* of Abū Dāwūd in the report of ʿAbdallāh b. ʿAmr b. al-ʿĀṣ, concerning the provision of camels for the army.[5]

What this brief review of Qur'anic and Prophetic texts shows is that the foundational elements of both public and private (individual and business) finance, as well as commercial and noncommercial finance, both debt and equity, are found in the texts of revelation. It would be a mistake, then, in formulating a purposive interpretation of Islamic law's approach to finance to reduce the *Sharīʿa*'s teachings to one set of financial tools to the exclusion of the others. The *Sharīʿa* endorses both profit-seeking modes of finance and altruistic modes of finance. It endorses voluntary acts of altruism—gifts (*hiba*) and charity (*ṣadaqa*)—as a means of transferring surpluses

5. According to this report, after ʿAbdallāh informed the Prophet (S) that there were insufficient camels in the public treasury to equip a proposed military expedition, the Prophet (S) ordered him to purchase additional camels on credit, purchasing one camel for two to be delivered at the time *zakāt* would be collected. Abū Dāwūd Sulaymān b. al-Ashʿath al-Sijistānī, 3 *Sunan Abī Dāwūd* (al-Maktaba al-ʿaṣriyya: Beirut, n.d.), hadith no. 3357, p. 250. ʿAlī b. ʿUmar al-Dāraquṭnī, 4 *Sunan al-Dāraquṭnī* (Muʾassasat al-Risāla: Beirut, 2004), hadith no. 3055, p. 37. See also, Sulaymān b. Aḥmad al-Ṭabarānī, 13 *al-Muʿjam al-kabīr* (Maktabat Ibn Taymiyya: Cairo, 1994), hadith no. 155, p. 63 (ʿAbdallāh b. ʿAmr b. al-ʿĀṣ was asked whether it was permitted to sell one camel for two, one cow for two, and one sheep for two, and he cited his experience equipping the Prophet's expedition). This report contradicts al-Ṭaḥāwī's claim that the original ruling permitting this kind of sale was abrogated. See Abū Jaʿfar Aḥmad b. Muḥammad al-Ṭaḥāwī, 4 *Sharḥ maʿānī al-āthār*, ed. Muḥammad Zuhrī al-Najjār and Muḥammad Sayyid Jād al-Ḥaqq (ʿĀlam al-kutub: Cairo, 1994), hadith no. 5737, p. 60.

to those in deficits, and it also endorses coercive means of redistribution of surplus assets—*zakāt* and *kharāj*—to those in need. Before formulating a general theory of the ethics of Islamic finance, therefore, it is crucial that we begin with understanding the purposes of each of the different financial tools that the *Sharīʿa* has recognized, and then consider, from a macro-perspective, how these micro-financial tools are to work together. A closely [25] related question is whether Muslims are restricted to the tools explicitly endorsed by revelation,[6] or whether the presumption of permissibility (*al-aṣl fī'l-ashyāʾ al-ibāḥa*) should apply to financial transactions. Finally, there is also the larger, systemic question of the macroeconomic environment, in which these individual contracts ought to be deployed and the overall relationship between individuals' pursuit of their own ends, including, commercial for-profit ends, with the public good, a question to which this essay will turn later.

We now turn to the more detailed question of analyzing the goals of each of the subareas of finance recognized in the basic texts of the *Sharīʿa*: commercial contracts; altruistic finance; and coercive public finance (*zakāt*).

C. COMMERCIAL CONTRACTS, THE PURSUIT OF PROFIT AND *MAQĀṢID AL-SHARĪʿA*

The jurists have recognized numerous contracts, the purpose of which is the realization of private gain for the contracting parties. The paradigmatic case of the profit-seeking contract in Islamic law is the sale (*al-bayʿ*). Jurists not only assume that the parties to a sale contract, provided they enjoy full capacity, are entitled to maximize their private gains from a commercial contract, but that they ordinarily do seek to maximize their private gains, at least to the best of their ability. For this reason, Muslim jurists generally allowed parties to determine freely the terms on which they would trade, and in contrast to medieval Church doctrine, they rejected a just price theory. Even contracts that evidenced off-market prices (*ghabn*) were valid, or at a minimum, were not invalid solely because the price was off-market.[7] This presumption that traders seek to maximize their private re-

6. For example, Mālikī jurists believe certain contracts are exceptional, for example *bayʿ al-salam* or *qirāḍ*, and accordingly, it is not permitted to derive new contractual forms by means of analogy to these contracts which are themselves deemed to be outside the operation of the ordinary principles of trade. See, for example, 3 *al-Sharḥ al-ṣaghīr*, Abū al-Barakāt Aḥmad b. Muḥammad b. Aḥmad al-Dardīr, ed. Muṣṭafā Kamāl Waṣfī (Dār al-maʿārif: Cairo, n.d.), p. 684 (rejecting the permissibility of using anything other than gold or silver coins as capital for a *qirāḍ* on the grounds that "the *qirāḍ* contract is a dispensation so its permissibility is restricted to what has been reported, and anything outside of that remains prohibited in accordance with the ordinary rule of prohibition [of a hire-contract for an indefinite wage]" (*li-ʾanna al-qirāḍ rukhṣa yuqtaṣar fīhā ʿalā mā warada wa yabqā mā ʿadāhu ʿalā al-aṣl min al-manʿ*).

7. 3 *Bulghat al-sālik*, p. 29 (*bayʿ al-ghabn jāʾiz*).

turns is manifested in the juristic presumption [26] that contracts of sale and other commercial contracts are governed by a presumption of mutual covetousness, *mushāḥḥa*, which requires holding the parties strictly to their bargain in light of the presumption that each party demands performance of exactly what was in the contract, in contrast to other contracts, such as marriage, which is governed by a presumption of generosity—*mukārama* or *musāmaḥa*—that results in a looser interpretation of contractual terms.[8] The assumption of profit maximization is also clearly manifested in the rules governing the obligations of an agent (*wakīl*) who is entrusted with selling the goods of his principal[9] or the duties of an investment agent (*al-ʿāmil*) in a *qirāḍ* or *muḍāraba*. The agent in a *qirāḍ*, for example, is prohibited from making gifts (other than de minimis gifts, such as a loaf of bread or the like) out of the capital of the investment partnership on the theory that he is working solely for the interests of the investor.[10] A partner in a general partnership is also limited in his right to act out of generosity: he is permitted, for example, to give discounts on debts owed to the partnership or make gifts, but only if such acts further the commercial interests of the partnership.[11]

The legitimacy of the private pursuit of profit is so ingrained in Islamic jurisprudence that the jurists over the centuries recognized numerous exceptions to their rules in order to facilitate the private pursuit of commercial gains. Indeed, the contract of the *qirāḍ* is itself considered to be exceptional insofar as it entails a contract for hire for an indefinite wage (*al-ijāra al-majhūla*). Despite this otherwise grave contractual defect, Islamic law declared it to be permissible because of necessity in light of the fact that many people with surplus funds lack the ability or

8. 2 *Bulghat al-sālik*, p. 445 (explaining that it is impossible to include commercial contracts, such as sales, partnerships, and *qirāḍ*, alongside a marriage contract, because the principles governing the two sets of contracts are incompatible, marriage being based on generosity and commercial contracts based on covetousness [*al-nikāḥ mabnī ʿalā al-mukārama wa'l-bayʿ wa mā maʿahu (al-qirāḍ wa'l-qarḍ wa'l-sharika wa'l-ṣarf wa'l-musāqāt wa'l-jiʿāla) mabnī ʿalā al-mushāḥḥa*]). Ibn Rushd the Grandfather illustrates the difference in the two kinds of contracts when he discusses the non-obligation of the guardian to disclose the moral defects of the bride, such as non-virginity, even if that would result in a reduction of the dower, while a seller is obliged to disclose any defects in the good if it would reduce the price of the good by noting that the marriage contract is governed by a presumption of generosity, *mukārama*, while a contract of sale reflects an adversarial relationship (*mukāyasa*). See 4 *al-Bayān wa'l-taḥṣīl*, Ibn Rushd al-Jadd, p. 263.

9. 3 *Al-Sharḥ al-ṣaghīr*, p. 508 (an agent entrusted with selling or purchasing a good must act for the benefit of the principal [*wa faʿala al-wakīl al-maṣlaḥa wujūban ... li-muwakkilihi*] and he may neither purchase for more, nor sell for less, than the market price [*thaman al-mithl*]).

10. 3 *Al-Sharḥ al-ṣaghīr*, p. 710 (*wa laysa li-ʿāmil ay yaḥrum ʿalayhi hiba ... wa law li'stiʾlāf)*.

11. 3 *Al-Sharḥ al-ṣaghīr*, p. 464 (*wa lahu ... al-tabarruʿ fī māl al-sharika bi-ghayri idhni sharīkihi bi-shayʾ ka-hiba wa ḥaṭīṭa li-baʿḍ thaman bi'l-maʿrūf in istaʾlafa bihi ... qulūb al-nās li'l-tijāra aw khaffa al-mutabarraʿ bihi ... wa dafʿ kisra li-faqīr*).

the opportunity to invest their property themselves.[12] A careful reader of the history of Islamic law will find numerous examples from the fatwas of the scholars that [27] evidence a principled willingness to recognize exceptions to various rules of *fiqh* in order to further the legitimate need of private parties to earn a profit. In addition to such exceptional contracts as *qirāḍ*, *bayʿ al-salam*, *muzāraʿa*, *bayʿ al-ʿariyya*, and *musāqāt*, all of which have some textual basis, jurists also recognized exceptions to their own rules in numerous instances. In the Mālikī school, for example, Andalusian jurists gave opinions permitting partnerships for the cultivation of silkworms (*tarbiyat al-dūd*) despite the fact that the customary arrangements were not in accordance with Mālikī teachings on labor partnerships.[13] Later Mālikīs, in an effort to enhance the rights of creditors, permitted the debtor to appoint the creditor his agent for the purpose of selling pledged property in the event the debtor defaulted in order to avoid the inconvenience of a judicial sale.[14] Mālikī jurists also recognized an exception to their rule regarding the requirement of immediate payment or performance of a binding contract of hire (*ijāra maḍmūna*) in the case of contracts for the advance hire of transportation for long distances, like the Pilgrimage, again on the grounds of necessity.[15] Muslim jurists also generally upheld the liability of artisans for the property of their customers (*taḍmīn al-ṣunnāʾ*) despite the fact that the customers willingly gave them their property, and thus the artisans would ordinarily be deemed to be bailees (*amīn*) and thus free of liability in the absence of proof of negligence.[16]

Another important example of the jurists relaxing the rules of *fiqh* in light of the need to pursue profit is found in an important opinion of the great Andalusian jurist al-Shāṭibī, in which he was asked about the legitimacy of another customary but controversial practice in Andalus that contradicted numerous rules of Mālikī *fiqh*, but strict application of the rules of Mālikī *fiqh* would have deprived average individuals of the [28] opportunity to earn a profit with their property.[17] Al-Shāṭibī explained the controversial practice as follows: a group of urban dwellers who own livestock, for example, sheep or goats, contract with one or more shepherds, who then

---

12. 3 *Bulghat al-sālik* Aḥmad b. Muḥammad al-Ṣāwī, ed. Muṣṭafā Kamāl Waṣfī (Dār al-maʿārif: Cairo, n.d.), p. 681. (*wa kāna [al-qirāḍ] fī'l-jahiliyya fa-aqarrahu al-muṣṭafā ʿalayhi al-ṣalāt wa'l-salām fī al-islām li-ʾanna al-ḍarūra daʿat ilayhi li-ḥājat al-nās ilā al-taṣarruf fī amwālihim wa laysa kull aḥad yaqdir ʿalā al-tanmiya bi-nafsihi wa huwa mustathnā li'l-ḍarūra min al-ijāra al-majhūla*).

13. *Al-Ḥadīqa al-mustaqilla al-naḍra*, ed. Jalāl ʿAlī al-Qadhdhāfī al-Jihānī (Dār Ibn Ḥazm: Beirut, 2003). See fatwas nos. 157 (pp. 97–98), 168–71 (pp. 102–6). This was known as *sharikat al-ʿalūfa*.

14. *Ibid*, fatwa no. 185 (p. 110). See also, 5 *al-Tāj wa'l-iklīl* (Dār al-fikr: Beirut, 1992), pp. 21–2 (discussing controversy regarding the bindingness of such a condition).

15. 4 *Al-Sharḥ al-ṣaghīr*, p. 15 ("*taʿjīl jāmiʿ al-ujra fī mithli dhalika yuʾaddī ilā ḍayāʿ amwāl al-nās bi-sabab hurūb al-jammālīn idhā qabaḍū al-ujra*").

16. 4 *Al-Sharḥ al-ṣaghīr*, p. 47.

17. *Al-Ḥadīqa al-mustaqilla al-naḍra*, fatwa no. 301 (pp. 170–73).

take the animals into the countryside to graze. While the animals are grazing, the shepherds milk the herd, and use the milk to manufacture cheese. When the shepherds return to the city, they distribute the cheese in proportion to the number of animals each partner contributed to the herd. He was also asked about the Andalusian practice of forming partnerships for the manufacture of cheese, with each partner contributing milk and the cheese being divided in proportion to the amount of milk contributed by each partner. Because the amount of cheese produced from milk is not uniform, that is, some milk yields more cheese than others, dividing the cheese in proportion to the milk contributed by each partner, for example, if A contributed 1/10th of the milk, he receives 1/10th of the cheese, does not result in a distribution of the cheese that in fact corresponds to the cheese produced by the partner's contribution of milk. Under standard principles of Mālikī law, such a transaction amounts to *muzābana*, as well as *ribā faḍl* and *ribā nasīʾa* insofar as it entails the unequal exchange of food combined with delay, that is, the exchange of milk for cheese on a deferred basis. Application of ordinary rules then would result in an invalidation of these two widespread customary transactions.

Nevertheless, al-Shāṭibī upheld this practice in reliance on an early opinion of Imam Mālik recorded in the *ʿUtbiyya* and explicated by Ibn Rushd the Grandfather in *al-Bayān wa'l-taḥṣīl*. Mālik is asked about a practice in his day, where people would meet at an oil press, and instead of each of them pressing his own seeds individually, they would combine their seeds together, press them together, and split the oil in proportion to [29] the amount of seeds that each person had contributed. Mālik stated that in principle this was impermissible because there is no guarantee that each set of seeds produces oil in equal amounts, thus leading to uncertainty in exchange (*gharar*) and *ribā faḍl* in the exchange of food. Nevertheless, Imam Mālik permitted the practice, saying:

> "This is disliked because some of it will produce more than the rest, but when the people need this, I hope it is a trivial thing because they must have which is necessary to improve their condition. Accordingly, I hope that there is a dispensation for those things which they cannot avoid, God willing, and I see no harm in it."[18]

According to Ibn Rushd, Saḥnūn rejected Mālik's view, and declared the practice forbidden on the basis of analogy, while Mālik permitted it "on the grounds of *istiḥsān*, necessity compelling him to that conclusion, since it is impossible to press a small amount

18. Ibn Rushd al-Jadd, *al-Bayān wa'l-taḥṣīl*, 12:16. ("*innamā yukrah hadhā li-ʾanna baʿḍahu yukhrij akthar min baʿḍ fa-idhā iḥtāja al-nās ilā dhalika fa-arjū an yakūna khafīfan li-ʾanna al-nāsa la budda lahum mimmā yuṣliḥuhum wa'l-shayʾ alladhī la yajidūna ʿanhu ghinā wa la budda fa-arjū an yakūna lahum fī dhalika sāʿa in shāʾa allāhu wa la arā bihi baʾsan*").

of seeds and in light of the opinion of some scholars that unequal exchange is permitted in those [commodities]."[19]

What is clear from the previous examples is that jurists, certainly in the Mālikī school, were willing to make exceptions to rules that would normally apply by force of analogy in favor of reasoning based on doctrines such as *maṣlaḥa mursala* and *istiḥsān*, usually claiming necessity (*ḍarūra*) to justify abandoning the rule that analogy would require. Necessity in these cases, however, is a far cry from the necessity that would be required to permit, for example, a person to eat carrion (*akl al-mayta*); rather, the jurists in commercial contexts use necessity loosely, treating legitimate commercial need (*ḥāja*) as the equivalent of necessity (*ḍarūra*) in other circumstances in order to justify a dispensation (*rukhṣa*) from the ordinarily applicable rule. In other words, simple need (*ḥāja*) is transformed into necessity [30] in the context of commercial dealings (*tunazzal al-ḥāja manzilat al-ḍarūra*).

I am not aware of any explicit discussion among the jurists that explains this anomaly. After all, the Mālikī jurists do not permit consumption of carrion except in circumstances where the person is starving. In the cases of the exceptions noted above, they did not require proof that the person seeking the dispensation was on the verge of starvation or poverty; it was sufficient that the transaction under consideration served a legitimate need, particularly the need for individuals to invest their property for a gain (*tanmiya*), or otherwise realize a profit. The different sense by which jurists use the term necessity (*ḍarūra*) in the two cases may be that the prohibition on eating carrion is owed to God exclusively (*ḥaqq Allāh*), while property rights belong to human beings (*ḥaqq ādamī*). All of the cases cited above involve exceptions to rules that regulate property rights, and thus belong primarily to the realm of the rights of human beings (*ḥuqūq al-ādamiyyīn*). Accordingly, and to the extent that they have consented to these practices, no violation is being committed against their property and so the lower standard for the *rukhṣa* is justified.[20]

We can conclude then by noting that in private, commercial transactions, legitimate need (*ḥāja*), not actual necessity (*ḍarūra*), is sufficient to justify an exception from a

---

19. Ibid. (*qawl Mālik istiḥsān dafaʿahu li'l-ḍarūra ilā dhālika idh lā yataʾattā ʿaṣr al-yasīr min al-juljulān wa'l-fijl ʿalā ḥidatihi [wa] murāʿātan li-qawl man yujīz al-tafāḍul fī dhālika min ahl al-ʿilm*).

20. See, for example, the 15th-century Mālikī jurist al-Mawwāq quoted Mālik as saying that a starving person (*al-muḍṭarr*) may not only eat carrion, but that he also may take excess meat with him for his journey to be consumed in the future (*yatazawwad*); however, if he takes food belonging to someone on account of his hunger, he is only permitted to take enough to fill his stomach but he is not permitted to take more as provisions (*lā yatazawwad*). This case arises in circumstances where the true owner of the food is not present to give the food to the starving person, something he is under an obligation to do. The narrowness of the exception in the case of another's property is on account of the need to respect the absent property's owner rights in that food. 3 al-Mawwāq, *al-Tāj wa'l-iklīl* (Dār al-fikr: Beirut, 1992), p. 233–34.

rule based on analogy. That is the inevitable conclusion that should be drawn from the various exceptions noted by the jurists to their own rules.

D. ALTRUISTIC FINANCE IN THE *SHARĪʿA*

In addition to utilizing the profit motive to encourage the transfer of surplus property to those who need it for immediate use, [31] the *Sharīʿa* cultivates an ethic of generosity and altruism (*īthār*) among its followers to share whatever surplus they have with those who are in greater need. For example, the Qur'an praised the Ansar—the Arabs of Yathrib at the time of the Prophet's *hijra* (S)—for their altruistic sharing with the Emigrants their properties, even though the Ansar themselves were needy.[21] Altruistic contracts include the contract of gift (*hiba*) as well as the loan (*qarḍ*). In each of these transactions, the person transferring the property to the other does so without any consideration, and indeed, in the case of a loan, the stipulation of a consideration nullifies the transaction's character as a loan and transforms it into a sale, which might or might not be valid depending on the terms of the sale.

The absolutely altruistic character of the loan is exemplified in the juristic rule invalidating self-interested loans, that is, *salaf jarra nafʿan*, and is reflected in its definition among the Mālikīs as the transfer of property from the transferor to the transferee for the exclusive benefit of the transferee.[22] Even though this juristic rule rests on a weak report, it is rationally consistent with the notion that a loan should be solely for the benefit of the borrower in order for it to qualify as an act of altruism. We have seen previously that the Muslim jurists were keen to separate profit-seeking contracts such as sales, the governing presumption for which is covetousness (*mushāḥḥa*), from other contracts that were governed by a norm of generosity (*mukārama*). This distinction is reinforced through the juristic rule invalidating self-interested loans. It is also consistent with the Qur'anic ethic of altruism: individuals are not obliged to be altruistic (except in the limited circumstances of necessity), but where they choose to act altruistically, they may not then act toward the recipient in a way that contradicts the original intention: [32] "A kind word and a prayer of forgiveness are superior to charity followed by vexation."[23]

Likewise, the charitable nature of the loan, that is, the fact that the lender receives no benefit from the borrower in consideration for the loan, explains why, unlike a sale, it is an act of obedience (*mandūb*) that entails divine reward.[24] A gift (*hiba* or *ṣadaqa*) is like a loan insofar that it is an uncompensated transfer of property, but with

21. 59:9, *al-Ḥashr*.
22. 3 *Al-Sharḥ al-ṣaghīr*, p. 291. ("*al-qarḍ iʿṭaʾ mutamawwal fī ʿiwaḍ mutamāthil*").
23. 2:263, *al-Baqara*.
24. 3 *al-Sharḥ al-ṣaghīr*, p. 292.

the important difference that the recipient is under no obligation to return the gift, unlike the case of a loan, but it shares with a loan the fact that it merits divine reward as a supererogatory duty (*mandūb*).[25]

They also share the requirement that a prerequisite for the validity of the loan or the gift that the lender or the giver, as applicable, have the capacity to engage in a donative act (*ahliyyat al-tabarruᶜ*) and be the owner of the property.[26] This means, for example, that agents lack the capacity to engage in donative acts without the consent of their principals. So, too, guardians are not allowed to engage in donative acts on behalf of their wards, and therefore, Mālikīs held that an orphan's guardian is not permitted to lend the orphan's property,[27] and a child is entitled to seek restitution from a parent who made gifts to others out of the minor child's property.[28]

Altruistic contracts also differ from commercial contracts in other important ways. For example, both contracts of loan (*qarḍ*) and gift (*ṣadaqa*) are binding only after they have been performed by the lender or the donor, respectively.[29] By contrast, the contract of sale is immediately effective in transferring title of the sold good to the purchaser. This feature of altruistic contracts further weakens their obligatory character relative to commercial contracts. On the other hand, because these are altruistic contracts, they tolerate a degree of indefiniteness (*gharar*) that is not permitted in contracts of sale that [33] entail mutual compensation.[30]

25. Ibid., p. 139.

26. Ibid., p. 141.

27. Muḥammad b. Muḥammad b. ᶜAbd al-Raḥmān al-Ḥaṭṭāb, 6 *Mawāhib al-Jalīl* (Dār al-fikr: Beirut, 1992), pp. 399–400. (Quoting several Mālikī authorities who rejected lending out an orphan's property but encouraging the guardian to give it out as commercial investment, and sharply criticizing the Ḥanafī position allowing orphan's property to be lent out).

28. Shihāb al-Dīn al-Qarāfī, 6 *al-Dhakhīra*, ed. Muḥammad Ḥajjī and Saᶜīd Aᶜrāb (Dār al-gharb al-islāmī: Beirut, 1994), p. 224.

29. 4 *al-Sharḥ al-ṣaghīr*, p. 143 (a gift is void if a legal obstacle arises preventing its completion prior to the donee taking possession [*ḥawz*]. Mālikīs consider both an unperformed gift and unperformed loan to be valid, meaning the donor or the borrower, as applicable, can sue the donor or the lender and compel his performance, but if something arises prior to performance, for example, the donor becomes bankrupt, then the obligation to perform the gift or lend the money lapses. Ibid. 3 *Bulghat al-sālik*, p. 295 (noting that every act of generosity, *maᶜrūf*, in the Mālikī system transfers title by virtue of the contract except that the transfer is not complete until possession takes place, although there is a controversy within the school whether the requirement of possession also applies to loans). Shāfiᶜīs and Ḥanafīs, by contrast, hold that possession is a condition of the contract's validity, not its perfection, meaning that until the donor delivers the gift, the donee has no rights to the gift. 5 *Bidāyat al-mujtahid*, p. 363.

30. 4 *Al-Sharḥ al-ṣaghīr*, p. 141 (an indefinite gift is valid). Likewise, a loan need not include a repayment date. 3 *al-Sharḥ al-ṣaghīr*, pp. 295–96.

To conclude, the *Sharīʿa* encourages acts of generosity, and altruistic modes of finance are certainly part of the financial tools recognized by the *Sharīʿa*. At the same time, however, it would be a mistake to limit finance in Islam to acts of altruism, which, according to the jurists themselves, are only recommended (*mandūb*) and not obligatory (*wājib*). Finally, with respect to a purposive approach to donative contracts, Muslim jurists must be careful to preserve the wholly altruistic nature of contracts such as *qarḍ* and *ṣadaqa* and not confuse them with profit-seeking contracts, or obligatory acts of transfer, namely *zakāt*, the next topic to which I now turn.

E. *ZAKĀT*, DISTRIBUTIVE JUSTICE AND THE GOAL OF A UNIVERSAL MINIMUM INCOME

So far, we have seen that Islamic law respects the private pursuit of profit, and that the jurists regularly made doctrinal concessions in furtherance of this goal in circumstances where it was clear that the concession (*rukhṣa*) at stake was beneficial to both parties. We also saw that while the *Sharīʿa* encourages an ethic of generosity, and rewards those who act altruistically toward those less fortunate, it does not compel generosity, but instead imposes it only as a supererogatory obligation (*mandūb*). Indeed, in many contexts, where the property is managed by an agent or guardian, such agent or guardian, as applicable, is effectively prohibited from acting out of generosity on the theory that this is not in the best interest of the principal or the beneficiary. This might suggest that the *Sharīʿa* is largely *laissez-faire* with respect to economics: it permits private parties to engage in commercial transactions and in so doing to maximize their returns from trade, provided [34] that they do so honestly, with no offsetting obligation to share their profits with others. This would be true but for the existence of the crucial institution of *zakāt*, which acts coercively to redistribute surplus from those having property in excess of their current needs to those lacking sufficient property to meet their current needs.[31]

From the perspective of purposive jurisprudence, the fundamental goal of the law of *zakāt* is to guarantee that each Muslim (or citizen, in the modern context) is guaranteed a minimum subsistence income. This is evidenced by the Mālikī rule that anyone lacking a year's worth of food is entitled to receive *zakāt* (*faqīr lā yamliku qūta ʿāmihi*).[32] Interestingly, there is no requirement that the able-bodied work in order to be eligible to receive *zakāt*[33] nor must an individual prove his poverty: it is enough in the absence of contrary

31. 1 *Al-Sharḥ al-ṣaghīr*, pp. 670–71.
32. Ibid, p. 657.
33. Ibid., p. 665.

circumstantial evidence that he claims eligibility according to the Mālikīs.[34] *Zakāt* funds were also to be used to free slaves and for debt relief[35] with the general rule being that priority should be given to the neediest.[36]

I say that the fundamental purpose is to relieve the needy and not the moral improvement of *zakāt* payers (although that is also an important goal of the *Sharīʿa*) in light of the fact that it can be coercively enforced against wealthy individuals who refuse to pay and that even minors who are otherwise not morally obligated are required to pay *zakāt* on their property if it exceeds the threshold amount (*niṣāb*).[37] This observation is also confirmed by the laws governing when it is obligatory to assist another in need. As a general rule, there is no duty to offer assistance to another (*muwāsāt*); however, if a person's need rises to that of dire and life-threatening necessity (*al-muḍṭarr*), a person who is able to help, but refuses is liable for his failure to offer assistance if the needy person dies.[38] Just as is the [35] case with *zakāt*, although the *Sharīʿa* desires to produce individuals who would voluntarily pay their obligations and offer assistance to those in desperate circumstances, where there is a conflict between the moral failures of the wealthy and the need of the poor or those under necessity, the latter are given legal priority, but only to the extent necessary to relieve their need, with *zakāt* providing food for a year, and the obligation to provide a person facing a dire necessity enough to relieve the immediate need, but no more.[39]

The *Sharīʿa*, viewed from a purposive perspective, endorses coercive redistribution based on need, with the goal of providing everyone in society a basic safety net, below which no one can fall. This is an absolute individual right, without proof that the person is morally worthy of our assistance, for example, that he has exerted sufficient diligence in feeding himself by working. At the same time, however, the *Sharīʿa* appears to limit mandatory assistance to individuals' basic needs, and in so

34. 1 *Bulghat al-Sālik*, p. 658 (*idhā iddaʿā shakhṣ al-faqr aw al-maskana li-yaʾkhudha min al-zakāt fa-innahu yuṣaddaq bi-lā yamīn illā li-rība bi-an yakūna ẓāhirahu yukhālifu mā yaddaʿīh*).

35. 1 *Al-Sharḥ al-ṣaghīr*, p. 661.

36. Ibid., p. 664.

37. The Ḥanafīs reconcile the public assistance aspect of *zakāt* (*muʾna*) with its status as a religious ritual (*ʿibāda*) in the case of minors by holding that it accrues with respect to their property during their minority, but it only becomes due, for example, the obligation matures, when the minor reaches majority. 2 *al-Mabsūṭ*, p. 162 and 3 *al-Mabsūṭ*, p. 103. The Shāfiʿīs and Mālikīs, by contrast, impose the obligation to pay *zakāt* on the property itself, so long as its owner is free (*ḥurr*), without regard to the owner's majority. 2 *al-Mabsūṭ*, p. 162 (attributing this view to the Shāfiʿīs) and 1 *al-Sharḥ al-ṣaghīr*, p. 589 (*zakāt* is obligatory on all free persons owning sufficient property, even if they are not of majority or otherwise are not morally bound by the law [*ghayr mukallaf*]).

38. If he negligently fails to offer assistance and the person dies, thinking, for example, that he is not bound to help, then he is only monetarily liable, but if he knows that he is obliged to help, and refuses, then he is subject to *qiṣāṣ*. 2 *Bulghat al-sālik*, pp. 169–70.

39. al-Mawwāq, p. 233 (*wa li'l-ḍarūra mā yasudd*).

doing, it also appears to encourage voluntary transactions, whether commercial or altruistic, as the primary means by which individuals are expected to satisfy their economic goals.[40]

F. EFFICIENCY AND HUMAN DIGNITY AS A META-ISLAMIC ETHICS OF FINANCE

In the discussion of *zakāt*, we emphasized its aspiration to provide all persons a minimum income that guarantees their survival without regard to whether they are prepared to sell their labor in the marketplace. The willingness of the jurists to guarantee access to a minimum entitlement without demanding any contribution of labor suggests an ideal of free labor, namely labor that is given not out of necessity but out of genuine freedom. [36] One finds corroboration for this idea particularly in the writings of the Ḥanafī jurists who openly worry about the prospects that paid employment renders the employee vulnerable to degradation (*dhull*) and is one reason why hire-contracts are deemed exceptional (*khilāf al-aṣl*). For this reason, Ḥanafīs prohibit a child from entering into a hire contract with either of his parents because it would put the child in a position to exploit his parents, something that is contrary to the parent–child relationship.[41] More generally, the great 19th century Damascene Ḥanafī jurist Ibn ʿĀbidīn explained in his *Radd al-muḥtār* that the Ḥanafī position that "self-effacement to other than God is sinful (*al-tawāḍuʿ li-ghayr Allāh ḥarām*)," means "degradation of the self in order to receive a worldly benefit (*ay idhlāl al-nafs li-nayl al-dunyā*)."[42] He also quoted the prominent companion Ibn Masʿūd as saying "Whoever humbles himself before a wealthy man and renders himself at his service to magnify him and out of covetousness for what he possesses loses two thirds of his manly self-respect and half of his religion."[43]

From the perspective of purposive jurisprudence, this value can be translated into an anti-subordination principle, meaning, that the *Sharīʿa* strives to eliminate all manner of avoidable subordination of one person to another. We will return to this goal of the *Sharīʿa* later in this essay when we discuss the principles of public finance in a modern context. Now, however, we must discuss the place of efficiency and its role in the Islamic ethics of finance and one of the goals of an Islamic financial system.

---

40. This is consistent with several hadiths that reveal the Prophet (S) to have been reluctant to interfere in market transactions, for example, his reluctance to set prices for goods traded in the public market, and his statement prohibiting city-dwellers from acting as selling agents for itinerant Bedouin selling in the city.

41. Muḥammad b. Aḥmad al-Sarakhsī (Dār al-maʿrifa: Beirut, 1993), 16 *al-Mabsūṭ*, p. 56 (*wa in istaʾjara al-ibn abāhu ... li-khidmatihi lam yajuz li-ʾannahu manhī ʿan istikhdām hāʾulāʾi li-mā fīhi min al-idhlāl*).

42. Muḥammad Amīn b. ʿUmar Ibn ʿĀbidīn, 6 *Radd al-muḥtār* (Dār al-fikr: Beirut, 1992), p. 384.

43. Ibid. ("*man khaḍaʿa li-ghaniyy wa waḍaʿa lahu nafsahu iʿẓāman lahu wa ṭamaʿan fī mā qibalahu dhahaba thuluthā murūʾatihi wa shaṭr dīnihi*").

Before asking whether Islamic ethics incorporates efficiency as a virtue, however, we first ought to ask what efficiency means. For economists, efficiency is a state of the world in which it is impossible to make one person better off without making another person worse off. This state, of course, is an ideal and is never actualized, but can only be approached.[44] Accordingly, [37] economists use the term efficiency and inefficiency to judge the relative ability of a society (or contract or institution) to produce a good without wasting resources. A financial system is more (less) efficient to the extent that it can produce the same amount of the good—the transfer of surpluses (savings) to those in deficit (users of savings, i.e., "borrowers" broadly understood)—at a lower cost. If the costs are lower, but the output of the good is reduced, or it produces greater misallocation of surpluses, it is not more efficient than a system with higher costs but produces better results. Likewise, a financial system that produces few losses, but also results in the hoarding of large amounts of surplus is not necessarily more efficient than an alternative financial system that produces more losses, but also produces more gains. In short, a system is efficient only when all resources available to it are optimally utilized. Essentially, maximizing efficiency is simply another way of saying minimizing waste, with waste including both realized losses arising from unwise uses of surpluses, for example, building too much private housing as was the case in the United States during the first decade of the 2000s, and unrealized losses arising from the failure to deploy surpluses to sectors of the economy that could use those resources productively, for example, as a result of hoarding.[45]

Fortunately, there is evidence in revelation that shows that efficiency, at least in this abstract sense, is indeed an important Islamic ethical value. God praises those who "When they spend, they are neither excessive nor are they miserly, and between these is prosperity." (*al-Furqān*, 67). The word *qawām* (also *qiwām*) includes the meaning of justice and stability, or to read the verse from the perspective of an economist, equilibrium.

---

44. This is the ideal of *Pareto* efficiency. A state of the world is described as being *Pareto optimal* when it is impossible to make one person better off without making another person worse off. Under the Pareto conception of efficiency, a redistribution of entitlements is efficient only if it makes both (or all) of the parties involved better off, and therefore, a commitment to Pareto efficiency usually entails a commitment to private trade and a reluctance to permit coercive transfers. Another conception of efficiency, known as *Kaldor-Hicks efficiency*, permits coercive redistributions whenever the gains realized by those made better off from the transfer are sufficiently large that they could reimburse the losses suffered by those who suffered a loss from the redistribution of property or rights, as applicable. The criterion of Kaldor-Hicks efficiency is more realistic from a public policy perspective than that of Pareto efficiency.

45. For example, according to statistics maintained by the Federal Reserve Bank of the United States, banks in the United States held $2.578 *trillion* of excess reserves (reserves beyond that required by law) and United States corporations as of the end of 2013 held $1.64 trillion in cash on their balance sheets, figures that suggest that vast amounts of social resources are sitting idle, doing nothing productive for the economy.

From this perspective, God praises those whose spending is neither more nor less than necessary, and is appropriate [38] for their needs, thus producing justice and stability. When all spending is directed to what is necessary and in the amount that is necessary, then a state of perfect efficiency is achieved, as it would be impossible to redirect spending without making someone worse off. By contrast, in an inefficient state, it is possible to redirect spending without making someone worse off.

This aversion to waste is affirmed in numerous verses of the Qur'an, where God makes clear that He does not impose obligations on humanity simply to burden them without a corresponding benefit. Thus, God negated the imposition of gratuitous difficulty (*ḥaraj*) in numerous verses of the Qur'an, (e.g. *al-Māʾida*, 6 and *al-Ḥajj*, 78); He stated that He intends ease in religion and not hardship (e.g. *al-Baqara*, 185) and that He did not overburden us with useless commands (*al-Baqara*, 220). For these reasons, Imam Mālik, may God be pleased with him, recognized "the removal of hardship" (*rafʿ al-ḥaraj*) as one of the foundational principles of his legal school. This recognition of efficiency as a consideration in a jurist's legal determinations left many traces in Imam Mālik's legal opinions, particularly with respect to monetary transactions, some of which were noted earlier in this essay.

The history of Islamic law no doubt provides other examples of cases where the jurists overrode the formal rules of *fiqh* in order to achieve the social goal of improved efficiency, and these examples are not limited to the Mālikī School. The existence of cash *waqf*s (*waqf al-nuqūd*) in the late Ottoman Empire, for example, is an important example of the jurists making exceptions to the formal rules of law in order to ensure that the law serves the goal of efficiency and does not result in waste. Indeed, one might make the argument that from a legal perspective, *ḥaraj* ought simply to be understood as any kind of expenditure that is not necessary to achieve the goal of [39] the transacting parties and thus produces a dead-weight loss in economic terms.

In the Andalusian case of the partnership for the production of cheese, for example, the Mālikī jurists might have relied on the famous hadith of Bilāl, in which the Prophet (S) told him to sell one kind of dates in the market and use the proceeds from that sale to purchase the different kind of dates that he had originally traded for in order to avoid the unequal exchange of dates, which violates the prohibition against *ribā al-faḍl*.[46] Had they applied this hadith to that transaction, they would have told the people to sell their milk in the market for cash, form a partnership with the cash obtained from its sale, repurchase milk from the partnership's capital, and then they could lawfully divide the cheese produced by the partnership in proportion to their respective cash contributions to the partnership's capital. By permitting them to avoid the intermediate steps of selling the milk and then repurchasing it, despite the formal violation of the

46. Aḥmad b. ʿAlī b. Ḥajar al-ʿAsqalānī, 4 *Fatḥ al-Bārī Sharḥ Ṣaḥīḥ al-Bukhārī* (Dār al-maʿrifa: Beirut, 1959), hadith no. 2201, p. 400.

rules against *ribā al-faḍl*, the jurists saved the partners the costs entailed in these two additional transactions. While that meant that the final distribution of the cheese would not be perfectly consistent with the actual productivity of the milk contributed by the various partners, the jurists recognized that the gains from forcing them to sell and then repurchase the milk with money were less than the costs such additional transactions would impose on them and thus represented dead-weight losses from the perspective of the parties.[47] This fact justified recognition of a *rukhṣa*.

Based on the foregoing, it follows that an overriding purpose of Islamic finance is to minimize dead-weight social losses, even if they arise in connection with practices that are formally compliant with the rules of Islamic law. In fact, one might say that whenever adherence to formal rules of Islamic law leads [40] to dead-weight social losses, the higher principles of Islamic law, in this case—*rafᶜ al-ḥaraj*—dictate the recognition of an exception, a *rukhṣa*, to the normally applicable rule, but only to the extent necessary to prevent the loss. This principle ought to be applied universally in the analysis of all contemporary private and public economic activity, and to the role of all financial institutions, whether for-profit or not-for-profit, with the goal of achieving a sustainable equilibrium that is reasonably stable—the state of *qiwām* that God praises in *Sūrat al-Furqān*, 67. We now turn to applying these principles in the light of the foregoing purposive analysis of finance in the *Sharīᶜa* to some contemporary problems.

G. ISLAMIC BANKS, FINANCIAL INTERMEDIATION AND THE PROBLEM OF THE GUARANTEE OF DEPOSITS FROM THE PERSPECTIVE OF PURPOSIVE *FIQH*

While the texts of revelation and the historical *fiqh* developed in light of revelation clearly established the necessity of finance to the social life of the community, neither revelation nor the jurists had developed advanced institutional means for financial intermediation. Most pre-modern tools of Islamic law that could be used for finance assumed direct relationships between the transferor and the transferee, the major exception being the *qirāḍ* or the *muḍāraba*, where savers gave their surplus to an entrepreneur who, in certain circumstances, could then invest those funds in a second venture. As a result,

47. The Andalusian case of partnerships for the production of cheese from milk also suggests that the analysis provided by the economist Mahmoud el-Gamal regarding the mark-to-market justification for the rules of *ribā al-faḍl* exists only in the special case where no market for the goods exists, or is only coming into existence, something that was no doubt the case in the early Islamic period. In cases where flourishing markets already exist, and traders can be presumed to know market prices, as must have been the case in a sophisticated urban setting such as 15th-century Granada, the need to apply the rules of *ribā al-faḍl* strictly lapses. Mahmoud El-Gamal, *Islamic Finance: Law, Economics and Practice* (Cambridge University Press: New York, 2006), p. 53.

banks, whether for profit or not-for-profit, did not develop indigenously in the Islamic world and were only introduced in the 19th century after contact with Europeans.[48]

Banks play a decisive role in modern financial systems by serving as efficient institutional intermediaries standing [41] between those persons with excess funds (savers) and those persons or entities in need of funds (borrowers). In the absence of a bank, any person with an excess of funds would have to expend substantial costs in order to find a person with whom he could invest his excess funds. At the same time, those persons needing funds also would have to expend substantial costs in identifying individuals with surplus funds that are available for investment. Banks, therefore, provide a convenient site for these two different social constituencies to meet: individuals with surpluses can place their money with the bank, and the bank can disburse those surplus funds to entrepreneurs and consumers who need the money immediately in exchange for repayment in the future. The bank also specializes in investigating the ability of the prospective borrowers to repay the funds borrowed from savers, resulting in further efficiency gains to society by reducing credit risk and thus lowering the risk of misallocated savings. Banks thus allow savings to be aggregated on a very wide scale and reallocated to productive uses throughout the economy, something that would be practically impossible if individual savers and individual borrowers had to find one another directly. Banks, therefore, perform tasks that would otherwise fall on savers and borrowers, respectively, but does so at a much lower aggregate (and in most cases, individual) cost than would be the case in their absence. Once the bank as an institution is developed, therefore, it would be socially wasteful to insist that the only permissible means of finance continue to be principal-to-principal contracting as had been largely assumed to be the case in pre-modern Islamic law.

Conventional, for-profit banking, however, poses at least two problems from the perspective of Islamic law. The first was that its profits were derived almost exclusively from interest income from loans. The second was that the bank guaranteed [42] the deposits of savers even as they gave savers a return, an "interest," on the funds that they deposited with the banks. The first principle violated the charitable nature of loans in Islamic law, which, as previously noted, characterized loans as purely *altruistic* transactions. The second principle violated the distinction between a deposit (*amāna*) and a debt (*dayn*): by guaranteeing the return of the deposit, the depositor's claim becomes transformed into a debt payable by the bank to the depositor, in which case it is prohibited for the depositor to receive a return in respect of that debt by virtue of the bank's guarantee of repayment.

---

48. Cash *waqf*s which proliferated in the late Ottoman Empire were not full-fledged banks because the contributors of surplus could not retrieve their money invested in the *waqf* in the future. Instead of being depositors or investors, their capital took the form of a charitable contribution, which was permanently alienated to the *waqf*. In other words, they could only get their surplus back in the form of a loan in the future from the *waqf* itself.

The depositor would only be entitled to the interest under classical juristic notions if the deposit was subject to loss, a possibility that was legally, if not practically, eliminated by virtue of the bank's guarantee of the deposit.[49]

In order to solve this problem, Muslim bankers and sympathetic jurists interested in creating an Islamic institution that acted like a conventional bank searched the Islamic tradition in order to find the closest analogue to financial intermediation that could function on a wide scale. They settled on the *muḍāraba* or *qirāḍ* for two principle reasons. First and unlike other kinds of Islamic partnerships, this contract contemplates passive investment on the part of individuals with surplus funds who invest the money with an entrepreneur pursuant to a pre-determined profit-sharing agreement between the entrepreneur and the investors. Because the entrepreneur could then invest the capital of the first *muḍāraba* in a second *muḍāraba*, known as *al-muḍārib yuḍārib*, this structure allows for financial intermediation akin to the function of modern banks. It is not surprising, then, that when for-profit, commercial Islamic banks first made their appearance in the mid-70s, they used the *muḍāraba* as the model for their operations.

Nevertheless, the so-called two-tiered *muḍāraba* has not [43] proven to be an ideal structure for financial intermediation. First, and in contrast to a conventional bank, the entrepreneur, that is, the Islamic bank, cannot guarantee the capital of the depositors, at least according to the historical doctrines of Islamic law:[50] if he guarantees the deposits, then the depositors would not be entitled to a return, and so therefore, deposits must be liable for investment losses in order for the depositors to be entitled as a formal legal matter to a return on their investment. This, however, is contrary to the expectations of those who deposit money with Islamic banks, even if they are nominally deemed to be investors (*rabb al-māl*) rather than depositors. As a practical matter, depositors in Islamic banks do not expect that the funds which they place with Islamic banks should be exposed to greater risk of loss than funds placed on deposit with conventional banks. And, as a matter of politics, no government would allow a major Islamic bank to fail if that meant that the average depositor would lose his savings. In short, strict application of the doctrine of *muḍāraba* to the deposits of Islamic banks would limit their effectiveness in mobilizing social savings, since they could only successfully attract funds which represent the risky portion of savers' portfolios. In practice, this risk is avoided using two strategies. The first is that the Islamic bank itself engages in a more conservative investment strategy in order to minimize the risk of loss—and thus the risk that depositors

49. This is a straightforward, even if mechanical, application of a bedrock principle of Islamic commercial law, namely that the right to profit is a function of the possibility of loss and is variously expressed as "*al-kharāj bi'l-ḍamān*" or "*al-ghunm bi'l-ghurm*." Jurists have not deemed the continued existence of credit risk to be sufficient to satisfy this principle.

50. 3 *Al-Sharḥ al-ṣaghīr*, pp. 687–88 (a *qirāḍ* in which the entrepreneur guarantees the capital to the investor is invalid [*fāsid*] and the condition is not enforced).

might lose their funds—and the second is reliance on either the existence of an explicit or implicit government guarantee of the bank's deposits.

These strategies to mitigate the problems inherent to the two-tiered *muḍāraba* structure produces at least three problems. First, assuming strict application of traditional doctrines of *muḍāraba*, investors would face a substantial risk of loss to their capital, which would mean that they would be willing to [44] give over to the Islamic bank only that portion of their savings that they are prepared to lose, and in the case of relatively poor individuals, they would be unwilling to give any of their meager savings to an Islamic bank. Since most Muslim countries are poor, it follows that a very small portion of societies' savings could be marshaled through Islamic accounts structured as *muḍāraba*. Secondly, and on the assumption that Muslim scholars continue to prohibit Islamic banks from guaranteeing their customers' funds while allowing a third party to guarantee deposits, for example, the state, Islamic banks will likely choose to invest in excessively risky projects, secure in their knowledge that if the investments fail, the government will bail out their depositors, leading to a situation of "privatized gains, socialized losses." Such a policy will inevitably lead to poor use of social savings where the bank will finance many projects that do not deserve to be financed. Thirdly, an Islamic bank could adhere strictly to traditional Islamic norms, and in response become more *risk averse* than a conventional bank by maintaining higher ratios of cash reserves than conventional banks, investing in less risky projects, or both. This last strategy, which is in fact commonly adopted, inevitably results in substantial efficiency losses insofar as the Islamic bank will refuse to fund prospectively profitable, but relatively risky, ventures, in order to maintain sufficient cash reserves to pay the depositors. All things being equal, then, the conventional bank, operating with deposit insurance whose premiums are paid by the bank, would be more efficient in deploying savings than a similarly situated Islamic bank that cannot guarantee its deposits.[51]

If the case can be made that Islamic ethics commands us to minimize dead-weight losses, then arguments contemplating the modification of traditional *muḍāraba* doctrine in the context of financial intermediation to make it more effective in the deployment of [45] savings could be accepted. Because of the ubiquitous use of leverage in banking in privately owned banks, whether Islamic or conventional, for-profit banks have a structural incentive to pursue gains for their shareholders at the expense of the public that will implicitly guarantee the liquidity and the solvency of these institutions.[52] The

51. For a detailed explanation of the problems with the two-tiered *muḍāraba* model for financial intermediation, see El-Gamal, pp. 165–69.

52. See, for example, the English language balance sheet of the 2013 Dubai Islamic Bank, p. 3 (listing its shareholder equity at approximately AED 16 billion and its liabilities at AED 96.9 billion, 79 billion of which is customer deposits). Note that the Arabic version of the same document appears to use different categories than that of the English language version, even though the totals are the same in both.

two-tier *muḍāraba* structure does nothing to solve the problem of moral hazard that permeates commercial banking.

The most radical solution to this problem would be to abandon the two-tier *muḍāraba* model in favor of a pure agency (*wikāla*) model of investment pursuant to which the role of the Islamic bank is understood simply as the investment agent of the investors (depositors), and in that capacity, it agrees to guarantee the performance of the borrower whose loan it arranges.[53] Because the bank in this case is an agent and never owns the funds that will be provided to the borrower, the problem of guaranteeing the capital sum does not arise. Under this arrangement, the Islamic bank would earn its returns for its services in arranging the transaction, and not pursuant to a dubious claim that it is profiting from trade. A less radical solution from a practical perspective—although it would represent a substantial departure from existing doctrine—would be to require the bank, in its capacity as the investment agent in the first-tier *muḍāraba*—to guarantee the deposits of the investors. This solution would be based on *istiḥsān* in light of the practical need to reduce the moral hazard involved in for-profit banking; it would also be fair to the bank insofar as the only economically valuable functions of Islamic banks is financial intermediation and evaluation of the creditworthiness of prospective borrowers, thus making the bank a better candidate for bearing the risk that the client defaults. Finally, a less drastic solution, at least in terms of doctrinal reform, would be to require the Islamic bank [46] to invest a certain amount of its own capital in the second-tier *muḍāraba*, for example, 10%.

The need (*al-ḥāja*) for an efficient system financial intermediation in the 21st century is just as legitimate as the need for 15th-century Andalusians to pool relatively small amounts of milk and small numbers of livestock in order to manufacture cheese efficiently. Likewise, applying the ordinary rule of *qirāḍ/muḍāraba* that would prohibit the entrepreneur from guaranteeing the funds would effectively prevent the benefits from financial intermediation from taking place, or it would require adoption of other solutions that themselves would substantially reduce the efficiency of the system of financial intermediation. The same problem faced the Andalusian Mālikī jurists when they considered the legality of customary partnerships for the production of cheese: applying the rules of *ribā* and *gharar* strictly would have prevented the achievement of efficient economies of scale and would have effectively prevented the people from pursuing their legitimate interest in realizing a gain from their own property, thus justifying a departure from the ordinary rules.

The same kind of reasoning ought to apply to the problem of guaranteeing the deposits of banks. Just as was the case for individuals who had small amounts of surplus milk, which they could not use to manufacture cheese except if they entered into partnerships with others, so too small-savers are not in a position to invest their surplus funds unless

53. Mahmoud el-Gamal proposed this solution previously. See, El-Gamal, pp. 159–61.

they are aggregated with the funds of others. However, they would be unwilling to invest those funds—given that they are rationally risk-averse given their liquidity constraints—except on terms that are guaranteed. While a third party could guarantee their investments, for example, the state, this solution, because of moral hazard, would be wasteful because it would lead to overinvestment [47] in risky projects. Accordingly, the entrepreneur—in this case, the bank—must be held liable for the loss in order to prevent wasteful investments in high-risk projects. Only by providing a guarantee to small depositors, and imposing liability on the entrepreneur, will the full benefits of financial intermediation be obtained, and in light of the principle of *rafʿ al-ḥaraj*, an exception to the rule that the entrepreneur is not liable to the investor for losses in capital ought to be recognized in the case of banks.

H. *ZAKĀT*, DISTRIBUTIVE JUSTICE AND ISLAMIC PUBLIC FINANCE IN A MODERN SETTING

I now wish to turn to questions of distributive justice in Islamic ethics, and how this should impact a modern conception of *zakāt* and public finance generally. As mentioned above, in principle, the law of *zakāt* provides that each Muslim (or citizen, in the modern context), is guaranteed a minimum subsistence income. This is evidenced by the previously cited Mālikī rule that anyone lacking a year's worth of food is entitled to receive *zakāt* (*faqīr lā yamliku qūta ʿāmihi*). The insistence that each person should, in principle, be entitled to a year's worth of provisions without being forced to sell his labor is consistent with the principle of anti-subordination that is reflected in many rules of *fiqh* and clearly works to support Islam's commitment to non-subordination. People are much less likely to accept humiliating conditions of employment if they are guaranteed a minimum income that at least allows them to live independently of others.

The strong commitment to establishing a minimum entitlement to subsistence is in tension, however, with the formalistic nature of most of the rules of *zakāt*, including, the rules establishing liability for *zakāt*. For example, a person may [48] simultaneously be liable for *zakāt* if he owns the minimum amount of property required (*niṣāb*) but nevertheless be eligible to receive *zakāt* to the extent that he also does not own enough to provide him with a year's worth of food, a rule that indicates the failure of the jurists to index the *niṣāb* to prevailing inflation rates. In short, many of the classical *fiqh* rules were formulated without giving adequate regard to the general policies of *zakāt* as an effective system of social justice.

The biggest obstacle to using *zakāt* as an effective tool for social justice is the fact that far from being a unified system of taxation, it provides substantially different rules depending on the nature of the property, a feature that has substantially reduced the Islamic tax base. As is well known, the jurists recognized three different categories for purposes of *zakāt*: livestock (*mawāshī*); agricultural output (*ḥarth*); and cash money (*ʿayn*), meaning gold and silver, or money's worth (*qīma*). The most important difference in the treatment of these various types of property is that agricultural products are liable for *zakāt* immediately upon harvest (after deduction of the *niṣāb*), while in the case of money, it is assessed only on savings, not income. This leads to substantially unfair results. Consider the case of a wheat farmer. At the end of the season, he successfully harvests his crop; he is entitled to keep the *niṣāb*—five *awsuq*, a year's worth of wheat—for himself—but he must pay *zakāt* on everything that exceeds this amount as of the day of the harvest. A person dealing in cash, however, whether a merchant or an employee, on the other hand, is only liable for *zakāt* with respect to what he has saved, and then only if he has held on to that savings for one year, and if the savings are in excess of the *niṣāb*, which in the case of cash is either 20 gold dinars or 200 silver dirhams, or their value in cash substitutes, for example, *fulūs* or goods held for sale (*ʿurūḍ*). This [49] leads to dissimilar treatment of the farmer and the merchant/employee: the farmer pays *zakāt* out of his income, while the merchant/employee pays his *zakāt* out of savings. A person dealing in cash, therefore, can always minimize his *zakāt* obligation simply by increasing his consumption! Such a perverse result hardly seems consistent with Islam's aspirations to achieve social justice; the Qur'an condemns excessive consumption as immoral and wasteful, but the rules of *zakāt* as historically elaborated seem to encourage consumption among those who deal in cash, at least at the margins.

Historically, those who dealt in cash—largely, the people who lived in cities—were also privileged by the rules of *zakāt* insofar as their property was deemed by many of the jurists to be *amwāl bāṭina*—hidden property—and accordingly, the state had no right to investigate the extent to which they held surplus cash. In other words, urban dwellers largely enjoyed the privilege of self-reporting their savings for purposes of liability for *zakāt*. By contrast, agricultural output and grazing livestock were considered *amwāl ẓāhira*—manifest property—and accordingly, the state had the right to calculate and compel owners of livestock and agricultural property to pay amounts due as *zakāt*.

From the perspective of modern tax theory, the treatment of cash in the rules of *zakāt* represents "leakage" from the tax base: property that ought to be taxed is not being captured in the rules that define the tax base. No system of taxation captures the tax base perfectly, and it is not surprising that the classical rules of *fiqh* should have suffered from some leakage as well. The important point to note, however, is that in pre-modern age, such leakage was relatively small because agricultural production was by far the largest sector of the economy. For us in the modern world, however, the cash economy is the largest [50] sector of the economy, and we tend to consider the rules governing the treatment of cash in the law of *zakāt* as the *aṣl*, the basic norm, and the other rules as secondary. Consider the case of Egypt: even though Egypt would hardly be considered an industrial powerhouse, the combined agricultural and livestock sectors represent only 14.5% of the country's annual economic output,[54] yet according to the rules of *zakāt*,

54. Central Intelligence Agency, The World Factbook: Egypt: Economy (2013).

cultivators would be the only Egyptians subject to *zakāt*-based liability on their income without first enjoying the right to satisfy their demands for consumption.

It is clear that a purposive approach to the rules of *zakāt*, taking into account that the goal of *zakāt* is to establish a minimally just distribution of the community's income, would require a radical revision in the rules of the tax base to which *zakāt* is applied, such that those who deal in cash are treated in line with those of agriculturalists: they should be allowed a deduction equivalent to a year's worth of subsistence level income, but they should then be liable for *zakāt* based on the rest of the income they earn during that year, regardless of how much they save.[55] Such a departure from historical doctrine would be justified by analogy to the treatment of agriculturalists: insofar as *zakāt* was an income tax and not a tax on savings with respect to agriculturalists, those who earn their living in cash ought to be subject to the same rules by virtue of the fact that they represent the largest portion of the tax base, just as agriculturalists represented the largest portion of the tax base in historical eras. A reorientation of *zakāt* to treat those who deal in cash similarly to agriculturalists would raise a substantial amount of revenue that could be used to fulfill the ambition of *zakāt* to guarantee every person a minimum subsistence level income, something that is a condition for achieving human dignity and freedom, something that is required by Islam's commitment to resist unnecessary subordination of one person to another. It would not, however, be enough on its own without increasing the rate of *zakāt* that is payable. The historical rate of 2.5% should be adjusted in the light of the needs of current Muslim states to achieve the goal of *zakāt*, namely a just distribution of the community's income while at the same time preserving incentives for private economic initiative. Unfortunately, the historical rules of *zakāt*, because of the jurists' formalism, have been unable to countenance revising the rates of *zakāt* that individuals must pay.[56] This is unfortunate, not only because it prevents *zakāt* from achieving its goals, but also because there is no textual authority that limits Muslims to the historical rates discussed in the books of *fiqh*. In fact, the textual evidence used to establish the basic rates that apply to private property derives from actions and decisions of the companions rather than express Prophetic (S) precedent or Qur'anic text.[57] And even if we assumed that the companions and successors were acting on the basis of Prophetic practice that was not explicitly attributed to the Prophet (S), it would be more

55. They would of course continue to be subject to *zakāt* on their savings that exceed a minimum threshold and is held for more than one year.

56. Even a jurist as willing to revise historical rules of *zakāt* such as Yūsuf al-Qaraḍāwī has been unwilling to consider changing the fixed-rate nature of *zakāt*. See *al-Nisbiyya wa'l-taṣāʿud bayn al-zakāt wa'l-ḍarība (inna al-zakāta bi'l-naẓar ilā ṭabīʿatihā farīḍa dīniyya khālida khulūd al-insān bāqiya baqāʾ al-islām lā tataghayyar bi-taghayyur al-ẓurūf wa'l-awḍāʿ wa'l-ḥājāt, bal yuṭālab bi-hā tadayyunan wa taʿabbudan kull muslim fī kull ʿaṣr wa fī kull bīʾa wa fī kull ḥāl)*.

57. See, for example, 2 *Sharḥ al-Zurqānī ʿalā Muwaṭṭaʾ Imām Mālik* (Dār al-maʿrifa: Beirut, 1987), pp. 107–118 (mentioning the precedents of ʿUmar b. ʿAbd al-ʿAzīz, Muʿādh b. Jabal and ʿUmar b. al-Khaṭṭāb).

appropriate to interpret the relevant precedents in the light of the role of the Prophet as Imam of the community (*taṣarruf bi'l-imāma*) rather than in his role as messenger of God (*taṣarruf bi'l-futyā*),[58] especially in light of the fact that the relevant precedents show that different kinds of properties were subject to different rates, a fact that strongly suggests that these rules were originally developed to further the public good (*al-maṣlaḥa al-ʿāmma*) and were not intended to be devotional rules (*taʿabbud*).

While *zakāt* is intended to further distributive justice within an economy, it is not sufficient in the absence of macroeconomic policies that promote sustainable economic growth: one cannot achieve distributive justice if there is no surplus to redistribute. *Zakāt* can only function, then, within an overall framework of [52] effective macroeconomic policy, an important pillar of which is public finance. The *fiqh*, however, provides very problematic limitations on the tools available for legitimate public finance, seemingly limiting permissible taxation to the taxes set forth in revelation, namely, *zakāt* and *kharāj*. Indeed, one Mālikī author claims a consensus for the proposition that levying taxes on a Muslim in excess of the textual rates is a matter of consensus, and whoever violates this consensus has abandoned Islam insofar as he has violated a cardinal Islamic principal.[59] When this rule is combined with the jurists' decision to fix the rates of *zakāt* and *kharāj*, the state is deprived of the financial tools necessary to manage flexibly the legitimate needs of the public, especially with respect to financing badly needed investments in public goods, such as education, health, and public infrastructure.

By tying the hands of the state with respect to taxation, the jurists were forced, in certain circumstances, to adopt second-best solutions that were far from optimal from the perspective of a rational system of public finance. For example, the Shāfiʿīs adopted a doctrine of compelled loans, whereby the state could force the rich to lend money to the state in circumstances where the treasury lacked sufficient resources to meet its obligations.[60] While most Muslim states today have attempted to establish rational systems of taxation in spite of these doctrinal limitations, and many modern jurists have permitted taxation beyond that of *zakāt* and *kharāj*, albeit reluctantly and on the assumption that they are exceptional measures,[61] it remains the case that many Muslims, scholars and

58. For the distinction between *al-taṣarruf bi'l-imāma* and *taṣarruf bi'l-futyā*, and their different effects in the *Sharīʿa*, see Shihāb al-Dīn al-Qarāfī, *al-Iḥkām fī tamyīz al-fatāwā ʿan al-aḥkām wa taṣarrufāt al-Qāḍī wa'l-Imām*, ed. ʿAbd al-Fattāḥ Abū Ghudda (Maktab al-Maṭbūʿāt al-Islāmiyya: Aleppo, 1967), *al-Suʾāl al-khāmis wa'l-ʿishrūn*, pp. 99–120.

59. 2 *Al-Sharḥ al-ṣaghīr*, p. 322 (*wa'l-ijmāʿ ʿalā ḥurmat al-akhdhi min al-muslimīn wa ʿalā kufri mustaḥillihi li-annahu min al-maʿlūm min al-dīn bi'l-ḍarūra*).

60. Zakariyya b. Muḥammad al-Anṣārī, 5 *Asnā al-maṭālib sharḥ rawḍ al-ṭālib*, ed. Muḥammad Tāmir (Dār al-kutub al-ʿilmiyya: Beirut, 2001), p. 617 (*fa-idhā ʿudima bayt al-māl ... iqtaraḍa ʿalayhi al-imām min aghniyāʾ baladihi ... fa-in taʿadhdhara al-iqtirāḍ qassaṭahā ʿalā al-aghniyāʾ qarḍan*).

61. See, for example, a variety of fatwas on the topic of the permissibility of modern taxes on the web site of Multaqa Ahl al-Hadith. For a detailed argument on the permissibility of collecting

laity, resent taxes, believe them to be inherently unjust and Islamic, and believe that it is Islamically permissible to engage in tax evasion, if such taxes are in excess of the obligations imposed by revelation.[62]

[53] From the perspective of the Islamic objectives of public finance, however, the classical position rejecting the legitimacy of taxation in excess of what is imposed in the law of *zakāt* and *kharāj* must be categorically rejected. What the Prophet (S) prohibited was *mukūs*, taxes taken coercively by a tyrant to fulfill his own private ends, not money taken by a legitimate state used to further the legitimate ends of the public. Indeed, to the extent that the state is pursuing ends that are morally obligatory for it to pursue from the perspective of Islamic law because they are constitutive of the public good (*al-maṣlaḥa al-ʿāmma*), that is, what the jurists call *furūḍ kifāya*, then one might say it is obligatory on individual Muslims to obey rational rules of taxation that are intended to provide the state with the means to fulfill those obligations. This is consistent with the principle of *uṣūl al-fiqh* that "what is an indispensable condition for the fulfillment of an obligation is itself an obligation" (*mā lā yatimmu al-wājib illā bihi, fa-huwa wājib*). The premodern jurists recognized quite a wide scope for communal obligations. For example, pursuit of all the secular arts (*al-ḥiraf al-muhimma*) that are related to achieving the public good was historically recognized as a communal obligation, just as religious goods such as teaching religious sciences was a communal obligation.[63] It should be recognized that where the state chooses to provide these goods, then the citizens have an obligation to pay taxes levied to finance the provision of those goods.

This forces us to consider whether the state should have a role in fulfilling these collective duties, or whether it is permissible to leave the field open to private individual Muslims to discharge these obligations. After all, while the jurists identified various activities as being collective obligations, they did not say that it was the responsibility of the state to achieve them; indeed, they make it clear that as long as someone fulfills [54] the obligation, then the community has fulfilled its duty. And given the broad class of actions that constitute collective obligations, for example, preparing the dead for prayer (*tajhīz al-mayyit*) and conducting funeral prayers (*ṣalāt al-janāza*), returning greetings of peace (*radd al-salām*), and praying for the one who sneezes (*tashmīt al-ʿāṭis*), it would be inconceivable to conclude that it is always, or even presumptively, the state's responsibility to discharge all collective obligations. What is needed, then, is a principle that

---

taxes in addition to the *zakāt* and the *kharāj*, see Yūsuf al-Qaraḍāwī, *al-Adilla ʿalā jawāz farḍ al-ḍarāʾib maʿ al-zakāt*.

62. Bin Baz, for example, has given the opinion that it is permissible for a Muslim to circumvent payment of customs duties levied by a Muslim government so long as he does it secretly and without an intention to overthrow that government (*yajūz bi-sharṭ an lā yakūna fī dhalika munābadha li'l-ḥukūma*). See *Fatāwā al-ʿulamāʾ fī ḥukm al-ḍarāʾib wa'l-jamārik al-mukūs allatī taʾkhudhuha al-duwal al-islāmiyya al-yawm*.

63. 3 *Al-Tāj wa'l-iklīl*, p. 348.

allows us to distinguish between which collective obligations ought to be fulfilled by the state in its capacity as representative of the Muslim community, and which collective duties can be left to individual Muslims to fulfill in their private capacities. Here, I would again suggest that Islamic ethics requires us to use considerations of efficiency, meaning, that those cases in which the state is in the best position to discharge the obligation at the lowest cost, responsibility should lie with the state, and the state can legitimately tax the population in order to fund the programs necessary to satisfy the obligation.

The provision of such basic tasks of modern government as universal education, universal health care, public infrastructure, for example, highways, bridges, railroads, and ports, constitute what most economists would call "public goods." Because they are public goods, the private market fails to produce them, or fails to produce them in an economically optimal quantity. To understand why, consider the case of education. If it were to be provided solely by the market, the only people who could acquire this good would be those who could afford it. The more wealth a person has, the more education he or she could buy. But unless it is the case that the cost of a minimally necessary education is less than the income of all the citizens of a particular state, the cost of education will have to [55] be subsidized to ensure that everyone in society receives a minimally adequate education. Otherwise, the law of supply and demand means that some people in society will be unable to pay the market-clearing price for education, and therefore they will be forced to forego education, causing a social loss. The public good, because it requires universal education, can only be achieved if the public subsidizes the cost of education for those lacking sufficient means to pay for it themselves. Taxes are the only reliable means to fund this public good.[64]

The same is true of health care: from a social perspective, it is always rational to treat a sick person when the benefits to be gained from curing, or even treating the sick person, exceed the costs of the treatment. Persons with chronic diseases, such as diabetes, high cholesterol, or high blood pressure, are good examples. Such persons gradually lose their ability to function as productive members of society if they are left untreated, and indeed, in some cases, their chronic conditions may develop into full-blown health crises that lead to substantial costs, for example, an untreated diabetic who may become blind or lose a limb, or a person with untreated high blood pressure or cholesterol may suffer a stroke or a heart attack. From a social perspective, it is rational to treat these individuals in order to prevent their conditions from deteriorating or leading to potentially catastrophic health consequences in the future for two reasons. The first is that as

64. A state might have its disposal vast mineral wealth, like the states of the Arabian Gulf, but at some point in time that wealth will disappear, and the state will have to have access to other, recurring sources of revenue. Indeed, it would be healthier even for such states to invest their mineral wealth for the long-term benefit of their people and rely only on tax revenue for the state's ordinary expenses, such as education and health care.

a result of the occurrence of a health catastrophe society loses the contributions such persons would have made to it. The second reason is the actual out-of-pocket costs that will have to be incurred by society as a result of the health catastrophe, including costs of medical care and post-event costs of recovery, such as increased monitoring and care, if the patient, for example, becomes bed-ridden or otherwise is incapable of taking care of himself or herself. Although it would [56] be rational for such persons to be treated to prevent these losses from occurring, it will inevitably be the case that many individuals will not be able to pay for the medication or other health care services necessary to treat their condition were it the case that such services or medications are provided exclusively by the private sector.

Because the private sector will only provide the service if it can do so for a profit, it will undersupply the required good of health care. The only solution is to have the government provide the care, as was the case for universal education. The government will only be able to do so, however, if it can collect revenue from the public in an efficient manner, and if the population believes that it is their duty to pay such taxes when the government demands them. Accordingly, whenever the government is reasonably viewed as the most efficient institution with respect to the discharge of a *farḍ kifāya*, Islamic ethics should be understood as requiring that this service be provided by the government and not the private sector; that the government be authorized to levy taxes in whatever amount necessary to allow it to discharge those obligations; and, that the citizenry is under a moral obligation to pay such taxes when they are levied.

Having established the legitimacy of taxation for the purpose of financing the legitimate collective goals of the community, the question then arises as to what methods of taxation and public finance should be used, and how to prioritize public spending. In this case, pre-modern Islamic law provides important principles in support of social justice. One of these is the legal principle of *darʾ al-mafāsid qabla jalb al-maṣāliḥ*, warding off harm is to be given priority to obtain additional benefits. While it is not completely clear how this principle can be applied in all cases, in general, I understand it as an Islamic version of [57] the American philosopher John Rawls' difference principle, namely, that inequality is to be justified to the extent, and only to the extent, that permitting inequality improves the welfare of the worst-off in society. One can find many statements from the jurists that support this proposition. Jalāl al-Dīn al-Suyūṭī, for example, wrote in his *al-Ashbāh wa'l-naẓaʾir* that "It is not permissible for the Imam to prefer anyone over the most needy with respect to spending the treasury's funds."[65] The Ḥanafī author of *Ghamz ʿuyūn al-baṣāʾir sharḥ al-ashbāh wa'l-naẓaʾir* quotes another Ḥanafī jurist for the proposition that the well-off have no claim to money from the treasury unless they are performing a specific task for the benefit of the community:

65. Jalāl al-Dīn al-Suyūṭī 1, *al-Ashbāh wa'l-naẓaʾir, al-Qāʿida al-khāmisa taṣarruf al-imām ʿalā al-raʿiyya manūṭ bi'l-maṣlaḥa*, p. 121 (*lā yajūz lahu an yuqaddima fī māl bayt al-māl ghayr al-aḥwāj ʿalā al-aḥwāj*).

> "al-Rāzī was asked about the treasury, whether the rich have a claim to its revenue; he said, 'No, unless he is a scholar or a judge and the jurists (*fuqahāʾ*) have no claim except for a jurist who spends his days teaching law or the Qur'an.'"[66]

I take from this principle that a fundamental principle of Islamic public finance is that government spending must be targeted to prioritize the requirements of the neediest sectors of society. Failure to adhere to this principle in countries such as Egypt, where substantial amounts of public revenues are spent on subsidies that benefit the wealthy, for example, energy subsidies and subsidies for university education, disproportionately benefit those Egyptians who are already well-off, and have had the effect of substantially reducing the state's commitment to public investment in favor of financing private consumption by the well-off. It should not be surprising, then, to learn that only 12.5% of Egypt's gross domestic product goes to savings, ranking it 125th in the world in 2013, while Malaysia, a country whose per-capita income is almost three times greater than Egypt, devotes nearly a third of its GDP to investment, giving it an impressive ranking of 19th in the world in 2013.[67] It also [58] follows that in raising revenue, the government should focus on the relatively well-off and not the poor, and accordingly, should adopt progressive taxation policies.[68]

The Islamic Development Bank (IDB) could play an important role in this context by encouraging Muslim countries to rationalize their public finances so that public money is spent more rationally to develop the human capital of Muslim countries by providing financing to assist these countries seeking to transition from inefficient subsidies toward public policies that prioritize human development, as well as encouraging Muslim countries to adopt effective progressive taxation schemes rather than relying on regressive sales taxes. Unfortunately, the IDB for the most part has functioned primarily to assist Muslim countries finance international trade rather than finance the development of indigenous human capital or encourage Muslim countries to reform their spending priorities or public finances in a fashion more consistent with Islamic values of distributive justice and the needs of national development.

---

66. Shihāb al-Dīn Aḥmad b. Muḥammad al-Ḥamawī, 1 *Ghamz ʿuyūn al-Baṣāʾir Sharḥ al-ashbāh wa'l-Naẓāʾir li-Ibn Nujaym* (Dār al-kutub al-ʿilmiyya: Beirut, 1985), p. 372.

67. Central Intelligence Agency, The World Factbook: Country Comparison: Gross National Saving (2013).

68. Modern jurists who endorse a general power of taxation have also endorsed a progressive theory of taxation.

I. EVALUATING THE PERFORMANCE OF THE FOR-PROFIT ISLAMIC FINANCIAL SECTOR FROM THE PERSPECTIVE OF PURPOSIVE JURISPRUDENCE

Much of the practice of the for-profit Islamic financial sector, instead of seeking to avoid dead-weight losses, or to minimize transaction costs as a purposive approach to Islamic law would require, engages in meaningless transactions that *increase* dead-weight losses for the sole purpose of giving the appearance of complying with Islamic law (and earning additional profits). This problem of adherence to forms simply for the sake of compliance with forms is at its furthest extreme with the *tawarruq* transaction, but it is also present in the vast majority [59] of contemporary Islamic financial transactions where credit transactions are being consciously disguised as contracts of sale or lease in order to avoid the accusation of *ribā*.

Such a strategy suffers from numerous defects, only one of which is that it generates dead-weight losses from a social perspective relative to their conventional, non-Islamic counterparts. More seriously, it risks undermining the public's confidence in Islam when they discover that the Islamic product is substantially no different from the conventional product, and in some cases, even more burdensome.[69] Islamic products, particularly in circumstances where the Islamic sector is small relative to the conventional sector, will generally be more expensive than the comparable conventional product by virtue of the lack of an economy of scale. Even where economies of scale exist, however, the Islamic product may be substantially worse in certain cases for the consumer than the conventional one, as the controversy around default under credit-sale financings (*bayᶜ bi-thaman ājil*) have proven in Malaysia. Because the classical *fiqh* deems the credit price of a good to be fixed at the time of the contract, and because it views the discount of a debt in exchange for early payment to be a kind of *ribā* (*ḍaᶜ wa taᶜajjal*), a debtor who has purchased property using the credit sale structure is worse off than he would have been had he financed the transaction using a conventional loan: under the classical *fiqh*, if the bankrupt debtor defaults, the entire, undiscounted amount of the debt, which in the Islamic contract is denominated as the contract price for the good sold (*al-thaman*), becomes due and payable. In a conventional loan, by contrast, because the debtor's obligation is divided into principal and interest, the debtor is only under an obligation to pay interest when it accrues. Accordingly, he is only required to repay the outstanding amount of the loan at the time of the [60] default as well as any accrued, but unpaid, interest as of the date of default. In the Islamic contract, by contrast, the debtor is under a categorical obligation to pay the "price," even if he defaults one day after entering into a 25-year credit sale.

69. Edib Smolo, *Journal of Islamic Banking and Finance* (January–March 2010), "*al-Bayᶜ bi-thaman ajīl* (BBA) As Practiced in Malaysia: A Critical Review," p. 69.

As a result, while the economic characteristics of an Islamic credit sale transaction and a conventional loan transaction are essentially the same, that is only true if the debtor performs the contract in full. If the debtor defaults and goes bankrupt, the debtor in the Islamic contract becomes liable for the entire amount of the contract, while the conventional debtor will only be liable for the principal plus interest accrued to the moment of default. The sooner the debtor defaults, moreover, the greater the loss will be. Accordingly, if the transaction entails a 25-year period of repayment, and the debtor defaults in year 3, the Islamic debtor's loss will be substantially magnified relative to the loss of a conventional creditor who also defaults in year 3, with the gap only gradually shrinking over the 25-year term.

This feature of Islamic credit law became extremely controversial in Malaysia when debtors discovered that upon default they were expected to pay the entire contract amount. The problem was only resolved when the Malaysian Central Bank intervened and forced Islamic banks to discount the debts owed by their debtors down to their present values.[70] Ironically, it was Malaysia's secular authorities that intervened to protect the Malaysian Muslim consumer, and not the *ʿulamāʾ* who continue, in too many cases, to adhere to the formal letter of historical doctrines without taking into account the real-world impact of those rules, and without taking into account advances in the sciences of finance, accounting, and risk modelling.

Islamic equity investing—the creation of Islamic equity indices such as the Dow Jones Islamic Index—poses fewer problems to the principle of reducing dead-weight losses than the [61] credit practices of Islamic banks, but it also is not free of difficulties. The biggest problem facing Islamic equity investing is the difficulty of constructing a reasonably diversified portfolio of shares using the various "Islamic" screens that scholars have stated must be met in order for an equity investment to be Islamically permissible. The first of these requirements, that the company be engaged in a permissible activity, is non-controversial and of course must be observed. What is more problematic are the financial screens that jurists insist on applying to any equity investment. The primary financial screens are those that test the leverage of a firm; the amount of income it receives from interest; and, the extent to which a firm's assets consist of accounts receivable rather than tangible assets.

The justification for the leverage screen is that a Muslim should not invest in a firm if it is substantially financed by debt, which for these purposes is defined as 1/3rd (i.e. there should be $2 dollars of equity for every $1 dollar of debt in the firm's capital structure).[71]

70. *Resolutions of Shariah Advisory Council of Bank Negara Malaysia*, BNM/RH/GL/012-2, pp. 89–92.

71. Note that if the corporation is taken to be a permissible form for doing business in analogy to the *qirāḍ/muḍāraba*, Mālikī jurists did not allow any debt to be incurred in the name of the *qirāḍ/ muḍāraba*, even with the permission of the investors. 3 *al-Sharḥ al-ṣaghīr* 698 (*wa lā yashtarī ... bi-nasīʾa ... wa in adhina rabbuhu*).

Presumably, for purposes of applying this leverage screen, it is irrelevant whether the debt is Islamic debt or conventional debt. While this rule has been criticized insofar as it is not clear why the jurists chose the 1/3rd benchmark, a more fundamental criticism is that it is not at all clear how this screen can be meaningfully applied. Should it be applied to the book value of a firm's debt and equity, that is, paid-up capital plus retained earnings, or should it be applied to the market valuation of the firm's debt and equity? While it gives a relative objective measure of a firm's value, book value loses its value over time as an accurate presentation of a firm's value, or even of its balance sheet. In the case of a successful firm, using the book value of the firm's equity will substantially understate its true worth in the market as measured by the profitability of the firm, which ultimately supports both a higher sale price for the [62] company if it were to be sold to a third party, and an ability to support a relatively large amount of debt in light of its ability to earn substantial profits in a sustainable fashion. In the case of a failing firm, however, book value may overstate the value of the equity. This reflects the general inability of the firm to earn substantial or sustainable profits with its assets, thus justifying a low price for the company and an inability to support substantial debt, which may, in fact, be one reason why the firm may have a relatively small amount of debt. On the other hand, the use of market capitalization is also not free of difficulties: when market prices are high, that is, price-to-equity ratios are high, then the universe of firms which pass the leverage screen will increase. If, on the other hand, market prices are low, then the universe of firms which pass the leverage screen will shrink.[72]

It might make more sense to reconcile the goal of encouraging reduced reliance on debt with the goal of having a reasonably diversified investment portfolio by linking the two concerns such that Muslim equity investors are allowed, for example, to invest in the least leveraged companies from each of the sectors that make up a diversified portfolio. Such modification—instead of relying on one measure of excessive debt (1/3rd)—would be more sensitive to the financing characteristics of various sectors of the economy. Where one sector supports relatively high level of debt because of regular and predictable cash flows, such as real estate or public utilities, the permitted leverage ratio would exceed 1/3, while in other sectors which do not tolerate high levels of debt, for example, the hi-tech sector, the permitted leverage ratio might be less than 1/3.

It is crucial, then, that in discussing Islamic finance, we judge it not by its adherence to formal doctrinal labels (although it would be found wanting in that respect as well), but rather by [63] reference to its substantive successes or failures in achieving the various goals of an Islamic economy, one of which is its effectiveness in channeling savings into productive uses. And in this respect, Islamic finance, at least with respect to its credit instruments, for example, *sukūk*, *murābaḥa*, and *ijāra-mutanāqiṣa* facilities, and *tawarruq* lines of credit, does little more than mimic conventional financial products

72. See generally, El-Gamal, pp. 125–9.

but with added expense and complication; instead of avoiding or reducing dead-weight losses—what we have argued should be the definition of *ḥaraj* for legal purposes—current Islamic finance products actually increase dead-weight losses relative to conventional products and thus produce an increase in *ḥaraj*. The relative inefficiency of Islamic financial solutions, moreover, is not limited to Islamic credit instruments but also extends to Islamic equity strategies. As long as Muslim jurists are unwilling to adopt a more functional approach to private, for-profit finance, however, the current practices of Islamic finance may nevertheless be defensible if they are successful in marshaling social savings to finance public and private investment and consumption. This would only be true if it could be shown that the creation of Islamic financial products—whether in the credit or the equity markets—have resulted in a net increase in banking deposits and equity investment in public companies, that is, it has convinced people who otherwise would not have deposited their surplus funds with conventional banks or to invest them in public equity markets, to place them with Islamic banks or Islamic investment funds, thus increasing the overall efficiency of the financial intermediation system. In the absence of such evidence, the existence of the Islamic financial system would simply divert resources from the conventional system to the Islamic system with no obvious efficiency gains to society, but raising the possibility of a decrease in overall efficiency in light [64] of the increased transaction costs associate with Islamic financial products.

Finally, we would be remiss if we smugly assumed that Islamic banks are exempt from the structural instability that plagues conventional for-profit banking. Conventional banks pursue high-risk, high-return investments because that is the optimal strategy for the maximization of their profits, insofar as they earn profits based on the "spread"—the difference between what they pay their depositors and what they receive from borrowers. For-profit, privately owned Islamic banks suffer from the same problem: they too earn their profit through the spread between what they pay investors in the first-tier *muḍāraba* and what they receive as their share of the profits earned from the second-tier *muḍāraba*. This structure not only poses structural risks to the safety and soundness of the banking system, but it also potentially distorts the allocation of savings away from socially desirable goals, such as public investment in favor of excessive private consumption. Particularly where there are few opportunities for private investment in profitable businesses, banks will gravitate toward consumer finance, which has very little positive impact on economic development. Muslim-majority states would be well-advised to consider strategies for bifurcating various institutions of financial intermediation, for example, by encouraging the spread of mutually owned banks or credit cooperatives for the purpose of financing private consumption, and limiting for-profit banking to the corporate or sovereign sectors.[73] By prohibiting for-profit ownership of consumer credit agen-

73. Mahmoud El-Gamal has discussed how mutual banking could help to revitalize Islamic banking and put it in the service of the needs of Muslim majority societies. El-Gamal, pp. 186–8.

cies, states can substantially reduce the risk that the profit-seeking incentive of banks will lead to a bubble in consumer credit.

CONCLUSION

[65] I have tried to show in this essay that Islamic ethics provide a rich body of teachings that promote the efficient use of social resources and support a conception of distributive justice that favors the poor while at the same time preserving substantial freedom for private exchange. The sources of Islamic law, the Qur'an and *Sunna*, provide important precedents for public and private finance, and when properly interpreted in the light of the goals of promoting growth, human dignity and a just distribution of wealth, can and should contribute to the development of Muslim countries. At the same time, however, I would be remiss if I did not point out that if the failures of Muslim states in sustaining real human development is not a product of their religious values, then it is a failure of their politics: without the political will to implement rational public policy that promotes human development, it is unlikely (and indeed, unfair) to believe that private investment, whether supported by conventional or Islamic finance, will succeed in achieving sustainable development. In other words, it is impossible to avoid politics: unless Muslim governments begin to adopt rational economic policies, or are forced to adopt such policies, I suspect that Muslim countries will continue to be economic laggards, whether or not private finance develops along Islamic or conventional lines. Theoretical discussion of Islamic finance, such as that encouraged at this workshop, can play an important role, however, in educating the government and the public about the importance of adopting rational economic policies that support development and social justice as not only a crucial part of Islamic ethics, but also indispensable to promoting national development.

Bibliography of Mohammad H. Fadel's Published Works

Books

2019. Mālik b. Anas. al-Muwaṭṭaʾ: *Recension of Yaḥyā b. Yaḥyā al-Laythī (d. 234/848)*. Edited and translated by Mohammad Fadel and Connell Monette. Cambridge: Harvard Islamic Legal Studies Program.

2017. Shihāb al-Dīn al-Qarāfī. *The Criterion for Distinguishing Legal Opinions from Judicial Rulings and the Administrative Actions of Judges and Rulers*. Edited and translated by Mohammad Fadel. New Haven: Yale University Press.

Peer-Reviewed Articles

2023. "Sovereignty, Territoriality, and Islamic Private International Law." *American Journal of Comparative Law* (forthcoming).

2022. "DNA Evidence and the Islamic Law of Paternity in Light of *Maqāṣid al-Sharīʿa*." *The Muslim World, Special Issue: Family Structure in the Wake of Genetic and Reproductive Technologies in the Muslim World* 112.3 (Summer).

2019. "Muslim Theologies of Solidarity and Disavowal and the Challenge of Religious Pluralism." *Political Theology* 21.4:303–17.

2018. "Political Legitimacy, Democracy and Islamic Law: The Place of Self-Government in Islamic Political Thought." *Journal of Islamic Ethics* 2:59–75.

2018."The Sounds of Silence: The Supreme Constitutional Court of Egypt, Constitutional Crisis, and Constitutional Silence." *International Journal of Constitutional Law* 16.3:936–51.

2016–2017. "Modern Islamic International Law between Accommodation and Resistance: the Case of Israel and BDS." *Yearbook of Islamic and Middle Eastern Law* 19:247–78.

2016. "Concluding Comments and Continuing Conversations." *Studies in Christian Ethics* 29.2:221–23.

2016. "Islamic Law and Constitution-Making: The Authoritarian Temptation and the Arab Spring." *Osgoode Hall Law Journal* 53:471–507.

2016. "Nature, Revelation and the State in Pre-Modern Sunni Theological, Legal and Political Thought." *The Muslim World* 106.2:271–90.

2014. "Had It Been from Other than God They Would Have Found Therein Much Contradiction: Legal Orthodoxy, Legal Heterodoxy, and Ibn Ḥazm's Quest for a Univocal Islamic Law." *Journal of Islamic Law and Culture* 15.

2013–2015. "Islamic Law Reform: Between Reinterpretation and Democracy." *Yearbook of Islamic and Middle Eastern Law* (2013–15)18:44–90. (Noel Coulson Memorial Lecture, School of Oriental and African Studies.)

2013. "Judicial Institutions, the Legitimacy of Islamic State Law, and Democratic Transition in Egypt." *International Journal of Constitutional Law* 11.3:646–65.

2013. "Secularism in Canada and Europe." *Journal of Parliamentary and Political Law* 7.2:179–88.

2013. "Theology, Torture and the United States: Do Abrahamic Religions Have Anything Meaningful to Say?" *The Muslim World* 103.2:223–28.

2012. "Muslim Reformists, Female Citizenship, and the Public Accommodation of Islam in Liberal Democracy." *Politics and Religion*, 5.1:2–35.

2011. "Is Legal History a Viable Strategy for Islamic Legal Reform? The Case of 'Never Shall a Folk Prosper Who Have Appointed a Woman to Rule Them.'" *Islamic Law & Society* 18:131–76.

2008. Commentator on "The Global Importance of 'Illiberal Moderates,' an Exchange: Partners in Peace to Precede a Concert of Democracies." By Amitai Etzioni et al. *Cambridge Review of International Affairs* 21.2:165–67.

2008."The True, the Good and the Reasonable: The Theological and Ethical Roots of Public Reason in Islamic Law." *Canadian Journal of Law and Jurisprudence* 21.1:5–69.

1997. "Two Women, One Man: Knowledge, Power and Gender in Medieval Sunni Legal Thought." International Journal of Middle East Studies." 29.2:185–204.

1996. "The Social Logic of *Taqlīd* and the Rise of the *Mukhtaṣar*." *Islamic Law and Society* 3.2:193–233.

1995. "Ibn al-Ḥajar's Hady al-Sārī: A Medieval Theory of the Structure of al-Bukhari's *Al-Jamiʿ al-Ṣaḥīḥ*, Introduction and Translation." *Journal of Near Eastern Studies* 54.3:161–97.

Chapters in Books

2021. "Pluralism, Authority and Islamophobia: Sharīʿa and its Discontents in North America." Pages 315–39 in *Overcoming Orientalism: Essay in Honor of John L. Esposito*. Edited by Tamara Sonn. New York: Oxford University Press.

2020. "The Challenges of Islamic Law Adjudication in Public Reason." Pages 115–42 in *Public Reason and Courts*. Edited by Silje Langvatn, Mattias Kumm, and Wojciech Sadurski. Studies on International Courts and Tribunals. Cambridge: Cambridge University Press.

2020. "Islamic Modernist Political Thought, Republicanism and Liberal Democracy: Civic Virtue, Negative Freedom and the Hope for Arab Democracy." Pages 47–64 in *Political Islam: Conceptualising Power Between Islamic States and Muslim Social Movements*. Edited by Naʿeem Jeenah. Craighall, South Africa: Afro-Middle East Centre.

2019. "Islam, Inequality, Morality, and Justice." Pages 181–210 in *Economic Inequality and Morality: Diverse Ethical Perspectives*. Edited by William Sullivan and Richard Madsen. Ethikon Series in Comparative Ethics. Washington: Brookings Institution Press.

2016. "Authority in Ibn Abî Zayd al-Qayrawânî's *Kitâb al-nawâdir wa al-ziyâdât 'alâ mâ fî al-mudawwana min ghayrihâ min al-ummahât*: The Case of the 'The Chapter of Judgments' (*Kitâb al-aqḍiya*)." Pages 228–48 in *The Heritage of Arabo-Islamic Learning: Studies Presented to Wadad Kadi*. Edited by Sean Anthony and Aram Shahin. Leiden: Brill.

2016. "Egyptian Revolutionaries' Unrealistic Expectations." Pages 28–40 in *Egypt beyond Tahrir Square*. Edited by Bessma Momani and Eid Mohamed. Bloomington: Indiana University Press.

2015. "The Implications of *Fiqh al-Aqalliyyat* for the Rights of Non-Muslim Minorities in Majority Muslim Countries,"Pages 83–106 in *The Question of Minorities in Islam: Theoretical Perspectives and Case Studies*. Edited by Mohamed El-Tahir El-Mesawi. Kuala Lumpur: The Other Press.

2015. "A Tale of Two Massacres: *Charlie Hebdo* and Utoya Island." Pages 29–42 in *After the Paris At-*

tacks: Responses in Canada, Europe and Around the Globe. Edited by Edward M. Iacobucci and Stephen J. Toope. Toronto: University of Toronto Press.

2014. "'*Istafti qalbaka wa in aftâka al-nâsu wa aftûka*': The Ethical Obligations of the Muqallid between Autonomy and Trust." Pages 105–26 in *Islamic Law in Theory: Studies on Jurisprudence in Honor of Bernard Weiss*. Edited by A. Kevin Reinhart and Robert Gleave. Leiden: Brill.

2014. "State and Shariʿa." Pages 93–107 in *The Ashgate Research Companion to Islamic Law*. Edited by Peri Bearman and Rudolph Peters. Surrey: Ashgate.

2012. "'No Salvation outside Islam': Muslim Modernists, Democratic Politics, and Islamic Theological Exclusivism." Pages 35–61 in *Between Heaven and Hell: Islam and the Fate of Others*. Edited by Mohammad Hassan Khalil. Oxford: Oxford University Press.

2012. "The Paternity of the Illegitimate Child and the 2004 Moroccan Family Law Code (*al-Mudawwana al-Jadīda*)." [Published in Morocco in Arabic along with other papers presented at the conference "The Mālikī Madhhab in Its Modern Contexts." Fez, Morocco, February 2012.]

2012. "Political Liberalism, Islamic Law and Family Law Pluralism." Pages 164–98 in *Marriage and Divorce in a Multi-Cultural Context: Multi-Tiered Marriage and the Boundaries of Civil Law and Religion*. Edited by Joel Nichols. New York: Cambridge University Press.

2004. "Too Far From Tradition." Pages 81–86 in *Islam and the Challenge of Democracy*. Edited by Joshua Cohen and Deborah Chasman. Princeton: Princeton University Press.

2002. "*Istihsan* Is Nine-Tenths of the Law: The Puzzling Relationship of *Usul* to *Furu'* in the *Maliki Madhhab*." Pages 161–76 in *Studies in Islamic Law and Society*. Edited by Bernard Weiss. Leiden: Brill.

1997. "Rules, Judicial Discretion and the Rule of Law in Nasrid Granada." Pages 49–86 in *Islamic Law: Theory and Practice*. Edited by Robert Gleave. London: I.B. Tauris.

Law Review Articles

2022. "Muslim Modernism, Islamic Law, and the Universality of Human Rights." *Emory International Law Review* 36.4:713–41.

2017. "Ethics and Finance: An Islamic Perspective in Light of the Purposes of the Islamic Sharīʿa." *Journal of the Center for Islamic Legislation and Ethics*. https://www.cilecenter.org/publications/publications/314-ethics-and-finance-islamic-perspective-light-purposes-islamic-sharia.

2015. "Religious Law, Family Law and Arbitration: Shariʿa and Halakha in America." *Chicago-Kent Law Review* 90:163–81.

2014. "Is There a Future for an Arab Human Rights Mechanism? Not Without Democracy." *Netherlands Quarterly of Human Rights* 32.1:5–7.

2014. "Prospects for Democratization in Egypt and the Arab World in the Wake of the Exclusion of Political Islam from the Political Terrain." *Cairo Institute for Human Rights* 65/66:157–71.

2013. "Overlapping, Not Separate: A Response to ʿAbdallahi an-Naʿim's *Complementary, Not Competing Claims of Law and Religion: an Islamic Perspective*." *Pepperdine Law Review* 39:1231–55.

2012–2013. "Islamic Law and American Law: Between Concordance and Dissonance." *New York Law School Law Review* 57:231–42.

2011. "Modernist Islamic Political Thought and the Egyptian and Tunisian Revolutions of 2011." *Middle East Last and Governance* 3:94–104.

2011. "Public Corruption and the Egyptian Revolution of January 25: Can Emerging International Anti-Corruption Norms Assist Egypt Recover Misappropriated Public Funds?" *Harvard International Law Journal* 52:292–300. http://www.harvardilj.org/2011/04/online_52_fadel/.

2009. "BCE and the Long Shadow of American Corporate Law." *Canadian Business Law Journal* 48:190–212.

2008. "Ribâ, Efficiency and Prudential Regulation: Preliminary Thoughts." *Wisconsin International Law Journal* 25.4:655–702.

2007. "Public Reason as a Strategy for Principled Reconciliation: The Case of Islamic Law and International Human Rights Law." *Chicago Journal of International Law* 8.1:1–20.

2004. "Classical Religious Perspectives of Adoption Law." *Notre Dame Law Review* 79:693–753. With Danil Pollack, Moshe Bleich, and Charles J. Reid Jr.

1998. "Reinterpreting the Guardian's Role in the Islamic Contract of Marriage: The Case of the Maliki School." *Journal of Islamic Law* 3:1–26.

Review Essays

2019. "Ideas, Ideology, and the Roots of the Islamic State." *Critical Review* 30.3–4:1–13.

2016. "The Priority of the Political: Politics Determines the Possibilities of Islam." *Marginalia.* https://themarginaliareview.com/priority-political-politics-determines-possibilities-islam-mohammad-h-fadel/.

2011. "A Tragedy of Politics or an Apolitical Tragedy?" *Journal of American Oriental Society* 131.1:109–.

2009–2010. "Islamic Politics and Secular Politics: Can They Co-Exist?" *Journal of Law and Religion* 25.1:101–118.

2009. "Back to the Future: The Paradoxical Revival of Aspirations for an Islamic State." *Review of Constitutional Studies* 14.1:105–23.

Encyclopedia Entries

2019. "Fiduciary Principles in Classical Islamic Law Systems." Pages 524–43 in *The Oxford Handbook of Fiduciary Law.* Edited by Evan J. Criddle, Paul B. Miller, and Robert H. Sitkoff. Oxford: Oxford University Press.

2019. "Islam, Constitutionalism and Democratic Self-Government." Pages 415–27 in *The Routledge Handbook of Islamic Law.* Edited by Khaled Abou el Fadl, Ahmad Atif Ahmad, and Said Fares Hassan. New York: Routledge.

2019. "al-Qāḍī," *The Oxford Handbook of Islamic Law.* Edited by Anver M. Emon and Rumee Ahmed. Oxford: Oxford University Press.

2009. "International Law, Regional Developments: Islam." In *Max Planck Encyclopedia of Public International Law.* Edited by Frauke Lachenmann.

Forthcoming. "International Law in General in the Medieval Islamic World." In *The Cambridge History of International Law. Volume VIII: International Law in the Islamic World, Part I: International Law in the Medieval Islamic World (622–1453).*

Index

A

adoption, xii, xxxvi–xxxviii, 273–75, 288–90
ʿAbd Allāh b. ʿAlī b. Samārā (d. 647/1249), 111, 113
Abrahamic religions, xiii, 4
abrogation (*naskh*), 9, 102, 111–12, 122, 342n5
Abū al-Faraj b. Ṭarār, 179, 179n101, 180–81, 186
Abū Bakra [Nufayʿ b. al-Ḥārith al-Thaqafī] (d. 51/671), 164–66, 168–69, 171, 173, 173n83, 175, 175n88, 176, 176n92, 177, 180–83, 183n112, 186, 186n129, 187–89, 189nn134–35, 190
Abū Ḥayyān Muḥammad b. Yūsuf al-Andalusī, (d. 745/1344), 186, 186n129
androcentrism, xxxvi, 172, 182, 184–85, 187–88
Abū Thawr [Ibrāhīm b. Khālid al-Baghdādī] (d. 124/742 or 124/757), 150n19, 170
acting on behalf of a third-party (*al-taṣarruf ʿan al-ghayr*), 41, 43
Adam and Eve, 255
adoption, pre-Islamic, 274, 289–90
ʿAḍud al-Dawla (d. 373/983), 179
affiliated jurist (*muntasib*), 93, 94n41, 97n54
age of majority, 221, 223, 276, 276n279, 277, 277n284, 279–80, 351n37
  adult, xxxvii, 229n39, 247, 282, 289–90
  adult daughter, xxxvii, 221, 249
  adult man, 221n6
  adult son, 221
  adult woman, 14, 49, 57n95, 221, 221n6, 223n13, 223n15, 226–28, 228nn34–35, 229, 231, 249
  physical maturity, 225–26
  physical puberty, xxxvii, 222, 222n10, 225n20, 257n95
  social maturity, 225, 225n22, 226nn25–26
agency (*wikāla*), xxxii–xxxiv, 18–19, 19n30, 20–22, 29–30, 30n17, 31, 35–36, 36nn30–31, 38–39, 39nn40–41, 40, 40n42, 40n46, 41, 41nn47–49, 42–45, 47, 47n72, 48, 59–60, 65–65, 147, 222–23, 226, 229–30, 230n40, 329, 329n195, 330n198, 344, 344n9, 345, 349–50, 352n40, 359
  authorized agent, 60
  government agent, 246n43
Ahmed, Leila, 195, 195nn1–2, 202, 216–17
ʿĀʾisha bint Abī Bakr al-Ṣiddīq (d. 57/677 or 75/694), 165–66, 173, 176, 176n92, 177, 183, 203, 203nn20–21
ʿAlī b. Abī Bakr, Nūr al-Dīn (d. 807/1405), 164
ʿAlī b. Abī Ṭālib (d. 41/661), 17, 183, 200, 278
ʿAlī [b. Aḥmad] al-ʿAdawī (d. 1189/1775), 119
al-kharāj bi-l-ḍamān, xxxviii, 52, 174, 284, 357n49
al-wāqifiyya, 168
alienage, 71–73
altruism (*īthār*), xxxix, 341–43, 348–50, 352, 356
al-Āmidī, Sayf al-Dīn (d. 631/1233), 125n11, 127n17, 129n22, 130n24, 131, 131n33, 137, 144n6, 146, 161n17, 170, 170n63, 189n133
analogy (*qiyās*), 10, 16, 37, 43–44, 48, 53, 56, 94, 94n40, 97, 97n54, 98, 98n60, 99n62, 102, 118, 127–28, 132, 134, 143, 145, 145n7, 147, 147n12, 150, 169n60, 181, 211n37, 220n3, 241, 297, 298n24, 309, 314n124, 339, 343n6, 346, 347, 348, 357, 362, 369n71
ʿaqd, 30, 34, 58n100, 70, 342
ʿaqd al-khilāfa (contract of the caliphate), 30, 34
Arab pagans, pre-Islamic, 171
Arabian family, pre-Islamic, 253
argument, weak, 206, 213n40
Ashʿarī, 6–7, 7n10, 8–9, 123–24, 125n12, 126, 128, 178–79, 338
Atatürk, Kamal, 78
attribution, certainty (*qaṭʿī al-thubūt*), 12
authors, pre-Islamic Christian, 184n121
al-ʿAynī, Badr al-Dīn (d. 855/1451), 175–76, 182

B

bailment (*amāna*), 150, 345, 356, 358
al-Bājī Abu al-Walīd Sulaymān b. Khalaf (d. 474/1081), 105, 129n23, 131n33, 144, 145n7, 146, 168n57, 211n36, 286n337, 330n197, 330n200
bank, 293, 314n122, 314n124, 322–23, 353n45, 356, 356n48, 357–60, 369, 371–72
  bankers, 294n4, 357
  banking, 295, 322, 325, 356, 358–59 371, 371n73
  Islamic banks, 325n182, 337–38, 355, 357–59, 369, 371
  The Islamic Development Bank (IDB), 337, 367
bankruptcy, 147–48, 225n23, 296–97, 322, 322n165, 323n173, 328n190, 329, 329n191, 334, 349n29, 368–69
al-Bāqillānī, Abū Bakr (d. 403/1013), 131, 179–80, 186
*bay*ᶜ *al-salam*, 343, 343n6, 345
*bay*ᶜ *al-*ᶜ*ariyya*, 307n75, 332, 345
al-Bayḍāwī (d. 685/1286), 106–7, 107nn87–88, 107n90
Bedouin, 126, 126n13, 286, 328n190, 329, 330n198, 352n40
Best Problem Solver, 232
British law, 237, 237n2, 238, 259n102
Buddhist, 81
al-Bukhārī, Muḥammad b. Ismāᶜīl (d. 255/869), 164, 165, 173–75, 175n88, 176, 176n92, 177, 182, 187–88, 215n46
al-Bunānī[, Muḥammad b. al-Ḥasan] (d. 1194/1780), 119–20,
al-Burzulī, Abū al-Qāsim b. Aḥmad (d. 841/1437), 120–21

C

Catholic, 72, 74–75, 259n105, 294n5
Catholicism, 4n3, 72–73
Caliph (*Khalīfa*), 17–19, 19n30, 20, 29–30, 34–35, 35n28, 36, 36nn30–31, 37–38, 43n58, 44, 44n61, 45, 45nn62–63, 48, 54, 54n89, 57, 60n105, 177, 178–80, 187–88, 215n45, 278, 281
Caliphate, xxxii, xxxiii, 17–19, 21, 30, 32–35, 37–38, 44, 46, 52, 60, 180, 215n45. *See also* ᶜ*aqd al-khilāfa*
Canada, vii, 157, 237, 259, 261, 261n112, 264, 265nn125–26, 267n132, 269, 271
Canadian, 240, 240n8, 261n112, 266n129, 269n146
Canadian Charter of Rights and Freedoms, 269
capitalism, vii, xxxii, 89
caregiver (*kāfil*), 276–77, 279–80, 286, 286n341, 287
carrion, consumption of (*akl al-mayta*), 171, 319n151, 347, 347n20
Carmathian, 195
cash waqf (*waqf al-nuqūd*), 354, 356n48
charity (*ṣadaqa*), 296n14, 304n59, 333, 342, 348–50
  capacity to engage in (*ahliyyat al-tabarru*ᶜ), 303, 349
child, xxvi–xxviii, xxviiin69, xxix–xxx, xxxn74, xxxviii, 41–42, 42n54, 43, 138, 174, 224–25, 227, 233, 234n47, 241, 243nn25–26, 247, 247nn48–49, 248–49, 253n80, 257, 267, 267n136, 273–75, 275n271, 275nn273–75, 276, 276n279, 277, 277nn283–84, 278, 278n291, 279–83, 283n320, 283n324, 283n326, 284, 285, 285n333, 286, 286n338, 287, 287n345, 287nn347–48, 288, 288nn350–51, 289, 289n356, 290, 341, 349, 352
  child's interests, xxxviii, 41–42, 42n54, 233, 260, 267, 274–76, 285n331, 286–88, 288n351, 290, 349
  illegitimate, 275n273, 276, 288–89
Christianity, xii, 5, 72, 258–59, 286, 317n143
Church of England, 73
citizen, xii, xvii, 16, 60, 70–71, 71n8, 72–74, 76–83, 238–42, 256, 260, 260n107, 263, 266, 268, 270, 350, 360, 364–66
citizenship, xxxiv, 70–78, 82–83
collateral (that may be secreted away [*mā yughāb* ᶜ*alayhi*] *and* that which cannot [*mā lā yughāb* ᶜ*alayhi*]), 146–49, 149n15, 149n17, 150–51, 151n21, 152–54, 154n31, 155, 155nn32–33
colonialism, 157, 161n20, 259n102

commenda (*qirāḍ* or *muḍāraba*), 307n77, 326, 338, 342, 343, 343n6, 344, 344n8, 345, 345n12, 355, 357, 357n50, 358, 358n51, 359, 369n71, 371
condition of contractual validity (*sharṭ al-ṣiḥḥa*), 147, 148
condition of perfection (*sharṭ al-tamām*), 147, 147n13, 148
conscription, Christians, 77
consensus (*ijmāʿ*), 10–11, 11n17, 16, 41n51, 42n55, 64, 91–92, 92n27, 97, 103, 105, 128, 131, 131n33, 134, 143, 145, 145n7, 147, 154, 162n22, 180, 211, 243n27, 363, 363n59
consent, xxxvii, 14, 56, 59–60, 64, 65n115, 200, 223, 223n15, 226–27, 227nn31–32, 228nn33–34, 229n38, 235, 245n37, 249, 265n126, 327, 347, 349
contract for hire for an indefinite wage (*al-ijāra al-majhūla*), 343n6, 344, 345n12
convert, 77, 333, 333n212
Copt, 78
credible individuals (*ʿudūl*), 212, 225n20
credit, xxix, 40, 152n22, 154n31, 250, 294n5, 295, 295n9, 297–98, 302n52, 312n112, 313, 313n115, 316, 321–22, 322nn164-65, 324–25, 325n180, 331n201, 334, 342, 342n5, 356, 357n49, 359, 368–72
creditor, xxxv, 147–48, 151–52, 152n22, 155, 295n9, 296–97, 297n19, 303n58, 314, 314n122, 316, 318, 318n147, 319n152, 320n158, 321, 323n173, 323n173, 324, 328, 328n190, 329n191, 334, 345, 369

D

dār al-ḥarb (enemy territory), 68, 79, 82
dār al-islām (Muslim territory), 68, 70, 79, 82
ḍarūra (necessity), xxix, xxx, 8, 11, 17, 25, 27, 30, 36, 37–38, 51n80, 76, 129, 135, 188, 306n69, 312, 317, 319n151, 344–45, 345n12, 346–47, 347n19, 348, 351, 351n39, 352, 355, 363n59
ḍaʿīf, "weak", 117, 170, 206, 213n40, 309
debt (*dayn*), xxxi, 146–48, 149n17, 150–52, 152n22, 153–54, 154n31, 155, 155n33, 191, 198, 234, 249n57, 250, 255n89, 261–62, 271, 285, 287n349, 295, 295n9, 296, 296n11, 296n14, 297, 297n19, 298, 303, 303n57, 313n115, 314, 314n122, 315, 315n128, 317, 317n137, 320n158, 322, 326, 328, 328nn189–90, 342, 344, 351, 356, 368–69, 369n71, 370
debtor, xxxv, 40, 146–48, 151, 154n31, 155, 155n33, 295, 295n9, 296, 296n14, 297, 314, 316–18, 318n147, 320n158, 321, 322n165, 323n173, 324, 324n177, 328, 328nn189–90, 329, 329n191, 334, 341, 345, 368–69
debts, pre-Islamic, 296–97
default, 147, 322, 322n165, 328, 328n190, 334, 345, 359, 368–69
delegation
  niyāba, 38–40
  tafwīḍ, 38, 38n40, 232
delegator (*al-munīb*), 39
democracy, xi–xii, xvii, xx, xxxii–xxxiii, xxxv, 25, 62, 65n115, 66, 72, 80–83, 159, 180n102, 237–38, 259, 269
designated successor/guardian (*waṣī*). *See under* successor; guardian
designation (*waṣiyya*), 213n41, 223, 223n13, 224nn18–19, 225n21, 274,
dhimma, 36n30, 67, 70–71, 83
  mustaghraq al-dhimma, ix
dhimmī, 47n71, 71–72, 77, 257
diploma (*ijāza*), 203
disobedience (*nushūz*), 22, 32, 76, 246, 250, 245n81, 262–63
dispositive (*qaṭʿī*), 11, 167
  certain with respect to its meaning (*qaṭʿī al-dalāla*), 12
  conclusive rules (*aḥkām qaṭʿiyya*), 11
  having certainty with respect to attribution (*qaṭʿī al-thubūt*), 12
divorce, xxi, xxvii, xxx, xxxin77, 13, 58, 64, 77, 83, 92n28, 208–9, 209n31, 235, 247–48, 248n52, 249–50, 250n65, 252–53, 253n78, 253n80, 254n81, 261, 261n112, 262–64, 264n123, 265, 265n127, 266–67, 267n132, 267n134, 267n136, 270, 270n149, 271
  divorce (*ṭalāq*), xxviin65, 213n41
  divorce (*khulʿ*), 64, 64nn113–14, 65, 250,
  dissolution of marriage, 65, 69, 247, 257, 262, 264, 265n127

final divorce (*bāʾin*), xxix, xxxn73
separation, xxix, xxx, 250, 264n123,
Dow Jones Islamic Index, 337–38, 369
dowry (*mahr*, *ṣadāq*), 234, 252, 253n78, 255n86, 262, 270, 270n149, 271

E

Ebrahim Moosa, xv, 157–58, 159, 161, 188, 191
education, 178, 180n193, 204, 234, 243n25, 279–80, 286, 287n347, 363, 365, 365n64, 366–67
Egypt, xv–xvii, 25, 56, 64, 64n114, 77–78, 109, 181, 221, 253, 276n282, 314n124, 317n143, 320n158, 321n159, 361, 367
emancipation (*tarshīd*), 221, 221n6, 225, 225nn21–22, 235, 275n275
emigrate, 70, 274, 348,
immigrate, 244n31, 333, 333n213
migrate, 82, 333, 333n212–13
Enlightenment, 4
equity, 320, 325n182, 326, 335, 338, 342, 358n52, 369–71
ethics, Islamic, 5, 124, 136, 140, 243, 243n26, 244, 244n33, 246, 248, 343, 352–53, 358, 360, 365–66, 372
European Court of Human Rights, 81
evidence, dispositive, 167
exegesis (*tafsīr*), 160n15, 185n125, 186, 190, 195–97, 197n8, 198–99, 202, 217–18, 274, 295
extrapolation (*takhrīj*), 97, 97n54, 98

F

al-Fārābī (d. 339/950), 5
al-Farrāʾ, Abū Yaʿlā (d. 458/1066), 18–19, 21, 30
father, xxvii, xxix, 14, 41–42, 42n54, 43, 55, 57n95, 175–76, 219, 221, 221n6, 222, 222nn9–12, 223, 223nn13–14, 223n17, 224, 224nn18–19, 225, 225n21, 226n24, 227, 227n31, 228n33, 233–36, 245n37, 247, 247n48, 249, 253n80, 273–75, 275n273, 275n275, 279–80, 282, 283n320, 285, 285n331, 287–88, 288n350, 289–90
fatwā, 53, 55, 63, 75, 96, 96n49, 96n52, 97–98, 98n60, 103, 105–6, 107n87, 108, 110–11, 113, 114n 124, 130, 133, 135, 137, 137n54, 138–39, 199–200, 202, 202n17, 203, 210, 212, 345, 365n61
Fazlur Rahman, 160, 160nn13–14
feminists, 241
Jewish, 178n94
Muslim, xxxvi, 158, 161n20, 163, 189n135, 191n140, 195, 197, 216
feminism. *See* woman, women
finance, xxxviii–xxxix, 208–9, 209n31, 211, 213, 221n6, 225, 250, 252, 262, 275n275, 276, 279, 279nn298–99, 280–81, 281n313, 284–85, 293–94, 294n5, 308n88, 312, 321, 321n159, 321n163, 322, 323n169, 325, 325nn181–82, 326, 326n183, 335, 337–38, 340–43, 350, 352, 355–58, 358n51, 359–60, 363–64, 366–72
financial system, 322, 340–41, 353, 356
Islamic finance, xxxviii–xxxix, 293–94, 294n5, 304n63, 312–13, 313n116, 334–35, 337–38, 340, 343, 355, 368, 370–72
Islamic financial system, 313n116, 352, 371
Finnis, John, 81
fiqh, xiv, xvi–xvii, xxiii–xxvi, xxviii–xxix, xxxi, xxxv, 3–6, 6nn6–7, 26, 28–29, 144n6, 146, 162n22, 197, 217–18, 220, 337–339, 345, 354–55, 360–63, 368. *See also* uṣūl al-fiqh
fiqhiyyāt, 128
fiqh al-Aqalliyyāt, xxxiv, 67, 70, 73, 76, 79–83
forged (*mawḍūʿ*), 12, 179, 188
foundling (*laqīṭ*), 273, 275–77, 277nn283–84, 277n287, 278, 278n293m 278n295, 279, 279nn296–99, 280, 280nn301–2, 281, 281n310, 281nn313–14, 282, 282n315, 282nn318–19, 283, 283n321, 283nn323–24, 283n326, 284–85, 285n331, 285nn334–35, 286, 286nn336–37, 286n341, 287, 287nn345–49, 288, 288n351
Christian, 285–86
Fukuyama, Francis, 159
fundamentalism, 157–58, 160–61, 188
furūʿ, 5, 125, 143, 145–46, 150, 222

G

gain (*tanmiya*), 316, 332, 343–44, 345n12, 347, 353, 353n44, 355–56, 358–59, 372
private, 332, 343

Gaudreault-DesBiens, 237n1, 268–69
al-Ghazālī, Abū Ḥāmid (d. 505/1111), xxiii, xxiiin41, xxxi–xxxii, 4n1, 5, 6nn6–7, 7, 7nn10–11, 8, 13–14, 92, 92n28, 93, 104, 123n1, 125, 126n15, 127–28, 129nn22–23, 130n25, 131, 131n31, 132, 133n41, 134–35, 135n47, 137, 137n54, 138–39, 144n6, 169–70, 183, 187, 254nn81–82, 256n90, 338
gender, vii–viii, xxxii, xxxvii–xxxviii, 157, 159–60, 162n22, 182, 184–85, 185n126, 187–88, 195, 195n2, 196, 196n6, 197, 200–201, 201n15, 202, 205, 207–10, 213–19, 221–22, 231, 243n25, 251n69, 256, 256n90, 258, 261–62
  gender equality, xxxii, 157–58, 160, 160n13, 184, 189, 195–97, 219, 239n7, 240, 242, 261n111
  gendered division of labor, 199, 241–42, 241n21, 242, 243
gift (*hiba*), 249, 249n57, 253n79, 255, 271, 279n299, 280, 341–42, 344, 344nn10–11, 348–49, 349nn29–30
grace, divine (*faḍl*), 8, 18, 186
Great Britain, 237, 237n2
guardian (*walī*), xxxvii, 38, 41–42, 42n54, 43–44, 46n69, 48–49, 54, 56, 57n95, 121, 181, 185n126, 219–20, 220n3, 221–22, 222nn7–8, 223, 223nn13–14, 223n17, 224, 224nn18–19, 225, 225n21, 226, 226nn25–27, 227, 227nn31–32, 228, 228nn33–34, 228n36, 229, 229nn38–39, 230–32, 232n44, 233–34, 282n318, 303n55, 308n87, 344n8, 349, 349n27, 350
  designated successor/guardian (*waṣī*), 41, 41n51, 49n74, 223, 223nn13–14, 224, 224nn18–19, 225, 225n21, 226n24
guardianship (*walā'*), xxxvii, 38–39, 48, 223, 225, 232, 282

H

ḥadd, 36n30, 68–69, 191, 247n47
  ḥadd of zinā, 68, 247n47
hadith, xvii, xxiiin40, 95, 96n50, 115, 123, 139, 149, 149n18, 150, 150n19, 152n24, 158, 158n7, 162, 162nn22–23, 163–65, 165n41, 166, 168–69, 171–72, 172n73, 173, 173n83, 174–75, 175n88, 176, 176n92, 177–78, 178n95, 179–83, 183n112, 184, 186, 186n129, 187–91, 197, 203–4, 204n22, 204n23, 205–6, 209–10, 212n39, 215n45–46, 216n48, 310n100, 337, 352n40, 354
ḥāja, 347, 359
  fundamental needs (*ḥāja ḍarūriyya*), 310
al-Ḥajawī, Muhammad b. al-Hasan al-Thaʿālibī (d. 1376/1956), 88, 88n8, 89n11, 93, 96n52
Hallaq, Wael, viii, xv, xvin8, xvii, xviiin11, xxivn48, xxxiii, 11n17, 26, 87n2, 88, 96nn49–50, 115n128, 117n136, 122n155, 144n2, 167n52, 169n60
Ḥanafī, xiv, xxi, xxin28, xxiv–xxvii, xxviin65, xxviii–xxxi, xxxviii, 19, 39, 40n42, 40n46, 43, 43n59, 46, 50n78, 52, 54, 56, 56n93, 69–70, 91n19, 93, 134, 148–51, 155n32, 167n53, 171, 178, 180–82, 82n110, 187, 206, 208n28, 209, 210n32, 211, 211nn36–37, 217, 243n26, 245n37, 246n44, 248–49, 249n53, 250–52, 254, 254n83, 255, 257, 257n92, 258, 264, 275n273, 276n282, 277–78, 278n293, 280, 282, 284, 287–88, 288n351, 298n26, 299–301, 301n47, 302–3, 303n55, 309, 309n93, 310–12, 312n108, 313, 314n124, 316, 318n146, 323–24, 324n177, 349n27, 349n29, 351n37, 352, 366
Ḥanbalī, xxii, 18–20, 50, 179, 212, 248, 276n282, 277, 277n284, 281, 287, 298n26
ḥaqīqa, 166
hardship (*ḥaraj*), 286, 308, 308n87, 354, 371
  hardship (*mashaqqa*), 133
  removal of hardship (*rafʿ al-ḥaraj*), 230n41, 308, 354–55, 360
ḥashwiyya, 127
al-Ḥaṭṭāb, Muḥammad b. Muḥammad (d. 954/1547), 42n54, 51n79, 57n95, 57n97, 154, 154n31, 204, 204n24, 211n36, 224n19, 225n21, 227n32, 232n44, 276n276, 280n300
health care, 365, 365n64, 366
Hindu, 81
historicist, 158–60, 60n13, 162,
  historicism, xxxiv, 157–63, 188, 190–91
  progressive historicism, 159–60, 160n13, 161–63 , 191
ḥudūd, applicability to Christians and Jews, 68

ḥukm (verdict), xxvn54, 6–7, 14, 17n27, 58, 58n100, 100n67, 116, 119, 177, 199–200, 202, 202n17, 207, 214n43, 244
particular rule (*ḥukm khāṣṣ*), 53
humiliation (*dhull*), 73, 352, 360

I

Ibn ʿAbbās, [ʿAbd Allāh] 318, 319n150
Ibn ʿAbd al-Salām or Ibn ʿAbdassalām, al-ʿIzz (ʿAbd al-ʿAzīz) (d. 660/1262), 7, 18, 32, 50n78, 106, 131, 131n36, 133, 135, 140, 298n25, 306n69, 338
Ibn ʿĀbidīn, [Muḥammad Amīn b. ʿUmar] (d. 1252/1836), 181n109, 257n95, 318n147, 352
Ibn Abī Shayba, [Abū Bakr] (d. 849/234), 164, 164n34, 172–73, 176–77, 183, 187–88
Ibn Abī Zayd al-Qayrawānī, [Abū Muḥammad ʿAbd Allāh b. ʿAbd al-Raḥmān] (d. 386/996), 111
Ibn al-ʿArabī, Abū Bakr (d. 1148/543), 47, 47n72, 97n54, 98, 178–80, 180n102, 186, 295n9, 296n11, 302n52, 327n187, 328n189
Ibn al-Bashīr, ʿAbd al-Ṣamad (d. 526/1131), 113
Ibn al-Furāt, Asad (d. 213/828), 109, 113, 113n116,
Ibn al-Ḥājib, [Abū ʿAmr ʿUthmān b. ʿUmar] (d. 646/1248), 107, 107n90, 108, 108n93, 110, 112, 112n115, 113–15, 115n126, 115n129, 116, 122, 144, 144n6, 146
Ibn Ḥanbal, Aḥmad (d. 240/855), 150n19, 164, 165n41, 174, 276n282
Ibn Kathīr, [Ismāʿīl b. ʿUmar] (d. 1373/774), 186
Ibn al-Ṣalāḥ, [Abū ʿAmr ʿUthmān b. ʿAbd al-Raḥmān] (d. 643/1245), 92n28, 93–94, 94nn40–41, 95, 104, 104n78, 105, 105n82, 111, 112n113, 202, 202n17
Ibn al-Shāṭṭ, [Qāsim b. ʿAbd Allāh] (d. 723/1323), 206, 206n26, 208n30
Ibn Farḥūn, [Ibrāhīm b. ʿAlī] (d. 799/1397) xvi–xvii, xxiii, 46n67, 97n54, 98n59, 103, 103n75, 104, 104n76, 105n82, 107, 107n90, 108, 108nn93–94, 109n97, 110–12, 112n115, 113–15, 115n126, 306, 306n74,
Ibn Ḥabīb, [ʿAbd al-Malik] (d. 238/852), 109, 109n98
Ibn Ḥajar al-ʿAsqalānī, [Aḥmad b. ʿAlī] (d. 1449/853), 175, 204n24, 215n45, 333n213
Ibn al-Humām, Kamāl al-Dīn Muḥammad (d. 1457/861), 181–82, 211n37, 285n333, 301n47, 303n55, 310n100, 311, 312n108
Ibn Masʿūd, 352
Ibn al-Mawwāz, Muḥammad (d. 269/882), 109, 111
Ibn Nujaym, Zayn al-Dīn (d. 969/1562), 181
Ibn Qayyim al-Jawziyya, [Muḥammad b. Abī Bakr] (d. 751/1350), 203n19, 212–13, 213nn40–41, 214, 214n43, 215, 215n44, 217, 232, 232, 253n79, 319nn149–51
Ibn Qudāma, [Muwaffaq al-Dīn ʿAbd Allāh b. Aḥmad] (d. 541/1147), 20, 20n33, 50–51, 51n79, 57nn96–97, 179n99, 211n36, 330nn199–200
Ibn Rushd the Grandfather, [Abū'l Walīd Muḥammad b. Aḥmad] (d. 520/1126), 255n86, 302n52, 334n8, 346
Ibn Rushd the Grandson, [Abū'l Walīd Muḥammad b. Aḥmad] (d. 594/1198), 145–46, 222n7, 227, 297, 297n20, 340
Ibn Shās, [ʿAbd Allāh b. Najm] 103–4, (d. 616/1219), 104n80
Ibn Sīnā (d. 428/1037), 5
ijāra-mutanāqiṣa, 370
ijtihād, xvin8, xvii, xix, xxv, xxvn53, 13n19, 15, 49n74, 57n97, 62, 87, 87n2, 88, 88n8, 89–90, 92, 95–97, 101, 103, 112, 112n113, 115, 117, 119, 122, 124, 126–27, 127n18, 128, 129n22, 131n34, 132–33, 136, 137n54, 340
mujtahid, xxvn54, xxxiv–xxxv, 11–12, 12n19, 15, 29, 63, 87, 87n2, 90, 92, 92n26, 92n28, 93, 93n30, 96n52, 102–3, 111–12, 119–21, 121n152, 122, 124–27, 127nn17–18, 128–29, 129n22, 130–33, 133n41, 134–35, 135n47, 136, 136n52, 137–40, 145, 200
Imam, xxv, xxvn54, 17–18, 18n29, 32, 34, 36–37, 43, 43n58, 46n70, 47, 47n72, 48, 49n74, 51, 51n79, 53–54, 54n89, 57n98, 61, 68–69, 91n21, 94, 98, 100, 100n68, 103, 112n113, 118–22, 128, 134, 177–78, 180, 221n5, 228n33, 232, 233n46, 244n31, 281, 281n311, 338, 346, 354, 363, 363n60, 366. *See also* al-taṣarruf bi'l-imāma

ʿaqd al-imāma, 34
independent jurist (*mustaqill*), 93, 93n30
indicant, weak, 170
infallibilism, 131, 131nn31–34, 135
infrastructure, 25, 363, 365
inheritance (*irth*), xxix, 208, 223, 247n48, 248, 253n80, 257n95, 274, 275n275, 276, 282n318, 284, 290
iftiyāt (vigilantism), 36n30, 46, 46n67
inḥiṭāṭ, 88
interpretations, feminist, 159
interpreter of the law. *See ijtihād, mujtahid*
investor (*rabb al-māl*), 41n48, 294n5, 326, 340, 344, 376n48, 357, 357n50, 358–60, 369n71, 370–71
Islam, orthodox, 159, 237–38, 238n5, 239–40, 245, 245n42, 246, 246n45, 258–60, 262–65, 269–71
Islamic Development Bank (IDB). *See* bank
Islamic family law. *See* law, family
Islamic state. *See* state, Islamic
Ismāʿīl b. Muḥammad al-Jarrāḥ (d. 1748/1161), 164
istiḥsān (juristic preference), xxxv, 143, 145, 151, 156, 346–47, 347n19, 359
istiṣḥāb al-ḥāl (presumption of continuity), 145, 145n7

J

Jāmiʿ al-ummahāt, 107, 108n93, 109–10, 112, 114, 114n124, 115, 117n135, 122, 146
Jew, 68, 81, 178n94, 237, 258, 261n112, 264, 264n121, 267, 267n134, 267n137, 271n151, 285, 285n333, 286
Judaism, xii, 258, 286, 317n143
  orthodox Jewish law, 240, 266
jizya (a tax), 67
judge (*qāḍī*), xiv, xvi, xxv, xxvn54, xxvi–xxx, 13–14, 14n21, 15–16, 16n26, 17, 19, 19n30, 21, 32, 35, 35n28, 37, 44, 44n61, 45, 45nn63–63, 46n69, 49–50, 50n78, 53, 53n86, 54, 54n88, 55, 55n91, 56, 57n95, 58, 58n100, 59, 59n104, 60, 60n105, 77, 91, 93, 93n29, 94, 97–99, 99n64, 100, 100n66, 100n68, 102–3, 103n75, 104n80, 105–6, 109–14, 117, 117n139, 118–21, 121n152, 122, 128, 131, 131n36, 134, 151n21, 166, 175, 177, 177n93, 178, 178n94, 179–82, 186–88, 199–202, 205, 209, 209n31, 210–11, 211nn36–37, 212–14, 214n43, 215, 217, 221n5, 223, 223n17, 224, 224n18, 226n24, 227–228, 228n34, 232, 232n44, 244, 244n35, 245, 249, 249n57, 250, 250n150, 279, 279nn296–97, 280, 280n301, 283, 287, 353, 367
jurisdictions (*wilāyāt*/s. *wilāya*), xxi, xxxi–xxxii, 19n30, 21, 29–31, 35, 36n30, 38, 40n46, 42, 42n55, 43, 44n61, 45n62, 45n64, 46, 46n67, 46n70, 47–49, 49n74, 52, 54–55, 55n91, 56–57, 57n95, 58, 58n100, 59–61, 80, 83, 96, 98, 119, 179, 181, 213n40, 225, 227, 231–32, 240, 246n45, 257, 259–60, 262–65, 265n126, 266, 270, 270n150, 271
al-Juwaynī, [Abū al-Maʿālī ʿAbd al-Malik b. ʿAbd Allāh] (d. 478/1085), 104, 133n41, 137–38

K

kafāʾa (sufficiency), 228, 228n36, 229, 229n38, 230, 249
kalām (rationalist theology), 3, 123–25. *See also* theology
Kaldor-Hicks, 295, 353n44
al-Kāsānī, Abū Bakr (d. 587/1191), 19, 19n30, 39, 39n40, 40n42, 40n46, 41, 41n48, 41n51, 43, 43n59, 44–47, 47n71, 52nn81–83, 57n97, 59–60, 280nn301–2, 281n314, 282n315, 284n328, 287, 287n347, 303n55, 303n57, 313n118
Khaled Abou el Fadl, xii, xviii, xixn21, xx, 63n111, 163, 173n83, 183n112, 188, 189n134
Khalīl, 89n11, 104n80, 106n86, 108n93, 114, 114n124, 115, 115n126, 115n129, 116, 116n130, 117nn135, 118–21, 121n152, 121n154, 122, 146
Kharāj, 17, 149, 180, 343, 363, 363n61, 364
  al-kharāj bi'l-ḍamān, xxxviii, 52, 154, 174, 284, 357n49
al-Kharshī, [Muḥammad b. ʿAbd Allāh] (d. 1101/1690) 61n106, 119–20, 275n273, 276n279, 277n283, 281n313
Khayr al-Dīn al-Tūnisī (1307/1890), 27–28
Khawārij, 17, 17n27, 18, 189

L

labor, reproductive, 242
law
Canadian, 237, 265n126, 266n129, 268, 269n147
commercial, vii–viii, xxiv, xxviin65, xxviii, xxxi, xxxv, xxxvii–xxxviii, 40, 198, 210, 255, 293, 305, 314, 314n122, 314n124, 315, 315n125, 316, 320, 322, 324–25, 325n182, 326n183, 335, 341–44, 344n8, 347, 349, 349n27, 350, 352, 357, 357n49, 359
common, xix, 64n114, 91, 122, 259, 259n100, 270n149, 327
family, xxviin65, xxxvii–xxxviii, 58, 64, 76, 237–39, 239n7, 240, 240n8, 242, 245–46, 248, 249n53, 251, 253, 255–59, 260n105, 261, 261n112, 263–64, 264nn123–24, 265, 265n126, 266–71
Islamic family law, xxxvii–xxxviii, 191, 237–40, 246, 246, 246nn45–46, 248, 251, 253, 257, 262–66, 271, 284, 290,
liberal family law, xxxviii, 238–40, 251, 258–59, 265–66, 268–69, 271
rule of, xxxii, xxxv, 15, 21, 27, 28, 38, 50, 52, 59n103, 90, 92, 116, 200, 244, 245–46, 258, 375
partnership law *(sharika)*, 326, 342, 344n8, 344n10, 345n13
school of (*madhhab*), xvn6, xvii, xxiin35, xxvn54, xxviiin70, xxixn71–72, xxxn73, xxxin77, xxxiv, xl, 21n36, 22n38, 47n72, 56n93, 58, 89n10, 90, 100, 106–8, 112n113, 113, 121, 143, 144n6, 146n10, 171n70, 178n96, 182n110, 200n13, 211n37, 245n36, 276n282, 281n311
substantive (*furūʿ*), xvi–xix, xxi, xxxiv–xxxv, xxxvii, xxxix, 5, 9, 15, 43n58, 45–46, 58, 73, 76, 96n49, 110n101, 110n104, 115n128, 117n136, 122, 125–26, 143, 145–46, 150, 162n22, 177–78, 182, 186, 191, 222, 248, 282, 308, 311n107
legal opinion (*al-fatwā*). *See fatwā*
legitimacy, vii, xxiii, xxivn50, xxvn53, xxxiv, 16–17, 21–22, 27–28, 31–32, 35, 37, 39, 56, 59–60, 62–66, 68, 70, 74–75, 79, 81, 83, 93, 93n29, 94, 99, 110, 115–16, 139, 158n5, 158n8, 162n22, 169n60, 181, 187, 200n12, 202, 204–5, 211n37, 212, 214n43, 231, 239, 247–48, 253, 258, 265, 268, 274–75, 282, 282n318, 283n321, 290, 295–96, 316, 317n144, 319, 319n152, 345, 347, 359, 363–66. *See also* illegitimate child
Islamic conception of, xxxiv, xxxviii, 17, 26–27, 30, 33, 37, 60–61, 63, 68–69, 72, 89–90, 92–93, 97, 99n64, 104, 127–28, 146, 160, 199, 247, 247n49, 258, 298, 299n33, 304, 320, 323, 337, 344–45, 364, 366
liability, strict, 247
liberalism, xii, xvii, xx, xxxviii, 237, 239–40, 240n8, 241–43, 251, 256, 258–59, 269n145, 270–71
liberal family law. *See* law, family
loan (*qarḍ*), xxxviii, 255, 281n312, 301n47, 303, 303nn53–58, 304n59, 313, 313n118, 314, 314n119, 314n124, 315–16, 318, 319n146, 320, 320n157, 321–22, 322n165, 325, 325n179, 331n201, 342, 344n8, 348, 348n22, 349, 349n29, 350, 356, 356n48, 359, 363, 368–69
Louisiana, 260
loyalty (*walāʾ*), 35, 36n31, 73–75, 79–80, 183, 254n82

M

Madina, 67, 82, 149, 179, 220, 276n282, 330n199, 331n201, 333, 333n212, 334
maintenance (*nafaqa*), xxvii, 54–55, 55n91, 235, 247–48, 248n52, 249, 249n57, 250–51, 251n69, 253n78, 257, 257n95, 261, 276, 280
majāz (metaphor), 167
Makka, 235, 333, 333n212–13
Malaysia, 367–69
Mālik b. Anas, viii, 144, 170, 220, 276n282, 279n299, 281,
Mālikī, viii, xiv–xvii, xxii, xxvi, xxviii–xxxi, xxxv, xxxvii–xxxviii, 4n1, 40n42, 40n46, 42, 42n54, 46, 46n67, 47–48, 54, 57n95, 57n98, 58–59, 61, 70, 89, 89n11, 91n19,

93–96, 100, 103, 103n75, 104–8, 108n95, 109, 109nn98–99, 110–12, 112n115, 113–14, 114n124, 115–16, 117n135, 118, 118n140, 120–22, 131n33, 134, 143–44, 144n6, 145–46, 148, 149n17, 150, 153–54, 154n31, 155–56, 178–79, 184, 201n15, 204, 210, 210n32, 211n36, 219–20, 220n4, 221, 221n6, 222–23, 223n17, 224–27, 227nn31–32, 228n34, 229, 232, 245n37, 246n44, 248–49, 249n53, 250–52, 254, 254n83, 255, 255n89, 257, 275n273, 276, 276n282, 278–79, 281–82, 286n337, 287, 298n26, 299–301, 301n42, 301n44, 301n47, 302, 302n52, 303, 303n56, 307n81, 309–10, 314, 314n124, 316, 324–25, 340, 340n6, 345–47, 347n20, 348–49, 349n27, 349n29, 350–51, 351n37, 354, 359–60, 363, 369n71

Mamlūk, 56, 58, 253

maqāṣid (ends), 9, 9n16, 83, 337–40, 340n3, 343
  universal ends (*al-Maqāṣid al-kulliyya*), 8, 167n53, 192n138, 338

maqāṣidī (purposive approach), xxxvi, 337–40, 342, 350–52, 355, 362, 368

marriage, Christian, 260

marital property. *See* property

market, prudential regulation of, xxxvii–xxxviii, 22, 293, 295, 323, 329–30, 334

marriage, xxiv, xxviii, xxxviii, xxxn75, xxxvii–xxxviii, 13–14, 42, 42nn54–55, 49, 54, 56, 56n93, 57n95, 64–65, 69, 92n28, 174, 191n139, 201n15, 208–9, 209n31, 219–21, 221n6, 222, 222n7–12, 223, 223nn13–15, 223n17, 224, 224nn18–19, 225–26, 226nn24–27, 227, 227nn31–32, 228, 228nn33–35, 229, 229nn38–39, 230, 230n41, 231, 233–35, 238, 238n6, 239–41, 241n11, 244n31, 245, 245n37, 246–47, 247nn48–49, 248–49, 251–52, 253nn79–80, 254, 254n82, 255–56, 256n90, 257, 257n95, 259, 259n100, 259nn104–105, 260, 260n106, 260nn108–109, 262, 264, 264n123, 265, 265n126, 269–71, 275, 275n271, 275n273, 276, 289n356, 339, 344, 344n8
  marriage contract, xiii, xxx, xxxvii–xxxviii, 14, 54, 64, 220–22, 227, 229–30, 230nn41–42, 231–35, 239, 244–45, 248, 250–53, 255–56, 258, 261, 264, 264n123, 267n137, 270–71, 344n8
  marriage contracted for a specific period of time (*mutʿa*), 251

Marx, Karl, 159

maṣāliḥ mursala (public welfare), 36, 338, 347

maṣlaḥa, 21, 30n17, 39n41, 49n74, 54, 54n90, 133, 145, 224nn18–19, 340–41, 341n9, 347, 363-66

al-maṣlaḥa al-ʿāmma (public good), 20n32, 21–23, 43, 43n59, 49n74, 54–55, 56n98, 58, 60, 62–64, 74, 343, 363–65

al-Māwardī, [Abū al-Ḥasan ʿAlī b. Muḥammad b. Ḥabīb] (d. 450/1058), 4n1, 15, 18–19, 21, 30, 33–35, 35n28, 36, 36n30–31, 37–38, 46–47, 80, 104, 178, 182, 216n48

meaning, certain (*qaṭʿī al-dalāla*), 12

Mehmet 'Ali Pasha (d. 1245/1849), 78

Mernissi, Fatima, 158n7, 160n13, 162n23, 163n25, 162n27, 188–89, 195, 195n1, 195n4, 196–97, 256n91

messenger (*rasūl*), 19, 45, 102, 103, 165, 187n126, 244n31, 296, 330, 330n199, 363

misogyny, 184, 184n121, 185–88

mispricing (*ghabn*), 302n52, 309–10, 343

mukallaf {moral agent), 129, 134, 140, 351n37

muʿāmala (transaction), xxxiii, 14, 39, 42n54, 171, 198, 209, 214, 230, 230n41, 295, 297, 299, 302n52, 303, 314n122, 316, 318n146, 319n150, 321, 321n162, 323n170, 324, 324n173, 325, 335, 340n3, 346–47, 354, 359, 368–69, 371

Muʿāwiya b. Abī Sufyān (d. 60/680), 17

muḍāraba (*commenda*). *See* commenda

muftī, 53n85–86, 54, 58–59, 88n2, 91, 96, 96n52, 97, 99–100, 105–6, 109–10, 113, 114n124, 117–18, 121, 124, 202, 202n17, 203n19, 210, 217, 307, 315n121

Muḥammad ʿAbduh (d. 1323/1905), 198, 198n10, 199

Muhammad (the Prophet), xvin8, xxiv, 10–12, 17–18, 48, 91, 123, 128, 139, 143, 162n22, 163–64, 167, 169, 170n63, 172–73, 173n83, 175–77, 188, 189n133, 203, 235, 243n27, 244n31, 247n47, 254n81, 274, 278, 278n291, 285n333, 289, 297, 297n22, 298,

Muhammad (*continued*)
299n33, 300, 305n68, 314nn124, 318, 330, 330n199, 333, 333n13, 334
murābaḥa (cost plus contract), 318, 370
musāmaḥa or *mukārama* (presumption of generosity), 255, 344, 344n8, 348
musāqāt (irrigation partnership), 342, 344n8, 345
mushāḥḥa or *mukāyasa* (presumption of mutual covetousness), 255, 302n52, 344, 344n8, 348
al-Muttaqī, ʿAlī b. ʿAbd al-Malik (d. 974/1567), 164
muzāraʿa (sharecropping contract), 326n183, 342, 345
Muslim territory (*dār al-Islām*). *See dār al-Islām*
mutakallim (speculative theologian), 3, 125, 204
Muʿtazilī, 7, 7n9, 8–9, 123–26, 128
al-Muzanī, [Ismāʿīl b. Yaḥyā] (d. 263/877), 170, 283n324

N

Nahḍa, 28–29
narrator (*rāwī*), 174, 188, 200–202, 202n17, 206
al-Nasāʾī, [Abū ʿAbd al-Raḥmān Shuʿayb b. ʿAli] (d. 915/302), 164, 166, 173–75, 175n88, 177, 188
naskh (abrogation). See abrogation
al-Nawawī, [Yaḥyā b. Sharaf] (d. 676/1277) 106, 107nn87–88, 107n90, 117n136, 139, 303n57, 325n179
necessity (*ḍarūra*). *See ḍarūra*
New Testament, 240
New York, xi, xiin3, 64n113, 240, 266–68, 269n146, 270–71
niyāba (delegation). *See* delegation
al-nukūl (refusal to swear), 214

O

oaths (*yamīn*), xxvn54, xxxi, xxxin77, 39, 52, 53n86, 170, 201n15, 214, 214n43, 235, 252, 255n89
obligation, moral, xxxi, 22, 58, 124, 126, 129, 131–33, 140, 185, 190, 239, 366
Ontario, 237, 237n1, 240, 264–65, 268, 269n147, 271
Ontarian law, 264nn123–24, 268
opinion
probable (*ẓann*), 11–13, 15, 92n27, 123, 132–33, 135, 147, 167, 208n27, 215n47, 223n17
valid (*al-ṣaḥīḥ*), 96, 136n52
weak (*ḍaʿīf*), 117, 309
well-established (*mashhūr*), xx, 56, 64, 93n34, 94, 96, 99–100, 107–8, 110–15, 117, 120, 122, 159, 220n4, 238
orientalism, xiii, xx, xxiii, 157
orthodox Jewish law. *See* Jew
Ottoman, 25–26, 56n93, 77
Empire, 25, 77, 316, 318, 354, 356n48
Era, 21, 56, 223n17, 317

P

parent, xxxviii, 42n54, 138, 247–49, 257, 262, 267n136, 273–74, 275n273, 276–77, 284–85, 285n333, 286, 286n336, 287, 287n347, 287n349, 288–89, 349, 352,
parental rights, 284–85, 288–90
paternity (*nasab*), 247n48, 275n273, 275n275, 277, 282, 268n338, 287, 287nn345–49, 287n349, 288, 288n351, 289, 289n356
pledgor (*al-rāhin*), 146, 146n11, 147–50, 152, 152n24, 155,
pledgee (*al-murtahin*), 146, 146n11, 147–48, 150–51, 151n21, 152, 152n24, 154–55
pluralism, legal, xx, xxxviii, 15, 27–40, 248, 253, 256–58, 263, 269–71, 89
poetry, pre-Islamic, xiv
polygamy, 259, 259nn100–103, 260, 260nn106–107, 265, 265n126, 270
pragmatism, 17, 27, 143, 167n53, 216–17
profligate (*safīha*), 225, 225n22, 226, 226n25
proof
detailed (*tafṣīlī*), 125–26
general (*ijmālī*), 125–26, 126n13
property (*māl*), xix, xxvi, xxix, xxxi, xxxv, 8, 19n30, 20, 20n32, 36n30, 40, 42, 42n54, 43, 44n61, 46–49, 49n74, 49n77, 50, 50n78, 51n79, 52, 52nn82–83, 57n97, 69, 71, 134, 137, 146, 148, 149n17, 150, 151n21, 152–53, 153n27, 153n29, 154n31, 155, 155n32, 169, 201, 219–20, 220n3, 221n6, 223n16, 225, 225n20, 225n22, 231, 235, 245, 247, 248,

250n65, 253n80, 254n82, 261, 262, 278, 278n295, 279n299, 280, 280nn301–302, 283n321, 283n326, 284n327, 285–86, 301, 303n55, 303n58, 306, 308n87, 310, 312, 315n125, 316, 319n151, 324n173, 330n199, 338–39, 341–42, 344n11, 345, 347, 347n20, 348–49, 349n27, 350–51, 351n37, 353n44, 357, 359–63, 363n60, 366n65, 368
Islamic property law, 52
marital property, 225, 225nn20–21, 246, 252–53, 262, 264n123
property law, xxxvi, 264n123, 284–85, 288–89
property rights, 22, 148, 151–53, 153n27, 154, 154n31, 220n3, 285, 347

Q

al-Qaraḍāwī, Yūsuf 75, 162n22, 163n24, 180n103, 183, 183n117, 187, 189, 189n136, 190, 362n56, 364n61
al-Qarāfī, Shihāb al-Dīn Aḥmad b. Idrīs (d. 684/1285), 14, 42n55, 48, 49n74, 49n77, 53, 53n84, 54, 54n89, 55–56, 58, 59, 89, 93–97, 97n54, 98–99, 99n62, 99n64, 100, 100n66–69, 104–6, 110, 123, 127, 127nn17–18, 131, 131n36, 133–35, 137, 140, 144, 144nn5–6, 146, 179n99, 184, 200n13, 201, 204–7, 209, 210n39, 216–17, 325, 363n58,
qarīna (extrinsic circumstance), 167
qasāma (collective oaths), 52
qāṭʿī al-dalāla (conclusive in meaning), 10, 12
qāṭʿī al-thubūt (conclusive in attribution), 10, 12
qirāḍ (*commenda*). *See commenda*
Quebec, 284
Qur'ān (*Quran*), xvii, xxv, xxviii, xxxviii, 160, 195, 196, 199, 243, 253, 260
feminist interpretation of, 159
interpretation of, 158n5, 171, 185, 191, 196, 214, 218, 273.
Quraysh, 34

R

rafʿ al-ḥaraj (removal of hardship), 230n41, 308, 354, 355, 360, 371
al-Rāghib al-Iṣfahānī, [Abū'l-Qāsim al-Ḥusayn b. Muḥammad] (d. 502/1108 or 503/1109), 5
Rashīd Riḍā, 27–28, 62–63, 198n10, 315–17, 319, 323
Rawls, John, vii, xix–xx, xxxviii, 239, 241, 241n17, 242, 242n21, 243n25, 260n107, 266, 268–69, 269n145, 270, 366
raʾy (practical reason), 27–28, 55, 125, 143, 216n48, 266, 340
al-Rāzī, Fakhr al-Dīn [Muḥammad b. ʿUmar] (d. 606/1210), 8, 123n1, 126, 126n15, 127n17, 138, 144n6, 146, 185, 185n125, 198, 198n9, 206, 367
rebels (*bughāt*), 17, 21, 35
Reformation, 73, 294n5
Reformer's Dilemma, 159, 163
reports
of individuals (*āḥād*, sing. *aḥad*), 10
solitary (or individual) (*khabar al-wāḥid* or *akhbār al-āḥād*), 11, 127, 209, 214n42
revealed law, pre-Islamic, 8
revelation, interpretation of, 15, 27, 29–30, 30n19, 55, 64, 66, 91, 100–102, 132, 136, 140, 185, 202–3, 243, 245, 275n273, 309, 342
ribā, xxxvii, xxxviii, xxxix, 171, 293–304, 306–29, 331–35, 346, 351n34, 354–55, 359, 368, 376
pre-Islamic, 314–15, 318–19, 320n158, 323n173, 327–28, 239n191
ribā al-faḍl (of excess), 293, 298, 298–302, 307, 310–12, 314, 321, 323–24, 327–29, 331–32, 346, 354–55
ribā al-jāhiliyya, 297
ribā al-nasāʾ or *nasīʾa* (of delay), 293, 300–302, 304, 307, 312, 314–15, 319–22, 323n173, 324–25, 327–29, 331, 346
ribā al-Qur'ān, 295–97
right of first refusal, neighbor's (*shufʿat al-jiwār*), 134, 246n44
rukhṣa (dispensation), 126, 171, 326, 343, 347, 350, 355
rule, explicit (*al-manṣūṣ*), 94, 94n40, 97–100, 110–11, 118, 225, 339
rules, conclusive (*aḥkām qaṭʿiyya*), 11
rules of conduct (*fiqhiyyāt*). *See fiqh*

S

Saḥnūn [b. Saʿīd] (d. 240/854-5), 109, 109n98, 113, 113n116, 155, 346
salaf (loan), 301–2, 302n47, 303n53, 348
sale (*al-bayʿ*), xxi, xxii, 58, 134, 147, 149, 149n15, 153–54, 171, 245, 246n44, 296, 298, 299n33, 302n52, 307n75, 308n88, 310–11, 314n124, 317–18, 319n151, 321–22, 322n165, 323, 233n173, 324, 325, 332, 334, 342–45, 348, 349, 354, 361, 368–70
al-Sanhūrī, ʿAbd al-Razzāq (d. 1391/1971), xxxiiin82, 78, 78n16, 79, 317, 317nn140–41, 318, 318n147, 319, 319nn149–52, 320, 320n158, 323, 325nn181–82
al-Sarakhsī, [Abū Sahl Muḥammad b. Aḥmad] (d. 483/1090), xxvin61, 20n32, 46, 275n273–74, 279n299, 282n319, 283n321, 284n327, 285n333, 287n346
Sayyid Quṭb (d. 1386/1966), 198, 198n9, 206
Schacht, Joseph, xvin7, xviii, xviiin15, xxn27, 25, 26nn5–6, 87nn1–2, 88, 91n22, 116–17, 143n1
Scott, Elizabeth, 260
Scott, Robert, 260
al-Shāfiʿī, Muḥammad b. Idrīs (d. 204/820), 50n78, 95, 95n43, 104, 107n87, 111, 112n113, 134, 143–44, 144n2, 145–46, 170–71, 276n282, 282n319, 338
Shāfiʿī, 4n1, 7, 8, 18, 19, 50n78, 58, 70, 91, 93, 94, 104–7, 111, 112n113, 117, 134, 144–46, 148–51, 152n24, 153–54, 162n22, 171, 178–79, 185, 248, 277–78, 280–81, 283–84, 287, 298n26, 299–303, 310–13, 314n124, 316, 318n147, 325, 338, 349n29, 351n37, 363
shahāda (testimony), 53n86, 128, 179, 181, 189n136, 197–202, 205–18, 225, 283, 287n349
Shaikh, Saʿdiyya, 161, 161n20, 163n27
Shajarat al-Durr (d. 655/1257), 181
Sharia, xvin7, xxxiiin82, 33n23, 237, 240n9
al-Shāṭibī, Abū Isḥāq Ibrāhīm b. Mūsā (d. 790/1388), 130n28, 131–32, 133n41, 134–35, 137–39, 167n53, 260n109, 307–8, 338, 340, 345–46
Shīʿa or Shīʿī, xxv, xxxix, 17–18, 91n21, 189, 237
siyāsa or *siyāsa sharʿiyya*, xxv, 16, 22, 27, 28, 29, 54, 245
slave, xxxi, 41n48, 94n40, 148–49, 176, 181, 199, 209, 212, 229, 234, 274, 275n271, 277, 283–84, 288
Spain, 72–73, 276n282
speech, normative, 200, 210, 212
sphere
  public, 4n3, 31, 37–38, 46–47, 162n22, 187
  private, 31, 38, 47, 221
state
  Christian or Jewish, 258
  Islamic, xxxiiin82, xxxiv, 16n26, 27n8, 33, 36n30, 65, 67–73, 76–83, 177–78, 183n117, 233, 245n42, 257, 283n32, 331n201, 333–34, 362–63, 372
successor
  designated successor/guardian (*waṣī*), 41, 41n51, 49n74, 223, 223nn13–14, 224, 224nn18–19, 225, 225n21, 226n24
  generation of, 149n18, 215n45, 362
  guardian, 223, 224n19, 226n24, 282n315
  head of state (*walī al-ʿahd*), 34, 36n31, 165
  judge, 118n140
  state, 25–26
  trustee, 42n56
Sufism, 195
al-Sulamī, Abū ʿAbd Allāh Muḥammad, 104, 111–12
Sunna, xvin8, 10, 75, 95, 97, 102–3, 135n47, 143–45, 149, 167, 243n27, 341–42, 372
Sunnī, xviii, xxiv–xxv, xxviiin65, xxxii–xxxiv, xxxvii, xl–xli, 3, 4–6, 10–13, 15–23, 29, 31–35, 37–39, 41, 43–46, 48, 52–53, 61, 63–64, 69, 88, 91n21, 123, 126, 128, 140, 159, 162, 164, 167, 172, 177n93, 180, 182n110, 184n120, 189, 195–97, 202, 207, 211n36–37, 216–17, 237, 238n5, 248, 251, 260n109, 276–77, 298, 309, 323, 338–39
supervisor of an endowment (*nāẓir al-waqf*), 41
suspicion (*tuhma*), 106, 151, 201, 210, 212n39, 277, 324
al-Suyūṭī, Jalāl al-Dīn [ʿAbd al-Raḥmān b. Abī Bakr] (d. 1505/910), 49n74, 149n16, 164, 366

T

al-Ṭabarī, Muḥammad b. Jarīr (d. 923/310), 178–79, 179n101, 197n8, 211, 211n36, 217, 295n9, 296n11
tadayyun (religious consciousness), 229
al-Ṭahṭāwī, Rifāʿa Rāfiʿ (1290/1873), 27–28
takhṣīṣ al-ʿāmm (specification of the general term), 159, 161, 162n22, 163, 166, 168–70, 188, 191
takhyīr, 100, 104–6, 109, 130n28, 131–35, 137, 140
Tanẓīmāt, 25–27, 78
taqlīd or *muqallid*, xxxiv–xxxv, 15–16, 21n35, 87–90, 92–93, 99n64, 100–101, 112, 115–16, 122, 124–30, 135, 139–41, 152n23,163n28
al-Ṭarābulusī, [ʿAlāʾ al-Dīn ʿAlī b. Khalīl] (d. 844/1440), 206, 206n27, 207, 209–10, 210n32, 217
tarjīḥ (weighing), 105, 131–33, 137–40
al-Ṭarṭūshī, Abū Bakr (d. 520/1126), 104, 104n80
taṣarruf bi'l-imāma (administrative act), 54, 56, 58, 60–61, 363
tawarruq, 368, 370
tawātur, 10, 137
Taʿlīmiyya, 127–28
taʿzīr (discretionary penalty), 68–69
thayyib (previously married woman), 222, 228n33
theology (*kalām*), xvin8, xviii, xx–xxi, xxiii, xxv, xxxiii, 3, 4, 9, 12, 91n22, 124–27, 140, 172, 261. *See also kalām*
    Christian, 4–5, 22–23, 261
al-Tirmidhī, [Abū ʿĪsā] Muḥammad b. ʿĪsā (d. 279/892), 164–66, 173–74, 175n88, 176, 176n9, 177
trade, xxii, 69, 294, 296n12, 299, 300–302, 306, 310–11, 313, 316–17, 319n151, 321, 323–24, 327–32, 334, 341–43, 350, 353, 359, 367
traditionalist, traditionalism, 3, 158–60, 255–56
trustee, 36n31, 42–43, 245
Turkey, 81n20–21

U

ʿUmar b. al-Khaṭṭāb (d. 23/644), 179
ʿUthmān b. ʿAffān (d. 36/656), 17, 215n45
Umm ʿAṭiyya, [Nusayba bt. al-Ḥārith al-Anṣāriyya] 215, 215n45, 215n47
Umm al-Dardāʾ, [Hujayma bt. Ḥuyay], d. 82/701, 215, 215n45, 215n47
United States, xi, xvii, 53, 61, 159, 219, 233, 238n4, 259, 261, 264, 265n126–27, 268n142, 270n149, 271, 313n115, 353
uṣūl al-fiqh (jurisprudence). *See fiqh*
uṣūlīs, xxvn53, 127n17, 129–31, 133, 135, 137, 139, 146
al-ʿUtbī, [Abū ʿAbd Allāh Muḥammad b. Aḥmad] (d. 255/868), 109, 109n98, 113n116

W

Wadud-Muhsin, Amina, 160n13, 162n21, 191n140, 195, 195n1, 195n3, 196, 196n6, 256n91
al-Wansharīsī, [Abū'l-ʿAbbās Aḥmad b. Yaḥyā] (d. 914/1508), 121, 328n190
ward (*mūlā ʿalayhi*), 38, 42, 48, 221, 222n8, 223n17, 224n19, 225–27, 282
weak. *See ḍaʿīf*
Weber, Max, 89, 89n15, 90
witnesses in court (*shuhūd*), 77
woman, women, xxviii–xxix, xxxn73–74, xxxiv, 14, 49, 54–55, 58, 77, 92n28, 149n15, 157–58, 160n13, 162, 164–65, 175–77, 179–83, 186, 189n134, 195, 196n6, 198, 202, 204–6, 208n30, 211n37, 212n37, 213–17, 219, 220n3, 221, 222n7, 224n19, 225–31, 232n44, 233, 234n47, 244n31, 245, 248n52, 249–52, 254n81, 254n83, 255n86, 256n91, 259n104, 260, 264, 268, 271, 275n273, 287n345
    female testimony, capacity to testify, xxxvii, 179, 181, 189n136, 197–98, 198n9, 200, 202–3, 205–8, 208n28, 208n30, 209, 210n32, 211, 211nn36–37, 213–15, 217–18, 225, 225n20, 225n22
    feminism, xiii, 218

Z

ẓāhir (presumptive), 43n59, 50–51, 51n79, 59n103, 107–8, 110n102, 114, 167, 170, 182,

ẓāhir (*continued*)
217, 221, 244, 267, 283n321, 311, 319n150, 320, 327, 364
Ẓāhirī, 298, 309, 339
Zakat, xxxi, 61, 310, 331–34, 338, 342–43, 350–52, 360–64
ẓannī al-dalāla (probable in meaning), 11–13, 15, 91–92, 115n126, 117, 123, 132–33, 135, 147, 167, 223n17
al-Zarkashī, [Badr al-Dīn Muḥammad b. ʿAbd Allāh], (d. 794/1392), 68n3, 171, 203n20, 314n119
Zayd b. Ḥāritha, (d. 8/629), 274
al-Zuḥaylī, Wahba (1436/2015), 79–80, 82, 297n21, 312, 312n111, 313–14, 314n120, 314n122, 314nn124–25, 323n173, 324n177, 325nn181–182
al-Zurqānī, [Muḥammad b. ʿAbd al-Bāqī] (d. 1122/1710), 119–20